THE AUTO BOOK

THIRD EDITION

WILLIAM H. CROUSE
DONALD L. ANGLIN

Gregg Division
McGraw-Hill Book Company

New York Atlanta Dallas
St. Louis San Francisco Auckland
Bogotá Guatemala Hamburg
Johannesburg Lisbon London
Madrid Mexico Montreal
New Delhi Panama Paris
San Juan São Paulo
Singapore Sydney
Tokyo Toronto

Sponsoring Editor: D. Eugene Gilmore
Editing Supervisors: Katharine Glynn and Larry Goldberg
Design and Art Supervisor/Cover Design: Caryl Valerie Spinka
Production Supervisor: S. Steven Canaris

Interior Design: Sharkey Design
Cover Graphic: Iversen Associates
Technical Studio: Vantage Art, Inc.

Library of Congress Cataloging in Publication Data

Crouse, William Harry (date)
  The auto book.

  Includes index.
  Summary: Describes the various parts of the automobile, how they
function, and how they can be repaired. Includes the latest developments
in the automotive field.
  1. Automobiles. 2. Automobiles—Maintenance and repair. [1. Automobiles. 2. Automobiles—Maintenance and repair.] I. Anglin, Donald L.
II. Title.
TI2 05.C85 1983   629.2'222   83-16206
ISBN 0-07-014571-7

The Auto Book, Third Edition

  3 4 5 6 7 8 9 0   VNHVNH   8 9 1 0 9 8 7 6 5

ISBN 0-07-014571-7

(M) 629.2 C

CONTENTS

PREFACE

Since the second edition of *The Auto Book* was published, tremendous changes have taken place in the automotive field. New automotive designs, new production techniques, and new service methods have been put into place. Now front-wheel-drive vehicles, as well as four-wheel-drive vehicles, are common. New suspension systems have been introduced. A new generation of smaller, fuel-efficient, transverse-mounted, four-cylinder engines has arrived. Turbochargers have come into widespread use, giving smaller engines almost the power of larger engines.

The automotive industry has caught up with the electronics revolution. Now, on many vehicles, electronic devices control the ignition system; the fuel system; the suspension system; and the transmission, braking, and emission-control systems.

Many cars now have talking computers which tell the driver that "A door is ajar"; or, "The key is in the ignition"; or, "Please fasten your seat belt." Some of these computers can now respond to oral requests such as "Open the window" and "Tune the radio." Where this electronics revolution will end no one can predict. So it is very important for all of us to keep up to date on automotive developments and service. For this reason the new edition of *The Auto Book* was being revised to include new material right up to press time. It is the most up to date text in the field of automotive science and service.

The basic aim of the book and its related materials remains the same: to provide a complete and flexible teaching program for students of automotive mechanics. These related materials include the *Auto Study Guide,* the *Auto Shop Workbook,* the *Auto Test Book,* the *Automotive Transparencies,* and the *Auto Instructor's Guide.*

ACKNOWLEDGMENTS

During the planning and preparation of the third edition of *The Auto Book,* the authors and publisher had the advice and assistance of many people—educators, researchers, artists, editors, automotive-industry service specialists, and automotive engineers. The authors gratefully acknowledge their indebtedness and offer their sincere thanks. All cooperated with the aim of providing accurate and complete information that would be useful in the training of automotive technicians.

Special thanks must go to the following: John Steck, Frank Derato, and John Flaherty, who took time out from busy schedules to attend the master planning sessions for the new edition of the book; and to Ron Dreucci, for reviewing the manuscript and offering many suggestions for improving it.

Special thanks are also owed to the following organizations for information and illustrations they supplied:

AC Spark Plug Division of General Motors Corporation; American Honda Motor Company, Inc.; American Motors Corporation; Ammco Tools Inc.; Bear Manufacturing Company; Bendix Corporation; B.F. Goodrich Company; Goodyear Tire and Rubber Company; Black and Decker Incorporated; British Motor Corporation, Limited; Buick Motor Division of General Motors Corporation; Cadillac Motor Car Division of General Motors Corporation; California Bureau of Automotive Repair; Carter Carburetor Division of ACF Industries; Champion Spark Plug Company; Chevrolet Motor Division of General Motors Corporation; Chrysler Corporation; Clevite Division of Gould, Inc.; Dana Corporation; Delco Moraine Division of General Motors Corporation; Delco-Remy Division of General Motors Corporation; Dow Corning Corporation; Echlin Manufacturing Company; Federal-Mogul Corporation; Fel-Pro Incorporated; Fiat Motors of North America, Inc.; Ford Motor Company; General Motors Corporation; Go-Power Systems; The Hearst Corporation; Hunter Engineering Company; K-D Manufacturing Company; Lisle Corporation; Loctite Corporation; The L.S. Starret Company; Mazda Motors of America, Inc.; McCord Replacement Products Division of McCord Corporation; Monroe Auto Equipment Company; Moog Automotive, Inc.; Motor Vehicle Manufacturers Association; McQuary-Norris Manufacturing Company; Nissan Motor Company, Ltd.; Oldsmobile Division of General Motors Corporation; Owatonna Tool Company; Pontiac Division of General Motors Corporation; Robert Bosch Corporation; Rockwell International Corporation; Rubber Manufacturers Association; Saab-Scania of America, Inc.; Schwitzer Division of Wallace-Murray Corporation; Sealed Power Corporation; Shelby International, Inc.; Silver Products Company, Inc.; Snap-on Tools Corporation; Standard Motor Products, Inc.; Stewart-Warner Corporation; Sun Electric Corporation; Sunnen Products Company; Texaco, Inc.; Tire Industry Safety Council; Trico Products Corporation; TRW, Inc.; United States Safety Service Company; United Technologies; Volkswagen of America, Inc.; Volvo of America Corporation; Walker Manufacturing Division of Tenneco, Inc.

William H. Crouse

Donald L. Anglin

PART 1

AUTOMOTIVE SHOP FUNDAMENTALS

This is your introduction to the automobile and to the automotive service shop. You will learn how to work safely in the shop so you can protect yourself and others from injury. As you use the *Auto Shop Workbook* along with *The Auto Book,* you will learn about the two systems of measurement used in the shop: the U.S. Customary System (USCS) and the metric system. You will also learn about gaskets and sealants and the different types of fasteners used to hold together automotive parts. Also, you will learn how to use and take care of the various measuring and hand tools you will use in the shop. When you finish Part 1 and the related jobs in the workbook, you will have the background you need to begin working in the automotive shop. There are five chapters in Part 1:

CHAPTER 1 You and the Automobile
       2 Auto Shop Safety
       3 Shop Measurements and Measuring Tools
       4 Fasteners, Gaskets, and Sealants
       5 Shop Tools and Equipment

CHAPTER 1

YOU AND THE AUTOMOBILE

After studying this chapter, you should be able to:
1. List the various types of automotive service businesses.
2. Describe the different jobs in the automotive service business.
3. List and describe the five major components of the automobile.
4. Discuss the various automotive service publications and explain how they differ.

The Auto Book tells you about automobiles. It tells you how automobiles run, how to tell when something is wrong, and how to fix troubles that may occur. As you study this book and perform the related shopwork on automobiles, you will learn what you need to know to begin a career in the automotive service business.

AUTOMOTIVE CAREERS

☐ 1-1 THE AUTOMOTIVE SERVICE BUSINESS

The automotive business is big—one of the biggest businesses in this country and in the world. In fact, one out of every six people working in the United States is employed in the motor vehicle industry (Fig. 1-1). More than 14 million people have jobs because of the manufacture, distribution, maintenance, and commercial use of cars, trucks, and buses!

Many types of automotive service businesses hire auto mechanics. Some of these include:

■ Dealerships, where motor vehicles are sold and serviced.
■ Service stations, where cars and trucks get fuel, oil, and related products and services.
■ Independent garages, where various types of vehicles are serviced.
■ Specialty shops, where wheel alignment, transmission, tuneup, engine repair, air conditioning, body repair, painting and refinishing, and racing and high-performance work is performed. Many of these

shops may be *franchises*. These are shops that carry a nationally known name but are locally owned.

- Diesel shops, where troubleshooting and repair of diesel engines, diesel fuel-injection systems, and turbochargers is performed.
- Fleet garages, where leasing and rental agencies, companies that operate five or more vehicles, and taxicab, truck, and bus lines have their own shops.
- Parts stores, where automotive parts are sold.
- Auto service centers in department stores, where the car owner can buy frequently needed parts for do-it-yourself (DIY) installation or for installation in the store's shop.
- Automotive machine shops, where some automotive parts are reconditioned.

Fig. 1-1 One out of every six people working in the United States is employed because of the manufacture, distribution, maintenance, and commercial use of cars, trucks, and buses.

☐ 1-2 CAREERS IN AUTOMOTIVE SERVICE

Nearly 160 million cars, trucks, and buses are rolling on our highways. These vehicles serve the transportation needs of the 220 million people in the United States. In addition, there are millions more off-the-road vehicles, such as tractors, power mowers, golf carts, dune buggies, all-terrain vehicles, motorcycles, and mopeds. It requires a large number of mechanics to service all these vehicles.

Maintaining these millions of vehicles is a huge and growing industry. Americans spend billions of dollars every year for automotive parts and service. In fact, more money is spent on service than is spent to buy vehicles!

Almost 300,000 businesses repair automobiles. In these businesses, about 900,000 people have good, well-paying jobs as auto mechanics. The government reports that 28 percent or more new job openings will be available for auto mechanics during the next 10 years. Older workers are retiring earlier (Fig. 1-2). Younger workers change jobs. The result is hundreds of thousands of job opportunities for you.

The automotive service business offers a wide range of interesting and profitable careers. However, to get and keep the job, you must acquire the necessary education, skill, and experience. On the job, you must become a skilled mechanic. This means job security, job versatility, and unlimited opportunity for advancement. So let's take a look at some of these jobs.

☐ 1-3 JOBS IN AUTOMOTIVE DEALER SHOPS

There are about 26,000 new-car dealers in the United States. Every one of these dealers has a service shop. Most mechanics work in shops that employ one to five mechanics. Other shops are large and employ 100 or more mechanics and other service people. Dealer shops generally are larger than independent shops. The dealer shops have general mechanics or service specialists who can usually do just about everything required to diagnose and repair cars. Using special tools and equipment if necessary, they can:

- Check for excessive exhaust emissions
- Diagnose car and truck troubles
- Repair gasoline and diesel engines
- Service turbochargers and fuel-injection systems
- Repair manual and automatic transmissions and transaxles
- Service drive shafts, universal joints, and axles

Fig. 1-2 Job openings occur when highly skilled older mechanics retire. (*Chrysler Corporation*)

Fig. 1-3 About 158,000 service stations supply fuel, oil, and lubricants needed to keep cars running.

- Balance wheels and align front ends
- Replace brake, suspension, and steering parts
- Service air conditioners, heaters, and radios
- Perform body and paint work, including collision repair and glass replacement

This is quite a list. It shows you the variety of jobs that may be performed in the service department of an automobile dealership.

□ 1-4 JOBS IN SERVICE STATIONS

There are about 158,000 service stations in the United States (Fig. 1-3). Their basic job is to supply fuel, oil, and lubricants needed to keep cars running. Many service stations also wash and wax cars, fix flat tires, balance wheels, and align front-ends. In addition, some service stations sell tires, batteries, and accessories (TBA) such as shock absorbers, seat covers, light bulbs, and car wax and polish.

□ 1-5 JOBS IN INDEPENDENT GARAGES

In the United States, there are about 90,000 independent garages, both large and small. The large garages do all the jobs that are done in the dealer service shop. Smaller shops may specialize.

There are many more independent garages than dealer service shops. Some people buy a car from a dealer and then never return the car there for service. These people may find a nearby independent garage more convenient. Or one of the mechanics may be a personal friend. Or they may prefer to take their car to a shop that specializes.

□ 1-6 JOBS IN FLEET GARAGES

Automotive service facilities—such as new-car dealers, service stations, and independent garages—basically are open to the public. Some of these shops will work on almost any vehicle that can be driven or towed in. Others work only on specific makes and models of cars. Some shops perform only certain types of jobs. However, who *owns* the vehicle is not important.

Some mechanics work in fleet garages. These are private service facilities for car, truck, and bus fleets. They may be owned by federal, state, and local governments or any company that repairs its own vehicles. Work for others usually is not permitted.

Many fleet garages are authorized by the vehicle manufacturer to do *warranty work*. This is the repair work that the manufacturer agrees to pay for—if it is required—while the vehicle is new. Then the manufacturer usually supplies the parts. Later the fleet owner is sent a check to pay for the mechanic's labor. With big fleets, warranty work can amount to a lot of money.

Some fleet cars are expected to go more than 100,000 miles [160,930 km]. Trucks and buses may be expected to last for 20 years and travel a million miles [1,609,300 km] or more. It is the fleet mechanic's job to see that this occurs. Maintenance and other services must be performed regularly. In addition, the fleet mechanic must do everything possible to prevent on-the-road breakdowns.

□ 1-7 JOBS IN PARTS STORES

The parts store stocks and sells automotive parts (Fig. 1-4). Many parts stores sell to "the trade" only. This means they sell—and usually deliver—parts only to automotive service shops. Other parts stores sell to anyone who wants to buy. These stores attract the car owner and do-it-yourselfer.

Working for a parts store is similar to working in a retail store. You must know the merchandise—automotive parts—and you must know where everything is located. There are hundreds of thousands of different automotive parts, so it is a big job to keep track of them all. Parts catalogs and "applications charts" help you identify the exact part needed. This is where training as an auto mechanic is useful. If you know automobiles, you already know a lot about automotive parts.

No parts store is big enough to stock *all* automotive parts. Usually, only *fast-moving parts* are on the shelves. These are the parts that most often require replacement. Spark plugs and oil filters are examples of fast-moving parts.

When a parts store gets an order for a part that is not in stock, it is ordered from a distributor's warehouse. Sometimes the part is ordered from the parts division of the automobile manufacturer. Many orders are placed over the phone or by computer for quick filling. Within hours the needed part may be located and shipped. The use of computer ordering and air-freight delivery has greatly reduced the time required to get a "special order" part.

If you have a driver's license, you might get a job driving a delivery truck for a parts store. When not driving, you might take phone orders and then get to "work the counter."

Many parts stores have an automobile machine shop. The automotive machinist may grind valves, resurface cylinder heads, and turn brake rotors and drums. Small garages and service stations usually remove and install the parts on the car. But for reconditioning, they take them to the nearby automotive machine shop.

□ 1-8 SUCCESS IN THE AUTOMOTIVE SERVICE BUSINESS

When you get your job in the automotive service business, you will become a member of the business community. This means you will have steady work and a steady income. There are well-paying jobs in the automotive service business, and there is always the chance for advancement—the chance to move up to a better job.

For example, in larger shops good mechanics who can communicate well may become *service advisors*. Their job is to greet customers, determine service needs, and write repair orders (Fig. 1-5). It is the labor instructions on the repair order that tell the mechanic what to do. For the good service advisor, the next step up is to service manager. The service

Fig. 1-4 Parts stores stock and sell automotive parts. *(Lisle Corporation)*

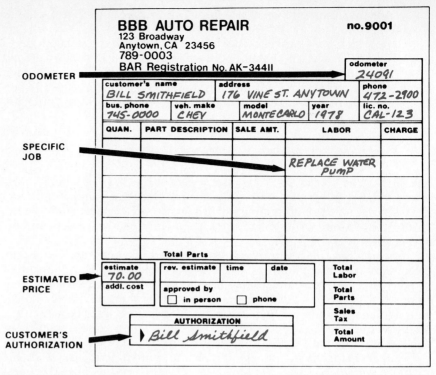

Fig. 1-5 Service advisors write labor instructions on the repair order that tell the mechanic what to do. *(California Bureau of Automotive Repair)*

manager runs the whole shop. And for the outstanding service manager, the opportunity to become a dealer often comes along!

How far you go and how much money you make are largely up to you. There are jobs and opportunities waiting for you in the automotive service business. One way to start your career is by taking classes in auto mechanics, by getting practical experience in the shop, and by studying *The Auto Book*. By getting this far, you have already made a good start.

COMPONENTS OF THE AUTOMOBILE

☐ 1-9 AUTOMOTIVE COMPONENTS

So far, you have been introduced to the automotive service business and the variety of jobs in it. Now let's take a quick look at the car and its major parts.

The automobile (Fig. 1-6) has five basic components, or parts:

1. The power plant, or engine, which is the source of power
2. The chassis, which supports the engine and body and includes the brake, steering, and suspension systems
3. The power train, or drive train, which is the power-transmission system that carries power from the engine to the drive wheels. It consists of the clutch (on vehicles with a manual transmission), transmission,

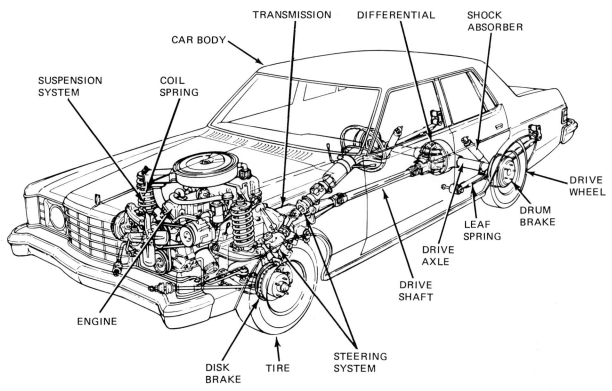

Fig. 1-6 Components of the automobile. The chassis includes the power plant, or engine; the frame, which supports the engine, wheels, and body; the power train, which carries the engine power to the drive wheels; and the brake, suspension, and steering systems. *(Ford Motor Company)*

transfer case (on vehicles with four-wheel drive), and drive-axle assembly. This unit includes the final drive, the differential, and the wheel axles.
4. The car body
5. The car-body accessories, which include the heater and air conditioner, lights, radio and tape player, windshield wiper and washer, and electric windows and seat adjusters

Many of these major components of the car are shown in Figs. 1-6 and 1-7. The construction, operation, and service of each system and component is covered in later chapters.

AUTOMOTIVE SERVICE PUBLICATIONS

☐ 1-10 AUTOMOTIVE MANUFACTURERS' SERVICE MANUALS

No one is born with the knowledge and skills needed to fix cars. These are learned by study and actual experience. The basic source of service infor-

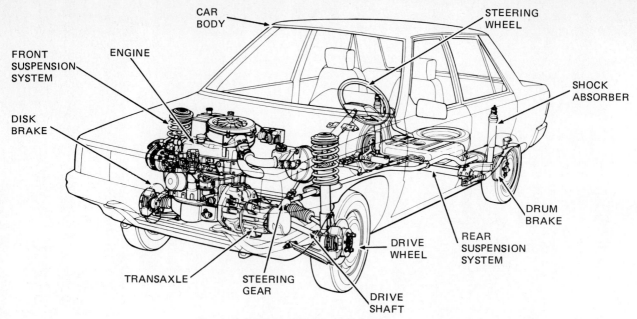

Fig. 1-7 Location of the major power-train components in a car with front-wheel drive. *(American Motors Corporation)*

mation for any car or truck is the manufacturer's shop manual (Fig. 1-8).

Every automobile manufacturer publishes shop manuals for its cars. These manuals—also called *service manuals*—are published every year when the new models come out. Service manuals:

- Cover all service procedures
- Provide the specifications
- Name the special tools needed for different jobs
- Explain how to diagnose and repair all kinds of car trouble on the manufacturer's new models

Figure 1-8 shows the service manuals published by one manufacturer to cover one model year. Two volumes—each more than an inch [25 mm] thick—contain all the servicing procedures that you will need. Some car manufacturers issue one large service manual each year. Other manufacturers require five or six volumes to completely cover all jobs on all their makes and models. Some service manuals are issued in large loose-leaf binders. This style allows any revisions issued during the model year to be easily inserted.

□ 1-11 AUTO REPAIR MANUALS

Manufacturers' service manuals provide the most complete service information available. However, it is often not practical to work out of them in the shop. Buying all the service manuals for each make and model of car sold in the United States costs a lot of money. In addition, sometimes manufacturers' service manuals are difficult to obtain. Since manufacturers' service manuals contain so much information that the average mechanic will never use, many independent shops don't get them. They prefer to use an *auto repair manual*.

Auto repair manuals (Fig. 1-9) are published by book companies such as Chilton, Motor, and Mitchell Manuals. The typical auto repair manual

Fig. 1-8 Service manuals are published each year by the car manufacturers. They provide complete service information for all vehicles built during that model year. *(ATW)*

includes specifications for all cars manufactured in the United States for about the last seven years. The manual has the key steps and illustrations for the most frequently performed mechanical repairs. Body and paint work is not covered. Separate manuals are published to provide similar coverage for imported cars and trucks.

☐ 1-12 OTHER SOURCES OF SERVICE INFORMATION

Many monthly automotive magazines contain information on servicing various cars. Automotive service magazines help explain how to do hard jobs, how to take service shortcuts, and how to become a better and better-paid auto mechanic.

Test-equipment manufacturers provide operating instructions or manuals on how to use their equipment. Parts makers, such as manufacturers of pistons, piston rings, and bearings, also provide booklets and service bulletins that are very helpful to the automotive mechanic.

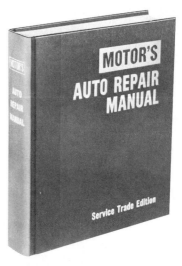

Fig. 1-9 An auto repair manual such as this includes the specifications, information, and illustrations for the most frequently performed repairs on all cars made in recent years in the United States. *(The Hearst Corporation)*

☐ 1-13 SPECIALIZED AUTOMOTIVE TEXTBOOKS

A textbook, such as *The Auto Book* which you are now studying, differs from service manuals and the auto repair manuals. They are written for the experienced working mechanic who already knows the basics. And they are very limited in coverage. The service manual covers only one model year. Auto repair manuals cover about seven model years, but many jobs are left out.

To learn the construction, operation, and service of automobiles, you need a textbook such as *The Auto Book*. Instead of being basically a book of "product knowledge," the textbook takes a different approach. The textbook assumes you are learning about something new. Names of parts are identified in illustrations. New words, and common words used with special meanings, are defined. Questions are provided at the end of the chapter for you to check up on yourself. At the end of the book, the answers are provided along with an index and a glossary of terms.

There are several specialized textbooks that cover in detail the various components of the automobile, such as engines, electrical equipment, transmissions, and brakes. For example, McGraw-Hill publishes the Automotive Technology Series, which includes such books as

> *Automotive Air Conditioning*
> *Automotive Automatic Transmissions*
> *Automotive Body Repair and Refinishing*
> *Automotive Brakes, Suspension, and Steering*
> *Automotive Electronics and Electrical Equipment*
> *Automotive Emission Control*
> *Automotive Engines*
> *Automotive Fuel, Lubricating, and Cooling Systems*
> *Automotive Manual Transmissions and Power Trains*
> *Automotive Tuneup*

If you want to dig deeper into any of these subjects, refer to the book covering the parts which especially interest you. These books cover the basics of construction, operation, troubleshooting, and servicing.

There is also the McGraw-Hill *Automotive Technician's Handbook,* which is a reference book covering all aspects of automotive service.

Select the *one* correct, best, or most probable answer to each question. Then check your answers against the correct answers given at the end of the book.

1. How many people in the United States work in the motor vehicle industry?
   a. 1,000,000
   b. 10,000,000
   c. 14,000,000
   d. 40,000,000

2. How many automotive vehicles are there on the highways in the United States?
   a. 5,000,000
   b. 50,000,000
   c. 100,000,000
   d. 160,000,000

3. In the United States, the total number of automotive repair facilities is about
   a. 900,000
   b. 300,000
   c. 26,000
   d. 145,000

4. Auto service centers often sell parts for use by
   a. the professional mechanic
   b. automotive machine shops
   c. the do-it-yourselfer
   d. fleet garages

5. Repair work that the car manufacturer agrees to pay for is called
   a. warranty work
   b. customer-pay labor
   c. machine-shop work
   d. retail selling

6. TBA stands for
   a. the Battery Association
   b. tool-box additive
   c. tires, batteries, and accessories
   d. none of the above

7. Good mechanics who communicate well may become
   a. new-car sales representatives
   b. automotive machinists
   c. parts sales representatives
   d. service advisors

8. The basic components of the car include
   a. the engine and chassis
   b. the drive train and car body
   c. the car-body accessories
   d. all of the above

9. The most complete source of service information for any car or truck is the
   a. auto repair manual
   b. manufacturer's service manual
   c. monthly automotive magazines
   d. daily newspaper

10. Specifications for cars manufactured in the United States in recent years are in
    a. auto repair manuals
    b. parts catalogs
    c. applications charts
    d. textbooks

CHAPTER 2
AUTO SHOP SAFETY

After studying this chapter, you should be able to:
1. Explain what good safety practice in the shop means.
2. Explain what you should do in an emergency.
3. Discuss fire prevention.
4. Describe the various types of fire extinguishers and the types of fires they are to be used on.
5. List the safety guidelines you should follow in the shop.

Shopwork is varied and interesting. The shop is where all the automotive service jobs are done. These jobs include grinding valves, replacing bearings, honing engine cylinders, checking and correcting wheel alignment, and so forth. These and many other jobs are discussed in later chapters of this book.

Before you start working in the shop, you should know about safety. Safety in the shop means protecting yourself and others from possible danger or injury. In this chapter, you will learn how to protect yourself and others by safely working with and handling tools.

□ 2-1 SAFETY IS YOUR JOB

Safety in the shop means protecting yourself and those around you from danger or injury. Safety is everybody's job. It is *your* job. When working in the shop, you are being "safe" if you are protecting your eyes, your fingers, your hands—your whole body—from danger at all times. And, just as important, safety also means looking out for those around you.

□ 2-2 LAYOUT OF THE SHOP

The first thing you should do when you go out into a shop is to find out where everything is located. A typical layout for an automotive shop is shown in Fig. 2-1. Study the layout of your shop. You should do this regardless of whether it is a school shop or a shop where you are going to work.

Fig. 2-1 Typical layout of an automotive shop. *(Motor Vehicle Manufacturers Association)*

You should note where the machine tools—the power tools—are located. Read the warning and caution signs posted on the walls. They are posted to warn you against potential danger. Learn where the fire extinguishers are located. Learn how to use them. Someday you might unexpectedly need a fire extinguisher quickly (Fig. 2-2).

☐ 2-3 ACTIONS IN EMERGENCIES

If there is an accident and someone gets hurt, notify your instructor at once! Your instructor will decide what to do—whether to call the school nurse, a doctor, or an ambulance. If there is a fire, get help at once. The quicker you fight a fire, the easier it is to control.

☐ 2-4 FIRE PREVENTION

Gasoline is such a familiar item in the shop that people often forget that it can be extremely dangerous. A spark or lighted match in a closed place filled with gasoline vapor can cause an explosion. Even the spark from a light switch can set off gasoline vapors. There have been explosions after employees washed the shop floor with gasoline—with the doors closed—and then turned off the lights. The spark from the light switch set off an

Fig. 2-2 Know where the shop fire extinguishers are located and how to use them. *(ATW)*

Fig. 2-3 Gasoline vapor and air can explode with enough force to blow a building apart. *(ATW)*

Fig. 2-4 Always store gasoline and other flammable liquids in approved safety containers. *(ATW)*

SAFETY GLASSES

SAFETY GOGGLES

FACE SHIELD

Fig. 2-5 Always wear safety glasses, safety goggles, or a face shield when there is any danger from flying particles. *(United States Safety Service Company)*

explosion of gasoline vapor that destroyed the building and also injured or killed the employees (Fig. 2-3).

Never pour gasoline down floor drains. Gasoline can form vapors in the sewer line. These vapors could be set off by a lighted match or cigarette thrown down a drain.

To prevent explosions, keep the shop doors open or the ventilator system going if there is gasoline vapor around. Wipe up spilled gasoline at once, and put the rags outside to dry. Never light or smoke cigarettes around gasoline. If you are working on a car with a leaky carburetor, fuel line, or fuel pump, catch the leaking gasoline in a container or with rags. Then put the rags outside as soon as possible. Fix the leak right away. Be very careful to avoid sparks around gasoline. Store gasoline in an approved safety container (Fig. 2-4). Never keep gasoline in a glass jug or a household type of thin plastic jug. The jug could break and cause an explosion or fire.

Oily rags are another possible source of fire. The oil on the rags might cause so much heat to develop that the rags ignite spontaneously, or catch fire. This is called *spontaneous combustion*. It results from a chemical action that produces heat and fire. Oily rags and waste should be put into special metal containers with lids. By keeping air out, fire is prevented.

□ *2-5 TAKING CARE OF YOURSELF IN THE SHOP*

Some people say, "Accidents will happen!" Safety experts do not agree. They say, "Accidents are caused"—caused by carelessness, by inattention to the job, by the use of damaged or incorrect tools, and sometimes by just not thinking. To help prevent accidents, follow these safety guidelines:

1. Work quietly and give the job your undivided attention.
2. Keep your tools and equipment under control.
3. Never indulge in horseplay or other foolish activities. You could cause someone to get seriously hurt.
4. Do not put sharp objects, such as screwdrivers, in your pocket. You could cut yourself or get stabbed.
5. Always remove all rings from your fingers and your watch from your arm before working in the shop. Also, remove any dangling chains and necklaces. Most jewelry is metal. It can accidentally short electric circuits and burn you severely.
6. Make sure your clothes are suitable for the job. Dangling sleeves or ties can get caught in machinery and cause serious injuries. Do not wear sandals or open-toe shoes. Wear full leather shoes with nonskid rubber heels and soles. Steel-toe shoes are best for shopwork.
7. Wipe excess oil and grease off your hands and tools so that you can get a good grip on tools or parts.
8. If you spill oil or grease or any liquid on the floor, clean it up so that no one will slip and fall.
9. Never use compressed air to blow dirt from your clothes, and never point a compressed-air hose at another person. Flying particles could put out an eye.
10. Always wear goggles or a face shield on any job where there is danger from flying particles (Fig. 2-5).
11. Watch out for flying sparks when you are using the grinding wheel or welding. The sparks can set your clothes on fire.
12. To protect your eyes, wear safety goggles when using chemicals, such as solvents or refrigerant (Fig. 2-6). If you get a chemical in your

SAFETY
GOGGLES

Fig. 2-6 Never work on an automotive air conditioner unless you are wearing safety goggles. *(Ford Motor Company)*

Fig. 2-7 If solvent or some other chemical splashes in your eye, immediately wash your eye with water.

eyes, wash them out with water (Fig. 2-7) and see the school nurse or a doctor at once.

13. Always use the right tool for the job. The wrong tool could damage the part being worked on and could also cause you to get hurt.

14. If you have to lift a heavy object, do it right. You can strain your back and injure yourself if you try to lift too much or lift improperly. When you must lift or move a heavy object, get help.

15. Never siphon gasoline from a tank using your mouth and a piece of hose. Swallowing even a small amount of gasoline can cause serious respiratory infection and pneumonia. Also, the lead in gasoline is poisonous. If you should get some gasoline in your mouth, spit it out, and rinse out your mouth several times. Avoid taking deep breaths. If you swallow some gasoline, do not try to vomit. Instead, get medical help at once. Your life may depend on it!

16. Never run an engine in a closed building that does not have an exhaust ventilating system (Fig. 2-8). The exhaust gases contain carbon monoxide. Carbon monoxide is a colorless, odorless, tasteless, poisonous gas that can kill you! Enough carbon monoxide to kill you can accumulate in a closed one-car garage in only 3 minutes.

17. When using a floor jack in the shop, make sure the jack is properly placed so that it won't slip. Never jack up a car while anyone is under it. People have been killed when the jack slipped and the car fell on them! Always place safety stands under a car before going under it (Fig. 2-9).

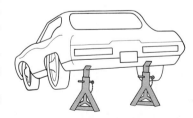

Fig. 2-8 Never run an engine inside a closed building unless the shop exhaust system is operating and attached to the car tail pipe. *(Sun Electric Corporation)*

☐ 2-6 DRIVING CARS IN THE SHOP

Cars have to be moved in the shop. They have to be brought in for service, and they may have to be moved from one work area to another. When the job is finished, they have to be moved out of the work area. You must be very careful when you drive a car in the shop. Make sure the way is clear. Make sure that no one is under a nearby car. The person might suddenly stick out an arm or leg. Make sure that there are no tools on the floor that you could run over.

When you take a car out on the street for a road test, *fasten your seat belt* even if you're going only a short distance.

CAUTION You should always fasten your seat belt when you are in a moving car. Use it whether you are the driver or a passenger. In accidents, seat belts save lives.

Fig. 2-9 Always use safety stands, properly located, to hold the car safely before going under it. *(ATW)*

Select the *one* correct, best, or most probable answer to each question. Then check your answers against the correct answers given at the end of the book.

1. Safety in the shop means protecting from danger or harm yourself and
   a. no one else
   b. those around you
   c. your boss
   d. none of the above

2. One of the most common causes of accidents in the shop is
   a. failure to follow instructions
   b. following instructions
   c. following the wrong instructions
   d. none of the above

3. One liquid that is used so much in the shop that people forget it is very dangerous if not handled properly is
   a. engine oil
   b. refrigerant oil
   c. gasoline
   d. brake fluid

4. Never store gasoline in
   a. an approved safety container
   b. a glass jug
   c. a metal tank
   d. none of the above

5. Oily rags must be stored in
   a. a closed metal container
   b. piles under the workbench
   c. the corner of the shop
   d. a plastic bag

6. After raising a car with a floor jack, never go under the car until
   a. all grease and oil is cleaned up
   b. you are sure the jack is filled with hydraulic jack oil
   c. you get a creeper
   d. safety stands are placed under it

7. If you splash solvent or other chemical in your eyes, you should
   a. rub your eyes vigorously
   b. immediately wash them with water
   c. close your eyes tightly and press them with a cloth
   d. call for a ride to your doctor's office

8. Before working in the shop, you should always remove all rings and your wristwatch to prevent
   a. getting them dirty
   b. scratching them
   c. accidental electrical shorts that may burn you
   d. oil and grease from causing them to rust and corrode

CHAPTER 3

SHOP MEASUREMENTS AND MEASURING TOOLS

After studying this chapter, you should be able to:

1. Describe the two basic systems of measurement used in the United States.
2. List the basic units of measurement in each system.
3. Define the prefixes *kilo-, centi-,* and *milli-.*
4. Demonstrate how to convert measurements from one system into the other system.
5. Explain how to use and read the inch micrometer.
6. Explain how to use and read the metric micrometer.
7. Explain how to use and read the vernier caliper.

Most parts used in automobiles and automobile engines have exact measurements for length, width, diameter, and thickness. When installed, many parts have extremely close fits. This requires the automotive mechanic to frequently measure parts to make sure they fit together correctly. Inaccurate measurements may result in parts failing after they are installed. In the shop, many measurements are made in inches or thousandths of an inch, or in metric measurements of meters and millimeters. This chapter covers both systems of measurement. Later sections describe the basic shop measuring tools.

SYSTEMS OF MEASUREMENT

☐ 3-1 BASIC MEASUREMENT SYSTEMS

Two different measuring systems are used in working with automobiles (Fig. 3-1). Most people brought up in the United States are familiar with U.S. Customary System (USCS) measurements. These measurements are inches, feet, and miles for length; pints, quarts, and gallons for volume; and ounces, pounds, and tons for weight. However, the United States is the only major country in the world still using this system. All other countries use the metric system.

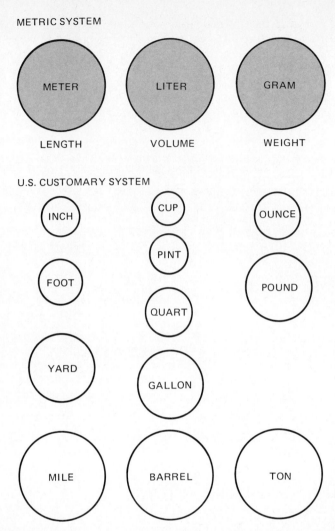

Fig. 3-1 Three metric units replace many different U.S. Customary System (USCS) units. *(ATW)*

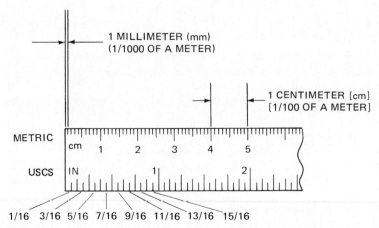

Fig. 3-2 Rule or steel scale marked in both inches (U.S. Customary System) and centimeters (metric system). *(ATW)*

Some cars and trucks built in the United States, and almost all imported vehicles, are dimensioned in the metric system. The metric unit of length is the meter, volume is the liter, and weight is the gram. The United States is gradually switching to the metric system. Some day all cars and trucks made in this country will be built to metric measurements. Whenever practical, all measurements in this book are dual-dimensioned. The USCS measurement is given first, followed by the metric equivalent in brackets: 1 inch [25.4 mm].

☐ 3-2 USCS MEASUREMENTS

Measurements in the U.S. Customary System include

Length	12 inches = 1 foot (ft) 3 feet = 1 yard (yd) 5280 feet = 1 mile (mi)
Capacity or Volume	16 fluid ounces (fl oz) = 1 pint (pt) 2 pints = 1 quart (qt) 4 quarts = 1 gallon (gal)
Weight	16 ounces (oz) = 1 pound (lb) 2000 pounds = 1 ton

Notice that many different units of measurement (such as inch, quart, pound) are used, with various numbers for each. Yet these are only a few of the many numbers and names in the U.S. Customary System.

☐ 3-3 METRIC SYSTEM

The metric system is based on multiples of 10, the same as our money system. Ten cents is one dime, and 10 dimes is one dollar. In the same way, 10 millimeters (mm) is 1 centimeter (cm), 10 centimeters is 1 decimeter (dm), and 10 decimeters is 1 meter (m) (Fig. 3-2). Note that *meter* is part of every word. This is because the meter is the unit of length in the metric system. A meter is 39.37 inches, or slightly longer than 1 yard (Fig. 3-3).

The names of metric units often include prefixes *(milli-, centi-, kilo-)* as in "milliliter," "centimeter," and "kilogram." These prefixes indicate multiples or submultiples of the units.

- ■ Kilo means 1000 (one thousand)
- ■ Deci means 0.10 (one-tenth)
- ■ Centi means 0.01 (one-hundredth)
- ■ Milli means 0.001 (one-thousandth)

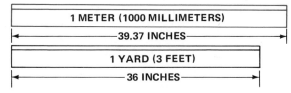

Fig. 3-3 The meter is the metric unit of length. It is a little longer than a yard. *(Ford Motor Company)*

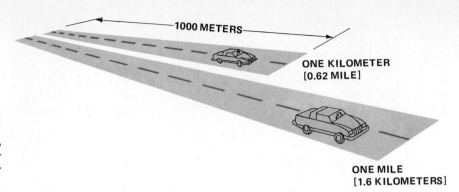

1000 METERS

ONE KILOMETER
[0.62 MILE]

ONE MILE
[1.6 KILOMETERS]

Fig. 3-4 In the metric system, road signs, maps, and car odometers show distance in kilometers. *(ATW)*

Therefore, 1 kilometer (km) is 1000 meters, which equals 0.62 mile (Fig. 3-4). Figure 3-5 is a table that compares many basic USCS measurements with metric measurements.

The metric unit of liquid measurement is the *liter* (L). It is the volume of a cube that measures 10 cm [$^1/_{10}$ m] on a side (Fig. 3-6). The liter is slightly larger than a quart (Fig. 3-7) and contains 1000 milliliters (mL). Five milliliters is about the same as 1 teaspoon.

The weight of a liter of water is called a *kilogram* (kg). It weighs about 2.2 pounds and contains 1000 grams (g). A gram is about $^1/_{28}$ ounce, which is about the weight of two or three paper clips.

Because of the way that cubic centimeter and milliliter are defined, they are equal. One gram is the mass of 1 cubic centimeter (cc) of water at its temperature of maximum density. A cubic centimeter is a cube that measures 1 cm [$^1/_{100}$ m] on each side (Fig. 3-6). Since both 1 cc and 1 mL are $^1/_{1000}$ of a liter, they have the same volume.

Length		
1 in (inch)	= 25.4 mm (millimeters)	= 2.54 cm (centimeters)
1 ft (foot)	= 304.8 mm	= 0.3048 m (meter)
1 mi (mile)	= 1.609 km (kilometers)	= 1609 m
1 mm	= 0.039 in	= 0.1 cm
1 cm	= 0.390 in	= 10 mm
1 m	= 3.28 ft	= 39.37 in
1 km	= 0.62 mi	= 3281 ft
Capacity and Volume		
1 cu in (cubic inch)	= 16.39 cc (cubic centimeters)	= 0.016 L (liter)
1 fl oz (fluid ounce)	= 29.57 cc	= 29.57 mL (milliliter)
1 qt (quart)	= 32 fl oz	= 0.946 L
1 gal (gallon)	= 4 qt	= 3.78 L
1 cc	= 0.061 cu in	= 1 mL
1 L	= 61.02 cu in	= 1.057 qt
Mass and Weight		
1 oz (ounce)	= 0.0625 lb (pound)	= 28.35 g (grams)
1 lb	= 16 oz	= 454 g
1 ton	= 2000 lb	= 908 kg (kilograms)
1 g	= 0.035 oz	= 1000 mg (milligrams)
1 kg	= 2.2 lb	= 35.2 oz

Fig. 3-5 Comparison of various USCS measurements with metric measurements. *(ATW)*

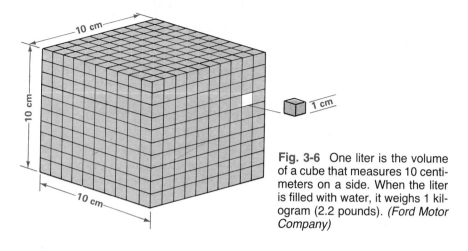

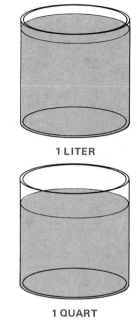

Fig. 3-6 One liter is the volume of a cube that measures 10 centimeters on a side. When the liter is filled with water, it weighs 1 kilogram (2.2 pounds). *(Ford Motor Company)*

1 LITER

1 QUART

Fig. 3-7 One liter is slightly larger than a quart. *(ATW)*

☐ 3-4 DECIMAL AND METRIC EQUIVALENTS

In the United States, many inch measurements are given as fractions (Fig. 3-2). Other measurements are given as decimals in the USCS and metric systems. The table of equivalents in Fig. 3-8 helps you change fractions to their decimal and metric equivalents. Comparisons of various USCS measurements to metric measurements are given in Fig. 3-5. Other conversion tables and formulas are available for finding the various equivalents. The ones needed most in the automotive shop are frequently found in the automotive manufacturers' service manuals.

Inches			Inches			Inches		
Fraction	**Decimal**	**mm**	**Fraction**	**Decimal**	**mm**	**Fraction**	**Decimal**	**mm**
1/64	0.0156	0.3969	23/64	0.3594	9.1281	11/16	0.6875	17.4625
1/32	0.0312	0.7938	3/8	0.3750	9.5250	45/64	0.7031	17.8594
3/64	0.0469	1.1906	25/64	0.3906	9.9219	23/32	0.7188	18.2562
1/16	0.0625	1.5875	13/32	0.4062	10.3188	47/64	0.7344	18.6531
5/64	0.0781	1.9844	27/64	0.4219	10.7156	3/4	0.7500	19.0500
3/32	0.0938	2.3812	7/16	0.4375	11.1125	49/64	0.7656	19.4469
7/64	0.1094	2.7781	29/64	0.4531	11.5094	25/32	0.7812	19.8438
1/8	0.1250	3.1750	15/32	0.4688	11.9062	51/64	0.7969	20.2406
9/64	0.1406	3.5719	31/64	0.4844	12.3031	13/16	0.8125	20.6375
5/32	0.1562	3.9688	1/2	0.5000	12.7000	53/64	0.8281	21.0344
11/64	0.1719	4.3656	33/64	0.5156	13.0969	27/32	0.8438	21.4312
3/16	0.1875	4.7625	17/32	0.5312	13.4938	55/64	0.8594	21.8281
13/64	0.2031	5.1594	35/64	0.5469	13.8906	7/8	0.8750	22.2250
7/32	0.2188	5.5562	9/16	0.5625	14.2875	57/64	0.8906	22.6219
15/64	0.2344	5.9531	37/64	0.5781	14.6844	29/32	0.9062	23.0188
1/4	0.2500	6.3500	19/32	0.5938	15.0812	59/64	0.9219	23.4156
17/64	0.2656	6.7469	39/64	0.6094	15.4781	15/16	0.9375	23.8125
9/32	0.2812	7.1438	5/8	0.6250	15.8750	61/64	0.9531	24.2094
19/64	0.2969	7.5406	41/64	0.6406	16.2719	31/32	0.9688	24.6062
5/16	0.3125	7.9375	21/32	0.6562	16.6688	63/64	0.9844	25.0031
21/64	0.3281	8.3344	43/64	0.6719	17.0656	1	1.0000	25.4000
11/32	0.3438	8.7312						

Fig. 3-8 Table for changing fractions of an inch to their decimal and metric equivalents.

Fig. 3-9 Measuring cylinder diameter with a steel scale. *(ATW)*

☐ 3-5 NEED FOR PRECISION MEASURING

Automobiles are built in factories by people using machinery to turn raw materials into finished parts. These parts, made to precision measurements, are then assembled into automobiles. However, the need for precision does not stop at the end of the assembly line. To service and maintain the car, you need the specifications, tolerances, and clearances for each part. But before the information can be useful, precision measurements must be made. Taking these many types of accurate measurements requires a variety of measuring tools.

☐ 3-6 RULES AND STEEL SCALES

Rules, or steel scales (Fig. 3-9), are marked in inches and fractions of an inch. Sometimes these markings are as small as 1/64 inch. Other rules or steel scales are dual-dimensioned. They are marked with both inches and centimeters. This is the type shown in Fig. 3-2. The top markings are the centimeter scale. Rules are also made with only metric markings.

☐ 3-7 THICKNESS GAUGES

Thickness gauges (Fig. 3-10) are strips or blades of hardened steel or other metal. They are ground or rolled with great accuracy so that they are the exact thickness marked on the blade. Thickness gauges are often called *feeler gauges*. Many thickness gauges are dual-dimensioned. For example, the 6 on the blade in Fig. 3-10 means that it is 0.006 inch [0.15 mm] thick.

Some thickness gauges have two steps or thicknesses. These are called *stepped thickness gauges,* or *go–no-go gauges.* The tip is thinner than the rest of the blade (Fig. 3-11). The thinnest gauge shown in Fig.

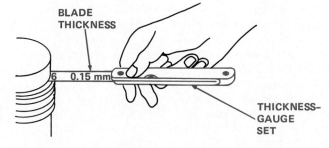

Fig. 3-10 Using a thickness gauge to measure piston-ring clearance.

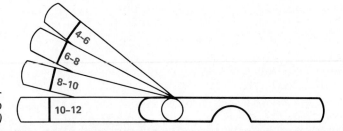

Fig. 3-11 A set of stepped thickness gauges. These are also called *go–no-go* gauges. *(ATW)*

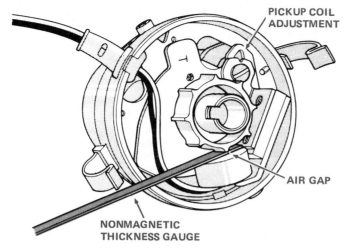

PICKUP COIL ADJUSTMENT

AIR GAP

NONMAGNETIC THICKNESS GAUGE

Fig. 3-12 Nonmagnetic thickness gauges made of brass are used for measuring the air gap in electronic distributors. *(Chrysler Corporation)*

3-11 is 0.004 inch [0.10 mm] at the tip and 0.006 inch [0.15 mm] thick over the rest of the blade.

Thickness gauges are used to measure small distances, or clearances, between objects that cannot be measured in any other way. For example, Fig. 3-10 shows a thickness gauge being used to check the clearance between the side of a piston ring and the ring groove in a piston. To determine the clearance, gauges of various thicknesses are tried until one is found that fits snugly. The number on that gauge is the clearance.

The stepped thickness gauge is preferred for use on some jobs where an adjustment is made. When the specifications call for a clearance of 0.005 inch [0.13 mm], select the 0.004–0.006-inch [0.10–0.15-mm] gauge. The clearance is adjusted so that the 0.004-inch [0.10-mm] tip fits, but the 0.006-inch [0.15-mm] part does not fit. The result is a clearance of 0.005 inch [0.13 mm].

Thickness gauges are made in many shapes and sizes. Some thickness-gauge blades are straight, as in Figs. 3-10 and 3-11. Other blades are bent at an angle. A thickness-gauge set usually consists of several blades which often range in size from 0.0015 to 0.040 inch [0.04 to 1.02 mm]. Sometimes you might need to measure a space that is a size for which your set does not have a blade. You can make up the gauge you need by combining blades of various thicknesses from the set.

Most thickness gauges are made of steel. However, sometimes you need a nonmagnetic thickness gauge. Brass thickness gauges are available for work around permanent magnets. One example is measuring the air gap in an electronic distributor (Fig. 3-12). A permanent magnet will attract the steel gauge and prevent an accurate measurement.

□ *3-8 WIRE THICKNESS GAUGES*

Wire thickness gauges (Fig. 3-13) are made of accurately drawn wire. They are used for checking spark-plug gaps (Fig. 3-14) and other measurements. Metric wire thickness gauges are also available. Sometimes specifications are given in the metric system when you do not have metric gauges. Then convert the measurements from metric to inches by using the conversion tables (Figs. 3-5 and 3-8).

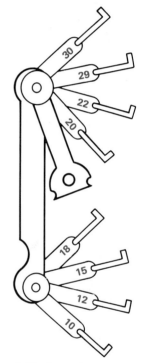

Fig. 3-13 A set of wire thickness gauges. *(ATW)*

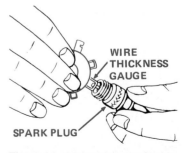

WIRE THICKNESS GAUGE

SPARK PLUG

Fig. 3-14 Measuring spark-plug gap with a wire thickness gauge.

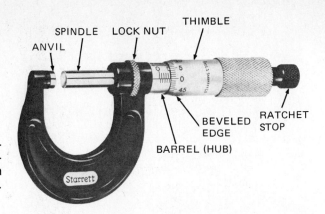

Fig. 3-15 A 1-inch outside micrometer. It measures thicknesses in thousandths of an inch from 0 to 1.000 inch. *(The L.S. Starrett Company)*

□ 3-9 MICROMETERS

Measurements made with a steel scale or ruler are not accurate enough for much automotive service work. A precision measuring tool such as an inside or outside micrometer (Fig. 3-15) must be used. It can measure the thickness and diameter of parts in thousandths ($\frac{1}{1000}$) or ten-thousandths ($\frac{1}{10,000}$) of an inch. Metric micrometers read in hundredths ($\frac{1}{100}$) of a millimeter. In the shop, the micrometer usually is called a "mike." Measuring something with the mike is called "miking."

Look at Fig. 3-15 and identify the thimble, hub, spindle, frame, and anvil. There are screw threads and a screw nut inside the thimble. As you turn the thimble, the threads move the spindle toward or away from the anvil.

To measure the diameter of a rod, place it between the end of the spindle and the anvil (Fig. 3-16). Turn the thimble gently to move the end of the spindle toward the rod. The rod should be touched lightly on one side of the anvil and on the other side by the end of the spindle. Never turn the spindle tight against anything. This can ruin the mike. Turn the thimble only until the spindle touches and you feel a light drag.

The mike in Fig. 3-16 has a small knob on the end of the thimble called a *ratchet stop*. When the spindle nears the part being measured, turn the ratchet stop instead of the thimble. Then, when the spindle touches the part with proper force, the ratchet will slip. This improves the accuracy of your measurements, especially when they must be repeated. It also prevents damage to the mike from overtightening.

CAUTION Never use the micrometer to measure a part that is moving, such as a rotating shaft. The mike might clamp onto the shaft, be whirled around, and break. You could be seriously injured by the mike or flying particles.

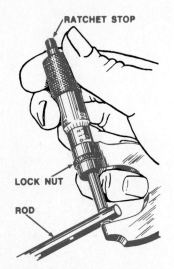

Fig. 3-16 Measuring the diameter of a rod with an outside micrometer.

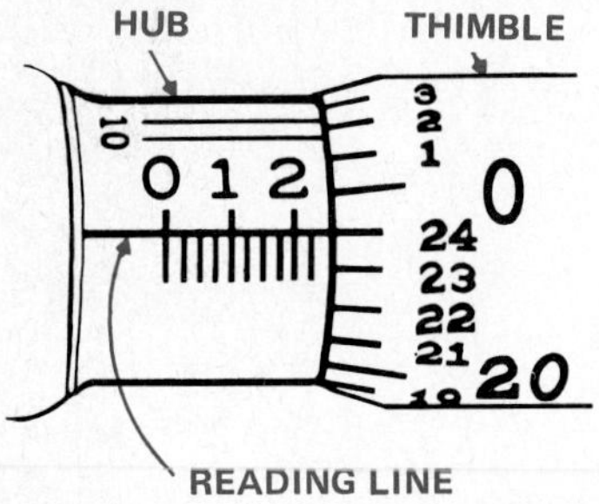

Fig. 3-17 Hub and thimble markings on a micrometer.

□ 3-10 READING THE INCH MICROMETER

After you have adjusted the mike, you have to *read* it. The micrometer reading is the thickness, or diameter, of the part being measured. Markings on the thimble and hub are added together to get the reading.

In Fig. 3-17, notice that the hub is marked with numbers that run from 0 to 9 along the reading line. Each number represents tenths (0.1) of an inch. For example, the numbered line 2 shown in Fig. 3-17 indicates two-tenths (0.2) inch. Each of the lines between the numbers represents twenty-five thousandths (0.025) inch. Every time the thimble is turned

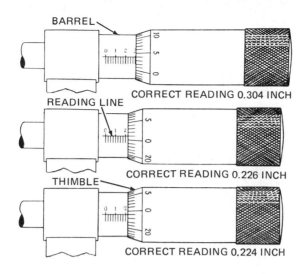

BARREL

CORRECT READING 0.304 INCH

READING LINE

CORRECT READING 0.226 INCH

THIMBLE

CORRECT READING 0.224 INCH

Fig. 3-18 Reading a micrometer.

one revolution, it moves exactly 0.025 inch. When the thimble is turned four times, it moves 0.1 inch ($4 \times 0.025 = 0.1$). Lines around the beveled edge of the thimble divide it into 25 parts. Therefore each thimble mark equals one-thousandth (0.001) inch.

Reading the micrometer requires you to do an addition problem. The values of the numbered lines and the intermediate lines exposed by the thimble are added together. To this sum, add the value of the thimble line that is even with (or slightly below) the reading line. Their total is the micrometer reading. Using the micrometer setting shown in Fig. 3-17 as an example:

Numbered lines (on hub)	$2 \times 0.100 = 0.200$ inch
Intermediate lines (between numbers)	$1 \times 0.025 = 0.025$ inch
Thimble lines (around thimble)	$24 \times 0.001 = 0.024$ inch
Micrometer reading	$= 0.249$ inch

Figure 3-18 shows three other micrometer settings for you to read. If you have trouble getting the correct reading, follow the procedure shown above. Write down the value of each line. Then add them together.

□ 3-11 READING THE METRIC MICROMETER

In the metric system, the "1-inch mike" becomes a "25-mm mike" (Fig. 3-19). They look alike, handle alike, and read the same way. The difference is in the graduations. On the metric micrometer, one revolution of the thimble moves the spindle 0.5 mm. The reading line on the sleeve is graduated in millimeters (1.0 mm). Above the reading line, the graduations are numbered by 5s from 0 to 25. Short vertical lines below the reading line divide each millimeter in half (0.5 mm). Therefore two revolutions of the thimble are required to move the spindle 1.0 mm.

The beveled edge of the thimble is divided into 50 parts. The lines are numbered by 5s from 0 to 50. One revolution of the thimble moves the spindle 0.5 mm. Therefore each line on the thimble equals $\frac{1}{50}$ of 0.5 mm, or 0.01 mm.

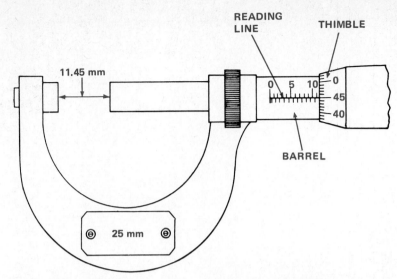

Fig. 3-19 A 25-mm metric micrometer. *(Volkswagen of America, Inc.)*

To read the metric micrometer, add the number of millimeters and half-millimeters visible on the sleeve. To that sum, add the number of hundredths of a millimeter shown on the thimble line that is even with (or slightly below) the reading line. The total is the micrometer reading. Using the micrometer setting shown in Fig. 3-19 as an example:

Millimeter lines (above reading line)	11×1.00 mm $= 11.00$ mm
Half-millimeter lines (below reading line)	0×0.50 mm $= 0.00$ mm
Thimble lines (around thimble)	45×0.01 mm $= 0.45$ mm
Micrometer reading	$= 11.45$ mm

☐ 3-12 INSIDE MICROMETERS

Many variations of the micrometer are used in the automotive shop. For example, inside micrometers are used to measure hole diameters such as the diameter, or *bore,* of an engine cylinder (Fig. 3-20). Extension rods of various lengths can be attached for measuring larger diameters. The markings on the hub and thimble correspond to those on the hub and thimble of the outside micrometer.

To measure a cylinder bore, first turn the thimble clockwise until the micrometer is shorter than the diameter of the cylinder bore. With one hand, hold the head end of the micrometer squarely against the cylinder wall. Then, with your other hand, turn the thimble to lengthen the micrometer. As you are doing this, feel for the maximum diameter by moving the rod end slightly from left to right and up and down. When no left-to-right movement of the rod end is possible and a light drag is felt as you move the rod end up and down, take the reading.

☐ 3-13 MICROMETER FEEDS

In the automotive shop, many power tools have micrometer-type adjustments. This is called a *micrometer feed.* Cylinder hones, boring bars,

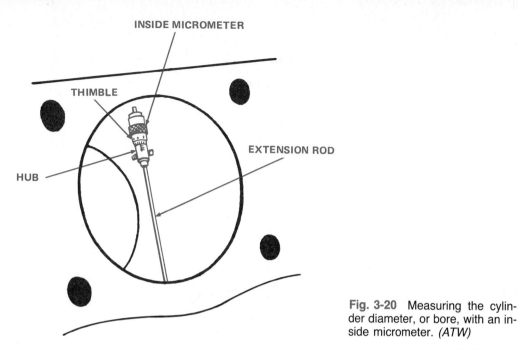

INSIDE MICROMETER

THIMBLE

EXTENSION ROD

HUB

Fig. 3-20 Measuring the cylinder diameter, or bore, with an inside micrometer. *(ATW)*

brake lathes, and valve refacers are some of the power tools that use it to ensure accurate machining of parts. These machines have adjusting knobs or dials marked like the micrometer. They move the machine's cutting or grinding tool in thousandths (0.001) of an inch or hundredths (0.01) of a millimeter. These adjustments are read in the same way as the micrometer setting.

☐ 3-14 DIAL INDICATORS

A *dial indicator* is a precision measuring tool that has a dial face and needle to register movement (Fig. 3-21). It is used to measure variations in dimensions and movements too small to be measured accurately by other tools. Typical measurements are shaft endplay, gear backlash, contact-point opening, brake-rotor runout, valve lift, valve-guide wear (Fig. 3-22), and cylinder wear.

The dial indicator has a contact point attached to a movable arm or plunger. As the arm moves, the needle rotates around the dial to show the distance. The dial usually is scaled in thousandths (0.001) of an inch or hundredths (0.01) of a millimeter.

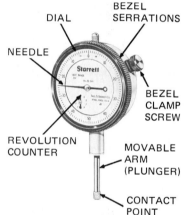

BEZEL
SERRATIONS

DIAL

NEEDLE

BEZEL
CLAMP
SCREW

REVOLUTION
COUNTER

MOVABLE
ARM
(PLUNGER)

CONTACT
POINT

Fig. 3-21 A dial indicator. This one has a range of 1.000 inch, with each mark around the dial representing 0.001 inch. *(The L.S. Starrett Company)*

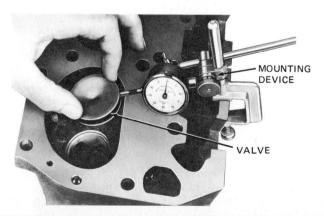

MOUNTING
DEVICE

VALVE

Fig. 3-22 Measuring valve-guide wear with a dial indicator. *(Chrysler Corporation)*

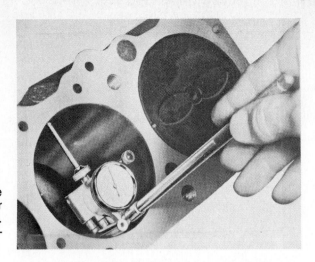

Fig. 3-23 A cylinder-bore gauge can measure cylinder wear, taper, and out-of-round. *(Pontiac Motor Division of General Motors Corporation)*

To use the dial indicator, assemble it in its mounting device. This may be a strong magnetic base or a type of C-clamp (Fig. 3-22). Then attach the mount securely to a stationary part near the part to be measured. Place the contact point of the dial indicator against the part to be measured. With your hand, press on the dial indicator until you see the indicator needle move around the dial. Then tighten the clamp screw to hold the dial indicator firmly in position.

With your fingers, rotate the bezel serrations until the needle is aligned with the 0 mark. Then move the part to be measured back and forth. Read the amount of needle movement on the dial. This is called *total indicator reading,* or TIR. On the dial indicators shown in Figs. 3-21 and 3-22, every mark on the dial equals 0.001 inch.

Figure 3-23 shows a cylinder-bore gauge being used to check an engine cylinder. The gauge is basically a dial indicator built into a special mounting device. As the gauge is moved up and down and around the cylinder, the gauge measures cylinder wear, taper, and out-of-round.

□ *3-15 VERNIER CALIPER*

The *vernier caliper* (Fig. 3-24) is basically two steel rules, the fixed rule and the sliding rule. The fixed rule, or "frame," has a fixed jaw attached to one end. The sliding rule, which moves along the frame, also has a jaw attached at one end. This jaw is called the *adjustable jaw,* or *sliding jaw*. On some calipers, both the inside and outside of the jaws are used as measuring surfaces. This allows you to measure outside and inside diameters with the same tool. Other calipers have two sets of jaws (Fig. 3-25).

To measure an outside diameter with a vernier caliper, place the object snugly between the jaws of the caliper (Fig. 3-24). The number of inches is read off the fixed scale on the frame. To this, add the number of tenths that are seen between the last inch reading and the 0 on the vernier scale. Then add the number of 0.025-inch marks seen between the last tenth reading and the 0 on the vernier scale. Finally, read the number of lines from 0 on the reverse scale to the point where the line on the vernier scale coincides exactly with a line on the fixed scale. Each of these lines represents $\frac{1}{1000}$ (0.001) inch. Some vernier calipers have slightly different scales or 0 marks for reading inside diameters.

Figure 3-25 shows a dual-dimensioned vernier caliper. On this caliper, the fixed metric scale is divided into 1-mm sections. Each mark on the movable vernier scale represents $\frac{1}{20}$ (0.05) mm. To read the metric

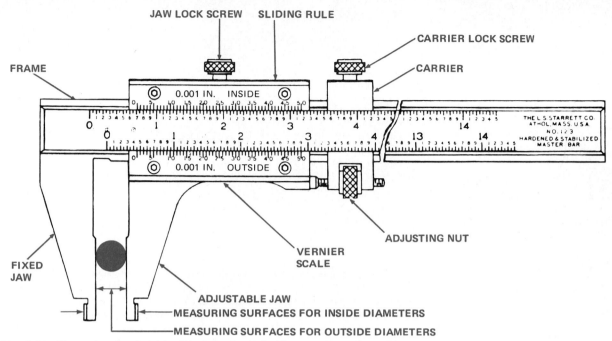

Fig. 3-24 Measuring the outside diameter of a rod with a vernier caliper. *(The L.S. Starrett Company)*

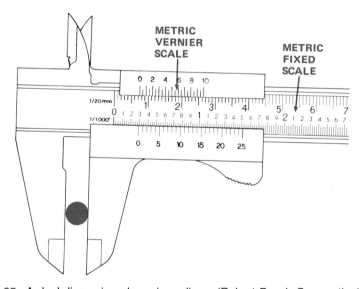

Fig. 3-25 A dual-dimensioned vernier caliper. *(Robert Bosch Corporation)*

vernier caliper, start with the fixed scale. Count the number of millimeters from the 0 on the fixed scale to the 0 on the vernier scale. Then look at the vernier scale. On it, each long line represents 0.10 mm. Each short line represents 0.05 mm. Find the line that matches exactly with a line on the fixed scale. When you have found it, count each long line on the vernier scale from 0 to the point where the two lines meet. Since each line is 0.10 mm, count by 10s. Now add 0.05, if it is a short line that matches exactly. Add this reading to the fixed-scale reading. Your answer for the measurement shown in Fig. 3-25 should be 7.40 mm.

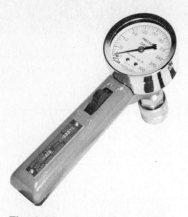

Fig. 3-26 A cylinder-compression tester, one type of gauge used to check pressures on the car. *(Sun Electric Corporation)*

☐ 3-16 PRESSURE GAUGES

Pressures that you measure on the car include tire pressure, fuel-pump pressure, and compression pressure (in the engine cylinders). In the U.S. Customary System, pressure measurements are given in *pounds per square inch* (psi). This is the force applied, in pounds, to each square inch of surface. In the metric system, pressure is measured in *kilopascals* (kPa). The conversion factor is

$$1 \text{ psi} = 6.895 \text{ kPa}$$

For everyday use, 1 psi = 7 kPa is close enough.

Figure 3-26 shows a cylinder-compression tester. It is attached to the cylinder after removing the spark plug. When the engine is cranked, the needle shows the compression pressure. If the cylinder has a compression pressure of 120 psi, this would be 840 kPa in the metric system (120 × 7 = 840).

☐ 3-17 VACUUM GAUGES

When the pressure in something is less than atmospheric pressure, this reduced pressure is called a *vacuum*. Many devices on the car are operated by vacuum. In fact, the engine itself acts as a "vacuum pump." Improper vacuum may indicate engine trouble and affect mileage and emissions. It may also affect the shifting of the automatic transmission, and the operation of the heater and air conditioner.

Vacuum is measured in *inches (or millimeters) of mercury*. Actually, there is no mercury in the vacuum gauge (Fig. 3-27). The gauge reading is the same as how high the vacuum would raise a column of mercury in a barometer. The gauge in Fig. 3-27 shows "20 inches," or "20 inches Hg." Hg is the symbol for mercury. In the metric system, vacuum is measured in millimeters. To convert inches of vacuum to millimeters of vacuum:

$$1 \text{ inch Hg} = 25.4 \text{ mm Hg}$$

However, in the shop, use 1 inch Hg = 25 mm Hg.

Fig. 3-27 A vacuum gauge with both inch and millimeter scales. *(Sun Electric Corporation)*

Select the *one* correct, best, or most probable answer to each question. Then check your answers against the correct answers given at the end of the book.

1. The bore of an engine cylinder is 3.400 inches. In the metric system the bore is
   a. 86.36 m (meters)
   b. 86.36 mm (millimeters)
   c. 86.36 cm (centimeters)
   d. 86.36 km (kilometers)

2. The contact-point gap for an imported car is given as 0.45 mm. In the U.S. Customary System, the points should be gapped at
   a. 0.018 inch
   b. 0.015 inch
   c. 0.180 inch
   d. 0.021 inch

3. Connecting-rod bearing clearance is given as 0.051 mm. In the U.S. Customary System, the clearance is
   a. 0.0002 inch
   b. 0.2000 inch
   c. 0.020 inch
   d. 0.002 inch

4. In the U.S. Customary System, the camshaft turns at ½ the crankshaft speed. Therefore, in the metric system, the camshaft turns at
   a. the crankshaft speed
   b. one-half the crankshaft speed
   c. one-fourth the crankshaft speed
   d. twice the crankshaft speed

5. The fuel-tank capacity is 21 gallons. In liters, the tank holds
   a. 7.5 L (liters)
   b. 75 cc (cubic centimeters)
   c. 79 L (liters)
   d. 750 cc (cubic centimeters)

6. A dual-dimensioned scale is marked in
   a. inches and meters
   b. inches and fractions of inches
   c. inches and centimeters
   d. centimeters and millimeters

7. A dual-dimensioned thickness gauge
   a. is marked in inches and millimeters
   b. has a blade with two thicknesses
   c. has a pair of blades
   d. none of the above

8. A stepped thickness gauge
   a. is marked in inches and centimeters
   b. has a blade with two thicknesses
   c. has a pair of blades
   d. none of the above

9. The two types of micrometers are:
   a. inside and outside
   b. direct and indirect
   c. parallel and circular
   d. upper and lower

10. The metric micrometer reads
    a. in fractions of an inch
    b. in meters
    c. in centimeters
    d. in millimeters and hundredths of a millimeter

11. The bore, or diameter, of an engine cylinder can be measured with
    a. an inside micrometer
    b. a vernier caliper
    c. both a and b
    d. neither a nor b

12. The dial indicator has a needle that rotates around the face to show
    a. valve-guide diameter
    b. engine cylinder diameter
    c. movements in thousandths of an inch
    d. force and pressure

13. TIR means
    a. total ignition resistance
    b. total indicator reading
    c. total irregular reading
    d. total instant reading

14. To measure the wear, taper, and out-of-round in an engine cylinder, you can use
    a. a steel scale
    b. a wire thickness gauge
    c. a vernier caliper
    d. none of the above

15. In the automotive shop, most measurements are given to the nearest
    a. thousandth ($\frac{1}{1000}$) of an inch
    b. hundredth ($\frac{1}{100}$) of a millimeter
    c. both a and b
    d. neither a nor b

CHAPTER 4
FASTENERS, GASKETS, AND SEALANTS

After studying this chapter, you should be able to:
1. Discuss screw threads and explain pitch, series, and classes.
2. Explain how bolts, nuts, screws, and studs are marked to indicate their strength.
3. Explain how metric threads differ from USCS threads.
4. Define *prevailing-torque fastener*.
5. List four types of nonthreaded fasteners and describe their use.
6. Explain why gaskets are needed and name the types used.
7. Describe the difference between RTV sealant and anaerobic sealant.

Fasteners are the parts that hold the engine and the automobile together. *Fastener* is the name given to any device that holds or joins other parts together. Many are threaded. Examples are the screw, the nut and bolt, and the stud and nut. All are widely used in the automobile. Washers and sealants are often used with threaded fasteners to prevent their loosening. Gaskets are frequently used to prevent leaks from between parts held together by threaded fasteners. Other types of fasteners include cotter pins, snap rings, keys, splines, and rivets.

☐ 4-1 THREADED FASTENERS

A fastener that has some form of screw thread on it is a *threaded fastener*. Threaded fasteners let you remove and disassemble parts that may need repair during the life of the car. These parts usually are held together by screws, bolts, and studs (Fig. 4-1).

All threaded fasteners are not the same just because they look alike. For example, many metric fasteners and USCS fasteners are similar in appearance. But using the wrong one may "strip the threads," break the fastener, or cause a failure later while the car is on the road.

When you must install a new fastener, try to get a duplicate of the original fastener. If a duplicate is not available, the replacement fastener

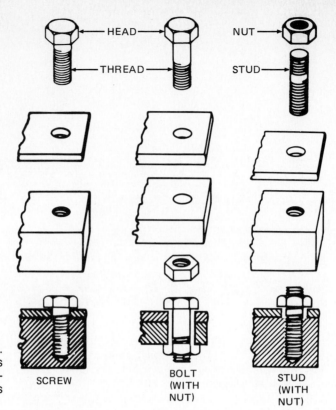

Fig. 4-1 Screw, bolt, and stud. Top shows the attaching parts separated, but aligned for assembly. Bottom shows the parts together.

SCREW

BOLT
(WITH
NUT)

STUD
(WITH
NUT)

you install *must* be equivalent to the one removed. Be careful when selecting a replacement fastener.

□ 4-2 SCREWS, BOLTS, AND STUDS

Screws and *bolts* are types of fasteners that have a head on one end and threads on the other. The screw is turned into a threaded hole in one of the parts being joined together. There are many different types and sizes of screws (Fig. 4-2). Most are turned, or "driven," with a screwdriver or wrench. Many engine and car parts are put together with *machine screws* and *cap screws*. These look like bolts. They are classed as screws because they do not use a nut. Most small screws have slotted heads. However, many Phillips-head and Reed-and-Prince-head screws are used in the car.

Bolts require nuts (Fig. 4-1). The parts that the bolt holds together have larger matching holes through which the bolt passes freely. Then a nut is turned onto the threaded end of the bolt and tightened. Sometimes bolts and screws look the same. If they are used with nuts, they are bolts. If they are turned into a threaded hole, they are screws. However, on the engine, the cylinder head is fastened to the cylinder block without the use of nuts. It is general shop practice to call these particular fasteners "head bolts." Most common bolts have a hexagonal (six-sided), or "hex," head (Fig. 4-2).

A *stud* is a short piece of rod with threads on one or both ends so that it looks like a headless bolt (Fig. 4-1). If the stud is threaded at both ends, one end is screwed into a threaded hole. Then a part to be held in place is installed over the stud. A nut is then turned onto the exposed end of the stud to hold the part in place. Many engines have rocker-arm studs that

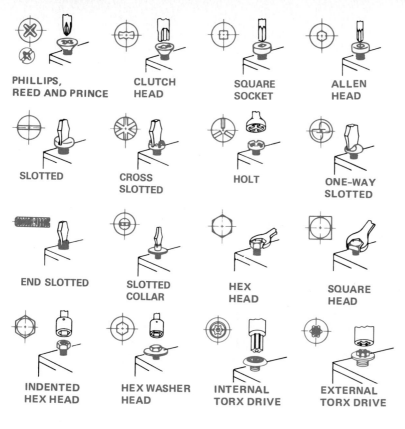

PHILLIPS, REED AND PRINCE

CLUTCH HEAD

SQUARE SOCKET

ALLEN HEAD

SLOTTED

CROSS SLOTTED

HOLT

ONE-WAY SLOTTED

END SLOTTED

SLOTTED COLLAR

HEX HEAD

SQUARE HEAD

INDENTED HEX HEAD

HEX WASHER HEAD

INTERNAL TORX DRIVE

EXTERNAL TORX DRIVE

Fig. 4-2 Screwdrivers and wrenches required to drive various types of screws. *(ATW)*

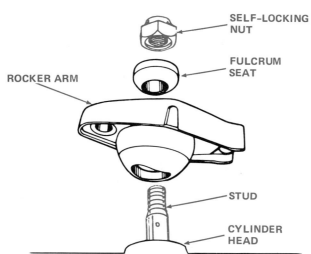

SELF-LOCKING NUT

FULCRUM SEAT

ROCKER ARM

STUD

CYLINDER HEAD

Fig. 4-3 An engine rocker-arm stud, threaded on only one end and using a self-locking nut. *(ATW)*

are threaded on only one end (Fig. 4-3). The other end is a *press-fit* into a hole in the cylinder head. The rocker arm and seat are placed over the stud. Then a nut is threaded onto it to hold the rocker arm in place.

□ 4-3 NUTS

A *nut* is a removable fastener used with a bolt or stud to hold parts together (Figs. 4-1 and 4-3). The nut is made by threading a hole through

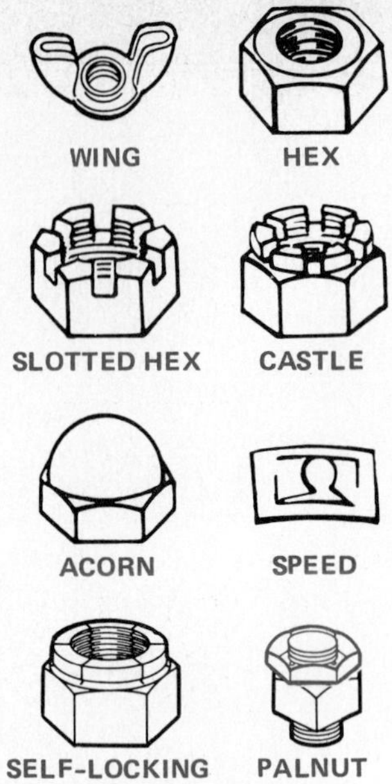

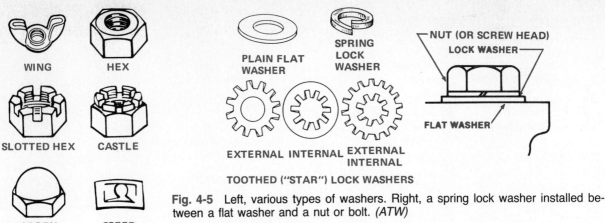

WING   HEX

SLOTTED HEX   CASTLE

ACORN   SPEED

SELF-LOCKING   PALNUT

Fig. 4-4 Nuts are made in various shapes and sizes. *(ATW)*

PLAIN FLAT WASHER   SPRING LOCK WASHER

EXTERNAL INTERNAL   EXTERNAL INTERNAL

TOOTHED ("STAR") LOCK WASHERS

NUT (OR SCREW HEAD)
LOCK WASHER
FLAT WASHER

Fig. 4-5 Left, various types of washers. Right, a spring lock washer installed between a flat washer and a nut or bolt. *(ATW)*

the center of a piece of material (usually metal) which has been shaped to a standard size. Nuts are made in various shapes and sizes (Fig. 4-4). However, like bolt heads, most nuts used on cars have a hexagonal, or six-sided, shape. Slotted and castle (or "castellated") nuts are locked with a cotter pin. Other nuts are locked with lock washers. Cotter pins and lock washers prevent the nuts from working loose and dropping off. Some nuts are designed to be self-locking (Figs. 4-3 and 4-4).

□ 4-4 WASHERS

A *washer* is a thin part with a hole in it for a screw, bolt, or stud to pass through. There are several types of washers (Fig. 4-5). The common types are the plain flat washer and the spring lock washer. The flat washer is used under nuts and bolt heads to provide a smooth bearing surface and to act as a shim. Flat washers are often used under lock washers (Fig. 4-5, right). This prevents them from damaging the surface of the part they are resting against.

Lock washers are used with screws and bolts. The lock washer is placed between the nut or screw head and a flat washer (Fig. 4-5). The edges at the split (in the spring lock washer) cut into the nut or screw head. This keeps it from turning and loosening. Toothed lock washers have many edges to improve the locking effect. Sometimes the flat washer is not used. The lock washer is placed directly against the part.

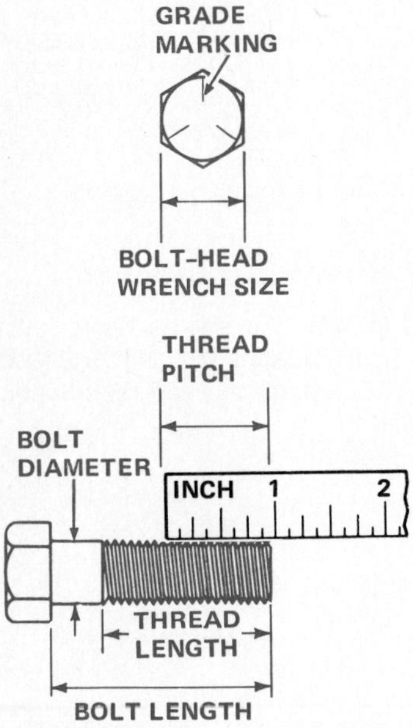

□ 4-5 SCREW THREADS

Screws, bolts, and studs all have threads on the outside (Fig. 4-1). These are called *external* threads. Nuts and threaded holes have threads on the inside, or *internal* threads (Fig. 4-4). Most threads are made by "roll-forming" during manufacture. Threads can also be cut with taps and dies (Chap. 5). Threads, or *screw threads,* are described or "designated" in several ways, according to whether the threads are USCS threads or metric threads.

There are other important measurements of a bolt (Fig. 4-6). These include the length of the bolt, diameter of the bolt, length of the thread, and size of the wrench required to turn the bolt head. Most bolts, screws, studs, and nuts have "right-hand threads." This means that you must turn the fastener clockwise (to the right) to tighten it.

GRADE MARKING

BOLT-HEAD WRENCH SIZE

THREAD PITCH

BOLT DIAMETER

INCH 1 2

THREAD LENGTH

BOLT LENGTH

Fig. 4-6 Various measurements of a bolt. *(ATW)*

☐ 4-6 THREAD PITCH

Nuts and bolts are made in many sizes, from very small to very large. Large nuts and bolts have *coarse* threads (Fig. 4-7). This means there are only a few threads per inch. Smaller nuts and bolts have *fine* threads, with more threads per inch. Very small nuts and bolts have *extra-fine* threads. These have even more threads per inch.

The number of threads per inch is called the *pitch*. On a bolt, you can find the pitch by counting the number of threads in 1 inch (Fig. 4-7). Or you can use a thread gauge to determine pitch. To use the thread gauge, find the blade that has the proper number of teeth to exactly fit the threads (Fig. 4-8). Then read the pitch from the blade. The number is marked on it.

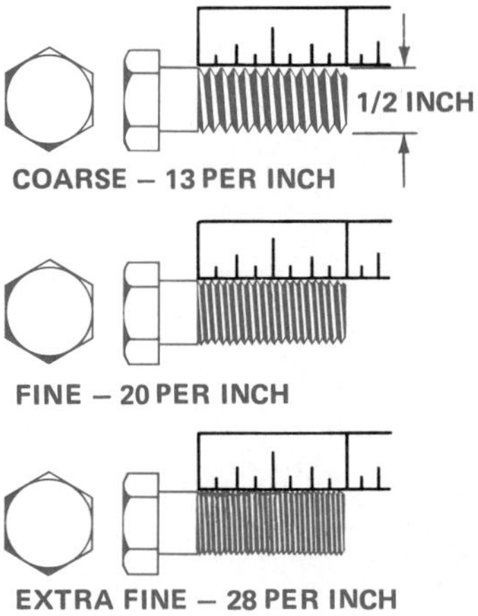

COARSE – 13 PER INCH

1/2 INCH

FINE – 20 PER INCH

EXTRA FINE – 28 PER INCH

Fig. 4-7 Thread series on a ½-inch bolt.

☐ 4-7 THREAD SERIES

There are three thread series: coarse, fine, and extra-fine. These classifications refer to the pitch (number of threads per inch) on each size of threaded fastener. Figure 4-9 shows the thread series for various sizes of screw, bolt, stud, and nut. For example, a ½-inch bolt could have coarse threads (13 threads per inch), fine threads (20 threads per inch), or extra-fine threads (28 threads per inch). A coarse thread shortens disassembly and reassembly time. Fewer turns are required to remove and install it. The fine and extra-fine threads are smaller than the coarse threads. Fine and extra-fine threads are used where greater bolt strength and additional accuracy of assembly are required.

☐ 4-8 THREAD CLASS

There are three thread classes. The difference is in the closeness of fit. Class 1 has the loosest fit. It is easiest to remove and install, even when the threads are dirty and battered. Class 2 has a tighter fit. Class 3 has a very close fit. An external thread, which is used on a bolt, screw, or stud, is called an A thread. An internal thread, which is used in a nut or threaded hole, is called a B thread.

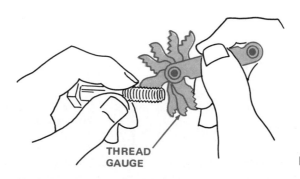

THREAD GAUGE

Fig. 4-8 Using a thread gauge.

Size	Diameter (Decimal)	Threads per Inch		
		Coarse (UNC or NC)	Fine (UNF or NF)	Extra-Fine (UNEF or NEF)
0	0.0600	. . .	80	
1	0.0730	64	72	
2	0.0860	56	64	
3	0.0990	48	56	
4	0.1120	40	48	
5	0.1250	40	44	
6	0.1380	32	40	
8	0.1640	32	36	
10	0.1900	24	32	
12	0.2160	24	28	32
¼	0.2500	20	28	32
⁵⁄₁₆	0.3125	18	24	32
³⁄₈	0.3750	16	24	32
⁷⁄₁₆	0.4375	14	20	28
½	0.5000	13	20	28
⁹⁄₁₆	0.5625	12	18	24
⅝	0.6250	11	18	24
¾	0.7500	10	16	20
⅞	0.8750	9	14	20
1	1.0000	8	12	20
1⅛	1.1250	7	12	18
1¼	1.2500	7	12	18
1⅜	1.3750	6	12	18

Fig. 4-9 Thread series for various sizes of screw, bolt, stud, and nut.

☐ 4-9 THREAD DESIGNATION

In the U.S. Customary System, threads are designated by size, pitch, series, and class. Figure 4-10 shows the complete thread designation for a ¼-20 UNC-2A bolt. The bolt is ¼ inch in diameter. It has coarse threads (20 threads per inch). And the thread is an external, class 2 thread. After the thread designation, a number or fraction may appear. For example, ¼-20x 1½. The 1½ is the bolt length in inches.

You cannot use a ¼-28 bolt with a ¼-20 nut because the threads do not match. The bolt size *and* the thread pitch must be the same for a bolt or screw to fit a matching nut or a threaded hole.

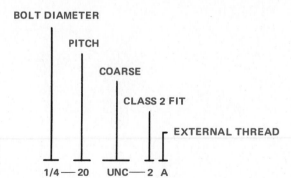

Fig. 4-10 Thread designation in the U.S. Customary System. *(ATW)*

Capscrew Head Markings	Capscrew Body Size Inches—Thread	SAE Grade 1 or 2 (Used Infrequently) Torque		SAE Grade 5 (Used Frequently) Torque		SAE Grade 6 or 7 (Used at Times) Torque		SAE Grade 8 (Used Frequently) Torque	
		ft-lb	N-m	ft-lb	N-m	ft-lb	N-m	ft-lb	N-m
Manufacturer's marks may vary. Three-line markings on heads shown below, for example, indicate SAE Grade 5.	¼–20 –28	5 6	6.7791 8.1349	8 10	10.8465 13.5582	10	13.5582	12 14	16.2698 18.9815
	⁵⁄₁₆–18 –24	11 13	14.9140 17.6256	17 19	23.0489 25.7605	19	25.7605	24 27	32.5396 36.6071
	⅜–16 –24	18 20	24.4047 27.1164	31 35	42.0304 47.4536	34	46.0978	44 49	59.6560 66.4351
	⁷⁄₁₆–14 –20	28 30	37.9629 40.6745	49 55	66.4351 74.5700	55	74.5700	70 78	94.9073 105.7538
	½–13 –20	39 41	52.8769 55.5885	75 85	101.6863 115.2445	85	115.2445	105 120	142.3609 162.6960
	⁹⁄₁₆–12 –18	51 55	69.1467 74.5700	110 120	149.1380 162.6960	120	162.6960	155 170	210.1490 230.4860
	⅝–11 –18	83 95	112.5329 128.8027	150 170	203.3700 230.4860	167	226.4186	210 240	284.7180 325.3920
	¾–10 –16	105 115	142.3609 155.9170	270 295	366.0660 399.9610	280	379.6240	375 420	508.4250 569.4360
	⅞–9 –14	160 175	216.9280 237.2650	395 435	535.5410 589.7730	440	596.5520	605 675	820.2590 915.1650
	1–8 –14	235 250	318.6130 338.9500	590 660	799.9220 894.8280	660	894.8280	910 990	1233.7780 1342.2420

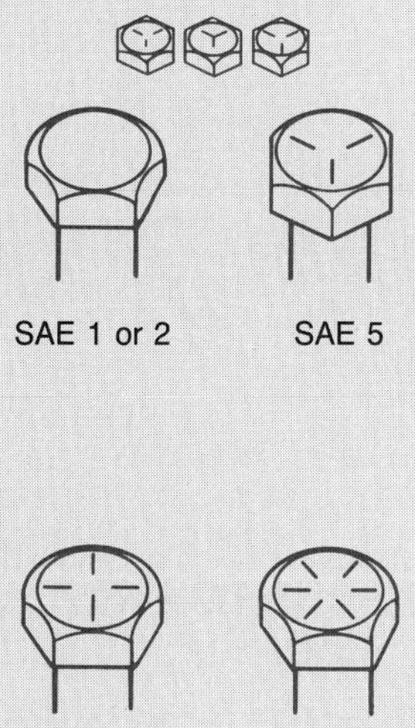

SAE 1 or 2   SAE 5

SAE 6 or 7   SAE 8

Fig. 4-11 Torque specifications and cap-screw head markings. *(American Motors Corporation)*

☐ 4-10 FASTENER STRENGTH MARKINGS

Bolts and hex-head screws are made of materials of different strengths. The table in Fig. 4-11 shows the head markings that tell the quality of the bolt or screw. The minimum tensile strength is the pull (in pounds) that a round rod with a cross section of 1 inch can stand before it breaks. High-quality screws are more expensive. They are used only where added strength is necessary.

METRIC FASTENERS

☐ 4-11 METRIC FASTENERS

Today many cars use metric fasteners. There are some similarities with USCS fasteners. For example, the wrench size for both types is determined by measuring across the flats of the bolt head (Fig. 4-12). Some metric fasteners are *almost* the same size as USCS fasteners. However,

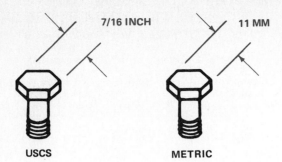

Fig. 4-12 Determining wrench size required for a bolt head.

USCS   METRIC

USCS Thread Size (Inch)	Metric Thread Size		USCS Thread Size (Inch)	Metric Thread Size		USCS Thread Size (Inch)	Metric Thread Size	
	Diameter (mm)	Pitch (mm)		Diameter (mm)	Pitch (mm)		Diameter (mm)	Pitch (mm)
	M1.5 x 0.35		¼-28				M22.0 x 2.50	
0-80				M7.0 x 1.00			M22.0 x 2.00	
	M1.6 x 0.35			M7.0 x 0.75			M22.0 x 1.50	
	M1.8 x 0.35		⁵⁄₁₆-18			⅞-9		
1-64			⁵⁄₁₆-24			⅞-14		
1-72				M8.0 x 1.25			M24.0 x 3.00	
	M2.0 x 0.45			M8.0 x 1.00			M24.0 x 2.00	
	M2.0 x 0.40			M9.0 x 1.25			M24.0 x 1.50	
2-56				M9.0 x 1.00			M25.0 x 2.00	
2-64			⅜-16				M25.0 x 1.50	
	M2.2 x 0.45		⅜-24			1-8		
	M2.3 x 0.40			M10.0 x 1.50		1-12		
	M2.5 x 0.45			M10.0 x 1.25			M26.0 x 3.00	
3-48				M10.0 x 1.00			M27.0 x 3.00	
3-56				M11.0 x 1.50			M27.0 x 2.00	
	M2.6 x 0.45		⁷⁄₁₆-14				M28.0 x 3.00	
4-40			⁷⁄₁₆-20				M28.0 x 2.00	
4-48				M12.0 x 1.75		1⅛-7		
	M3.0 x 0.60			M12.0 x 1.50		1⅛-12		
	M3.0 x 0.50			M12.0 x 1.25			M30.0 x 3.50	
5-40			½-13				M30.0 x 3.00	
5-44			½-20				M30.0 x 2.00	
	M3.5 x 0.60			M14.0 x 2.00		1¼-7		
6-32				M14.0 x 1.50		1¼-12		
6-40				M14.0 x 1.25			M32.0 x 3.50	
	M4.0 x 0.75		⁹⁄₁₆-12				M32.0 x 2.00	
	M4.0 x 0.70		⁹⁄₁₆-18				M33.0 x 3.50	
8-32				M15.0 x 1.50			M33.0 x 3.00	
8-36			⅝-11				M33.0 x 2.00	
	M4.5 x 0.75		⅝-18				M34.0 x 3.50	
10-24				M16.0 x 2.00		1⅜-6		
10-32				M16.0 x 1.50		1⅜-12		
	M5.0 x 1.00			M17.0 x 1.50			M36.0 x 4.00	
	M5.0 x 0.90			M18.0 x 2.50			M36.0 x 3.00	
	M5.0 x 0.80			M18.0 x 2.00			M36.0 x 2.00	
12-24				M18.0 x 1.50			M38.0 x 4.00	
12-28				M19.0 x 2.50				
	M5.5 x 0.90		¾-10					
	M6.0 x 1.00		¾-16					
	M6.0 x 0.75			M20.0 x 2.50				
	M6.3 x 1.00			M20.0 x 2.00				
¼-20				M20.0 x 1.50				

Fig. 4-13 Chart comparing USCS thread sizes with metric sizes.

INCH		METRIC	
⁵⁄₁₆-18		M8x1.25	
Thread major diameter in inches	Number of threads per inch	Thread major diameter in millimeters	Distance between threads in millimeters

Fig. 4-14 Metric and USCS thread designations. *(Chrysler Corporation)*

they are not interchangeable! The threads are not the same. Metric threads are measured in millimeters.

□ 4-12 METRIC FASTENER SIZES

The sizes of metric fasteners are not as completely standardized as in the U.S. Customary System. Many manufacturers follow the standard metric fastener sizes defined by the International Standards Organization (ISO). These are shown in Fig. 4-13. This system reduces the number of different metric fasteners, while retaining the best strength qualities in each thread size. For example, the USCS ¼-20 and ¼-28 screws are replaced by the metric M6.0x1 screw. It has nearly the same diameter and 25.4 threads per inch. This places the thread pitch between the USCS coarse and fine.

□ 4-13 METRIC THREAD DESIGNATION

Metric and USCS thread designations differ slightly. The difference is shown in Fig. 4-14. In the metric system, the "M8" indicates the bolt is 8 mm in diameter. The "1.25" is the distance between the threads. On the bolt designation shown in Fig. 4-14, the distance between each thread is 1.25 mm. This measurement is made from the crest of one thread to the crest of the next thread (Fig. 4-15).

□ 4-14 METRIC FASTENER STRENGTH

Both USCS and metric bolts have head markings to show bolt strength. Slash marks on the head of a USCS bolt indicate its strength (Fig. 4-11). The more slash marks on the head, the stronger the bolt. Metric bolts

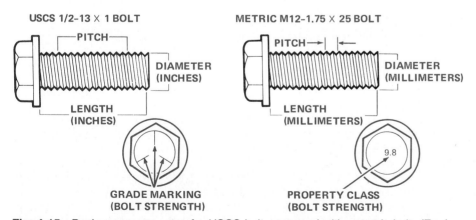

Fig. 4-15 Basic measurements of a USCS bolt compared with a metric bolt. *(Ford Motor Company)*

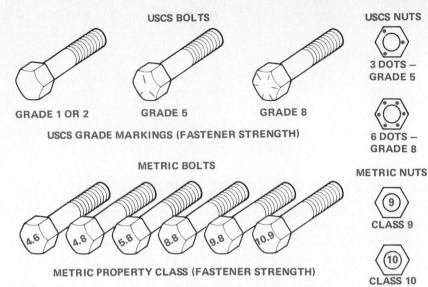

USCS BOLTS

GRADE 1 OR 2   GRADE 5   GRADE 8

USCS GRADE MARKINGS (FASTENER STRENGTH)

METRIC BOLTS

4.6   4.8   5.8   8.8   9.8   10.9

METRIC PROPERTY CLASS (FASTENER STRENGTH)

USCS NUTS

3 DOTS – GRADE 5

6 DOTS – GRADE 8

METRIC NUTS

9
CLASS 9

10
CLASS 10

Fig. 4-16 Fastener strength markings. *(Ford Motor Company)*

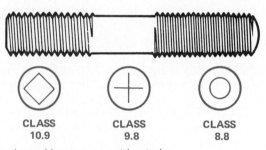

CLASS 10.9   CLASS 9.8   CLASS 8.8

Fig. 4-17 Strength markings on a metric stud.

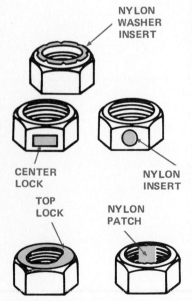

NYLON WASHER INSERT

CENTER LOCK

NYLON INSERT

TOP LOCK

NYLON PATCH

Fig. 4-18 Various types of prevailing-torque nuts. *(General Motors Corporation)*

have the "property class" number (Fig. 4-15, right) on the bolt head (Fig. 4-16). The higher the number, the greater the strength. Common metric bolt markings are 9.8 and 10.9. Nut strength markings are also shown in Fig. 4-16. Large studs may have the property class number stamped on them. Smaller studs are stamped on the end with a geometric code (Fig. 4-17).

☐ 4-15 PREVAILING-TORQUE FASTENERS

Many nuts and bolts are designed to have a continuous resistance to turning. This type of fastener is called a *prevailing-torque fastener*. No lock washer is required. The *interference fit* of the threads prevents the fastener from loosening.

For example, a prevailing-torque nut is designed to have an interference between the nut (Fig. 4-18) and the bolt threads. As a result, the nut resists loosening, even if it is not tightened down. The interference is often caused by distortion of the top of an all-metal nut. Another method is by using a nylon patch on the threads in the middle of the held flat. A nylon insert may also be used between the nut and bolt threads.

A prevailing-torque bolt (Fig. 4-19) is designed to have an interference between the bolt and the nut threads or the threads of a tapped hole. The interference is caused by distorting some of the bolt threads or by using a patch of nylon or adhesive on the threads.

DRY ADHESIVE COATING   THREAD PROFILE DEFORMED   NYLON STRIP   OUT-OF-ROUND THREAD AREA

Fig. 4-19 Various types of prevailing-torque bolts. *(General Motors Corporation)*

☐ 4-16 REUSE OF PREVAILING-TORQUE FASTENERS

Prevailing-torque fasteners which are rusty or damaged should be replaced with new ones of equal or greater strength. However, sometimes clean unrusted prevailing-torque nuts and bolts may be reused. Before installation, inspect each one as follows:

1. Clean any dirt and other foreign material off the nut or bolt.
2. Inspect the nut or bolt for cracks, elongation, or other signs of misuse or overtightening. If there is any doubt, discard the fastener.
3. Assemble the parts, and hand-start the nut or bolt.
4. Before the fastener seats, check that the specified torque is required to overcome the resistance to turn. The torque specifications for most common sizes of prevailing-torque nuts and bolts are given in Fig. 4-20. If the fastener turns too easily, replace it. If installed, it will work loose.
5. Tighten the fastener to the installed torque specified in the manufacturer's service manual.

Prevailing Torque for Metric Fasteners								
	Millimeters	**6 & 6.3**	**8**	**10**	**12**	**14**	**16**	**20**
Nuts and all-metal bolts	N-m	0.4	0.8	1.4	2.2	3.0	4.2	7.0
	in-lb	4.0	7.0	12	18	25	35	57
Adhesive- or nylon-coated bolts	N-m	0.4	0.6	1.2	1.6	2.4	3.4	5.6
	in-lb	4.0	5.0	10	14	20	28	46

Prevailing Torque for USCS Fasteners								
	Inch	**¼**	**⁵⁄₁₆**	**³⁄₈**	**⁷⁄₁₆**	**½**	**⁹⁄₁₆**	**⁵⁄₈**	**¾**
Nuts and all-metal bolts	N-m	0.4	0.6	1.4	1.8	2.4	3.2	4.2	6.2
	in-lb	4.0	5.0	12	15	20	27	35	51
Adhesive- or nylon-coated bolts	N-m	0.4	0.6	1.0	1.4	1.8	2.6	3.4	5.2
	in-lb	4.0	5.0	9.0	12	15	22	28	43

Fig. 4-20 Torque specifications for common sizes of prevailing-torque nuts and bolts. *(General Motors Corporation)*

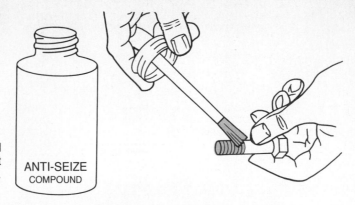

Fig. 4-21 Antiseize compound should be used on any bolt that goes into aluminum threads. *(ATW)*

ANTI-SEIZE COMPOUND

□ 4-17 ANTISEIZE COMPOUND

The specifications for tightening a fastener are usually given for clean dry threads. However, most bolts are steel. Sometimes they fit into aluminum threads cut into an aluminum cylinder head or block. Cylinder-head bolts and main-bearing-cap bolts have high torque specifications. When such a bolt is removed from an aluminum part, the aluminum threads may be damaged or even pulled out by the bolt. This is because of corrosion, and because steel bolts tend to lock, or "seize," in aluminum threads.

To prevent this, an *antiseize compound* should be used on any bolt that goes into aluminum threads (Fig. 4-21). A coating of antiseize compound on the threads prevents corrosion, seizing, galling, and pitting. Later, the bolt may be removed easily without damage to the threads.

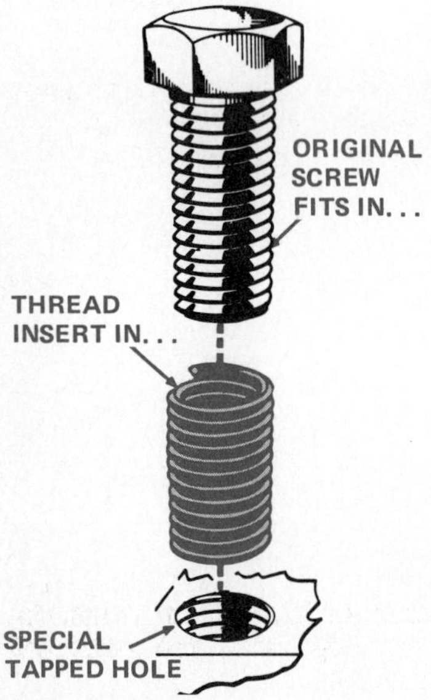

□ 4-18 THREAD INSERTS

Damaged or worn threads in a cylinder block, cylinder head, or other part can often be replaced with a thread insert (Fig. 4-22). To make the repair, you need a thread repair kit. First, drill out the hole using the same size drill that is equal in diameter to the bolt. For example, for a ¼-inch bolt, use a ¼-inch drill. Then tap the hole with the special tap from the thread repair kit. These taps cut the special threads for the insert.

Using the inserting tool from the thread repair kit, install the thread insert into the hole (Fig. 4-22). This brings the hole back to its original thread size. Now the original bolt can be used in it. After the thread insert is installed, apply antiseize compound to the inside thread of the insert. Then install the bolt and tighten to the specified torque.

ORIGINAL SCREW FITS IN. . .

THREAD INSERT IN . . .

SPECIAL TAPPED HOLE

Fig. 4-22 Installing a thread insert into a tapped hole. *(Chrysler Corporation)*

MECHANICAL FASTENERS

□ 4-19 COTTER PINS

A *cotter pin* is a split soft-steel pin with a loop at one end for a head (Fig. 4-23). The cotter pin is inserted in a drilled hole (Fig. 4-24). The split ends are spread to lock the pin in position. This usually secures a castle nut (Fig. 4-24) or other type of pin. To use the cotter pin with a castle nut, tighten the nut until the nut slots are aligned with the hole. Then insert the cotter pin and bend the legs outward. One method is shown in Fig. 4-24.

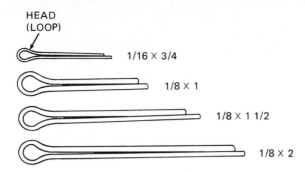

HEAD (LOOP)

1/16 × 3/4

1/8 × 1

1/8 × 1 1/2

1/8 × 2

Fig. 4-23 Various sizes of cotter pins. *(ATW)*

□ *4-20 RIVETS*

A *rivet* (Fig. 4-25) is a headed metal fastener which joins parts together when a head is formed on the headless end. In the car, rivets hold the brake lining on the brake shoes. They also keep the clutch lining in place. Rivets are used to hold some transmission linkage together and to attach trim and upholstery to the car.

One end of the rivet has a head (Fig. 4-25). After the rivet is in place, a driver or a hammer-and-rivet set is used to form the head on the other end.

Blind rivets, or "Pop" rivets (Fig. 4-26), are special rivets for blind holes. These are holes where one end of the rivet cannot be reached to flatten it. To install a blind rivet, load the stem of the rivet into the rivet

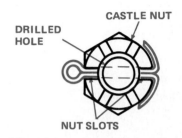

DRILLED HOLE

CASTLE NUT

NUT SLOTS

Fig. 4-24 A cotter pin is installed through a drilled hole to secure a castle nut in place. *(ATW)*

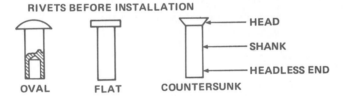

RIVETS BEFORE INSTALLATION

HEAD

SHANK

HEADLESS END

OVAL   FLAT   COUNTERSUNK

RIVETS AFTER INSTALLATION

OVAL   COUNTERSUNK

Fig. 4-25 Rivets before installation (top) and after installation (bottom).

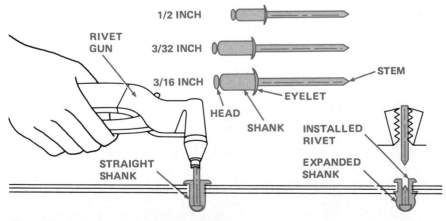

RIVET GUN

1/2 INCH

3/32 INCH

3/16 INCH

STEM

EYELET

HEAD

SHANK

INSTALLED RIVET

STRAIGHT SHANK

EXPANDED SHANK

Fig. 4-26 Installing a blind rivet. *(ATW)*

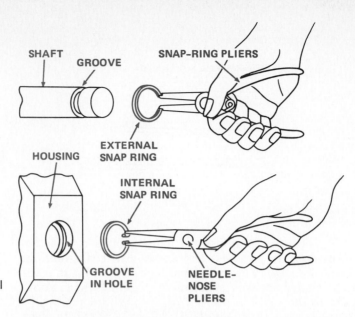

Fig. 4-27 Internal and external snap rings. *(ATW)*

gun. Then insert the shank of the rivet into the hole. Squeeze the handle of the rivet gun. This pulls the stem of the rivet out until it breaks off. Now the rivet is set in place.

The head on the blind side of the hole is formed as the stem is pulled out. The small stem head pulls against the soft metal shank on the blind side of the hole. The shank collapses and expands before the stem breaks off. This secures the blind rivet in place.

Rivets are usually removed by cutting off one end with a chisel. They can also be driven out with a punch or drilled out.

□ *4-21 SNAP RINGS*

External retaining rings, or "snap rings," prevent end-to-end movement of a gear or bearing on a shaft (Fig. 4-27). Internal snap rings are used in housings to keep shafts or other parts in position. The external snap ring must be expanded, or stretched, with *snap-ring pliers*. Then it is slipped over the end of a grooved shaft and released to seat in the groove (Fig. 4-27, top). The internal snap ring must be squeezed so it can slip into the hole and then expand into a groove in the housing (Fig. 4-27, bottom). Many types of snap rings are used in automobiles. Some can be removed and installed with needle-nose pliers (Fig. 4-27). Others require the use of various types of snap-ring pliers (Figs. 4-27 and 4-28).

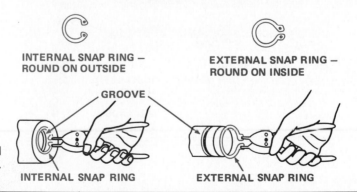

Fig. 4-28 Installing internal and external Truarc retaining rings. *(ATW)*

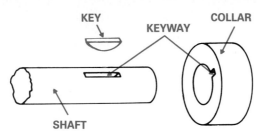

Fig. 4-29 A key locks parts together by fitting into slots called *keyways*.

The Truarc retaining ring is a special type of snap ring. Its two lips have holes for the pin ends of special snap-ring pliers (Fig. 4-28). With the pins securely in the holes, there is less chance of the ring slipping off the pliers during removal and installation.

☐ 4-22 KEYS AND SPLINES

Keys and splines are used to lock gears, pulleys, collars, and other similar parts to shafts so that they will rotate together. Figure 4-29 shows a typical key installation. The key is wedge-shaped and fits into slots called *keyways*. The keyways are cut in the shaft and collar (or other part being installed). The key locks the shaft and collar together.

To install the key, place the key into the keyway in the shaft (Fig. 4-29). Then slide the collar over the key until the collar is in place. If the collar or gear is to be installed on the end of the shaft, the keyway often extends to the end of the shaft. With this type of assembly, the collar is placed on the shaft so that the keyways match. Then a wedge-shaped key is driven into the two keyways for a tight fit. No other holding device is required to fasten the collar firmly to the shaft.

Splines are internal and external teeth cut in both the shaft and the installed part (Fig. 4-30). When the gear, pulley, or collar is installed on the shaft, it is the same as having many keys between the two parts. In many assemblies, the splines fit loosely so that the gear or other part is free to move back and forth on the splines. However, the splines force both parts to rotate together. Splines may be straight or curved (Fig. 4-30).

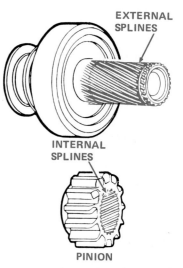

Fig. 4-30 Internal and external splines.

GASKETS

☐ 4-23 GASKETS

A *gasket* is a thin layer of soft material such as paper, cork, rubber, or copper. It is placed between two flat surfaces to make a tight seal (Fig. 4-31). When the gasket is squeezed by the tightening of fasteners, the soft material fills any small irregularities in the mating surfaces. This prevents any leakage of fluid, vacuum, or pressure from the joint. Sometimes the gasket is used as a shim to take up space.

Various types of gaskets are used throughout the automobile, especially in the engine. They seal joints between engine parts, such as between the oil pan, manifolds, or water pump and the cylinder head or block. A complete *engine-overhaul gasket set* for an in-line six-cylinder engine is shown in Fig. 4-32. In most joints, holes through the gasket allow it to seal in fuel, oil, or coolant. At the same time, it keeps out dirt, water, and air.

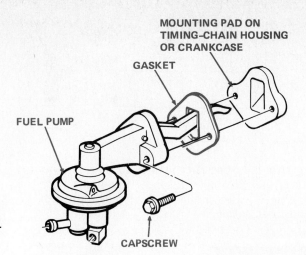

MOUNTING PAD ON
TIMING–CHAIN HOUSING
OR CRANKCASE

GASKET

FUEL PUMP

CAPSCREW

Fig. 4-31 Installation of a gasket. *(Chrysler Corporation)*

□ 4-24 FORMED-IN-PLACE GASKETS

Today many gaskets are "formed-in-place." This means that instead of using a preshaped layer of cork, rubber, or paper, the gasket is formed by a bead of plastic gasket material (Fig. 4-33). Formed-in-place gaskets are found on valve covers, thermostat housings, water pumps, axle covers, and other parts. When the car manufacturer uses formed-in-place gaskets, the material is applied by a machine. When the mechanic uses the gasket material, it is applied by squeezing a tube (Fig. 4-33). This provides a continuous bead of material which forms the gasket.

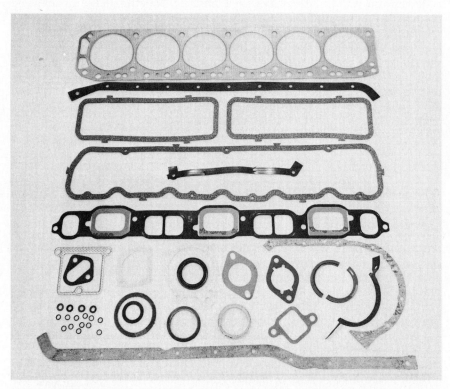

Fig. 4-32 Engine-overhaul gasket set for a six-cylinder engine, showing all the gaskets and seals used in the engine. *(McCord Replacement Products Division of McCord Corporation)*

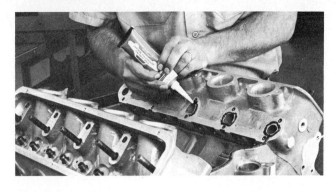

Two types of materials are used for formed-in-place gaskets. These are *aerobic* and *anaerobic*. Aerobic material is also known as "self-curing" or "room-temperature-vulcanizing (RTV)" silicone rubber. RTV and anaerobic materials are different. They cannot be used interchangeably.

SEALANTS

☐ 4-25 RTV SILICONE-RUBBER SEALANTS

Figure 4-33 shows a mechanic making a gasket by squeezing a tube of RTV silicone-rubber sealant. The bead of sealant forms a skin within 15 minutes after it is exposed to the air. The room-temperature air causes the sealer to "vulcanize," or "cure." A material that cures only in the presence of air is called *aerobic*. The bead is dry to the touch in about 1 hour. Full curing takes about 24 hours.

RTV sealant is normally used on surfaces that flex or vibrate, such as a valve cover. The sealant may be used with or without a separate gasket. If a gasket is used, apply the sealant to both sides and assemble immediately. If no gasket is used, apply the sealant to one surface and allow a skin to form. Then assemble the parts. The RTV sealant will act as a formed-in-place gasket.

☐ 4-26 ANAEROBIC SEALANT

An anaerobic material cures only when subjected to pressure and the *absence* of air. This means it hardens when squeezed tightly between two surfaces. It will not cure if left in the uncovered tube.

Anaerobic material may be used as an adhesive, sealer, and locking cement. Applied to machined surfaces between parts, it may eliminate the separate gasket. However, anaerobic material should not be used on parts that flex.

Figure 4-34 shows an anaerobic material being applied to the outside of a bushing. When the bushing is installed, the anaerobic material fills the small spaces between the outside of the bushing and the hole. Deprived of air, the material hardens. This locks the bushing in place. Anaerobic material is frequently used on bolts, nuts, and screws.

To remove a small screw that has been locked in place with anaerobic material, you must first soften the material. Heat the area around the screw with an electric soldering gun. Never use a torch or other open flame. Sometimes applying fresh anaerobic material to the hard material will soften it.

Fig. 4-34 Applying an anaerobic material to the outside of a bushing. *(Loctite Corporation)*

Select the *one* correct, best, or most probable answer to each question. Then check your answers against the correct answers given at the end of the book.

1. Fasteners that have threads on the outside are
   a. nuts, bolts, and screws
   b. screws, bolts, and studs
   c. threaded holes and nuts
   d. splines, rivets, and screws

2. Pitch is the
   a. number of threads per inch
   b. depth of the threads
   c. thread series
   d. thread classes

3. The three thread series are
   a. class 1, 2, and 3
   b. series 1, 2, and 3
   c. coarse, fine, and extra-fine
   d. pitch, series, and class

4. An external thread is called
   a. an A thread
   b. a B thread
   c. a C thread
   d. none of the above

5. The most common bolts
   a. have hexagonal heads
   b. have six-sided heads
   c. have hex heads
   d. all of the above

6. The purpose of the cotter pin is to
   a. fasten the cotter safely
   b. prevent the cotter from loosening
   c. prevent the nut from loosening
   d. prevent the splines from loosening

7. To keep the nut from loosening, use
   a. a Palnut
   b. a cotter pin
   c. a lock washer
   d. any of the above

8. The two types of snap rings are
   a. threaded and with teeth
   b. internal and external
   c. split and solid
   d. retainer and locking

9. Keys and splines
   a. lock nuts to bolts
   b. lock plates and shafts together
   c. lock gears, pulleys, and collars to shafts
   d. fasten screws or studs in place

10. Thread inserts are used to
    a. repair damaged internal threads
    b. repair damaged external threads
    c. replace faulty screws or studs
    d. repair damaged nuts

11. A gasket is used to
    a. seal in fuel, oil, or coolant
    b. seal out dirt, water, and air
    c. take up space
    d. all of the above

12. Gaskets that are made by squeezing material from a tube are called
    a. precut gaskets
    b. preshaped gaskets
    c. framed-by-the-part gaskets
    d. formed-in-place gaskets

13. An aerobic material is also known as
    a. RTV (room-temperature-vulcanizing)
    b. self-curing silicone rubber
    c. both a and b
    d. neither a nor b

14. To make a gasket on a valve cover, you should use
    a. RTV silicone rubber
    b. anaerobic sealant
    c. antiseize compound
    d. none of the above

15. To loosen a screw held with anaerobic sealant, you should
    a. hit the screw with a hammer
    b. heat the sealant with an electric soldering gun
    c. spray the sealant with oil
    d. soak the area with water

CHAPTER 5
SHOP TOOLS AND EQUIPMENT

After studying this chapter, you should be able to:

1. List and describe the basic hand tools used in the shop and explain how each is used.

2. List and describe the purpose of cutting tools used in the shop and explain how to use them.

3. List and describe power tools used in the shop.

4. Explain how to clean parts safely using a parts washer or solvent tank.

You may be a highly skilled auto mechanic. But when something breaks on the car, you need tools to fix it. A *tool* is almost any device you can use to do work or to make working easier. Even with advanced electronic equipment in the shop, the mechanic still relies on tools. Therefore, you must *have, choose,* and *use* the correct tools to perform a job properly. Without the proper tools, or without knowing how to use them, you will waste time and lower your productivity. You may even injure yourself or damage the car.

HAND TOOLS

□ 5-1 TYPES OF SHOP TOOLS

Two main types of tools are used in the auto shop. One type is called *hand tools* (Fig. 5-1). Your hand supplies the energy needed to operate them. The hammer and the wrench are good examples of hand tools (Fig. 5-2). The other type is called *machine tools,* or *power tools.* Electricity or compressed air supplies the energy for these tools. An example of a power tool that uses electricity is the electric drill (Fig. 5-3). Tools using compressed air as the energy source are called *pneumatic tools,* or *air tools.* "Pneumatic" means of or pertaining to air. The air-powered impact wrench used to remove and install nuts and bolts is an example (Fig. 5-4).

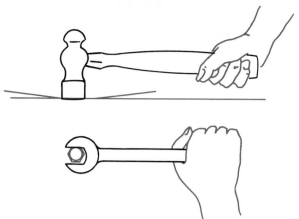

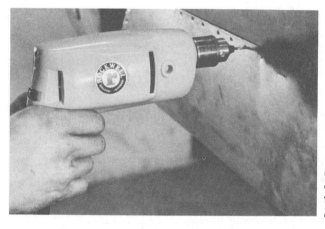

Fig. 5-2 The hammer and wrench are examples of hand tools. *(ATW)*

Fig. 5-1 A complete set of mechanic's hand tools *(Snap-on Tools Corporation)*

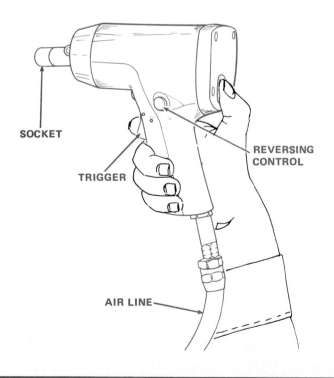

Fig. 5-3 An electric drill is an example of an electric power tool. *(Rockwell International)*

SOCKET

REVERSING CONTROL

TRIGGER

AIR LINE

Fig. 5-4 An air-powered impact wrench is an example of a pneumatic tool. *(ATW)*

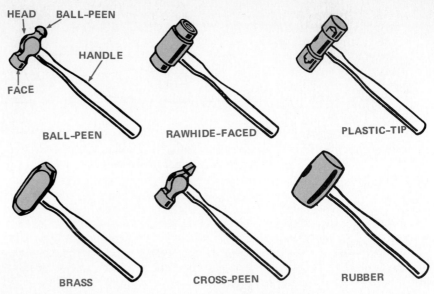

Fig. 5-5 Various types of hammers used in the auto shop.

Some hand tools are used to cut and remove metal. These are called *cutting tools*. Common mechanic's hand tools, cutting tools, and shop equipment are described in the following pages. Later chapters cover the special power tools that are used for jobs such as grinding valves, honing engine cylinders, and refinishing disk-brake rotors.

☐ 5-2 HAMMER

A *hammer* (Fig. 5-5) is a hand tool used for striking. It usually is made by attaching a shaped head of steel, plastic, or other material to one end of a wood handle. There are several kinds of hammers (Fig. 5-5). However, the ball-peen hammer is the most used by mechanics. It is a general, all-purpose hammer made in various weights from 2 ounces [57 g] up to 2½ pounds [1.1 kg]. The size of a ball-peen hammer is given as the weight of the head.

Rawhide-faced, rubber, plastic-tipped, and brass hammers are "soft" hammers designed for special jobs. They are used for striking on easily scratched surfaces. The cross-peen hammer is used in metalwork, such as body work on damaged cars.

Figure 5-6 shows the right and wrong ways to grip a hammer. When using a hammer, grip the end and swing the hammer so that the head strikes the surface squarely. The swinging action should come from your elbow, not from your wrist or shoulder.

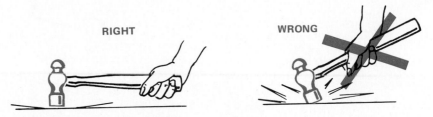

Fig. 5-6 Right and wrong ways to use a hammer.

CAUTION Always make sure that the hammerhead is firmly wedged on the handle. A loose head could fly off and hurt someone. The head is held on by a wedge (Fig. 5-7) or screw in the end of the handle.

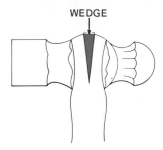

Fig. 5-7 Wedge installation in a ball-peen hammer.

□ 5-3 SCREWDRIVERS

A tool used for driving, or turning, screws is a *screwdriver*. Screwdrivers are made in a variety of sizes, shapes, and special-purpose designs. Figure 5-8 (top) shows a typical slotted-head screwdriver. Figure 5-9 shows how the screwdriver blade should completely fill the screw slot to avoid damaging the head. When the screw is turned clockwise (to the right), it goes into the hole. When the screw is turned counterclockwise (to the left), it backs out.

Four sizes of screwdrivers are used most frequently in automotive work. Probably the handiest is the "stubby," which has a blade about 1 to 1½ inches [25 to 38 mm] long. The others have blades that are 4, 6, and 8 inches [100, 150, and 200 mm] long. Wood handles and square shanks are preferred by some mechanics. A wrench can be used on the square shank to help turn stubborn screws.

The slotted-head screw is only one of many types of screw. Other types are shown in Figs. 4-2 and 5-8. The Phillips-head screw (Fig. 5-8) has two slots that cross at the center. It is widely used on automobile trim and molding. There is less chance that the Phillips screwdriver will slip out of the slots and damage the finish. The differences between the Phillips and the Reed-and-Prince screwdrivers are shown in Fig. 5-10. Both types are cross-slotted, but the angles are different.

Figure 4-2 shows other screw heads and the special screwdrivers needed to turn them. Some screws have hex heads. They are turned with wrenches.

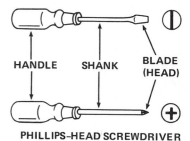

SLOTTED-HEAD SCREWDRIVER

HANDLE   SHANK   BLADE (HEAD)

PHILLIPS-HEAD SCREWDRIVER

Fig. 5-8 Two basic types of screwdrivers. *(ATW)*

□ 5-4 PLIERS

Pliers are hand tools that have a pair of pivoted jaws. These jaws can be used for holding, bending, or cutting. There are two basic types of pliers, gripping pliers and cutting pliers (Fig. 5-11). All pliers are a type of adjustable wrench. The jaws are adjustable because the two legs move on a pivot. This opens and closes the jaws, allowing an object to be gripped or cut.

Channellock pliers (Fig. 5-11) are a type of utility pliers. They have wide-opening jaws and extra-long handles to make them a strong gripping tool. Channellock pliers have a "tongue-and-groove" (or "groove-

Fig. 5-9 The tip of the screwdriver blade should completely fill the slot in the screw head.

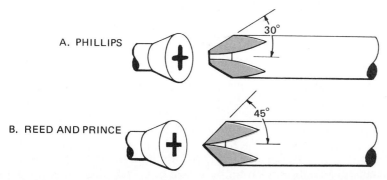

A. PHILLIPS

30°

B. REED AND PRINCE

45°

Fig. 5-10 Difference between the Phillips and the Reed-and-Prince screwdrivers.

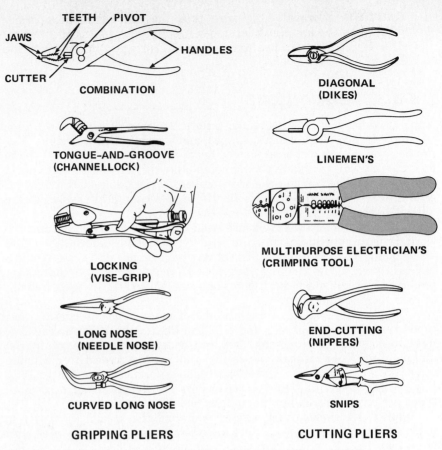

Fig. 5-11 Various types of gripping pliers and cutting pliers. *(ATW)*

and-land") design. The tongues, or lands, are on one jaw, and the grooves are in the other. To change the distance the jaws can open, the relative positions of the grooves and lands are changed. The design permits the jaws to be parallel to each other at any setting. This makes the pliers less likely to slip when gripping an object.

Vise-Grip pliers (Fig. 5-11) are locking-jaw pliers, sometimes called a *locking-pliers wrench.* They are a combination tool that can be used as pliers, a wrench, and a clamp or small vise. The jaws can be locked onto an object. A screw in the end of the primary handle is turned to adjust the size of the jaw opening. When the jaws are adjusted to grip an object, closing the handles will lock the jaws in place. They are released by pulling on the release lever.

> **CAREFUL** Never use gripping pliers on hardened steel surfaces. This dulls the teeth in the jaws. Pliers must never be used to turn nuts or bolt heads. The jaws will slip, rounding off the edges of the hex. Then a wrench will no longer fit the nut or bolt head properly.

Cutting pliers (Fig. 5-11) are used to cut wire and strip insulation from it. Instead of jaws with teeth, nippers have cutting edges. They are used to cut wire, thin sheet metal, and small bolts. However, most sheet-metal cutting is done with snips. Some gripping pliers include a small cutter close to the pivot.

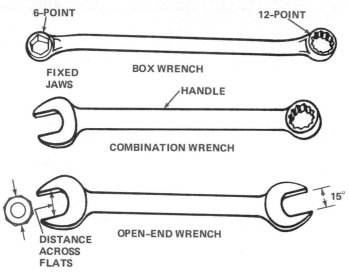

Fig. 5-12 Box, combination, and open-end wrenches. *(ATW)*

□ 5-5 WRENCHES

A *wrench* is a long-handled tool with fixed or adjustable jaws (Fig. 5-12). It usually is used for turning nuts, bolts, or screws with hex heads. The long handle provides leverage to increase the turning force. Today the name "wrench" is used for a great variety of turning or twisting tools, such as the *impact wrench* (Fig. 5-4).

Three types of wrenches that a mechanic needs are the open-end wrench, the box wrench, and the combination wrench (Fig. 5-12). Open-end wrenches usually have the jaw opening at a 15 degree angle to the handle. This permits turning in a tight place. The nut or bolt is turned as far as possible. Then the wrench can be flipped over to permit further turning. Most open-end wrenches have a different size opening on each end.

> **CAREFUL** Never use an open-end wrench to final-tighten a nut or bolt or to free a frozen bolt. The jaws may spread enough to allow the wrench to slip. A box wrench or a socket (□ 5-7) should be used.

The box wrench (Fig. 5-12) has an opening that surrounds, or "boxes," the nut or bolt head. The advantage of this wrench is that it will not slip off. However, the box must be lifted completely off and then placed back on for each swing. A thin head allows the box wrench to be used in restricted places. The typical box wrench has 12 notches, or "points," in the head. Using this wrench, you can install a nut or bolt in a place where the wrench can be swung only about 15 degrees. The six-point end can be used on many nuts and bolt heads that have been rounded off. On these, the 12-point end (which has less contact area) would slip off. Some box wrenches have the head set at an angle of 15 degrees to the handle. This provides clearance for your hand while swinging the wrench.

A combination wrench (Fig. 5-12) combines a box wrench with an open-end wrench. One end of the combination wrench has a box opening. The other has an open end. Both are usually the same size. The open end is used for running the nut or bolt on or off. The box end is used for the final tightening or breaking loose of a nut or bolt. This lets you use first one type and then the other by reversing ends.

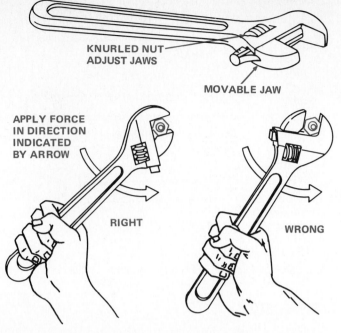

KNURLED NUT ADJUST JAWS

MOVABLE JAW

APPLY FORCE IN DIRECTION INDICATED BY ARROW

RIGHT

WRONG

Fig. 5-13 How to use an adjustable wrench. *(Ford Motor Company)*

□ 5-6 ADJUSTABLE WRENCHES

An adjustable wrench (Fig. 5-13) has a movable jaw that can be adjusted to fit nuts and bolt heads of various sizes. Figure 5-13 shows the wrong way and the right way to use an ajustable wrench. The jaws must be tight against the flats of the nut or bolt before you apply force.

□ 5-7 SOCKET WRENCHES

A socket set (Fig. 5-14) is one of the most versatile sets of tools in the auto mechanic's toolbox. Basically, the *socket wrench* is similar to the box wrench (□ 5-5). However, the head, or "socket," is detachable. You make up the socket wrench that you need from the set in your toolbox. Select a handle, or "driver." Several types of drivers are shown in Fig. 5-14. Then select the socket that will fit the bolt head or nut. There are several kinds and many sizes of sockets (Fig. 5-15). Attach the socket to the driver (Fig. 5-16). The 12-point socket is the most common. If an extension or a universal joint is needed, it is attached to the driver before the socket is attached.

A typical socket set is shown in Fig. 5-14. It consists of several different types of drivers, extensions, a universal joint, and a variety of sockets. Many socket sets are packaged in a case with a special place for each piece in the set. By checking the case, you can see immediately which pieces are missing. In addition, the case makes the socket set easier to clean and store without danger of losing pieces. With every tool in its place, little time is lost trying to find a small tool in a large toolbox.

The drive end of the socket, which snaps onto the handle, is square and always sized in fractions of an inch. The "drive size" is determined by the width of the square driving lug on the driver or handle (Fig. 5-16). Commonly used socket sets are the ¼-inch, ⅜-inch, and ½-inch drive. In

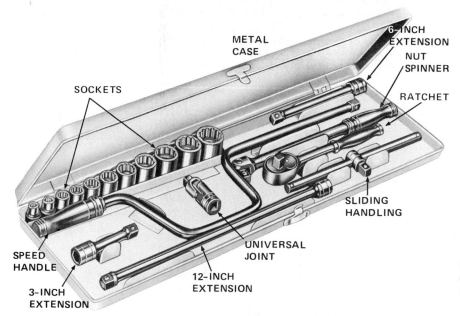

Fig. 5-14 A socket set in a metal case, with handles, extensions, and universal joint. *(Snap-on Tools Corporation)*

a ⅜-inch-drive set, for example, all the drivers have a ⅜-inch square driving lug. To fit this, all the sockets have a ⅜-inch square drive-end opening (Fig. 5-16). For work on imported and domestic cars made to metric measurements, you need metric sockets. USCS sockets will not properly fit metric nuts and bolts.

Figure 5-15 shows three common types of socket openings. The 12-point socket is the most widely used. However, it may slip off nuts and

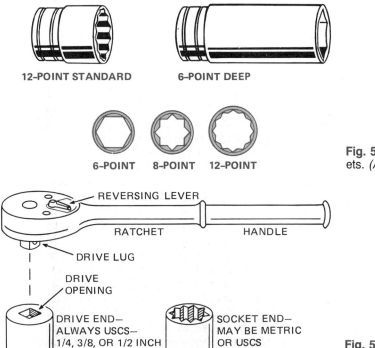

Fig. 5-15 Various types of sockets. *(ATW)*

Fig. 5-16 Attaching the socket to the ratchet handle. *(ATW)*

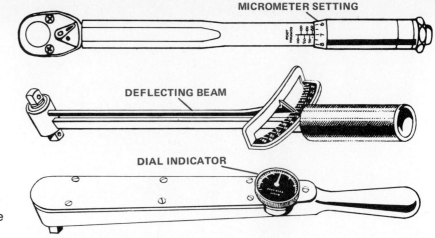

MICROMETER SETTING

DEFLECTING BEAM

DIAL INDICATOR

Fig. 5-17 Types of torque wrenches.

Fig. 5-18 Using a torque wrench to tighten cylinder-head bolts. The numbers indicate the order in which the bolts should be tightened. *(Snap-on Tools Corporation)*

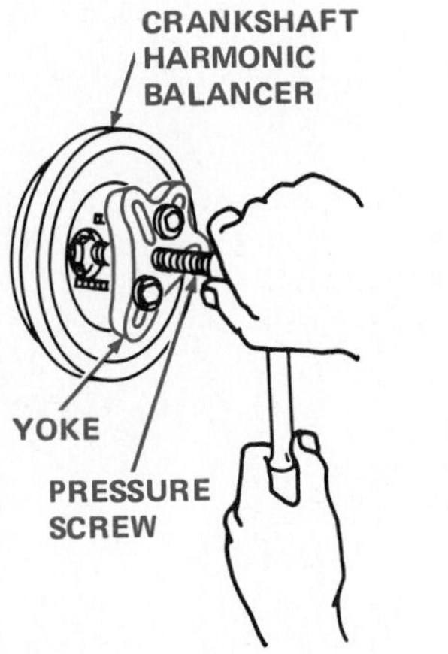

CRANKSHAFT HARMONIC BALANCER

YOKE

PRESSURE SCREW

Fig. 5-19 Using a pressure-screw puller to remove the harmonic balancer from the front of the engine crankshaft. *(Lisle Corporation)*

bolts that have rounded corners. The six-point sockets is used on these. The eight-point socket is used for turning square heads, such as pipe plugs. Deep sockets are used for nuts on studs or bolts that are too long for the standard socket. Spark plugs are removed and installed with a special *spark-plug socket*. Basically, it is a six-point deep socket with a rubber insert in it. The drive end has a hex shape for turning with a wrench or other socket.

A variety of handles are used with sockets. The *ratchet handle* has a mechanism that permits motion in one direction only (Fig. 5-16). It releases in one direction but catches in the other. To tighten a nut with a ratchet, flip the reversing lever on the handle head. This makes the ratchet turn the socket only in the tightening direction.

Extensions of various lengths are used to increase the distance from the socket to the handle, when needed. Commonly used extensions are 3 inch [76 mm], 6 inch [152 mm], and 12 inch [305 mm]. Any number of extensions can be attached together between the socket and the driver.

A universal joint (Fig. 5-14) is used if you must turn a nut or bolt head while holding the handle at an angle. The universal joint is attached between the handle and the socket. For some jobs, the separate universal joint and socket may be too long and awkward to use. A one-piece, combined universal joint and socket is available.

Adapters permit a handle of one size to be used to drive a socket of a different size. Allen wrenches, Phillips screwdrivers, and other types of blades and sockets of different sizes are available for use with the socket-set handles.

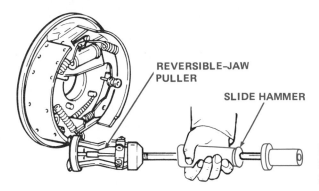

REVERSIBLE–JAW PULLER

SLIDE HAMMER

Fig. 5-20 Removing an axle seal with a slide-hammer puller. *(Ford Motor Company)*

□ 5-8 TORQUE WRENCHES

A *torque wrench* (Fig. 5-17) is basically a special handle for a socket set (□ 5-7). It measures the torque, or twisting force, being applied to a nut or bolt while tightening it. Almost every nut and bolt on the car must be tightened the correct amount—not too little or too much (Fig. 5-18). Nuts and bolts that are too tight cause distortion of parts and danger of stripped threads or broken bolts. Too little tightening may permit the nut or bolt to loosen. By using a torque wrench, the fastener can be tightened to within the limits specified by the manufacturer.

For example, a manufacturer might specify tightening a bolt to "20 lb-ft" (in the U.S. Customary System). This means that you have to apply a 20 pound (lb) pull or force at a distance of 1 foot (ft) from the bolt. The torque wrench lets you do this. Snap the correct socket on the torque wrench, fit the socket on the bolt head, and pull the wrench handle. When the torque wrench indicates the specified torque, you know you have tightened the bolt correctly. This procedure is called *torquing* the bolt.

Most torque wrenches measure the torque in pound-feet (lb-ft). Some torque wrenches used on small nuts and bolts measure torque in pound-inches (lb-in). Twelve pound-inches equals 1 pound-foot. In the metric system, torque wrenches are scaled in kilogram-meters (kg-m), kilogram-centimeters (kg-cm), and newton-meters (N-m). Newton-meters is the preferred metric unit, although the others are still used in some manufacturers' specs. To convert pound-feet to kilogram-meters, multiply the pound-feet by 0.138. To convert to newton-meters, multiply pound-feet by 1.35.

NOTE Threads must be clean and in good shape. Dirty or damaged threads put an unwanted drag on the threads as the fastener is turned. This prevents tightening of the bolt to the proper torque. Therefore, when torquing bolts or nuts, make sure that the threads are clean and in good condition.

□ 5-9 PULLERS

Pullers are used to remove parts assembled with an interference fit such as gears and hubs from shafts, bushings from blind holes, and cylinder liners from engine blocks. A complete puller set has many pieces that can fit together to form different pullers. There are three basic types: the pressure screw (Fig. 5-19), the slide hammer (Fig. 5-20), and the combination (Fig. 5-21). In the pressure-screw type, turning a screw applies the pulling force. In the slide-hammer type, the slide hammer hitting the end of the handle provides the pulling force.

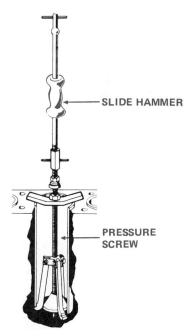

SLIDE HAMMER

PRESSURE SCREW

Fig. 5-21 Combination puller being used to remove a sleeve from an engine cylinder. *(Owatonna Tool Company)*

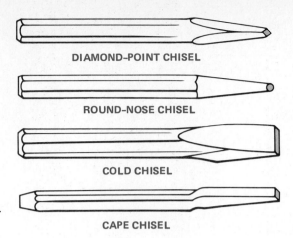

DIAMOND–POINT CHISEL

ROUND–NOSE CHISEL

COLD CHISEL

Fig. 5-22 Various types of chisels.

CAPE CHISEL

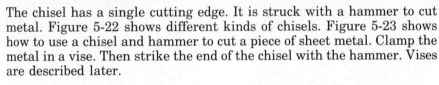

□ 5-10 CHISELS

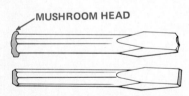

Fig. 5-23 How to use a chisel and hammer to cut sheet metal.

The chisel has a single cutting edge. It is struck with a hammer to cut metal. Figure 5-22 shows different kinds of chisels. Figure 5-23 shows how to use a chisel and hammer to cut a piece of sheet metal. Clamp the metal in a vise. Then strike the end of the chisel with the hammer. Vises are described later.

> **CAUTION** Always wear safety goggles or a face shield to protect your eyes when using a chisel. A flying chip could injure an unprotected eye.

After a chisel has been used for a while, the cutting edge gets chipped and dull. Also, the head tends to flatten, or "mushroom" (Fig. 5-24). The mushroom must be ground off on a grinding wheel. A piece of the mushroomed metal could break off when the chisel is struck. The chip could fly into your hand and cut you. Figure 5-25 shows how to grind the cutting edge of the chisel.

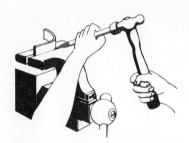

MUSHROOM HEAD

Fig. 5-24 Top, worn chisel with mushroomed head and dented cutting edge. Bottom, new or properly "dressed" chisel.

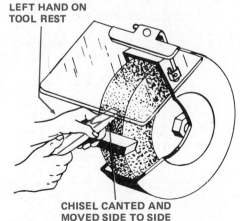

LEFT HAND ON TOOL REST

CHISEL CANTED AND MOVED SIDE TO SIDE

Fig. 5-25 Dressing the chisel by grinding the mushroom from the head.

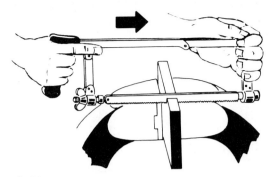

Fig. 5-26 How to hold and use a hacksaw.

□ 5-11 HACKSAWS

The hacksaw (Fig. 5-26) has a steel blade with a series of sharp teeth. Each tooth acts like a tiny chisel. When the blade is pushed over a piece of metal, the teeth cut fine shavings, or filings, off the metal. Each forward, or cutting, stroke should be full and steady and not jerky. On the back stroke, the saw blade should be lifted slightly so the teeth do not drag along the metal. If they drag, it could dull their cutting edges.

When using a hacksaw, select a blade with the right number of teeth for the material to be cut. The teeth must be close enough so that at least two teeth will be cutting at the same time. If the teeth are too fine, they will clog and stop cutting.

□ 5-12 FILES

The *file* (Fig. 5-27) is a cutting tool with a large number of cutting edges, or teeth. Each tooth acts like a tiny chisel. There are many types and shapes of files. The flat file is the most common. Files range in coarseness, or size of individual teeth, from "rough" or "course-cut," through "bastard" and "second-cut," to "smooth" and "dead-smooth." Some of these are shown in Fig. 5-28. Also, files can be single-cut or double-cut. The single-cut file has a series of teeth that are parallel to each other. The double-cut file has two sets of cuts on the face of the file that are at an angle to each other. The teeth on the double-cut file are pointed.

Figure 5-29 shows how to use a file. Strokes should be steady and made with the right amount of force. Excessive force will clog the file teeth and could break the file. Insufficient force will not cut the metal properly. It can also cause the file to chatter, or vibrate.

> **CAUTION** Always use a file handle (Fig. 5-27). Tighten the file in the handle by tapping the end of the handle on the workbench. Don't use a file without the handle. You could ram the file tang into your hand. Never hammer on the file or try to use it as a pry bar. A file is brittle and will shatter.

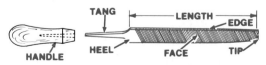

Fig. 5-27 Typical file and handle, with the parts named.

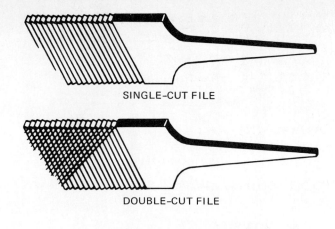

SINGLE-CUT FILE

DOUBLE-CUT FILE

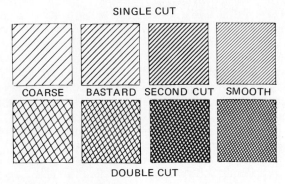

SINGLE CUT

COARSE   BASTARD   SECOND CUT   SMOOTH

DOUBLE CUT

Fig. 5-28 Types of files and file cuts.

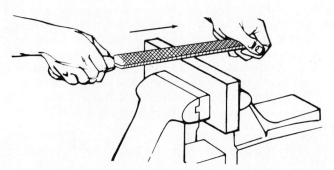

Fig. 5-29 Correct way to hold and use a file. *(Ford Motor Company)*

☐ *5-13 PUNCHES*

Punches are used to knock out rivets and pins and to align parts for assembly. They are also used to mark where holes are to be drilled.

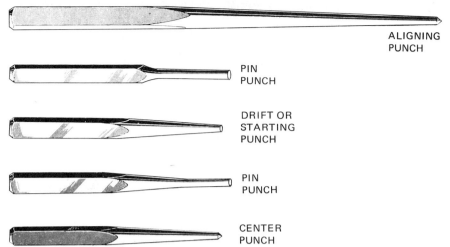

ALIGNING PUNCH

PIN PUNCH

DRIFT OR STARTING PUNCH

PIN PUNCH

CENTER PUNCH

Fig. 5-30 Various kinds of punches. *(General Motors Corporation)*

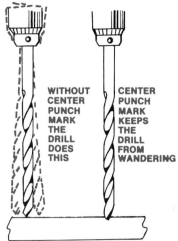

WITHOUT CENTER PUNCH MARK THE DRILL DOES THIS

CENTER PUNCH MARK KEEPS THE DRILL FROM WANDERING

Fig. 5-31 Center-punching a hole location will keep the drill from wandering.

Punches for knocking out rivets and pins are of two kinds, the drift and the pin punch (Fig. 5-30). The rivet head is ground off or cut off with a chisel. Then the tapered drift punch is used to break the rivet loose. The pin punch is then used to drive the rivet out.

The center punch (Fig. 5-30) is handy for marking hole locations for drilling. Unless the hole location is punched before a hole is drilled, the drill may wander, or move around, on the piece to be drilled (Fig. 5-31). If the hole location is first center-punched, the drill will not do this. The center punch is also used for marking parts before they are disassembled. Then they can be reassembled in the same position.

☐ 5-14 DRILLS

Drills are tools for making holes. The typical drill used in the automotive shop is called a *twist drill* (Fig. 5-31). It has a point and two cutting edges, or lips. When the drill is rotated against a material, the cutting edges shave off material. It is sent back up in the spiral grooves and out of the hole. Twist drills can be used with an air drill or with an electric drill (Fig. 5-3). Twist drills are made in many sizes. They are numbered according to the size of the hole they make.

☐ 5-15 TAPS AND DIES

Taps are used to cut threads in drilled holes (Fig. 5-32). Dies are used to cut threads on rods (Fig. 5-33). Also, taps and dies can be used to clean up battered threads. For example, the threads in tapped holes in a cylinder block can often be cleaned by running a tap of the right size into it. There are also special thread straighteners, called *thread chasers,* to clean up damaged threads.

☐ 5-16 STUD EXTRACTORS

When a stud or bolt breaks off, it has to be removed. Cover the threads with penetrating oil. If the break is above the surface, attach Vise-Grip or locking pliers to the threads (Fig. 5-34). Then turn the broken bolt out of

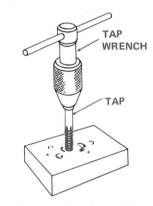

TAP WRENCH

TAP

Fig. 5-32 A tap is used to cut threads in a hole. *(ATW)*

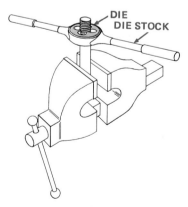

DIE
DIE STOCK

Fig. 5-33 A die is used to cut threads on a rod. *(ATW)*

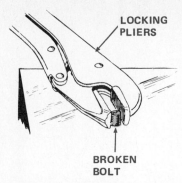

Fig. 5-34 Removing a broken bolt with locking pliers.

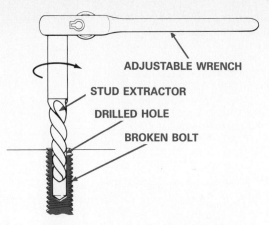

Fig. 5-36 Using a stud extractor to remove a broken stud.

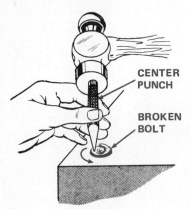

Fig. 5-35 Removing a broken bolt with a center punch and hammer.

the hole. If the break is close to the surface, try removing the broken bolt with a center punch (Fig. 5-35). Place the point of the punch on the bolt, but off center. Then tap the punch lightly with a hammer. By moving the punch and tapping it, you should be able to back out the broken bolt.

If the break is below the surface, or if other methods fail, you may need a *stud extractor* (Fig. 5-36). First, center-punch the broken bolt. Then drill a small hole in it. Next, drill a larger hole almost as big as the small diameter of the threads. Leave only a thin shell. Turn, or drive, a stud extractor into the hole. One type of stud extractor is the *Ezy-Out* (Fig. 5-36). It has coarse spiral threads. As the extractor is turned, the threads bite into the shell of the bolt, removing it. There are other ways and tools for removing a broken stud or bolt.

SHOP EQUIPMENT

☐ 5-17 BENCH VISE

The bench vise (Fig. 5-37) is used to hold a part that is being worked on. When the handle is turned, a screw moves the movable jaw toward or away from the stationary jaw. To protect the surfaces of parts clamped in the vise, caps of soft metal are placed over the steel jaws of the vise. These are called "soft jaws."

☐ 5-18 SHOP PRESSES

A strong, steady, force is needed for many automotive service jobs, such as installing bearings or bushings and pressing pulleys on or off shafts. Trying to do such jobs with a hammer can ruin the parts. For relatively light force, a hand-operated arbor press can be used (Fig. 5-38). It has a handle that rotates a gear which is meshed with a rack. The lower end of the rack has a tool- or arbor-holding device. Pulling down on the handle can exert considerable force on the device. For greater force, a hydraulic press is used (Fig. 5-39). The hydraulic press has a cylinder filled with oil. Operating a pump forces additional oil into the cylinder. As the oil enters, it pushes the ram of the press down with great force.

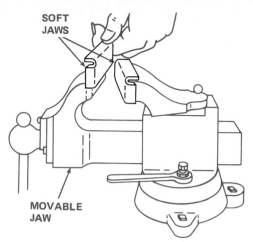

Fig. 5-37 A bench vise showing soft jaws being put into place on the vise jaws.

SOFT JAWS

MOVABLE JAW

☐ 5-19 BENCH GRINDER

A bench grinder (Fig. 5-40) has one or more grinding wheels made of abrasive material bonded together. When the wheel is rotated by the electric motor, objects held against the wheel are ground down. Therefore, the grinder can be used to shape and sharpen tools (Fig. 5-25).

There are many different sizes and grades of wheels. For coarse work, the abrasive particles are relatively large. They cut material rapidly. An example is the grinding wheel used to take the rough edges off castings. For fine work, such as sharpening small tools, a relatively fine grinding wheel is used.

Many grinders have a combination of one grinding wheel and one wire wheel. The wire wheel has hundreds of wires fastened to a central core. When the wire wheel revolves, objects held against it are cleaned and polished.

> **CAUTION** When using a grinder, always wear goggles or a face shield to protect your eyes from flying sparks and metal chips. Be sure the wheel guards are in place. The light must be on and aimed at the surface you are about to grind. Do not use the grinder until your instructor has explained how to use it and has given you permission to begin. Grinders are safe if used properly. But if you use a grinder improperly, you could hurt yourself!

☐ 5-20 CLEANING EQUIPMENT

Proper cleaning of the parts to be serviced is a very important step in automotive service. Not even the most experienced mechanic can always tell if a dirty part is good or bad. Without proper cleaning, the most expensive overhaul job can be ruined by dirt left in during assembly. Parts cleaning is one of the most important jobs in auto repair. It is so important that many professional mechanics never let anyone else clean their parts. Important clues to the cause of failure might be washed away or overlooked by an inexperienced person. Parts cleaning is a dirty job. But shop cleaning equipment and liquid cleaners reduce the time and mess.

To thoroughly clean parts quickly, auto shops have some type of parts washer, or *solvent tank* (Fig. 5-41). It uses a cold liquid cleaner to wash away grease and dirt. Most solvent tanks have a tray or basket for soaking parts. A small pump and motor continually circulates the solvent. Filters and sediment trays remove dirt and grease from the solvent.

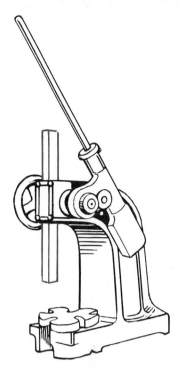

Fig. 5-38 An arbor press can be used when a light force is needed.

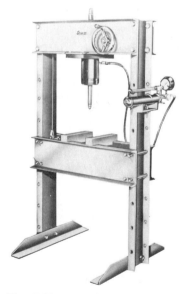

Fig. 5-39 A hydraulic press is used when a heavy force is required. *(Snap-on Tools Corporation)*

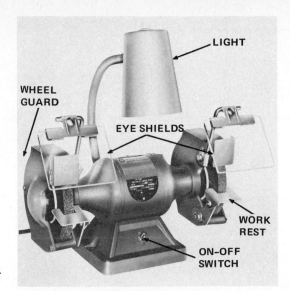

Fig. 5-40 A bench grinder. *(Rockwell International)*

Before placing parts in the solvent tank, first remove any heavy deposits of dirt and grease with a wire brush and scraper. Then place the parts in the basket and lower it into the solvent. Many solvent tanks have a nozzle or spray that can be used with a brush to clean parts or to rinse them after soaking (Fig. 5-42).

> **CAUTION** Some cleaning solutions and solvents are *toxic* and *caustic*. This means they are poisonous and will burn your eyes and skin. Always wear eye protection while using the shop cleaning equipment. Avoid overexposure of your skin to cleaning solutions. After using a cleaning solution, wash your hands and arms to prevent possible skin irritation.

□ 5-21 USING POWER TOOLS

The auto shop has a variety of power tools. These are tools operated by electricity or compressed air. Always carefully follow the instructions for using any of these tools. Keep your hands and clothes away from moving machinery, such as the engine fan, the drive belt, and the grinding wheel. Keep your hands out of the way when using power cutting tools, such as cylinder-refinishing equipment and brake lathes.

Never attempt to feel the finish while the machine is running. There may be slivers of metal on the surface of the workpiece that could cut your hand. When working on equipment with compressed springs, such as clutches or valves, use care to keep the springs from slipping. They could fly off at high speed and hurt someone. Never oil or adjust moving machinery unless the instructions specifically tell you to do so.

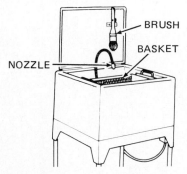

Fig. 5-41 A typical parts washer or solvent tank. *(Ford Motor Company)*

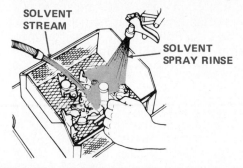

Fig. 5-42 Rinsing parts in a solvent tank. *(Ford Motor Company)*

CHAPTER 5
REVIEW QUESTIONS

Select the *one* correct, best, or most probable answer to each question. Then check your answers against the correct answers given at the end of the book.

1. The two main types of tools used in the auto shop are
   a. pneumatic and electric
   b. machine and power
   c. hand and power
   d. direct and mechanical

2. The hammer used most often in the auto shop is the
   a. ball-peen hammer
   b. claw hammer
   c. brass hammer
   d. plastic hammer

3. The two basic types of pliers are
   a. channellock pliers and Vise-Grip pliers
   b. diagonal pliers and needle-nose pliers
   c. combination pliers and utility pliers
   d. cutting pliers and gripping pliers

4. The main difference between the box wrench and the socket wrench is that the socket wrench
   a. is larger
   b. does not have an attached handle
   c. has more points in the head
   d. is a combination-type wrench

5. The most frequently used socket is the
   a. 6 point
   b. 9 point
   c. 12 point
   d. 16 point

6. The purpose of the torque wrench is to
   a. enable you to apply torque to a nut
   b. measure the torque applied while tightening a nut or bolt
   c. check the torque required to turn the engine crankshaft
   d. loosen cylinder-head bolts in the correct sequence

7. Various types of handles used with sockets include
   a. speed, ratchet, and sliding
   b. 6 point and 12 point
   c. box and combination
   d. hex and slotted

8. The three basic types of pullers are
   a. speed, ratchet, and sliding
   b. pressure screw, slide hammer, and combination
   c. micrometer setting, dial indicator, and torque
   d. needle-nose, side-cutting, and combination

9. When the head of a chisel mushrooms, it should be
   a sharpened
   b. discarded
   c. hammered flat
   d. ground off

10. The most common type of file is the
    a. flat
    b. round
    c. second-cut
    d. dead-smooth

11. Normally, the blade is put in the hacksaw frame so the
    a. blade cuts on the forward stroke
    b. blade cuts on the back stroke
    c. blade cuts on both strokes
    d. none of the above

12. To knock out rivets and pins, use a
    a. drift punch and a pin punch
    b. pin punch and an aligning punch
    c. center punch and a pin punch
    d. drill punch and a starting punch

13. To cut internal threads in a hole, use a
    a. die
    b. threaded insert
    c. stud extractor
    d. tap

14. If a bolt breaks off flush with the surface of the cylinder block, to remove it you need a
    a. threaded insert
    b. die
    c. stud extractor
    d. screwdriver

15. The main caution or cautions you must observe when using a grinding wheel are to
    a. always wear goggles or a face shield.
    b. make sure the wheel guards are in place.
    c. make sure the light is on and aimed at the surface you are about to grind.
    d. all of the above

PART 2

AUTOMOTIVE ENGINE FUNDAMENTALS

Part 2 of *The Auto Book* describes the construction and operation of automobile engines, including the support systems needed for the engine to run. These systems include the lubricating, cooling, and fuel systems for spark-ignition and diesel engines. You will learn about the parts that go together to make the engine and how they all work together to produce power. In addition, you will learn about engine fuels and oils. There are 12 chapters in Part 2:

CHAPTER 6
ENGINE OPERATION

After studying this chapter, you should be able to:

1. Explain the ways in which automotive engines are classified.
2. Describe how the crankshaft and connecting rod change reciprocating motion to rotary motion.
3. Describe valve arrangements used in engines.
4. Explain how the four-cycle engine works.
5. Describe the various types of valve trains.
6. Explain valve timing.

An *engine* is a machine that converts heat energy into mechanical energy. The engine burns fuel to produce mechanical power. For this reason, the engine is sometimes called the "power plant." There are gasoline engines, diesel engines, Wankel engines, steam engines, gas-turbine engines, jet engines, and rocket engines. However, the two most commonly used in cars and trucks are the gasoline engine and the diesel engine.

□ 6-1 INTERNAL-COMBUSTION AND EXTERNAL-COMBUSTION ENGINES

There are two kinds of engines: internal-combustion and external-combustion. Internal-combustion engines burn fuel inside the engine. All automobiles built today have internal-combustion engines.

External-combustion engines burn fuel outside the engine. Steam engines are external-combustion engines. These engines run on steam that is produced by boiling water outside the engine.

BASIC PISTON ENGINE

□ 6-2 RECIPROCATING AND ROTARY ENGINES

Internal-combustion, or IC, engines are classified in two ways, according to the *motion* of the internal parts. In most automotive engines, the main parts reciprocate, or move up and down (Fig. 6-1A). In other engines, such as the gas turbine and the Wankel, the main parts spin, or rotate (Fig. 6-1B). The parts that move up and down in automotive engines are called *pistons*. For this reason, reciprocating internal-combustion engines are often referred to as *piston engines*. The gas turbine and Wankel engines are known as *rotary engines*.

□ 6-2 TWO KINDS OF PISTON ENGINES

There are two kinds of piston engines: *spark-ignition* and *compression-ignition*. The difference is in the type of fuel used, the way the fuel is introduced into the engine cylinders, and how the fuel is "ignited," or set on fire.

The spark-ignition engine uses gasoline (or *gasohol*). The compression-ignition engine is more commonly known as the "diesel engine." It burns *diesel fuel*.

□ 6-4 ENGINE CYLINDERS

Pistons move up and down in engine cylinders. Most automobile engines have four, five, six, or eight cylinders. The same action takes place in each cylinder. We will study just one cylinder to find out how the engine works. Figure 6-2 shows a four-cylinder engine partly cut away to show the pistons and cylinders. Figure 6-3 shows how this type of engine is mounted sideways, or "transversely," in a front-wheel-drive car. The arrangement includes the transmission and power train to drive the front wheels.

The cylinder and the piston look like two soft-drink cans, one slightly smaller than the other (Fig. 6-4A). The larger can is open at the bottom. The smaller can fits into the larger can (Fig. 6-4B). If you push the smaller can up into the larger can, you will "compress" the air into a smaller volume. The bigger can is the *engine cylinder*. The smaller can is the *piston*.

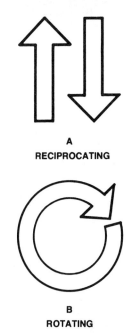

A
RECIPROCATING

B
ROTATING

Fig. 6-1 Reciprocating motion is up-and-down or back-and-forth motion as contrasted with rotary (rotating) motion.

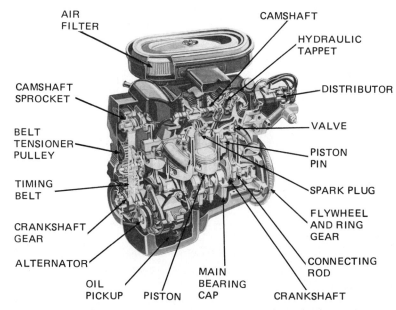

Fig. 6-2 A four-cylinder engine, partially cut away to show the internal parts. *(Ford Motor Company)*

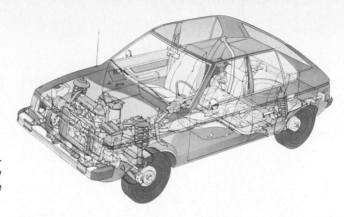

Fig. 6-3 Installation of a four-cylinder engine, transversely mounted in a front-wheel-drive car. *(Chrysler Corporation)*

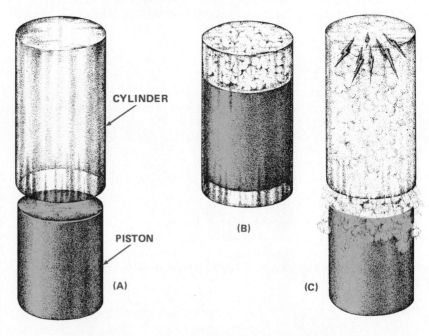

CYLINDER

PISTON

(A)

(B)

(C)

Fig. 6-4 Three views showing the actions in the engine cylinder. (A) The piston is a metal plug that fits inside the cylinder. (B) When the piston is pushed up into the cylinder, air is trapped and compressed. (C) When the fuel ignites and burns, the pressure increases. This forces the piston down in the cylinder.

When the piston is pushed up into the cylinder, the air in the cylinder is compressed. Suppose there is some fuel vapor in the compressed air. Then a spark inside the cylinder will cause an explosion. The piston will be forced down the cylinder (Fig. 6-4C).

☐ 6-5 CONNECTING ROD AND CRANKSHAFT

Forcing a piston out of a cylinder just once is not enough to make a car move. The piston must remain in the cylinder and move up and down rapidly. Then this up-and-down, or reciprocating, motion must be turned into rotary motion to rotate the car wheels. The connecting rod and crankshaft do the job of changing the reciprocating motion of the piston into rotary motion.

Figure 6-5 is a picture of a piston. The piston is about 4 inches [100 mm] in diameter and weighs about 1 pound [0.45 kg]. Figure 6-6 shows the piston with the connecting rod attached. Figure 6-7 shows a crankshaft. The part of the crankshaft that changes the reciprocating motion of the piston into the rotary motion of the wheels is called the *crank*, or *crankpin*. Figure 6-8 shows how the piston, connecting rod, and

Fig. 6-5 A piston for a piston engine. *(ATW)*

74

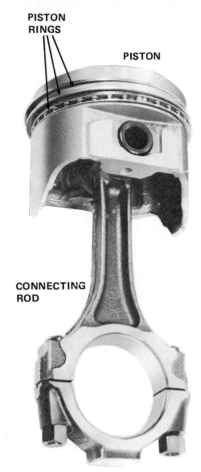

Fig. 6-6 Piston with connecting rod attached and piston rings installed. *(Ford Motor Company)*

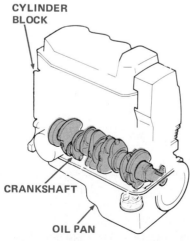

Fig. 6-7 Crankshaft for a four-cylinder engine. *(Federal-Mogul Corporation)*

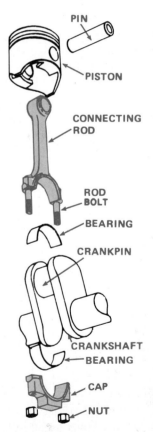

Fig. 6-8 Parts that make up the piston-and-connecting-rod assembly.

Fig. 6-9 Piston-and-connecting-rod assembly attached to the crankpin on the crankshaft.

crankshaft work together. Only part of the crankshaft is shown in Fig. 6-8. The connecting rod is attached to the piston by a *piston pin*. It fits through two holes in the piston and one hole in the connecting rod (Fig. 6-9). The other end of the connecting rod is attached to a crankpin on the crankshaft (Fig. 6-9). This combination changes the reciprocating motion of the piston into the rotary motion of the crankshaft.

☐ 6-6 CRANKPIN

As the crankshaft rotates, the crankpin swings around in a circle (Fig. 6-10). During this circular motion, the piston is moving up and down, or reciprocating (Fig. 6-11). While the piston moves up and down in the cylinder, the piston, connecting rod, and crankpin go through the positions shown in Fig. 6-12. The connecting rod tilts first in one direction and then in the other. The lower end of the connecting rod moves in a

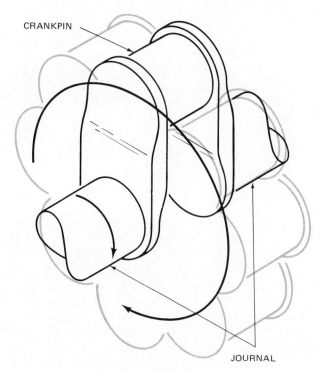

Fig. 6-10 As the crankshaft rotates, the crankpin swings in a circle around it.

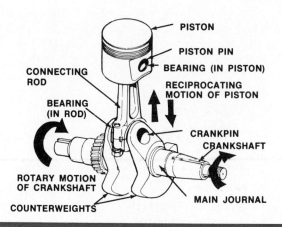

Fig. 6-11 The crankpin moves in a circle around the crankshaft while the piston moves up and down.

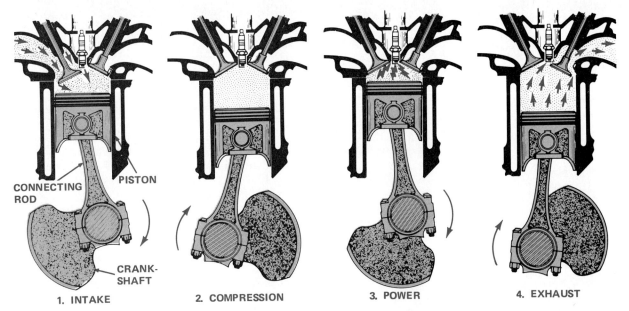

CONNECTING ROD PISTON CRANK-SHAFT

1. INTAKE   2. COMPRESSION   3. POWER   4. EXHAUST

Fig. 6-12 The sequence of actions as the piston travels through one complete cycle of engine operation. This requires two complete revolutions of the crankshaft.

circle with the crankpin. Figure 6-12 shows how the reciprocating motion of the piston is changed into the rotary motion of the crankshaft.

NOTE The crankpin is also called the *crank throw,* or *connecting-rod journal*.

☐ 6-7 PISTON STROKE

When the piston moves from top to bottom of the cylinder, or from bottom to top, it completes a *stroke*. The piston completes *two strokes* as it travels through the positions shown in Fig. 6-12. In position A, the piston starts from the top of the cylinder and moves down. When the piston reaches the bottom of its travel down the cylinder, the piston has completed one *piston stroke*. As the crankshaft continues turning, the piston starts moving up in the cylinder (Fig. 6-12B). When the piston reaches the top, it has completed a second piston stroke.

When the piston is at the top of the cylinder, this position is called *top dead center* (TDC). The bottom position is called *bottom dead center* (BDC). TDC and BDC are referred to many times in this book and in shop manuals. These are the reference points for ignition timing and valve timing.

☐ 6-8 FOUR STROKES

Automobile engines are called "four-stroke engines" or "four-cycle engines." This means that automobile engines are *four-stroke-cycle engines*. It takes four piston strokes for the engine to go through one complete "cycle" of operation. This requires two revolutions of the crankshaft.

A *cycle* is a series of events that repeat themselves. For example, the four seasons—spring, summer, fall, and winter—form a cycle. In the au-

Fig. 6-13 An engine valve is a long metal stem with a flat top.

tomobile engine, the four-stroke cycle is made up of the intake stroke, compression stroke, power stroke, and exhaust stroke. These are described later in this chapter.

□ 6-9 MAKING THE ENGINE RUN

There are two kinds of piston engines—spark-ignition and compression-ignition (□ 6-3). In the spark-ignition engine, the fuel vapor is mixed with air *outside* of the engine cylinder. This mixture of fuel vapor and air goes into the cylinder. Then the piston is pushed up to compress the mixture. Next, a spark occurs in the cylinder. The spark ignites the mixture (*spark ignition*) and it burns rapidly. The rapid burning is called *combustion*. As combustion takes place, it creates a high pressure in the cylinder. This pressure forces the piston down. As a result, the crankshaft turns and the car wheels rotate. Then the piston moves up, clearing the burned gases out of the cylinder. This happens rapidly and repeatedly to produce a flow of power.

In the compression-ignition (diesel) engine, the fuel (diesel fuel) is sprayed into the air *inside* the engine cylinder. As the piston moves up, it compresses air only. This makes the air very hot. Then the diesel fuel is sprayed into the cylinder. The hot air (or "heat of compression") ignites the fuel. This is what is meant by *compression ignition*. The heat produced by compressing the air ignites the fuel. As the fuel burns, it produces a high pressure. The pressure forces the piston down so the crankshaft turns and the car moves.

These two methods of igniting the fuel are described in later chapters.

□ 6-10 ENGINE VALVES

In a running engine, the piston is moving up and down and the crankshaft is rotating. The piston moves because fuel is being burned in the engine cylinder. However, to make the engine run, *valves* in the cylinder must open and close. A valve is any device that can be opened and closed to control the flow of a liquid or gas.

The cylinder has an opening in the top so that the air or air-fuel mixture can get in. A second opening is needed for the burned gas to get out. These openings are called *ports*. They are opened and closed at the proper time by the engine valves.

A valve has a long metal stem and a flat top (Fig. 6-13). The stem moves up and down in a *valve guide* (Fig. 6-14), which is a round hole in the cylinder head. The *cylinder head* is the engine part that encloses the top of the cylinder. The guide keeps the valve moving up and down in a straight line. When the valve moves up, its head fits into the valve port in the cylinder head. This closes the port so no air or gas can enter or leave the cylinder.

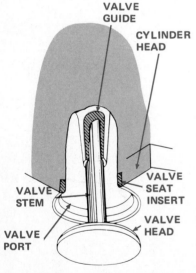

Fig. 6-14 Cylinder head and valve guide, partly cut away to show valve, valve guide, and valve seat.

HOW THE ENGINE OPERATES

□ 6-11 ENGINE OPERATION

The basic operation of the engine can be described by the actions of the crankshaft, piston, and valves. First, one valve opens to let the air or air-fuel mixture into the cylinder. The fuel is burned in the cylinder, pushing the piston down. This forces the crankshaft to rotate. Then the other valve opens to let the burned gas out. To keep the engine running, the cycle must be quickly repeated. The complete cycle of events—the four strokes of the four-stroke-cycle engine—are described in the following pages.

□ 6-12 THE INTAKE STROKE

The four-stroke cycle begins with the piston at TDC. To start the intake stroke, the piston moves down the cylinder (Fig. 6-15). As the piston moves down, it produces a vacuum in the cylinder. A *vacuum* is the absence of air or any other substance. Outside air will try to rush in to fill the vacuum in the cylinder.

During this piston stroke, one of the valves—the *intake valve*—is open (Fig. 6-15). This allows the air or air-fuel mixture to pass the valve and enter the cylinder. The downward movement of the piston while the intake valve is open is called the *intake stroke*. This is because the cylinder is *taking in* air or a mixture of air and fuel.

In the compression-ignition (diesel) engine, air alone enters the cylinder. In the spark-ignition engine, the fuel is first mixed with the air outside the cylinder. A carburetor or a fuel-injection system is used. Then the air-fuel mixture enters the cylinder. Operation of the carburetor and fuel-injection systems are described in later chapters.

At the end of the intake stroke, the piston is at the bottom of the cylinder at BDC (bottom dead center). The cylinder is filled with air or air-fuel mixture. Now the intake valve closes. When the piston starts up the cylinder, the compression stroke begins.

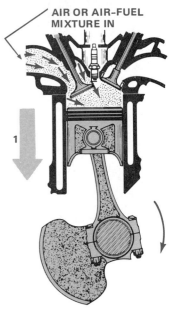

Fig. 6-15 The intake stroke. The intake valve has opened. The piston is moving downward, drawing the air or air-fuel mixture into the cylinder.

□ 6-13 THE COMPRESSION STROKE

After the piston passes BDC at the end of the intake stroke, it starts to move up. Both valves are closed, so the air or air-fuel mixture has no place to go. It is pushed, or compressed, into a smaller volume (Fig. 6-16). The amount that the mixture of air and gasoline vapor is compressed is called the *compression ratio*.

In a typical spark-ignition engine, the air-fuel mixture is compressed into about one-eighth of its original volume (Fig. 6-17). This is like squeezing 1 quart into ½ cup. The volume before compression is 8 times the volume after compression. When the mixture is compressed down from 8 to 1, the compression ratio is 8 to 1. Usually, the compression ratio is written as 8 : 1. You read this as "eight to one."

In the compression-ignition, or diesel, engine, the compression ratio is much higher. In some diesel engines, the compression ratio is 20 : 1 or higher (Fig. 6-18). The reason for this higher compression ratio is that the compressed air must be very hot. This heat of compression is used to ignite the diesel fuel when it is sprayed into the cylinder. The more the air is compressed, the hotter it gets. In the diesel engine, the air reaches temperatures above 1000 degrees Fahrenheit [535 degrees Celsius]. When the fuel spray hits the very hot air, the fuel ignites almost instantly.

As the piston travels from BDC to TDC, the air or air-fuel mixture is compressed. This stroke is called the *compression stroke*. When the piston begins to move down the cylinder again, the power stroke begins. Compression ratio is discussed further in Chap. 7.

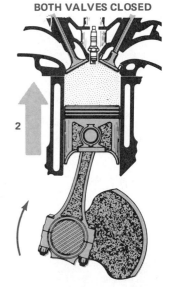

Fig. 6-16 The compression stroke. The intake valve has closed. The piston is moving upward, compressing the air or air-fuel mixture.

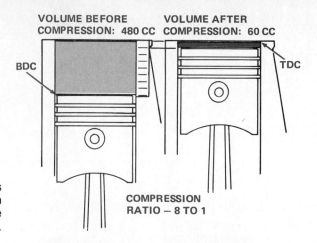

VOLUME BEFORE
COMPRESSION: 480 CC

VOLUME AFTER
COMPRESSION: 60 CC

BDC

TDC

COMPRESSION
RATIO – 8 TO 1

Fig. 6-17 Compression ratio is the volume in the cylinder with the piston at BDC divided by the volume with the piston at TDC.

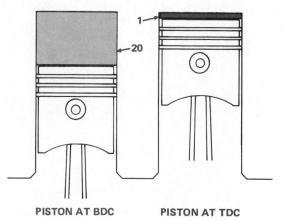

1

20

Fig. 6-18 Compression ratio in a diesel engine may be 20:1 or higher.

PISTON AT BDC   PISTON AT TDC

☐ 6-14 THE POWER STROKE

As the piston nears TDC at the end of the compression stroke, a spark occurs in the *combustion chamber* (spark-ignition engine). This is the space at the top of the cylinder and above the piston in which the burning of the fuel takes place (Fig. 6-19). Combustion chambers vary in shape.

The spark plug makes the spark that starts the *combustion,* or burning. (How the spark plug makes this happen is described in Chap. 22.) When the spark occurs in the compressed air-fuel mixture, there is a very rapid burning. The pressure and temperature of the mixture suddenly go up. Every square inch of the piston head gets a push of up to 600 pounds [2669 N] or more. This adds up to as much as 2 tons—4000 pounds [17,792 N]—pushing down on the piston head! As a result, the piston is forced down the cylinder, the crankshaft turns, and the car moves.

This downward movement of the piston caused by the combustion pressure is called the *power stroke* (Fig. 6-19). As the piston reaches BDC, the exhaust valve opens. Now the exhaust stroke begins.

☐ 6-15 THE EXHAUST STROKE

As the piston reaches BDC on the power stroke, the exhaust valve opens. Then, when the piston moves up again, the burned gases escape through the exhaust port. This upward movement of the piston is called the *exhaust stroke.* The remaining burned gases are pushed out, or *exhausted,* from the engine cylinder (Fig. 6-20).

COMBUSTION CHAMBER

3

Fig. 6-19 The power stroke. After the fuel is ignited, it burns, creating a high pressure which forces the piston down.

☐ *6-16 THE FOUR-STROKE CYCLE*

As the piston reaches TDC on the exhaust stroke, the exhaust valve closes and the intake valve opens. The piston moves down once more on another intake stroke. The cycle of events in the cylinder is then repeated: intake stroke, compression stroke, power stroke, exhaust stroke. This four-stroke cycle (☐ 6-8) continues as long as the engine runs.

The actions in the cylinder are the same for spark-ignition and diesel engines. Both types of automotive engine operate on the four-stroke cycle. However, there are two exceptions:

1. The way the fuel gets into the cylinder
2. The way that the fuel is ignited

In the spark-ignition engine, the fuel is mixed with air before the air enters the cylinder. The compressed mixture is then ignited by an electric spark. In the diesel engine, the fuel is sprayed into the compressed air. Then the heat of compression ignites the fuel.

☐ *6-17 MULTIPLE-CYLINDER ENGINES*

A single-cylinder engine provides only one power impulse for every two crankshaft revolutions. The engine is delivering power only one-fourth of the time. To provide a more continuous flow of power, automobile engines have multiple cylinders. With four, five, six, or eight cylinders, the power impulses follow one another, or *overlap* (Fig. 6-21). This gives a more even flow of power from the engine. The car runs smoother.

EXHAUST GAS OUT

Fig. 6-20 The exhaust stroke. The exhaust valve opens, allowing the burned gases to escape as the piston moves up the cylinder.

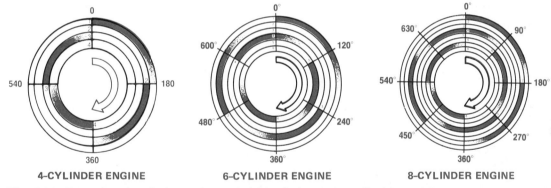

4-CYLINDER ENGINE **6-CYLINDER ENGINE** **8-CYLINDER ENGINE**

Fig. 6-21 Power impulses in four-, six-, and eight-cylinder engines. Each complete circle represents two complete crankshaft revolutions, or 720 degrees. Less power is delivered toward the end of the power stroke because cylinder pressure falls off. This is shown by the lightening of the shaded areas that show the power impulses. Notice how the power impulses overlap in six- and eight-cylinder engines.

VALVE OPERATION

☐ *6-18 THE VALVE TRAIN*

During the four-stroke cycle, the intake valve is open during the intake stroke. The exhaust valve is open during the exhaust stroke. Typical engine valves are shown in Fig. 6-22. Notice that the intake valve is larger.

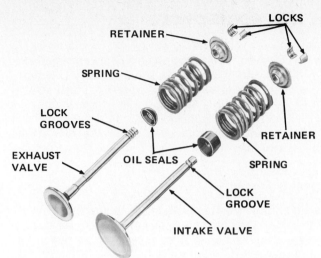

Fig. 6-22 Engine valves, springs, seals, and related parts. *(Chrysler Corporation)*

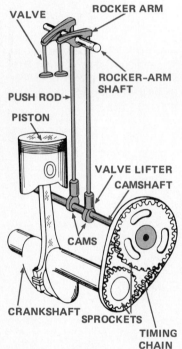

Fig. 6-23 Basic valve-operating mechanism for one cylinder of an overhead-valve engine.

The parts that operate the valves are called the *valve train*. Two basic types of valve trains are used in car engines today. These are the overhead-valve (OHV) type and the overhead-camshaft (OHC) type. In both, the valves are in the cylinder head. The basic difference is where the camshaft is located. In the overhead-valve engine, the camshaft is in the cylinder block. In the overhead-camshaft engine, the camshaft is on the cylinder head.

NOTE Some cars have the Wankel rotary engine. It operates on the four-stroke cycle. But no valve train or valves are used. The Wankel engine is described in □ 8-22.

□ 6-19 OVERHEAD-VALVE ENGINE

The overhead-valve (OHV) engine is also called the *I-head*, or *valve-in-head*, engine. All automotive piston engines built today—both spark-ignition and diesel—are this type. As the name implies, the valves are located above the piston in the cylinder head. Figure 6-23 shows the complete valve train for one cylinder of an overhead-valve engine. Valve action starts at a *cam lobe* on the *camshaft*. The camshaft is the shaft in the engine with lobes which operate the valves. It is driven from the crankshaft by sprockets and a toothed belt or chain, or by gears. When the crankshaft turns, the camshaft turns. This brings the cam lobes into action.

Figure 6-24 shows a cam. The lobe is a bump or high spot on the cam. Riding on the cam is a round cylinder called the *lifter,* or *tappet.* When the

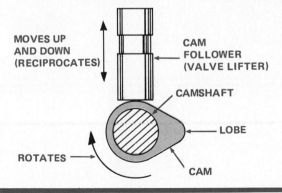

Fig. 6-24 Cam and valve lifter. As the cam rotates, the lifter follows the cam surface. This causes the lifter to move up and down. *(ATW)*

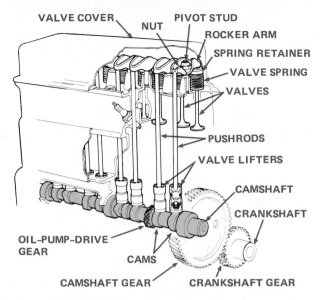

VALVE COVER
NUT
PIVOT STUD
ROCKER ARM
SPRING RETAINER
VALVE SPRING
VALVES
PUSHRODS
VALVE LIFTERS
CAMSHAFT
CRANKSHAFT
OIL–PUMP–DRIVE GEAR
CAMS
CAMSHAFT GEAR
CRANKSHAFT GEAR

Fig. 6-25 Valve train in an in-line engine. *(Federal-Mogul Corporation)*

lobe comes up under the lifter, the lobe causes the lifter to move up. The cam and lifter change the rotary motion of the camshaft back into reciprocating motion. This is the action needed to open and close the valves.

In the overhead-valve engine, the camshaft is located in the cylinder block. As the camshaft rotates, the upward movement of the valve lifter forces the pushrod up (Fig. 6-23). The pushrod pushes on one end of the *rocker arm*. The rocker arm has a pivot near its center. The pivot may be a shaft (Fig. 6-23) or a ball-and-stud arrangement (Fig. 4-3). When one end of the rocker arm moves up, the other end moves down. As the rocker arm moves down, it pushes down on the valve stem. This pushes the valve head off its seat, opening the valve.

The valve is normally held closed by a valve spring (Figs. 6-22 and 6-25). The lower end of the spring rests against the cylinder head. The upper end of the spring rests against a valve-spring retainer (Fig. 6-22). The retainer (Fig. 6-26) is similar to a washer. It is locked by valve locks,

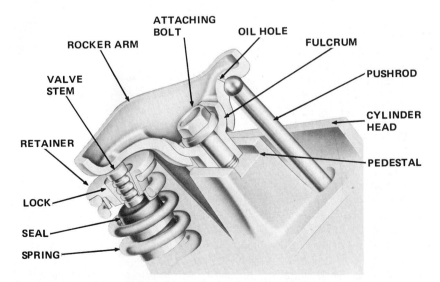

ATTACHING BOLT
OIL HOLE
ROCKER ARM
FULCRUM
PUSHROD
VALVE STEM
CYLINDER HEAD
RETAINER
PEDESTAL
LOCK
SEAL
SPRING

Fig. 6-26 Pushrod, rocker arm, and valve-stem assembly for an overhead-valve engine. *(Ford Motor Company)*

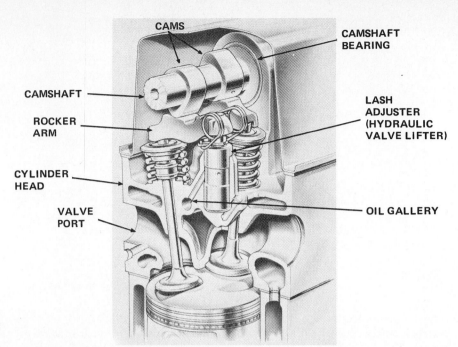

CAMS

CAMSHAFT BEARING

CAMSHAFT

LASH ADJUSTER (HYDRAULIC VALVE LIFTER)

ROCKER ARM

CYLINDER HEAD

VALVE PORT

OIL GALLERY

Fig. 6-27 Valve train for one cylinder of an overhead-camshaft engine using rocker arms. *(Ford Motor Company)*

or "keepers," to the valve stem. When the valve is pushed open, the spring is compressed. It stays compressed until the cam lobe moves out from under the valve lifter. Then the valve spring expands, pulling the valve back up into its seat. This closes the valve port.

Engines with overhead valves and pushrods such as shown in Figs. 6-25 and 6-26 are often called *pushrod engines*. Many automobile engines are this type.

☐ 6-20 OVERHEAD-CAMSHAFT ENGINE

The overhead-camshaft engine is a variation of the overhead-valve engine. The difference is that the camshaft is on the cylinder head, instead of in the cylinder block. The cams work directly on rocker arms (Fig. 6-27) or valve tappets (Fig. 6-28). Long pushrods are not used.

Two types of overhead-camshaft valve trains are made. If the engine has only one camshaft (Fig. 6-27), the engine is a *single-overhead-camshaft* (SOHC) engine. Some engines have two camshafts (Fig. 6-28). One camshaft is for the intake valves. The other operates the exhaust valves. This is called a *double-overhead-camshaft* (DOHC) engine. With this arrangement, a V-type engine has four camshafts.

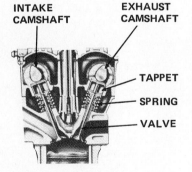

INTAKE CAMSHAFT

EXHAUST CAMSHAFT

TAPPET

SPRING

VALVE

Fig. 6-28 A dual-overhead-camshaft engine has two camshafts, one for the intake valves and one for the exhaust valves. *(Chevrolet Motor Division of General Motors Corporation)*

☐ 6-21 VALVE TIMING

Valve timing is the relation between valve action and piston position. The valves must move "in time" with the piston. The intake valve must be open during the intake stroke. The exhaust valve must be open during the exhaust stroke. During the compression and power strokes, both valves must be closed.

To complete the four piston strokes, the crankshaft must rotate twice. One-half (180 degrees) of crankshaft rotation is needed for each piston stroke. With four piston strokes, the crankshaft must rotate two full revolutions, or 720 degrees. During these two crankshaft revolutions,

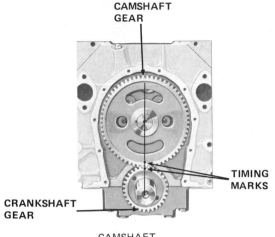

CAMSHAFT
GEAR

TIMING
MARKS

CRANKSHAFT
GEAR

Fig. 6-29 Crankshaft and camshaft gears for a V-type engine. Notice the timing marks on the gears. *(Chevrolet Motor Division of General Motors Corporation)*

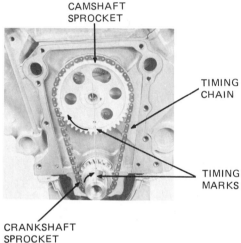

CAMSHAFT
SPROCKET

TIMING
CHAIN

TIMING
MARKS

CRANKSHAFT
SPROCKET

Fig. 6-30 Crankshaft and camshaft sprockets driven by a timing chain. *(Chrysler Corporation)*

the camshaft must rotate once. Each time the camshaft rotates, both valves open and close. This means that the camshaft turns at one-half crankshaft speed. To get this ratio, the gear or sprocket on the camshaft is twice as large as the gear or sprocket on the crankshaft.

So that the valves open and close at the proper time, there are *timing marks* on the gears and sprockets (Figs. 6-29 to 6-31). These must be properly aligned when the engine is assembled. This assures that the timing of the valves and piston will be correct.

☐ 6-22 DRIVING THE CAMSHAFT

Three different ways of driving the camshaft are used in automobile engines. One method is by two gears, one on the crankshaft and the other on the camshaft (Fig. 6-29). The camshaft is also driven by sprockets and a chain (Fig. 6-30) or by sprockets and a toothed belt (Fig. 6-31). The gears are called *timing gears*. The chain is the *timing chain*. The toothed belt is the *timing belt*. They all "time" the valve action.

There is one difference between driving the camshaft by a chain or toothed belt and driving it by gears. When a chain or toothed belt is used, the camshaft and crankshaft both turn in the same direction. With gears, the camshaft rotates in the opposite direction from the crankshaft. The directions of rotation are shown in Figs. 6-29 to 6-31.

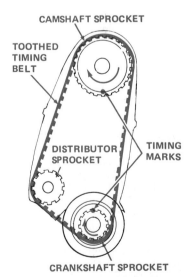

CAMSHAFT SPROCKET

TOOTHED
TIMING
BELT

DISTRIBUTOR
SPROCKET

TIMING
MARKS

CRANKSHAFT SPROCKET

Fig. 6-31 Crankshaft and camshaft sprockets using a toothed timing belt to drive the camshaft. *(ATW)*

Select the *one* correct, best, or most probable answer to each question. Then check your answers against the correct answers given at the end of the book.

1. The two kinds of piston engines are
   a. reciprocating and rotary
   b. spark-ignition and compression-ignition
   c. compression-ignition and diesel
   d. internal-combustion and external-combustion

2. To change reciprocating motion to rotary motion, the engine uses a
   a. crankshaft and camshaft
   b. crankpin and crank
   c. connecting rod and a crank
   d. piston and a connecting rod

3. The smallest number of cylinders in automobile engines built in the United States is
   a. two
   b. four
   c. six
   d. eight

4. In the spark-ignition engine
   a. fuel is mixed with air outside the engine cylinders.
   b. the air-fuel mixture is ignited by an electric spark.
   c. both *a* and *b*
   d. neither *a* nor *b*

5. In the compression-ignition engine
   a. fuel is mixed with air inside the engine cylinders.
   b. the air-fuel mixture is ignited by the heat of compression.
   c. both *a* and *b*
   d. neither *a* nor *b*

6. Rapid compression of air in diesel-engine cylinders raises the air temperature above
   a. 100 degrees Fahrenheit (37.8 degrees Celsius)
   b. 1000 degrees Fahrenheit (538 degrees Celsius)
   c. 2000 degrees Fahrenheit (1093 degrees Celsius)
   d. 5000 degrees Fahrenheit (2760 degrees Celsius)

7. The type of engine using valve lifters, pushrods, and rocker arms is
   a. a V-type engine
   b. an overhead-valve engine
   c. an L-head engine
   d. a T-head engine

8. The type of engine which always uses pushrods is
   a. a T-head engine
   b. an overhead-valve engine
   c. an overhead-camshaft engine
   d. an L-head engine

CHAPTER 7
ENGINE MEASUREMENTS

After studying this chapter, you should be able to:
1. Explain what bore and stroke mean.
2. Explain what piston displacement is and how it is calculated.
3. Explain what compression ratio is and how it is calculated.
4. Define *horsepower, volumetric efficiency, torque, friction horsepower, brake horsepower,* and *engine efficiency.*

To compare one engine to another, you have to know various measurements. It doesn't mean much to say that one engine is "powerful" and another engine is "weak." This chapter describes the ways in which engines and engine performance are measured. These include physical measurements such as the cylinder bore and piston stroke. They also include performance measurements such as torque and horsepower.

ENGINE MECHANICAL MEASUREMENTS

☐ 7-1 BORE AND STROKE

Engine measurements begin with the engine cylinder. There are two basic cylinder measurements—*bore* and *stroke*. The bore is the diameter of the cylinder (Fig. 7-1). The stroke is the distance the piston travels from BDC to TDC (Fig. 7-2). These measurements are used to figure *piston displacement* (☐ 7-2).

Some engines are called *oversquare* engines. This means that the bore is greater than the stroke. An engine with a 4- by 3.5-inch [102- by 89-mm] cylinder is oversquare. A 4- by 4-inch [102- by 102-mm] cylinder is square. Many engines are oversquare. With a shorter stroke, the piston and rings don't travel as far for each crankshaft revolution.

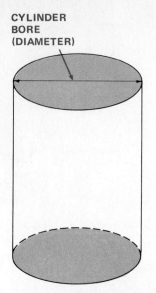

CYLINDER BORE (DIAMETER)

Fig. 7-1 The bore is the diameter of the engine cylinder.

☐ 7-2 PISTON DISPLACEMENT

When the piston moves up from BDC to TDC, it sweeps, or *displaces,* a certain volume. This volume forms a cylinder as shown in Fig. 7-2. The top and bottom are the piston head at TDC and at BDC. The volume of the cylinder is called the *piston displacement* or *swept volume.*

For example, an engine cylinder measures 4 inches [102 mm] in diameter. The distance the piston moves from BDC to TDC is 3.5 inches [89 mm]. The displacement of this engine cylinder is the volume of a cylinder 4 inches [102 mm] in diameter and 3.5 inches [89 mm] in length. To calculate the volume, let D stand for diameter and L for length. The symbol π is called *pi.* It equals 3.1416. Working the formula

$$\text{Piston displacement} = \frac{\pi \times D^2 \times L}{4} = \frac{3.1416 \times 4^2 \times 3.50}{4}$$

$$= \frac{3.1416 \times 16 \times 3.50}{4}$$

$$= 43.98 \text{ cubic inches}$$

The displacement of one cylinder of the engine is 43.98 cubic inches (720.1 cc [cubic centimeters]). For comparison, 1 quart contains about 61 cubic inches. So 43.98 cubic inches is about equal to ¾ quart. That's for one cylinder. To find the displacement of an eight-cylinder engine, multiply 43.98 cubic inches [720.1 cc] by 8. The result is the engine displacement of 351.84 cubic inches [6.76 L (liters)]. Many technicians don't always say "cubic inches." Instead, they say "It's a 351." This means that the engine has a displacement of 351 cubic inches.

Today engine size is often given in metric measurements of liters or cubic centimeters. For example, a typical four-cylinder engine may be called a "2300 cc" engine or a "2.3 liter" engine.

☐ 7-3 COMPRESSION RATIO

The compression ratio of an engine is a measure of how much the air or air-fuel mixture is compressed during the compression stroke in the en-

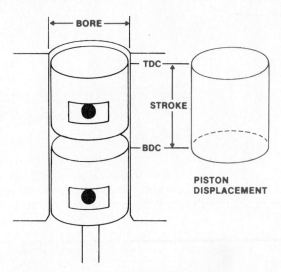

BORE
TDC
STROKE
BDC
PISTON DISPLACEMENT

Fig. 7-2 The bore and stroke of an engine cylinder. Piston displacement is the volume the piston displaces as it moves from BDC to TDC.

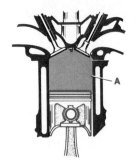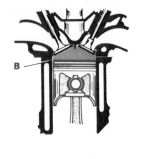

PISTON AT BDC **PISTON AT TDC**

Fig. 7-3 Compression ratio is the volume in the engine cylinder with the piston at BDC divided by the volume with the piston at TDC, or A divided by B.

gine cylinder. Compression ratio was described in Chap. 6. It is calculated by dividing the volume above the piston at BDC by the volume remaining above the piston at TDC. (This is basically the combustion-chamber volume.)

For example, suppose in a spark-ignition engine that volume A is 45 cubic inches and volume B is 5 cubic inches (Fig. 7-3). Then the ratio between A and B—which is the compression ratio—is 45 divided by 5, or 9. The compression ratio is 9 : 1. The volume B above the piston when it is at TDC is called the *clearance volume*. The volume A, with the piston at BDC, is called the *air volume*.

Increasing the compression ratio of a spark-ignition engine usually increases the power output. For example, when the compression ratio is raised from 6 : 1 to 8 : 1, power output is increased by 12 percent. At the same time, fuel consumption is reduced by 9 percent. Engines with 12 : 1 compression ratios have been built. However, these engines usually require premium gasoline, which may contain lead. (Lead in gasoline is discussed in Chap. 13). Most compression ratios today are in the 8.5 : 1 range. This allows the engine to run on regular unleaded gasoline.

The compression ratio of a diesel engine usually is never less than 16 : 1. Below this ratio, too little heat is produced during the compression stroke to ignite the fuel after it is injected. Compression ratios usually do not exceed 22 : 1 or 23 : 1. Above this, the high pressures may overstress engine parts. Light and less expensive diesel engines can be built if the compression ratio is not raised too high.

ENGINE PERFORMANCE MEASUREMENTS

□ 7-4 ENERGY

Energy is the capacity or ability to do work. The most common forms of energy are heat, mechanical, electrical, and chemical. Energy in one form can be changed into a different form. For example, in the engine, gasoline or diesel fuel is burned to create heat. Then the heat energy is changed into the mechanical energy of the crankshaft, which moves the car.

When work is done on an object, energy is stored in that object. (Work is described in □ 7-5.) Lift a 10-pound [4.54-kg] weight 5 feet [1.5 m]. Now you have stored energy in the weight (Fig. 7-4). When dropped, the energy in the weight can do 50 foot-pounds (ft-lb) of work. If a spring is

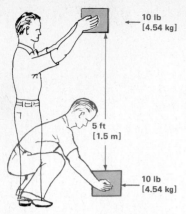

Fig. 7-4 When you lift an object against the opposing force of gravity, you are doing work on the object.

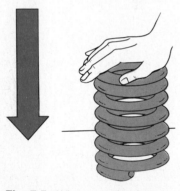

Fig. 7-5 When a spring is compressed, work is done on the spring and energy is stored in it.

compressed, energy is stored in it. When released, it also can do work (Fig. 7-5).

☐ 7-5 WORK

Work is the moving of an object against an opposing force. The force can be a pull (such as gravity), a push, or a lift. For example, when a coil spring is compressed, work is done on the spring (Fig. 7-5). The spring will "give back" the work when you release it.

Work is measured in terms of distance and force. The *foot-pound* is the basic unit of work. For example, 50 ft-lb (foot-pounds) of work is required to lift a 10-pound [4.54-kg] weight 5 feet [1.5 m]. *Work equals force times distance.*

In the metric system, the unit of work is the *joule* (J). One joule is the amount of work done by a force of 1 newton (N) when it acts through a distance of 1 meter (m). Therefore, 1 joule equals 1 meter-newton (m-N). Multiply foot-pounds by 1.35 to get joules.

☐ 7-6 TORQUE

Torque is twisting or turning force (Fig. 7-6). You apply torque to the steering wheel when you steer a car around a turn. The engine applies torque to the car wheels to make them rotate. However, torque must not be confused with *power* (☐ 7-7). Applying torque to an object *may* or *may not* result in motion. Torque is the *ability* to do work, or the ability to cause something to rotate.

Torque is measured in pound-feet (lb-ft) or in newton-meters (N-m). *Work* is measured in foot-pounds (ft-lb) and in joules (J). For example, suppose you pushed on the crank in Fig. 7-6 with a 20-pound force. If the crank is 1.5 feet long, you are applying 20 × 1.5 = 30 lb-ft of torque to the crank. You are applying this amount of torque whether or not the crank is turning. The torque is there as long as you continue to apply the 20-pound push to the crank handle.

☐ 7-7 POWER

Work can be done slowly, or it can be done rapidly. The rate at which work is done is called *power*. An engine that can do a lot of work in a short time is a "high-powered" engine.

During a power stroke in the engine (☐ 6-14), the high-pressure gas pushes on the piston head with a force of up to 4000 pounds [17,792 N]. The automobile is the opposing force. The 4000-pound force must overcome the opposing force of the car to move it. This is work (☐ 7-5). The repeated power strokes in all engine cylinders do the work necessary to move the car. Therefore, power results from the work done on the pistons by the burning gases in the cylinders.

Fig. 7-6 Torque is measured in pound-feet (lb-ft) and in newton-meters (N-m). It is calculated by multiplying the applied force times the distance from the rotating shaft.

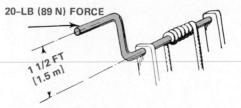

20–LB (89 N) FORCE

1 1/2 FT [1.5 m]

For example, let's say that the 4000 pounds of force pushes the piston down 3 inches, or ¼ foot, as shown in Fig. 7-7. This means the force has produced ¼ × 4000 = 1000 ft-lb of work.

When the power strokes follow one another very rapidly, the engine is "working hard." It is doing a lot of work in a short time. The engine is putting out a lot of *power*. When there are fewer power strokes per minute, the engine is doing less work in the same amount of time. Therefore, it is producing less power.

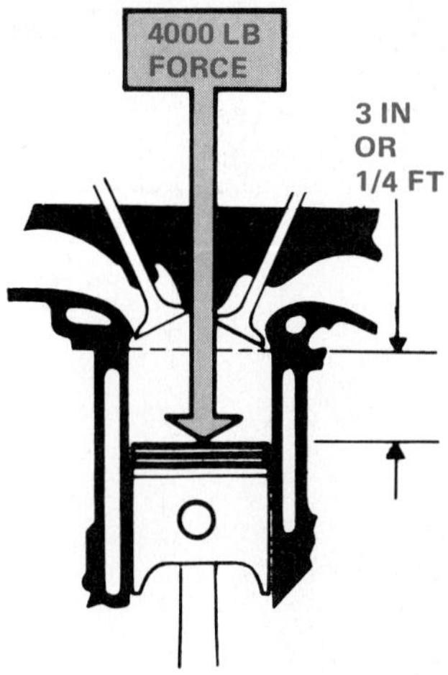

☐ 7-8 ENGINE POWER

Engine power is the power available from the crankshaft to do work. The most common units of measure for power are the *horsepower* (hp) and the *kilowatt* (kW). One horsepower equals 33,000 ft-lb of work per minute. It is the power necessary to raise 33,000 pounds 1 foot in 1 minute. One horsepower equals 746 watts [0.746 kW].

The average horse can raise a 200-pound weight a distance of 165 feet in 1 minute. Figure 7-8 shows how this measurement can be made. The horse walks 165 feet in 1 minute. The cable, running over the pulley, raises the 200-pound weight 165 feet. Therefore, the amount of work done in 1 minute is 165 × 200, or 33,000 ft-lb. This is 1 hp. If the horse took 2 minutes to do the same amount of work (33,000 ft-lb), it would be working only half as hard. It would be producing only ½ hp.

A formula for finding horsepower is

$$\text{hp} = \frac{\text{ft-lb/minute}}{33,000} = \frac{L \times W}{33,000 \times t}$$

where hp = horsepower
  L = length, in feet, through which W is exerted
  W = force, in pounds, exerted through distance L
  t = time, in minutes, required to move W through L

Here is another formula for finding horsepower. It uses engine speed and torque.

$$\text{hp} = \frac{\text{torque} \times \text{rpm}}{5252}$$

where   hp = horsepower
  torque = torque available at crankshaft
  rpm = crankshaft speed, in revolutions per minute

When you work in the shop, you can use the shop *dynamometer* to measure engine power. This formula is more convenient for dynamometer testing. You can measure torque and horsepower with the dynamometer.

Fig. 7-7 To move the piston, the force on top of the piston must overcome the opposing force of the automobile. This is work.

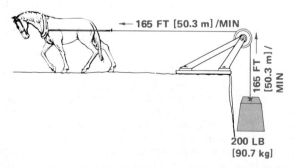

Fig. 7-8 When a horse does 33,000 ft-lb of work in 1 minute, the horse is working at the rate of 1 hp [0.746 kW].

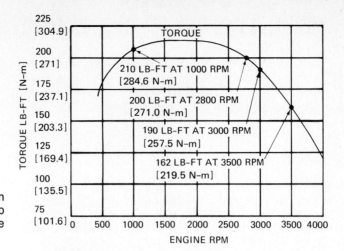

Fig. 7-9 Torque curve of an engine showing the relationship between torque and engine speed (rpm).

☐ 7-9 ENGINE TORQUE

Engine torque comes from the pressure of the burning gases in the cylinders. This force pushes down on the pistons and causes the crankshaft to turn. The greater the force, the greater the torque. *Torque* is the twisting force that the pistons apply to the crankshaft. It is the torque of the engine that provides acceleration and "performance."

The torque that an engine can develop changes with engine speed. An engine can develop more torque at intermediate speeds than at high speeds (Fig. 7-9). This is because there is more time for air-fuel mixture to enter the cylinders (in a spark-ignition engine). Volumetric efficiency is high. (Volumetric efficiency is described in ☐ 7-12.) There will be a greater amount of air-fuel mixture to burn during the power stroke and higher combustion pressures will develop. This means, in turn, that greater torque will be applied to the crankshaft.

☐ 7-10 BRAKE HORSEPOWER

The power available from the engine crankshaft to do work is the *brake horsepower* (bhp) of the engine. It is called "brake" horsepower because some type of brake is used to measure it. The brake places a load on the engine crankshaft (Fig. 7-10). Today most measurements of engine power are made with a *dynamometer*. It can measure the power that a running engine is producing. If the engine is out of the car, an *engine dynamometer* is used (Fig. 7-11). A *chassis dynamometer* can measure the engine power reaching the drive wheels (Fig. 7-12).

The amount of power that an engine produces depends on its torque and speed (rpm). As speed goes up, horsepower goes up. And as torque goes up, horsepower goes up. This is shown in the second formula in ☐ 7-8. The horsepower calculated by that formula is actually brake horsepower.

☐ 7-11 FRICTION HORSEPOWER

Friction horsepower (fhp) is the power that an engine uses to overcome its own internal friction. Friction is the resistance to motion between two objects in contact with each other. For example, place a book on a table and then push on the book. Some force is required to move it. If you put oil

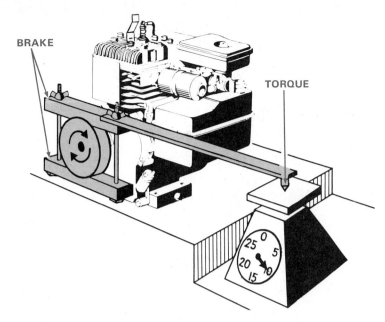

Fig. 7-10 An engine dynamometer is used to measure engine torque and brake horsepower.

Fig. 7-11 Dynamometer used for testing engines and measuring their power output. (Go-Power Systems)

Fig. 7-12 Automobile in place on a chassis dynamometer. The drive wheels rotate the dynamometer rollers, which measure the power available at the wheels. (Sun Electric Corporation)

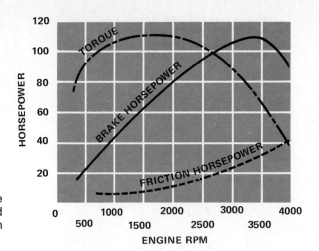

Fig. 7-13 Comparison of the torque, friction-horsepower, and brake-horsepower curves of an engine.

on the table, you could move the book much more easily. The oil reduces the friction between the table and the book.

In the engine, all moving parts are covered with oil. The oil lubricates the parts so they will easily slide over one another. Even so, some power is used up just to overcome the friction. This power is called "friction" horsepower.

Friction horsepower increases as engine speed increases. The graph in Fig. 7-13 shows this. At low speeds, it takes only a few horsepower to overcome the friction in the engine. But as speed increases, the friction loss goes up. At 4000 rpm, friction is using up 40 hp.

□ 7-12 VOLUMETRIC EFFICIENCY

The word *volumetric* means having to do with volume. *Efficiency* generally refers to how well a job is done. The two words used together refer to how completely the engine cylinder fills up on the intake stroke of a spark-ignition engine. As the piston moves down on the intake stroke, the air-fuel mixture tries to fill the cylinder. But there isn't much time. At high engine speed, the intake stroke takes less than 0.01 second. So before the cylinder fills completely, the intake valve closes and the compression stroke begins.

If the cylinder fills up almost completely, the volumetric efficiency (VE) is high. If the cylinder is only partly filled, the volumetric efficiency is low. There is less air-fuel mixture to be compressed and burned, so the power stroke is weaker. This is why engine speed cannot be increased indefinitely. As engine speed increases, the intake-stroke time gets shorter and shorter. Less and less air-fuel mixture gets in. Volumetric efficiency gets lower and lower. Finally the power strokes get so weak that they cannot increase the engine speed any further.

The formula for volumetric efficiency is

$$VE = \frac{actual\ amount\ of\ air\ that\ enters\ cylinder}{theoretical\ amount\ that\ could\ enter}$$

Suppose that at a certain speed 40 cubic inches [656 cc] of mixture enters the cylinder. However, to completely fill it, 50 cubic inches [819 cc] should enter. The volumetric efficiency is 40 divided by 50, which is 0.8, or 80 percent.

☐ 7-13 IMPROVING VOLUMETRIC EFFICIENCY

To improve volumetric efficiency, intake valves can be made larger. The number of valves per cylinder can be increased. (Some engines have three or four valves per cylinder.) The lobes on the camshaft can be made larger so that the valves open wider. The passages carrying the air-fuel mixture into the cylinder can be made larger. They should be as straight, short, and smooth as possible (Fig. 7-14). This procedure is called *porting and polishing*. Long, curved, rough surfaces tend to restrict the flow of the air-fuel mixture.

"Two-barrel" and "four-barrel" carburetors are used on some engines. The extra barrels are additional air passages that let the engine "breathe" easier. This gives the engine a higher volumetric efficiency. In turn, this allows the engine to develop more power, especially at high speeds.

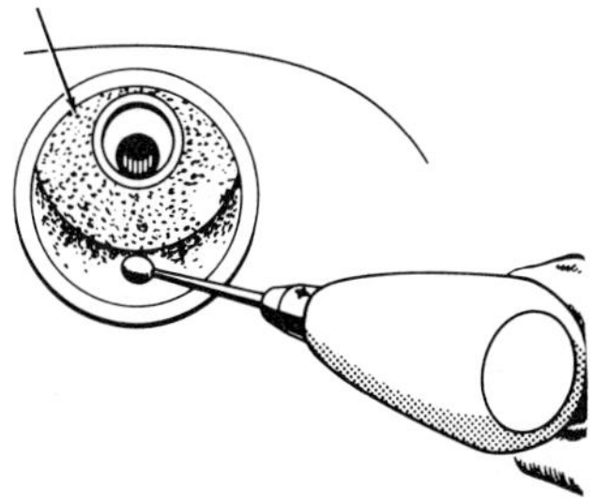

VALVE PORT

Fig. 7-14 Smoothing the inside surfaces of the ports improves the volumetric efficiency of the engine.

☐ 7-14 ENGINE EFFICIENCY

In an engine, efficiency is the relationship between the effort exerted and the results obtained. *Engine efficiency* is the ratio of the power actually delivered to the power that could be delivered if the engine operated without any power loss.

Unfortunately, there is considerable power loss in an engine. Power is lost during the combustion process. Only part of the energy in gasoline is converted to power (Fig. 7-15). A large part of the energy in gasoline is lost as heat. The engine cooling system, which is described in Chap. 12, removes about a third of the heat energy of the gasoline. Another third is lost because the exhaust gases are very hot when they leave the engine. This escaping heat energy does not do any work. More power is lost because of engine friction. The result is that only about 20 percent of the energy in the fuel is available to move the car.

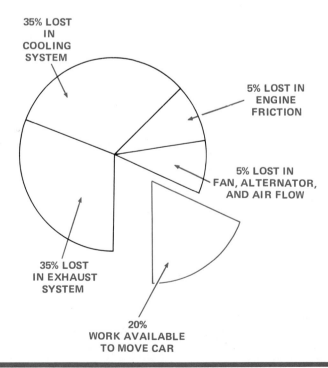

35% LOST IN COOLING SYSTEM

5% LOST IN ENGINE FRICTION

5% LOST IN FAN, ALTERNATOR, AND AIR FLOW

35% LOST IN EXHAUST SYSTEM

20% WORK AVAILABLE TO MOVE CAR

Fig. 7-15 Only about 20 percent of the energy in gasoline is available to move the car. *(Ford Motor Company)*

Select the *one* correct, best, or most probable answer to each question. Then check your answers against the correct answers given at the end of the book.

1. The size of an engine cylinder is referred to in terms of its
   a. bore and length
   b. bore and stroke
   c. diameter and bore
   d. displacement and radius

2. Piston displacement is calculated from the
   a. bore and stroke
   b. piston length and diameter
   c. cylinder diameter and length
   d. ring width and depth

3. The air volume above the piston with the piston at TDC is called the
   a. compression ratio
   b. clearance volume
   c. piston displacement
   d. bore

4. The air volume in the cylinder with the piston at BDC divided by the clearance volume is called the
   a. piston displacement
   b. cylinder ratio
   c. compression ratio
   d. compression pressure

5. One horsepower is
   a. 3300 ft-lb of work per minute
   b. 33,000 ft-lb of work per minute
   c. 330,000 ft-lb of work per minute
   d. 16,500 ft-lb of work per minute

6. The measure of how completely the engine cylinders fill up on the intake strokes is
   a. thermal efficiency
   b. actual efficiency
   c. volumetric efficiency
   d. compression ratio

7. In a typical engine-torque curve, the torque peaks at
   a. around 500 rpm
   b. top speed
   c. maximum horsepower
   d. intermediate speed

8. Friction horsepower is the amount of power required to
   a. overcome road friction
   b. produce maximum torque
   c. overcome friction in the engine
   d. accelerate the car

9. Engine horsepower drops off at higher speeds due to
   a. increased friction and reduced torque
   b. loss of compression ratio
   c. increased reciprocating losses
   d. reduced friction and increased torque

10. The ratio of power actually delivered to the power that could be delivered if the engine operated without any power loss is the
   a. brake horsepower
   b. engine horsepower
   c. engine efficiency
   d. compression ratio

CHAPTER 8
ENGINE TYPES AND CLASSIFICATIONS

After studying this chapter, you should be able to:

1. Explain the various ways in which automotive engines are classified.
2. Explain why the four-cylinder engine has become more popular.
3. Describe the various engine cylinder arrangements.
4. Explain what a turbocharger is and how it works.
5. Describe the various valve arrangements used in engines.
6. Explain the differences between spark-ignition and diesel engines.
7. Explain what firing order is.
8. Explain how the Wankel engine works.

Earlier chapters have already mentioned some of the different types of automotive engines—overhead valve, overhead camshaft, reciprocating, and rotary. However, there are other engine classifications. Automotive piston engines can be classified in at least eight different ways:

1. Number of cylinders
2. Arrangement of cylinders
3. Arrangement of valves
4. Type of cooling system
5. Number of piston strokes per cycle
6. Type of fuel burned
7. Method of ignition
8. Firing order

This is not a complete list. But it shows some of the many ways that engines can be classified.

ENGINE TYPES

☐ 8-1 NUMBER AND ARRANGEMENT OF CYLINDERS

Figure 8-1 shows some of the various ways that engine cylinders can be arranged. Almost all automotive piston engines have either four, five,

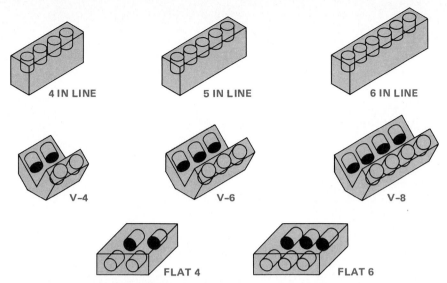

Fig. 8-1 Several cylinder arrangements. *(ATW)*

Fig. 8-2 Four-cylinder in-line engine, with a belt-driven overhead camshaft. *(Chrysler Corporation)*

six, or eight cylinders. The cylinders, in four-, five-, and six-cylinder engines are often arranged in a single row, or line. These are called *in-line* engines. In V-type engines, the cylinders are placed in two rows set at an angle to each other. Flat four- and six-cylinder engines have also been made. In these, the cylinders are in two rows across from each other.

☐ 8-2 FOUR-CYLINDER IN-LINE ENGINES

Figure 8-2 shows a cutaway four-cylinder in-line engine. The cylinders are arranged in one row, or line. The four-cylinder engine has become increasingly popular in recent years. One reason is the trend toward small, lightweight cars. This trend has been encouraged by the oil shortage. It has also been helped by government regulations requiring cars to get increased fuel mileage.

There is another reason for the increasing popularity of the four-cylinder in-line engine. It is small enough to fit sideways, or transversely, at the front of the car. Figures 6-3 and 8-3 show how a four-cylinder engine is mounted between the front wheels. It is attached to a *transaxle,*

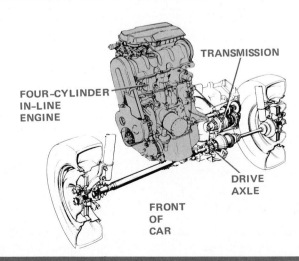

Fig. 8-3 In-line four-cylinder engine mounted transversely between the wheels of a front-wheel-drive car. *(Chrysler Corporation)*

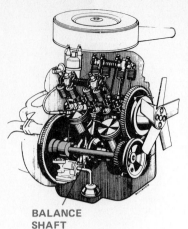

BALANCE
SHAFT

Fig. 8-4 A V-4 engine using a balance shaft to make the engine run smoother. *(Ford Motor Company)*

which is a combination *trans*mission and drive *axle*. The transaxle is described in Chaps. 33 and 34.

☐ 8-3 V-4 ENGINES

The V-4 engine has two rows, or "banks," of two cylinders each (Fig. 8-4). The rows are set at an angle to each other so the banks form a V. The crankshaft has only two cranks. Each crankpin has two connecting rods attached to it.

This type of engine may be difficult for engine designers to *balance*. A "balanced" engine runs smoothly and does not vibrate or shake. In the engine shown in Fig. 8-4, a *balance shaft* is used to make the engine run smoother. The balance shaft turns in a direction opposite to the crankshaft. Some in-line four-cylinder engines also use a balance shaft.

☐ 8-4 FLAT-FOUR ENGINES

Figure 8-5 shows the opposed, or "flat," four-cylinder engine used in the Volkswagen Beetle. The four cylinders are arranged in two opposing rows of two cylinders each. The engine is mounted at the rear of the car, which has rear-wheel drive. The flat design is sometimes called a "pancake" engine. It requires very little room, so the engine compartment can be very compact.

The Volkswagen engine is air-cooled. The cylinders are surrounded by flat metal rings called *fins*. The fins provide large surfaces from which

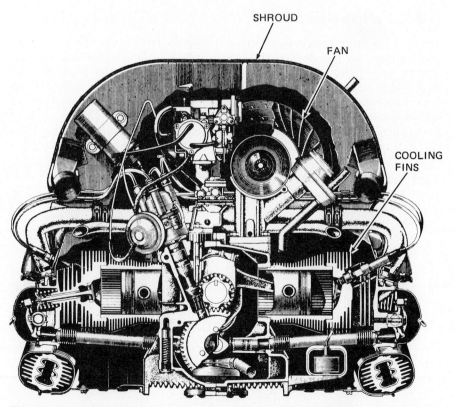

SHROUD

FAN

COOLING
FINS

Fig. 8-5 A flat-four-cylinder engine with two banks of two cylinders each, opposing each other. This is an air-cooled engine. *(Volkswagen of America, Inc.)*

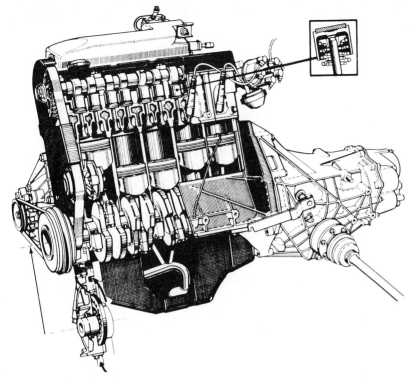

Fig. 8-6 A five-cylinder in-line engine with overhead camshaft, for a front-wheel-drive car. *(Volkswagen of America, Inc.)*

heat is carried away. This prevents engine overheating. Other flat-four engines are liquid-cooled. The two types of engine cooling—air cooling and liquid cooling—are described in Chap. 12.

□ 8-5 FIVE-CYLINDER ENGINES

Some cars have five-cylinder in-line engines. Mercedes-Benz has a five-cylinder diesel engine. Audi uses a five-cylinder overhead-camshaft spark-ignition engine (Fig. 8-6). The five-cylinder engine is a compromise between a four- and a six-cylinder engine. It produces more power than a four. But it is not as long or heavy as a six.

The Audi engine (Fig. 8-6) is for a front-wheel-drive car. Compare Fig. 8-6 with Fig. 8-2, which shows the same view of a similar four-cylinder engine. All five-cylinder automotive engines are in-line engines.

□ 8-6 SIX-CYLINDER IN-LINE ENGINES

Most six-cylinder engines are in-line engines. The six cylinders are arranged in a single row, or line. Figure 8-7 shows a six-cylinder in-line spark-ignition engine. It has overhead valves. This engine is a "slant six." The cylinders are slanted to one side so the car can have a lower hood.

□ 8-7 V-6 ENGINES

Many cars are equipped with V-6 engines. These engines have two rows, or banks, of three cylinders each. The banks are set at an angle to form a

Fig. 8-7 Slant-six in-line over-head-valve engine. The cylinders are slanted to permit a lower hood line. *(Chrysler Corporation)*

V. Figure 8-8 shows two views of a V-6 spark-ignition engine. Figure 8-9 shows a V-6 engine with its power train—the transaxle—attached. This engine is mounted transversely between the front wheels. The car has front-wheel drive.

In a V-6 engine, the angle for the V may be either 60 or 90 degrees, depending on the engine design. When the angle is 60 degrees, the engine is "even firing." This means that one cylinder fires every 120 degrees of crankshaft rotation. But in the basic design of a 90 degree V-6, the firing intervals are unevenly spaced. They occur at 150 and 90 degrees instead of evenly every 120 degrees. This causes an out-of-balance condition in the engine. One way to balance a 90 degree V-6 is by using a *splayed crankshaft*. The splayed crankshaft is described in Chap. 9.

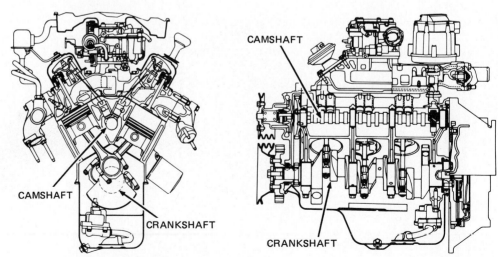

Fig. 8-8 Two views of a V-6 overhead-valve engine. *(Chevrolet Motor Division of General Motors Corporation)*

Fig. 8-9 A V-6 overhead-valve engine with attached power train, mounted transversely between the wheels of a front-wheel-drive car. *(Chevrolet Motor Division of General Motors Corporation)*

□ 8-8 FLAT-SIX ENGINE

The flat-six engine is very similar to the flat-four (□ 8-4) except that one more cylinder has been added to each bank. A flat-six engine is used in the Chevrolet Corvair. This engine is air-cooled and mounted at the rear of the car. The car and engine are no longer manufactured.

□ 8-9 V-8 ENGINES

All eight-cylinder automotive engines made today are V-8s. They have two rows, or banks, of cylinders, with four cylinders in each bank. The two banks are set at an angle to form a V. Figure 8-10 shows one model of V-8 engine. At one time, in-line eight-cylinder engines were common.

Fig. 8-10 A V-8 overhead-valve engine. *(Ford Motor Company)*

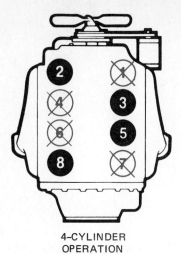

4-CYLINDER OPERATION

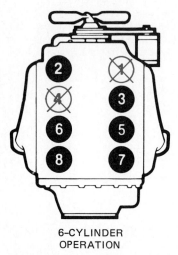

6-CYLINDER OPERATION

Fig. 8-11 A variable-displacement V-8 engine which can selectively cut out two or four cylinders at a time. *(Sun Electric Corporation)*

But V-8 engines took their place. The V-8 engine is a shorter, more rigid engine.

Now the V-8 engine is losing its popularity. It is being replaced by six- and four-cylinder engines. One reason is the trend toward smaller, lighter cars. These cars give good performance and fuel mileage with smaller engines.

☐ 8-10 MULTIPLE-DISPLACEMENT ENGINES

Some cars have a *multiple-*, or *modulated-, displacement* engine. As used by Cadillac, this is basically a V-8 engine with electronic controls that selectively cut out two or four cylinders at a time (Fig. 8-11). The number of cylinders that the controls cut out depends on the power requirements.

When the engine is idling or cruising at a steady speed on a level highway, the controls cut out four cylinders. Only four cylinders are needed to provide sufficient power for these operating conditions. However, when the car encounters a hill, additional power is needed. So the electronic controls put additional cylinders to work. The same thing happens when the driver "steps on the gas" to increase speed. Additional cylinders are put to work. The number of cylinders that go back to work depends on the amount of additional power needed.

☐ 8-11 SUPERCHARGERS

Many engines use some type of air pump to force more air or air-fuel mixture into the engine cylinders. This "supercharge" allows more fuel to be burned during each power stroke. When more fuel is burned, higher pressures develop in the cylinders during the power strokes. As a result, the engine can do more work. An engine with any type of supercharger is called a *blown engine.* Engines without superchargers are sometimes classed as *normally-aspirated* engines. This means that they "breathe," or take in air, at normal atmospheric pressure.

There are two types of superchargers. One type is mechanically driven by a belt, a chain, or gears from the engine crankshaft. Figure

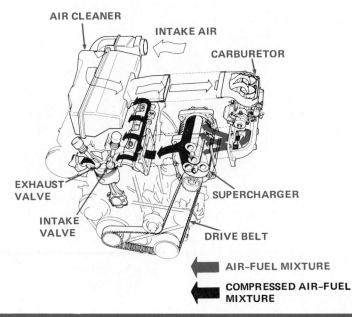

Fig. 8-12 Engine using a two-rotor belt-driven supercharger. *(Fiat Motors of North America, Inc.)*

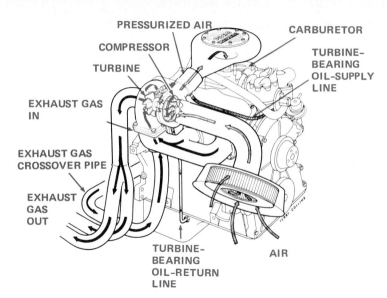

Fig. 8-13   A turbocharged Ford 182-cubic-inch (3-L) V-6 engine. *(Ford Motor Company)*

8-12 shows an engine equipped with a "Roots-type" supercharger. It has two rotors, each with two lobes. As the rotors spin, air or air-fuel mixture is carried around in the spaces between the lobes and the housing. The air or air-fuel mixture is then forced into the intake manifold, raising the manifold pressure.

☐ 8-12 TURBOCHARGERS

The other type of supercharger is the *turbo-supercharger,* or *turbocharger* (Fig. 8-13). It is driven by the exhaust gas from the engine. The turbocharger has two basic parts. These are two rotors, called the *compressor* and the *turbine,* mounted on opposite ends of a shaft. Exhaust gas is routed through the turbine so that it spins at high speed. Since the compressor is on the same shaft, it also spins at high speed. As the compressor spins, it sends compressed air or air-fuel mixture into the engine cylinders. With more fuel to burn, the engine produces more power. On many turbocharged engines, power output is boosted 30 percent or more. For example, a 100-horsepower (hp) engine could produce 130 hp with a turbocharger. Both spark-ignition and diesel engines can be turbocharged. Chapter 14 further describes the operation and controls of the turbocharger.

ENGINE CLASSIFICATIONS

☐ 8-13 ARRANGEMENT OF VALVES

Another way to classify engines is according to the arrangement of the valves and valve trains. Various arrangements are shown in Fig. 8-14. They are described in Chap. 6. For example, an engine might be classed as an "overhead-valve engine"or as an "overhead-cam engine." Then an overhead-cam engine might be classified further as a "single-overhead-cam engine" or a "double-overhead-cam engine." Valves and valve trains are covered in detail in Chap. 10.

L-HEAD (FLAT-HEAD)

I-HEAD (OVERHEAD VALVE)

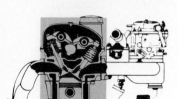

V-TYPE OVERHEAD VALVE

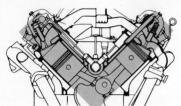

SINGLE OVERHEAD CAM

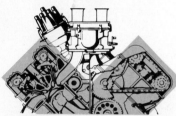

DOUBLE OVERHEAD CAM

Fig. 8-14 Various valve arrangements. Compare these drawings with the illustrations of different engines shown in the book.

☐ 8-14 METHOD OF COOLING

There are two methods of engine cooling: liquid-cooling and air-cooling. Almost all automotive engines are liquid-cooled. The liquid is called the *coolant*. It is a mixture of antifreeze and water. The cylinder block and cylinder head have water jackets through which the coolant can circulate to carry away excess heat. Figure 8-15 is a cutaway V-8 engine. The arrows show how the coolant circulates through the water jackets. Operation of the liquid-cooling system is described in Chap. 12.

The Volkswagen flat-four and Chevrolet Corvair flat-six engines are both air-cooled. Also, most of the small engines used in power mowers and other garden equipment are air-cooled. Figure 8-5 shows the Volkswagen flat-four air-cooled engine. Fins circle the cylinder block and head. These fins have large surface areas that carry heat away from the cylinders. Automotive air-cooled engines are equipped with *shrouds*. These are shields that direct air from a fan driven by the engine crankshaft. The air circulates past the fins and helps to keep the engine cool. Most motorcycle engines are air-cooled. They do not use fans or shrouds.

☐ 8-15 CLASSIFICATION BY PISTON STROKES

Engines can be classified according to the number of piston strokes needed to complete one cycle of engine operation (Fig. 8-16). The four strokes of the four-cycle engine were described in Chap. 6. This engine requires four piston strokes to make one complete cycle. Many small engines in equipment such as chain saws and lawn mowers, and in motorcycles, use the *two-stroke cycle*. In the two-cycle engine, the complete cycle takes place in only two piston strokes. Two-cycle engines are described in *Small Engine Mechanics* and in *Motorcycle Mechanics*. These are two other books in the McGraw-Hill Automotive Technology Series.

☐ 8-16 TYPE OF FUEL BURNED

Automotive engines can be classified according to the type of fuel they use. Most automobile engines run on gasoline. Some have made use of

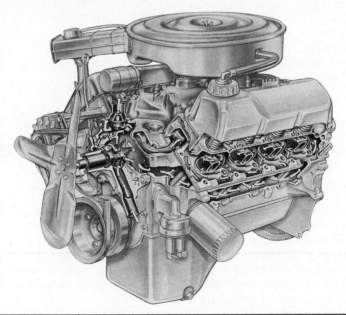

Fig. 8-15 Cutaway V-8 engine, showing the cooling system. The arrows show the direction of coolant flow through the water jackets. *(Ford Motor Company)*

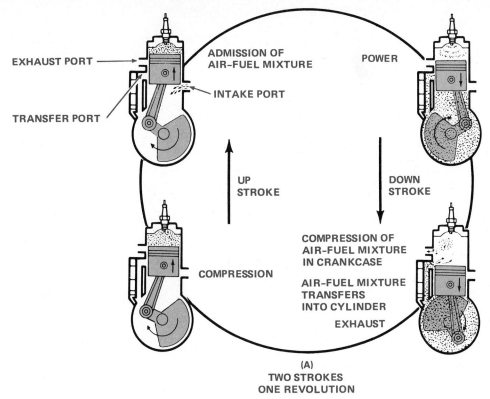

EXHAUST PORT

ADMISSION OF AIR-FUEL MIXTURE

POWER

INTAKE PORT

TRANSFER PORT

UP STROKE

DOWN STROKE

COMPRESSION OF AIR-FUEL MIXTURE IN CRANKCASE

AIR-FUEL MIXTURE TRANSFERS INTO CYLINDER

COMPRESSION

EXHAUST

**(A)
TWO STROKES
ONE REVOLUTION**

ADMISSION OF AIR-FUEL MIXTURE

EXHAUST

INTAKE VALVE OPEN

EXHAUST VALVE CLOSED

COMPRESSION

POWER

INTAKE VALVE CLOSED

HEAD

BOTH VALVES CLOSED

BOTH VALVES CLOSED

EXHAUST VALVE OPEN

INTAKE PORT

SPARK PLUG

EXHAUST PORT

CYLINDER

PISTON

CONNECTING ROD

DOWN STROKE

UP STROKE

DOWN STROKE

UP STROKE

CRANKSHAFT

**(B)
FOUR STROKES
TWO REVOLUTIONS**

Fig. 8-16 Comparison of the operation of a two-cycle engine with a four-cycle engine.

gasohol, which is a mixture of gasoline and alcohol. However, these are considered gasoline engines. Some truck and bus engines, and a few car engines, run on liquefied petroleum gas (LPG) such as *propane.* Others use compressed natural gas (CNG). These are called *gas engines* because they use a gas (*not* a liquid) for fuel. Diesel engines use diesel fuel oil. Engine fuels are described more fully in Chap. 14.

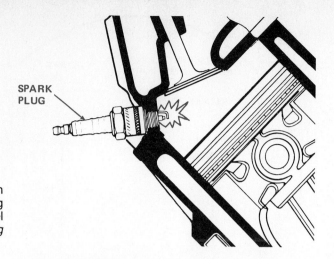

SPARK
PLUG

Fig. 8-17 In a spark-ignition engine, a spark at the spark plug ignites the compressed air-fuel mixture. *(Champion Spark Plug Company)*

□ *8-17 METHOD OF IGNITION*

Engines may be classified as spark-ignition or compression-ignition engines. The difference is in how the fuel is ignited in the cylinder. In the spark-ignition engine, a spark occurs at the spark plug (Fig. 8-17). The heat from this spark ignites the compressed air-fuel mixture. In the compression-ignition or diesel engine, the heat of compression ignites the fuel (Fig. 8-18). During the compression stroke, the air is raised to a temperature of 1000 degrees Fahrenheit [538 degrees Celsius] or higher. When the fuel is sprayed into the hot compressed air, the heat of compression ignites the fuel.

□ *8-18 FIRING ORDER*

Another way of classifying engines is by their *firing order*. This is the sequence in which the cylinders deliver their power strokes. Engines are designed to deliver the power strokes to the crankshaft in a certain pattern. Two adjacent cylinders are usually not allowed to fire one after the other. When an end cylinder fires, the next cylinder to fire should be near the center or toward the other end of the crankshaft. The purpose of carefully scattering the power strokes along the crankshaft is to avoid

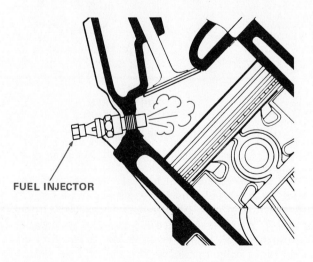

FUEL INJECTOR

Fig. 8-18 In a diesel engine, the heat of compression ignites the fuel as it is sprayed into the hot compressed air. *(ATW)*

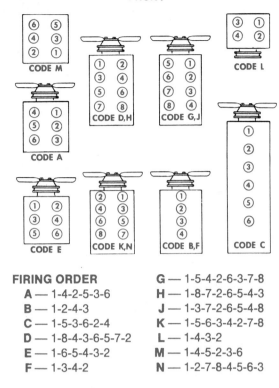

FIRING ORDER

A — 1-4-2-5-3-6
B — 1-2-4-3
C — 1-5-3-6-2-4
D — 1-8-4-3-6-5-7-2
E — 1-6-5-4-3-2
F — 1-3-4-2

G — 1-5-4-2-6-3-7-8
H — 1-8-7-2-6-5-4-3
J — 1-3-7-2-6-5-4-8
K — 1-5-6-3-4-2-7-8
L — 1-4-3-2
M — 1-4-5-2-3-6
N — 1-2-7-8-4-5-6-3

Fig. 8-19 Firing orders for various cylinder arrangements. *(Standard Motor Products, Inc.)*

stress on any one part of the crankshaft. If two or three adjacent cylinders are fired one after the other, this places a strain on the crankshaft. It may break. A proper firing order prevents this.

Figure 8-19 shows the possible firing orders for various cylinder arrangements. In four-cylinder engines, adjacent cylinders do fire one after another. This is because there are only two reasonable firing orders: 1–3–4–2 or 1–2–4–3. In the 1–3–4–2 firing order, number 1 cylinder fires, followed in order by number 3, 4, and 2 cylinders. Cylinders are numbered from front to back.

It is easier to keep the power strokes scattered in a six-cylinder in-line engine. Two firing orders are possible in these engines: 1–5–3–6–2–4 and 1–4–2–6–3–5. However, all these engines today fire 1–5–3–6–2–4 (Fig. 8-19).

In both four-cylinder and six-cylinder engines, the cylinders are numbered from front to back. The cylinders in V-type engines are numbered in various ways. One engine manufacturer numbers them from front to rear in this way:

■ Right bank: 2–4–6–8
■ Left bank: 1–3–5–7

The right bank is the right-hand row as viewed from the driver's seat. The firing order of this engine is 1–8–4–3–6–5–7–2. Firing order is also discussed in later chapters.

NOTE The firing order is built in by the engine designer. It cannot be changed without major redesign of the engine. However, in some engines the firing order can be changed by installing a different camshaft. Then the ignition must be rewired.

□ 8-19 ROTARY ENGINES

Until now, we have been talking about reciprocating engines. These engines have pistons that move up and down, or reciprocate, in cylinders. There is another type of engine that has no pistons. Instead, it has a rotor that is spun by force from the burning fuel in the engine. There are two general types of rotary engines: the gas turbine and the Wankel.

□ 8-20 GAS TURBINES

Gas turbines have been used in a few buses and trucks. But some engineers think we may never see them as a mass-produced car engine. Figure 8-20 shows the airflow through an automotive gas-turbine engine. There are two sections to the gas-turbine: the gasifier section, where the fuel is burned, and the power section, where the power from the burned fuel is produced. The gas turbine can burn gasoline, kerosene, or oil for fuel.

The compressor in the gasifier section has an impeller with a series of blades on it. When the impeller spins, it acts as an air pump and supplies the burner with high-pressure air. This is shown by the arrows at the left in Fig. 8-20. In the burner, fuel is sprayed into the compressed air, where the fuel is ignited and burned. The burned gases then flow, at higher pressures, through the blades of the power turbine. This causes the turbine rotor to spin. Then the rotary motion is carried through shafts and gears to the vehicle drive wheels.

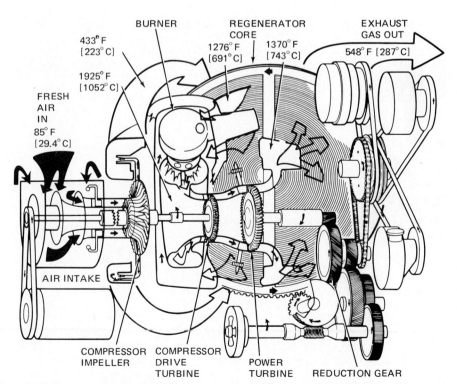

Fig. 8-20 Air flow through an automotive gas-turbine engine. *(Chrysler Corporation)*

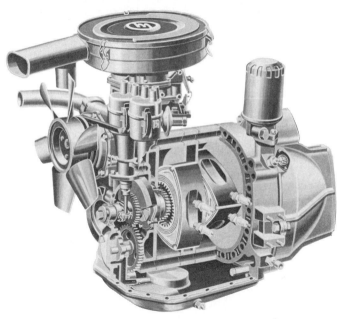

Fig. 8-21 Cutaway of a Mazda two-rotor Wankel engine. *(Mazda Motors of America, Inc.)*

□ 8-21 WANKEL-ENGINE CONSTRUCTION

The *Wankel engine* (Fig. 8-21) has a rotor that spins in an oval housing shaped like a fat figure 8. This shape is called an *epitrochoid*. The Japanese firm of Toyo Kogyo has produced more than 1 million Mazda cars powered by Wankel engines. Other manufacturers have also produced Wankel-powered cars. General Motors spent many millions of dollars on the Wankel engine but then decided not to use it.

The Wankel is also called a *rotary-combustion,* or RC, engine. This is because the combustion chambers rotate, or move in somewhat circular paths. The engine uses a three-lobe rotor (Fig. 8-22) that rotates eccentrically in an oval housing. The three lobes always have *apex seals* in contact with the oval housing. These seals compare with the seals formed by the piston rings against the cylinder wall in the reciprocating engine.

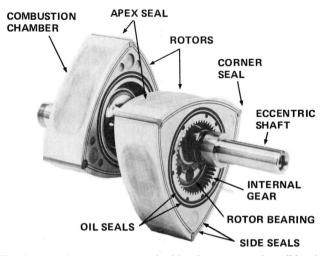

Fig. 8-22 The three main moving parts of a Mazda rotary engine. *(Mazda Motors of America, Inc.)*

111

□ 8-22 WANKEL-ENGINE OPERATION

The Wankel engine is a four-cycle engine. The four actions—intake, compression, power, and exhaust—are going on at the same time around the rotor as long as the engine is running. Figure 8-23 shows how the Wankel engine works. The rotor lobes A, B, and C seal tightly against the housing. The rotor has recesses in its three faces between the lobes. These are the combustion chambers. They are shown by the dashed lines on the rotors in Fig. 8-23. The spaces between the rotor lobes are where intake, compression, power, and exhaust take place.

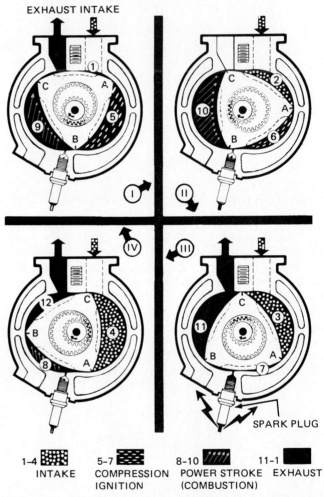

Fig. 8-23 Actions in a Wankel engine during one complete revolution of the rotor.

Select the *one* correct, best, or most probable answer to each question. Then check your answers against the correct answers given at the end of the book.

1. What are three ways to classify automotive engines?
    a. by valve number, cylinder arrangement, and valve arrangement
    b. by cylinder ports, cylinder arrangement, and valve arrangement
    c. by number of cylinders, cylinder arrangement, and valve arrangement
    d. none of the above

2. The cylinders in a four-cylinder engine can be arranged in three ways: two opposed rows of two cylinders each,
    a. two rows in a V, and in line
    b. in a circle, and radially
    c. end to end, and radially
    d. all of the above

3. The supercharger is an air pump that
    a. delivers more air or air-fuel mixture to the engine
    b. increases the power output of the engine
    c. improves the full-power performance of the engine
    d. all of the above

4. The type of supercharger driven by exhaust gas is called a
    a. charger
    b. supercharger
    c. turbocharger
    d. power charger

5. The multiple-displacement V-8 engine selectively cuts out
    a. one or two cylinders
    b. two and three cylinders
    c. two and four cylinders
    d. four and six cylinders

6. The two firing orders for four-cylinder in-line engines are
    a. 1–2–3–4 and 4–3–2–1
    b. 1–4–3–2 and 1–3–4–2
    c. 1–3–4–2 and 1–2–4–3
    d. 4–2–3–1 and 4–3–2–1

7. Two types of rotary engines are
    a. piston and Wankel
    b. piston and turbine
    c. turbocharger and Wankel
    d. gas turbine and Wankel

8. The Wankel engine has
    a. a three-lobed rotor
    b. two rotary pistons
    c. a rhombic drive
    d. a gasifier and a power section

9. By the method of cooling, engines are classified as
   a. air-cooled and liquid-cooled
   b. water-cooled and liquid-cooled
   c. air-cooled and oil-cooled
   d. none of the above

10. The two-cycle engine produces a power stroke
   a. every four crankshaft revolutions
   b. every three crankshaft revolutions
   c. every two crankshaft revolutions
   d. every crankshaft revolution

CHAPTER 9
ENGINE CONSTRUCTION

After studying this chapter, you should be able to:

1. Explain the function of the cylinder block and cylinder head in the engine.

2. Name the parts attached externally to the block and describe the function of each.

3. Name the parts installed internally in the block and describe the function of each.

Earlier chapters described basic engine operation and the various types of engines used in cars. This chapter covers the construction of typical automotive engines. It takes a close look at the various engine components, how they are made, and what they do in the engine. Unless otherwise noted, the engine is liquid-cooled. The discussion begins with the cylinder block. This is followed by sections covering the parts that are attached to it. Later sections then discuss the parts that are installed in it. Valves and valve trains are described in Chap. 10.

☐ 9-1 CYLINDER BLOCK

The cylinder block of a liquid-cooled engine is the basic part—the foundation—of the engine. Every other part is put inside the block or attached to it. Figure 9-1 shows the major components that are placed in and attached to a V-8 engine cylinder block. Only one piston-and-connecting-rod assembly and one cylinder head are shown. Figure 9-2 shows a disassembled cylinder-block assembly for a V-8 engine. Again, only one piston assembly is shown.

The cylinder block is a complicated casting made of gray iron ("cast iron") or aluminum. It contains the cylinders and the water jackets that surround them. Figure 9-3 shows one bank of a V-6 cylinder block cut away to show the internal construction. To make the cylinder block, a sand form—called a *mold*—is made. Then molten metal is poured into the mold. When the metal has cooled, the sand mold is broken up and removed. This leaves the rough cylinder-block casting. The casting is

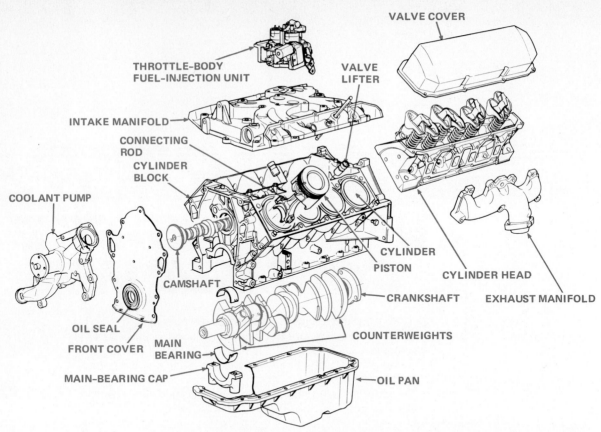

THROTTLE-BODY
FUEL-INJECTION UNIT

VALVE COVER

VALVE LIFTER

INTAKE MANIFOLD

CONNECTING ROD

CYLINDER BLOCK

COOLANT PUMP

CYLINDER PISTON

CYLINDER HEAD

EXHAUST MANIFOLD

CAMSHAFT

CRANKSHAFT

OIL SEAL

FRONT COVER

MAIN BEARING

COUNTERWEIGHTS

MAIN-BEARING CAP

OIL PAN

Fig. 9-1 Major components that are placed in and attached to a V-8 engine cylinder block. *(Cadillac Motor Car Division of General Motors Corporation)*

then cleaned and machined to make the finished block. Core clean-out holes are needed (Fig. 9-3) so that the sand cores that were originally in place can be cleaned out. This leaves the water jackets (Chap. 12). Liquid coolant flows through these spaces to prevent the engine from overheating.

Cylinder blocks for diesel engines are very similar to those for spark-ignition engines. The basic difference is that the diesel-engine cylinder block is heavier and stronger. This is because of the higher pressures developed in the diesel-engine cylinders.

☐ 9-2 ALUMINUM CYLINDER BLOCKS

Several engines have aluminum cylinder blocks. Aluminum is a relatively light metal, weighing much less than cast iron. Also, aluminum conducts heat more rapidly than cast iron. This means there is less chance for hot spots to develop. However, aluminum is too soft to use as cylinder-wall material. It wears too rapidly. Therefore, aluminum cylinder blocks must have cast-iron cylinder liners or be cast from an aluminum alloy which has silicon particles in it.

Mercedes-Benz, Porsche, and other manufacturers make an aluminum cylinder block that does not have cylinder liners, or sleeves. Instead, the aluminum is loaded with silicon particles. Silicon is a very hard mate-

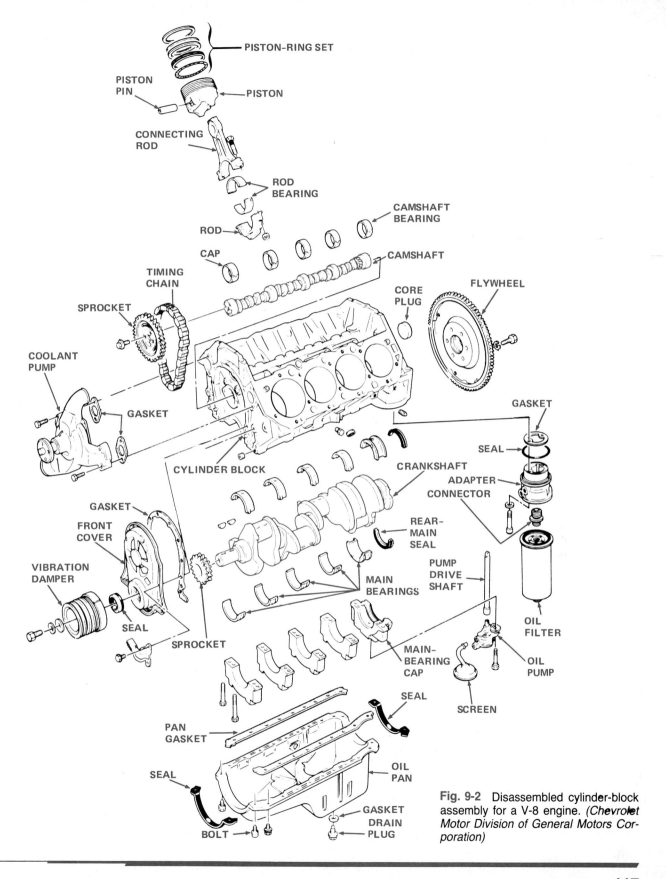

PISTON-RING SET

PISTON PIN

PISTON

CONNECTING ROD

ROD BEARING

CAMSHAFT BEARING

ROD

CAP

CAMSHAFT

TIMING CHAIN

SPROCKET

CORE PLUG

FLYWHEEL

COOLANT PUMP

GASKET

CYLINDER BLOCK

GASKET

SEAL

CRANKSHAFT

ADAPTER CONNECTOR

GASKET

FRONT COVER

REAR-MAIN SEAL

VIBRATION DAMPER

MAIN BEARINGS

PUMP DRIVE SHAFT

OIL FILTER

SEAL

SPROCKET

MAIN-BEARING CAP

OIL PUMP

SEAL

PAN GASKET

SCREEN

SEAL

OIL PAN

BOLT

GASKET DRAIN PLUG

Fig. 9-2 Disassembled cylinder-block assembly for a V-8 engine. *(Chevrolet Motor Division of General Motors Corporation)*

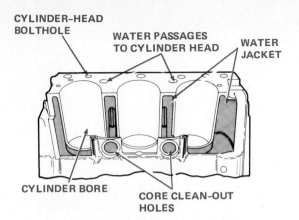

Fig. 9-3 One bank of a V-6 engine partly cutaway to show the internal construction.

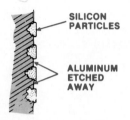

Fig. 9-4 Greatly enlarged view of a cylinder-wall surface in an aluminum alloy block with silicon particles in it.

rial. After the cylinder block is cast, the cylinders are honed. Then they are treated with a chemical that etches—or eats away—the surface aluminum. This leaves only the silicon particles exposed (Fig. 9-4). The piston and rings slide on the silicon with minimum wear.

□ 9-3 CYLINDER LINERS, OR SLEEVES

Cylinder liners are sleeves that are either cast into the block or installed later. With the cast-in type, the cylinder liners are installed in the mold and the aluminum is poured around them. They then become a permanent part of the cylinder block.

Two kinds of liners, dry and wet, can be installed later in either cast-iron or aluminum blocks. The dry liner is forced, or driven, into the cylinder block (Fig. 9-5). This type touches the cylinder block along the liner's full length. The wet liner touches the cylinder block only at the top and bottom (Fig. 9-6). The rest of the liner is in direct contact with the coolant. Wet and dry liners are removable. They can be replaced if they become worn or damaged.

Fig. 9-5 Installing a dry liner in a cylinder block.

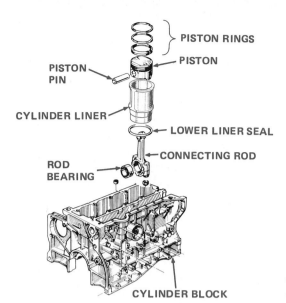

PISTON RINGS

PISTON

PISTON PIN

PISTON

CYLINDER LINER

LOWER LINER SEAL

CONNECTING ROD

ROD BEARING

CYLINDER BLOCK

Fig. 9-6 Cylinder block using wet liners. *(American Motors Corporation)*

EXTERNAL ENGINE PARTS

□ 9-4 PARTS ATTACHED TO THE BLOCK

Parts that are attached to the block when the engine is assembled are shown in Fig. 9-1. The cylinder head or heads are mounted on top of the block. Valve covers, intake and exhaust manifolds, carburetor or throttle body, and other parts are installed at the top of the engine. The crankshaft is hung underneath the block by bearings and bearing caps (Fig. 9-2). The oil pan attaches to the bottom of the block. Together, the lower part of the cylinder block and the pan form the engine *crankcase* (□ 9-5).

The timing chain (Fig. 9-2) is mounted on the crankshaft and camshaft sprockets so that the crankshaft can drive the camshaft. Other engines use a toothed belt, or a pair of gears, to drive the camshaft. The timing cover, or *front cover,* and water pump are attached to the front of the block. The clutch housing, or automatic transmission or transaxle, is attached at the rear of the block.

□ 9-5 OIL PAN

The oil pan (Figs. 9-1 and 9-2) is attached to the bottom of the cylinder block. The pan is formed from pressed steel or plastic. It usually holds from 4 to 9 quarts [4 to 8.5 L] of oil, depending on engine design. Bigger engines require more oil. The oil pan and the lower part of the cylinder block form the *crankcase*. This is a box, or case, that encloses, or encases, the crankshaft. Therefore the enclosure is called the crankcase.

Gaskets (□ 4-23) are used to seal the joint between the cylinder block and the oil pan. The gaskets prevent loss of oil from the pan. When the engine is running, the oil pump sends oil from the oil pan up to the moving engine parts. The engine lubricating system is described in Chap. 11.

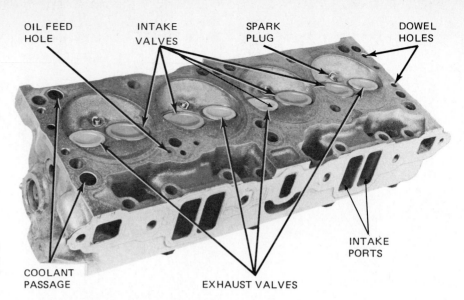

OIL FEED HOLE · INTAKE VALVES · SPARK PLUG · DOWEL HOLES · INTAKE PORTS · COOLANT PASSAGE · EXHAUST VALVES

Fig. 9-7 A cylinder head for a V-8 overhead-valve spark-ignition engine. *(Chrysler Corporation)*

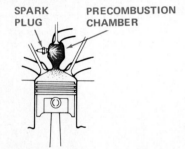

SPARK PLUG · PRECOMBUSTION CHAMBER

Fig. 9-8 One type of precombustion chamber for a spark-ignition engine.

□ 9-6 CYLINDER HEAD

The cylinder head is cast in one piece from gray iron or aluminum alloy. The casting method uses sand molds. The process is similar to casting cylinder blocks (□ 9-1). Each head includes water jackets and passages from the valve ports to the openings in the *manifolds*. On a V-type engine, there are two cylinder heads.

A typical cylinder head for a spark-ignition V-8 engine is shown in Fig. 9-7. It is a complex casting. Many machining operations are required to convert the rough casting into a finished cylinder head. Some cylinder heads include a *precombustion chamber*. This is a small chamber connected to the main combustion chamber. The precombustion chamber in a spark-ignition engine is shown in Fig. 9-8. In this engine, the precombustion chamber is directly above the main combustion chamber. Combustion of the air-fuel mixture begins when the spark occurs at the spark plug. It is located in the precombustion chamber.

Diesel-engine cylinder heads have a hole for the fuel-injection valve, or *fuel injector,* instead of the spark plug. Cylinder heads for automotive diesel engines usually have a precombustion chamber (Fig. 9-9). The fuel

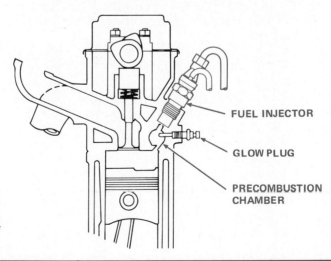

FUEL INJECTOR · GLOW PLUG · PRECOMBUSTION CHAMBER

Fig. 9-9 A diesel-engine precombustion chamber showing the locations of the glow plug and the fuel injector. *(Volkswagen of America, Inc.)*

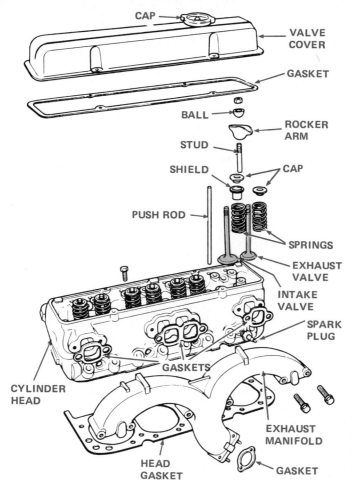

CAP

VALVE COVER

GASKET

BALL

ROCKER ARM

STUD

SHIELD

CAP

PUSH ROD

SPRINGS

EXHAUST VALVE

INTAKE VALVE

SPARK PLUG

GASKETS

CYLINDER HEAD

EXHAUST MANIFOLD

HEAD GASKET

GASKET

Fig. 9-10 Parts attached to a cylinder head for a V-8 engine. The valves and related parts for one cylinder are shown disassembled. *(Chevrolet Motor Division of General Motors Corporation)*

is sprayed into the precombustion chamber and starts burning there.

The cylinder heads also carry the valve assemblies. Figure 9-10 shows one of the two cylinder heads for a V-8 engine, with one set of valves removed. This head is for a pushrod engine, which has the camshaft in the cylinder block. Only one pushrod is shown. Actually, there are eight, one for each valve in the head.

Figure 9-11 shows the cylinder head for an overhead-camshaft engine. The camshaft and camshaft bearings (located in the cylinder head)

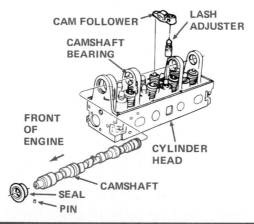

CAM FOLLOWER

LASH ADJUSTER

CAMSHAFT BEARING

FRONT OF ENGINE

CYLINDER HEAD

CAMSHAFT

SEAL

PIN

Fig. 9-11 Cylinder head for an overhead-camshaft engine, showing the bearings to support the camshaft. *(Ford Motor Company)*

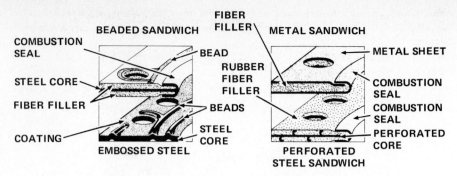

Fig. 9-12 Various types of head gaskets. *(Fel-Pro Incorporated)*

are shown. Also shown is the cam follower (rocker arm) and lash adjuster for one valve. None of the valves have been removed. Valves and valve trains are described in Chap. 10.

☐ 9-7 HEAD GASKETS

The joints between the cylinder block and the cylinder head must be tight. They must hold in the high pressure caused by combustion. The block and head cannot be machined flat enough to provide the necessary seal. Therefore, a *head gasket* is installed between the cylinder block and cylinder head (Fig. 9-10). The head gasket is shaped to fit the block, with all openings cut out.

The two types of head gaskets for automotive engines are the *embossed steel,* or "shim," type and the *sandwich* type (Fig. 9-12). Many of the newer engine designs use the embossed steel gasket. It is basically a beaded sheet of steel shim that is 0.020 inch [0.51 mm] thick. Various coatings, such as Teflon, are applied to it during manufacture. These aid in sealing. The perforated sandwich gasket has a thin sheet-steel core with tangs or perforations. These hold facing or filler material to both sides of the core. The soft surfaces provide sealing for the coolant and oil passages. Metal reinforcements are used to seal around the combustion chambers.

When the engine is assembled, the head gasket is placed between the block and the head. Then the head bolts are installed and tightened. This squeezes the gasket between the head and the block, sealing the joint. Some types of sandwich gaskets do not require later retorquing of the cylinder-head bolts.

The Volkswagen four-cylinder air-cooled engine (Fig. 8-5) does not use a head gasket. Instead, a *sealing ring* is installed between a shoulder on the cylinder and the cylinder head (Fig. 9-13).

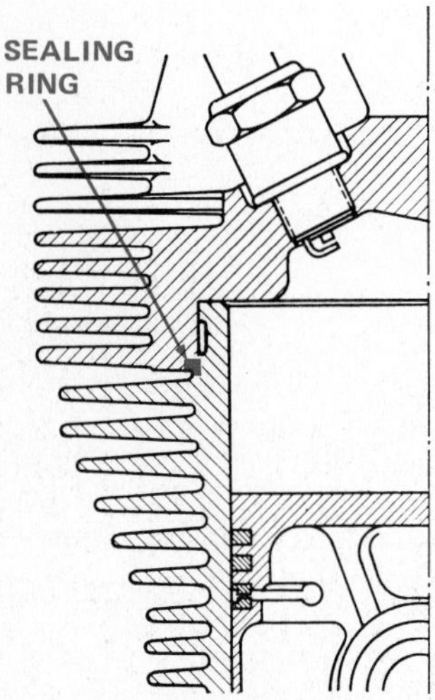

Gaskets are also used between the block and the other parts that are attached to it. Figure 4-32 shows a complete gasket set for a six-cylinder in-line engine. Other types of gaskets and gasket materials are described in Chap. 4.

Fig. 9-13 Instead of a head gasket, a sealing ring is used to prevent combustion leakage from an air-cooled engine. *(Volkswagen of America, Inc.)*

☐ 9-8 INTAKE MANIFOLD

The *intake manifold* (Figs. 9-1 and 9-14) is a casting with a series of passages that attaches to the cylinder head. In a spark-ignition engine, the passages carry air or air-fuel mixture. It flows from the carburetor or throttle body (fuel-injection system) through the intake manifold to the intake-valve ports in the cylinder head. On most in-line engines, the intake manifold is mounted on the same side of the engine as the exhaust

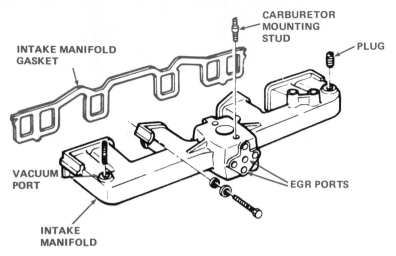

Fig. 9-14 Intake manifold for a six-cylinder in-line engine. *(American Motors Corporation)*

manifold. A gasket (Fig. 9-14) is used between the intake manifold and the mounting surface on the cylinder head. On V-type engines, the intake manifold is mounted between the cylinder banks (Fig. 9-1).

In diesel engines, only air flows to the cylinders. Therefore, the intake manifold carries only air. The fuel is injected directly into the cylinders by the fuel-injection system after the air is compressed.

□ 9-9 EXHAUST MANIFOLD

The *exhaust manifold* (Fig. 9-15) is a set of tubes which carry the burned exhaust gases away from the engine cylinders. Passages in the exhaust manifold connect to the exhaust ports in the cylinder head. A gasket is not always used between them. When the exhaust valve opens, the exhaust gases flow from the cylinder past the valve into the port. Then the exhaust gases pass through the exhaust manifold and into the car exhaust system.

On in-line overhead-valve engines, the exhaust manifold is bolted to the cylinder head. The exhaust manifold shown in Fig. 9-15 mounts underneath the intake manifold shown in Fig. 9-14. On V-type engines there are two exhaust manifolds, one for each bank of cylinders (Fig. 9-1). The exhaust manifolds are bolted to the outsides of the two heads. The exhaust system carries the exhaust gases from the exhaust manifold to the outside air. The exhaust system is described in Chap. 14.

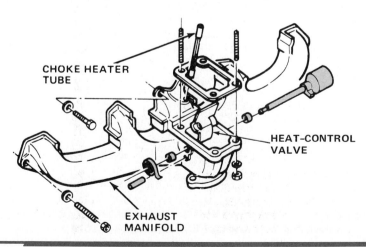

Fig. 9-15 The exhaust manifold for a six-cylinder in-line engine. The heat-control valve and parts are shown disassembled. *(American Motors Corporation)*

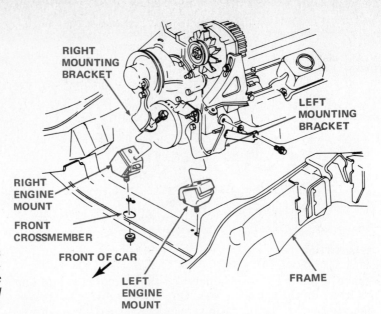

Fig. 9-16 Front engine mounts that support and insulate the engine from the frame. *(Cadillac Motor Car Division of General Motors Corporation)*

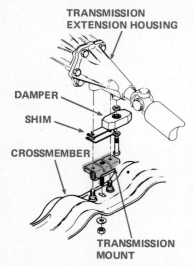

Fig. 9-17 Location of the rear engine mount, or transmission mount, between the transmission extension housing and a body or frame cross member. *(Buick Motor Division of General Motors Corporation)*

□ 9-10 ENGINE MOUNTS

If the engine is bolted directly to the car body or frame, the car vibrates too much. Passengers complain and parts fail early. To prevent these problems, the engine is bolted through flexible rubber insulators, or *engine mounts*. This places insulating collars, or pads, between the engine and the mounting brackets.

Many engines have a three-point mounting arrangement. One mount is placed on each side of the cylinder block (Fig. 9-16). The third mount is located between the transmission extension housing and a body or frame cross member (Fig. 9-17). Other engines have four mounting points.

Engines that are transversely mounted also may use three-point mounting. There usually is a right and left mount at each end of the engine (Fig. 9-18). These mounts carry the weight of the engine and the attached transaxle. The third mount is attached from the side of the engine to a reinforced section of the body. When the engine "torques," or attempts to move sideways, the mount limits the movement.

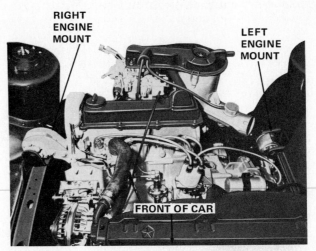

Fig. 9-18 On a transverse engine, the weight is supported by a mount at each end of the engine. *(Chrysler Corporation)*

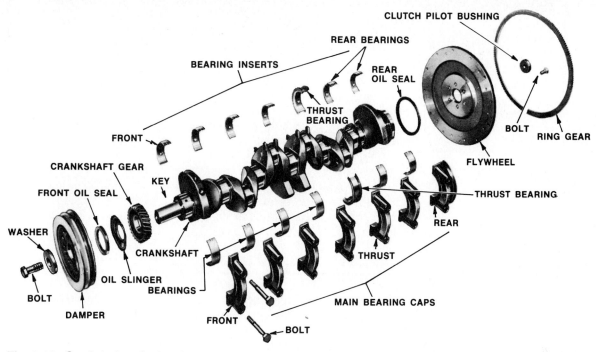

Fig. 9-19 Crankshaft and related parts for a six-cylinder engine. *(Ford Motor Company)*

☐ 9-11 CRANKSHAFT

The *crankshaft* is the main rotating member, or shaft, in the engine (Fig. 9-19). It has *crankpins* (Fig. 9-20) to which the connecting rods from the pistons are attached. During the power strokes, the connecting rods force the crankpins and therefore the crankshaft to rotate. The reciprocating motion of the pistons is changed to rotary motion as the crankshaft spins. This rotary motion is transmitted through the power train to the car wheels.

The crankshaft is a strong, one-piece casting, or forging, of heat-treated alloy steel. It must be strong enough to take the downward force

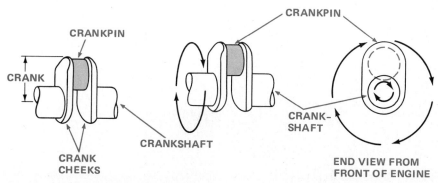

Fig. 9-20 The crankpins are offset from the center line of the crankshaft.

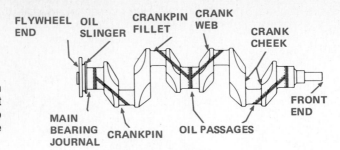

Fig. 9-21 Oil flows through holes drilled in the crankshaft from the main-bearing journals to the crankpins to lubricate the connecting-rod bearings.

of the power strokes without excessive bending. It must be balanced so the engine will run without excessive vibration (□ 9-12). It must distribute oil from the main bearings through drilled passages to the connecting-rod bearings (Fig. 9-21).

□ 9-12 CRANKSHAFT BALANCE

The crankpins are offset from the center line of the crankshaft (Fig. 9-20). As the crankpins rotate, they cause an out-of-balance condition. In addition, the lower ends (the "big ends") of the connecting rods are moving in circles along with the crankpins. At the same time, the upper ends of the connecting rods, the piston pins, and the pistons and rings are rapidly moving toward and away from the crankshaft center line. These reciprocating and rotating forces could cause serious vibrations while the engine is running. However, *counterweights* (Figs. 9-1 and 9-2) on the crankshaft tend to counterbalance these forces.

Some four-cylinder engines achieve balance by using one or two balance shafts (Figs. 8-4 and 9-22). The engine shown in Fig. 9-22 has two balance shafts which rotate at twice crankshaft speed. The balance shafts have additional counterweights. At the same time that the engine tries to move in one direction, the balance shafts are trying to move it equally in the opposite direction. This cancels any out-of-balance condition that could cause engine vibration.

A crankshaft with *splayed* crankpins is used to balance some V-6 engines that have a 90 degree angle between the banks (□ 8-7). This engine does not fire evenly. The uneven firing causes vibration. By splaying, or "spreading apart," the crankpins, each rod has its own crankpin (Fig. 9-23). This reduces the engine vibration.

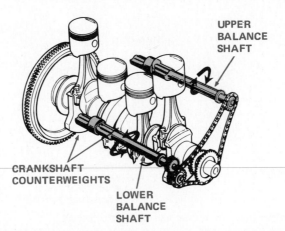

Fig. 9-22 How a four-cylinder engine uses two balance shafts to reduce engine noise and vibration. *(Chrysler Corporation)*

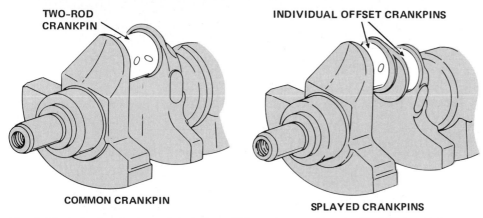

TWO-ROD CRANKPIN

INDIVIDUAL OFFSET CRANKPINS

COMMON CRANKPIN

SPLAYED CRANKPINS

Fig. 9-23 Left, standard crankshaft for a V-6 engine compared with (right) a V-6 crankshaft with splayed crankpins. *(Buick Motor Division of General Motors Corporation)*

□ 9-13 ENGINE BEARINGS

Bearings are needed at every point in the engine where there is rotary motion between engine parts. Bearings are parts that transmit a load to a support. In doing this job, they take most of the friction and wear of the moving parts. Bearings usually are replaceable. When they wear, they can be removed and new bearings installed. This costs much less than replacing major parts.

In the engine, bearings are used with three basic components (Fig. 9-24). These bearings are the crankshaft bearings (□ 9-14), the connecting-rod bearings (□ 9-15), and the camshaft bearings (Chap. 10). The bearing is named for the part or shaft that it supports. For example, the crankshaft bearings support the crankshaft.

□ 9-14 MAIN BEARINGS

Figure 9-25 shows a crankshaft and bearings. The bearings that support the crankshaft are called *main bearings,* or "mains." These are thin shells, or *inserts,* that fit into bores made in the cylinder block and main-bearing caps. The round sections along the center of the crankshaft that rest on the bearings are called the crankshaft *journals.* They rotate in the bearings.

The crankshaft shown in Fig. 9-25 has five main bearings. There is one at each end of the engine, and between each connecting rod. The

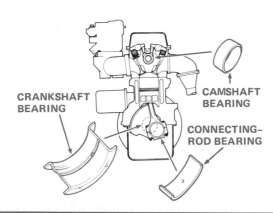

CRANKSHAFT BEARING

CAMSHAFT BEARING

CONNECTING-ROD BEARING

Fig. 9-24 In the engine, bearings are used with the crankshaft, connecting rods, and camshaft. *(Federal-Mogul Corporation)*

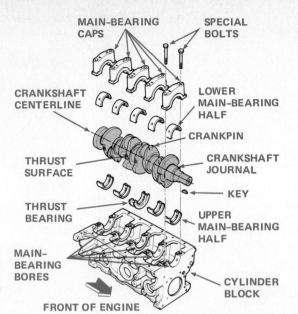

MAIN–BEARING CAPS   SPECIAL BOLTS

CRANKSHAFT CENTERLINE

LOWER MAIN–BEARING HALF

CRANKPIN

THRUST SURFACE

CRANKSHAFT JOURNAL

KEY

THRUST BEARING

UPPER MAIN–BEARING HALF

MAIN–BEARING BORES

CYLINDER BLOCK

FRONT OF ENGINE

Fig. 9-25 Disassembled engine "bottom end" showing the crankshaft and bearings. Arrows on caps should point toward front of engine. *(Ford Motor Company)*

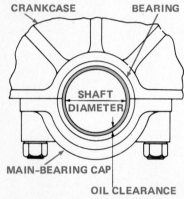

CRANKCASE   BEARING

SHAFT DIAMETER

MAIN–BEARING CAP

OIL CLEARANCE

Fig. 9-26 Oil clearance between the main bearing and the crankshaft journal. *(Clevite)*

upper half of the main bearing is installed in the cylinder block. The lower half is installed in the main-bearing cap. Then the cap is installed with special bolts to hold the bearing assembly in place. The space between the bearing and the shaft is called the *oil clearance,* or *bearing clearance* (Fig. 9-26).

To prevent the crankshaft from moving forward or backward in the block, one main bearing has flanges on the sides (Figs. 9-19 and 9-25). This bearing is called the *thrust bearing.* When the crankshaft tries to shift, machined surfaces on both sides of a main-bearing journal come up against the thrust-bearing flanges. This limits the forward or rearward movement of the crankshaft.

Figure 9-27 shows a typical bearing half, or insert, with the parts named. Each bearing half is usually made of a steel back. Then one or more layers of lining material are applied (Fig. 9-28). The bearing lining is relatively soft. As wear takes place, the lining wears instead of the more expensive crankshaft or other engine parts.

Some bearing inserts have an oil groove, or *annular groove* (Fig. 9-27). This groove helps distribute oil around the bearing. How the engine bearings are lubricated and operation of the engine lubricating system are described in Chap. 11.

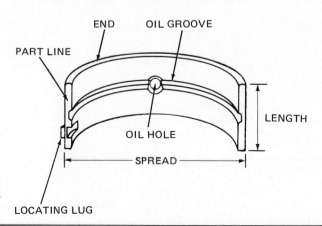

END   OIL GROOVE

PART LINE

LENGTH

OIL HOLE

SPREAD

LOCATING LUG

Fig. 9-27 Typical bearing half, or insert. *(McQuay-Norris Manufacturing Company)*

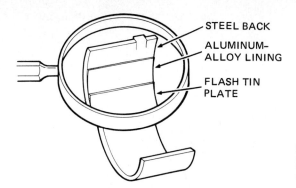

Fig. 9-28 Construction of a bearing insert. *(Federal-Mogul Corporation)*

□ 9-15 CONNECTING-ROD BEARINGS

Connecting-rod bearings (Fig. 9-29), or "rod bearings," are similar to main bearings, only smaller. Both are insert-type split bearings, which must be assembled around the crankshaft. The offset section of the crankshaft that fits inside the connecting-rod bearing is called the *crankpin* (Fig. 9-25), or "rod throw." Connecting-rod bearings are installed in about the same way as main bearings (Fig. 9-29). The upper bearing half is placed in the rod. The lower half is installed in the rod cap. Then the cap is bolted in place with the crankpin between the two bearing halves and torqued to specifications.

□ 9-16 CRANKSHAFT SEALS

In the engine, the crankshaft sticks out from the front and rear of the cylinder block. To prevent oil from leaking out of the crankcase past the rotating crankshaft, oil seals are installed at the front and rear. Figure 9-19 shows the crankshaft oil seals.

The *front-oil seal* is usually installed in the front cover (or *timing cover*) of the engine (Fig. 9-1). The *rear-main seal* prevents oil leakage past the flywheel end of the crankshaft (Figs. 9-2 and 9-19). Many engines also have an *oil slinger* at the front or rear (Fig. 9-19). This throws off excessive oil moving toward the seal.

□ 9-17 FLYWHEEL

The flow of power from the engine cylinders is not smooth. The power impulses overlap on six- and eight-cylinder engines. This is shown in Fig.

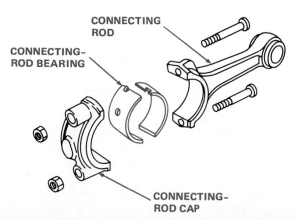

Fig. 9-29 Connecting-rod and bearing assembly. *(Federal-Mogul Corporation)*

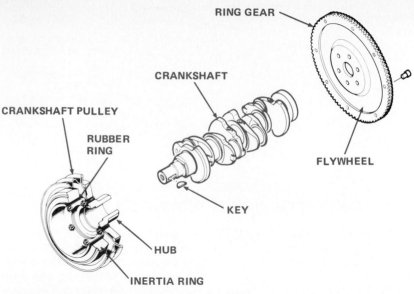

RING GEAR

CRANKSHAFT

CRANKSHAFT PULLEY

RUBBER RING

FLYWHEEL

KEY

HUB

INERTIA RING

HARMONIC BALANCER (VIBRATION DAMPER)

Fig. 9-30 In the engine, the crankshaft has a flywheel attached to the rear end and a vibration damper installed on the front end. *(ATW)*

6-21. When more power is being delivered, the crankshaft tries to speed up. While less power is being delivered, the crankshaft tries to slow down.

The *flywheel* (Fig. 9-30) helps keep the crankshaft turning at a steady speed. The flywheel is a heavy plate bolted to the rear end of the crankshaft. Because the flywheel is so heavy, it tends to turn at constant speed. The flywheel absorbs energy as the crankshaft tries to speed up. Then the flywheel gives back the energy as the crankshaft tries to slow down.

There are teeth around the outer rim of the flywheel (Fig. 9-30). This ring of teeth (the "ring gear") meshes with teeth on the starting-motor drive to crank the engine. The rear face of the flywheel also serves as the driving member of the clutch in cars with manual transmissions. (Clutches are described in Chap. 32.) In a car with an automatic transmission (Chap. 34), a light *flex plate* is bolted to the rear of the crankshaft. The automatic-transmission *torque converter* is then bolted to the flex plate. This serves the same function as the flywheel in stabilizing engine speed.

☐ 9-18 VIBRATION DAMPER

The front end of the crankshaft carries three devices. These are not actually "internal" engine parts. They are parts that form an assembly which is attached to the crankshaft, and not externally to the engine. First, there are the drive-belt pulleys. Belts running in these pulleys drive the engine fan, water pump, power-steering pump, air pump, air-conditioner compressor, and alternator. Second, there is some method of driving the camshaft (☐ 6-22). This may be gears, or sprockets and a chain or toothed belt. The third device on the front end of the crankshaft is the *harmonic balancer,* or *vibration damper* (Fig. 9-30).

As the engine runs, the power impulses hit the crankshaft in one place and then another. When a power impulse hits a crankpin toward the front of the engine, the crankshaft tries to "wind up" or twist a little. When that power stroke ends, the crankshaft unwinds. This twist-untwist action sets up an *oscillating* (back-and-forth) motion called *torsional vibration* (Fig. 9-31). If not controlled, it can break the crankshaft.

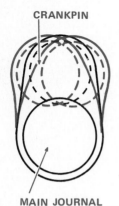

CRANKPIN

MAIN JOURNAL

Fig. 9-31 Torsional vibration causes the crankpin to flex with and then against crankshaft rotation.

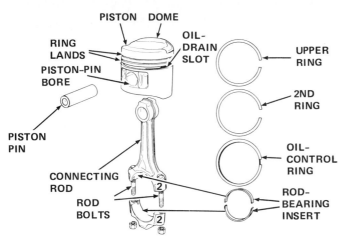

Fig. 9-32 Disassembled piston-and-connecting-rod assembly. *(Ford Motor Company)*

A vibration damper (Fig. 9-30) is mounted on the front end of the crankshaft to control torsional vibration. The vibration damper has a small flywheel, or "inertia ring." It is bonded through a rubber ring to a hub keyed to the crankshaft. While the engine is running, the inertia ring acts like a small flywheel. As the front of the crankshaft tries to speed up or slow down, the inertia ring resists any change of speed. By tending to hold the hub to a constant speed, torsional vibration of the crankshaft is kept to a minimum.

☐ 9-19 PISTON-AND-CONNECTING-ROD ASSEMBLY

The job of the piston-and-connecting-rod assembly (Fig. 9-32) is to carry the force caused by combustion from the piston through the connecting rod to the crankshaft. The force spins the crankshaft so that the car moves. The piston and connecting rod were introduced in Chap. 6. The following sections take a closer look at the parts that make up the piston-and-connecting-rod assembly.

☐ 9-20 CONNECTING ROD

The connecting rod (Fig. 9-32) is made of forged high-strength steel. It transmits force and motion from the piston to the crankpin on the crankshaft. A steel *piston pin*, or "wrist pin," connects the rod to the piston. The pin usually is pressed into the small end of the connecting rod (Fig. 9-33A). Some rods have a lock bolt in the small end (Fig. 9-33B). As the piston moves up and down the cylinder, the pin rocks back and forth in the hole, or bore, in the piston. The piston, which is made of aluminum alloy, acts as the bearing surface.

Another method of installation is to have a *bushing* in the small end of the rod (Fig. 9-33C). A bushing is a round, single-piece sleeve bearing. Then the pin is free to turn in both the rod or the piston. Some type of retainer or snap ring must be installed in grooves in the piston-pin bores to prevent the pin from sliding out.

The big end of the connecting rod is attached to a crankpin by a rod-bearing cap (Fig. 9-32). These are similar to main-bearing caps (☐ 9-14). Bearing inserts are installed in the rod and cap. Then assembly

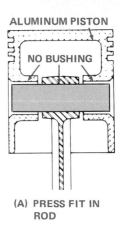

(A) PRESS FIT IN ROD

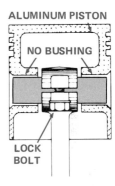

(B) LOCKED TO ROD

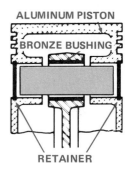

(C) FREE FLOATING

Fig. 9-33 Commonly used piston-pin arrangements. *(Sunnen Products Company)*

is completed. The bearing is lubricated by oil flowing from oilholes drilled through the crankshaft (Fig. 9-21). These oilholes go from the main-bearing journal to the crankpin.

Connecting rods and rod-bearing caps are assembled during manufacture. Then the hole for the bearing is bored with the cap in place. This is called *line-boring*. It makes each rod and its cap a matched set. Usually, the same number is stamped on the rod and cap (Fig. 9-32). This prevents the caps getting mixed during engine service. If the caps are mixed, the bearing bore will not be round. An engine assembled with the rod-bearing caps switched will probably lock the crankshaft. If the crankshaft turns, the bearing will probably have improper clearance and early bearing failure will result.

Another reason for keeping the cap and rod matched is to prevent engine unbalance and unwanted vibration. All connecting rods in an engine must be as light as possible. But they must all weigh the same. If one rod is heavier than the others, the engine will vibrate. This could damage the engine.

□ 9-21 PISTON-PIN LUBRICATION

The piston pin must be lubricated. In some engines, the connecting rod has a hole drilled up through it. Oil flows from the crankpin up to the piston pin. However, in most engines, the piston pin is lubricated from oil thrown off the rotating crankpin and rod big end. Some of the oil splashes onto the cylinder walls. The oil lubricates the walls and also the piston and piston rings. This oil is scraped off the cylinder walls by the piston rings. Some of the oil that is scraped off passes through holes or slots in the lower piston-ring groove (Fig. 9-32). This oil lubricates the piston pin.

□ 9-22 PISTONS

In the engine, the bottom of the combustion chamber is formed by the top of the piston (Fig. 7-7). The *piston* is the round plug that slides up and down in the cylinder. Force applied to the top of the piston by the high pressures of combustion pushes the piston down the cylinder. The piston transmits the force through the connecting rod to the crankpin. This causes the crankshaft to rotate. Therefore, the piston performs three jobs in the engine:

1. With the rings installed, the piston-and-ring assembly forms a sliding gastight seal in the cylinder.
2. The piston transmits the force of combustion through the piston pin to the connecting rod.
3. The piston provides bearing surfaces for the piston pin.

Pistons for automobile engines are made of aluminum. They are about 4 inches [100 mm] in diameter and weigh about 1 pound [454 g]. They are a loose sliding fit in the engine cylinders. A piston is shown attached to the connecting rod in Fig. 9-34. The piston pin is a press-fit in the connecting rod. Figure 9-32 shows all the parts separated.

The top surface of the piston is called the *head* (Fig. 9-34). The head may be flat (Fig. 9-34) or have a raised section, or *dome* (Fig. 9-32). Or the head may have flycuts or recesses for valve clearance, or even a cup shape. The upper section of the piston contains three or more *grooves* for piston rings. The areas between the ring grooves are called *ring lands*. The section under the rings is called the *skirt*. *Thrust faces* on the skirt guide the piston up and down the cylinder bore. A piston-pin *boss* is cast

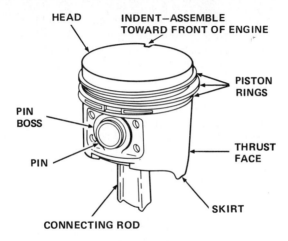

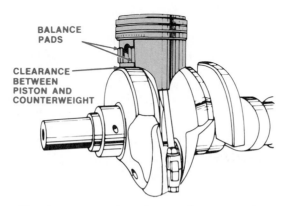

Fig. 9-34 Piston with rings installed, attached to the connecting rod.

Fig. 9-35 Slipper piston and connecting rod assembled to the crankshaft. *(Chevrolet Motor Division of General Motors Corporation)*

into each side of the piston. The boss is machined smooth to provide a bearing surface for the piston pin.

New pistons are often *plated.* During manufacture, they are coated with a thin layer of tin or other material. This plating helps prevent *scuffing* when the engine is first started and during break-in. Scuffing is a type of wear that occurs when parts slide against each other without lubrication. It shows up as pits and grooves in the mating surfaces.

☐ 9-23 PISTON TYPES

Two types of pistons are used in car engines. These are the *full skirt,* or *trunk, piston* (Fig. 9-33) and the *slipper piston* (Figs. 9-33 and 9-35). Most car engines use the slipper piston. Cutting away part of the skirt makes the piston lighter. This still leaves adequate surface, or *thrust face,* for normal operation. The thrust faces (Fig. 9-34) prevent the piston from tilting as it moves up and down the cylinder.

The shape of the slipper piston provides clearance for the crankshaft counterweights (Fig. 9-35). This allows a shorter engine with shorter connecting rods. Other engines, and especially heavy-duty engines, use the trunk piston with a full skirt (Fig. 9-33). It provides the larger thrust surface needed to control piston wear.

☐ 9-24 PISTON CLEARANCE

There must be some space between the piston and the cylinder wall (Fig. 9-36). This space, called the *piston clearance,* allows the piston to move up

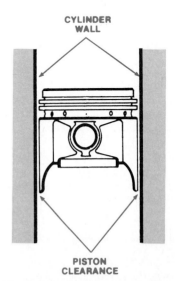

Fig. 9-36 Piston clearance is the space between the piston and the cylinder wall.

133

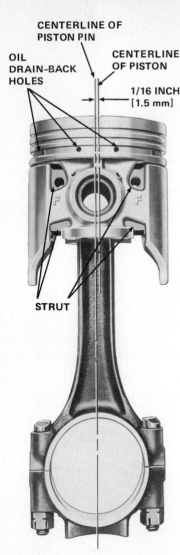

CENTERLINE OF PISTON PIN

CENTERLINE OF PISTON

OIL DRAIN-BACK HOLES

1/16 INCH [1.5 mm]

STRUT

Fig. 9-37 The center line of the piston pin is offset slightly from the center line of the piston to minimize piston slap.

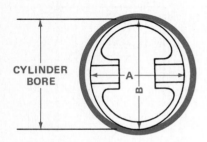

CYLINDER BORE

A

B

Fig. 9-38 A cam-ground piston is made slightly oval in shape. As the piston warms up, it becomes round.

and down easily in the cylinder. The clearance is 0.001 to 0.004 inch [0.03 to 0.10 mm] in most engines.

As cylinder walls wear, the clearance increases. When piston clearance gets excessive, the piston fits too loosely. Then *piston slap* occurs. There is so much clearance that the piston shifts from one side of the cylinder wall to the other when the power stroke starts. As the piston hits the other side of the cylinder wall, it makes a hollow, bell-like sound. When you hear this sound, you know the engine is in need of repair.

Piston slap usually is a problem only in older engines with worn cylinder walls and worn, or "collapsed," piston skirts. In many engines, the piston pin is slightly offset to one side (Fig. 9-37). This also minimizes piston slap.

☐ 9-25 PISTON EXPANSION CONTROL

A piston expands when it gets hot. The cylinder walls expand, too, but not nearly as much as the piston. If the piston were perfectly round, it could expand so much that all clearance would be gone. Then the piston would "seize." This could happen easily because the cylinder is cast-iron and the piston is aluminum. Aluminum expands more rapidly than iron with increasing temperature.

To prevent seizure, most automotive pistons have steel struts cast in (Fig. 9-37). These struts control the expansion of the piston. Other pistons are *cam-ground* (Fig. 9-38). They are slightly oval in shape. As the piston warms up, it becomes round.

☐ 9-26 PISTON RINGS

Piston rings are essential to the operation of an engine. The piston cannot be fitted close enough to seal the cylinder by itself. So grooves are cut in the top of the piston (Fig. 9-39). Metal rings called *piston rings* are installed in the grooves. Piston rings have three jobs:

1. They seal the combustion chamber, preventing gas leakage past the piston.
2. They scrape oil off the cylinder walls, preventing it from entering the combustion chamber.
3. They transfer heat from the hot piston to the cooler cylinder wall.

There are two types of piston rings, *compression rings* and *oil-control rings,* or simply "oil rings." Figure 9-39 shows a typical set of piston rings. Most automotive pistons have three rings. The two upper rings are the compression rings. They seal in the compression pressure and prevent *blowby.* Blowby is the leakage of compressed air-fuel mixture and burned gases (from combustion) past the piston rings into the crankcase. The bottom ring is the oil-control ring. It scrapes the excess oil off the cylinder walls, returning it to the crankcase. Only enough oil is left on the cylinder walls to provide piston and ring lubrication.

The piston rings are made a little larger than the cylinder bore. They are cut at one point (Figs. 9-40 and 9-41). This allows the ring to expand without breaking as it gets hot. The gap also allows the mechanic to expand the ring slightly so it can be slipped over the head of the piston. Then the ring can be slid down into the piston-ring groove. Figure 9-34 shows the rings in place in the piston grooves. The distance between the

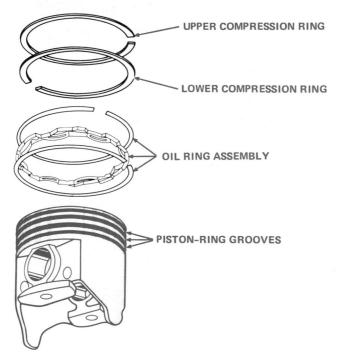

UPPER COMPRESSION RING

LOWER COMPRESSION RING

OIL RING ASSEMBLY

PISTON–RING GROOVES

Fig. 9-39 Piston and ring set.

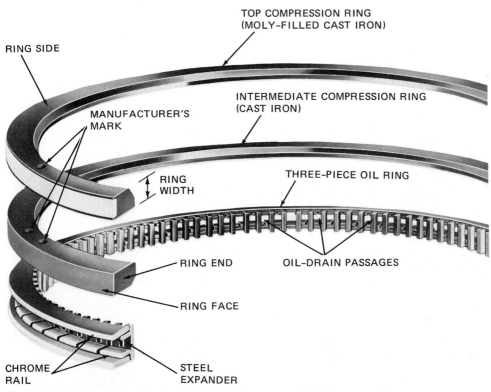

TOP COMPRESSION RING
(MOLY–FILLED CAST IRON)

RING SIDE

INTERMEDIATE COMPRESSION RING
(CAST IRON)

MANUFACTURER'S
MARK

THREE-PIECE OIL RING

RING
WIDTH

RING END

OIL-DRAIN PASSAGES

RING FACE

CHROME
RAIL

STEEL
EXPANDER

Fig. 9-40 Set of piston rings for a late-model engine. *(TRW, Inc.)*

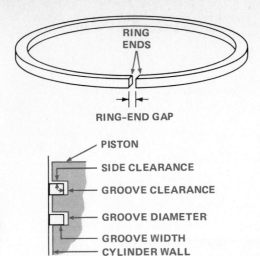

Fig. 9-41 Compression ring, showing the end gap and how the two compression rings fit into the grooves in the piston.

ends of the ring after the ring is installed is called the *ring end gap* (Fig. 9-41). Compressing the ring into the cylinder places an initial tension on the ring. This makes it press snugly against the cylinder wall.

□ 9-27 COMPRESSION RINGS

Compression rings (Fig. 9-42) usually are made of cast iron. They seal, scrape, and cool as described in □ 9-26. Some have an inside corner cut out. This is called a *chamfer*. It causes the ring to twist slightly so a sharp edge rides against the cylinder wall. Other rings have a *taper face* or a *barrel face*. The curvature of a barrel-face ring is very slight. You cannot see it. However, the face has a radius of 0.0003 to 0.0005 inch [0.008 to 0.013 mm].

While the piston is moving down on the intake stroke, the lower edge of the rings scrapes off any excess oil left by the oil ring (Fig. 9-43). As the piston moves up on the compression and exhaust strokes, the rings tend to skim over the oil film. This prevents the oil from being scraped into the combustion chamber. During the power stroke, combustion pressure on the compression rings is very high (Fig. 9-44). It causes them to untwist. Some of the high-pressure gas gets in back of the rings. This forces the ring face into full contact with the cylinder wall. The combustion pressure also holds the bottom of the ring tightly against the bottom of the ring groove. Therefore, high combustion pressure causes a tighter seal between the ring face and the cylinder wall.

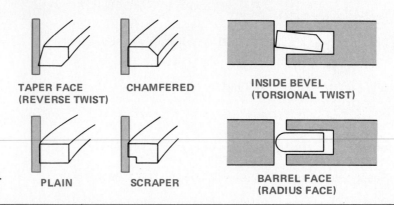

Fig. 9-42 Various types of compression rings. *(ATW)*

136

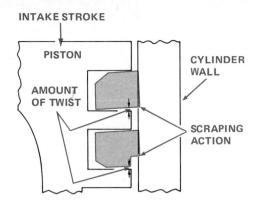

Fig. 9-43 Action of the compression rings during the intake stroke. *(ATW)*

Some of the high-pressure gas from combustion gets by the upper ring. One reason is that the ring has an opening, or end gap (□ 9-26). Most of the gas that gets by the top compression ring is caught and contained by the second compression ring. The two compression rings work together. They hold in the combustion pressures, thereby preventing excessive blowby.

□ 9-28 COMPRESSION-RING COATINGS

Various types of coatings are used on the face of cast-iron compression rings (Fig. 9-45). Cast-iron rings have a tendency to scuff when run directly against cast-iron cylinder walls. To prevent this, the ring face is coated with a thin layer of iron oxide, or *ferrous oxide* (Fig. 9-45A). Abrasive wear of the cylinder wall is greatly reduced by coating the ring face with *chromium,* or hard chrome (Fig. 9-45B).

Some "chrome" rings are so hard that the engine uses excessive oil before the rings seat, or wear-in. A soft chrome layer has been added over the hard chrome to aid in ring seating (Fig. 9-45C). High-temperature scuffing in late-model engines is controlled by a coating or inlay of *molybdenum* (Fig. 9-45D). "Moly" rings can operate at higher temperatures than chrome rings. They do this while providing better upper-cylinder lubrication. The upper compression rings in most new engines are coated with either chrome or moly.

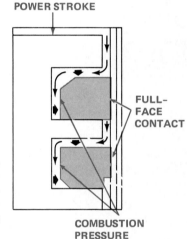

Fig. 9-44 Action of the compression rings during the power stroke. *(ATW)*

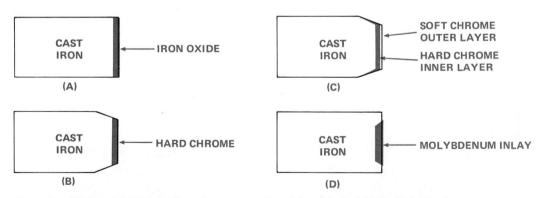

Fig. 9-45 Various types of coatings for compression rings. *(Perfect Circle Division of Dana Corporation)*

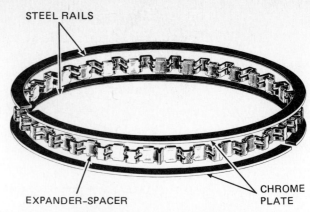

Fig. 9-46 Segmented, or three-piece, type of oil-control ring.

□ 9-29 OIL RINGS

While the engine is running, oil is continually sprayed and splashed on the cylinder walls. This provides lubrication. It also helps wash away any carbon and dirt particles, while slightly cooling the cylinder walls. However, the compression rings cannot scrape off all the excess oil during the downward strokes of the piston.

To provide oil control, most automotive engines now use a *segmented,* or three-piece, oil ring (Fig. 9-46). The oil is scraped into the expander-spacer by steel rails above and below it (Fig. 9-47). The oil passes through the open spaces in the expander-spacer. Then the oil goes through holes or slots in the back of the oil-ring groove (Fig. 9-37). The oil lubricates the piston pin (□ 9-21). Then the oil drains back into the crankcase.

Like the compression rings, oil rings also are plated (Figs. 9-46 and 9-47). Chrome is used to reduce wear and improve scuff resistance. Some three-piece oil rings have the sides of the rails chrome-plated.

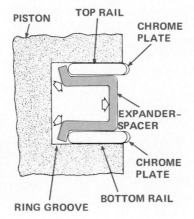

Fig. 9-47 Action of the expander-spacer in a three-piece oil ring. As shown by the arrows, the expander-spacer forces the rails out against the cylinder wall and up and down against the sides of the ring groove. *(Service Parts Division of Dana Corporation)*

Select the *one* correct, best, or most probable answer to each question. Then check your answers against the correct answers given at the end of the book.

1. The oil pan, crankshaft, and cylinder head are attached to the
   a. car frame
   b. engine cylinder block
   c. manifolds
   d. transmission

2. The flat pieces that are put between the engine block and those parts attached to it are
   a. studs
   b. fasteners
   c. gaskets
   d. flatteners

3. The water pump is attached to the block at the
   a. front
   b. side
   c. back
   d. top

4. The part that carries the burned gases from the engine cylinders is called the
   a. gas manifold
   b. intake manifold
   c. exhaust manifold
   d. manifold control

5. The V-6 engine has
   a. a single exhaust manifold
   b. two exhaust manifolds
   c. two intake manifolds
   d. three exhaust manifolds

6. The V-6 engine has
   a. one intake manifold
   b. two intake manifolds
   c. one exhaust manifold
   d. no exhaust manifolds

7. The most complicated cylinder head, considering the number of parts attached to or installed in it, is the
   a. L head
   b. flat head
   c. overhead-valve head
   d. overhead-camshaft head

8. The parts that bear the weight of the crankshaft are called the
   a. weights
   b. crankpins
   c. bearings
   d. journals

9. The purpose of the oilholes drilled in the crankshaft is to oil the
   a. main bearings
   b. connecting-rod bearings
   c. crankshaft bearings
   d. valve mechanisms

10. Attached to the rear end of the crankshaft is the
    a. vibration damper
    b. drive pulley
    c. timing gear
    d. flywheel

11. Attached to the front of the crankshaft is (are) the
    a. vibration damper
    b. flywheel
    c. connecting rod
    d. journals

12. The purpose of the main bearing with flanges on sides of it is to
    a. keep the bearing from moving in its bore
    b. control endplay of the crankshaft
    c. prevent oil throwoff to the cylinder walls
    d. reduce the twisting of the crankshaft

13. The difference in diameters between a crankshaft journal and the main bearing is called
    a. bearing clearance
    b. oil clearance
    c. both a and b
    d. neither a nor b

14. Power overlap occurs in
    a. four-cylinder engines
    b. six- and eight-cylinder engines
    c. both a and b
    d. neither a nor b

15. The purpose of the vibration damper is to
    a. smooth out the engine power impulses
    b. control crankshaft torsional vibration
    c. prevent crankshaft twist.
    d. prevent crankshaft endplay

16. In the piston-and-connecting-rod assembly, the piston pin may be
    a. free or locked to the piston or rod
    b. free or locked to the crankpin or rod
    c. free or locked to the head or camshaft
    d. none of the above

17. The escape of burned gases from the combustion chamber past the piston rings and into the crankcase is called
    a. gas loss
    b. blowby
    c. bypass
    d. passed gas

18. Pistons for automotive engines are made of
    a. cast iron
    b. steel
    c. aluminum
    d. brass

19. Excessive piston clearance can cause
    a. excessive compression pressure
    b. piston slap
    c. reduced oil pressure
    d. excessive oil pressure

20. Pistons become round as they warm up because
    a. they are cam-ground
    b. they have a steel strut cast in
    c. both a and b
    d. neither a nor b

21. Offsetting the piston pin
    a. reduces piston heating
    b. reduces piston slap
    c. improves engine power
    d. eliminates the need for oil-control rings

22. The two types of piston rings are
    a. oil-control and compression
    b. oil-compression and expander
    c. rail and expander
    d. compression and expansion

23. An aluminum cylinder block has a sleeve in it. Mechanic X says the sleeve is made of aluminum. Mechanic Y says the sleeve is made of cast iron. Who is right?
    a. X only
    b. Y only
    c. both X and Y
    d. neither X nor Y

24. Mechanic X and Mechanic Y are discussing precombustion chambers. Mechanic X says that in a spark-ignition engine the spark plug is located in the precombustion chamber. Mechanic Y says that in a diesel engine the fuel injector is located in the precombustion chamber. Who is right?
    a. X only
    b. Y only
    c. both X and Y
    d. neither X nor Y

25. All of the following statements about piston-ring coatings are true *except*
    a. a thin layer of iron oxide prevents scuffing.
    b. a thin layer of chrome prevents abrasive wear.
    c. a thin layer of molybdenum prevents scuffing.
    d. a thin layer of soft chrome prevents abrasive wear.

CHAPTER 10

VALVES AND VALVE TRAINS

After studying this chapter, you should be able to:
1. Describe the construction and operation of overhead valve trains and their component parts.
2. Describe the construction and operation of overhead-camshaft valve trains.
3. Explain the arrangements for driving the camshaft.
4. Explain what valve timing means and why valves are timed to open early and close late.
5. Explain how hydraulic valve lifters and valve rotators work.

Regardless of engine design, the valves must open and close at the proper time as long as the engine runs. They must allow fresh air or air-fuel mixture into the cylinders, and then allow the burned gases to escape from the cylinders. A valve opens and closes as many as 2000 times per mile [1.6 km]. In fact, each valve has opened and closed up to 200 million times in an engine that has gone 100,000 miles [160,900 km]! This chapter describes the valves and valve-train parts that provide this action.

☐ 10-1 VALVE-TRAIN TYPES

The valve-operating mechanism in an engine is called the *valve train*. It includes all components from the camshaft to the valve. There are two basic valve-train arrangements:

1. Camshaft in the cylinder block
2. Camshaft in or on the cylinder head

These basic arrangements are described in ☐ 6-18 to 6-20 and illustrated in Fig. 8-14.

Figure 10-1 shows the basic parts of a valve train used in an engine with the camshaft in the cylinder block. This type of engine is often called a *pushrod engine* because it uses pushrods in the valve train. Figure 10-1 shows how the valve train operates. As the cam lobe comes up under the

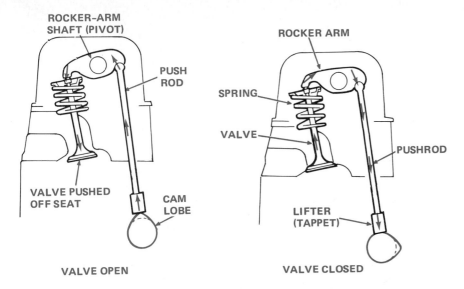

valve lifter (left), the pushrod is pushed up. This causes the rocker arm to pivot and push down on the valve, opening it. As the valve opens, it overcomes the valve-spring tension and compresses the spring. When the cam lobe passes out from under the lifter, the spring pulls the valve up to the closed position. Then the rocker arm rocks back forcing the pushrod and lifter down to the valve-closed position (Fig. 10-1, right).

The overhead-camshaft (OHC) engine uses various means of transmitting cam-lobe action to the valve. One arrangement is shown in Fig. 10-2. The cam is directly under the rocker arm. As the lobe comes around under the end of the rocker arm (left in Fig. 10-2), the lobe causes the rocker arm to move. This movement pushes down on the valve stem so the valve is opened. Then, when the lobe passes out from under the rocker

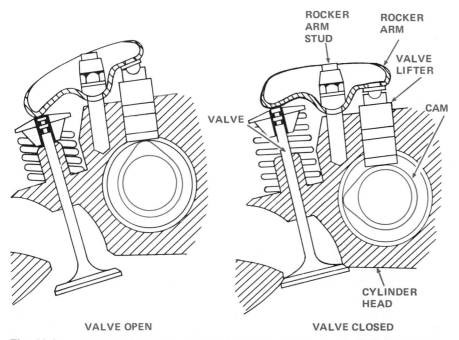

Fig. 10-2 Overhead-camshaft arrangement using a rocker arm between the valve lifter and valve stem.

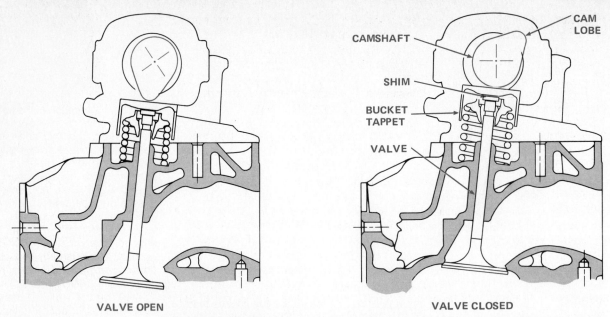

VALVE OPEN

VALVE CLOSED

CAM LOBE

CAMSHAFT

SHIM

BUCKET TAPPET

VALVE

Fig. 10-3 Overhead-camshaft arrangement using a bucket tappet. The cam works directly on the tappet.

arm, spring force pulls the valve back up to the closed position. As the valve stem rises, it forces the rocker arm back to the valve-closed position (Fig. 10-2, right).

In some OHC engines, the rocker arm is eliminated. The cam lobe works directly on the valve stem through an inverted valve tappet, sometimes called a *bucket tappet* (Fig. 10-3).

CAMSHAFTS

☐ 10-2 THE CAMSHAFT

Figure 10-4 shows a camshaft, with bearings, for a V-8 engine. This camshaft is located in the cylinder block and driven from the crankshaft by

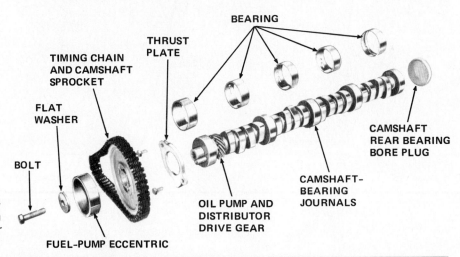

BEARING

THRUST PLATE

TIMING CHAIN AND CAMSHAFT SPROCKET

FLAT WASHER

BOLT

CAMSHAFT REAR BEARING BORE PLUG

CAMSHAFT-BEARING JOURNALS

OIL PUMP AND DISTRIBUTOR DRIVE GEAR

FUEL-PUMP ECCENTRIC

Fig. 10-4 The camshaft and related parts for a V-8 engine with overhead valves. *(Ford Motor Company)*

sprockets and a chain. The arrangement is shown from the front end of the engine in Fig. 6-30. The camshaft sprocket is twice as large as the crankshaft sprocket. This causes the camshaft to turn at one-half the speed of the crankshaft. The reason for this 1 : 2 ratio is that each valve opens only once for every two revolutions of the crankshaft (□ 6-21).

When the camshaft is in the cylinder block, the camshaft is driven by either sprockets and a chain (Fig. 10-5) or by gears (Fig. 10-6). Overhead-camshaft engines use either chain and sprockets (Fig. 10-7) or toothed belt and sprockets (Fig. 10-8) to drive the camshaft. The belt is reinforced with fiberglass cords and has a facing of woven nylon fabric on the toothed side. The teeth in the belt fit the grooves on the sprockets. To prevent the belt or chain from slipping, or "jumping time," most overhead-camshaft engines have some type of *tensioner* (Fig. 10-8). The tensioner is either spring-loaded or adjusted to press lightly against the belt or chain. This prevents excess play in the belt or chain from allowing it to skip a tooth and jump time. Driving the camshaft is discussed further in □ 6-22.

Opening the valves is the primary job of the camshaft. However, it may also provide one or more auxiliary drives. For example, the camshaft shown in Fig. 10-4 has an integral spiral gear to drive the oil pump and ignition distributor. This drive arrangement is shown in Fig. 10-9. A camshaft may also have an extra lobe, or an attached eccentric (as shown in Fig. 10-4), to operate the fuel pump. When the camshaft is in the crankcase, the cam lobes are lubricated by the crankcase oil mist. Engines with overhead camshafts have oil pumped up to the head to lubricate the cam lobes.

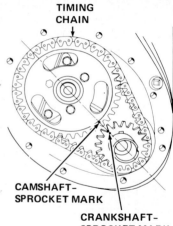

Fig. 10-5 Camshaft in the cylinder block, driven by sprockets and chain from the crankshaft. Timing marks on the sprockets must be aligned during installation so the valves will open and close in proper relation to piston position.

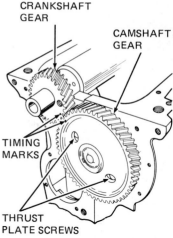

Fig. 10-6 Camshaft in the block, driven by timing gears. Note that the camshaft gear is twice the size of the crankshaft gear.

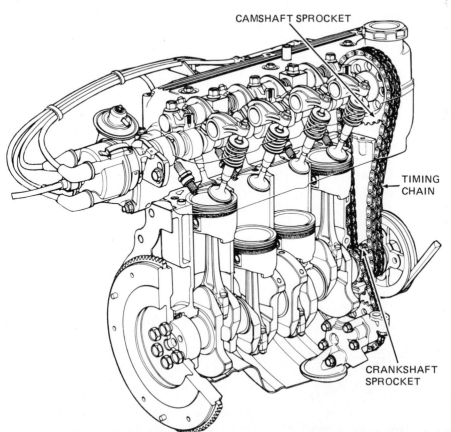

Fig. 10-7 An overhead-camshaft engine using a timing chain to drive the camshaft. *(Mazda Motors of America, Inc.)*

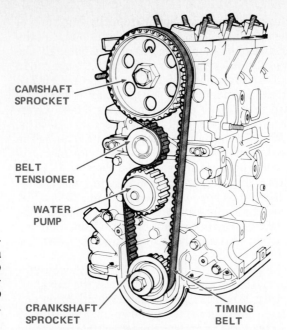

CAMSHAFT
SPROCKET

BELT
TENSIONER

WATER
PUMP

CRANKSHAFT
SPROCKET

TIMING
BELT

Fig. 10-8 Front end of an over-head-camshaft engine using a toothed belt and sprockets to drive the camshaft. A belt tensioner presses against the belt to prevent it from jumping time. *(Ford Motor Company)*

□ 10-3 CAMSHAFT BEARINGS

In the engine, *camshaft bearings* are installed between the camshaft-bearing journals (Fig. 10-4) and the cylinder block or head. Each camshaft bearing is a full-round sleeve bearing that supports the camshaft and holds it in position. The bearing is usually made of two-layer construction. Typically, it has a lining of "babbitt" (a soft bearing material) on a steel backing layer. The bearing journals on the camshaft are larger than the cams. This allows the camshaft to be installed and removed through the bearing bores. Camshaft bearings are usually replaced when the engine is overhauled. Engine bearings are described further in □ 9-13.

While the camshaft is turning, it may try to move out of its proper position. If the camshaft moves too far to the front or rear, the cams will not line up with the valve lifters. Also, the bearing journals will no longer be centered in the camshaft bearings. To prevent excessive movement to the front or rear, some camshafts have a *thrust plate* bolted to the front of the cylinder block (Fig. 10-4). The thrust plate acts as the camshaft

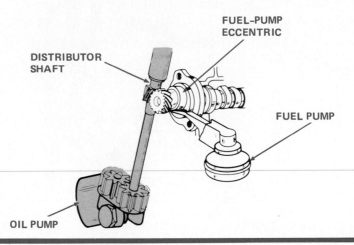

DISTRIBUTOR
SHAFT

FUEL-PUMP
ECCENTRIC

FUEL PUMP

OIL PUMP

Fig. 10-9 Oil-pump, distributor, and fuel-pump drives. The gear on the camshaft drives the distributor, and it drives the oil pump. An eccentric on the front of the camshaft operates the fuel pump.

thrust bearing (□ 9-14). If the camshaft tries to move back, the hub of the sprocket runs against the thrust plate. This limits rearward movement of the camshaft. If it tries to move forward, the front camshaft-bearing journal contacts the thrust plate. This stops forward movement of the camshaft.

When the camshaft drive mechanism is properly assembled, the correct clearance is automatically obtained. There is a necessary running clearance between the sprocket hub and the front of the thrust plate. Also, a clearance is required between the rear of the thrust plate and the front camshaft-bearing journal.

The camshaft bearings are lubricated by oil flowing from passages in the bearing bores. Holes or slots in the camshaft bearings must align with the openings in the bores to allow the oil to flow through. The bearings or journals may be grooved to distribute the oil. More about engine bearing lubrication is described in Chap. 11.

TIMING THE VALVES

□ 10-4 VALVE TIMING

Valve timing is the relation between valve action and piston position. It was described earlier in □ 6-21. The timing is expressed as the number of crankshaft degrees before or after the top dead center (TDC) or bottom dead center (BDC) position of the piston. This number indicates the open or closed position of the valve in relation to piston travel. A valve-timing diagram, such as shown in Fig. 10-10, is used to show valve timing of a camshaft.

Previous discussions of engine and valve action used a very basic explanation: The intake valve opens when the intake stroke starts and closes when the intake stroke ends. The exhaust valve opens when the exhaust stroke starts and closes when the exhaust stroke ends. Actually, the valves are *not* timed to open and close at these points. The intake valve starts to open before the intake stroke starts. Then the intake valve stays open for some time after the intake stroke ends and the compression stroke starts. The exhaust valve opens before the exhaust stroke starts and remains open for some time after the exhaust stroke ends.

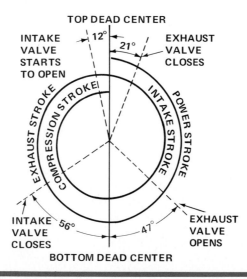

Fig. 10-10 A valve-timing diagram shows the positions of the crankshaft when the valves open and close.

147

Valve timing varies for different engines. It depends on the shape of the cam lobe that operates the valves. It also depends on the relationship between the gears or sprockets on the crankshaft and camshaft.

☐ 10-5 INTAKE-VALVE TIMING

The intake valve does not open instantly. It takes time for the cam lobe to start moving the valve train to open the valve. For this reason, the cam is positioned on the camshaft so that the lobe starts opening the intake valve well before the piston reaches TDC at the end of the exhaust stroke. By the time the piston reaches TDC and starts down on the intake stroke, the intake valve is wide open.

As the piston moves down on the intake stroke, the air-fuel mixture flows into the cylinder. However, the air-fuel mixture takes time to enter the cylinder (☐ 7-12). Holding the intake valve open past BDC on the intake stroke gives the mixture more time to enter the cylinder. The result is that more air-fuel mixture enters the cylinder, giving a stronger push on the power stroke.

How long the intake valve remains open after BDC varies with different engine designs. Typical timing for the intake valve is shown in Fig. 10-10. The intake valve starts to open 12 degrees before TDC at the end of the exhaust stroke. It stays open past BDC after the intake stroke and does not completely close until 56 degrees into the compression stroke. This gives the air-fuel mixture more time to enter so that volumetric efficiency is improved.

☐ 10-6 EXHAUST-VALVE TIMING

The exhaust valve starts to open before the power stroke ends and stays open after the exhaust stroke ends. This gives the exhaust gases more time to get out of the cylinder. Typical exhaust-valve timing for one engine is shown in Fig. 10-10. The exhaust valve starts to open 47 degrees before BDC on the power stroke. It stays open 21 degrees after the beginning of the intake stroke.

The early opening of the exhaust valve does not waste power. By the time the piston has moved down to 47 degrees before BDC, the pressure in the cylinder has already dropped. The purpose of getting the exhaust valve open early is to start the exhaust gases moving out.

In Fig. 10-10, notice that the exhaust valve does not completely close until 21 degrees after TDC on the intake stroke. The upward movement of the piston during the exhaust stroke helps clear the exhaust gases from the cylinder. The exhaust gases continue to flow out even after the piston reaches TDC and starts moving down on the intake stroke. However, by leaving the exhaust valve open a little longer, most of the remaining exhaust gases escape from the cylinder.

☐ 10-7 VALVE OVERLAP

Figure 10-10 shows that the two valves are both open for a short time. This is called *valve overlap*. It is the number of degrees of crankshaft rotation during which the intake and exhaust valves are open together. In Fig. 10-10, both valves are open a total of 33 degrees (12 degrees plus 21 degrees) at the end of the exhaust stroke and at the start of the intake stroke. This provides a valve overlap of 33 degrees. During this time, the exhaust gases are leaving the cylinder, creating a partial vacuum. The vacuum helps the cylinder to fill with fresh air-fuel mixture which is being pushed in by atmospheric pressure. The result of proper valve overlap is improved volumetric efficiency (□ 7-12), especially at higher speeds.

□ 10-8 VALVE GUIDES

The valves slide up and down in *valve guides* in the cylinder head. In some engines, the valve guides are metal tubes that are pressed, or driven, into the cylinder head (Fig. 10-11). In other engines, the valve guides are *integral* with the cylinder head (Fig. 6-27). Integral guides are basically holes bored in the cylinder head.

Valve guides must provide a close fit with the valve stems. This prevents excessive oil from getting into the combustion chambers. At the same time, there must be enough clearance between the valve stems and guides so that the valves can freely move up and down.

□ 10-9 VALVES

In most engines, each cylinder has two valves: an intake valve and an exhaust valve (Fig. 10-11). When the valve is seated, the valve face must fully contact the seat (□ 10-10). This match is necessary for two reasons: First, to prevent combustion pressure from leaking out between the valve face and the valve seat; second, to help conduct heat away from the valve head.

When the engine is running, the exhaust valve gets very hot. It is repeatedly passing the hot exhaust gases. Exhaust-valve temperature can reach 1600 degrees Fahrenheit [871 degrees Celsius]. Some heat flows up the valve stem to the valve guide (□ 10-8). The valve guide is cooled by the coolant circulating in the cylinder head. But much more heat is transferred from the head, through the face, to the seat while the

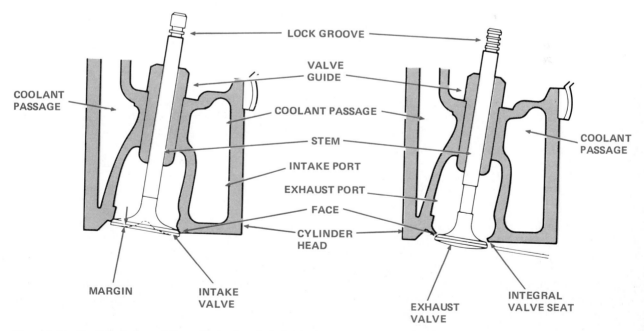

Fig. 10-11 Sectional view of the cylinder head showing the valves installed.

valve is closed. The valve is closed nearly three-fourths of the time. With a tight seal between the valve face and the valve seat, the maximum amount of heat can be transferred to the seat. The seat is also cooled by the circulating coolant.

If the contact between the valve face and the valve seat is poor, less heat will flow to the seat. Then the valve will run hotter. Also, hot exhaust gases will leak out between the valve and seat at the points of poor contact. The escaping hot exhaust gases will overheat the valve and may burn it and the seat. Poor contact, or poor seating, can be caused by dirt and other conditions. This is explained in greater detail in Chap. 29.

□ 10-10 VALVE SEATS

The valve seat is the surface against which the valve face rests when the valve closes (Fig. 10-11). With the valve closed, the seat and face form a seal to prevent compression and combustion leakage from the combustion chamber. Valve seats may be either *integral* or *replaceable*. Many automotive engines using cast-iron cylinder heads have integral seats. They are ground into the combustion-chamber side of the cylinder head (Fig. 10-11). Integral exhaust-valve seats are usually hardened by a special electric-heating process called *induction hardening*. This improves exhaust-valve-seat durability. It also allows the engine to run on lead-free fuels without valve and seat damage (Chap. 13).

When the cylinder heads are made of aluminum, a valve-seat insert must be installed in the head. This is because the steel valve face will wear the aluminum seat excessively. Figure 10-12 shows the complete valve assembly in a typical aluminum cylinder head. The valve-seat insert is shown installed in the left illustration and removed in the right illustration.

Some cast-iron cylinder heads have valve-seat inserts for the exhaust valves. This is because the exhaust-valve seat is subjected to the high temperature of the exhaust gas. The valve-seat insert, made of heat-resistant steel alloy, holds up better than the cast iron. Also, when the valve-seat insert becomes worn so much that it cannot be refaced again with a valve-seat grinder or cutter, the insert can be replaced.

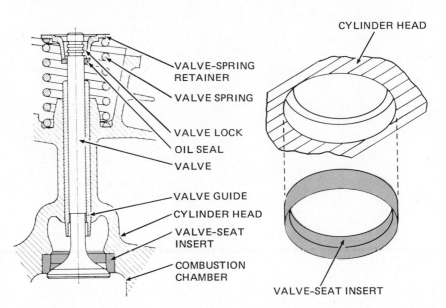

Fig. 10-12 Valve assembly showing how the valve seat insert fits in a counterbore in the cylinder head. *(Volkswagen of America, Inc.)*

☐ 10-11 VALVE-SPRING RETAINERS AND LOCKS

The valve spring is held between the cylinder head and the end of the valve stem by a spring retainer and a pair of split-collar locks called *valve keepers* (Fig. 10-12). The *retainer* is basically a large, thick washer with a slightly tapered hole in the center. Two types of locks are shown in Fig. 10-13. To install the locks, the spring is compressed. Then the locks are fitted into the mating slots, or grooves, in the valve stem. The outside of the locks forms a tapered collar around the valve stem. When the spring is released, the locks wedge themselves in the retainer, which holds the locks in place. This maintains valve-spring tension on the valve stem and securely holds the assembly together.

On some engines, the locks butt together to provide a slight clearance around the valve stem. This allows the valve to rotate in operation. The result is more even valve and seat wear.

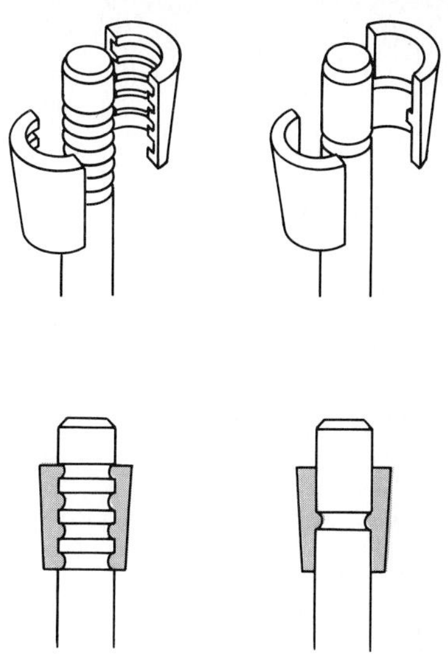

☐ 10-12 VALVE-STEM OIL SEALS

Most engines with valves in the cylinder head use some type of oil seal on the valve stem. The seal prevents excess oil on the rocker arms or valve train from reaching the valve stem. Without the seal, excess oil is drawn through the valve guide and into the combustion chamber. Too much oil in the combustion chamber will foul the spark plugs and cause the piston rings to stick in their grooves. Excessive oil on the hot valve stems could form deposits. Then, instead of opening and closing freely, the valves could stick in a partly open position. Oil on the valve seats could burn, causing deposits that prevent proper valve seating. When valves fail to close when they should, or fail to seat properly, they will overheat and burn.

To protect the valve stems from excessive oil, oil seals and shields or shedders are used. The seal may be a cup type that fits over the end of the valve guide (Fig. 6-22) or an O-ring that fits in a valve-stem groove below the valve locks. Some shields or shedders cover the top two turns of the spring. The nylon shedder shown in Fig. 10-14 is installed on the inside of the spring. The purpose of both the shield and the shedder is to prevent excessive oil from running down the valve stem past the locks and retainer.

FOUR GROOVE   SINGLE GROOVE

Fig. 10-13   Types of valve-spring-retainer locks, or valve keepers. *(ATW)*

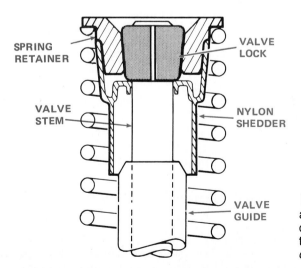

Fig. 10-14   A valve-and-spring assembly that uses a nylon shedder inside the spring for oil control. *(Cadillac Motor Car Division of General Motors Corporation)*

151

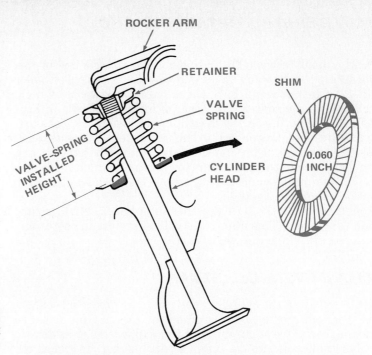

Fig. 10-15 Shims are installed under the valve spring to adjust the valve-spring installed height.

☐ 10-13 VALVE SPRINGS

The cam lobe opens the valve. But when the lobe rotates away from the lifter, or tappet, the valve spring (Fig. 10-15) has the job of closing the valve. Each valve spring is made from thick steel wire wound into a coil. The ends are ground flat so that the valve spring stands square. This eliminates any tendency for the spring to cock the valve and cause wear in the guide. In many engines, each valve uses only one spring (Figs. 10-14 and 10-15). In other engines, two valve springs are used for each valve. One spring is inside the other.

Valve springs are relatively strong because they must force the lifter to follow the cam. As engine speed increases, greater force is necessary. If the springs get "weak," the valves tend to "float." This means the valves do not close completely, or fail to close at the proper time. The result is lost power and burned valves. However, spring force must be limited. Springs that are too strong cause excessive cam-lobe and lifter wear. Also, they increase the frictional losses in the engine, which reduces fuel economy.

Since springs often get weaker in use, they should be checked with a *valve-spring tester* during a valve job or engine overhaul. A good spring must provide the specified tension at its normal *installed height* (Fig. 10-15). This is the spring length measured between the retainer and the cylinder head with the valve fully closed. When valve faces and seats are refinished, the installed height increases slightly. This reduces valve-spring tension. Then shims should be installed under the springs to compress them to the correct installed height (Fig. 10-15).

☐ 10-14 ROCKER ARMS

The *rocker arm* (Figs. 6-26 and 10-16) is the device in overhead valve trains that pivots to open the valve as the cam moves the pushrod. In doing this, the rocker arm performs two functions. First, it reverses the direction of lift. The pushrod moves up, raising one end of the rocker arm.

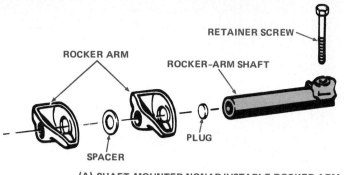

(A) SHAFT-MOUNTED NONADJUSTABLE ROCKER ARM

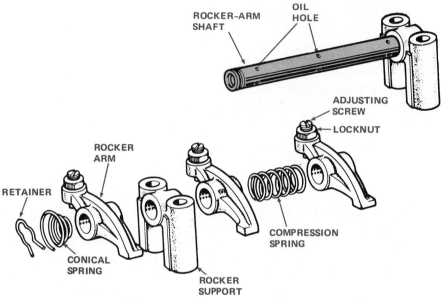

(B) SHAFT-MOUNTED ADJUSTABLE ROCKER ARM

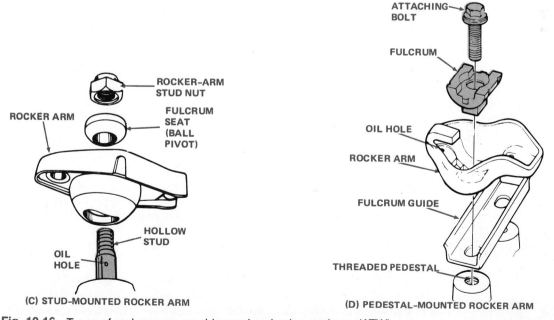

(C) STUD-MOUNTED ROCKER ARM

(D) PEDESTAL-MOUNTED ROCKER ARM

Fig. 10-16 Types of rocker arms used in overhead-valve engines. *(ATW)*

But by pivoting, the other end of the rocker arm moves down to force the valve open. Secondly, the rocker arm changes the cam-lobe lift to get the valve opening desired by the engine designer. This results from locating the pivot point off center. The ratio of cam-lobe lift to valve lift is called the *rocker-arm ratio*.

There are several types of rocker arms (Fig. 10-16). Some rocker arms have means of adjustment. The purpose of the adjustment is to have a minimum *valve clearance* (□ 10-15), or small gap, in the valve train of an engine using mechanical, or "solid," lifters. On valve trains using hydraulic valve lifters, this is not important (□ 10-19). Some rocker arms have an adjusting screw that can be turned in or out to change the valve clearance. The stud-mounted rocker arm is adjusted by turning the stud nut up or down.

Overhead-camshaft engines may also use rocker arms as shown in Fig. 10-2. This type is mounted on a rocker-arm stud. A different arrangement for an overhead-camshaft engine is shown in Fig. 6-27. The rocker arm floats. It is attached at one end to an automatic valve-lash adjuster which is like a hydraulic valve lifter (□ 10-19). The other end of the rocker arm rests on the tip of the valve stem. Midway, a hump on the rocker arm rests on a cam on the camshaft. As the cam lobe moves around, it pushes down on the rocker arm. This forces the valve open. When the cam lobe moves out from the rocker arm, the valve spring closes the valve. Meantime, the automatic valve-lash adjuster automatically takes up any clearance, or *valve lash*. Operation of the hydraulic valve lifter is described in □ 10-19.

□ 10-15 VALVE CLEARANCE

Either of two different types of valve lifters may be used in an engine with overhead valves: hydraulic (□ 10-19) and solid (or mechanical) lifters. When solid lifters are used, there must be a small clearance in the valve train when the valve is closed. This clearance is called *valve clearance, tappet clearance, valve lash,* and *valve-tip-to-rocker-arm clearance.* Its purpose is to ensure that the valve can close tightly against the seat. If there is no clearance, the valve will be held slightly off the seat. Then the valve will not seal and will burn quickly.

Excessive clearance allows the valve-train parts to hammer against each other. The result is a regular clicking noise called *tappet noise.* The clearance adjustment on most overhead-valve engines is made at the rocker arm (Fig. 10-16). Valve clearance must be checked and adjusted periodically on engines with solid lifters. The clearance changes as parts in the valve train wear.

Figure 10-3 shows an overhead-camshaft valve train using a bucket tappet. Clearance is adjusted by changing the thickness of the shim between the valve-stem tip and the tappet. The overhead-camshaft valve train shown in Fig. 10-17 has an adjusting screw inside the tappet. The screw has a tapered flat on one side which rests against the valve stem. Clearance adjustment is made by turning the screw full turns (so the flat always ends up resting on the valve stem). Various ways of adjusting valve clearance are described in Chap. 29.

□ 10-16 VALVE ROTATION

In some engines, the rocker arm is slightly offset from the center line of the valve. This causes the rocker arm to rotate the valve slightly each time it opens. The action helps clean any deposits from the valve face and

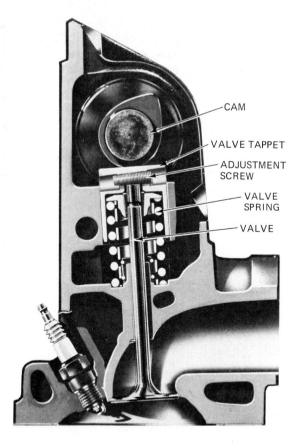

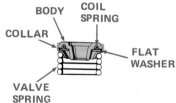

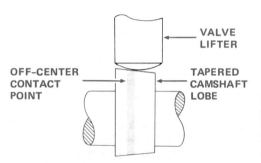

Fig. 10-17 Location of the adjustment screw in the valve train of an overhead-camshaft engine. *(Chevrolet Motor Division of General Motors Corporation)*

seat. This prevents valve burning. Many engines have *valve rotators,* especially on the exhaust valves (Fig. 10-18). These devices are installed in place of the valve-spring retainer. They turn the valve slightly as it opens. The turning motion is carried through the valve locks to the valve stem.

☐ 10-17 VALVE LIFTERS

Valve lifters are also called *valve tappets,* or *cam followers.* There are two types: solid, or mechanical, and hydraulic (☐ 10-19). The solid lifter is a round cylinder installed between the cam lobe and pushrod of an overhead-valve engine (Fig. 10-1). Basically, the solid lifter is a hollow piece of machined metal with no moving parts.

While the engine runs, the valve lifter rotates slightly each time it moves up and down. The turning action is provided by off-center contact

Fig. 10-18 A positive valve rotator is installed in place of the valve-spring retainer. *(Oldsmobile Division of General Motors Corporation)*

Fig. 10-19 Some cam lobes are ground slightly tapered so that the off-center contact with the lifter will cause it to rotate. *(Ford Motor Company)*

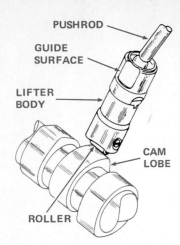

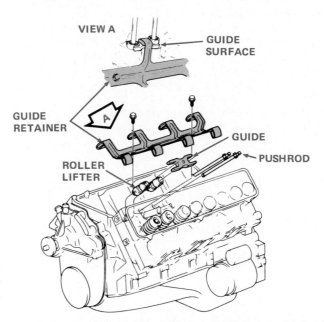

with the cam lobe or by grinding the cam lobe slightly tapered (Fig. 10-19). Rotating the lifter distributes the wear more evenly. Rotation also prevents sludge from accumulating in the lifter bore in the cylinder block. At the same time, the turning valve lifter rotates the pushrods, keeping the pushrod ends clean. A rough or worn cam lobe can be pinpointed on some engines by seeing which pushrod is not turning or is turning slower than the other pushrods.

☐ 10-18 ROLLER TAPPETS

The valve lifters described above are "flat tappets." The face contacting the cam lobe is ground either flat or slightly convex as shown in Fig. 10-19. However, some engines such as diesel engines and racing engines often use *roller tappets,* or *roller lifters* (Fig. 10-20). These have a hardened steel roller on the end. The roller rolls over the cam lobe instead of sliding over it. This reduces the friction between the valve lifter and the camshaft lobe. The body of a roller lifter must *not* rotate in its bore. If it did, the roller could turn sideways or even slide off the cam lobe. To prevent this, guides are used (Fig. 10-21). They hold the lifter body in position while allowing it to move up and down freely.

☐ 10-19 HYDRAULIC VALVE LIFTERS

Hydraulic valve lifters (Fig. 10-22) are used in engines to reduce noise and eliminate valve adjustments. With the hydraulic valve lifter, all clearance in the valve train is taken up by the oil in the lifter every time the valve closes. Then, when the valve train starts to open the engine valve, there is no clearance between metal parts. The valve opens silently because there is no clearance to be taken up.

Figure 10-22 shows how the lifter works. The principle of operation is that the lifter is kept filled with oil from the engine lubricating system. This takes up all the clearance. The left illustration in Fig. 10-22 shows the conditions when the valve is closed. Notice that the lobe of the cam has passed out from under the valve lifter. Oil from the lubricating sys-

Fig. 10-20 A roller-type valve lifter, or roller tappet, has rolling contact with the cam lobe instead of sliding contact. *(Oldsmobile Division of General Motors Corporation)*

Fig. 10-21 Guides and guide retainers are used with roller lifters to prevent them from turning in the lifter bores. *(Oldsmobile Division of General Motors Corporation)*

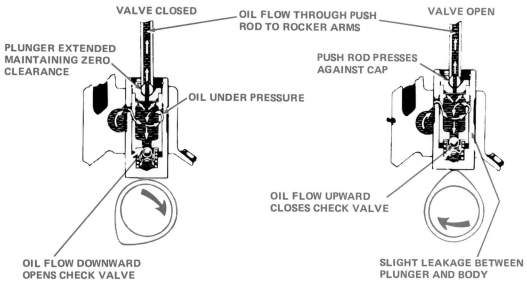

VALVE CLOSED

OIL FLOW THROUGH PUSH ROD TO ROCKER ARMS

VALVE OPEN

PLUNGER EXTENDED MAINTAINING ZERO CLEARANCE

PUSH ROD PRESSES AGAINST CAP

OIL UNDER PRESSURE

OIL FLOW UPWARD CLOSES CHECK VALVE

OIL FLOW DOWNWARD OPENS CHECK VALVE

SLIGHT LEAKAGE BETWEEN PLUNGER AND BODY

Fig. 10-22 Operation of a hydraulic valve lifter. *(Cadillac Motor Car Division of General Motors Corporation)*

tem is flowing through holes in the valve-lifter body and plunger. This oil is under pressure from the engine oil pump. As the oil flows inside the plunger, most of the oil flows up through the hollow pushrod to lubricate the rocker arms.

Some of the oil pushes down on the check valve (Fig. 10-22, left), opening it. Then the oil flows under the plunger. The oil raises the plunger enough to take up clearance—usually only a few thousandths of an inch—in the valve train. Figure 10-22 shows a ball-type check valve. Other hydraulic lifters use a flat disk-type check valve. Both work as described above.

When the cam lobe moves under the lifter (Fig. 10-22, right), the lobe pushes the lifter up. The increase in pressure under the check valve closes it. Now the lifter acts like a solid lifter and moves up, forcing the pushrod up. The pushrod operates the rocker arm and opens the engine valve. During this interval, some of the oil may leak out from under the plunger. This allows the plunger to drop slightly in the body. The amount of oil that leaks out is called the *lifter leak-down rate*. The leakage is necessary to prevent the lifter from "pumping up" and acting like a solid lifter (□ 10-17) with no clearance. It also compensates for heat expansion in the valve train parts. However, if the lifter leaks down too much, valve lift is reduced.

As soon as the cam lobe moves out from under the lifter and the engine valve closes, oil flows into the lifter. This takes up any clearance in the lifter once again.

Select the *one* correct, best, or most probable answer to each question. Then check your answers against the correct answers given at the end of the book.

1. One major difference between an overhead-valve engine and an overhead-camshaft engine is that the overhead-camshaft engine
   a. uses no pushrods
   b. has no valve lifters
   c. has no valve train
   d. uses four valves per cylinder

2. Comparing the crankshaft and camshaft gears or sprockets, the camshaft gear or sprocket is
   a. the same size as the crankshaft gear or sprocket
   b. smaller than the crankshaft gear or sprocket
   c. twice as large as the crankshaft gear or sprocket
   d. larger than the crankshaft gear or sprocket

3. The valves are closed by
   a. mechanical action of the cam lobes
   b. valve-spring force
   c. the pushrods
   d. piston action

4. To keep the valve from overheating, the most important part of the valve is the
   a. valve tip
   b. stem
   c. face
   d. spring

5. Valve overlap is the number of degrees of crankshaft rotation during which
   a. each valve is open
   b. each valve is closed
   c. both valves are open at the same time
   d. both valves are closed at the same time

6. Some engines use valve-seat
   a. clearances
   b. insulators
   c. knurling
   d. inserts

7. Some OHC engines
   a. use rocker arms
   b. do not use rocker arms
   c. use bucket valve tappets
   d. all of the above

8. As the hydraulic valve lifter moves up, opening the valve, the check valve in the plunger is
   a. closed
   b. open
   c. closing
   d. opening

9. The purpose of the hydraulic valve lifter is to
   a. reduce engine noise
   b. eliminate valve clearance
   c. eliminate valve adjustments
   d. all of the above

10. The purpose of the oil shedders and seals on valve stems is to prevent excessive oil from
    a. lubricating the valve stems
    b. getting into the combustion chambers
    c. excessively cooling the valves
    d. all of the above

11. The purpose of valve overlap is to
    a. prevent valve bounce
    b. prevent valve burning
    c. improve volumetric efficiency
    d. improve cold-engine starting

12. Too much valve clearance in an engine with solid lifters will cause the valves to
    a. open late and close early
    b. open early and close early
    c. open late and close late
    d. open early and close late

13. In an engine that drives the camshaft by sprockets and a chain, the purpose of the tensioner is to
    a. reduce noise
    b. prevent the camshaft from moving forward and back
    c. prevent the engine from "jumping time"
    d. all of the above

14. In an overhead-valve engine, the valves may be rotated by
    a. valve rotators
    b. off-center contact with the rocker arm
    c. both a and b
    d. neither a nor b

15. To prevent rotation of a roller lifter, the engine has
    a. roller tappets
    b. lifter guides and retainers
    c. center contact with the cam lobe
    d. off-center contact with the pushrod

CHAPTER 11
ENGINE LUBRICATING SYSTEMS

After studying this chapter, you should be able to:

1. List the five jobs the lubricating oil does in the engine.

2. Explain how automotive engine oil is rated as to viscosity and service.

3. Describe the various engine-oil additives and their purpose.

4. Describe the operation of the engine lubricating system.

5. List the components in the engine lubricating system and describe how each works.

6. Explain the difference between an oil-level indicator and an oil-pressure indicator.

The engine has many moving parts. If these parts rub against one another, they will wear out quickly. A "frozen," or seized, engine may result. The purpose of the engine lubricating system is to minimize friction and wear. The lubricating system performs this job by supplying oil to prevent metal from rubbing against metal. This chapter explains how oil works as a lubricant and how it gets to the moving parts in the engine.

☐ 11-1 MOVING PARTS IN THE ENGINE

Figure 11-1 shows the moving parts in an engine. First, there is the crankshaft, which spins in stationary *main bearings* in the cylinder block and must be lubricated. The bearings are the replaceable parts that bear the weight of the crankshaft. When bearings wear, they can be removed and new bearings installed. (Engine bearings are described in Chap. 9)

Second, there is the connecting rod. The lower end of the connecting rod—the rod big end—is attached to a crankpin on the crankshaft by *rod bearings* and a rod cap. The upper end of the rod—the small end—is attached to the piston by a piston pin. Various attachment methods are described in Chap. 9. Regardless of the method, the surfaces or bushings in which the piston pin moves must be lubricated.

Third, there is the camshaft, which rotates in the *cam bearings*. In most engines, valve lifters move up and down in bores in the cylinder

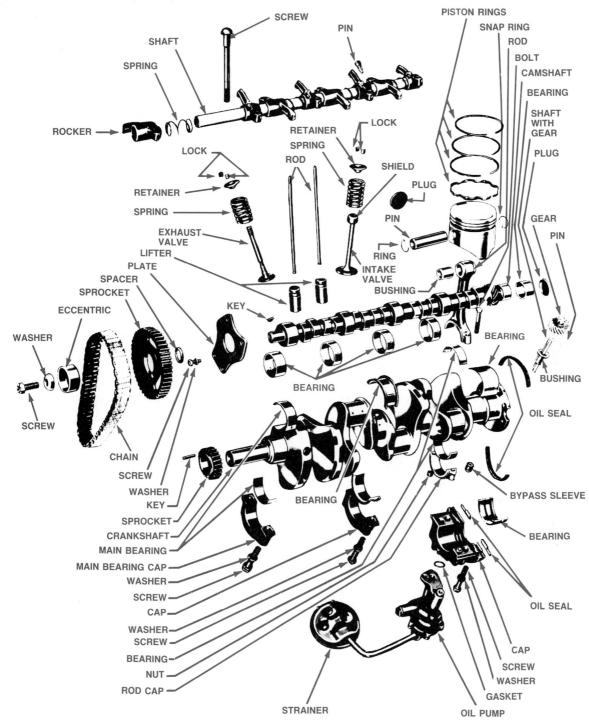

Fig. 11-1 The moving parts in a V-8 engine that must be lubricated. *(Chrysler Corporation)*

block or head. Also, the engine may have rocker arms that rock back and forth as the valves move up and down in the valve guides.

Fourth, and most important for engine operation, are the pistons and the piston rings. They move up and down in the cylinders.

All these parts—and many others—must be covered with oil so that they can move with relative ease and without metal-to-metal contact. This is the job of the engine lubricating system. It sends oil to all engine parts that have relative motion (Fig. 11-1). The oil reduces the friction between the moving parts. It allows the parts to move over each other easily while keeping their wear to a minimum. In the engine, the oil has other jobs to do. These are covered in the following pages.

ENGINE OIL

□ 11-2 PURPOSE OF ENGINE OIL

Oil flows in slippery layers onto engine parts, preventing metal-to-metal contact. Figure 11-2 shows two surfaces that are highly magnified. If you look at a part that is made of very smooth metal (such as a crankpin) under a microscope, you will see tiny rough edges sticking up from the surface of the metal. If two such dry metal surfaces rub against each other, the irregular edges catch on each other. Particles of metal are worn off. This action consumes energy and wastes power.

What is worse is that the rubbing and tearing action, or friction, produces heat. Rub your hands together very fast and hard. They get hot. The same thing would happen in the engine if it ran without oil. Metal parts would be moving against each other at very high pressure. Without oil, these parts would quickly get so hot that the metal would melt. Then the engine would seize.

The oil prevents this because layers of oil cover the metal surfaces, as shown in Fig. 11-2. The layers of oil hold the metal surfaces away from each other. Only the oil layers must slip as the two metal parts move. The oil greatly reduces power loss and wear of moving metal parts. In addition, oil does other jobs which are described below.

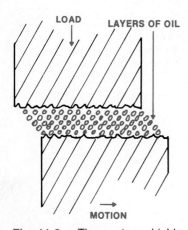

Fig. 11-2 These two highly magnified surfaces show irregularities that you could not see without a microscope. When the surfaces move in relation to each other, the layers of oil prevent metal-to-metal contact.

□ 11-3 OTHER JOBS FOR ENGINE OIL

The oil reduces friction and wear. It also does other jobs in the engine:

■ It removes heat from the engine.
■ It absorbs shocks between bearings and other engine parts.
■ It forms a seal between the piston rings and the cylinder wall.
■ It acts as a cleaning agent.

Let's look at each of these jobs in detail.

1. REMOVING HEAT

The engine oil is pumped up from the oil pan at the bottom of the engine through various oil passages to the moving engine parts. As the oil circulates through the engine, the oil picks up heat from the engine parts. Then the oil flows back down into the oil pan. The oil pan is much cooler than the engine. The pan is below the engine and in the path of the air flowing under the moving car. The hot oil therefore loses heat to the air passing under the oil pan. The circulation of the oil between the engine and the oil pan keeps taking heat away from the engine. This helps keep the engine cool.

2. ABSORBING SHOCKS

The layers of oil between moving engine parts help to absorb shocks. For example, let's look at the bearing in the big end of the connecting rod. This bearing rests on a crankpin of the crankshaft. When combustion of the compressed air-fuel mixture takes place, a load of up to 4000 pounds [1814 kg] is suddenly put on the rod (Fig. 11-3). This load is carried through the rod bearing to the crank journal. The only thing that prevents metal-to-metal contact is a layer of oil between the bearing and the journal. The layer of oil resists "squeezing out." It acts as a cushion to absorb the sudden shock of the load as combustion takes place.

3. FORMING A SEAL

The cylinder walls are covered with oil which lubricates the piston rings as they slide up and down. If you put a drop of oil between your finger and thumb, you can feel how slippery it is. But notice, also, how sticky it is. The oil tends to resist your attempts to separate your finger and thumb. It is the quality of stickiness that allows the oil to form a seal between the piston rings and the cylinder wall. The layer of oil on the cylinder wall fills in most of the irregularities so that there is a good seal.

4. ACTING AS A CLEANING AGENT

The oil circulates through the engine and then flows back down into the oil pan. As the oil passes through the engine, the oil picks up particles of carbon, metal, and dirt. The oil carries all these particles back down to the oil pan. The larger particles fall out. Smaller particles are filtered out by the oil filter.

□ 11-4 PROPERTIES OF ENGINE OIL

Oil is the liquid used in the lubricating system. For many years, the only oil used in engines was made from natural crude oil which came from oil wells drilled deep into the earth. Much of the engine oil used today still comes from crude oil. This crude oil was formed underground millions of years ago in various parts of the world. It must be refined to make it usable. In the refining process, gasoline, kerosene, lubricating oil, and many other products are made.

In recent years, synthetic oils have been developed. These are oils made by chemical processes and do not necessarily come from petroleum. Some oil manufacturers claim that these synthetic oils have superior lubricating properties. Actually, there are several types of synthetic oils. The type most widely used now is produced from organic acids and alcohols (from plants of various types). A second type is produced from coal and crude oil. Tests have shown that these synthetics do have certain superior qualities. However, no automotive manufacturer has given them unqualified approval yet.

Not all oil is the same. There are several grades of oil and several ratings. Oil made for automobiles contains a number of additives (chemical compounds that are added to the oil) that improve the performance of the oil. Oil ratings and additives are described below.

□ 11-5 OIL VISCOSITY

Viscosity refers to the ability of a liquid to flow. An oil with high viscosity is very thick and flows slowly. An oil with low viscosity flows easily. Oil gets thicker as it becomes colder. Therefore, starting a car in cold weather

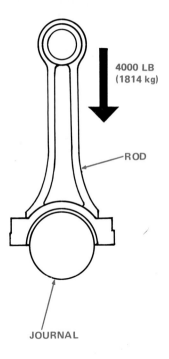

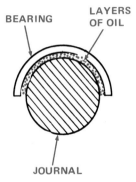

Fig. 11-3 The layers of oil between the journal and the rod bearing help to absorb the shock of the sudden load when combustion starts.

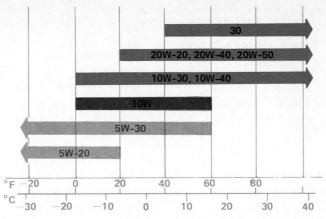

Fig. 11-4 Selecting engine oil based on outside temperature. *(Chevrolet Motor Division of General Motors Corporation)*

TEMPERATURE RANGE ANTICIPATED BEFORE NEXT OIL CHANGE

is more difficult than starting it in warm weather. The cold has increased the viscosity of the oil.

Oil viscosity is rated in two ways by the Society of Automotive Engineers (SAE). It is rated for (1) winter driving and (2) summer driving. Winter-grade oils are packaged in three grades: SAE5W, SAE10W, and SAE20W. The "W" stands for winter grade. For other than winter use, the grades are SAE20, SAE30, SAE40, and SAE50. The higher the number, the higher the viscosity (the thicker the oil). All these grades are called *single-viscosity oils*.

Many oils are rated as *multiple-viscosity oils*. For example, one oil of this type has the same viscosity as an SAE10W oil when cold and as an SAE40 oil when hot.

Car manufacturers specify the viscosity of the oil that should be used in their engines. Figure 11-4 is a chart showing how outside temperature affects the viscosity requirements of the engine. For example, a 5W-20 oil is recommended if the temperature will be 20 degrees Fahrenheit [− 8 degrees Celsius] or less. This oil is good for starting and driving in these low outside temperatures. If the weather is going to warm up, a different oil should be used, such as a 10W-30 or 10W-40. These oils will hold their viscosities in the higher temperatures. They will not thin out too much. However, they are thin enough for easy initial starting and cold-engine operation.

☐ 11-6 SERVICE RATINGS FOR SI-ENGINE OILS

The service rating indicates the type of service for which the oil is best suited. For spark-ignition (SI) engines, the service ratings are SA, SB, SC, SD, SE, and SF. Here is a brief description of each of these ratings:

SA—Acceptable for engines operated under the mildest conditions (not for use in automobile engines).

SB—Acceptable for minimum-duty engines operated under mild conditions (not for use in automobile engines).

SC—Meets requirements of gasoline engines in 1964–1967 model passenger cars and trucks.

SD—Meets requirements of gasoline engines in 1968–1970 model passenger cars and some trucks.

SE—Meets requirements of gasoline engines in 1972 and later cars and certain 1971 model passenger cars and trucks.

SF—Meets requirements of gasoline engines in 1981 and later cars and some trucks and certain 1980 models. This oil provides more protection against sludge, varnish, wear, oil-screen plugging, and engine deposits.

Notice that this is an open-end series. When the car manufacturers and oil producers see the need for other types of oil, they can bring out SG and SH service-rated oils. SA and SB oils are not recommended for use in automobile engines. These are nondetergent oils. Detergent oils (□ 11-8) are required in modern automotive engines.

□ 11-7 SERVICE RATINGS FOR DIESEL-ENGINE OILS

Diesel-engine oils must have different properties than oils for spark-ignition engines. The CA, CB, CC, and CD ratings indicate oils for increasingly severe diesel-engine operation. For example, CA oil is for light-duty service. CD oil is for severe-duty service. This oil should be used in turbocharged high-output diesel engines operating on fuel oil with a high sulfur content.

Modern high-speed automotive diesel engines require a special "combination" type of lubricating oil. For example, General Motors specifies that the oil for their 1978 model V-8 passenger-car diesel engine should be oil which has the service designation SE/CD marked on the can. For 1979 and later models, the can must be marked SE/CC. Do *not* use oil labeled only SE or CD. These oils could cause engine damage. General Motors states that a single-viscosity grade oil such as SAE20W or SAE30 is better for their V-8 automotive diesel engines than multiviscosity oils. However, this recommendation is for sustained high-speed driving.

□ 11-8 OIL ADDITIVES

Certain chemical compounds, called *additives*, are added to the oil. Their purpose is to give the oil certain properties it does not have in its original refined state. The refining process determines the viscosity and other basic properties of the oil. The additives give the oil other desirable properties. Some additives and what they do are described below.

1. VISCOSITY IMPROVER
The viscosity improver is a compound that lessens the tendency of the oil to thin out as it gets hot. Without this additive, the oil would not be safe for high-temperature, high-speed operation because it might thin out too much. However, a 10W-40 oil could be used in outside temperatures of 0 to 100°F [−17.8 to 37.8°C].

Multiple-viscosity oils are made by adding a viscosity improver.

2. POUR-POINT DEPRESSANTS
Pour-point depressants are compounds that help prevent the oil from getting too thick at low temperatures. These additives help the oil to flow at low temperatures. Their action is to depress the tendency of the oil to thicken.

3. INHIBITORS
Inibitors are compounds that fight potential oil and lubricating-system troubles. Several inhibitors are used in engine oil. Some fight corrosion

and rust. Others fight oxidation of the oil. Oil oxidation takes place because, at fairly high temperatures, the oil is constantly being agitated, or stirred up, in the engine crankcase. The oil is not hot enough to burn. But the oil is hot enough to react with the oxygen in the air. When this happens, oxidation occurs. Oil oxidation results in the formation of new compounds that are harmful to the engine. One compound formed by oil oxidation is a sticky, tarlike material called *sludge* that can clog oil lines. It also causes valves and piston rings to hang up and not work properly. Another compound formed by oil oxidation is similar to varnish. This compound can also cause trouble in the engine.

Another oil additive—an antifoaming compound—helps to prevent the oil from foaming. The oil in the crankcase is constantly being stirred up by the rotation of the crankshaft. This action tends to make the oil foam, just as the action of an egg beater causes egg whites to foam. Foaming prevents normal oil circulation and results in loss of lubrication and engine damage.

4. DETERGENT-DISPERSANTS

A detergent is similar to soap. When you wash your hands with soap, the soap surrounds and loosens the particles of dirt. You can then rinse off the dirt with water. Similarly, the detergent in the oil loosens the particles of carbon, gum, and dirt on engine parts and carries them away. Some of the particles drop to the bottom of the crankcase, where they are drained away when the oil is changed. Other particles are trapped in the oil filter.

The dispersant action *disperses,* or *scatters,* the particles. This prevents the particles from clotting, or forming clumps, which could clog oil passages and bearings.

5. EXTREME-PRESSURE AGENTS

In automotive engines, the lubricating oil is subjected to very high pressures in the bearings and valve train. To prevent the oil from squeezing out, extreme-pressure agents are added to the oil. These agents react chemically with metal surfaces to form very strong, slippery films, which may be only about one molecule thick. Therefore, these additives supplement the oil by providing protection during periods of extreme pressure during which the oil itself is likely to be squeezed out.

6. ANTIFRICTION MODIFIERS

Certain chemicals when added to oil in effect tend to plate the metal surfaces that the oil is lubricating. This layer allows the oil to pass through the space between the parts more easily. As a result, the friction in the engine is reduced, and fuel consumption is decreased. When added to the oil, a friction modifier dissolves completely and becomes part of the oil itself.

7. GRAPHITE AND MOLYBDENUM MODIFIERS

Some oils now have small particles of molybdenum ("moly") held in suspension in the oil. These particles are very slippery, much more slippery than the oil they are in. As a result, the amount of engine power required to overcome the internal friction of the engine is reduced. One theory is that the small particles actually support part of the load, thereby reducing the friction between moving metal surfaces. In the oil, the small particles do not dissolve. They are held in suspension to prevent their settling out while the engine is stopped and the oil is stored.

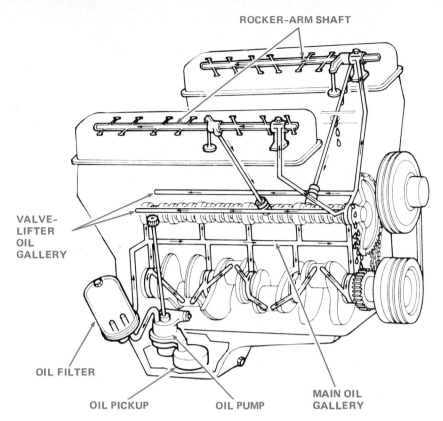

ROCKER-ARM SHAFT

VALVE-
LIFTER
OIL
GALLERY

OIL FILTER

OIL PICKUP   OIL PUMP

MAIN OIL
GALLERY

Fig. 11-5 Lubricating system for an overhead-valve V-8 engine with five main bearings. *(Chrysler Corporation)*

ENGINE LUBRICATING SYSTEMS

☐ 11-9 OIL PUMP

The main purpose of the engine lubricating system is to supply oil to all the moving parts in the engine. The engine-driven oil pump does this job. It sits in or near the engine oil pan and pumps oil from the pan up to the engine parts. Many illustrations of engines in this book show the location of the oil pump and the gears that drive it. Figure 11-5 shows the lubricating system in a V-8 engine.

The pump sends oil from the oil pan through the oil filter, as shown by the arrows in Fig. 11-5. (The oil filter is described in ☐ 11-13.) The oil then flows through oil passages to the crankshaft bearings, camshaft bearings, valve lifters, pushrods, rocker arms, and valves. Oil is sprayed or splashed onto the cylinder walls to lubricate the pistons and rings. Then the oil drains back down to the oil pan.

☐ 11-10 OIL-PUMP OPERATION

The two common types of oil pumps are the gear type (Fig. 11-6) and the rotor type (Fig. 11-7). The gear type pump uses a pair of meshing gears. As the gears rotate, the spaces between the gear teeth open by moving apart. This draws oil in from the oil inlet. The gear teeth seal to the housing and carry the oil around it to the oil outlet. Then, as the teeth

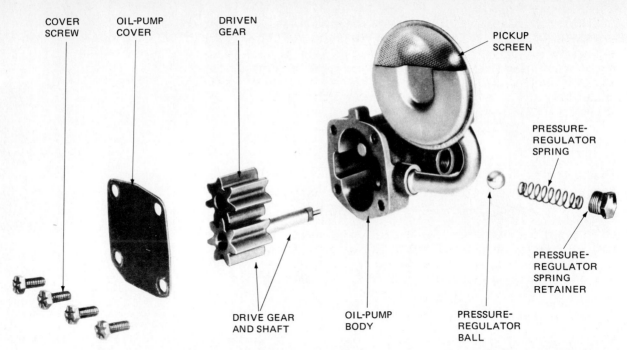

COVER
SCREW

OIL-PUMP
COVER

DRIVEN
GEAR

PICKUP
SCREEN

PRESSURE-
REGULATOR
SPRING

PRESSURE-
REGULATOR
SPRING
RETAINER

DRIVE GEAR
AND SHAFT

OIL-PUMP
BODY

PRESSURE-
REGULATOR
BALL

Fig. 11-6 A disassembled gear-type oil pump. *(Pontiac Motor Division of General Motors Corporation)*

mesh, the oil is forced out through the oil outlet. The rotor type uses an inner and outer rotor. The inner rotor is driven and causes the outer rotor to turn with it. As this happens, the spaces between the rotor lobes become filled with oil. When the lobes of the inner rotor move into the spaces of the outer rotor, oil is squeezed out through the outlet.

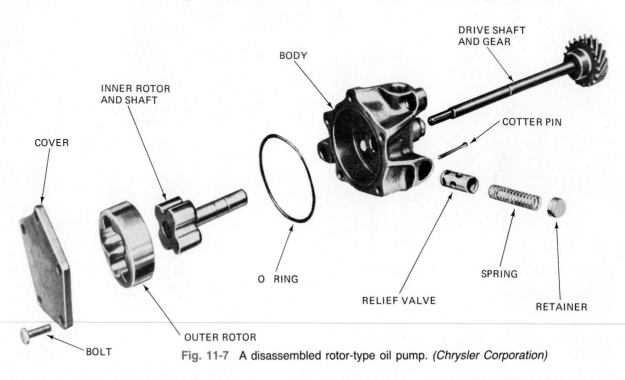

DRIVE SHAFT
AND GEAR

BODY

INNER ROTOR
AND SHAFT

COTTER PIN

COVER

O RING

SPRING

RELIEF VALVE

RETAINER

BOLT

OUTER ROTOR

Fig. 11-7 A disassembled rotor-type oil pump. *(Chrysler Corporation)*

Oil pumps are usually driven from the engine camshaft from the same spiral gear that drives the ignition distributor (Fig. 10-9). In most engines, the oil intake for the oil pump is a rigidly mounted screen assembly. It is mounted to the oil pump or engine block and positioned just above the bottom of the pan (Fig. 11-5). The screen prevents large dirt and metal particles from entering the pump. They could damage or jam the pump gears or rotor.

☐ 11-11 RELIEF VALVES

The faster the engine runs, the faster the gears or rotors turn in the oil pump. This means that, without relief, the oil pressure would go very high. To prevent too much pressure, oil pumps contain a relief valve. This valve contains a ball (Fig. 11-6) or a plunger (Fig. 11-7), which is held in place by a spring. When the pressure starts to go too high, the relief valve pushes the ball or the plunger back against the spring tension. This opens up a relief hole, which allows part of the oil to flow back down into the oil pan. Therefore the pressure is relieved so it does not go too high.

☐ 11-12 OIL COOLERS

Some engine lubricating systems include an oil cooler. Oil coolers are used on almost all automotive air-cooled engines and on Mazda Wankel engines (☐ 8-21). One type of oil cooler is a small heat exchanger mounted on the side of the engine block. Oil and engine coolant circulate through separate circuits in the heat exchanger. As the coolant circulates, it picks up heat. The heat is carried by the coolant to the radiator, where the heat is transferred to the cooler air flowing through. This process helps cool the oil and keeps it at its normal operating temperature.

Another type of oil cooler uses a small section of the cooling-system radiator. A separate heat exchanger is not required. The oil cooler for air-cooled engines consists of a small heat exchanger much like the radiator used in the liquid-cooled engine cooling system. Air flows through the oil cooler to remove heat from the oil.

☐ 11-13 OIL FILTERS

The oil filter is the engine's main protection against dirt. The oil from the oil pump must first pass through an oil filter (Fig. 11-5) before the oil goes up to the engine. The filter removes particles of carbon and dirt so they do not get into the engine and damage engine bearings and other parts. The filter contains a filtering element made of pleated paper or fibrous material. The oil passes through the filter, and the paper or fibers trap the dirt particles.

Figure 11-8 is a cutaway view of an oil filter. The filter element is housed in a disposable can. It is removed and thrown away at periodic intervals specified by the manufacturer. The filter has a bypass valve. If the filter element becomes so clogged that all the oil needed by the engine cannot pass through the filter, the increased pressure from the oil pump causes the valve to open. Now, some of the oil from the pump can bypass the filter and go directly to the engine to prevent oil starvation. However, this is unfiltered oil. The filter should be changed before this happens.

The filter shown in Fig. 11-8 is called a *single-stage* filter. It uses folded, or pleated, paper as the filtering element. Dirty oil enters the filter around the outside of the filtering element as shown by the heavy

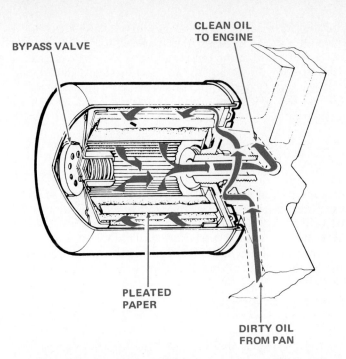

BYPASS VALVE

CLEAN OIL
TO ENGINE

PLEATED
PAPER

DIRTY OIL
FROM PAN

Fig. 11-8 An oil filter cut away to show the built-in bypass valve. *(Chrysler Corporation)*

black arrows. Then the oil is forced through the pleated paper, which filters out the dirt and contaminants by trapping them in the paper. The paper has fine pores through which the oil can pass. However, the dirt particles are too large to pass through these tiny pores.

Some filters have what is called a *depth-type* filtering element. These filters do not use a pleated-paper element. Instead, the filtering is done by a different type of material, usually a fiber such as cotton, wool, rayon, and nylon. The dirty oil passes through the packed fiber, and the dirt is trapped in it.

Another type of filter that is sold in stores today is the *dual filter*. This filter has two different kinds of filtering material. One claim for the dual filter is that it can be used longer and does not need to be changed so often.

The oil filter should be replaced before it stops working properly. Car manufacturers recommend that oil filters be replaced periodically. The usual recommendation is that the filter be replaced at the first oil change and then every other oil change after that.

☐ 11-14 OIL GALLERIES

The cylinder block has oilholes called *oil galleries* drilled into it. They carry the oil from the oil pump to the main bearings (Fig. 11-5). Long holes, drilled from the front to the back of the block, are connected by short holes drilled in the half-round supports for the crankshaft. These short holes match the holes in the bearings that are installed in the support. The oil flows through the oil galleries to the holes in the bearings. Then the oil flows through the bearing holes and onto the crankshaft journals rotating in the bearings. Therefore the crankshaft is "floating" on layers of oil. Relatively little force is required to spin the crankshaft. As a result, little engine power is lost and metal-to-metal contact is prevented.

However, some power is required to force the crankshaft to rotate on its layers of oil. Friction horsepower—the power lost because of friction in the engine—was described in □ 7-11. It includes the power that is used to overcome the friction between the layers of oil as they slip over one another.

□ 11-15 OIL-PRESSURE INDICATORS

Cars are equipped with some means of showing the driver the oil pressure in the engine. If the pressure drops too low, the engine is not being properly lubricated. Continued operation at low oil pressure will ruin the engine. The driver must be warned of low pressure so that the engine can be stopped.

There are two general types of oil-pressure indicators. In one, a dial on the car instrument panel shows the oil pressure. In the other, a light comes on if the oil pressure drops too low. Both of these indicating systems are discussed in Chap. 23.

□ 11-16 OIL-LEVEL INDICATORS

A *dipstick* is used to check the level of the oil in the oil pan (Fig. 11-9). To use the dipstick, allow the engine to sit 1 minute after running. This allows the oil to drain back to the pan. Then pull the dipstick out, wipe it off, and put it back in place. Then pull it out again so that you can check the level of the oil shown on the dipstick. Figure 11-10 shows the markings on different engine-oil dipsticks.

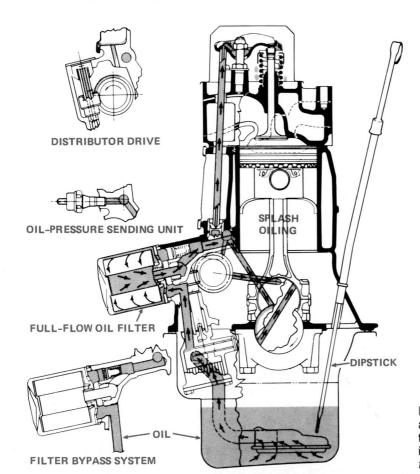

DISTRIBUTOR DRIVE

OIL-PRESSURE SENDING UNIT

SPLASH OILING

FULL-FLOW OIL FILTER

DIPSTICK

OIL

FILTER BYPASS SYSTEM

Fig. 11-9 Lubricating system for an in-line engine. Arrows show the flow of oil to the moving parts in the engine. *(Chrysler Corporation)*

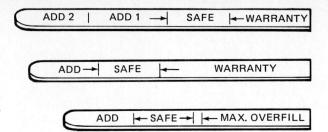

Fig. 11-10 Typical markings on an engine-oil dipstick. *(Chrysler Corporation)*

On engines with a positive crankcase ventilating (PCV) system, the dipstick tube is sealed at the top when the dipstick is in place. This keeps unfiltered air from entering the crankcase and blowby gases from escaping. (The PCV system is described in Chap. 24.)

□ 11-17 ENGINE LUBRICATING SYSTEM OPERATION

The automobile engine has a *pressurized,* or *pressure-fed,* lubricating system (Fig. 11-11). In this system, most moving engine parts are lubricated by oil fed to them under pressure from the oil pump (Fig. 11-11). Other parts are lubricated by *splash oiling.*

Oil is picked up from the "sump," or reservoir, in the oil pan by the oil pump (□ 11-9). The pump has a strainer over the oil intake to prevent large particles from getting into the engine oil supply. The pump then sends the oil to the oil filter (Figs. 11-8 and 11-11). As the cleaned oil leaves the filter, the oil flows to the main oil gallery in the cylinder block. Other passages branch off from the main oil gallery. They send oil to the crankshaft, camshaft, hydraulic lifters, and valve train.

From the main oil gallery, oil flows to the crankshaft main-bearing supports. These are ribs in the bottom of the cylinder block which have been drilled so oil can flow through. A hole (and sometimes a groove) in the upper half of the main bearing allows oil to reach the crankshaft journal (Fig. 9-27). Rotation of the journal carries the oil around to the

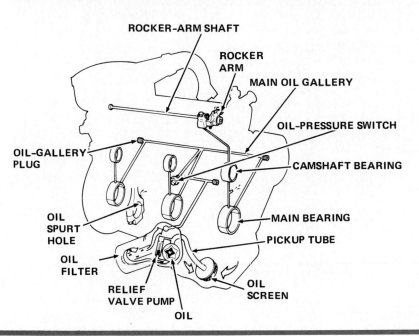

Fig. 11-11 Engine lubricating system showing the oil galleries and spurt holes. *(Federal-Mogul Corporation)*

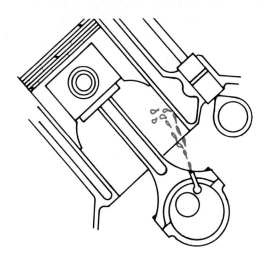

Fig. 11-12 When a hole in the connecting rod aligns with a hole in the crankpin, oil is sprayed onto the cylinder walls to lubricate the piston and rings. *(Ford Motor Company)*

lower bearing half. In this way, the complete bearing is lubricated. The oil flows from holes in the cylinder block, through the oilhole in the bearing, into the space between the shaft and the bearing. Then the oil flows from the center of the bearing to the edges. There the oil drops off, falling back into the oil pan.

Part of the oil flowing to the main bearings takes an additional path. It goes through holes drilled in the crankshaft to reach the connecting-rod bearings (Fig. 9-21). Every time the hole in the crankshaft main journal passes the hole in the main bearing, a spurt of oil flows through the drilled hole to the crankpin. The oil flows over the crankpin to lubricate the connecting-rod bearing. Then the oil flows out from the center and drops off the edges of the bearing back into the oil pan. In this way, the oil cleans as it lubricates.

Some of the oil still has not finished its trip through the engine. Oil thrown off the connecting-rod bearings covers the cylinder walls. This is called *splash oiling* as shown in Fig. 11-9. It provides an oily mist that lubricates the pistons, piston rings, piston pins, and camshaft lobes.

Many engines further ensure adequate lubrication by having spit holes in the connecting rod (Fig. 11-12). Some of the oil feeding through the crankshaft holes to the connecting-rod bearings spurts through these holes and onto the cylinder walls. The spurt takes place every time the hole in the connecting rod aligns with the hole in the crankpin. This supplies the pistons, piston rings, piston pins, and camshaft lobes with the oil they need.

In some engines, the camshaft bearings receive oil directly from the main oil gallery (Fig. 11-5). The oil flows through passages to the bearings. Each bearing must be installed with its oilhole aligned with the passage in the bearing bore. Then a continuous flow of oil is supplied to lubricate the camshaft-bearing journals. In other engines, the oil first flows to the main-bearing journals (Fig. 11-11). Another set of passages allows the oil to flow on to the camshaft bearings.

□ 11-18 BEARING LUBRICATION

The engine lubricating system pumps oil to the moving parts in the engine. This oil covers all the moving parts, so that they "float" on layers of oil. The layers of oil are very thin. However, they are thick enough to prevent metal-to-metal contact. When metal-to-metal contact occurs in an engine, damage can result. Metal rubbing on metal will scratch surfaces, waste power, overheat the metal, and cause engine seizure. To avoid these problems, a large volume of oil must reach the bearings in which the crankshaft turns.

Lubrication of the bearings allows the moving part to slide easily on layers of oil. The journal must be slightly smaller than the bearing to provide *oil clearance* (Fig. 9-26). Typically, this is about 0.001 inch [0.03 mm]. Oil feeds through the bearing oilhole into this clearance. The oil flows across the bearing and then drops off the edges. This movement of the oil cleans the bearings and helps cool them. As the oil moves across the bearing, it picks up heat along with particles of dirt. The oil drops into the oil pan, where it loses heat. The oil pump continuously sends oil through the oil filter to the engine parts. The filter removes dirt from the oil. Then the oil goes back through the engine. This continuous circulation of oil allows the oil to both clean and cool the engine while lubricating it.

☐ 11-19 VALVE-TRAIN LUBRICATION

The valve-train oiling arrangement is shown in Fig. 11-5. Some of the oil from the oil pump flows through an oil gallery to all the valve lifters. This oil lubricates the valve lifters and fills hydraulic valve lifters (Fig. 10-22). Some oil flows from the lifters up to the cylinder head through hollow pushrods (Fig. 11-9). As the oil reaches the top of the pushrods, it spurts out to lubricate the rocker arms, the rocker-arm shaft or ball pivots, and the valve stems. Drain holes allow the oil to flow down into the oil pan.

Not all engine lubricating systems operate exactly as described above. One common variation is how the rocker arms get oil. Instead of oiling through hollow pushrods, many rocker arms get oil through the hollow stud on which they pivot (Fig. 10-16). Others receive oil through hollow rocker-arm shafts (Fig. 11-5). As the rocker arms pivot, holes in the shaft align with holes in the rocker arm. This allows a spurt of oil to lubricate the valve-and-spring assembly (Fig. 11-11).

☐ 11-20 OVERHEAD-CAMSHAFT LUBRICATION

In the overhead-camshaft engine, additional lubrication must be furnished to the cylinder head for the camshaft bearings (Fig. 6-27). Usually, there is an oil gallery running the length of the cylinder head (Fig. 6-27). It supplies oil to the camshaft bearings. The gallery also supplies oil to the hydraulic valve lifters and other valve-train parts.

Select the *one* correct, best, or most probable answer to each question. Then check your answers against the correct answers given at the end of the book.

1. In addition to providing lubrication and acting as a cooling agent, the engine oil must
   a. clean, dry, and absorb shocks
   b. oxidize, carbonize, and clean
   c. absorb shocks, seal, and clean
   d. reduce oil consumption and keep the engine dry

2. The latest service rating for gasoline-engine oil is
   a. SC
   b. SB
   c. SF
   d. SE

3. Viscosity refers to the ability of a liquid to
   a. thicken
   b. thin out
   c. flow
   d. all of the above

4. The purpose of the relief valve in the lubricating system is to
   a. ensure adequate pressure
   b. prevent excessive pressure
   c. prevent insufficient lubrication
   d. ensure adequate oil circulation

5. The purpose of the dipstick is to
   a. check the quality of oil
   b. check the level of oil in the oil pan
   c. measure the oil pressure
   d. help the oil-filter action

6. The purpose of the oilholes drilled in the crankshaft is to
   a. lubricate the piston pins
   b. lubricate the main journals
   c. lubricate the connecting-rod bearings
   d. none of the above

7. Two types of engine oil pumps are
   a. pressure-feed and force-feed
   b. gear and rotor
   c. centrifugal and impeller
   d. splash and free-flow

8. Most manufacturers recommend that the oil filter be replaced
   a. at 10,000 mile [16,000 km] intervals
   b. every year
   c. every 6 months
   d. every other oil change

9. Oil for use in automotive diesel engines must be marked
   a. high sulfur or low viscosity
   b. heavy-duty or synthetic
   c. SE/CC or SE/CD
   d. none of the above

10. Two types of oil filters used in automotive engines are
   a. single-stage and depth-type
   b. open and closed
   c. low-pressure and high-pressure
   d. full-flow and flow-through

CHAPTER 12
ENGINE COOLING SYSTEMS

After studying this chapter, you should be able to:
1. Describe the operation of the engine cooling system.
2. Explain the construction and operation of the water pump.
3. Define *variable-speed fan* and *fan-clutch drive*.
4. Discuss the flow of coolant through the two types of radiators.
5. Explain why cars with an automatic transmission have a transmission-oil cooler.
6. Explain the operation of the thermostat.
7. Explain the purpose of pressurizing the cooling system and how this is done.

The burning of fuel in an engine produces a large quantity of heat. But only about one-third of this heat is used to create the pressure that forces the piston down the cylinder. A small amount is removed by the lubricating oil (Chap. 11). Another third leaves the engine unused in the hot exhaust gas. And about a third is removed through the combustion chamber and cylinder walls by the engine cooling system. It has the job of regulating engine temperature so that the engine is neither too hot nor too cold. This chapter describes how the engine cooling system works.

☐ 12-1 PURPOSE OF THE COOLING SYSTEM

The cooling system must cool the engine properly. If the cooling system cools too much, fuel will be wasted. The engine will not have normal power. If the cooling system does not cool the engine enough, it will overheat. An overheated engine loses power. Also, overheating can burn off the film of lubricating oil from the cylinder walls. This will cause damage to the cylinder walls, pistons, and piston rings. The result could be a seized engine.

The heat comes from the fuel being burned in the combustion chambers. Combustion temperatures in the cylinders can momentarily reach 4000 degrees Fahrenheit [2200 degrees Celsius] or higher. That is hot enough to melt the cylinder block. Therefore, the excess heat must be taken away from the engine before the heat causes damage. The cooling system does this. It must withdraw heat when the engine is hot. But while the engine is cold or warming up, it must withdraw little or no heat.

☐ 12-2 TYPES OF COOLING SYSTEMS

There are two kinds of cooling systems: air-cooling and liquid-, or water-, cooling. In the air-cooled engine, air passing the cooling fins on the cylinders and the cylinder heads carries away the excess heat. This system is described in ☐ 8-14 and illustrated in Fig. 8-5. In the liquid-cooled engine, water mixed with antifreeze circulates around the combustion chambers to carry away excess heat. The mixture of water and antifreeze—called *coolant*—cools the engine. Several liquid-cooled engines are shown in Chap. 8.

☐ 12-3 OPERATION OF THE LIQUID-COOLING SYSTEM

In liquid-cooled engines, the cylinder block and cylinder head have water jackets through which the coolant can circulate to carry away heat. Figure 12-1 shows the operation of the liquid-cooling system in an in-line six-cylinder engine. The arrows show the direction of coolant flow. The coolant is pumped through the water jackets by a water pump mounted

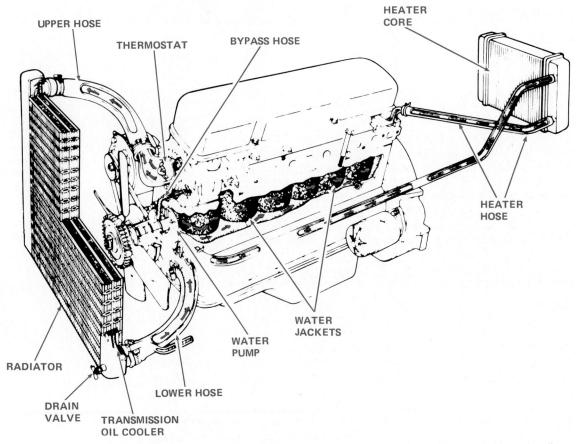

Fig. 12-1 Operation of the liquid-cooling system. The small arrows show the direction of coolant flow. *(Chrysler Corporation)*

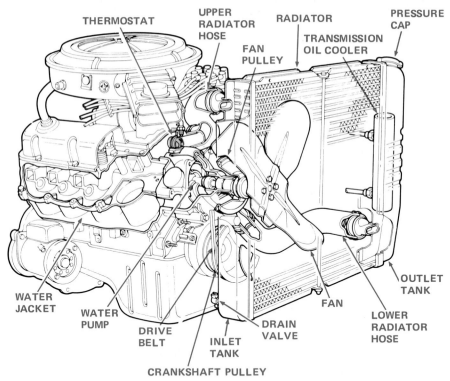

THERMOSTAT UPPER RADIATOR HOSE RADIATOR TRANSMISSION OIL COOLER PRESSURE CAP FAN PULLEY WATER JACKET WATER PUMP DRIVE BELT INLET TANK DRAIN VALVE FAN OUTLET TANK LOWER RADIATOR HOSE CRANKSHAFT PULLEY

Fig. 12-2 A V-8 engine cut away to show the cooling system. *(Ford Motor Company)*

on the front of the engine. As the coolant flows through the water jackets, it picks up heat. The coolant gets very hot, almost to the boiling point. Then the coolant flows into the radiator.

The radiator has a series of coolant passages and a series of air passages. The arrows in Fig. 12-1 show how the coolant circulates. It leaves the bottom of the radiator and goes up to the water pump. The pump forces the coolant through the water jackets in the cylinder block. From there, the coolant flows up through the water jackets in the cylinder head. Then the coolant leaves the head and returns to the top of the radiator by flowing through the upper radiator hose (Fig. 12-2). The coolant then flows through the radiator and loses heat to the air passing through it. When the car is not moving, or is moving slowly, the engine fan helps maintain airflow through the radiator. It is this continuous circulation of coolant between the engine and the radiator that prevents the engine from overheating.

□ *12-4 WATER JACKETS*

Water jackets are spaces surrounding the combustion chambers and cylinders walls through which coolant flows. Figure 12-3 shows the water jackets in a cylinder block and head. In the block, the water jackets are open spaces between the outside of the cylinder and the inside of the block. In the cylinder head, the water jackets surround the openings for the spark plugs and valve guides. Water jackets are watertight, so coolant can flow through them without leaking out. The coolant passes first through the cylinder-block water jackets and then through the cylinder-head water jackets, picking up heat. Then the hot coolant flows into the

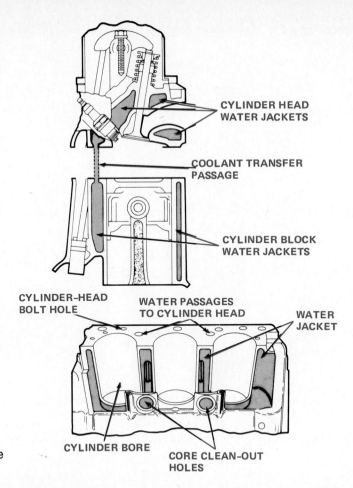

CYLINDER HEAD
WATER JACKETS

COOLANT TRANSFER
PASSAGE

CYLINDER BLOCK
WATER JACKETS

CYLINDER-HEAD
BOLT HOLE

WATER PASSAGES
TO CYLINDER HEAD

WATER
JACKET

CYLINDER BORE

CORE CLEAN-OUT
HOLES

Fig. 12-3 Water jackets in the cylinder head and block.

radiator. As the coolant flows through the radiator, the coolant loses heat. The cooled coolant then flows back into the bottom of the cylinder-block water jackets to start another trip through the engine.

□ 12-5 WATER PUMP

The *water pump* is a small centrifugal pump that forces coolant to flow through the cooling system. The pump is located at the front of the engine between the block and radiator (Fig. 12-1 and 12-2). The pump is usually driven by a belt from the front of the crankshaft. The pulley that drives the pump also carries the engine fan (□ 12-6).

The pump consists of a housing, with a coolant inlet and outlet, and an impeller (Fig. 12-4). The *impeller* is a flat plate mounted on the pump shaft with a series of flat or curved blades, or vanes. When the impeller rotates, the coolant between the blades is thrown outward by centrifugal force. This forces the coolant through the pump outlet and into the cylinder-block water jacket. The pump inlet is connected by a hose to the bottom of the radiator. Coolant from the radiator is drawn into the pump to replace the coolant forced through the outlet. Figure 12-5 shows the coolant flow through the water pump.

The impeller shaft is supported on one or more bearings. A seal (Fig. 12-4) prevents coolant from leaking out around the bearings. Most water pumps use sealed bearings which never need additional lubrication. With a sealed bearing, grease cannot leak out. Also, dirt and water cannot get

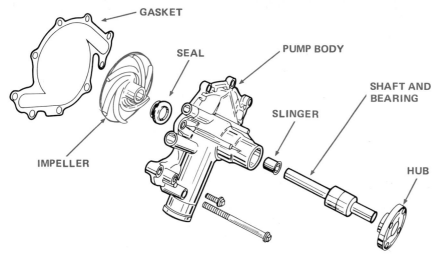

Fig. 12-4 A disassembled water pump. *(Chrysler Corporation)*

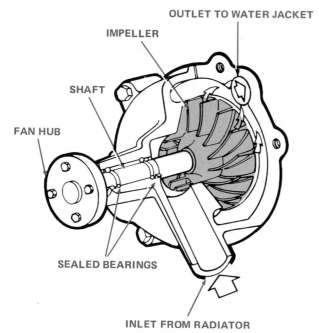

Fig. 12-5 A cutaway water pump showing the impeller action. *(Chrysler Corporation)*

in. Older water pumps had bearings that required a water-pump lubricant, such as soluble oil, mixed with the coolant for lubrication.

□ *12-6 ENGINE FAN*

The engine fan usually mounts on the water-pump shaft (on engines that are *not* installed transversely). Therefore, the fan is driven by the belt that drives the water pump (Fig. 12-6). The purpose of the fan is to pull air through the radiator. This improves cooling at slow speeds and idle. At car speeds above about 40 miles per hour (mph) [64 kilometers per hour (km/h)], the air rammed through the radiator by the forward motion of the vehicle provides all the cooling air that is needed.

Fig. 12-6 The fan is driven through a fan-drive clutch by a belt from the crankshaft. *(Ford Motor Company)*

181

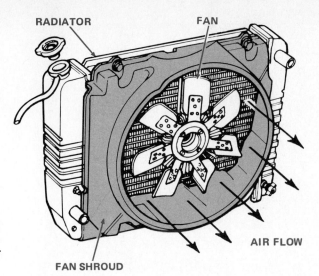

RADIATOR   FAN

AIR FLOW

FAN SHROUD

Fig. 12-7 A shroud is attached to the back of the radiator to improve fan performance. *(Chrysler Corporation)*

The fan usually has from four to six blades which, in turning, pull air through the radiator. Some cars have a *fan shroud* (Fig. 12-7) to direct the airflow. Use of the shroud assures that all air pulled back by the fan passes through the radiator, and not around it.

> **CAUTION** Fan blades can break and fly off. Whenever the engine is running, never stand directly in line with the rotating fan. Also, avoid allowing your clothing, hands, or tools to get near the fan blades or fan belt.

□ 12-7 VARIABLE-SPEED AND FLEXIBLE-BLADE FANS

Many engines have a variable-speed fan. It is driven through a fan clutch (Fig. 12-6). The clutch drive increases fan speed as the engine gets hot and reduces fan speed as the engine gets cooler. The advantage of the variable-speed fan is that it saves power. When full fan speed is not needed, it turns slower. The fan is also quieter when it runs slower.

One type of variable-speed fan drive has a small fluid coupling (Fig. 12-6). The driving force passes through a fluid in the coupling. When the engine gets hot, more fluid is forced into the coupling. Then the fan runs faster. When the engine is cool, less fluid goes into the coupling. Therefore, the fan runs slower.

Another type of fan has flexible blades that reduce both the power needed to drive the fan and fan noise at high speed (Fig. 12-8). With this fan, centrifugal force causes the pitch of the blades to decrease as fan speed increases. As the pitch changes, each blade takes a smaller "bite" of air. Therefore, less engine power is required to drive the flex fan at higher speeds. Fan noise is less, also.

□ 12-8 ELECTRIC FAN

Cars with front-wheel drive usually have the engine mounted transversely, or crosswise, at the front of the car (Fig. 6-3). Most of these cars use a fan driven by an electric motor to pull air through the radiator. Figure 12-9 shows a typical arrangement. A thermostatic switch turns on the motor only when the fan is needed. The switch turns the fan motor off

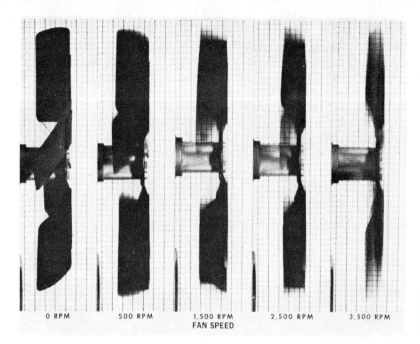

Fig. 12-8 The fan blades change pitch as fan speed increases.

0 RPM   500 RPM   1,500 RPM   2,500 RPM   3,500 RPM
FAN SPEED

if the engine begins to cool down too much. However, on cars with air conditioning, the fan motor may run as long as the air conditioner is turned on.

The electric fan requires less power and makes less noise than other types. There is no fan belt to inspect, adjust, and replace periodically. Therefore, the cooling system requires less maintenance.

CAUTION Electrically operated and thermostatically controlled fans may or may not be shut off when the ignition switch is turned to OFF. Because the coolant temperature switch turns the fan motor on and off solely on the basis of coolant temperature, the fan may start and run even with the engine stopped. When working near an electric fan, disconnect the lead to the fan motor to avoid injury should the fan start.

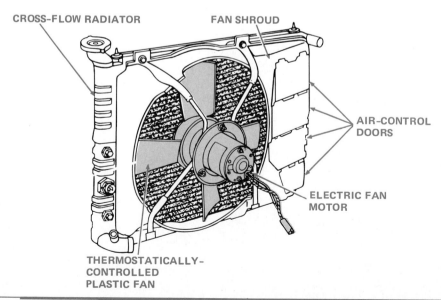

CROSS-FLOW RADIATOR

FAN SHROUD

AIR-CONTROL DOORS

ELECTRIC FAN MOTOR

THERMOSTATICALLY-CONTROLLED PLASTIC FAN

Fig. 12-9 An electric fan used with a transversely mounted engine in a car with front-wheel drive. *(Chrysler Corporation)*

☐ 12-9 DRIVE BELTS

All engine cooling systems include a fan. It may be either electric
(☐ 12-8) or mechanical (☐ 12-6 and 12-7). The mechanical fan is driven
by a belt from the crankshaft. Figures 12-2 and 12-6 show two different
types of belt drives. The fan belt, or drive belt, shown in Fig. 12-2 is a
V-belt. When the belt is properly tightened, it wedges into the pulley
groove. There is friction between the sides of the belt and the sides of the
groove. This friction transmits power from the crankshaft, through the
belt, to the fan pulley. An engine may require as many as five or six
V-belts to drive all the engine-driven accessories.

Figure 12-6 shows a *serpentine belt,* which is used on some newer
cars. It is a wide belt with a series of small V-shaped ridges and grooves
on the inside surface. The pulleys used with a serpentine belt have a
matching series of grooves and ridges. On the engine, one serpentine belt
turns all engine-driven accessories. It may replace the several V-belts
otherwise required.

☐ 12-10 RADIATOR

The radiator is a *heat exchanger* (Figs. 12-1 and 12-2). It removes heat
from the coolant passing through it. The radiator does this by holding
some of the hot coolant close to a large volume of cooler air. The hot
coolant enters the radiator, loses heat, and comes out cooler. The heat is
transferred from the coolant to the air passing through the radiator (Fig.
12-7).

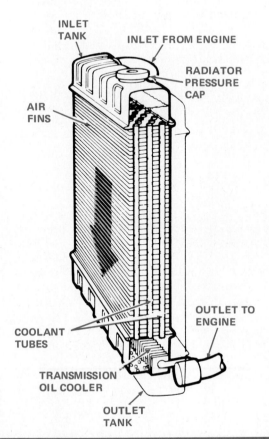

Fig. 12-10 Construction of a
down-flow type of tube-and-fin
radiator. *(Chrysler Corporation)*

Figure 12-10 shows the construction of a radiator. Basically, it is a core made of tubes and fins with an inlet and an outlet tank attached. The tubes and fins divide the core into two separate sections. Coolant passes through one, and air passes through the other. Several types of radiator cores have been used. The most common is the tube-and-fin type (Fig. 12-10). It has a series of coolant tubes that run from the radiator inlet tank to the outlet tank. Surrounding these tubes and fastened to them are air fins. Air passes between the fins and around the outside of the coolant tubes. As the cooler air passes by, it absorbs heat from the coolant in the tubes.

The coolant leaves the radiator from the outlet tank and returns through the inlet tank. The inlet tank may be at the top (Fig. 12-10) or at the side (Fig. 12-2) of the radiator. The outlet tank is located on the bottom (Fig. 12-10) or at the other side of the radiator (Fig. 12-2). This tank receives the coolant after it has been cooled by passing through the radiator core. A filler cap, called a *radiator cap,* may be removed to add coolant to the coolant system. Coolant may be lost because of evaporation or leakage.

In cars with an automatic transmission, a *transmission-oil cooler* is located in the outlet tank (Fig. 12-10). The oil cooler prevents overheating of the automatic-transmission fluid which could damage the transmission. Radiators used in cars with factory-installed air conditioning are larger or have extra fins. This provides more cooling surface. Air conditioning tends to make the engine run hotter.

☐ 12-11 DOWN-FLOW AND CROSS-FLOW RADIATORS

Radiators can be classified according to the direction that the coolant flows through them. In the *down-flow radiators,* the coolant flows from a tank at the top of the radiator to a tank at the bottom of the radiator. Figure 12-11 shows a radiator of this type. It was used in most cars until about 1970.

Most later-model cars have a *cross-flow radiator* (Fig. 12-12). It is basically a down-flow radiator turned on its side. This makes the radiator shorter from top to bottom so cars can be designed with lower hood lines. In the cross-flow radiator, coolant flows horizontally from the inlet tank on one side to the outlet tank on the other side.

☐ 12-12 RADIATOR PRESSURE CAP

The cooling systems of most engines are sealed. When the engine gets hot, pressure develops in the cooling system. The increasing pressure increases the boiling temperature of the coolant. At normal air pressure, water boils at 212 degrees Fahrenheit (°F) [100 degrees Celsius (°C)]. If the air pressure is increased, the temperature at which water boils is also increased. For example, if the pressure is raised 15 pounds per square inch (psi) [103 kilopascals (kPa)] over normal pressure, the boiling point is raised to about 260°F [127°C].

This is what happens in the sealed cooling system. As pressure goes up, the boiling point goes up. This means the coolant can be safely used at a temperature higher that 212°F [100°C] without its boiling. The higher the coolant temperature, the greater the difference between the coolant temperature and the air temperature. The difference in temperatures is what causes the cooling system to work. The hotter the coolant, the faster the heat moves from the radiator to the cooler passing air. A pressurized

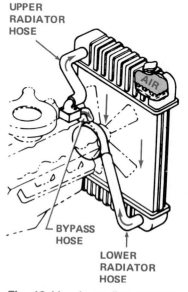

UPPER RADIATOR HOSE

BYPASS HOSE

LOWER RADIATOR HOSE

Fig. 12-11 A cooling system using a down-flow radiator.

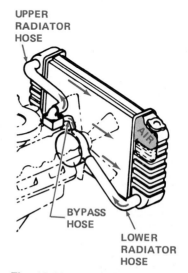

UPPER RADIATOR HOSE

BYPASS HOSE

LOWER RADIATOR HOSE

Fig. 12-12 A cooling system using a cross-flow radiator.

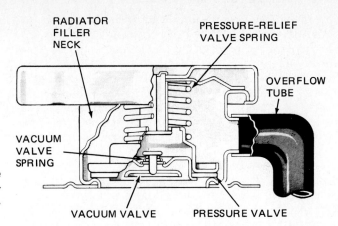

Fig. 12-13 Radiator pressure cap cut away to show the pressure valve and the vacuum valve. *(Ford Motor Company)*

RADIATOR FILLER NECK

PRESSURE-RELIEF VALVE SPRING

OVERFLOW TUBE

VACUUM VALVE SPRING

VACUUM VALVE

PRESSURE VALVE

sealed cooling system can take heat away from the engine faster. Therefore the cooling system works more efficiently under higher pressure.

However, the cooling system can be pressurized too much. If the pressure goes too high, it could damage the radiator. To prevent this, the radiator cap has a pressure-relief valve (Figs. 12-13 and 12-14). When the pressure goes too high, it raises the valve so that the excess pressure can escape (right, Fig. 12-15).

The radiator cap also has a vacuum valve. This valve lets air or coolant from the expansion tank into the cooling system if a vacuum occurs (left, Fig. 12-15). This can happen when the engine stops and cools off. The pressure falls in the cooling system. If it falls too much below outside air pressure, the vacuum could cause a partial collapse of the radiator. To prevent this, the vacuum valve opens. On cars without an expansion tank, outside air enters to equalize the pressure. On cars with an expansion tank, coolant from the expansion tank flows into the radiator to equalize the pressure (□ 12-13).

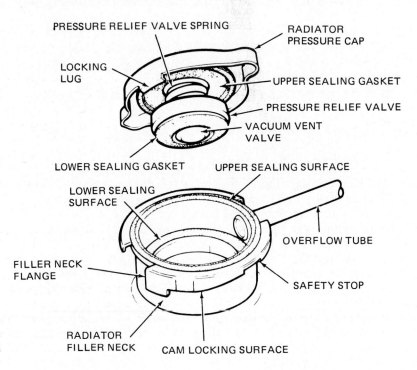

PRESSURE RELIEF VALVE SPRING

RADIATOR PRESSURE CAP

LOCKING LUG

UPPER SEALING GASKET

PRESSURE RELIEF VALVE

VACUUM VENT VALVE

LOWER SEALING GASKET

UPPER SEALING SURFACE

LOWER SEALING SURFACE

OVERFLOW TUBE

FILLER NECK FLANGE

SAFETY STOP

RADIATOR FILLER NECK

CAM LOCKING SURFACE

Fig. 12-14 A radiator pressure cap removed from the radiator filler neck. *(Chrysler Corporation)*

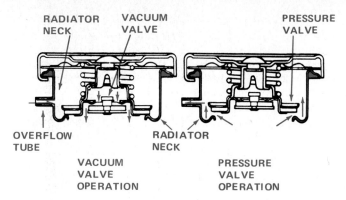

RADIATOR NECK   VACUUM VALVE   PRESSURE VALVE

OVERFLOW TUBE   RADIATOR NECK

VACUUM VALVE OPERATION   PRESSURE VALVE OPERATION

Fig. 12-15 Valve actions in a radiator pressure cap. *(American Motors Corporation)*

□ 12-13 EXPANSION TANK

Many cooling systems have a separate plastic *coolant reservoir,* or *expansion tank* (Fig. 12-16). The expansion tank is partially filled with coolant and connected to the overflow tube in the radiator filler neck. As the coolant is heated, it expands and the pressure in the cooling system goes up. When the pressure reaches the specified value, it pushes the pressure valve open, as shown to the right in Fig. 12-15. Enough coolant then flows into the expansion tank to prevent further pressure increase.

When the engine cools off, the coolant in the cooling system contracts. This produces a partial vacuum in the cooling system. Now the vacuum valve in the radiator cap opens (left in Fig. 12-15). Coolant from the expansion tank flows back into the radiator. The entire operation works to keep the cooling system filled with coolant at all times. Figure 12-16 shows how the expansion tank is connected to the radiator.

Coolant level is checked by looking at the level in the expansion tank. The radiator cap is not removed to check coolant level on cars with a cooling-system expansion tank. You can see the level marks in Fig. 12-16.

□ 12-14 PURPOSE OF THERMOSTAT

A thermostat is placed in the coolant passage between the cylinder head and the top of the radiator (Figs. 12-1 and 12-2). Its purpose is to close off this passage when the engine is cold. Then coolant circulation is restricted, causing the engine to reach normal operating temperature more quickly. This reduces the formation of acids, moisture, and sludge in an engine. Also, after warm-up, the thermostat keeps the engine running at a higher temperature than it would without a thermostat. The higher operating temperature improves engine efficiency and reduces exhaust emissions (Chap. 24).

□ 12-15 TYPES OF THERMOSTATS

The thermostat (Fig. 12-17) is a valve that automatically opens and closes in response to changes in coolant temperature. There are several types of thermostats. All operate the same way. When the engine is cold, the thermostat valve is closed. This prevents coolant from flowing through the upper hose to the radiator. As the engine and coolant warm up, the valve starts to open. Now coolant flows to the radiator so that the cooling system can remove the heat.

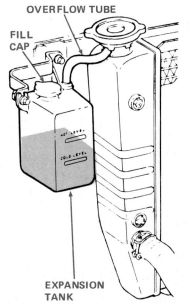

OVERFLOW TUBE

FILL CAP

EXPANSION TANK

Fig. 12-16 Cooling system using an expansion tank. *(Ford Motor Company)*

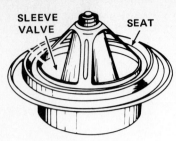

SLEEVE VALVE

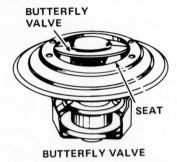

BUTTERFLY VALVE

Fig. 12-17 Two types of thermostats used in engine cooling systems. *(Chrysler Corporation)*

The valve in most thermostats is operated by a wax pellet (Fig. 12-18). When heated, the wax expands and squeezes a rubber diaphragm against a stationary steel piston. This causes the piston to move downward, compressing the return spring and opening the valve. When the wax cools, it contracts. Now the return spring closes the valve.

Thermostats are designed to open at specific temperatures. This temperature is known as the *thermostat rating,* and it may be stamped on the thermostat. Two frequently used thermostats have ratings of 185°F [85°C] and 195°F [91°C]. Most thermostats begin to open at their rated temperature. They are fully open about 20°F [11°C] higher. For example, a thermostat with a rating of 195°F [91°C] starts to open at that temperature. It is fully open at about 215°F [102°C].

☐ 12-16 COOLANT BYPASS PASSAGE

Figures 12-1, 12-11, and 12-12 show a small water-pump *bypass hose.* It is connected from the top of the water pump to just below the thermostat. The purpose of the bypass hose is to allow coolant flow within the engine when the thermostat is closed. This is needed to provide equal cooling of the cylinders and to prevent hot spots. As the engine warms up, the bypass passage may be closed or restricted.

One type of thermostat that controls the bypass passage and the coolant flow to the radiator is shown in Fig. 12-19. This type of thermostat is called a *blocking-bypass thermostat.* It has two valves—a primary thermostat valve and a bypass valve. When the engine is cold, the thermostat valve is closed, as shown to the left in Fig. 12-19. At the same time, the bypass valve is open. This permits coolant flow from the engine to pass directly into the water-pump inlet. The water pump then sends the coolant back into the engine.

When the engine warms up, the thermostat valve opens. Now coolant from the engine can flow to the radiator, as shown to the right in Fig. 12-19. At the same time, opening of the thermostat valve has caused the bypass valve to close. This shuts off the bypass flow to the water pump. Now all the coolant must flow to the radiator. Both valves work together because they are attached to the same stem.

Fig. 12-18 Operation of a wax-pellet thermostat. *(Chrysler Corporation)*

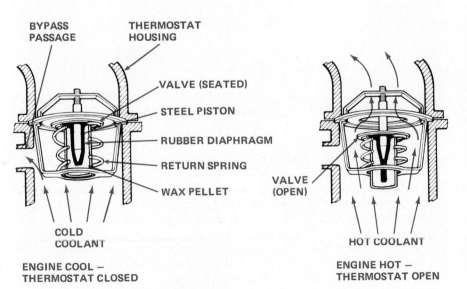

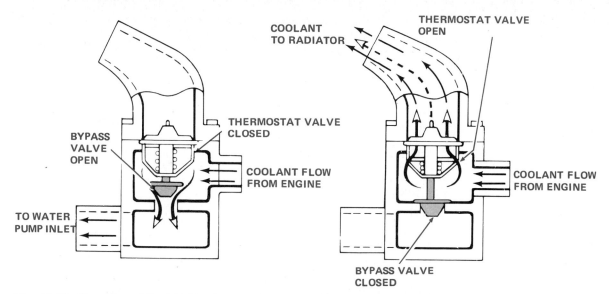

Fig. 12-19 Operation of the blocking-bypass thermostat. *(Chrysler Corporation)*

☐ 12-17 ANTIFREEZE AND COOLANT

Water freezes at 32°F [0°C]. If water freezes in the engine cooling system, it stops coolant circulation. Some parts of the engine will overheat. This could seriously damage the engine. What is worse is that water expands when it freezes. Water freezing in the cylinder block or cylinder head could expand enough to crack the block or head. Water freezing in the radiator could split the radiator seams. In either case, there is serious damage. A cracked block or head cannot be repaired satisfactorily. A split radiator is difficult and expensive to repair.

To prevent freezing of the water in the cooling system, antifreeze is added to form the coolant. The most commonly used antifreeze is ethylene glycol, although an alcohol-base antifreeze has been used in the past. A mixture of half water and half ethylene glycol freezes at −34°F [−36.7°C]. This is 34°F below zero. It seldom gets that cold in the United States, except in Alaska. A higher concentration of antifreeze will prevent coolant freezing at temperatures as low as −84°F [−64.4°C].

Some antifreeze solutions have been sold that seal small leaks in the cooling system. These antifreeze compounds contain tiny plastic beads or inorganic fibers which circulate with the coolant. When a leak develops, the beads or fibers jam in the leak and plug it. This is the same action provided by adding "stop-leak" or "sealer" to the cooling system in an emergency. However, if the leak is too large, no chemical can stop it. A chemical additive cannot stop leaks in hoses, cylinder-head gaskets, or water-pump seals. The only permanent repair for a leak in a cooling-system component is to repair or replace it.

Antifreeze solutions also provide corrosion protection. Compounds are added that fight corrosion inside the engine water jackets and radiator. Antifreeze solutions also serve a purpose during hot-weather operation. They raise the boiling point of the coolant so it does not boil away in hot weather. Also, they continue to fight corrosion.

The engine cooling system should be filled with coolant (antifreeze and water) year-round. One recommendation is that the cooling system be drained, flushed with plain water, and filled with a fresh mixture of antifreeze and water. This should be done every two years.

Automotive cooling systems should never be filled with water only. The temperature indicator light (□ 12-18) does not come on until well above the boiling point of water. Severe engine damage could occur before the driver is aware of the overheating problem if only water is used. Unlike water, a mixture of water and antifreeze will not boil until a higher temperature is reached, which will turn on the light.

□ 12-18 TEMPERATURE INDICATORS

The driver should know the temperature of the coolant in the cooling system at all times. For this reason, a temperature indicator is installed in the instrument panel, or "dash," of the car. An abnormal heat rise is a warning of abnormal conditions in the engine. The indicator warns the driver to stop the engine before serious damage is done.

There are two kinds of temperature indicators: lights and a gauge. The light system includes a light that comes on when the engine temperature goes too high. The other system has a gauge on the car instrument panel. A needle or pointer moves across the face of the gauge. This shows the actual temperature of the coolant in the engine. Temperature indicators are described in detail in Chap. 23.

Select the *one* correct, best, or most probable answer to each question. Then check your answers against the correct answers given at the end of the book.

1. The water-pump part that rotates to cause coolant circulation between the radiator and engine water jackets is the
   a. impeller
   b. fan
   c. body
   d. thermostat

2. The part of the cooling-system thermostat that functions to open and close the valve is the
   a. seater
   b. wax pellet
   c. pressure valve
   d. vacuum valve

3. The device in the cooling system that raises the boiling point of the coolant is called the
   a. water jacket
   b. radiator
   c. vacuum valve
   d. pressure cap

4. The radiator has two separate sections:
   a. vacuum section and pressure section
   b. coolant section and air section
   c. tube-and-fin
   d. ribbon-cellular

5. The pressure cap contains two valves:
   a. pressure valve and blowoff valve
   b. atmospheric valve and vacuum valve
   c. pressure valve and vacuum valve
   d. relief valve and pressure valve

6. Two types of radiators are the
   a. expansion-tank and sealed
   b. cross-flow and down-flow
   c. pressurized and pressure-capped
   d. none of the above

7. The two valves in the blocking-bypass thermostat are the
   a. primary thermostat and secondary thermostat
   b. pressure valve and vacuum valve
   c. bypass valve and vacuum valve
   d. bypass valve and thermostat valve

8. What is the main purpose of the water-pump bypass hose in the engine cooling system?
   a. to reduce pressure at the water-pump outlet during high engine speed
   b. to allow coolant flow within the engine when the thermostat is closed
   c. to prevent air pockets in the water-pump housing
   d. to prevent collapse of the lower radiator hose

9. As the engine cools down, coolant does *not* flow from the expansion tank into the radiator. The cause is probably a defective
   a. pressure-relief valve
   b. vacuum-relief valve
   c. thermostat
   d. bypass passage

10. If it collapses, which of the following can restrict coolant flow to the water-pump inlet?
    a. lower radiator hose
    b. upper radiator hose
    c. heater hose
    d. bypass hose

CHAPTER 13
ENGINE FUELS

After studying this chapter, you should be able to:
1. Describe the composition of gasoline and its additives.
2. Explain what volatility is and how it affects engine operation.
3. Discuss engine detonation and what is done to prevent it.
4. Explain why lead has been removed from some gasolines.
5. Explain the relationship between compression ratio and detonation.
6. Define *gasohol*.
7. Describe the characteristics of diesel fuel oil.

The most common fuel for automotive engines is gasoline. This fuel is for spark-ignition engines. Some vehicles are now using gasohol, a mixture of alcohol and gasoline. Also, some vehicles with spark-ignition engines are using gaseous fuels such as liquefied petroleum gas (LPG) or compressed natural gas (CNG). These vehicles require a special fuel system. Diesel engines, which are compression-ignition engines, use diesel fuel. This is a light oil. All of these fuels are discussed in this chapter.

☐ 13-1 PROPERTIES OF GASOLINE

Gasoline is a hydrocarbon (HC). It is made up of mostly hydrogen and carbon. These two elements readily unite with oxygen, a common element that makes up about 20 percent of the air. When hydrogen unites with oxygen, water is formed. (The chemical formula for water is H_2O.) When carbon unites with oxygen, carbon monoxide (CO) and carbon dioxide (CO_2) are formed.

If the gasoline in an engine burned completely, only water and carbon dioxide would remain. However, perfect combustion never occurs. Not all the gasoline burns completely. As a result, hydrocarbons (gasoline vapor) and carbon monoxide come out of the tail pipe to pollute the air. Chapter 24 tells more about air pollution and automotive emission controls.

□ 13-2 SOURCE OF GASOLINE

Gasoline is made from crude oil, from which engine lubricating oil and diesel fuel are also made. The crude oil goes through a process called *refining*. From the refining process come gasoline, lubricating oil, grease, fuel oil, and many other products.

During the refining process, several compounds, called *additives,* are added to gasoline to give it the characteristics of good gasoline. Good gasoline should have

1. Proper volatility, which determines how quickly gasoline vaporizes
2. Resistance to spark knock, or detonation
3. Oxidation inhibitors, which prevent formation of gum in the fuel system
4. Antirust agents, which prevent rusting of metal parts in the fuel system
5. Anti-icers, which fight carburetor icing and fuel-line freezing
6. Detergents, which help keep the carburetor clean
7. Dye for identification

Let's talk about volatility and antiknock value first.

□ 13-3 VOLATILITY

After gasoline is mixed with air in the carburetor, the gasoline must vaporize quickly, before it enters the engine cylinders. If the gasoline is slow to vaporize, tiny drops of liquid gasoline will enter the cylinders. Because these drops do not burn, some of the fuel is wasted. It goes out the tail pipe and helps create *smog* (Chap. 24). Also, the gasoline drops tend to wash the lubricating oil off the cylinder walls. This increases the wear on the cylinder walls, piston rings, and pistons.

The ease with which gasoline vaporizes is called its *volatility*. A high-volatility gasoline vaporizes very quickly. A low-volatility gasoline vaporizes slowly. A good gasoline should have just the right amount of volatility for the temperature. If the gasoline is too volatile, it will vaporize in the fuel pump. The result will be a condition called *vapor lock*. It prevents the flow of gasoline to the carburetor. Vapor lock causes the engine to stall from lack of fuel.

□ 13-4 ANTIKNOCK VALUE

Spark knock is also called *detonation*. If you have ever been in a car that had detonation, you know the sound. The engine pings, usually under light load. It sounds like someone is tapping on the cylinder walls with a hammer. Look at Fig. 13-1. The horizontal row at the top of the figure shows what happens during normal combustion. The fuel charge—the mixture of air and fuel—starts burning as soon as the spark occurs at the spark plug. The flame sweeps smoothly and evenly across the combustion chamber. Now look at the horizontal row at the bottom. The spark starts combustion in the same way. However, before the flame can reach the far side of the combustion chamber, the last part of the charge explodes. The result is a very quick increase in pressure. This is detonation, and it gives off a pinging sound.

Detonation can ruin an engine. The heavy shocks on the piston put a great strain on the engine parts. Continued detonation can cause pistons to chip and parts to break. So detonation must be avoided.

NORMAL COMBUSTION

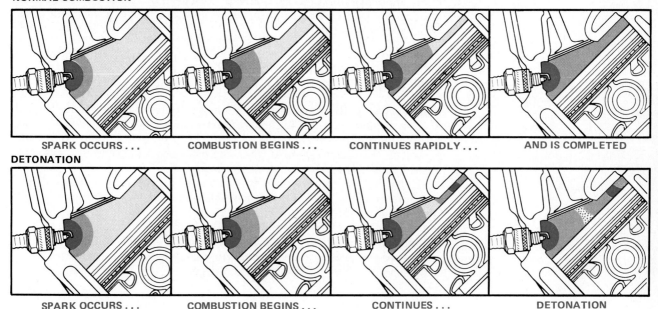

SPARK OCCURS . . . COMBUSTION BEGINS . . . CONTINUES RAPIDLY . . . AND IS COMPLETED

DETONATION

SPARK OCCURS . . . COMBUSTION BEGINS . . . CONTINUES . . . DETONATION

Fig. 13-1 Normal combustion without detonation is shown in the top row. The fuel charge burns smoothly from beginning to end, providing an even, powerful force on the top of the piston. Detonation is shown in the bottom row. The last part of the fuel explodes or burns almost instantly to produce detonation, or spark knock. *(Champion Spark Plug Company)*

Gasoline refiners have various ways to make gasoline that does not detonate easily. A gasoline that detonates easily is called a *low-octane* gasoline. A gasoline that resists detonation is called a *high-octane* gasoline.

□ 13-5 INCREASING THE OCTANE RATING

One way to increase the octane rating is to change the refining process. Another way is to add a small amount of tetraethyl lead, also known as "lead," "ethyl," or "tel." This additive tends to prevent the last part of the fuel charge from detonating. However, there are two problems with using tetraethyl lead.

One problem is that when gasoline containing lead is burned, some of it gets into the air. Lead is a poison, and breathing air containing lead can cause lead poisoning. Lead poisoning can cause illness and death. The other problem is that the lead keeps exhaust emission controls from working properly. These are two reasons why gasoline without lead is now required for most new cars.

□ 13-6 TWO KINDS OF GASOLINE

One of the emission controls is a *catalytic converter* (Chap. 24). The exhaust gases from the engine flow through this device. It reduces the amount of unburned gasoline vapor (HC) and carbon monoxide (CO) in the exhaust gases. However, it will stop doing its job if leaded gasoline is used in the engine. That is the reason most service stations now have pumps labeled "No Lead" or "Unleaded." These pumps dispense gasoline without lead for cars with catalytic converters. Other pumps may dispense leaded gasoline.

☐ 13-7 COMPRESSION RATIOS AND DETONATION

Over the years the compression ratios of automobile engines have gone up. The reason is that higher compression ratios give engines more power. *Compression ratio* is the amount that the air-fuel mixture is compressed on the compression stroke. The more the air-fuel mixture is compressed, the higher the compression ratio.

But a high compression ratio can cause a problem. It increases the temperature of the air-fuel mixture. The higher heat of compression may cause the remaining air-fuel mixture to explode before normal combustion is completed. This is detonation. The compression ratio must be kept low enough to make sure that the fuel charge will not ignite early from the heat of compression. Also, the higher combustion temperatures cause increased amounts of another exhaust-gas pollutant, nitrogen oxides (NO_x).

☐ 13-8 REDUCING COMPRESSION RATIOS

Increasing the combustion temperature increases the formation of NO_x. To have cleaner air, it is desirable to reduce the combustion temperature. One method is to reduce compression ratios to slightly less than 9 : 1 (for spark-ignition engines). A lower compression ratio means lower combustion temperatures. Then less NO_x is formed during the combustion process. This has also reduced engine performance and fuel economy. Other methods of lowering combustion temperature are also used. These are discussed in Chap. 24.

☐ 13-9 GASOHOL

Gasohol is gasoline to which a small amount of alcohol has been added. Usually, the alcohol is about 10 percent of the fuel. The alcohol can be made from corn or other agricultural products. Advocates of gasohol say that it reduces our dependance on foreign sources of oil.

Gasohol can be used in engines without any changes in the fuel system. However, when fuel with a larger percentage of alcohol is used, the carburetor or fuel-injection system must be recalibrated.

☐ 13-10 LIQUEFIED PETROLEUM GAS (LPG)

Propane is a type of liquefied petroleum gas (LPG) made from crude oil. When pressure is applied to a container of propane, the gas becomes a liquid. When the pressure is released, the liquid propane turns into a gas. Some car manufacturers offer a propane fuel system as an option (Fig. 13-2). Other vehicles have been equipped with it.

One advantage to using propane as an engine fuel is that it has an octane rating of well over 100. This allows the engine compression ratio to be raised for greater power and efficiency. Another advantage is that propane burns cleanly. Less engine wear occurs. Therefore, less maintenance is required. Also, no fuel pump and little emission control equipment is used. However, a special fuel system is needed to handle the

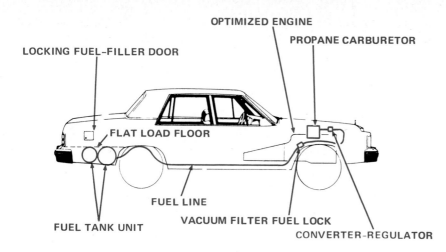

Fig. 13-2 Layout of a propane fuel system on a new car. *(Ford Motor Company)*

LOCKING FUEL-FILLER DOOR

OPTIMIZED ENGINE

PROPANE CARBURETOR

FLAT LOAD FLOOR

FUEL LINE

FUEL TANK UNIT

VACUUM FILTER FUEL LOCK

CONVERTER-REGULATOR

pressurized liquid and gas. The system includes special fuel tanks to hold reserve supplies of propane under pressure. The converter-regulator (Fig. 13-2) allows the liquid propane to become a vapor. A special carburetor controls the flow of the propane vapor into the engine.

□ 13-11 DIESEL-ENGINE FUELS

Diesel engines use diesel fuel oil. The fuel is sprayed, or injected, into the engine cylinders near the end of the compression stroke (Fig. 13-3). The heat of compression heats the air enough so that the fuel oil ignites as it enters the cylinder.

Diesel fuel is made from crude oil. It is a light oil with the proper volatility, viscosity, and cetane number.

1. Volatility is a measure of how easily a liquid evaporates. Diesel fuel has a relatively low volatility. It boils at a temperature of 700 degrees Fahrenheit [371 degrees Celsius] or less. There are two grades used in automobile engines, number 1 diesel and number 2 diesel. Number 1 diesel is more volatile. It is used in vehicles where the temperature is very low. Most automotive diesel engines normally run on number 2 die-

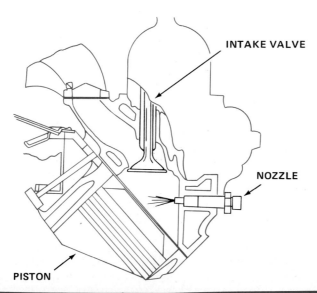

INTAKE VALVE

NOZZLE

PISTON

Fig. 13-3 In a diesel engine, diesel fuel is injected into the combustion chamber.

sel. This less volatile fuel is preferred for most driving conditions. It has a higher heating value and can deliver better fuel mileage.

2. Viscosity refers to the ease with which a liquid flows. Gasoline has a very low viscosity. It flows very easily. A light oil has a fairly low viscosity so it flows rather easily. A heavy oil has a high viscosity so it flows slowly.

Diesel fuel oil must have a relatively low viscosity. It must flow through the fuel-system lines easily and must spray into the engine cylinders with little resistance. If the oil has excessive viscosity, it will not break up into fine particles. The particles will not burn rapidly enough. Therefore, engine performance will be poor. If the viscosity is too low, the fuel oil will not properly lubricate the moving parts in the fuel pump and fuel injectors. Damage may result. Number 2 diesel has the proper viscosity for most driving conditions. Number 1 diesel has a lower viscosity. It will flow and spray properly in low temperatures.

3. Cetane number is a measure of the ignition quality of the fuel, or how high a temperature is required to ignite it. The lower the cetane number, the higher the temperature required to ignite the fuel. As the fuel is sprayed into the cylinder, the fuel ignites due to the high temperature of the compressed air (heat of compression). Fuel with a high cetane number ignites almost instantly.

If the fuel has a low cetane number, it takes a little longer for ignition to start. This is called *ignition lag*. During this slight delay (measured in very small fractions of a second), fuel continues to be sprayed into the cylinder. Then, when ignition does occur, all the accumulated fuel ignites at once. The pressure suddenly goes up and a combustion knock results. This is similar to detonation in a spark-ignition engine (□ 13-4).

With the higher-cetane-number fuel, there is no accumulation of fuel in the cylinder before ignition. The fuel ignites as soon as it enters the cylinder. The resulting pressure rise is smooth and no combustion knock takes place.

Select the *one* correct, best, or most probable answer to each question. Then check your answers against the correct answers given at the end of the book.

1. Gasoline is made up mostly of
   a. hydrogen and oxygen
   b. hydrogen and carbon
   c. hydrogen and carbon monoxide
   d. alcohol

2. Hydrocarbon (HC) is another name for
   a. water
   b. gasoline
   c. air
   d. exhaust gas

3. If all the gasoline burned completely in the engine, all that would remain is
   a. water and carbon monoxide
   b. carbon monoxide and hydrocarbon
   c. water and carbon dioxide
   d. carbon dioxide and alcohol

4. The ease with which gasoline vaporizes is called its
   a. oxidation
   b. octane rating
   c. cetane rating
   d. volatility

5. When the last part of the air-fuel mixture in the combustion chamber explodes before being ignited by the flame traveling from the spark plug, this condition is called
   a. detonation
   b. preignition
   c. stalling
   d. vaporization

6. A gasoline that detonates easily is called a
   a. high-octane gasoline
   b. low-octane gasoline
   c. gasohol
   d. blended gasoline

7. The cetane number of diesel fuel refers to the
   a. ease with which it knocks
   b. ease with which the fuel ignites
   c. rate of flame propagation
   d. viscosity of the fuel

8. Usually, the amount of alcohol in gasohol is about
   a. 50 percent
   b. 40 percent
   c. 20 percent
   d. 10 percent

9. The device that reduces the amount of hydrocarbons and carbon monoxide in the exhaust gases is called the
   a. tail pipe
   b. muffler
   c. catalytic converter
   d. none of the above

10. Most automobile diesel engines normally operate on
    a. number 2 diesel fuel
    b. number 3 diesel fuel
    c. number 4 diesel fuel
    d. number 1 diesel fuel

CHAPTER 14
FUEL AND EXHAUST SYSTEMS

After studying this chapter, you should be able to:

1. Explain the difference between carbureted fuel systems and fuel-injected systems.
2. List the components in the carbureted fuel system and describe the purpose and operation of each.
3. List the components in the exhaust system and describe the purpose and operation of each.
4. Describe the operation of the turbocharger and explain how it is controlled.

The spark-ignition engine must have a continuous supply of air-fuel mixture delivered to the cylinders to keep running. The system that supplies this mixture is the *fuel-induction system*. It is often called simply the "fuel system." After the air-fuel mixture is burned in the combustion chambers, the exhaust gases must be removed from the cylinders. The *exhaust system* collects the exhaust gases and discharges them into the air.

FUEL SYSTEMS

☐ 14-1 TWO FUEL-INDUCTION SYSTEMS

For many years, the spark-ignition engine has used a carburetor. This is a mixing device which mixes air and gasoline vapor in the proper ratios to produce a combustible mixture (Fig. 14-1). The air passing through the carburetor creates a vacuum which draws out a metered amount of fuel. The mixture then flows through the intake manifold to the cylinders.

A different type of fuel system, called *fuel injection,* is now installed on many engines. In this system, the carburetor is replaced with a *throttle body*. It controls only the amount of air entering the intake manifold.

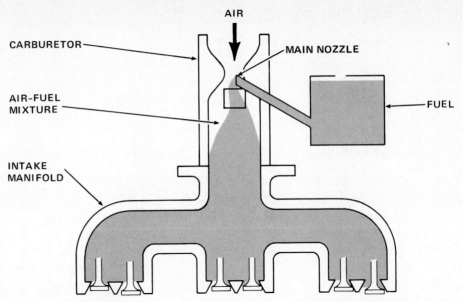

Fig. 14-1 Simplified view of a carbureted fuel system, showing carburetor action.

Fuel injectors, or *injection nozzles,* are located either opposite each intake valve (Fig. 14-2) or above the throttle body. The injectors spray a metered (or *measured*) amount of fuel into the air flowing through the intake manifold. There the air and fuel mix to form the air-fuel mixture. Then, when the intake valve opens, the air-fuel mixture enters the cylinders.

The basic difference between using a carburetor and using fuel injection is in how the fuel is metered. The carburetor uses vacuum. With fuel injection, the fuel is pressurized in the line to the injector. Then fuel sprays out as long as the injector is held open, or according to engine power demands.

Chapter 15 describes the construction and operation of various types of carburetors. Fuel-injection systems for spark-ignition engines are covered in Chap. 16.

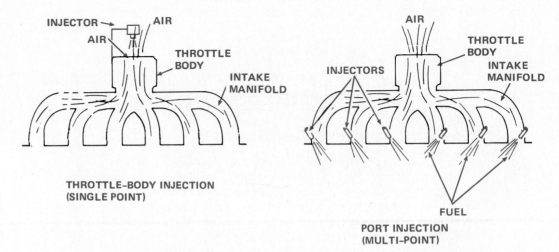

THROTTLE–BODY INJECTION
(SINGLE POINT)

PORT INJECTION
(MULTI–POINT)

Fig. 14-2 Basic fuel-injection systems for spark-ignition engines *(ATW)*

□ 14-2 THE CARBURETED FUEL SYSTEM

The carbureted fuel system is made up of

1. The fuel tank, which stores the liquid gasoline
2. The fuel filter, which filters out dirt particles from the gasoline
3. The fuel pump, which delivers the gasoline from the tank to the carburetor
4. The carburetor, which mixes the gasoline with air and delivers the combustible mixture to the intake manifold
5. The intake manifold, which delivers the air-fuel mixture from the carburetor to the engine cylinders
6. The fuel lines between the tank and the fuel pump and between the fuel pump and the carburetor
7. The evaporative emission control system, which prevents gasoline-vapor loss to the atmosphere (described in Chap. 24)

A typical fuel system for an automobile with an engine using a carburetor is shown in Fig. 14-3. Following sections discuss each component. Intake manifolds are described in □ 9-8.

FUEL-SYSTEM COMPONENTS

□ 14-3 FUEL TANK

The fuel tank is usually located at the rear of the car (Fig. 14-3). The tank is made of plastic or sheet metal and has two main openings. Gasoline enters the tank through one opening and leaves the tank through the other opening. The evaporative control system (Chap. 24) prevents the escape of gasoline vapor from the fuel tank. Any vapor is sent through an additional line from the tank to a charcoal canister or to the engine crankcase. Then the vapor cannot get out of the car and pollute the air.

□ 14-4 FUEL FILTER

The fuel system includes a fuel filter. It is located in the fuel-supply line (the "fuel line"), ahead of the carburetor float bowl (Fig. 14-3). The job of

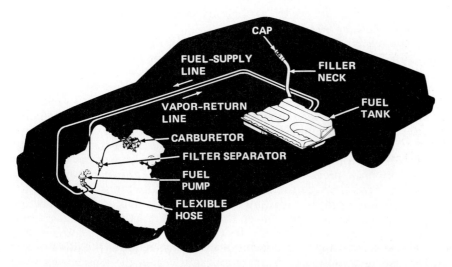

Fig. 14-3 Typical fuel system for an automobile with an engine using a carburetor. *(Chrysler Corporation)*

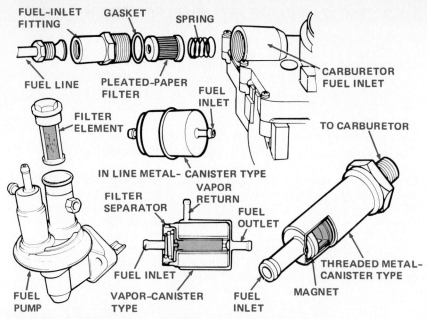

Fig. 14-4 Various types of fuel filters. *(Chrysler Corporation)*

the filter is to remove dirt, water, and other contaminants from the fuel passing through it. This protects the small fuel passages in the carburetor from becoming plugged with foreign material. It also helps prevent water from getting into the carburetor float bowl.

The filter is made of special pleated paper or other material that lets gasoline flow through while trapping the contaminants. Several types of fuel filters are shown in Fig. 14-4. Some are threaded into the carburetor and connected to the fuel line. Others are located in the carburetor fuel inlet or in the fuel pump. Some fuel filters contain a small magnet to trap any metal particles in the fuel.

□ 14-5 FUEL PUMP

The fuel system uses a fuel pump (Fig. 14-5) to deliver fuel from the tank to the carburetor. There are two types of fuel pumps, mechanical and electric. Electric fuel pumps are usually mounted in the fuel tank. These are described in □ 14-8.

The mechanical fuel pump is mounted on the engine. The fuel pump has two one-way check valves and a flexible diaphragm (Fig. 14-6). The diaphragm is alternately pulled up and pushed down. This action alternately produces a vacuum and then pressure in the fuel chamber of the pump. When the diaphragm is pulled up (Fig. 14-6), a partial vacuum is created that opens the inlet valve. Fuel flows from the tank, past the inlet valve, and into the chamber below the diaphragm. Next, the diaphragm is pushed down by spring force, producing pressure in the fuel chamber (Fig. 14-7). This pressure closes the inlet valve and opens the outlet valve. Then the pressure forces the gasoline out of the fuel chamber. The gasoline flows through the fuel line to the carburetor.

The diaphragm is pulled up by a rocker arm that rests on an eccentric, or special fuel-pump lobe, on the camshaft. As the camshaft rotates, the lobe pushes down against the fuel-pump rocker arm, forcing it to pivot. When one end of the rocker arm is pushed down, the other end of the rocker arm pulls up on the diaphragm. When the lobe moves away

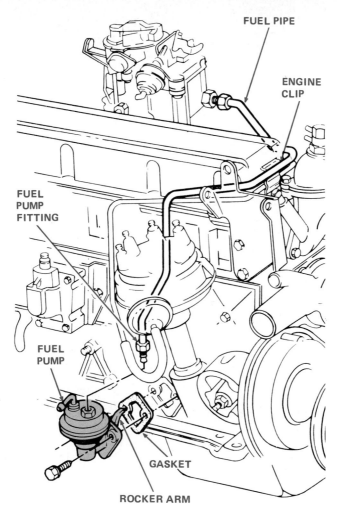

FUEL PIPE

ENGINE CLIP

FUEL PUMP FITTING

FUEL PUMP

GASKET

ROCKER ARM

Fig. 14-5 Installation of a fuel pump on an in-line engine. *(Chevrolet Motor Division of General Motors Corporation)*

from the rocker arm, the return spring pushes the diaphragm back down.

Compare Figs. 14-6 and 14-7. These two illustrations show how the rotation of the camshaft causes movement of the rocker arm to provide the pumping action.

□ 14-6 VAPOR-RETURN LINE

Many cars have a vapor-return line (Fig. 14-3). It runs from the fuel pump (Figs. 14-6 and 14-7) or fuel filter back to the fuel tank (□ 14-7). The line allows any vapor that has formed in the fuel pump to return to the tank. Since the pump can only handle liquid, fuel delivery stops if vapor forms and is not removed.

Vapor can be a problem in fuel systems using a mechanical fuel pump without a vapor-return line. Vapor may form from the combination of vacuum and heat. The fuel pump, located on the engine, creates a partial vacuum and gets very hot. These conditions encourage vapor formation. If vapor remains in the fuel pump, *vapor lock* can result. This prevents normal pump action. Then the carburetor does not receive enough fuel. When this happens, the engine stalls from lack of fuel, or *fuel starvation*.

The fuel pump can only handle liquid fuel. It cannot pump vapor. However, when the fuel system includes a vapor-return line, the fuel

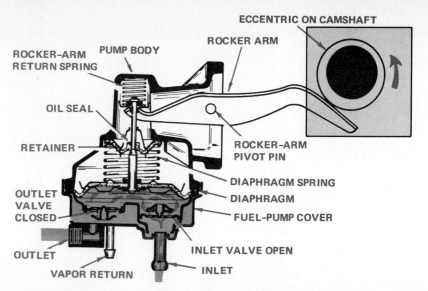

Fig. 14-6 When the eccentric rotates so that it pushes the rocker arm down, the arm pulls the diaphragm up. This pulls fuel into the chamber under the diaphragm. The inlet valve opens so fuel can enter.

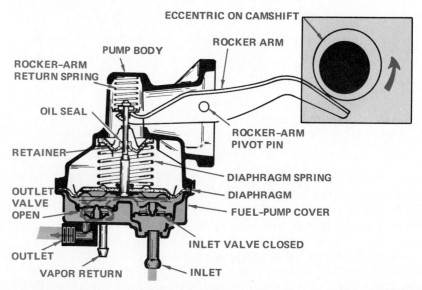

Fig. 14-7 When the eccentric rotates to allow the rocker arm to move up under it, the diaphragm is released. Now the spring pushes down on the diaphragm, creating pressure on the fuel under it. This pressure closes the inlet valve and opens the outlet valve. Now fuel flows to the carburetor.

pump can send any vapor back through the line to the fuel tank. Actually, the fuel pump keeps some fuel flowing through the vapor-return line continuously. The liquid fuel flows from the fuel tank, through the fuel pump and vapor-return line, and then back to the fuel tank. Since the fuel is cool, it cools the fuel pump. Therefore, vapor is less likely to form.

Some vapor-return lines have an in-line check valve (Fig. 14-8). This check valve prevents fuel from feeding back to the carburetor through the vapor-return line. If fuel does attempt to feed back, the pressure of the

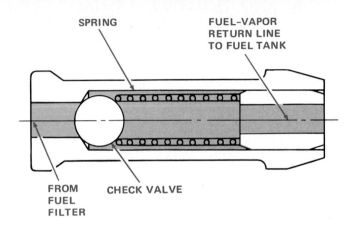

SPRING

FUEL–VAPOR
RETURN LINE
TO FUEL TANK

FROM
FUEL
FILTER

CHECK VALVE

Fig. 14-8 In-line check valve which is located between the fuel filter and the fuel tank. *(American Motors Corporation)*

fuel forces the ball to seat. This blocks the line. Normally, the pressure of the fuel vapor from the fuel pump unseats the ball and allows the fuel vapor to flow to the fuel tank.

> **NOTE** Fuel systems using an in-tank electric fuel pump do not require a vapor-return line (□ 14-8). This system maintains pressure on the fuel all the way from the tank to the carburetor. Since there is no vacuum in the line anywhere, vapor lock is less likely to occur.

□ 14-7 FILTER SEPARATOR

Some cars have a combination fuel filter and vapor separator (or *filter separator*). It is located between the fuel pump and the carburetor (Fig. 14-3). Gasoline from the fuel pump enters the filter separator through the inlet tube and exits through the outlet tube. The fuel is filtered, and any bubbles or vapor enter the return tube. It is connected to the vapor-return line so that the vapor flows back to the fuel tank.

□ 14-8 ELECTRIC FUEL PUMPS

Electric fuel pumps use either an electric motor or a solenoid to draw fuel from the tank and deliver it to the carburetor. The electric motor delivers a continuous supply of fuel. The solenoid provides pulses, or spurts, of fuel. This is similar to the operation of the mechanical fuel pump (□ 14-5). There are two basic types of electric fuel pumps. One type mounts inside the fuel tank and is called an *in-tank fuel pump*. The other type mounts anywhere in the fuel line, such as along the frame or in the engine compartment. This is an *in-line fuel pump*.

Figure 14-9 shows a typical in-tank fuel pump. It mounts on the same support that holds the fuel gauge. Pumping action is provided by a small electric motor that drives an impeller (Fig. 14-10). The impeller has a series of blades that force the fuel through the outlet pipe as the impeller spins.

An in-line fuel pump is shown in Fig. 14-11. This unit has a *solenoid*, or electromagnet. When the ignition switch is turned on, the electromagnet is connected to the car battery. Later chapters describe electromagnets and batteries. When the electromagnet is connected to the battery, the electromagnet pulls on an iron armature. The armature is a flat piece of iron. When the electromagnet pulls on the armature, the armature moves. The armature pulls down on a metal bellows, which produces a partial vacuum in the bellows (Fig. 14-11). There are two valves above

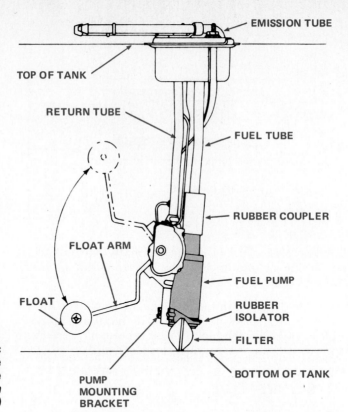

EMISSION TUBE

TOP OF TANK

RETURN TUBE

FUEL TUBE

RUBBER COUPLER

FLOAT ARM

FUEL PUMP

RUBBER ISOLATOR

FLOAT

FILTER

PUMP MOUNTING BRACKET

BOTTOM OF TANK

Fig. 14-9 The in-tank electric fuel pump is combined with the same support as the fuel-gauge tank unit. *(Cadillac Motor Division of General Motors Corporation)*

the bellows—an inlet valve and an outlet valve. The partial vacuum opens the inlet valve and pulls fuel into the bellows.

The downward movement of the armature disconnects the electromagnet from the battery. Current flow stops. Therefore the electromagnet loses its magnetism which can no longer pull on the armature. Now the armature return spring pushes the armature up. This produces a pressure in the bellows, which closes the inlet valve and opens the outlet valve. Fuel is then pushed into the carburetor.

This type of electric fuel pump works the same way as the mechanical fuel pump operated by the camshaft (Figs. 14-6 and 14-7). The only difference is how the vacuum and pressure in the pump chamber are produced. However, an electric fuel pump is not affected by camshaft wear. In addition, an electric fuel pump can be located so that it is not affected by engine heat. Some electric fuel pumps can be adjusted to change the outlet pressure.

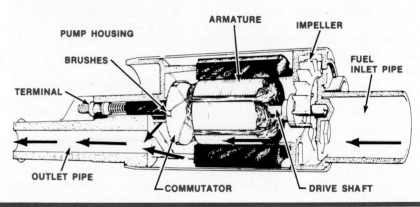

PUMP HOUSING

ARMATURE

IMPELLER

BRUSHES

FUEL INLET PIPE

TERMINAL

OUTLET PIPE

COMMUTATOR

DRIVE SHAFT

Fig. 14-10 An in-tank electric fuel pump, cut away to show the motor and the flow of fuel through it.

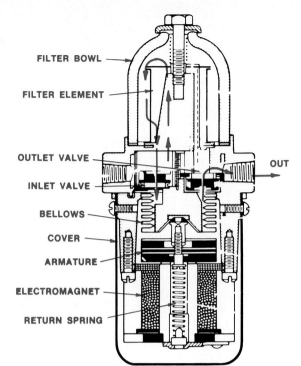

FILTER BOWL

FILTER ELEMENT

OUTLET VALVE

INLET VALVE

BELLOWS

COVER

ARMATURE

ELECTROMAGNET

RETURN SPRING

OUT

Fig. 14-11 A solenoid type of electric fuel pump that is connected in the fuel line between the fuel tank and the carburetor.

□ *14-9 AIR CLEANER*

Air mixes with gasoline vapor to make the combustible mixture that the spark-ignition engine needs for fuel. In operation, the engine requires a large volume of air. It uses about 10,000 gallons [37,854 L] of air for every gallon [3.78 L] of gasoline. That is a lot of air. And since air has dirt in it, that is also a lot of dirt. Dirt can ruin an engine and must be kept out. To do this job, all engines have an air cleaner (Fig. 14-12). It traps the dirt while allowing the needed volume of cleaned air to flow through.

The air cleaner is frequently mounted on top of the carburetor. All air going through the carburetor and into the engine must first pass through the air cleaner. Most cars have an air cleaner that uses a filter

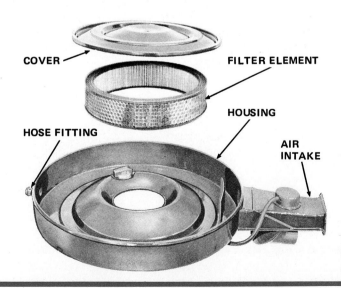

COVER

FILTER ELEMENT

HOUSING

HOSE FITTING

AIR INTAKE

Fig. 14-12 A carburetor air cleaner that uses a paper element. *(Chrysler Corporation)*

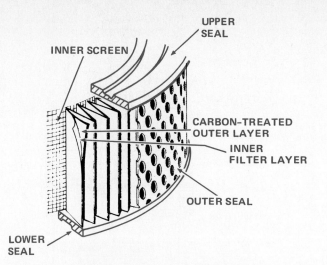

Fig. 14-13 Construction of a pleated-paper type of filter element made with two-ply paper. *(Chrysler Corporation)*

INNER SCREEN

UPPER SEAL

CARBON-TREATED OUTER LAYER

INNER FILTER LAYER

OUTER SEAL

LOWER SEAL

element made of specially treated pleated paper (Fig. 14-13). It lets the air through but traps the dirt particles. Then after long use, the filter element becomes filled with dirt and must be cleaned or replaced. The air cleaner also reduces the noise made by the air entering the engine. In addition, the air cleaner helps prevent fires in the carburetor, if the engine should backfire.

☐ 14-10 THERMOSTATIC AIR CLEANER

Most cars today have a *thermostatic air cleaner,* or *heated-air system* (Fig. 14-14). While the engine is cold and warming up, the system provides preheated air to the carburetor. This allows the engine to run on a leaner air-fuel mixture which reduces exhaust emissions (Chap. 24). In addition, the preheated air improves engine driveability and prevents ice forming in the carburetor.

The thermostatic air cleaner includes a temperature sensor, a vacuum motor, a control damper or *door,* and vacuum hoses. A metal shroud, or *heat stove,* surrounds the exhaust manifold (Fig. 14-14). A hot-air pipe connects the heat stove to the fresh-air duct, or *snorkel,* on the air cleaner.

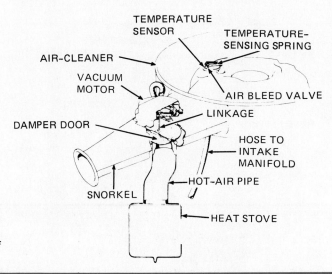

Fig. 14-14 A thermostatic air cleaner, showing the heat stove that surrounds the exhaust manifold. *(Chevrolet Motor Division of General Motors Corporation)*

TEMPERATURE SENSOR

TEMPERATURE-SENSING SPRING

AIR-CLEANER

VACUUM MOTOR

AIR BLEED VALVE

LINKAGE

DAMPER DOOR

HOSE TO INTAKE MANIFOLD

HOT-AIR PIPE

SNORKEL

HEAT STOVE

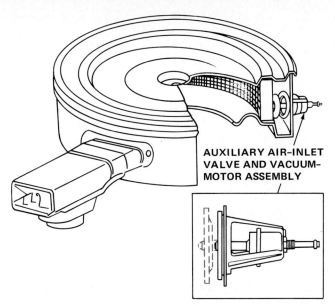

Fig. 14-15 Air cleaner with auxiliary air-inlet valve and vacuum motor. *(Ford Motor Company)*

The vacuum motor is controlled by the temperature sensor. When the engine is cold, manifold vacuum passes through the temperature sensor and raises the diaphragm in the vacuum motor. This closes the damper door, preventing the flow of cool air into the air-cleaner snorkel. Now all air to the carburetor first flows over the exhaust manifold, which heats quickly. Then this preheated air flows through the hot-air tube to the air cleaner. In this way, hot air is supplied to the carburetor almost as soon as the engine starts. The fuel vaporizes more completely, and more of it is burned. Therefore the exhaust gas is cleaner because it contains fewer hydrocarbons.

As the engine warms up, an air-bleed valve in the temperature sensor opens. This allows less vacuum to reach the vacuum motor, so the damper door opens. Now cool, fresh air enters through the fresh-air duct, not from the heat stove. When the engine is warmed up, no additional heat is needed to ensure good fuel vaporization. The thermostatic air cleaner is discussed further in Chap. 24 on automotive emission controls.

□ 14-11 AUXILIARY AIR INLET

Some air cleaners have another vacuum motor that opens and closes an extra hole in the air-cleaner housing (Fig. 14-15). The vacuum motor operates if a partial vacuum develops in the air cleaner. During cold-engine acceleration, not enough air may flow through the heat stove. If this happens, the partial vacuum operates the vacuum motor, and it opens the auxiliary air-inlet passage. Now extra air goes into the air cleaner, and the engine runs properly.

EXHAUST SYSTEMS

□ 14-12 EXHAUST-SYSTEM COMPONENTS

When combustion ends in each cylinder, the exhaust gas must be collected, cleaned, quieted, and then discharged into the air. This is the job

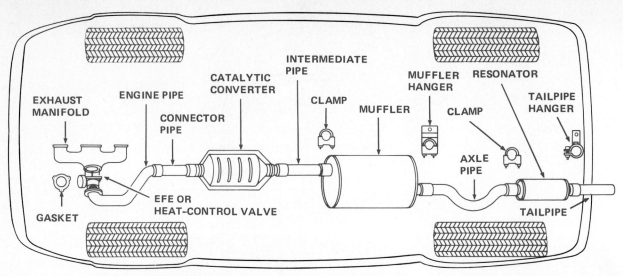

Fig. 14-16 Components in a typical exhaust system. *(Walker Manufacturing Division of Tenneco Inc.)*

of the *exhaust system* (Fig. 14-16). It performs these tasks while carrying the exhaust gases from the cylinders to the atmosphere.

The exhaust gases are collected in the exhaust manifold (□ 9-9). It bolts onto the cylinder head. Passages in the exhaust manifold match the size and shape of the exhaust ports in the head. On V-type engines, there is an exhaust manifold for each bank of cylinders. A *dual-exhaust system* has a complete exhaust system for each bank.

In a typical exhaust system, the exhaust gas flows from the exhaust manifold into an *exhaust pipe*. It connects the exhaust manifold to the muffler or catalytic converter. The muffler has a series of passages through which the exhaust gas must flow. This softens, or muffles, the engine exhaust noise. In addition, some cars have a *resonator*. This is a second muffler used with some engines to make them quieter.

Since the 1975 models, cars manufactured in the United States have been equipped with catalytic converters (Fig. 14-16). These devices are installed in the exhaust system, usually between the exhaust manifold and the muffler. Their purpose is to reduce the amounts of pollutants in the exhaust gas. Catalytic converters and other emission control devices are described in Chap. 24.

□ 14-13 MANIFOLD HEAT-CONTROL VALVE

During cold-engine operation, the gasoline must be vaporized before entering the cylinders. If the fuel is not properly vaporized, drops of gasoline will enter the cylinders. They will wash down the cylinder walls and remove the oil. This causes the walls, pistons, and piston rings to wear quickly. One way to improve fuel vaporization is to transfer some of the exhaust-gas heat to the intake air. There are two different methods of doing this. One is the heated-air system (□ 14-10). The other is use of a *manifold heat-control valve* (Fig. 14-17).

NOTE If the intake air is heated too much, it can cause detonation. Most late-model cars have a thermostatic air cleaner. Other cars may have a heat-control valve. However, both systems are generally not used on the same engine.

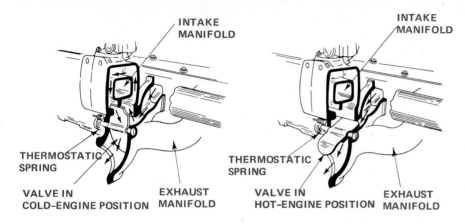

INTAKE MANIFOLD

INTAKE MANIFOLD

THERMOSTATIC SPRING

VALVE IN COLD-ENGINE POSITION

EXHAUST MANIFOLD

THERMOSTATIC SPRING

VALVE IN HOT-ENGINE POSITION

EXHAUST MANIFOLD

Fig. 14-17 Intake and exhaust manifolds of an in-line engine, cut away so that the action of the manifold heat-control valve can be seen. Left, the heat-control valve is in the cold-engine, or HEAT-ON, position. This directs hot exhaust gases up and around the intake manifold. *(Ford Motor Company)*

The purpose of the heat-control valve is to put heat into the air passing through the carburetor while the engine is cold. This helps vaporize the cold gasoline. Engines with a heat-control valve warm a section of the intake manifold by directing some of the exhaust gases through it. This is done by placing a butterfly-type valve between the exhaust manifold and the exhaust pipe (Fig. 9-15). Opening and closing of the valve is controlled by a thermostatic spring (Fig. 14-18) or by a vacuum motor. When a thermostatic spring is used, a weight is installed on the valve shaft. The weight minimizes valve flutter caused by the pulses of exhaust gas from the cylinders striking the valve.

When the valve is operated by a vacuum motor, the system is called an *early-fuel evaporation (EFE)* system. It is described in Chap. 24 with emission control devices.

☐ *14-14 TURBOCHARGER OPERATION*

In a spark-ignition engine, the amount of air-fuel mixture that enters the cylinders is determined by the difference in pressures. This is described in Chap. 15. Atmospheric pressure is forcing air into the carburetor. At the same time, intake-manifold vacuum is creating a low pressure area

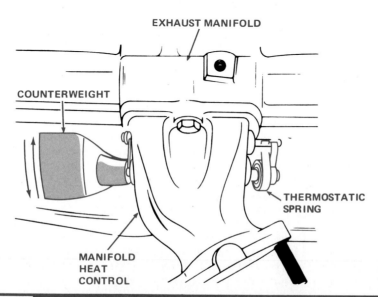

EXHAUST MANIFOLD

COUNTERWEIGHT

THERMOSTATIC SPRING

MANIFOLD HEAT CONTROL

Fig. 14-18 Manifold heat-control valve. *(Ford Motor Company)*

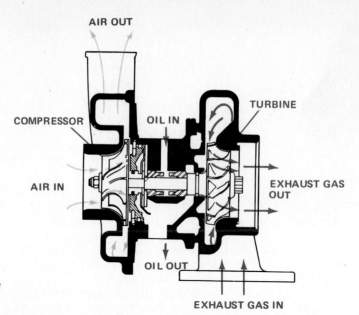

AIR OUT

COMPRESSOR   OIL IN   TURBINE

AIR IN

EXHAUST GAS OUT

OIL OUT

EXHAUST GAS IN

Fig. 14-19 Operation of a turbo-charger. *(Schwitzer Division of Wallace-Murray Corporation)*

below the throttle valve. The force acting on the air is the difference between the atmospheric pressure and the intake-manifold vacuum. Although atmospheric pressure stays relatively constant, intake-manifold vacuum varies according to throttle-valve opening. When the throttle valve is closed, the engine is idling. Little air is getting into the intake manifold. Therefore intake-manifold vacuum is high. As the throttle valve opens, more air enters and there is less intake-manifold vacuum. Ideally, at wide-open throttle (WOT), the intake-manifold vacuum will have dropped to zero.

To get more air-fuel mixture into the engine, a turbocharger can be used. This is a rotary air pump driven by the exhaust gas (Fig. 14-19). The basic construction and operation is described in □ 8-12. It has two basic parts, a turbine and a compressor. These are bladed wheels, sometimes called *impellers,* or *rotors.* They are attached to opposite ends of a rotating shaft.

The exhaust gas drives the turbine. When the exhaust gas hits the turbine blades, the turbine spins. This, in turn, spins the compressor which is on the opposite end of the same shaft. As the compressor spins, its blades scoop up and then throw out air at a higher pressure. Now more air is available for mixing with fuel. When the intake valves open, a larger amount of air-fuel mixture enters the cylinders. Combustion then produces a greater force on the pistons, and the engine produces more power.

As the compressor begins to force the additional air-fuel mixture into the cylinders, a pressure develops in the intake manifold. The amount of pressure increase is called the *manifold pressure,* or *boost pressure.* On automotive engines, maximum boost pressure may range from about 5 to 12 psi (34 to 83 kPa). In some engines, this increases the power output by 30 percent or more.

On a carbureted engine, the turbocharger may be installed two different ways. It may be located between the air cleaner and the carburetor, as shown in Fig. 8-13. The turbocharger compresses only air and then forces it through the carburetor. Figure 14-20 shows an engine with the turbocharger installed between the carburetor and the intake mani-

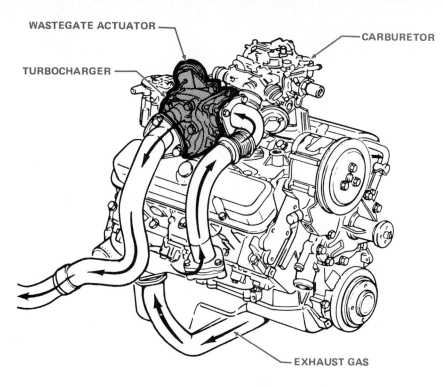

WASTEGATE ACTUATOR

TURBOCHARGER

CARBURETOR

EXHAUST GAS

Fig. 14-20 Turbocharger installation on a V-type engine. The wastegate prevents excessive boost pressure which could damage the engine. *(Pontiac Motor Division of General Motors Corporation)*

fold. All the air-fuel mixture from the carburetor is compressed by the turbocharger.

The turbocharger has two operating phases, the *atmospheric phase* and the *boost phase*. During light-load and cruising conditions, the compressor is idling. It is rotating too slowly to pressurize the intake air. The engine operates about the same as an engine of similar size without a turbocharger. As the throttle valve is opened wider, intake-manifold vacuum drops. The flow of exhaust gas increases. This speeds up the turbine and compressor until the compressor is providing boost. Now additional air-fuel mixture is delivered to the cylinders and the engine delivers more power.

A turbocharged engine operates in the atmospheric phase most of the time. The turbocharger does not add power during cruising at normal highway speeds. It usually provides boost only when acceleration or full power is required. Typically, this is about 5 percent of the operating time. However, the advantage to using a turbocharger is that a smaller engine which has good fuel economy can produce high power when needed.

NOTE A turbocharged engine is sometimes referred to as a "blown" engine. The turbocharger is "blowing" more air into the engine. However, an engine sometimes "blows." Here the word means that the engine has seized or quit abruptly because of internal damage.

☐ 14-15 CONTROLLING THE TURBOCHARGER

A turbocharger can produce so much power that it damages or destroys the engine. To prevent this, turbocharged engines have various types of control and safety systems. For example, as the boost pressure increases, severe detonation may occur. If allowed to continue uncontrolled, engine and turbocharger damage could result. To limit boost pressure, most turbochargers have a control device called the *wastegate* (Fig. 14-20).

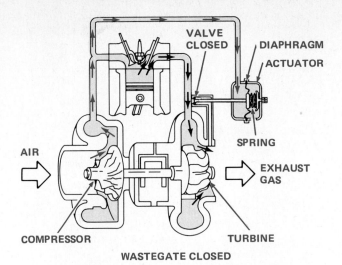

WASTEGATE CLOSED

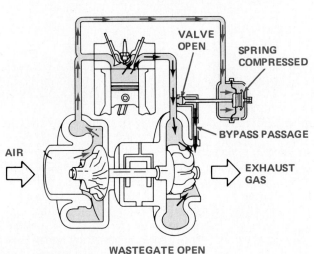

WASTEGATE OPEN

Fig. 14-21 Operation of the wastegate, which limits turbocharger boost pressure. *(ATW)*

Figure 14-21 shows the operation of the wastegate. Basically, it is a diaphragm-operated valve. A calibrated spring in the actuator holds the valve closed, up to the maximum allowable boost pressure. A tube connects one side of the diaphragm to the boost pressure. The other side is open to atmospheric pressure. When the boost pressure goes too high, it forces the diaphragm to compress the spring in the actuator. This opens the wastegate valve. Now some of the exhaust gas bypasses the turbine by flowing through the passage opened by the valve. This prevents any further increase in turbine speed, thereby limiting boost pressure.

NOTE Never change the spring or tamper with the setting of the wastegate. Excessive boost pressure will damage the engine and turbocharger.

Many turbocharged engines have an electronic *detonation control system*. It prevents excessive detonation by slightly retarding the ignition timing until the detonation stops.

Select the *one* correct, best, or most probable answer to each question. Then check your answers against the correct answers given at the end of the book.

1. The two basic fuel systems used with spark-ignition engines are
   a. gasohol and gasoline
   b. fuel-injected and carbureted
   c. diesel and gasoline
   d. LPG and gasoline

2. The system that prevents the escape of gasoline vapor from the fuel tank is called the
   a. gasoline-saver system
   b. carburetor system
   c. evaporative control system
   d. fuel-injection system

3. The fuel pump has
   a. two two-way valves
   b. one two-way valve
   c. one one-way valve
   d. two one-way valves

4. The manifold heat-control valve is located in the
   a. intake manifold
   b. exhaust manifold
   c. crankcase
   d. cylinder block

5. Fuel-pump pressure is controlled by the
   a. speed of the engine
   b. size of the pump
   c. tension of the diaphragm spring
   d. length of the diaphragm stroke

6. The heated-air system uses
   a. a thermostat
   b. a thermostatic air cleaner
   c. a heat-control valve
   d. an air pump

7. The most widely used fuel pump is operated by
   a. electric current
   b. vacuum from the intake manifold
   c. an eccentric on the camshaft
   d. none of the above

8. The vapor-return line has the job of
   a. returning fuel vapor from the fuel pump to the fuel tank
   b. turning vapor into liquid gasoline
   c. feeding auxiliary fuel to the fuel pump
   d. preventing vapor lock in the carburetor

CHAPTER 15
CARBURETORS

After studying this chapter, you should be able to:

1. Describe the operation of the six basic systems in the fixed-venturi carburetor.
2. Explain how the air-fuel ratio can be controlled electronically.
3. Discuss the operation of the idle solenoid and the dashpot.
4. Describe the difference between a two-barrel carburetor and a four-barrel carburetor.
5. Describe the construction and operation of the two types of variable-venturi carburetors.

The *carburetor* is the device in the engine fuel system that mixes fuel with air and then delivers the combustible mixture to the intake manifold. As air passes through the carburetor, gasoline is fed into the air through various fuel-metering systems. The gasoline enters the passing air as a fine spray. This causes it to evaporate very quickly. The result is a combustible mixture of gasoline vapor and fuel.

☐ 15-1 CARBURETOR TYPES

There are two basic types of carburetor: fixed-venturi and variable-venturi. The *venturi* is the restricted place in the air passage through which the air must flow. This restriction produces a partial vacuum that causes a fuel nozzle to discharge gasoline. The gasoline mixes with the air to produce the combustible mixture that the engine needs to run.

FIXED-VENTURI CARBURETORS

☐ 15-2 CARBURETOR OPERATION

The carburetor, regardless of type, is a sort of mixing valve. In the carburetor, gasoline is mixed with air. The mixture then goes through the intake manifold to the engine cylinders. There, the air-fuel mixture is compressed and burned to make the engine run.

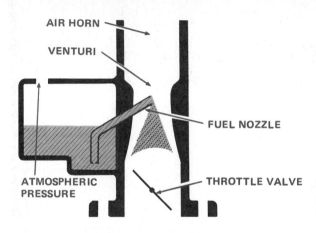

Fig. 15-1 A simple carburetor consists of an air horn, a fuel nozzle, and a throttle valve.

The fixed-venturi carburetor is basically an air horn, a fuel nozzle, and a throttle valve (Fig. 15-1). The air horn is a round tube, or barrel. The venturi is a narrow section below the air horn. The fuel nozzle is a small tube through which fuel can flow from the float bowl, or reservoir, in the side of the carburetor. The throttle valve is a round disk mounted on a shaft (Fig. 15-2). When the shaft is turned, the throttle valve is tilted. When it is tilted into the position shown by the dotted lines in Fig. 15-2, the throttle valve is open. Now air can flow through the air horn freely.

When the throttle valve is tilted into the position shown by solid lines in Fig. 15-2, the throttle valve is closed. Little or no air can get through the air horn. The throttle valve determines how much air gets through the carburetor. It is the amount of air passing through the carburetor that determines how much fuel flows to the cylinders.

□ 15-3 CONTROLLING THE THROTTLE VALVE

The throttle valve is connected to an accelerator pedal in the passenger compartment (Fig. 15-3). The linkage may consist of a series of interconnected levers and rods, or levers and a cable. The cable has a flexible outer covering and an inner sliding wire. With either arrangement, movement of the accelerator pedal causes the throttle valve to change its position in the throttle body. Therefore, the driver can position the throttle valve to suit operating requirements. On some cars, the throttle linkage performs other functions such as producing a down-shift of the automatic transmission under the right operating conditions. The kickdown rod for the automatic transmission is shown in Fig. 15-3.

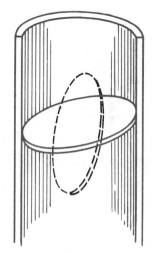

Fig. 15-2 Throttle valve in the air passage of a carburetor. When the throttle valve is closed, as shown, little air can pass through. But when the throttle valve is opened, as shown dashed, there is little throttling effect.

□ 15-4 VENTURI EFFECT

The venturi causes fuel to flow out of the fuel nozzle when air flows through the carburetor. The reason is that the air has to flow faster through the venturi than through the rest of the carburetor. This faster flow of air produces a partial vacuum in the venturi. The partial vacuum then causes fuel to flow from the fuel nozzle (Fig. 15-4). The more air that flows through the venturi, the greater the vacuum. The greater the vacuum, the more fuel is discharged by the fuel nozzle. There is a relationship between the amount the throttle valve is open, the amount of air going through the venturi, and the amount of fuel being discharged. This relationship keeps the ratio of air to fuel fairly constant. However, other

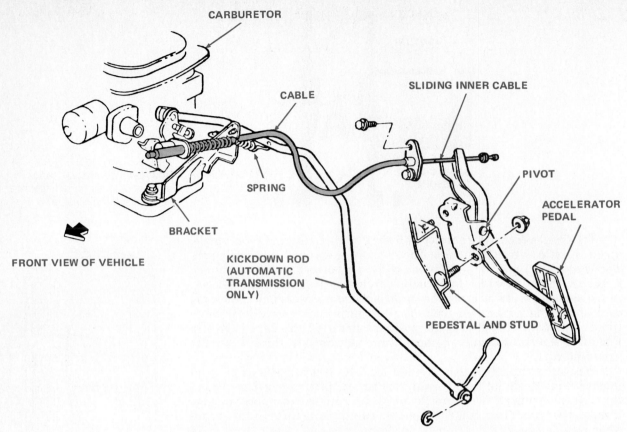

Fig. 15-3 A typical linkage arrangement between the accelerator pedal and the throttle valve in the carburetor. *(Ford Motor Company)*

systems and devices are needed to change the ratio for different operating conditions.

☐ 15-5 AIR-FUEL RATIOS

When the engine is started, the air-fuel mixture must be rich. This means that the mixture must have more fuel in it. A mixture of about 9 pounds

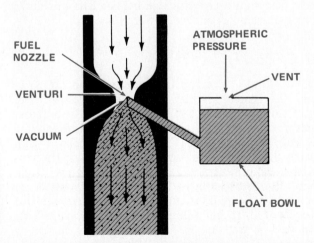

Fig. 15-4 The venturi, or constriction, causes a vacuum to develop in the air stream just below the constriction. Then atmospheric pressure pushes fuel up and out of the fuel nozzle.

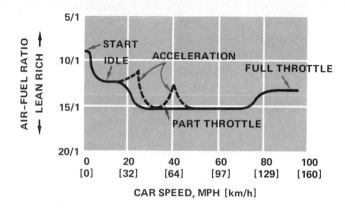

Fig. 15-5 A graph of air-fuel ratios for different car speeds. The graph shows only typical ratios. Car speeds at which the various ratios are obtained vary with different cars. Also, actual ratios will vary.

[4.1 kg] of air to 1 pound [0.45 kg] of fuel, or a ratio of 9:1, is required for starting a cold engine. The reason is that only part of the gasoline vaporizes when the engine is cold. Therefore the engine has to be given more than enough fuel to make sure enough will vaporize to ensure starting.

When the engine is idling, a less rich mixture is needed—about 12:1. During intermediate-speed, part-throttle operation, a relatively lean mixture of about 15:1 is needed. During high-speed, wide-open-throttle operation, a richer mixture of about 13:1 is needed.

The graph in Fig. 15-5 shows various air-fuel–ratio requirements for different operating conditions. These ratios are only typical. Different engines require different ratios for various operating conditions. Additional devices and systems are required on the carburetor to produce the changing air-fuel ratios that are needed for different operating conditions.

NOTE Many late-model engines are equipped with electronic carburetors, or *feedback carburetors*. These have electronic systems that control the air-fuel ratio of the mixture that the carburetor delivers. They are described in □ 15-12.

□ 15-6 CARBURETOR SYSTEMS

The fixed-venturi carburetor has six systems and several devices that provide the correct air-fuel mixture for different operating conditions. These include

1. Float system
2. Idle system
3. Main-metering system
4. Power system
5. Accelerator-pump system
6. Choke system

Following pages describe each system in detail.

□ 15-7 FLOAT SYSTEM

The float system (Figs. 15-6 and 15-7) maintains a constant level of gasoline in the float bowl. The fuel nozzle feeds fuel from the float bowl to the air passing through the venturi. It is important that the fuel level in the float bowl be held at a constant level. If the fuel level is too high, fuel will continue to flow from the fuel nozzle. The air-fuel mixture will be far too

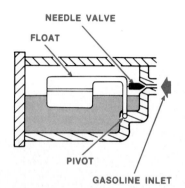

Fig. 15-6 A simple carburetor float system.

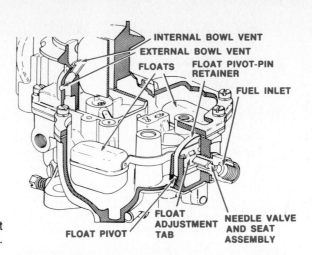

Fig. 15-7 A carburetor partly cut away to show the float system.

INTERNAL BOWL VENT
EXTERNAL BOWL VENT
FLOATS
FLOAT PIVOT-PIN RETAINER
FUEL INLET
FLOAT PIVOT
FLOAT ADJUSTMENT TAB
NEEDLE VALVE AND SEAT ASSEMBLY

rich. Fuel will be wasted, the engine will run poorly or stall, and the exhaust gas will contain excessive hydrocarbons and carbon monoxide.

If the fuel level in the float bowl is too low, the vacuum in the venturi will not pull enough fuel out of the float bowl. The mixture will be too lean, and the engine will run poorly or stall.

The float system includes a float that is pivoted at one end. The pivot is on the side of the float bowl. A needle valve is located at the float-bowl fuel inlet. As fuel flows into the float bowl, the float rises. This pushes the needle valve into its seat in the fuel inlet. When the level is high enough, the valve is tightly seated. Then no additional fuel can enter. When the fuel level drops, the float also drops. This allows the valve to move away from the valve seat. Now more fuel can flow into the float bowl.

In actual operation the float and the needle valve stay in a position that allows just enough fuel to enter the float bowl to maintain a constant level of fuel. The fuel entering the float bowl just balances the fuel leaving.

Figure 15-7 is a cutaway view of a carburetor, showing an actual float system. Two floats are connected to a single lever. This lever is pivoted on the side of the float bowl. The end of the lever rests against the end of the needle valve. Many carburetors use only one float.

□ 15-8 IDLE AND LOW-SPEED SYSTEM

When the throttle valve is closed or only slightly open, only a small amount of air can pass through the air horn. With low air speed, there is very little vacuum in the venturi. No fuel will feed from the fuel nozzle. To supply fuel during idle and low speeds, an idle system is built into the carburetor (Fig. 15-8). The system has an opening in the side of the carburetor below the throttle valve. This hole is called the *idle port*. In addition to the idle port, there is an idle-mixture screw, located behind the idle port. The port is connected by a passage to the float bowl.

When the throttle valve is closed and the engine is running, a high vacuum develops in the intake manifold. The pistons are repeatedly moving down on their intake strokes, which means they are demanding air-fuel mixture. If the pistons don't get enough air-fuel mixture, then a vacuum develops. This vacuum is great enough, when the throttle valve is closed, to cause fuel to flow through the fuel passage from the float bowl to the idle port.

Figure 15-8 shows the idle system in action. Air flows down through a passage in the side of the air horn. The air mixes with the gasoline

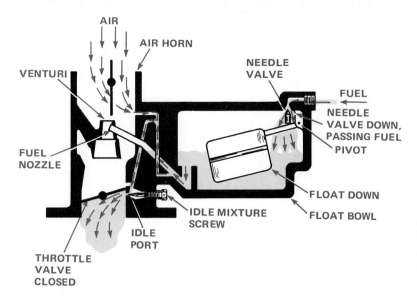

flowing out of a connecting passage from the float bowl. This mixture moves down to the idle port and discharges in the lower part of the carburetor. Some air gets past the throttle valve. This air mixes with the air-fuel mixture coming from the idle port to form the mixture going to the cylinders.

In older carburetors, the idle-mixture screw can be turned in or out to change the amount of air-fuel mixture discharging from the idle port. If the screw is turned out, more mixture can discharge. This makes the idle mixture richer. If the screw is turned in, the mixture is made leaner. However, on many carburetors, the screw has a special cap called an *idle limiter*. It allows only a small adjustment of the screw, which is properly set at the factory. Other carburetors cannot be adjusted after they leave the factory, except by disassembling the carburetor and removing a steel plug.

□ 15-9 LOW-SPEED OPERATION

If the throttle valve is open just a little for low-speed operation, the edge of the throttle valve moves past the idle port, as shown in Fig. 15-9. More air can flow past the throttle valve now, reducing the vacuum in the

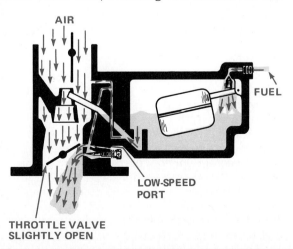

Fig. 15-9 Low-speed operation. The throttle valve is slightly open. Fuel is being discharged through the low-speed port.

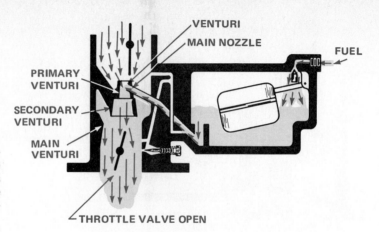

VENTURI
MAIN NOZZLE
PRIMARY VENTURI
SECONDARY VENTURI
MAIN VENTURI
FUEL
THROTTLE VALVE OPEN

Fig. 15-10 Main-metering system in a carburetor. The throttle valve is almost wide open. Fuel is being discharged through the high-speed nozzle, or main nozzle.

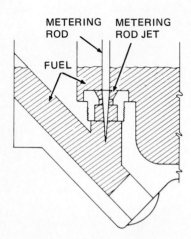

METERING ROD
METERING ROD JET
FUEL

TAPERED METERING ROD

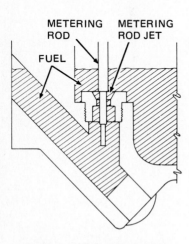

METERING ROD
METERING ROD JET
FUEL

STEP-TYPE METERING ROD

Fig. 15-11 Two types of metering rods used for controlling fuel flow through the metering rod into the power system.

intake manifold. So less fuel flows from the idle port. However, the low-speed port now comes into action. The throttle valve has moved past and above the low-speed port. The vacuum in the intake manifold can act on this port as well as on the idle port. Both ports discharge fuel to maintain the required amount of air-fuel mixture.

□ 15-10 MAIN-METERING SYSTEM

If the throttle valve is opened farther, more air will flow through. This means that there will be less vacuum in the intake manifold. As a result, the idle and low-speed ports stop discharging fuel. However, with more air flow, there is a vacuum in the venturi. This causes the fuel nozzle to discharge fuel. Therefore, enough fuel enters the carburetor and mixes with the air passing through. Figure 15-10 shows the main-metering system in action.

□ 15-11 POWER SYSTEM

When a driver wants full power, the accelerator pedal is pushed to the floor. This causes the throttle valve to open wide. Another system in the carburetor comes into action to deliver additional fuel. This system includes a metering rod and a hole, called the *metering-rod jet,* in which the rod hangs. The metering rod either has two or more steps of different diameters or is tapered at its lower end (Fig. 15-11). At intermediate throttle, the larger diameter, or step, is in the metering-rod jet. This restricts the fuel flow by partly blocking the jet. However, enough fuel flows to provide the proper air-fuel—mixture ratio during part-throttle operation.

When the throttle is fully opened, the metering rod is raised enough so the smaller diameter, or step, is lifted up out of the metering-rod jet (Fig. 15-12). Now the passage is larger. Therefore more fuel flows through. A richer air-fuel mixture results, so that the engine can develop maximum power.

The system shown in Fig. 15-12 is a mechanical system. The metering rod is lifted by a mechanical linkage to the throttle. In some carburetors a vacuum piston or diaphragm is used to lift the metering rod (Fig. 15-13). In this system, a flexible diaphragm is linked to the metering rod. The space above the diaphragm is connected by a vacuum passage to the intake manifold. When there is vacuum in the intake manifold, the vacuum holds the diaphragm up. In this position the metering rod is up, and the fuel flow is restricted. The up position is normal for

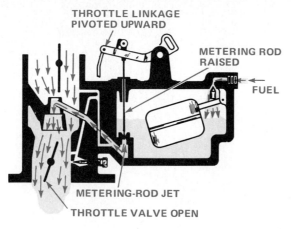

THROTTLE LINKAGE
PIVOTED UPWARD

METERING ROD
RAISED

FUEL

METERING-ROD JET

THROTTLE VALVE OPEN

Fig. 15-12 A mechanically operated power system. When the throttle valve is opened, as shown, the metering rod is raised. This allows the smaller diameter of the rod to clear the jet so additional fuel can flow.

part-throttle operation when the vacuum is fairly high in the intake manifold.

However, when the throttle is opened wide, the vacuum is lost and can no longer hold the diaphragm up. A spring pushes the diaphragm down. This lowers the metering rod so that additional fuel can flow into the carburetor. A richer mixture is delivered to the engine for full-power operation.

□ 15-12 ELECTRONIC CONTROL OF AIR-FUEL RATIO

The systems described above supply varying air-fuel ratios for different operating conditions. However, they are mechanical systems which may not be accurate enough. The exhaust gas may contain more pollutants than allowed by law. To reduce exhaust emissions, many carburetors now have electronic control systems. They continuously measure the amount of oxygen in the exhaust gas. Then this information is used to adjust the amount of fuel being delivered to the engine.

The ideal air-fuel–mixture ratio of 14.7:1 is called the *stoichiometric ratio*. It comes closest to providing complete combustion. As a result, at

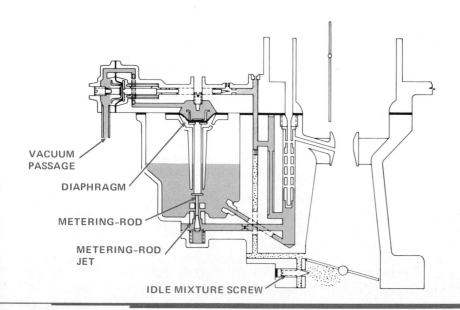

VACUUM
PASSAGE

DIAPHRAGM

METERING-ROD

METERING-ROD
JET

IDLE MIXTURE SCREW

Fig. 15-13 A carburetor with a metering rod controlled by a vacuum-operated diaphragm. *(Pontiac Motor Division of General Motors Corporation)*

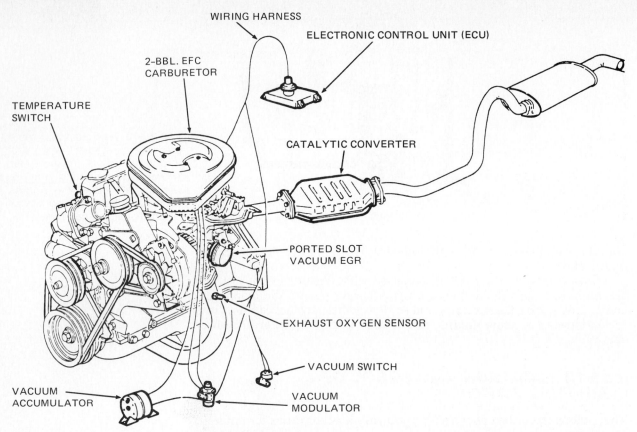

WIRING HARNESS

ELECTRONIC CONTROL UNIT (ECU)

2-BBL. EFC CARBURETOR

TEMPERATURE SWITCH

CATALYTIC CONVERTER

PORTED SLOT VACUUM EGR

EXHAUST OXYGEN SENSOR

VACUUM SWITCH

VACUUM ACCUMULATOR

VACUUM MODULATOR

Fig. 15-14 An electronic fuel control (EFC) system. *(Chevrolet Motor Division of General Motors Corporation)*

this air-fuel ratio the exhaust gas has the least pollutants (Chap. 24). If the exhaust gas is too low in oxygen, the air-fuel mixture is too rich. More than the normal amount of fuel is used up during combustion. If the exhaust gas is too high in oxygen, the air-fuel mixture is too lean. There is not enough fuel to use up enough of the oxygen in the air. When the amount of oxygen in the exhaust gas is not correct, the system immediately changes the air-fuel ratio. This is called a *feedback system*.

Figure 15-14 shows the feedback system on an engine. The oxygen-measuring device is called the *exhaust oxygen sensor*. Figure 15-15 shows how the oxygen sensor is mounted in the exhaust pipe. The oxygen sensor sends a varying voltage signal to the electronic control unit (ECU). The voltage depends on the amount of oxygen in the exhaust gas. If the percentage of oxygen is not correct, the ECU sends a signal to the carburetor. It then adjusts the air-fuel ratio as necessary.

For example, suppose the oxygen content is low. This means that the mixture is too rich. Then the ECU signals a vacuum switch for the carburetor. The signal works through a vacuum modulator to apply vacuum to a flexible diaphragm in the carburetor (Fig. 15-16). This diaphragm is called the *main-metering-system feedback diaphragm*. It controls the position of the metering rod in the main-metering system. When the mixture is too rich, the metering rod is moved to partly block off the metering-rod jet. Less fuel flows through and the mixture is leaned out.

If the mixture is too lean, as indicated by the oxygen sensor, the ECU changes the amount of vacuum on the flexible diaphragm. This causes the metering rod to move, opening the jet so more fuel can flow.

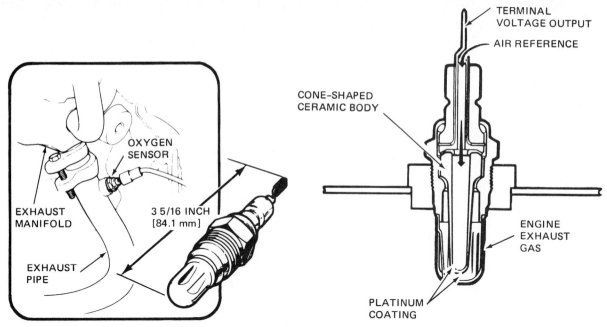

Fig. 15-15 An oxygen sensor, showing its construction and operation. *(AC Spark Plug Division of General Motors Corporation)*

□ 15-13 ACCELERATOR-PUMP SYSTEM

There is another operating condition that needs a richer air-fuel mixture. This condition occurs when the accelerator pedal is pushed down to increase speed, up to about 30 mph [48 km/h]. To get the power needed, the engine has to momentarily be fed a richer mixture. The accelerator-pump system handles this job. The system includes a pump (Fig. 15-17) that is operated when the accelerator pedal is depressed. The movement causes the pump plunger to be pushed down, as shown in Fig. 15-18. Pushing the pump plunger down forces a charge of fuel out through the pump jet. The fuel discharges into the air-fuel mixture that is moving through the carburetor. This further enriches the air-fuel mixture.

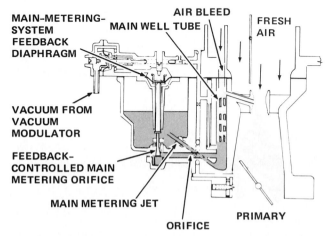

Fig. 15-16 Sectional view of the carburetor for the EFC system, showing the main-metering system with feedback diaphragm. *(Pontiac Motor Division of General Motors Corporation)*

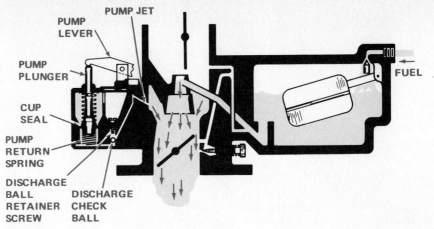

Fig. 15-17 The accelerator-pump system in a carburetor which uses a pump plunger.

□ 15-14 CHOKE SYSTEM

When a cold engine is being cranked for starting, extra fuel must be delivered to the engine. The choke valve does this job. The choke is a round disk located in the air horn (Fig. 15-19).

When the choke valve is turned to the closed position, as shown in Fig. 15-19, very little air can get past the choke into the air horn. Intake-manifold vacuum reaches the fuel nozzle. During cranking, this vacuum is great enough to cause the fuel nozzle to deliver fuel. This fuel mixes with the air passing through the carburetor to get the engine started. After the engine starts, the air-fuel mixture must immediately be leaned. In most engines an automatic choke (□ 15-15) leans the mixture.

□ 15-15 AUTOMATIC CHOKES

An automatic choke is shown in partial cutaway view in Fig. 15-20. It includes a thermostatic spring that winds up or unwinds with changing temperature. When the engine is cold, the spring winds up, closing the

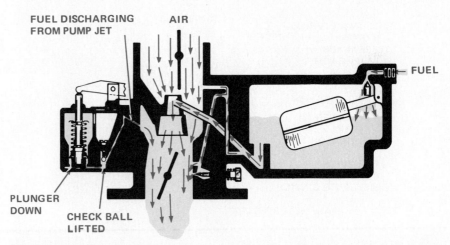

Fig. 15-18 When the throttle valve is opened, the pump lever pushes the pump plunger down. This forces fuel to flow through the accelerator-pump system and out the jet.

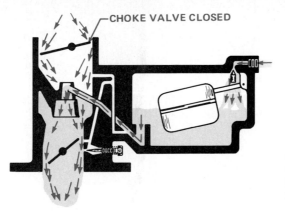

—CHOKE VALVE CLOSED

Fig. 15-19 With the choke valve closed, intake-manifold vacuum reaches into the carburetor air horn. This causes the main nozzle to discharge fuel.

choke valve. Then the cold engine gets a rich mixture for starting. As the engine warms up, the thermostatic spring unwinds, opening the choke valve.

During warm-up, the choke piston comes into action. When the engine is idling, the piston is pulled down by the intake-manifold vacuum. This partly opens the choke valve which prevents too rich an idle mixture. Then, when the throttle valve is opened for acceleration, intake-manifold vacuum decreases. This releases the choke piston so that the

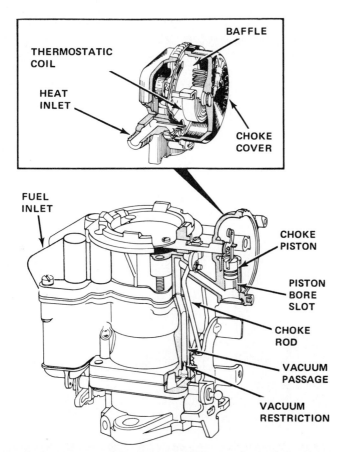

BAFFLE

THERMOSTATIC COIL

HEAT INLET

CHOKE COVER

FUEL INLET

CHOKE PISTON

PISTON BORE SLOT

CHOKE ROD

VACUUM PASSAGE

VACUUM RESTRICTION

Fig. 15-20 Choke system using a choke piston and a thermostatic coil spring mounted on the carburetor. *(American Motors Corporation)*

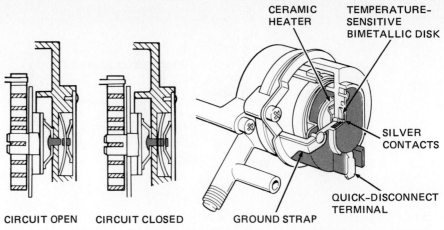

CERAMIC HEATER TEMPERATURE-SENSITIVE BIMETALLIC DISK

SILVER CONTACTS

QUICK–DISCONNECT TERMINAL

CIRCUIT OPEN   CIRCUIT CLOSED   GROUND STRAP

Fig. 15-21 Operation of the electric-assist choke. At low temperature, the ceramic heater turns on, adding heat to the choke so that the choke valve opens more quickly. *(Ford Motor Company)*

choke valve moves toward the closed position. This action enriches the mixture for acceleration.

During closed-choke operation, the air-fuel mixture is rich. The result is that more unburned hydrocarbon goes out the tail pipe. To reduce the time the choke is closed, some automatic chokes use an electric heating element (Fig. 15-21). The electric heating element speeds up the unchoking action. There is more information on electric chokes in Chap. 24.

Another type of automatic choke is shown in Fig. 15-22. The thermostat is located in a well on the exhaust manifold. A rod connects the thermostatic coil to the choke valve. This causes faster action because the exhaust-manifold heat does not travel to the coil through a heat tube. Many chokes use a vacuum diaphragm (Fig. 15-22) instead of a vacuum piston to pull open the choke valve.

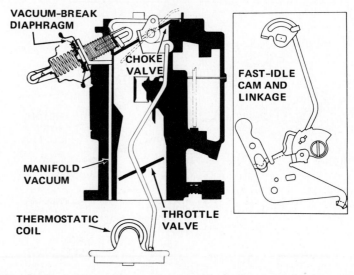

VACUUM–BREAK DIAPHRAGM

CHOKE VALVE

FAST–IDLE CAM AND LINKAGE

MANIFOLD VACUUM

THERMOSTATIC COIL

THROTTLE VALVE

Fig. 15-22 Choke system using a vacuum-break diaphragm and a thermostatic coil spring mounted in a well in the exhaust manifold. *(Chevrolet Motor Division of General Motors Corporation)*

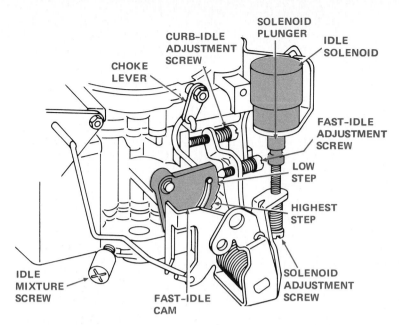

Fig. 15-23 Carburetor with an idle solenoid. The fast-idle cam is operated by the choke linkage. *(Chrysler Corporation)*

□ *15-16 FAST IDLE*

When the engine is cold, the throttle valve must be kept partly open so that the engine can idle fast. If a cold engine slows to normal hot-idle speed (or *curb idle*), the engine will stall. To get fast idle with a cold engine, there is a fast-idle cam on the carburetor (Fig. 15-23). This cam is linked to the choke valve. When the engine is cold, the automatic choke holds the choke valve closed. The linkage holds the fast-idle cam in the fast-idle position. In this position, the linkage has turned the fast-idle cam so that the adjusting screw rests on the highest step of the cam. Therefore, the throttle cannot close, and the engine idles fast. Then, as the automatic choke opens the choke valve, the linkage turns the fast-idle cam so that the high step moves out from under the fast-idle adjustment screw. Now the throttle valve can close to its normal hot-idle position as the engine warms up.

□ *15-17 CONTROL DEVICES ON CARBURETORS*

Carburetors have other devices to improve driveability, improve fuel economy, and lower air pollution. Some of these devices are described in Chap. 24. Others are listed and described briefly below.

1. IDLE SOLENOID

Some engines have a tendency to continue running after the ignition switch is turned off. This is called *run-on,* or *dieseling,* because the engine runs like a diesel, without electric ignition. The carburetors for these engines are equipped with an antidieseling solenoid or *idle solenoid* (Fig. 15-23). When the engine is running normally, the solenoid is connected to the battery. This causes the solenoid plunger to extend. The plunger serves as the idle stop and prevents complete closing of the throttle valve. Therefore, normal hot-idle speed results when the driver releases the accelerator pedal. However, when the engine is turned off, the solenoid plunger retracts. Now the throttle can close completely, shutting off all airflow. The engine stops running.

2. DASHPOT

If the throttle valve closes too rapidly after the driver releases the accelerator pedal, the air-fuel mixture can be momentarily excessively enriched. This happens because the fuel nozzle dribbles fuel for a moment even though the airflow has been shut off. The idle system will also feed a rich air-fuel mixture. This is due to the high vacuum that results when the engine is running fast with the throttle closed. An excessively rich mixture can cause the engine to stumble or stall. Also, the rich mixture can damage the catalytic converter. To prevent these problems, many carburetors are equipped with a throttle-return check, or *dashpot* (Fig. 15-24). It slows the throttle-valve closing to prevent the momentary excessive richness.

3. VACUUM VENTS

The carburetor and intake manifold have a vacuum in them when the engine is running. This vacuum is used by various other devices on the engine and elsewhere:

a. Ignition-distributor vacuum-advance mechanism. This advances the spark during part-throttle operation (Chap. 22).
b. Positive crankcase ventilating system. This is a system for ventilating the crankcase without polluting the atmosphere (Chap. 24).
c. Evaporative control system. This system traps gasoline vapor from the fuel tank and carburetor float bowl (Chap. 24).

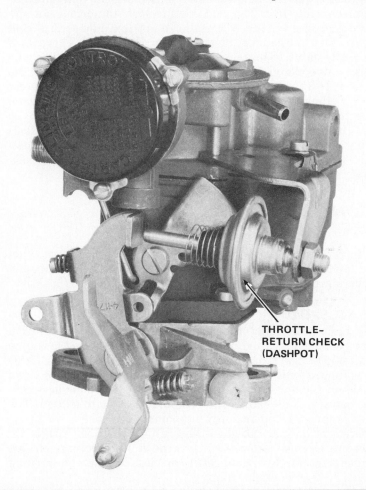

THROTTLE-RETURN CHECK (DASHPOT)

Fig. 15-24 The dashpot on a carburetor slows the closing of the throttle valve. *(Carter Carburetor Division of ACF Industries)*

d. Thermostatic air cleaner. This system ($\square$ 14-10) provides rapid heating of the air entering the carburetor when the engine is cold. This improves cold-engine performance.

e. Exhaust-gas recirculation system. The exhaust-gas recirculation (EGR) system introduces some exhaust gas into the air-fuel mixture going into the engine cylinders (Chap. 24). This reduces the formation of one of the air pollutants (NO_x).

$\square$ 15-18 TWO-BARREL AND FOUR-BARREL CARBURETORS

Many four-cylinder engines use carburetors with a single barrel (Figs. 15-1 and 15-24). These carburetors have one barrel, one main fuel nozzle, one venturi, and one throttle valve (Fig. 15-25). They work well with four-cylinder and some six-cylinder engines. However, for better performance, many six-cylinder and all eight-cylinder engines are equipped with carburetors having either two or four barrels.

A *two-barrel carburetor* is like two single-barrel carburetors combined into a single unit (Fig. 15-26). The purpose of the additional barrel is to improve engine breathing. This improves engine performance and driveability. Engine breathing, or volumetric efficiency, is described in $\square$ 7-12 and 7-13. Adding the extra barrel allows more air-fuel mixture to enter the engine. The second barrel in the dual carburetor is used in two different ways, according to the carburetor design. In one type, both barrels are the same size, and both operate all the time that the engine is running. In some engines, the intake manifold is open to all cylinders.

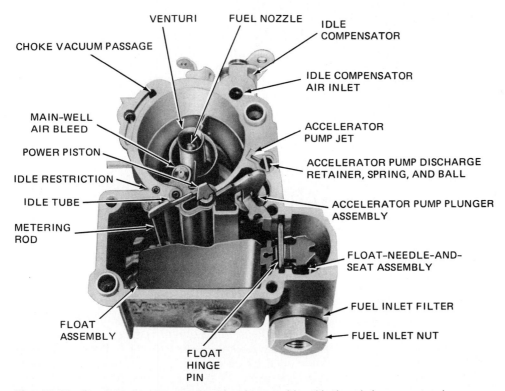

Fig. 15-25 One-barrel-carburetor float-bowl assembly with the air horn removed. *(Oldsmobile Division of General Motors Corporation)*

233

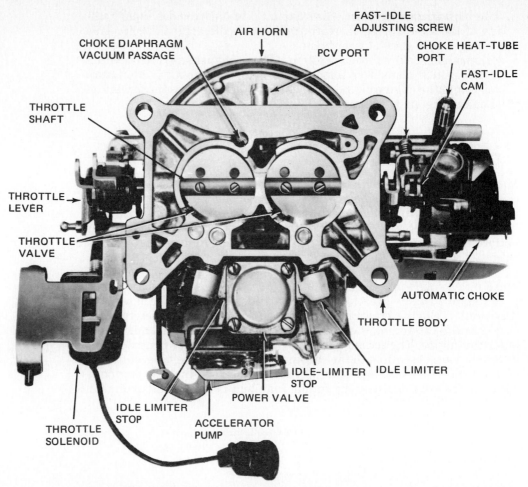

Fig. 15-26 A two-barrel carburetor, showing the locations of the two throttle valves.

Both barrels feed into this common manifold. In other engines, the manifold is split, or divided, into two parts. Each barrel feeds one part which takes care of half the engine cylinders.

In the second type, one barrel is the *primary barrel*. It takes care of the air-fuel requirements for all cylinders during idle, low-speed, and intermediate-speed operation. When the throttle is opened wide, the *secondary barrel* comes into operation. Then it supplies the additional air-fuel mixture for full power.

The *four-barrel carburetor,* or *quad carburetor* (Fig. 15-27), is like two two-barrel carburetors combined into a single unit. The carburetor has four barrels and four main nozzles. One pair of barrels, the primary barrels, makes up a primary dual carburetor. The other pair of barrels, with their main fuel nozzles, makes up a secondary dual carburetor.

The primary barrels handle all engine requirements under most operating conditions. Each barrel feeds half the cylinders. When the throttle is moved toward wide open for acceleration or full power, the secondary barrels come into operation. Their throttle valves are opened mechanically or by vacuum-operated linkage. Then the secondary barrels supply additional air-fuel mixture so the engine can produce more power.

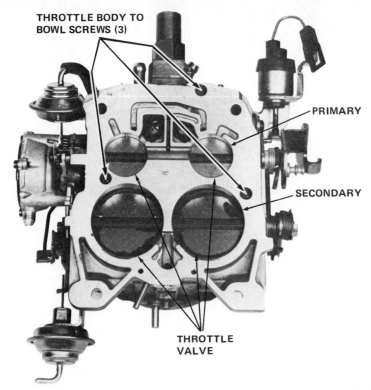

THROTTLE BODY TO
BOWL SCREWS (3)

PRIMARY

SECONDARY

THROTTLE
VALVE

Fig. 15-27 The throttle valves of a four-barrel carburetor. *(Oldsmobile Division of General Motors Corporation)*

□ 15-19 MULTIPLE CARBURETORS

Some engines use more than one carburetor. The use of more than one carburetor requires a special intake manifold. The additional carburetors supply more air-fuel mixture to improve performance.

VARIABLE-VENTURI CARBURETORS

□ 15-20 TYPES OF VARIABLE-VENTURI CARBURETORS

In the fixed-venturi carburetor, the venturi produces a partial vacuum when air flows through it (□ 15-4). This partial vacuum then causes the fuel nozzle to discharge fuel into the air passing through. The venturi in the variable-venturi (VV) carburetor does the same thing. The basic difference is that in the VV carburetor, the size of the venturi can vary. In the fixed-venturi carburetor, the venturi is located in the center of the carburetor air passage and cannot change in size.

There are two basic types of VV carburetors, the round-piston, or slide-valve, type and the rectangular-venturi-valve type. The slide-valve type has been used on some imported cars and many motorcycles for years. The rectangular venturi valve type is a relatively new design used by Ford. Both types of VV carburetors have float systems similar to those used in fixed-venturi carburetors.

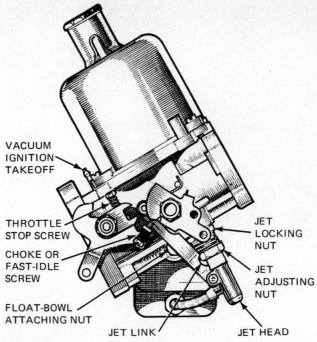

Fig. 15-28 A slide-valve type of variable-venturi carburetor. *(British Motor Corporation, Limited)*

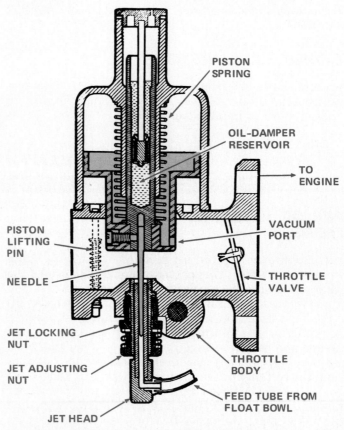

Fig. 15-29 Sectional view of the slide-valve VV carburetor. *(British Motor Corporation, Limited)*

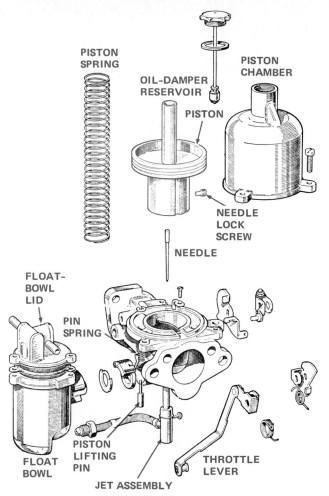

PISTON SPRING

OIL-DAMPER RESERVOIR

PISTON CHAMBER

PISTON

NEEDLE LOCK SCREW

NEEDLE

FLOAT-BOWL LID

PIN SPRING

PISTON LIFTING PIN

FLOAT BOWL

JET ASSEMBLY

THROTTLE LEVER

Fig. 15-30 A disassembled slide-valve VV carburetor. *(British Motor Corporation, Limited)*

☐ 15-21 ROUND-PISTON VV CARBURETOR

In this carburetor, the round piston and throttle body form the variable venturi. Figures 15-28 to 15-30 show assembled, sectional, and disassembled views of the carburetor. The piston moves up and down as the vacuum between it and the throttle valve changes. When the throttle is closed so that the engine is idling, there is very little vacuum on the air-cleaner side of the throttle valve. So the piston spring pushes the piston down to its lowest point. The space between it and the lower floor of the throttle body is small. Only a little air can get through. At the same time, the tapered needle is well down in the fuel jet so only a little gasoline can feed through to the passing air. The resulting air-fuel mixture is right for engine idling.

When the throttle is opened, the intake-manifold vacuum enters the throttle body. This vacuum draws air from the space above the piston, acting through the vacuum port in the lower part of the piston.

The piston is raised by the vacuum, partly lifting the needle out of the fuel jet. Now more air can flow through the carburetor and more fuel can feed into it. The amount of fuel delivered increases to match the additional air flowing through. The wider the throttle opens, the greater the vacuum working on the piston. So it moves up still more. It carries the needle up with it so that the air-fuel ratio stays the same throughout the operating range of the engine. Figure 15-31 shows how the size of the venturi changes as the piston moves up and down.

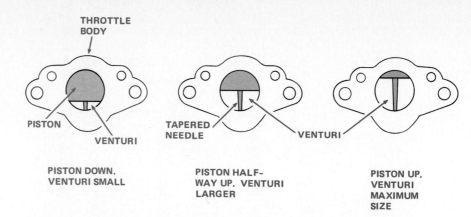

Fig. 15-31 Looking into the throttle body to see how the up-and-down movement of the piston changes the size of the venturi.

□ 15-22 FORD VARIABLE-VENTURI CARBURETOR

This carburetor (Fig. 15-32) was introduced on some 1978 Ford cars. The piston is rectangular. It is called the *venturi valve*. It slides back and forth across the opening above the throttle valve (Fig. 15-33). Its position is controlled by the amount of vacuum, and this depends on throttle-valve opening. The vacuum control includes a spring-loaded vacuum diaphragm which is connected by a rod to the venturi valve (Fig. 15-34). When the throttle is opened, the intake-manifold vacuum can act on the vacuum diaphragm. This causes the venturi valve to move back to increase the venturi opening. Now more air can flow through. At the same time, the tapered metering rod (the needle) is pulled out from the fuel jet, allowing more fuel to flow through. This additional fuel matches the additional air flowing through so that the proper air-fuel ratio is maintained.

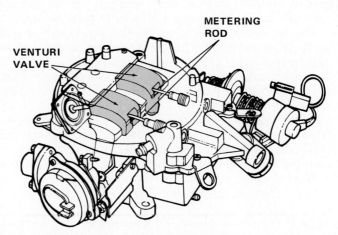

Fig. 15-32 A partially cut away Ford variable-venturi carburetor which uses rectangular-shaped venturi valves. *(Ford Motor Company)*

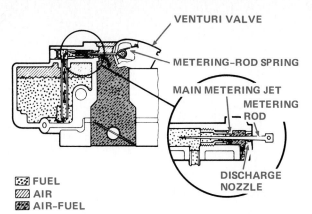

FUEL
AIR
AIR-FUEL

Fig. 15-33 Main-metering system of the Ford VV carburetor. *(Ford Motor Company)*

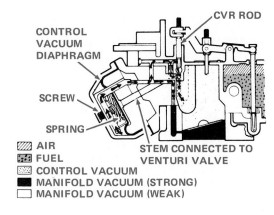

AIR
FUEL
CONTROL VACUUM
MANIFOLD VACUUM (STRONG)
MANIFOLD VACUUM (WEAK)

Fig. 15-34 Control vacuum system of the Ford VV carburetor. *(Ford Motor Company)*

Select the *one* correct, best, or most probable answer to each question. Then check your answers against the correct answers given at the end of the book.

1. The carburetor operates on the principle of
   a. atmospheric pressure
   b. fuel-pump pressure
   c. pressure differential
   d. none of the above
2. When operating under a heavy load or wide-open throttle, the power system of a carburetor must be able to supply
   a. leaner mixtures
   b. more vacuum
   c. richer mixtures
   d. more pressure
3. The purpose of the choke-system is to
   a. supply a leaner mixture for starting
   b. supply a richer mixture for starting
   c. aid the accelerator-pump system
   d. prevent dieseling after shutoff
4. The float system operates with all but one system in the carburetor. This system is
   a. the idle system
   b. the choke system
   c. the main-metering system
   d. none of the above
5. Fast idle is set with the fast-idle adjusting screw on which step of the fast-idle cam?
   a. lowest step
   b. second step
   c. third step
   d. highest step
6. Four-barrel carburetors have a
   a. primary side
   b. secondary side
   c. choke on the primary side
   d. all of the above
7. The secondary throttle valves in a four-barrel carburetor are controlled by
   a. the driver of the car
   b. mechanical or vacuum linkage
   c. engine speed
   d. none of the above
8. The metering rod used in the power system
   a. controls the idling system
   b. prevents overfilling of the float bowl
   c. has two or more steps, or is tapered
   d. is operated only by vacuum

CHAPTER 16
GASOLINE FUEL-INJECTION SYSTEMS

After studying this chapter, you should be able to:
1. Discuss the types of fuel injection for gasoline engines.
2. Define *injection valve.*
3. Describe the operation of the timed electronic fuel-injection system.
4. Explain the operation of the continuous injection system.
5. Locate the components of a gasoline fuel-injection system on various cars.
6. Explain the difference between timed injection and continuous injection.
7. Describe the operation of a throttle-body injection system.

Regardless of the type of fuel-injection system used on a spark-ignition engine, fuel injection eliminates many problems with carburetion and distribution of the air-fuel mixture. With fuel injection, exhaust emissions can be greatly reduced. Many driveability problems can be eliminated. For example, fuel injection can provide a complete fuel shutoff when the throttle valves close and the car decelerates. This eliminates exhaust emissions during deceleration. It also saves fuel, thereby improving fuel economy.

☐ 16-1 INTRODUCTION TO GASOLINE FUEL INJECTION

There are two basic types of gasoline fuel-injection systems, single-point and multiple-point (Fig. 14-2). The difference is in how many places fuel (under pressure) is injected into the engine. In the single-point system (also called *throttle-body injection,* or *TBI*), fuel enters the intake air at only one place. This is usually the throttle body on the intake manifold. Throttle-body injection is described later.

In the multiple-point, or *port-injection,* system, fuel is injected into the intake air for each cylinder. Therefore only air enters the intake manifold. Then as the air approaches the intake valves, injection valves open to spray fuel into the air stream (Fig. 16-1). In the carburetor, a

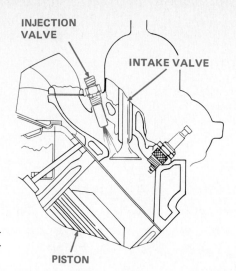

Fig. 16-1 Basic method for injecting fuel into the intake manifold near the intake valve.

vacuum draws, or "pulls," the amount of fuel the engine needs from nozzles in the carburetor. In the fuel-injection system, fuel is pressurized by a pump. Then the fuel is forced into the intake air when the injection valve is opened.

□ 16-2 CLASSIFYING FUEL-INJECTION SYSTEMS

There are several ways to classify gasoline fuel-injection systems. One way is according to where in the engine the fuel is injected. Another way is according to whether injection is continuous or intermittent.

Fuel can be injected directly into the combustion chamber (Fig. 16-2) or into the intake manifold (Fig. 16-1). Direct injection is used in diesel engines (Chap. 17). Injecting fuel into the air before it gets into the combustion chamber is the system used for spark-ignition engines.

The second classification of fuel-injection systems is the injection procedure. The fuel may be injected intermittently (*pulsed,* or *timed, injection*) or continuously. Electronic fuel-injection (EFI) systems usually have intermittent injection. The fuel sprays from the injection valves in a series of short "pulses." When the injection pulses occur in the engine firing order (as in a diesel engine), this is called *sequential injection.*

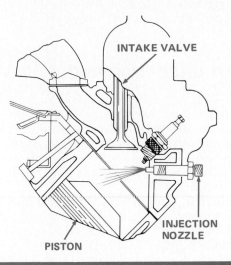

Fig. 16-2 Basic method for injecting fuel directly into the combustion chamber.

To change the amount of fuel being injected, the length of each pulse is lengthened or shortened. Pulse length (and therefore injection time) is controlled by the electronic control unit (ECU). It signals the injection valves when to open and close.

In a continuous injection system (CIS), fuel sprays continuously from the injection valves into the intake manifold. The amount of fuel sprayed varies with engine speed and power demands. Continuous injection systems do not require a control system to change the length of injection as operating conditions change.

All types of gasoline fuel-injection systems on new cars include an oxygen sensor (□ 15-12). It provides electronic control of the air-fuel mixture when used with a feedback carburetor. With gasoline fuel injection, the oxygen sensor and feedback control are often called the *Lambda Sond* system.

ELECTRONIC FUEL INJECTION

□ 16-3 ELECTRONIC FUEL INJECTION (EFI)

In 1968, Volkswagen began installing an electronic fuel-injection system built by Robert Bosch Corporation on some cars imported into the United States. In 1975, a version of the system appeared on some Cadillacs. This system was basically the Bosch D type (Fig. 16-3). In it a high-pressure electric fuel pump is located in or near the fuel tank. The pump sends fuel from the tank through the fuel-pressure regulator to the injectors. In

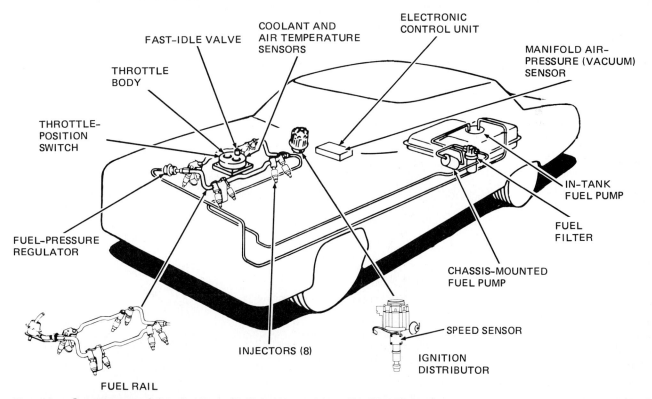

Fig. 16-3 Components of the electronic fuel-injection system. *(Cadillac Motor Car Division of General Motors Corporation)*

most systems, fuel is delivered to the injectors at a pressure of 39 psi [269 kPa]. Various sensors located on the engine send signals to the electronic control unit (ECU). It processes the information. Then the ECU computes when and for how long the injectors should be opened.

The primary signals the ECU uses for determining the amount of fuel to be injected are *engine speed* and *engine load*. The information on engine speed is provided by a speed sensor in the ignition distributor (Fig. 16-3). Intake-manifold vacuum indicates the load on the engine. The *manifold-air-pressure* sensor is used to measure the absolute pressure (which we call a vacuum) in the intake manifold. Then this information is sent to the ECU. The Bosch D system is described further in □ 16-4 to 16-6.

Later, Bosch developed the L-type electronic fuel-injection system. It was introduced by Porsche and Volkswagen in 1974. The system is similar in appearance and operation to the D type. Both have an injector near each intake valve. However, in the L type, fuel metering is controlled primarily by engine speed and by measuring the amount of air that actually enters the engine. This is called *air-mass metering,* or *airflow metering*. The airflow sensor in the air intake measures the actual amount of air that enters the engine. The L-type system is discussed further in □ 16-7.

Throttle-body injection (TBI), or *digital fuel injection* (DFI), was first used on some 1980 model cars (Fig. 16-4). In this system, one or two fuel injectors are mounted in the throttle body on the intake manifold. There they spray fuel into the airstream passing through. The operation and construction of these systems are described in □ 16-8 and 16-10.

□ 16-4 OPERATION OF THE TIMED EFI SYSTEM

Figure 16-3 shows the components of the electronic fuel-injection system used on some 1975 to 1980 model Cadillacs. Many imported cars used the

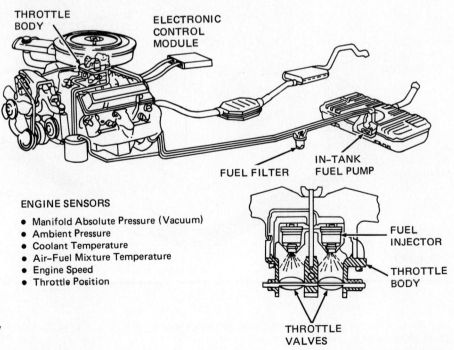

ENGINE SENSORS
- Manifold Absolute Pressure (Vacuum)
- Ambient Pressure
- Coolant Temperature
- Air–Fuel Mixture Temperature
- Engine Speed
- Throttle Position

Fig. 16-4 Typical throttle-body injection system.

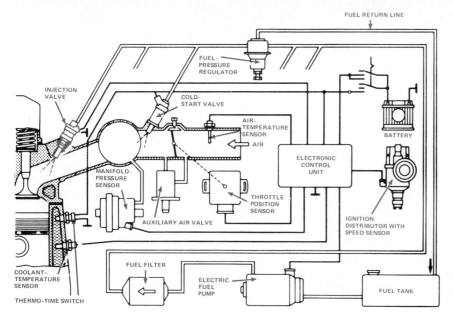

FUEL RETURN LINE

FUEL-PRESSURE REGULATOR

INJECTION VALVE

COLD-START VALVE

AIR-TEMPERATURE SENSOR

AIR

BATTERY

ELECTRONIC CONTROL UNIT

MANIFOLD-PRESSURE SENSOR

THROTTLE POSITION SENSOR

AUXILIARY AIR VALVE

IGNITION DISTRIBUTOR WITH SPEED SENSOR

COOLANT-TEMPERATURE SENSOR

THERMO-TIME SWITCH

FUEL FILTER

ELECTRIC FUEL PUMP

FUEL TANK

Fig. 16-5 Bosch D type of electronic fuel-injection system. *(Robert Bosch Corporation)*

same basic system. The various sensors that feed information to the electronic control unit (ECU) are shown in Fig. 16-3. (The ECU is described further in Chaps. 22 and 24.) Figure 16-5 shows a schematic view of the Bosch D system.

Figure 16-6 is a block diagram showing (to the left) the sensors that send information to the ECU. The absolute-manifold-pressure sensor provides an electric signal that changes with the pressure. (*Absolute pressure* is the same as intake-manifold vacuum.) A second sensor signals electrically the engine speed in revolutions per minute (rpm) of the crankshaft. A third sensor sends a changing electric signal as the engine coolant temperature changes. A fourth sensor signals intake-manifold air temperature. A fifth sensor signals the throttle position.

The ECU takes in all these varying signals (and sometimes more). Using this information, the ECU computes how long the injection valves should be held open. Then the ECU sends a *voltage pulse* to the injectors. The voltage pulse causes the injectors to remain open for the required

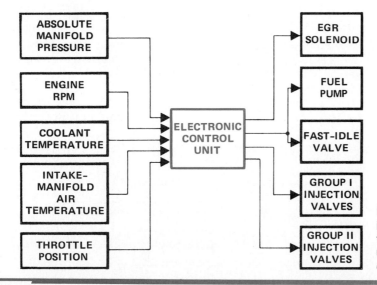

ABSOLUTE MANIFOLD PRESSURE

ENGINE RPM

COOLANT TEMPERATURE

INTAKE-MANIFOLD AIR TEMPERATURE

THROTTLE POSITION

ELECTRONIC CONTROL UNIT

EGR SOLENOID

FUEL PUMP

FAST-IDLE VALVE

GROUP I INJECTION VALVES

GROUP II INJECTION VALVES

Fig. 16-6 Block diagram showing sensors (left) that provide information to the electronic control unit. *(Cadillac Motor Car Division of General Motors Corporation)*

245

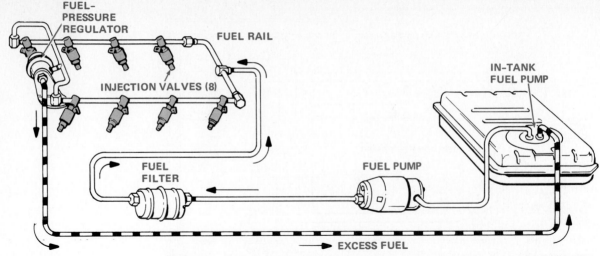

FUEL-PRESSURE REGULATOR

FUEL RAIL

IN-TANK FUEL PUMP

INJECTION VALVES (8)

FUEL FILTER

FUEL PUMP

EXCESS FUEL

Fig. 16-7 Fuel system for the Bosch D type of electronic fuel injection. *(Cadillac Motor Car Division of General Motors Corporation)*

time. To increase engine speed, the pulse width increases so that injectors stay open longer. If less fuel is needed, the pulse width decreases. Therefore the injectors close earlier and engine speed decreases.

☐ 16-5 FUEL DELIVERY SYSTEM

Figure 16-7 shows the fuel delivery system for the Cadillac electronic fuel-injection system. It includes eight fuel-injection valves, one for each engine cylinder. Each fuel-injection valve is placed so that it points at the intake valve for the cylinder. The injection valves are connected to fuel rails that are connected through a fuel filter to an electric fuel pump. Fuel at constant high pressure is available to the injector valves all the time the engine runs. The fuel-pressure regulator prevents excessive pressure.

Each injection valve is operated by a small electric solenoid (Fig. 16-8). When the solenoid is connected to the battery, it pulls back on the nozzle needle, opening the valve. Now fuel can spray out of the valve.

How long the valve stays open is determined by the ECU. It puts together the various signals from the sensors (Fig. 16-6) to determine this. For example, if the manifold-pressure sensor signals the ECU that the pressure is high (low vacuum), then the ECU will signal the injection valves to stay open longer. More fuel is needed because more air is entering the intake manifold.

The timing of the injection valves (*when* they open) is determined by the engine-speed sensor. It is located in the ignition distributor

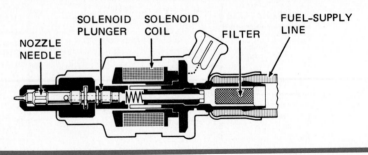

NOZZLE NEEDLE

SOLENOID PLUNGER

SOLENOID COIL

FILTER

FUEL-SUPPLY LINE

Fig. 16-8 Solenoid-operated injection valve. *(Robert Bosch Corporation)*

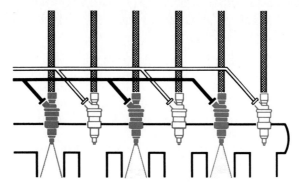

Fig. 16-9 Injection-valve grouping. *(Robert Bosch Corporation)*

(Fig. 16-3). This device includes two reed switches and two magnets. The magnets revolve with the distributor shaft. Every time a magnet passes a reed switch, the switch closes. This signals the ECU to actuate one set of injection valves. When the other switch is operated, the ECU actuates the other set of injection valves.

The speed with which the switches are opened and closed tells the ECU how fast the engine is running. The ECU needs this information so it can adjust the injection-valve actions to suit the operating conditions.

□ 16-6 GROUPING INJECTION VALVES

The injection valves do *not* open individually in time with the cylinder intake-valve opening. Instead, the injection valves are divided into two groups. Half the valves open together. In a four-cylinder engine, each group includes two injection valves; in a six-cylinder, three injection valves; in an eight-cylinder (like the Cadillac), four valves.

In any version of the Bosch D system, the solenoid injection valves are not actuated individually. Some of the injection valves are opening many degrees of crankshaft rotation before the intake valves open. For example, Fig. 16-9 shows the injection-valve grouping for a six-cylinder engine. Three injection valves open together. Figure 16-10 shows the injection timing chart for this engine. The individual intake valves open at varying times (crankshaft degrees) after injection. The top line in Fig. 16-10 is for number 1 cylinder. Injection takes place at 300 degrees of crankshaft rotation. Almost 60 degrees later (near 360 degrees), the number 1 intake valve opens and the intake stroke starts. Number 5 cylinder is next in the firing order. Its intake valve opens near 480 degrees, or about 180 degrees after injection. The intake valve for number 3 cylinder opens near 600 degrees, or about 300 degrees of crankshaft rotation after injection. During these varying intervals between fuel injection and intake-valve opening, the fuel is being "stored" in the intake manifold.

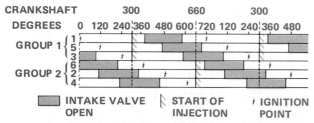

Fig. 16-10 Injection timing chart for a six-cylinder engine. *(Robert Bosch Corporation)*

☐ 16-7 FUEL METERING BY MEASURING AIRFLOW

In the Bosch L type of electronic fuel injection (Fig. 16-11), fuel metering is controlled primarily by engine speed and by measuring the intake airflow. The injection valves, which all open and close at the same time, are actuated twice for every camshaft revolution. This allows the injection pulses to be triggered directly by the ignition distributor. A separate speed sensor is not needed.

The amount of intake air is measured by the *airflow sensor* as the air passes through it (Fig. 16-11). A pivoted flap is placed in the air passage of the airflow sensor. Attached to the flap is a small spring and a voltage sensor. As airflow increases, the spring allows the flap to move according to the amount of air passing through. As the flap moves, the voltage sensor signals the ECU exactly how much air has entered. This information is then used by the ECU to determine the length of the injection pulse which holds the injectors open. Now the injection valves will deliver the exact amount of fuel needed for complete combustion with that amount of air.

☐ 16-8 THROTTLE-BODY INJECTION (TBI)

In 1980, *throttle-body injection* (TBI), or *central fuel injection* (CFI), was introduced (Fig. 16-4). It replaces the carburetor on some engines with a fuel-injection system that sprays fuel down through the throttle body into the intake manifold (Fig. 16-12). The system has one or two small injection valves positioned just above the throttle valves in the throttle body. The throttle body is similar to the carburetor throttle body.

Fuel pressure in the injectors is constant. In many TBI systems, the pressure is 10 psi [69 kPa]. The amount of fuel injected is determined by how long the injection valves are open. Various sensors keep track of throttle opening, coolant temperature, engine speed, and other conditions (Fig. 16-13). These signals are fed to an *electronic control module* (ECM). It then controls how much fuel is delivered.

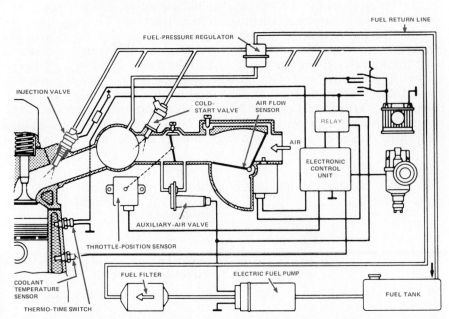

Fig. 16-11 Bosch L type of electronic fuel injection which meters fuel delivery by measuring the amount of air that enters the engine. *(Robert Bosch Corporation)*

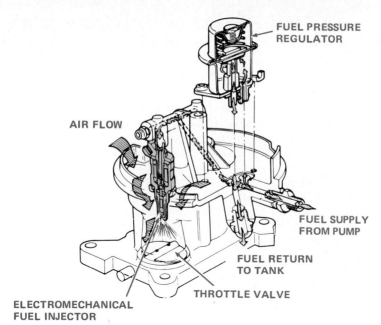

FUEL PRESSURE REGULATOR

AIR FLOW

FUEL SUPPLY FROM PUMP

FUEL RETURN TO TANK

THROTTLE VALVE

ELECTROMECHANICAL FUEL INJECTOR

Fig. 16-12 Cutaway throttle body and fuel injector used by Ford in its throttle-body injection system. *(Ford Motor Company)*

NOTE The computer that is on the car is an *on-board computer*. It controls the electronic fuel-injection system and may perform other functions. Some manufacturers call it the *electronic control unit* (ECU), or the *electronic control module* (ECM). Both mean the system computer.

The fuel-injection system shown in Fig. 16-13 includes an oxygen sensor. This feeds back to the ECM information on the amount of oxygen in the exhaust gas. The ECM then adjusts the amount of fuel being delivered so that exhaust emission standards can be met. Chapter 24 covers automotive emission controls. Electronic control of the air-fuel ratio by use of an oxygen sensor and a feedback system are described in □ 15-12.

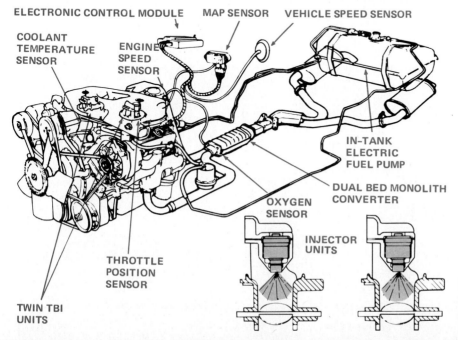

ELECTRONIC CONTROL MODULE **MAP SENSOR** **VEHICLE SPEED SENSOR**

COOLANT TEMPERATURE SENSOR

ENGINE SPEED SENSOR

IN-TANK ELECTRIC FUEL PUMP

DUAL BED MONOLITH CONVERTER

OXYGEN SENSOR

INJECTOR UNITS

THROTTLE POSITION SENSOR

TWIN TBI UNITS

Fig. 16-13 Engine with a throttle-body injection (TBI) system that includes an oxygen sensor. *(General Motors Corporation)*

☐ 16-9 CONTINUOUS INJECTION SYSTEM (CIS)

Figure 16-14 shows a continuous injection system (CIS). This is basically a mechanical system. Fuel metering is not dependent on electronics to time and meter fuel delivery. Instead, fuel sprays continuously from the injection nozzles as long as the engine runs.

To control the amount of fuel injected, an *airflow sensor plate* continuously measures the amount of air flowing into the intake manifold. As the airflow increases, it lifts the sensor plate higher. This causes a lever to lift the control plunger in the fuel distributor. The action increases the amount of fuel that flows to the injector nozzles. The proper air-fuel ratio results. To meet emission standards on late-model cars, the system includes an oxygen sensor and an electronic control unit (Fig. 16-14). However, fuel metering is still primarily a mechanical process performed by the airflow sensor plate.

☐ 16-10 CONTINUOUS-FLOW ELECTRONIC FUEL INJECTION

Another type of throttle-body injection is shown in Fig. 16-15. It is an electronic continuous injection system used by Chrysler. The air-fuel

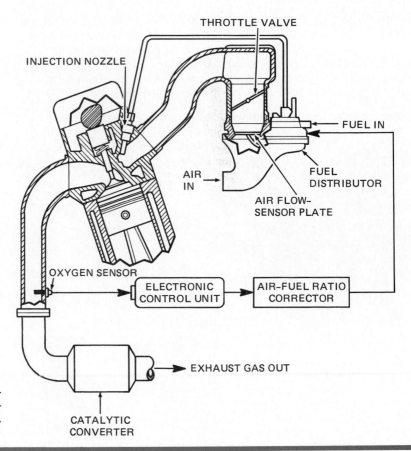

Fig. 16-14 A mechanical continuous injection system that includes an oxygen sensor. *(Saab-Scania of America, Inc.)*

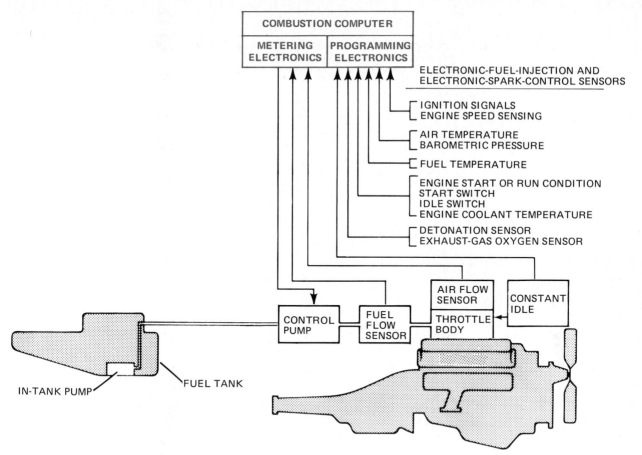

Fig. 16-15 Electronic continuous injection system that includes an oxygen and a detonation sensor. *(Chrysler Corporation)*

ratio is controlled by varying the pressure on the fuel spraying from the injector bars in the throttle body.

In this system, an in-tank fuel pump delivers fuel at a constant pressure to the control pump. Then the control pump boosts the fuel pressure, varying it as required to achieve the desired air-fuel ratio. The fuel, under varying pressure, sprays continuously from two sets of injector bars in the throttle body. The system includes an oxygen sensor (☐ 15-13) and a detonation sensor (☐ 14-15).

Select the *one* correct, best, or most probable answer to each question. Then check your answers against the correct answers given at the end of the book.

1. In the gasoline fuel-injection system, the gasoline is sprayed into the air
   a. in the combustion chambers
   b. in the intake manifold
   c. in the carburetor
   d. in the exhaust manifold

2. Gasoline fuel-injection systems can be classified in two ways, according to whether they are
   a. timed or pulsed
   b. continuous or controlled
   c. intermittent or continuous
   d. none of the above

3. The Bosch D-type fuel-injection system is controlled primarily by
   a. throttle position and electronic devices
   b. engine speed and intake-manifold vacuum
   c. timers and glow plugs
   d. none of the above

4. An engine has a Bosch D type of EFI system. The pressure in the fuel line is 39 psi [269 kPa]. This is
   a. normal operation
   b. too low
   c. too high
   d. excessive volume

5. In an EFI system, the ECU sends a voltage pulse to the injection valves. As pulse width increases,
   a. engine speed increases
   b. engine speed decreases
   c. engine load decreases
   d. none of the above

6. The amount of fuel injected by the timed injection system depends on
   a. when the injection valves open
   b. how far the injection valves open
   c. how long the injection valves stay open
   d. all of the above

7. Four factors that control the length of time the fuel-injection valves stay open are throttle position and
   a. intake-manifold vacuum, intake-air temperature, and coolant temperature
   b. intake-manifold temperature, manifold pressure, and oil temperature
   c. amount of oxygen in the exhaust gas, intake-manifold pressure, and coolant level
   d. none of the above

CHAPTER 17
DIESEL FUEL-INJECTION SYSTEMS

After studying this chapter, you should be able to:
1. Define *glow plug.*
2. Discuss the difference in operation of diesel and gasoline (compression-ignition and spark-ignition) engines.
3. Describe diesel-engine fuel-injection systems.
4. Locate the components of a diesel-engine fuel-injection system on various engines and explain the purpose and operation of each component.

Diesel engines have been used for many years in trucks, buses, and off-the-road equipment. The diesel has established a reputation as a reliable heavy-duty power plant. In recent years, several automotive manufacturers have begun to install four-cycle diesel engines in new cars. In basic construction, many of these engines are similar to spark-ignition engines. The big difference is in the fuel-injection system that times and meters fuel delivery to the cylinders. This chapter covers the diesel-engine fuel system and the two types of fuel-injection pumps used on most automotive diesel engines.

☐ 17-1 DIFFERENCES BETWEEN SPARK-IGNITION AND DIESEL ENGINES

The diesel (compression-ignition) engine is more heavily constructed than a gasoline (spark-ignition) engine. This is because a diesel engine has higher pressures acting on the pistons during the compression and combustion strokes.

NOTE All automotive diesel engines are the four-stroke-cycle type. There are also two-stroke-cycle diesels. However, they are used mostly in heavy-duty trucks and industrial equipment.

The actions during the four strokes of the four-stroke cycle used in spark-ignition engines are described in Chap. 6. The same four basic strokes—intake, compression, power, exhaust—are also used in the diesel engine. However, the actions in the cylinders of the two engines are

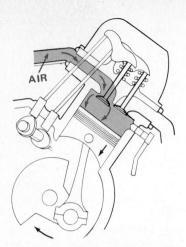

Fig. 17-1 Intake stroke in a diesel engine. *(Oldsmobile Division of General Motors Corporation)*

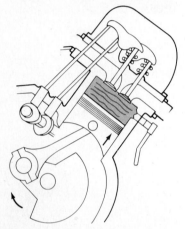

Fig. 17-2 Compression stroke in a diesel engine. *(Oldsmobile Division of General Motors Corporation)*

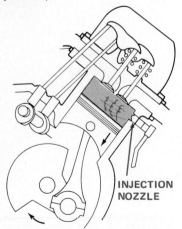

Fig. 17-3 Power stroke in a diesel engine. *(Oldsmobile Division of General Motors Corporation)*

not the same for all strokes. The four strokes of the diesel cycle are described below.

1. *Intake Stroke.* The intake valve is open and the piston is moving down (Fig. 17-1). Air moves through the air cleaner directly into the engine cylinder past the opened intake valve. The cylinder is filled with air only.
2. *Compression Stroke.* During the compression stroke, both valves are closed. The air is compressed as the piston moves up (Fig. 17-2). Compression ratios of diesel engines may be as high as 22:1. This means that the air is compressed to less than a twentieth of its original volume. Compression ratios are described in Chap. 7. When air is compressed, its temperature rises. The compressed air reaches 1000 degrees Fahrenheit [558 degrees Celsius] or more.
3. *Power Stroke.* As the piston nears TDC on the compression stroke, the diesel-engine fuel-injection system starts to spray fuel into the hot air in the cylinder (Fig. 17-3). The heat ignites the fuel and ignition starts. Pressure goes up in the cylinders. This forces the piston down on the power stroke.
4. *Exhaust Stroke.* The exhaust stroke is similar to that in the spark-ignition engine. As the piston moves up, the burned gases are pushed out past the opened exhaust valve (Fig. 17-4).

Several basic differences between diesel and spark-ignition engines are listed below. The diesel:

1. Has no throttle valve to restrict airflow into the engine
2. Compresses only air on the compression stroke
3. Has a much higher compression ratio
4. Ignites the fuel by heat of compression
5. Usually has glow plugs to help start the engine when it is cold
6. Has engine power and speed controlled by the amount of fuel sprayed into the cylinders

The following sections describe the fuel system and fuel-injection pumps used on diesel engines.

□ 17-2 DIESEL-ENGINE FUEL SYSTEM

The fuel system for an automotive diesel engine includes the fuel tank, fuel pump, fuel filters, transfer pump, injection pump, injection lines, and the injection nozzles, or injectors (Fig. 17-5). In addition, the fuel system may include a water detector in the tank and a *water-in-fuel* indicator light on the instrument panel (Fig. 17-6). The diesel engine *must* have clean fuel to operate properly.

In the diesel fuel system, the fuel pump is similar to the mechanical or electric fuel pump used with the spark-ignition engine (Chap. 14). The fuel pump draws fuel from the tank. Then the fuel pump pressurizes the fuel to about 7 to 15 psi [48 to 103 kPa] and delivers it to the fuel filter. The filter element is often made of pleated paper.

After the fuel is cleaned by passing through the filter element, the fuel flows to the *transfer pump* (Fig. 17-5). It increases fuel pressure to about 60 to 100 psi [413 to 690 kPa]. Then the transfer pump (which is usually part of the injection-pump assembly) delivers the fuel to the *injection pump.* This high-pressure pump meters the fuel and delivers it to the nozzle for each engine cylinder. Then the *nozzle* (Fig. 17-5) atomizes and delivers the pressurized fuel into the hot compressed air in the combustion chamber.

Special high-pressure lines called *fuel-injection tubing* connect the injection pump to the nozzles. At the right time, the injection pump pressurizes the fuel in each injection line to up to 4000 psi [27,579 kPa]. This forces the proper amount of fuel the engine needs to spray from the injection nozzle into the cylinder.

Most automotive diesel engines use one of two types of fuel-injection pumps to time and meter fuel delivery. These are discussed in following sections.

□ 17-3 TYPES OF DIESEL FUEL-INJECTION SYSTEMS

The compressed air in the diesel-engine cylinder, at the end of the compression stroke, is under high pressure. Therefore the fuel must be at a higher pressure for it to be injected into the compressed air. The diesel-engine fuel system (□ 17-2) includes a high-pressure injection pump or similar arrangement to inject fuel into the cylinders (Fig. 17-5).

There are two basic types of diesel-engine fuel-injection systems. In one, a centrally located pump pressurizes the fuel, meters it, and times it. Then the pump delivers the fuel at high pressure to the injection nozzles in the engine cylinders. This is the system used in cars and in many trucks and buses.

The other system sends the fuel at relatively low pressure to the fuel injectors. These injectors have cam-operated plungers which cause the injectors to spray the fuel, at high pressure, into the engine cylinders. This system is used on some heavy-duty diesel engines.

The centrally located pump system can be further divided into the following:

1. Cam-operated in-line plunger type
2. Rotary distributor type, now the most common system for passenger cars

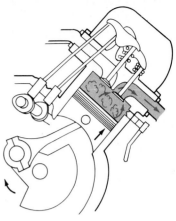

Fig. 17-4 Exhaust stroke in a diesel engine. *(Oldsmobile Division of General Motors Corporation)*

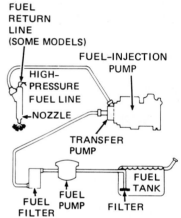

Fig. 17-5 Diesel-engine fuel system. *(ATW)*

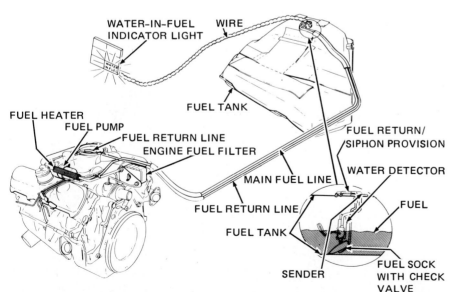

Fig. 17-6 Fuel-system layout for a transversely mounted engine. The system includes a water separator and a water-in-fuel indicator light. *(Oldsmobile Division of General Motors Corporation)*

□ 17-4 CAM-OPERATED IN-LINE PLUNGER PUMP

This pump has a barrel-and-plunger assembly for each engine cylinder. Figure 17-7 is a partial cutaway view of a fuel-injection pump for a six-cylinder engine. It has six plungers working in six barrels, one for each engine cylinder. The pump has a camshaft which is driven from the engine. The camshaft has a cam under each plunger. When the lobe of a cam comes up under a plunger, the plunger is raised. This forces fuel at high pressure to the injection nozzle in the engine cylinder (Fig. 17-8).

The quantity of fuel injected into the cylinder during each plunger lift is adjusted by turning the pump plungers. The top of each plunger has an inclined *helix* machined in it (Fig. 17-9). As the plunger is turned, its effective stroke is varied. The plungers are turned by moving the control rod. It is connected to the accelerator pedal through the *governor* and linkage (Fig. 17-8). When the accelerator pedal is pressed down, the pedal travel is converted to a corresponding control-rod travel.

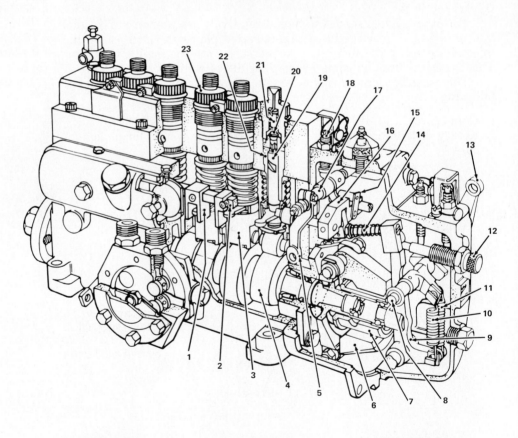

1 CONTROL FORK	9 CRANK LEVER	17 EXCESS FUEL DEVICE
2 CONTROL ROD	10 GOVERNOR MAIN SPRING	18 MAXIMUM FUEL STOP SCREW
3 **TAPPET ASSEMBLY**	11 GOVERNOR IDLING SPRING	19 PLUNGER
4 CAMSHAFT	12 DAMPER	20 DELIVERY VALVE
5 STOP CONTROL LEVER	13 SPEED CONTROL LEVER	21 VOLUME REDUCER
6 GOVERNOR FLYWEIGHT	14 TELESCOPIC LINK	22 BARREL
7 GOVERNOR SLEEVE	15 TRIP LEVER	23 DELIVERY VALVE HOLDER
8 SPEED LEVER SHAFT	16 BRIDGE LINK	

Fig. 17-7 In-line plunger pump for a six-cylinder diesel engine. *(CAV Limited)*

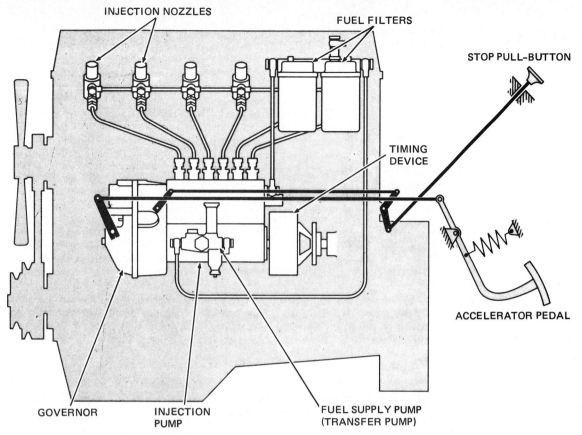

Fig. 17-8 Components of a fuel-injection system on an engine using a plunger pump. *(Robert Bosch Corporation)*

□ *17-5 GOVERNORS FOR FUEL-INJECTION PUMPS*

The fuel-injection pump on a diesel engine always includes a governor. This is a device on the engine that uses feedback—signals of changes in speed, load, or other conditions—to provide automatic control of fuel delivery. Actually, it is the governor that directly controls the amount of fuel injected into the engine. Movement of the accelerator pedal only changes the setting of the governor.

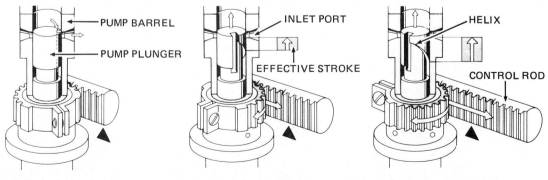

Fig. 17-9 Movement of the toothed control rod turns the pump plunger to vary the amount of fuel injected. *(Robert Bosch Corporation)*

Without a governor, a diesel engine will stall at low speed or run so fast that it will self-destruct. This is called *engine runaway*. Automotive diesel engines may use either a *mechanical* (or *centrifugal*) *governor* or a *pneumatic governor*. Both are types of *variable-speed governors*. *Constant-speed governors* are used when the engine must be held at a constant speed, regardless of load. This is required, for example, in the operation of a diesel-powered generator.

The governor (Fig. 17-7) performs three basic jobs. These are:

1. To maintain a certain engine speed regardless of load
2. To prevent the engine from overspeeding
3. To prevent the engine from stalling during idling or when the load is suddenly removed

The governor does these jobs by controlling the amount of fuel injected into the engine. As the amount of fuel needed changes, the governor automatically moves the control rod to vary the effective stroke of the plunger (Fig. 17-9).

Some diesel engines are turbocharged. These engines have a tube or hose from the intake manifold to the governor. This allows the governor to match fuel delivery with the pressure (or amount of air) in the intake manifold. Air-fuel ratios in a diesel engine range from about 100:1 at idle to about 20:1 under full load. The governor keeps the air-fuel ratio within these limits. If the air-fuel ratio gets richer than about 20:1, the diesel engine usually begins to produce unacceptable amounts of exhaust smoke.

The construction of a mechanical governor is shown in Fig. 17-7. The governor flyweights (6 in Fig. 17-7) spin with the camshaft. The faster they spin, the further out they swing. This acts on the control rod to adjust fuel delivery.

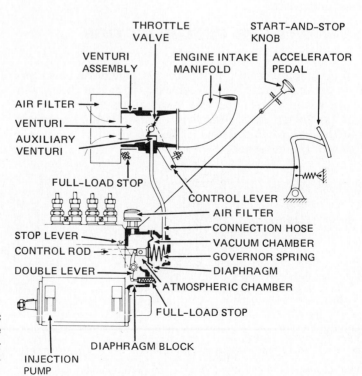

Fig. 17-10 When a pneumatic governor is used, a throttle valve is placed in the intake-air passage into the intake manifold. *(Robert Bosch Corporation)*

Figure 17-10 shows the basic layout of an engine with a pneumatic governor. It *has* a throttle valve in the intake manifold to create a vacuum. However, the purpose of the throttle valve is to provide a vacuum signal to the governor. The throttle valve is not used primarily for control of airflow into the engine.

A hose connects from a venturi section in the intake manifold to the vacuum chamber of a diaphragm assembly (Fig. 17-10). The control rod is attached to the vacuum-chamber diaphragm. This allows the governor to sense any changes in vacuum. As the throttle valve opens and closes, the varying vacuum causes the diaphragm and control rod to move. This adjusts fuel delivery as needed. Mercedes-Benz uses the pneumatic governor on some automotive diesel engines.

DISTRIBUTOR PUMP

☐ 17-6 ROTARY DISTRIBUTOR PUMP

The rotary distributor pump is used on most automotive diesel engines. Figure 17-11 is a schematic view of the fuel system using a distributor

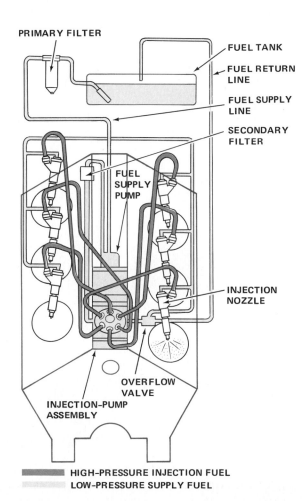

Fig. 17-11 Distributor-pump system for a V-6 diesel engine. *(General Motors Corporation)*

259

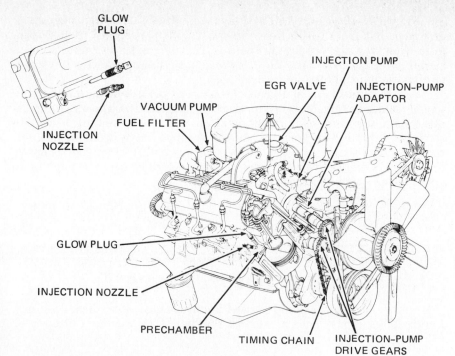

Fig. 17-12 V-8 diesel engine using a distributor pump, showing the pump drive arrangement. *(Oldsmobile Division of General Motors Corporation)*

Labels for Fig. 17-12:
- GLOW PLUG
- INJECTION NOZZLE
- VACUUM PUMP
- FUEL FILTER
- EGR VALVE
- INJECTION PUMP
- INJECTION–PUMP ADAPTOR
- GLOW PLUG
- INJECTION NOZZLE
- PRECHAMBER
- TIMING CHAIN
- INJECTION–PUMP DRIVE GEARS

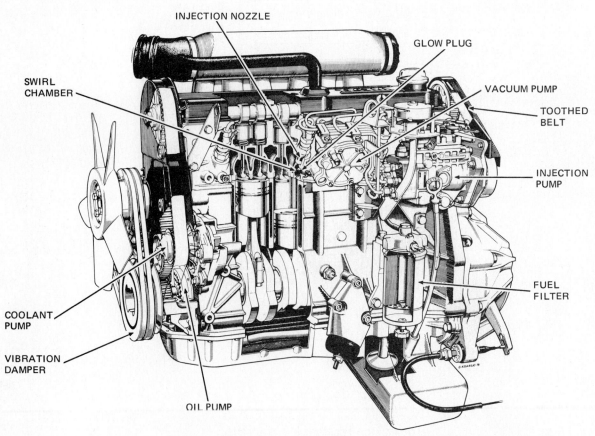

Labels for Fig. 17-13:
- INJECTION NOZZLE
- GLOW PLUG
- SWIRL CHAMBER
- VACUUM PUMP
- TOOTHED BELT
- INJECTION PUMP
- COOLANT PUMP
- VIBRATION DAMPER
- OIL PUMP
- FUEL FILTER

Fig. 17-13 Installation of a distributor pump on an in-line engine. *(Volvo of America Corporation)*

260

pump on a V-6 engine. Figure 17-12 shows a V-8 engine using the distributor pump. On General Motors V-type engines, the pump is driven by gears from the camshaft. Figure 17-13 shows how the pump is mounted on an in-line six-cylinder engine. In this installation, the pump is driven by a toothed belt from the back of the camshaft.

The distributor pump is similar in operation to the distributor in the ignition system. However, instead of electric sparks, the pump sends spurts of fuel to the engine cylinders in the proper firing order.

□ 17-7 FUEL-INJECTION NOZZLE

The fuel-injection nozzle (Fig. 17-14) is a pressure-operated valve. It serves to feed and atomize the fuel injected into the cylinders of a diesel engine. Each fuel-injection nozzle has a spring-loaded check valve, or delivery valve. The valve is closed except when high pressure is applied to the fuel. Then the check valve opens, allowing fuel to pass through. As the valve is pushed down off its seat, fuel begins to spray into the engine cylinder. There the fuel is ignited by the hot compressed air.

When the fuel pressure drops, the spring closes the valve. This stops injection of the fuel. The nozzle must close quickly to prevent "dribble." This is unwanted leakage of fuel into the cylinder following the end of the main injection.

□ 17-8 OPERATION OF THE ROTARY DISTRIBUTOR PUMP

Figure 17-15 shows the rotary distributor pump. Figures 17-16 and 17-17 show how the pump works. The pump has a rotor (Fig. 17-18) that includes a pair of cam rollers and plungers. These rollers roll on an internal cam (Fig. 17-19). As the rotor rotates, the rollers roll on the inner surface of the cam. They move in and out as they roll on the cam lobes. When they move out, they cause the plungers to move out. This causes the internal chamber to increase in size. Now fuel flows into the chamber.

When the rollers move in, they push the plungers into the chamber. This applies high pressure on the fuel in the internal chamber. At this instant, a port in the internal chamber aligns with a port connected by a high-pressure line to an engine cylinder. This cylinder is near the end of the compression stroke and ready for fuel to be injected (Fig. 17-17).

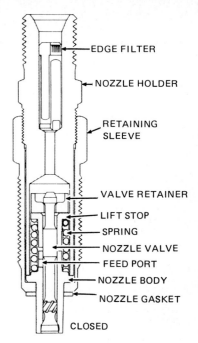

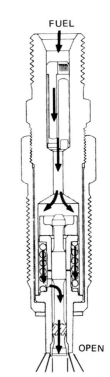

Fig. 17-14 Typical automotive diesel fuel-injection nozzle. *(General Motors Corporation)*

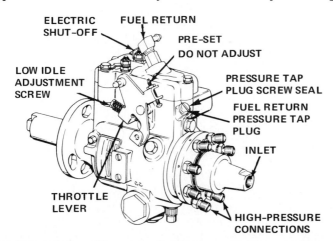

Fig. 17-15 External view of the rotary distributor pump. *(Chevrolet Motor Division of General Motors Corporation)*

261

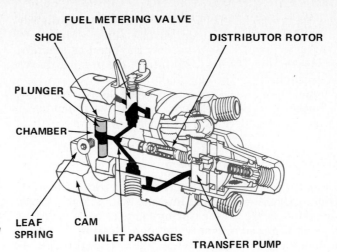

Fig. 17-16 Charging cycle in the distributor pump. The two plungers move apart to provide space for fuel to enter the chamber. *(Oldsmobile Division of General Motors Corporation)*

The amount of fuel injected is controlled by a mechanical governor (□ 17-5). It allows the correct amount of fuel to be injected. The proper engine speed and power result, as determined by the accelerator-pedal position.

□ 17-9 AUTOMATIC ADVANCE OF INJECTION TIMING

When injection occurs, the fuel is not delivered all at once. Fuel injection starts, continues for a fraction of a second, and then stops. The fuel begins to burn almost as soon as it is injected into the hot compressed air. However, the delay in time between the injection of the fuel and the start of combustion is called *ignition lag*. At slow speed, ignition lag is relatively

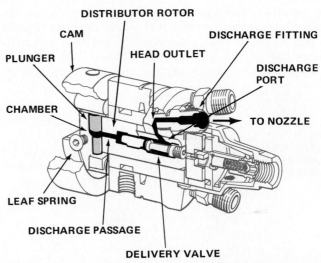

Fig. 17-17 Discharge cycle. The plungers are moving together, forcing fuel from the chamber, past the delivery valve, and through the discharge port. The rotor has turned so that the port in the rotor aligns with the next discharge port. This port is connected through a fuel line to the injection nozzle in the cylinder in which the piston is approaching TDC on the compression stroke. *(Oldsmobile Division of General Motors Corporation)*

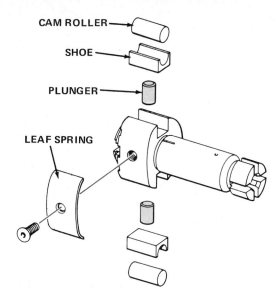

Fig. 17-18 Parts of the injection-pump rotor. *(Chevrolet Motor Division of General Motors Corporation)*

unimportant. But the faster the engine runs, the more ignition lag affects engine performance.

The fuel-injection pump includes an advance system to automatically provide earlier fuel injection as engine speed increases. Earlier ignition gives the fuel additional time to ignite and burn before the piston is too far down the cylinder on the power stroke. This compares with the advance system in the ignition distributor used on spark-ignition engines (Chap. 22). The advance allows the fuel to ignite and burn early enough so that maximum power results. Without advance, at high speed the piston is over TDC and moving down the cylinder before maximum combustion pressure occurs. If the piston stays ahead of the pressure increase, most of the energy in the fuel is wasted.

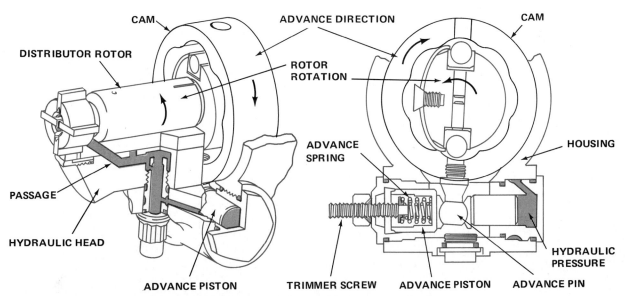

Fig. 17-19 Two views of the automatic advance system which provides automatic advance of injection timing. Hydraulic pressure, which increases with speed, moves the cam ahead. *(Oldsmobile Division of General Motors Corporation)*

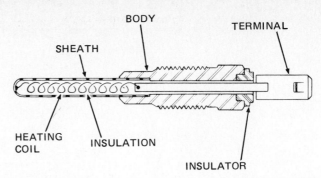

Fig. 17-20 Construction of a glow plug. *(General Motors Corporation)*

The advance mechanism is shown in Fig. 17-19. Its action depends on the hydraulic pressure—the pressure on the fuel coming from the transfer pump. As engine speed increases, the pressure on the transfer-pump fuel increases. This hydraulic pressure shifts the position of the internal cam, as shown in Fig. 17-19. As a result, the cam lobes move ahead and cause the rollers and plungers to move earlier. This advances the timing of fuel injection.

STARTING AIDS

□ 17-10 GLOW PLUGS

For easier starting, especially in cold weather, many diesel engines have *glow plugs*. Glow plugs have an electric heating element that becomes very hot when connected to the battery (Fig. 17-20). Figure 17-21 shows the location of a glow plug in an engine cylinder. It is located in the precombustion chamber. This chamber is where the fuel is injected and where ignition starts. After ignition and combustion start, the burning air-fuel mixture streams out into the main combustion chamber. There, it

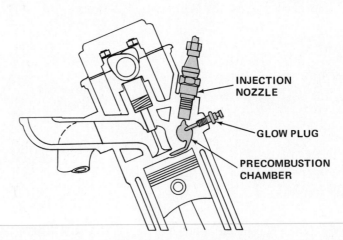

Fig. 17-21 The locations of the glow plug and injection nozzle in the precombustion chamber of a diesel engine. *(Volkswagen of America, Inc.)*

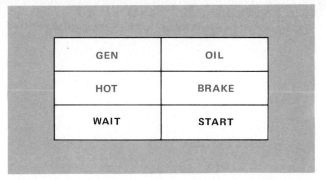

GEN	OIL
HOT	BRAKE
WAIT	START

Fig. 17-22 The instrument panel has two special lights, WAIT and START. *(Oldsmobile Division of General Motors Corporation)*

mixes with the combustion-chamber air and combustion is completed. Many diesel engines have precombustion chambers.

The position of the glow plug (Fig. 17-21) allows it to heat the precombustion chamber. Within a few seconds after the glow plug is turned on, the air in the precombustion chamber becomes hot. This assures ignition as soon as the fuel is injected.

☐ 17-11 DIESEL-ENGINE STARTING PROCEDURE

On some engines, the glow plugs can be turned on manually if they are needed for starting. In other engines, the system is semiautomatic. On these, the instrument panel has two special lights, WAIT and START (Fig. 17-22). The starting procedure is:

1. Put the transmission lever in PARK.
2. Turn the ignition switch (Fig. 17-23) to RUN. Do not turn it to START. When you turn the switch to RUN, an amber WAIT light comes on (if the engine is cold). This tells you that the glow plugs are on, heating the precombustion chambers in the engine.
3. After the precombustion chambers have been sufficiently heated (usually only a few seconds), the WAIT light will go out and the green START light will come on.
4. Now, push the accelerator pedal halfway down and hold it there. Turn the ignition switch to START. If the engine does not start after about 15

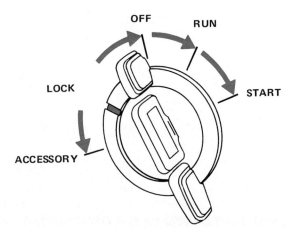

Fig. 17-23 Ignition-switch positions. *(Oldsmobile Division of General Motors Corporation)*

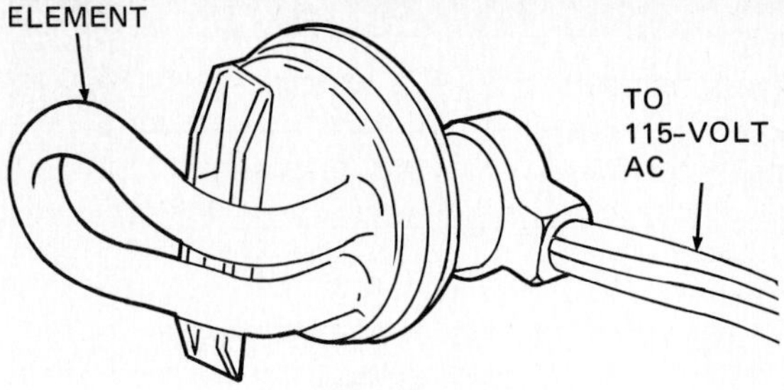

Fig. 17-24 Block heater, which is installed in a core-plug hole. When plugged into a 115-volt line, the heating element heats the coolant to make the engine easier to start in cold weather. *(Phillips Temro, Inc.)*

COOLANT HEATING ELEMENT

TO 115-VOLT AC

seconds of cranking, release the ignition switch. If the WAIT light comes on again, wait until the WAIT light goes off and the START light comes on again. Now try the starting procedure again.

NOTE Pumping the accelerator pedal will not aid in starting a diesel engine. There is no accelerator pump to force fuel into the air passing through the intake manifold on its way to the cylinders.

The starting instructions given above are for the General Motors automotive diesel engines. Other manufacturers have different starting instructions. These are given in the owner's manual and in the service manual.

□ 17-12 DIESEL FUEL HEATER

Cars that will be operated in cold weather can be equipped with an in-line diesel fuel heater (Fig. 17-6). The purpose of the heater is to warm the fuel so that the fuel filter does not plug with wax. This allows the use of number 2 diesel fuel in most cold-weather operations.

□ 17-13 BLOCK HEATER

For very cold weather where the temperatures are 0 degrees Fahrenheit [−18 degrees Celsius] and below, block heaters are often used to assist starting. This type of heater has an electric heating element that works from 115-volt house current (Fig. 17-24). The heater is installed in a freeze-plug hole in the engine block. To operate the heater, plug the electric cord into a regular electric outlet. The heater keeps the engine coolant warm so that starting is relatively easy. Without some type of heater, a diesel engine can be difficult to start in very cold weather.

ELECTRONIC FUEL INJECTION

□ 17-14 ELECTRONIC DIESEL FUEL INJECTION

Figure 17-25 shows a distributor type of electronic fuel-injection pump for use on diesel engines. The pump is controlled by a microprocessor. Sensors monitor the engine while it is running. Then actual engine performance is compared to the specifications which are programmed into the system memory. Timing, quantity, and duration of fuel injection are then automatically adjusted for maximum performance and fuel efficiency. This is similar to the operation of electronic fuel injection for spark-ignition engines (Chap. 16).

The system can be programmed to provide the driver with fuel-usage information and engine-service requirements. These are displayed on the instrument panel. The system also has a self-diagnostic capability. In addition, it can control other devices such as electronic fuel-injection nozzles, turbochargers, exhaust-gas recirculation valves, and automatic-transmission shifting.

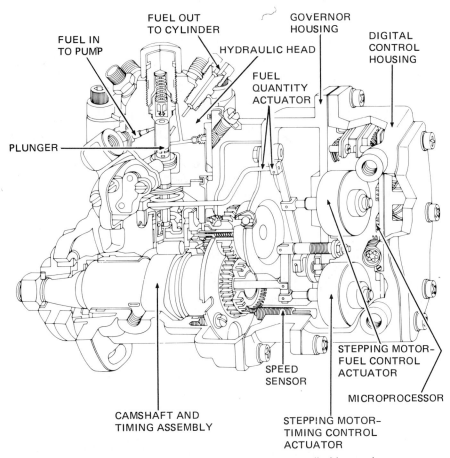

Fig. 17-25 An electronic diesel fuel-injection pump controlled by a microprocessor. *(United Technologies)*

Select the *one* correct, best, or most probable answer to each question. Then check your answers against the correct answers given at the end of the book.

1. A basic difference between the spark-ignition and the diesel engine is that
   a. air alone is compressed in the diesel
   b. the spark-ignition engine is heavier
   c. the diesel has a lower compression ratio
   d. fuel alone is compressed in the spark-ignition engine

2. In the diesel engine, engine power and speed are controlled by the
   a. position of the throttle valve
   b. amount of fuel sprayed into the cylinders
   c. amount of fuel sprayed into the intake manifold
   d. amount of air taken into the cylinders

3. In the diesel engine, the fuel is ignited by
   a. the ignition system
   b. the glow plugs
   c. heat of compression
   d. spark plugs

4. The most common type of fuel-injection system for automotive diesel engines uses a
   a. cam-operated in-line plunger pump
   b. set of cam-operated plungers in the injectors
   c. rotary distributor pump
   d. carburetor

5. In the distributor pump, the transfer pump sends fuel to the
   a. fuel injectors
   b. fuel-return line
   c. fuel filter
   d. fuel distributor

6. The distributor pump used on many automotive diesel engines sends
   a. air-fuel mixture to the cylinders
   b. compressed air to the injectors
   c. diesel fuel to the injectors
   d. gasoline to the cylinders

7. In the distributor the amount of fuel delivered to the cylinders is controlled by
   a. throttle-valve position
   b. manifold vacuum
   c. governor action
   d. none of the above

8. The distributor pump uses a speed-advance mechanism which controls the position of the
   a. cam ring
   b. injectors
   c. camshaft
   d. pistons

PART 3

AUTOMOTIVE ELECTRICAL SYSTEMS

Part 3 covers the various electrical systems used in automobiles. To provide an understanding of these systems, we first discuss electricity and electronics. Then we describe some of the actions of electricity, magnetism, diodes, and transistors. Next, we cover batteries, starting systems, charging systems, and ignition systems. For each of these, we describe their construction, operation, trouble diagnosis, and servicing. Part 3 ends with a look at other electrical units in the automobile. These include the lights, instruments, and signaling systems. There are six chapters in Part 3:

CHAPTER 18
ELECTRICITY AND ELECTRONICS

After studying this chapter, you should be able to:

1. Explain current flow and how electrons are made to move in a conductor.
2. Describe electromagnets and explain how they produce magnetism.
3. Define *amperes, voltage,* and *resistance* and explain how they are related in an electric current.
4. Explain how diodes and transistors work.

Electricity does many things for us. It gives us light. It runs much of the machinery around us (refrigerators, factory equipment, television sets, subway trains). It heats our homes. In the car, electricity does several jobs. It starts the engine when the ignition switch is turned on. It makes the sparks that ignite the compressed air-fuel mixture in spark-ignition engines. It operates the radio, the electric gauges, and the lights. Figure 18-1 shows the major parts of the automotive electrical system. This chapter describes all these electrical devices and the flow of electricity that makes them operate.

ELECTRICITY AND MAGNETISM

☐ 18-1 WHAT IS ELECTRICITY?

Nobody has ever seen what composes electricity. So we have to rely on the description of scientists. Electricity is composed of tiny particles. The particles are so tiny that it would take billions upon billions of them, all piled together, to make a spot big enough to be seen through a microscope. These particles are called *electrons*. Electrons are all around us in fantastic numbers. In 1 ounce [28 g] of iron, for example, there are about 22 million billion billion electrons. Electrons are normally locked into the elements that form everything in our world.

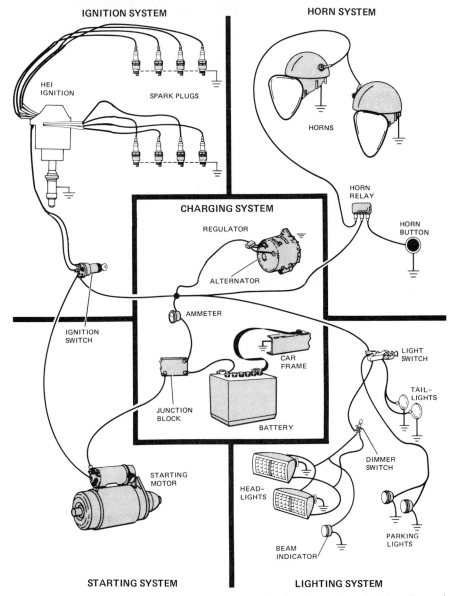

IGNITION SYSTEM

HEI IGNITION

SPARK PLUGS

HORN SYSTEM

HORNS

HORN RELAY

HORN BUTTON

CHARGING SYSTEM

REGULATOR

ALTERNATOR

AMMETER

IGNITION SWITCH

CAR FRAME

JUNCTION BLOCK

BATTERY

LIGHT SWITCH

TAIL-LIGHTS

DIMMER SWITCH

STARTING MOTOR

HEAD-LIGHTS

PARKING LIGHTS

BEAM INDICATOR

STARTING SYSTEM

LIGHTING SYSTEM

Fig. 18-1 Typical automobile electric system, showing the major electric units and the connections between them. The symbol ⏚ or ⌐⊤ means *ground,* or the car body, frame, or engine. By using these as the return circuit, only half as much wiring is needed. *(Delco-Remy Division of General Motors Corporation)*

☐ 18-2 ELECTRIC CURRENT

If electrons are forced to move together in the same direction, there is a flow, or current, of electrons. This flow is called an *electric current.* The job of the battery and the alternator is to get the electrons to flow in the same direction. When many electrons are moving, the current is high. When relatively few electrons are moving, the current is low.

☐ 18-3 MEASURING ELECTRIC CURRENT

The movement of electrons, or electric current, is measured in *amperes,* or *amps.* One ampere of electric current is a very small amount of current. A battery can put out 200 to 300 amperes as it operates the starting motor. Headlights draw 10 amperes or more. One ampere is the flow of 6.28 billion billion electrons per second.

We cannot count electrons to find out how many amperes are flowing in a wire. We must use an *ammeter* to find this out. The ammeter uses an effect of electron flow. This effect is that any flow of electrons, or electricity, produces magnetism.

☐ 18-4 MAGNETISM

There are two forms of magnetism: natural and electrical. Natural magnets are made of iron or other metals. Electrically produced magnets are called *electromagnets*. Natural and electromagnets act in the same way. They attract iron objects. Here are two important facts about magnets:

■ Magnets can produce electricity.
■ Electricity can produce magnets.

Magnets and electromagnets, and how they act, are described in later sections.

☐ 18-5 THE AMMETER

The ammeter measures electric current. A simple ammeter is shown in Fig. 18-2. It is used in the instrument panel of some cars. Its purpose is to tell the driver if the charging system is operating properly.

The ammeter works by magnetism. The conductor (in Fig. 18-2) is connected at one end to the battery. The pointer is mounted on a pivot. There is a small piece of oval-shaped iron mounted on the same pivot. This oval-shaped piece of iron is called the *armature*. A permanent magnet, almost circular in shape, is positioned so its two ends are close to the armature. The permanent magnet attracts the armature and tends to hold it in a horizontal position. In this position, the pointer or needle points to zero. When the alternator starts sending current to the battery, the current passing through the conductor produces magnetism. The magnetism attracts the armature and causes it to swing clockwise. This moves the pointer to the "charge" side. The more current that flows, the stonger the magnetism and the farther the pointer moves. The meter face is marked to show the number of amperes flowing.

Suppose the alternator is not working and the car lights are turned on. Current will flow from the battery to the lights. Now current will flow in the reverse direction through the conductor in the ammeter. Therefore, the armature is attracted in the opposite direction. It swings in a counterclockwise direction. This moves the pointer to the "discharge" side of the ammeter. The more current that flows out of the battery, the farther the pointer moves across the discharge side of the ammeter.

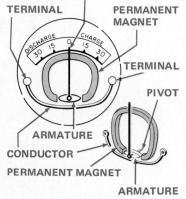

Fig. 18-2 Simplified drawing of a car ammeter, showing its interior construction.

☐ 18-6 MAKING ELECTRONS MOVE

Electrons on the move make up electric current. When too many electrons are gathered in one place, they try to move away. The battery and the alternator are devices that collect electrons. They collect electrons at one terminal by taking them away from the other. If the two terminals are connected by a conductor, electrons flow from the "too many" terminal to the "too few" terminal.

☐ 18-7 VOLTAGE

Suppose there are many electrons at one terminal. And suppose there is a shortage of electrons at the other terminal. When there is a great excess and a great shortage, we say that the electrical pressure is high. This means that there is a high pressure on the electrons to move from the "too many" terminal to the "too few" terminal.

Electrical pressure is measured in *volts*. High pressure is high voltage. Low pressure is low voltage. Car batteries are 12-volt units. Twelve volts is considered low pressure. The spark at the spark-plug gap is a flow of electrons at high pressure or voltage. The voltage at the spark-plug gap can be 35,000 volts or more. That's high, but not nearly as high as the voltage on cross-country power lines. The voltage in these lines may be several hundred thousand volts.

☐ 18-8 INSULATION

If electrons escape from the wire in which they are flowing, electric power is lost. That is the reason that electric wires are insulated. That's also the reason why power lines are hung from long insulators on power poles or towers. In addition to power loss, electrons can be dangerous. For example, if the insulation on the wire to a household appliance or a lamp is damaged, a fire could result. A person who touches the wire or appliance could get an electric shock.

In the car, the wires and cables between the battery, the alternator, and other electrical devices are all covered with insulation (Fig. 18-3). The insulation is a *nonconductor*. This means that it is extremely difficult for electrons, or electric current, to flow through it. But if the insulation goes bad, electric current will go where it is not supposed to. It could take a shortcut through the metal of the car frame and the engine. Such a shortcut is called a *short circuit*. It can cause trouble, as discussed later.

Insulation has the job of keeping the electrons, or the electric current, moving in the proper path, or circuit. Circuits include the wires and the electrical devices in the car.

☐ 18-9 MAGNETS

Magnets (☐ 18-4) act through *lines of force*. These lines of force stretch between the ends of the magnet. The two ends of the magnet are called

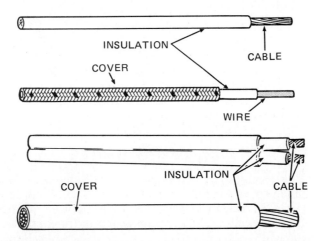

Fig. 18-3 Various types of automotive wiring, showing the insulation and outer cover. *(ATW)*

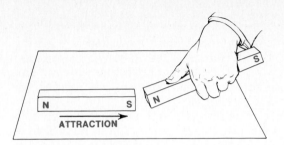

Fig. 18-4 Unlike magnetic poles attract each other.

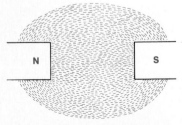

Fig. 18-5 Magnetic lines of force between two unlike magnetic poles try to shorten. This pulls together the two unlike poles.

the *magnetic poles*, or the *poles*. One pole is called the *north pole*. The other pole is called the *south pole*. The area surrounding the poles is called a *magnetic field*.

☐ 18-10 LINES OF FORCE

The lines of force have two characteristics. First, the lines of force try to shorten themselves. If you hold the north pole of one magnet close to the south pole of another magnet, the two magnets will pull together (Fig. 18-4). If we drew the lines of force between the two poles, the picture would look something like Fig. 18-5. The lines of force, stretching between the two poles, try to shorten. This tends to pull the two poles together.

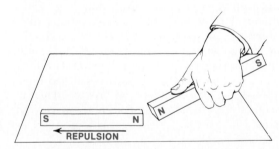

Fig. 18-6 Like magnetic poles repel each other.

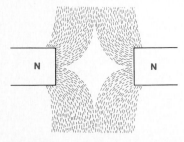

Fig. 18-7 Magnetic lines of force between two like magnetic lines of force tend to parallel one another. This forces the two like poles apart.

The second characteristic is that the lines of force run more or less parallel to each other. At the same time they try to push away from one another. Suppose we bring like poles together—two north poles, for example (Fig. 18-6). The lines of force run parallel to one another and try to push away (Fig. 18-7). The magnet that is free to move will move away as the same pole of the other magnet is brought closer.

We can draw these conclusions:

■ Like magnetic poles repel each other. North repels north. South repels south.
■ Unlike magnetic poles attract each other. North attracts south. South attracts north.

☐ 18-11 ELECTROMAGNETS

Electromagnets act just like natural magnets. An electromagnet can be made by wrapping a wire around a tube (Fig. 18-8). We saw what happened in the ammeter when current flowed one way or another through the conductor. The current produced magnetism, or magnetic lines of force.

Current flowing through a single wire, or conductor, will not produce much magnetism. But suppose you wind a conductor, or wire, around a rod. Then connect the ends of the wire to a source of electric current (or electrons). A strong magnetic field will develop around the coil of wire.

With current flowing through the winding, the winding acts just like a bar magnet. You can point one end of the winding toward a pole of a bar magnet. The winding will either attract or repel the bar-magnet pole. One end of the winding is a north pole. The other end is a south pole. You can change the poles by reversing the leads to the source of current. When the electrons flow through in one direction, one of the poles becomes north. But when the electrons flow through in the opposite direction, the poles reverse. The north pole becomes the south pole, and the south pole becomes the north pole.

An electromagnet such as the one made by winding wire around a tube is also called a solenoid. It is used in several places in the electrical system of the automobile. Solenoids are explained in more detail in later chapters.

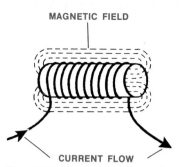

Fig. 18-8 Current flow through a wire coiled around a tube produces a magnetic field.

☐ 18-12 RESISTANCE

An insulator has a high resistance to the movement of electrons through it. A conductor, such as a copper wire, has a very low resistance. Resistance is found in all electric circuits. In some circuits a high resistance is needed to keep down the amount of current flow. In other circuits we want as little resistance as possible so that a high current can flow.

Resistance is measured in *ohms*. For example, a 1000-foot [305-m] length of wire that is about 0.1 inch [2.5 mm] in diameter has a resistance of 1 ohm. A 2000-foot [610-m] length of the same wire has a resistance of 2 ohms. The longer the path, the greater the resistance.

A 1000-foot [305-m] length of wire that is about 0.2 inch [5.1 mm] in diameter has a resistance of only ¼ ohm. The heavier the wire, the lower the resistance. The longer the path, or circuit, the farther the electrons have to travel. Therefore, the higher the resistance to the electric current. With the heavier wire, the path is larger. This means that the resistance is lower.

With most conductors, copper for example, resistance goes up with temperature. A hot copper wire will carry less current than a cold wire. The reverse is true for a few materials. The material in the engine sending unit of the cooling-system temperature indicator, for example, loses resistance as the temperature goes up.

☐ 18-13 OHM'S LAW

There is a definite relationship between amperes (electron flow), voltage (electrical pressure), and resistance. As the electrical pressure goes up, more electrons flow. Increasing the voltage increases the amperes of current. However, increasing the resistance decreases the amperes of current. These relationships are summed up in a formula known as *Ohm's law:*

Voltage is equal to amperage times ohms.
$$V = I \times R$$

where V = voltage
I = current in amperes
R = resistance in ohms

The important point about Ohm's law is that increasing the amount of resistance cuts down on the current flowing.

□ 18-14 ONE-WIRE SYSTEMS

For electricity to flow, there must be a complete path, or circuit. The electrons must flow from one terminal of the battery or the alternator, through the circuit, and back to the other terminal. In the automobile, the engine, car frame, and metal body are used to carry the electrons back to the other terminal. Therefore, no separate wires are required for the return circuit from the electrical device to the battery or the alternator. The return circuit is called the *ground*. It is indicated in wiring diagrams by the symbol ⁄⁊⁊ or ⏚ . Look at Fig. 18-1 and you will see many of these symbols. The ground—the engine, car body, and frame—is the other half of the circuit. It is the return circuit between the source of electricity (battery or alternator) and the electrical device.

□ 18-15 ALTERNATING CURRENT AND DIRECT CURRENT

Most of the electricity generated and used is alternating current (ac). The current flows first in one direction and then in the opposite direction. It alternates. The current you use in your home is ac. It alternates 60 times per second and therefore is called 60-cycle [Hz] ac. In the metric system, cycles per second are called *hertz,* abbreviated Hz.

The automobile cannot use ac. The battery is a direct-current (dc) unit. When you discharge the battery by connecting electrical devices to it, you take current out in one direction only. The current does not alternate, or change directions. Most electrical devices in the car operate on dc only.

ELECTRONICS

□ 18-16 FUNDAMENTALS OF ELECTRONICS

The words *electronics* and *solid-state* are key words today in the study of electricity and electronics. *Electronics* refers to any electrical assembly, circuit, or system that uses solid-state electronic devices such as transistors and diodes. A *solid-state* device is one that has no moving parts except electrons. Diodes and transistors are such devices.

Before electronics, all electric circuits were turned on and off by some type of mechanical switch. Now, electric circuits can be turned on and off electronically by devices that have no moving parts. An example is the primary circuit in the automotive ignition system. The old-style system used a set of contact points, which acted as a mechanical switch. The new electronic systems use a transistor to do this. The transistor acts faster, more accurately, and has no moving parts to wear. Ignition systems are described in Chap. 22.

Our interest is in what electronics do in the automobile and how it is done. First, we look at semiconductors, diodes, and transistors—the electronic devices that are the heart of electronic equipment. Basically, diodes are one-way valves that permit electricity to flow through in only one direction. Transistors can be electrical switches that start and stop current flow. Both diodes and transistors use materials called *semiconductors*.

Semiconductors are materials that are halfway between a conductor and a nonconductor. Sometimes they conduct, sometimes they act like insulators. This action is described when we discuss diodes and transistors in □ 18-17 and 18-18.

□ 18-17 DIODES

The *diode* is a device that permits electricity to flow through in one direction but not in the other. Figure 18-9 shows this. The alternator is the device in the automotive electrical system that produces current to charge the battery and operate electrical devices. However, the current from the alternator is alternating. So diodes are used to change it to direct current. You cannot use alternating current to charge the battery or operate most automotive electrical equipment. Direct current is required. Chapter 21 describes alternators and the diodes used in them.

□ 18-18 TRANSISTORS

The *transistor* is a diode with some additional semiconductor material. This added material makes it possible for the transistor to amplify current. In operation, a small signal current allows a large main current to flow. Figure 18-10 and 18-11 show this. In Fig. 18-10 a small current of 0.35 ampere is flowing to the base marked *n*. The *n* means that this slice of semiconductor material has extra electrons which have negative charges. When the extra electrons flow in (after the switch is closed), they form a path through which current can flow from one *p* slice to the other. This is shown by the arrows in Fig. 18-10. The *p* means that the material lacks electrons and therefore, in effect, has a positive charge.

When the switch is opened (Fig. 18-11), no current (electrons) flows into the *n* slice. Therefore, there is no path through the slice for electrons to flow from one *p* to the other.

In the transistor, a small current to the controlling slice of semiconductor material allows a large current to flow through the transistor. When this small current flows (which is called the *signal,* or *trigger current*), the large current flows. When the signal current stops, the large current stops.

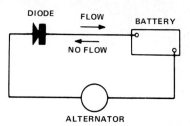

Fig. 18-9 Alternating current from an alternator can be rectified, or changed to direct current, by a diode so that the current can charge the battery.

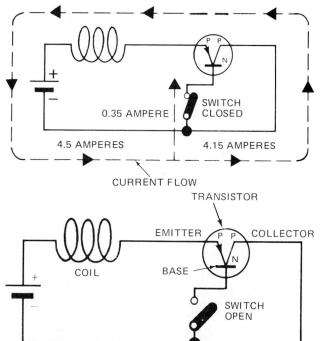

Fig. 18-10 When the switch is closed, current flows through the transistor.

Fig. 18-11 When the switch is open, no current flows.

□ 18-19 INTEGRATED CIRCUITS

Scientists and engineers have found ways to make diodes and transistors extremely small. This makes it possible to group large numbers of these semiconductor devices together in a small space. Such groups are called *integrated circuits* because many components are put together, or integrated, into a very small package called a *chip*. Integrated-circuit chips are used in computers and complex controlling devices. Examples in the automobile are the electronic ignition system, electronic fuel injection, and electronic engine-system controls, all described in other chapters.

□ 18-20 MICROPROCESSORS AND MICROCOMPUTERS

Many late-model cars have a small on-board solid-state electronic device called a *microprocessor*. This device combines logic and control circuits on a single integrated-circuit chip (□ 18-19). The chip acts as a central processing unit (CPU). Sensors provide input information to the microprocessor. Using this information, the CPU determines the desired response (if any) and provides the necessary output signal.

Figure 18-12 shows a *microcomputer* used in the General Motors Computer Command Control (CCC) system (Chap. 25). A microcomputer is basically a small but complete computer system that can receive, process, and present information in some usable form. It has a central processing unit made up of one or more chips, a memory, input/output devices, and a power supply. *Interface* devices allow its inputs and outputs to be connected to other devices.

The computer can do very complicated mathematics in a fraction of a second. For example, consider the electronically controlled fuel system (□ 15-12). The oxygen sensor in the exhaust system continuously reports to the electronic control unit (ECU) the amount of oxygen in the exhaust gas. The chip in the ECU compares this input signal with the information stored in its memory. If the oxygen content is not correct, the memory signals other components of the chip. The ECU then sends out a signal to the carburetor. This adjusts the air-fuel ratio so the amount of oxygen in the exhaust gas is corrected.

□ 18-21 ELECTRONIC DEVICES IN THE AUTOMOBILE

There are several electronic controls using chips or integrated circuits in automobiles. A partial list of automotive components using electronic controls includes:

1. Alternator voltage regulator (Chap. 21)
2. Electronic ignition system (Chap. 22)
3. Seat-belt interlock system (no longer used)
4. Air bags
5. Antilock braking system (Chap. 39)
6. Anticollision radar (still experimental)
7. Electronic fuel injection (Chap. 16)
8. Electronic engine control systems (Chap. 25)
9. Automatic level control (Chap. 41)
10. Accessories such as solid-state clocks, radios, and tape players, headlight dimmer, automatic on-off headlight control, speed controls, automatic temperature controls, and antitheft systems (Chap. 23)

Fig. 18-12 The electronic control module, or digital microcomputer, used in the General Motors Computer Command Control system. *(Pontiac Motor Division of General Motors Corporation)*

☐ 18-22 ELECTRICAL SYMBOLS

In the wiring diagrams in this book, and in the manufacturers' service manuals, you will find many electrical symbols. Figure 18-13 shows most of these symbols. As you examine wiring diagrams and schematics, become familiar with the symbols and their meanings.

ELECTRICAL SYMBOLS			
SYMBOL	REPRESENTS	SYMBOL	REPRESENTS
(ALT)	ALTERNATOR	HORN	HORN
(A)	AMMETER		LAMP OR BULB (Preferred)
—‖—	BATTERY-ONE CELL		LAMP OR BULB (Acceptable)
—‖‖—	BATTERY-MULTICELL	(MOT)	MOTOR-ELECTRIC
12 V +—‖‖—−	(Where required, battery voltage or polarity or both may be indicated as shown in example. The long line is always positive polarity.)	—	NEGATIVE
BAT	BATTERY-VOLTAGE BOX	+	POSITIVE
⊓⊓⊓	BI-METAL STRIP		RELAY
—◆—	CABLE-CONNECTED	—⋁⋁⋁—	RESISTOR
—‖—	CABLE-NOT CONNECTED		RESISTOR-VARIABLE
—)‖—	CAPACITOR	IDLE STOP	SOLENOID-IDLE STOP
	CIRCUIT BREAKER	B SOL / STARTING MOTOR	STARTING MOTOR
—<	CONNECTOR-FEMALE CONTACT		
—→	CONNECTOR-MALE CONTACT		
—≫—	CONNECTORS-SEPARABLE-ENGAGED		
—▶|—	DIODE	—o⁄o—	SWITCH-SINGLE THROW
DISTRIBUTOR H E I	DISTRIBUTOR	—o ⁄o—	SWITCH-DOUBLE THROW
⌒⌒	FUSE	(TACH)	TACHOMETER
(FUEL)	GAUGE-FUEL	—●	TERMINATION
(TEMP)	GAUGE-TEMPERATURE	(V)	VOLTMETER
—⊥	GROUND-CHASSIS FRAME (Preferred)		
—‖⫯	GROUND-CHASSIS FRAME (Acceptable)	⌒⌒⌒ OR ⌒⌒⌒	WINDING-INDUCTOR

Fig. 18-13 Electrical symbols used in automotive wiring diagrams. *(General Motors Corporation)*

Select the *one* correct, best, or most probable answer to each question. Then check your answers against the correct answers given at the end of the book.

1. Movement of electrons in one direction in a wire is called
   a. voltage
   b. electric current
   c. insulation
   d. watts

2. Electric current is measured in
   a. volts
   b. current flow
   c. amperes
   d. watts

3. Materials that strongly oppose the movement of electrons through them are called
   a. metals
   b. insulators
   c. conductors
   d. volts

4. Magnetic lines of force
   a. are a flow of electrons
   b. never exist in a dc circuit
   c. can be seen
   d. none of the above

5. When a great many electrons crowd around one alternator terminal and there is a shortage of electrons at the other terminal, the result is
   a. higher voltage
   b. lower voltage
   c. greater resistance
   d. higher alternator speed

6. Two basic facts about magnets are
   a. like poles attract, unlike poles repel
   b. unlike poles attract, like poles repel
   c. lines of force cross and shorten
   d. lines of force merge and lengthen

7. A solenoid
   a. is an electromagnet
   b. becomes magnetic when current flows through it
   c. includes a coil, or winding
   d. all of the above

8. Most electrical devices in the car operate
   a. on dc
   b. on dc or ac
   c. use neither ac nor dc
   d. are electro-mechanical

CHAPTER 19
BATTERIES

After studying this chapter, you should be able to:

1. Explain the construction and operation of automotive batteries.

2. Discuss battery efficiency and variations in terminal voltage.

3. Explain the chemical actions in the battery during charge and discharge.

4. Describe the various battery ratings and explain what they mean.

5. Describe battery maintenance and the various ways that batteries can be tested.

The battery supplies current to operate the starting motor and the ignition system when the engine is being started. It also supplies current for the lights, radio, and other electric accessories when the alternator is not handling the electric load. The amount of current the battery can supply is limited by the *capacity* of the battery. This, in turn, depends on the amount of chemicals it contains. Therefore, the battery is an *electrochemical device*. It produces electricity by converting chemical energy into electrical energy. This chapter explains how the battery works and how to keep it working.

BATTERY CONSTRUCTION AND OPERATION

☐ 19-1 BATTERY CONSTRUCTION

The 12-volt automobile battery has a series of six cells in the battery case (Fig. 19-1). Each cell has a number of battery plates with separators between them. When battery liquid, called *electrolyte*, is put into each cell, the cell produces an electrical pressure of 2 volts. The six cells in the battery produce a total of 12 volts. More exactly, each cell has a voltage of 2.1 volts when the electrolyte has a specific gravity of 1.250 and its temperature is 80 degrees Fahrenheit [27 degrees Celsius]. Specific gravity is described later in the chapter.

Many batteries have vent plugs on the cover of each cell. These vent plugs let gas escape from the battery when the battery is being charged.

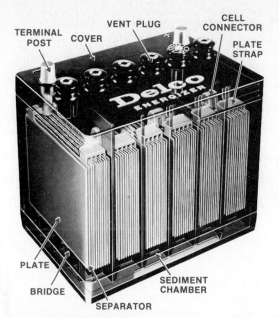

Fig. 19-1 A 12-volt automotive battery, shown as though the case is transparent so cell construction can be seen. *(Delco-Remy Division of General Motors Corporation)*

The vent plugs can be removed so that water can be added when the electrolyte level is low.

Some batteries are sealed. Because sealed batteries never need water, they do not need vent plugs. These batteries are often called *maintenance-free batteries* (Fig. 19-2). Many batteries have the terminals on the side instead of on top (Fig. 19-3). Figure 19-4 shows how this type of battery is mounted and how the cables are connected.

NOTE Delco-Remy calls its batteries "Energizers."

☐ *19-2 BATTERY ELECTROLYTE*

The battery electrolyte is made up of about 60 percent water and 40 percent sulfuric acid (in a fully charged battery). Here is what happens when electric current is taken out of a battery: The sulfuric acid gradually goes into the battery plates, which means the electrolyte gets weaker. As this happens, the battery runs down, or goes "dead." It then has to be recharged. The recharging job requires a battery charger. On the car, the alternator (Chap. 21) is the battery charger. The charger

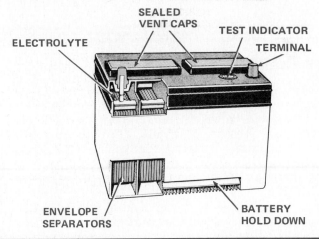

Fig. 19-2 A sealed maintenance-free battery with post-type terminals on top. *(Chrysler Corporation)*

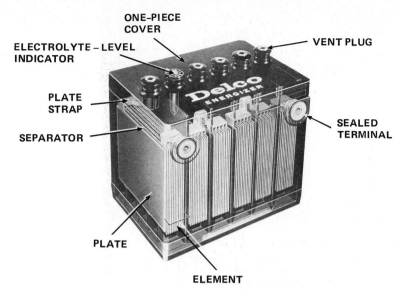

Fig. 19-3 A 12-volt battery with screw-type terminals in the side of the battery case. *(Delco-Remy Division of General Motors Corporation)*

ONE-PIECE COVER
ELECTROLYTE – LEVEL INDICATOR
VENT PLUG
PLATE STRAP
SEPARATOR
SEALED TERMINAL
PLATE
ELEMENT

pushes a current of electricity through the battery, restoring the battery to a charged condition. The current is pushed into the battery in a direction opposite to the direction in which it was taken out. There's more on this later.

☐ 19-3 BATTERY RATINGS

The amount of current that a battery can deliver depends on the total area and volume of active plate material. It also depends on the amount and strength of the electrolyte. This is the percentage of sulfuric acid in it. Factors that influence battery capacity include the number of plates per cell, the size of the plates, cell size, and quantity of electrolyte. The ratings most commonly used in referring to battery capacity are described below.

1. RESERVE CAPACITY

Reserve capacity is the length of time in minutes that a fully charged battery at 80 degrees Fahrenheit (°F) [27 degrees Celsius (°C)] can deliver 25 amperes. A typical rating would be 125 minutes. This figure tells how long a battery can carry the electrical operating load when the alternator quits. Some battery manufacturers rate their batteries in ampere-hours. To find the ampere-hour capacity of a battery, multiply the number of

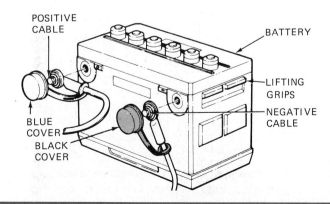

POSITIVE CABLE
BATTERY
LIFTING GRIPS
NEGATIVE CABLE
BLUE COVER
BLACK COVER

Fig. 19-4 Cable connections for a side-terminal battery. *(Cadillac Motor Car Division of General Motors Corporation)*

amperes by the number of hours. For example, the 125-minute rating means the battery is a 52.1 ampere-hour unit.

$$25 \times \frac{125}{60} = 52.1$$

2. COLD CRANKING RATE

One of the two cold cranking rates is the number of amperes that a battery can deliver for 30 seconds when it is at 0°F [−18°C] without the cell voltages falling below 1.2 volts. A typical rating for a battery with a reserve capacity of 125 minutes would be 430 amperes. This figure indicates the ability of the battery to crank the engine at low temperatures. The second cold cranking rate is measured at −20°F [−29°C]. In this case, the final voltage is allowed to drop to 1.0 volt per cell. A typical rating for a battery with a reserve capacity of 125 minutes would be 320 amperes.

Other battery ratings include overcharge life units, charge acceptance, and watts. They are described in detail in *Automotive Electronics and Electrical Equipment,* a book in the McGraw-Hill Automotive Technology Series.

BATTERY SERVICE AND TESTING

□ 19-4 BATTERY MAINTENANCE

Battery failure is one of the more common car troubles. In most cases, battery failure can be avoided if the battery is checked regularly. Here are the maintenance checks you should make:

1. Check the electrolyte level in all cells.
2. Add water if the electrolyte level is low.
3. Clean off corrosion around the battery terminals.
4. Check the battery condition with a tester.

These maintenance steps are described in the following sections.

□ 19-5 CHECKING ELECTROLYTE LEVEL AND ADDING WATER

To check electrolyte level, remove the vent caps on the battery and look into the cells. If the electrolyte level is low, add water.

NOTE You can't check battery cells on sealed batteries. But you can make sure that connections are clean and tight at the terminals. Some sealed batteries have a charge indicator in the cover (Fig. 19-3).

Many batteries have split rings in the cell covers. These rings show whether the battery needs water. Figure 19-5 shows how the electrolyte and split ring look when the electrolyte level is too low and when it is correct.

NOTE Don't add too much water! Too much water causes the electrolyte to leak out. The electrolyte will corrode the battery carrier and any other metal it touches.

ELECTROLYTE LEVEL LOW

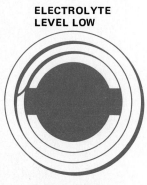

ELECTROLYTE LEVEL NORMAL

Fig. 19-5 The appearance of the electrolyte and split ring when the electrolyte level is too low and when it is correct. *(Delco-Remy Division of General Motors Corporation)*

☐ *19-6 CLEANING OFF CORROSION*

Battery terminals, especially those located on top of the battery, tend to corrode (Fig. 19-6). Corrosion builds up around the terminals and the cable clamps. To remove corrosion and clean the battery, mix some baking soda in a can of water. Brush on the solution. Wait until the foaming stops, and then flush off with water. If corrosion is bad, use a battery terminal cleaner to clean the terminal posts and cable clamps (Fig. 19-7).

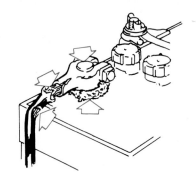

CAUTION The vent caps must be in place before cleaning the battery. Don't wash the top of the vent cap with either the baking-soda solution or the flushing water. Some of the baking soda might get down into the electrolyte through the vent hole in the cap. If this happens, the battery may be permanently damaged.

Fig. 19-6 Corroded battery cable and terminal post.

Don't be in a hurry for the battery to dry! If you can't wait for the battery to dry by itself, use a throwaway rag or paper towel. Then throw the rag or paper towel into the trash. Never use shop towels for wiping a battery. The shop air hose must never be used to air-dry the battery. The air stream might pull electrolyte out of the cell through the vent cap. Someone nearby could be seriously injured by this spray of battery acid.

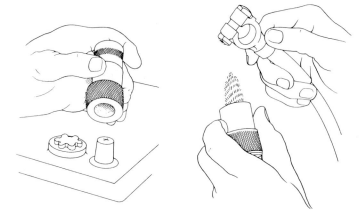

Fig. 19-7 Using a battery-cleaning brush to clean battery terminal posts and cable clamps. *(Buick Motor Division of General Motors Corporation)*

☐ *19-7 CHECKING BATTERY CONDITION*

There are several methods of testing the battery to find out its condition and state of charge. The hydrometer test and the high-discharge, or battery-capacity, test are the most common. When you work in the shop, your instructor will show you how to use the testers available. In the following sections, we cover only the main points of the tests.

☐ *19-8 HYDROMETER TESTS*

The hydrometer tests the specific gravity of the battery electrolyte. By measuring how much of the sulfuric acid remains in the water, the battery state of charge can be determined. There are two types of hydrometer. One contains a series of plastic balls, the other a glass float with a marked stem on it (Fig. 19-8). Both are used the same way. Insert the end of the rubber tube into the battery cell so the tube is in the electrolyte

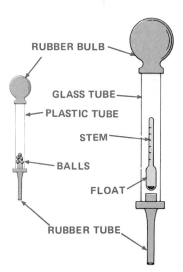

Fig. 19-8 Two types of battery hydrometers.

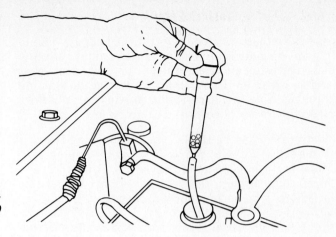

Fig. 19-9 Using a ball-type hydrometer to check a battery. *(K-D Manufacturing Company)*

(Fig. 19-9). Then squeeze and release the bulb. This draws electrolyte up into the glass tube. In the ball-type hydrometer, the number of balls that float indicate the state of charge of the battery cell. If all float, the cell is fully charged. If none float, the battery cell is run-down, or dead. Test all cells.

To use the float-type hydrometer (right in Fig. 19-8), place the end of the rubber tube in the electrolyte. Then squeeze and release the bulb to draw electrolyte up into the glass tube. On most hydrometers, the float will stick out above the electrolyte. The distance it sticks out above the electrolyte indicates the state of charge of the battery (Fig. 19-10). Take the reading at eye level (Fig. 19-11).

If the reading on the stem is between 1.260 and 1.290, the battery is fully charged. If the reading is between 1.200 and 1.230, the battery is only half charged. If the reading is around 1.140, the battery is almost dead and needs a recharge.

NOTE We do not usually refer to the decimal point in speaking of specific gravity. For example, we say the specific gravity is twelve-sixty (1.260) or eleven twenty-five (1.125).

CAUTION The electrolyte contains sulfuric acid! This is a dangerous acid that can give you serious skin burns. If it gets in your eyes, it can cause blindness. Sulfuric acid will eat holes in clothing, make spots on car paint finishes, and corrode any metal it touches. Be very careful when using the hydrometer to avoid spilling the electrolyte.

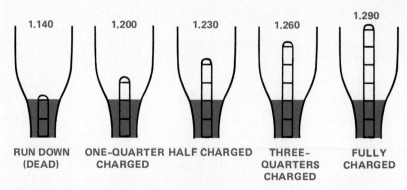

Fig. 19-10 Various specific-gravity readings.

If you get battery acid on your skin, flush it off *at once* with plenty of water. If you get acid in your eyes, flush your eyes with water over and over again (Fig. 2-7). Then get to a doctor at once! Acid can blind you.

After you have checked the electrolyte in the battery cell, squeeze the bulb to return the electrolyte to the cell from which you drew it.

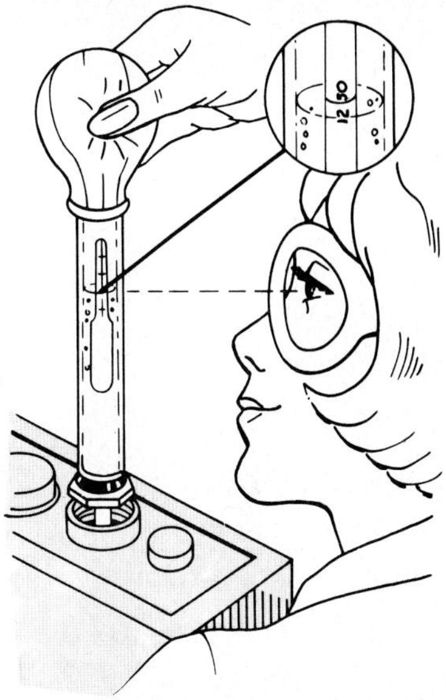

□ 19-9 BATTERY-CAPACITY TEST

The battery-capacity test is also called a *high-load test*. In this test, the tester puts a very heavy discharge on the battery for 15 seconds. The load should be 3 times the ampere-hour rating of the battery. Then the battery voltage is measured. If the battery voltage falls below 9.6 volts during this heavy load, then the battery is either discharged or worn-out. If it is worn-out, it should be replaced with a new battery. If the battery is only discharged, then it can be recharged and used again.

□ 19-10 CHARGING A BATTERY

If a battery is run-down but is otherwise in good condition, it can be given a charge with a battery charger and then put back into operation. The two ways to charge a battery are (1) by the slow-charge method, which may require taking the battery out of the car; and (2) by the quick-charge method, which can be done with the battery in the car. Figure 19-12 shows a battery ready to be charged with a quick charger. Certain precautions must be taken, regardless of which charger is used. With the quick charger, it is especially important not to overcharge the battery. If used in the wrong way, this charger can quickly ruin a battery.

CAUTION The gases that form in the tops of battery cells during charging are very explosive. For this reason, never have an open flame or lighted cigars or cigarettes around the battery. An explosion could occur that would blow the battery apart and you could be seriously injured.

Fig. 19-11 Using a float-type hydrometer to check a battery cell. Reading must be taken at eye level.

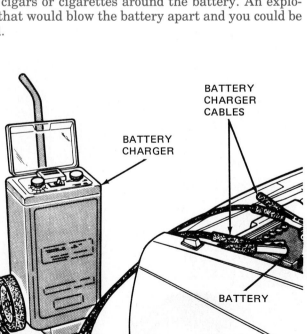

BATTERY CHARGER CABLES

BATTERY CHARGER

BATTERY

Fig. 19-12 Battery charger connected to a battery in the car and ready for charging. The grounded battery cable should be disconnected before the charger cables are connected. *(Chrysler Corporation)*

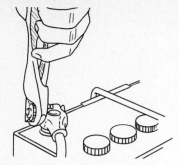

Fig. 19-13 Using battery pliers to loosen the nut-and-bolt type of battery-cable clamp.

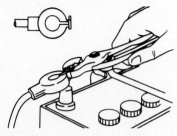

Fig. 19-14 Using pliers to loosen the spring-ring type of cable clamp from a battery terminal.

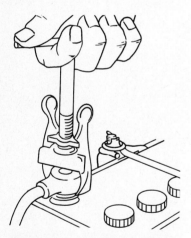

Fig. 19-15 Using a battery-clamp puller to pull the cable from the battery terminal.

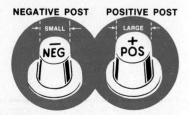

Fig. 19-16 The positive terminal post of the battery is larger than the negative terminal post.

☐ 19-11 IMPORTANCE OF KEEPING A BATTERY CHARGED

There are many reasons why it is important to keep a battery charged. A run-down battery will not start the engine. A discharged, or partly discharged, battery goes bad more quickly. Also, a discharged battery will freeze at about 18°F [−8°C]. But it takes −95°F [−35°C] to freeze a fully charged battery. Because a run-down battery can freeze, it is important to recharge it if it is low in cold weather.

☐ 19-12 REMOVING A BATTERY

When removing a battery from the car, be careful to avoid damaging the battery. Two types of battery terminals are used on automotive batteries. They are lead posts (Figs. 19-13 to 19-15) and side screws (Fig. 19-3). The battery with lead posts on top can be ruined if too much force is applied to the terminals as the clamps are loosened.

There are two types of battery-cable clamps: the nut-and-bolt type (Fig. 19-13) and the spring type (Fig. 19-14). Use battery pliers (Fig. 19-13) to loosen the nut-and-bolt type. If either type of clamp sticks to the post, don't pry the clamp off. This can break internal connections in the cable and battery. Instead, use a battery-cable puller (Fig. 19-15). If you hammer or apply force on the battery terminals, or lift the battery by the terminals, internal connections may break. This will ruin the battery.

CAREFUL When replacing a battery, don't install it backward. Don't connect the negative terminal to the cable clamp that should be connected to the positive terminal. This can cause serious damage. The negative terminal post of the battery is smaller than the positive terminal post (Fig. 19-16). Also, don't carry the battery by the terminal posts. Use a case-type battery carrier.

CAUTION Always disconnect the ground battery cable first. The ground battery cable is the cable or uninsulated strap fastened from the negative terminal of the battery to the car frame or engine. If you don't disconnect the ground cable first, you could accidentally ground the pliers or puller. This would cause a direct short across the battery. The result would be sparks and possible damage to the tool or the cable, or injury to yourself.

Select the *one* correct, best, or most probable answer to each question. Then check your answers against the correct answers given at the end of the book.

1. Which specific-gravity reading indicates a charged battery?
   a. 1.140
   b. 1.200
   c. 1.230
   d. 1.265

2. To check the state of charge of the battery, you should
   a. make a hydrometer test
   b. make a battery-capacity test
   c. both *a* and *b*
   d. neither *a* nor *b*

3. A battery is being tested by having a battery-capacity test made on it. Mechanic A says the battery voltage should not drop below 9.6 volts while the load is applied for 15 seconds. Mechanic B says the load should be 3 times the ampere-hour capacity of the battery. Who is right?
   a. A only
   b. B only
   c. both A and B
   d. neither A nor B

4. Reasons for keeping the battery charged include
   a. a run-down battery cannot start the car.
   b. a run-down battery can go bad more quickly.
   c. a low battery can freeze at low temperatures.
   d. all of the above

5. In a fully-charged battery, the electrolyte is
   a. 60 percent water and 40 percent acid
   b. 40 percent water and 60 percent acid
   c. 30 percent water and 70 percent acid
   d. 50 percent water and 50 percent acid

6. Maintenance-free batteries usually
   a. have no vent plugs
   b. are sealed
   c. never need watering
   d. all of the above

7. Two important battery ratings are
   a. size of plates and separators
   b. reserve capacity and cold cranking rate
   c. reserve capacity and hot cranking rate
   d. size and weight of battery

8. Be careful when working around batteries because
   a. they contain sulfuric acid
   b. the electrolyte can burn your skin
   c. the electrolyte can blind you if it gets in your eyes
   d. all of the above

CHAPTER 20
STARTING SYSTEMS

After studying this chapter, you should be able to:

1. Describe the construction and operation of starting motors.

2. Explain the purpose of the overrunning clutch and how it works.

3. Describe the construction and operation of magnetic switches and solenoids used in the starting system.

4. List the possible causes of trouble if the starting motor does not operate or if it operates slowly but the engine does not start.

Starting motors are also called *cranking motors* and *starters*. They are small but powerful electric motors that convert electrical energy from the battery into mechanical energy. When starting motors are working, they spin the crankshaft to start the engine. Starting motors are not very complicated, and they seldom need service.

STARTING-SYSTEM COMPONENTS AND OPERATION

☐ 20-1 STARTING-MOTOR OPERATION

The starting motor is operated by electromagnetism. Electricity flowing through wires and through coils of wire, or windings, produces electromagnetism. This leads to two important facts about magnets:

■ Like magnetic poles repel each other.
■ Unlike magnetic poles attract each other.

When current moves through a conductor, a magnetic field builds up around the conductor. If the conductor is in a magnetic field, as from a horseshoe magnet, a force is exerted on the conductor. Figure 20-1 shows the conductor in end view, with the resulting magnetic field indicated. The cross in the center of the conductor indicates that the current is flowing away from you.

Magnetic lines of force try to shorten themselves. Therefore, the bent lines of force in the magnetic-field pattern in Fig. 20-1 try to straighten

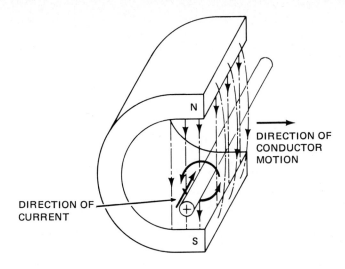

Fig. 20-1 Conductor held in the magnetic field of a magnet. The direction of current flow and the encircling magnetic field around the conductor are shown by arrows.

DIRECTION OF CONDUCTOR MOTION

DIRECTION OF CURRENT

out. As they do, they exert a push on the conductor. This is the principle upon which most electric motors operate.

If the conductor is bent into a U and the two ends connected to the two halves of a split copper ring, a simple electric motor is formed. Stationary *brushes,* connected to a battery and resting on the split ring, and the two poles of a magnet complete the motor. The brushes are carbon blocks that form sliding contacts with the *commutator.* In Fig. 20-2, the split ring is the commutator. It rotates with the U-shaped loop. Current flows from the battery through the right-side brush and segment of the commutator. The current flows through the conductor and left-side segment of the commutator and brush and back to the battery. This causes the left-side part of the conductor to be pushed upward and the right-side part to be pushed downward (Fig. 20-2). The result is that the loop rotates out from under the poles of the magnet.

When current flows through the loop, the magnetic field caused by the current opposes the magnetic field from the magnet. The result is that the magnet forces the loop out. In an electric motor, and in the start-

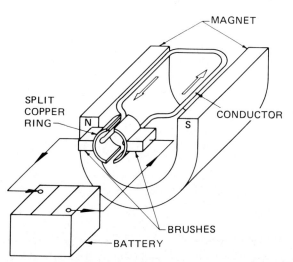

MAGNET

SPLIT COPPER RING

CONDUCTOR

BRUSHES

BATTERY

Fig. 20-2 Basic electric motor with a two-segment commutator.

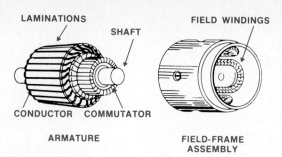

LAMINATIONS
SHAFT
FIELD WINDINGS
CONDUCTOR COMMUTATOR
ARMATURE
FIELD-FRAME
ASSEMBLY

Fig. 20-3 The two major parts of the starting motor: the armature and the field-frame assembly.

ing motor, there are many loops. The magnetic field they move in is very strong. So a strong force is applied to each loop.

☐ *20-2 STARTING-MOTOR CONSTRUCTION*

The basic parts of the starting motor are the armature and the field-frame assembly (Fig. 20-3). The armature has a series of wire loops, or conductors, mounted in a circle around the supporting shaft. The ends of the conductors are connected to the commutator. The purpose of the commutator is to connect the loops (through the brushes) to the battery as the loops rotate.

The field-frame assembly has windings. They produce the magnetic field in which the loops move.

The starting motor has other parts (Fig. 20-4). It has supports for the two ends of the armature shaft. It also has a drive gear to mesh with the flywheel ring gear. When the drive gear meshes with the flywheel ring gear and the armature spins, the flywheel and the engine crankshaft are rotated.

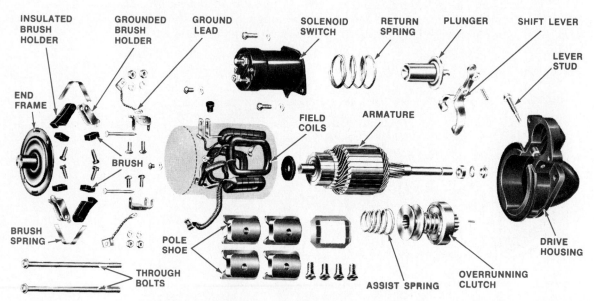

INSULATED BRUSH HOLDER GROUNDED BRUSH HOLDER GROUND LEAD SOLENOID SWITCH RETURN SPRING PLUNGER SHIFT LEVER LEVER STUD END FRAME FIELD COILS ARMATURE BRUSH BRUSH SPRING POLE SHOE DRIVE HOUSING THROUGH BOLTS ASSIST SPRING OVERRUNNING CLUTCH

Fig. 20-4 A disassembled starting motor. *(Delco-Remy Division of General Motors Corporation)*

□ 20-3 STARTING-MOTOR WIRING CIRCUIT

Figure 20-5 shows the basic wiring circuit of a starting motor. The current flows into the motor terminal and through the two field windings. From there, it flows through one brush and then through the armature conductors to the other brush. This brush is connected to ground, which is the return circuit to the battery. Ground is explained in Chap. 18. The brushes make sliding contact with the armature commutator. The commutator is made up of separate pieces, or segments, each connected to the end of one of the loops, or conductors. The armature conductors are not shown in Fig. 20-5.

When current flows through the starting motor, a very strong magnetic field is produced by the field windings. Another powerful magnetic field is produced by the armature conductors. The field-winding magnetic field tries to push the armature magnetic field out of the way. The result is a powerful downward push on the loops, which causes the armature to revolve. When the armature is connected to the engine flywheel through the meshing gears, it spins the engine crankshaft so that the engine starts.

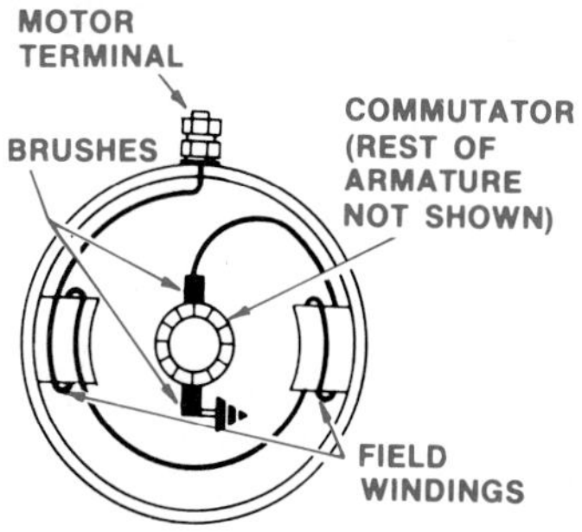

Fig. 20-5 Wiring diagram for a starting motor.

□ 20-4 STARTING-MOTOR DRIVES

The drive gear on the end of the armature shaft has only about 12 teeth. It is also called a *drive pinion*. The ring gear on the flywheel has about 15 times as many teeth. Therefore, the armature must turn 15 times in order to turn the flywheel once. In actual operation, the armature will spin about 3000 rpm (revolutions per minute). The spinning turns the flywheel and crankshaft about 200 rpm. This is fast enough to start the engine.

Now consider what would happen if the gears remained meshed when the engine started. If the engine were to speed up to 3000 rpm, the armature would be spun up to 45,000 rpm. That speed is fast enough to damage the armature and burn out the armature-shaft bearings. To prevent this from happening, the starting motor has an *overrunning-clutch drive*. This device meshes the drive gear for starting but demeshes it once the engine has started.

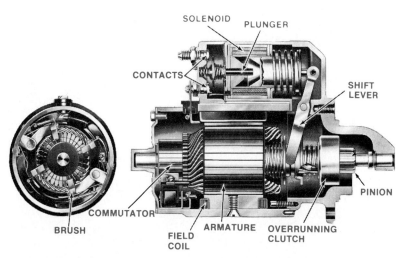

Fig. 20-6 End and sectional views of a starting motor using an overrunning clutch and solenoid. *(Delco-Remy Division of General Motors Corporation)*

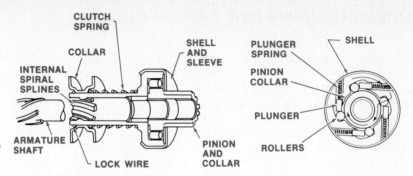

Fig. 20-7 Cutaway and end views of an overrunning clutch. *(Delco-Remy Division of General Motors Corporation)*

☐ *20-5 OVERRUNNING CLUTCH*

The *overrunning clutch* (Fig. 20-6) is a drive unit that transmits rotary motion in only one direction. This is from the starting-motor armature to the engine flywheel. When the engine starts and begins picking up speed, the teeth on the flywheel ring gear try to turn the overrunning-clutch pinion backwards. But as the rotary motion attempts to pass through the overrunning clutch, the pinion spins freely and fails to lock up. No motion is transmitted. This protects the starting-motor armature from damage after the engine starts. A solenoid on top of the starting motor operates to move the clutch-pinion teeth in and out of mesh with the flywheel ring gear.

Two views of an overrunning clutch are shown in Fig. 20-7. The clutch shown has four rollers positioned between the shell and the pinion and collar. The shell is attached to a sleeve. The sleeve has internal spiral splines that mesh with spiral splines on the end of the armature shaft. The sleeve and the shell can move back and forth along the shaft, but they must turn when the shaft turns. When the sleeve turns, the shell turns with it. As the shell turns, it causes the rollers to be pushed along in the notches in the shell. These notches are smaller at one end. As the rollers are pushed along, they jam in the smaller notches. The collar and pinion are locked to the rollers so that the pinion must rotate with the shell and the armature.

Figure 20-8A shows the pinion disengaged from the flywheel ring gear. To crank the engine, the solenoid must be connected to the battery. This connection is made through the ignition switch. When the key is inserted and turned past ON to START, current flows through the solenoid

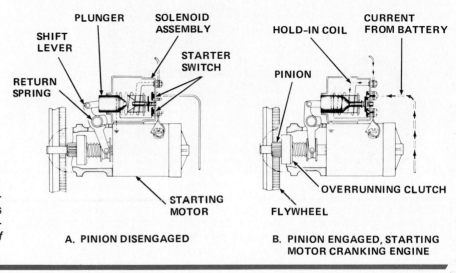

Fig. 20-8 Operation of the solenoid and overrunning clutch as the pinion meshes with the flywheel. *(Delco-Remy Division of General Motors Corporation)*

A. PINION DISENGAGED

B. PINION ENGAGED, STARTING MOTOR CRANKING ENGINE

and produces a magnetic field. The magnetic field pulls the iron plunger into the hollow center of the solenoid. This causes the overrunning-clutch assembly to be pushed along the armature shaft until the pinion engages with the flywheel ring gear.

As the plunger completes its movement into the solenoid (Fig. 20-8B), the plunger pushes a copper disk against two heavy contacts in the inner ends of the solenoid terminals. Now current flows from the battery, through the disk and terminals, and into the starting motor. The starting-motor armature begins to spin. The spinning armature spins the clutch sleeve. The rollers jam between the sleeve shell and the collar on the pinion. The pinion rotates and spins the flywheel, and the engine starts.

When the engine starts, the flywheel spins the overrunning-clutch pinion much faster than it originally was spinning. The pinion collar turns the rollers back out of the jamming part of the notches in the sleeve. Now the pinion and collar can spin freely without causing the armature speed to increase.

☐ 20-6 SOLENOID WINDINGS

There are two separate windings in the solenoid: a pull-in winding and a hold-in winding (Fig. 20-8). The pull-in winding has a few turns of a heavy wire. The hold-in winding has many turns of a relatively fine wire. The pull-in winding takes a high current through it and produces a strong magnetic field. A strong field is needed to pull the plunger in and shift the pinion into mesh. After the shift has been completed, a much smaller amount of magnetism is required to hold the plunger in. The pull-in winding is connected to the two heavy contacts. When the copper disk hits the two contacts to connect the starting motor to the battery, the copper disk shorts out the pull-in winding. However, the hold-in winding continues to do its job. It is connected from one contact to ground.

The purpose of the pull-in winding is to provide enough magnetism to shift the pinion into mesh. Then the pull-in winding is killed to reduce the load on the battery. The hold-in winding continues to hold the plunger in. This allows the battery to crank the engine without having to waste current where it is no longer needed.

☐ 20-7 GEAR REDUCTION

The starting-motor shown in Fig. 20-9 has a gear reduction which increases cranking torque. The shifter fork, when actuated by the solenoid, shifts the overrunning-clutch pinion into mesh with the flywheel. The gear ratio between the armature and the flywheel, because of the extra gears in the starting motor, is 45:1. The armature turns 45 times to turn the flywheel and crankshaft once. This provides high cranking torque for starting.

STARTING-SYSTEM SERVICE

☐ 20-8 STARTING-SYSTEM TROUBLE DIAGNOSIS

The following sections describe how to locate troubles in the starting system. If the trouble is in the starting motor, remove it from the car.

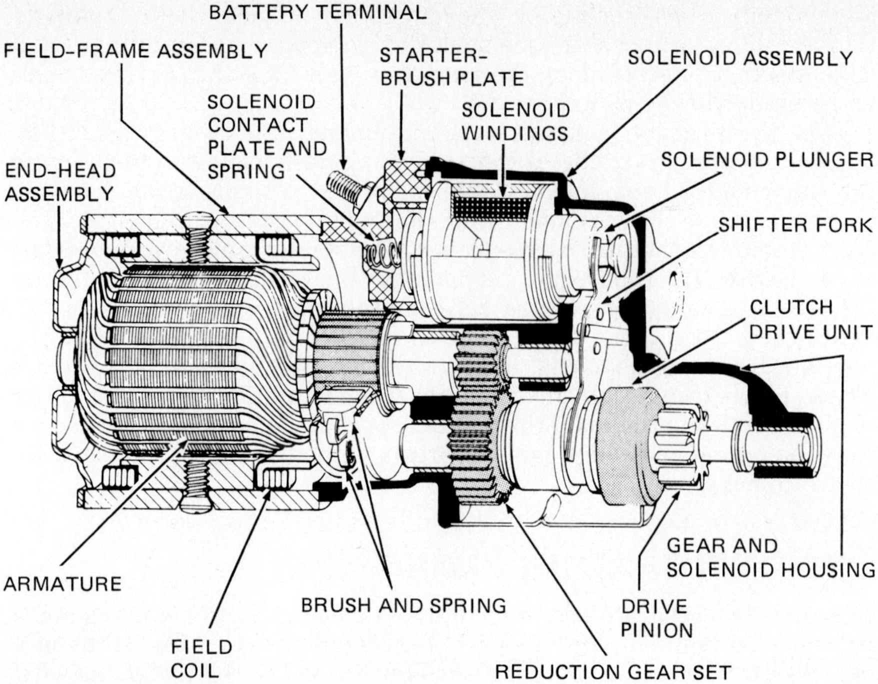

Fig. 20-9 Sectional view of a gear-reduction, overrunning-clutch starting motor. *(Chrysler Corporation)*

Then check the starting motor on the bench. Starting-motor service is often done in shops that specialize in automotive electrical work. In many shops, trouble in starting motors is fixed by "R and R." This means that the defective starting motor is *removed* and *replaced* with a new or rebuilt starting motor.

The basic starting-motor problems are:

■ The starting motor does not crank the engine.
■ The starting motor cranks slowly, but the engine does not start.
■ The starting motor cranks the engine at normal speed, but the engine does not start.

The last problem cannot be blamed on the starting motor. If it turns the crankshaft at normal cranking speed, the starting motor has done its job.

□ 20-9 STARTING MOTOR DOES NOT CRANK ENGINE

When you turn the ignition key to START and nothing happens, the first thing you probably think about is a dead battery. You may be right. But before you check the battery, do this. Turn on the headlights and try cranking. Five things could happen.

1. NO CRANKING, NO LIGHTS

When you try to start, if the starting motor does not do anything and the lights do not come on, either the battery is dead or a connection is bad. If you think there may be a bad connection, check the connections at the battery, at the starting-motor solenoid, and at the starter switch or relay.

2. NO CRANKING, LIGHTS GO OUT AS YOU TURN THE KEY

If the lights go out as you turn the key, there may be a bad connection at the battery. The bad connection lets only a little current through—enough for the lights to go on. But when you try to start, all the current goes to the starting motor because the starting motor has much less resistance than the lights. Therefore the lights go out. Try wiggling the battery connections to see if this helps.

3. NO CRANKING, LIGHTS DIM ONLY SLIGHTLY WHEN YOU TRY TO START

The trouble probably is in the starting motor. Either the pinion is not engaging with the flywheel, or there is an open circuit inside the starting motor. If you hear the starting-motor armature spin, then the overrunning clutch is slipping.

4. NO CRANKING, LIGHTS DIM HEAVILY WHEN YOU TRY TO START

This is most likely due to a run-down battery. The battery has sufficient charge to burn the lights, but not enough charge to deliver 200 to 300 amperes to the starting motor. Low temperatures place an added load on the battery. The starting motor needs more current to start a cold engine because the engine oil is thicker. The battery must be in good condition and fully charged in the winter to ensure starting. However, when the battery is charged and the starting motor fails to operate while the lights dim heavily, the starting motor or the engine may be seized or dragging.

5. NO CRANKING, LIGHTS STAY BRIGHT WHEN YOU TRY TO START

The trouble probably is either in the starting motor or in the circuit between the ignition switch and the solenoid. You have to check to find the problem. If the trouble is not in the wiring, then it is in the starting motor.

☐ 20-10 ENGINE CRANKS SLOWLY BUT DOES NOT START

This condition probably is due to a discharged battery. The battery cannot crank the engine fast enough for starting. Low temperature could be a factor here, as it was in number 4 above.

Also, the driver may have run down the battery trying to start the car. For example, there might be a problem in the engine, ignition, or fuel system that is preventing the engine from starting. The driver continued to crank until the battery ran down.

> **NOTE** Never operate the starting motor continuously for more than 30 seconds. Then pause for a few minutes to allow it to cool. It takes a very high current to crank the engine. This can overheat the starting motor if it is used for too long a time. Overheating can damage the starting motor.

Test the battery and replace it or recharge it, if necessary. Or, connect a booster battery and then try to start. If the engine will not start, the trouble is in the engine, not in the battery. As long as the starting motor cranks the engine normally, the starting motor is working properly. However, to start the engine the battery voltage must not fall below 9.6 volts during cranking (☐ 19-9).

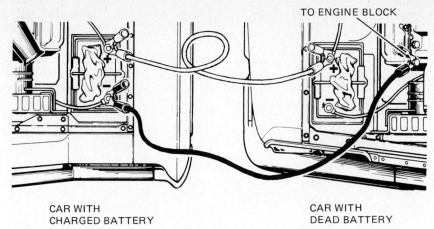

TO ENGINE BLOCK

CAR WITH
CHARGED BATTERY

CAR WITH
DEAD BATTERY

Fig. 20-10 Jumper-cable connections between the booster battery and the dead battery for starting a car with a dead battery.

CAUTION Use care in connecting a booster battery, to avoid hurting yourself or damaging the car electrical equipment. The correct connections for using jumper cables between two cars are shown in Fig. 20-10.

1. Remove the vent caps from both batteries. Cover the holes with cloths to prevent splashing of the electrolyte in case there is an explosion.
2. Shield your eyes.
3. Do not allow the two cars to touch each other.
4. Make sure all electrical equipment except the ignition is turned off on the car you are trying to start.
5. Connect the end of one cable to the positive (+) terminal of the booster battery. Connect the other end of this cable to the positive terminal of the dead battery.
6. Connect one end of the second cable to the negative (−) terminal of the booster battery.
7. Connect the other end of the second cable to the engine block of the car you are trying to start. *Do not connect it to the negative (−) terminal of the car battery!* This could damage electrical equipment.
8. Now start the car that has the booster battery. Then start the car that has the low battery. After the disabled car is started, disconnect the booster cable from the engine block. Then disconnect the other end of this (the negative) cable. Finally, disconnect the positive cable.

☐ 20-11 STARTING-MOTOR REPAIR

Repairing a starting motor is a job often performed by a tuneup technician. Other shops handle starter trouble by replacing the old starting motor with a new or rebuilt one. Figure 20-4 shows a completely disassembled starting motor. The major steps in rebuilding a starting motor are:

■ Replace bushings supporting the armature.
■ Test the armature and the field coils.
■ Turn the commutator if required.
■ Replace the field coils if they are damaged.
■ Check the solenoid.
■ Replace the brushes.

Select the *one* correct, best, or most probable answer to each question. Then check your answers against the correct answers given at the end of the book.

1. The three basic parts of the starting motor are the starting-motor drive and the
   a. armature and armature shaft
   b. armature and field-frame assembly
   c. field frame and switch
   d. field frame and armature shaft

2. A conductor that is carrying current in a magnetic field will
   a. resist attempts to move
   b. move to north pole
   c. move to south pole
   d. tend to move

3. The armature spins as the result of
   a. two opposing fields
   b. the armature magnetic field opposing the field-winding magnetic field
   c. current flow through the armature and field coils
   d. all of the above

4. In the starting motor, the armature windings and field windings are connected
   a. in parallel
   b. in series
   c. to separate terminals
   d. to the commutator

5. Comparing the number of teeth on the starting-motor drive pinion and on the flywheel ring gear, the
   a. ring gear has about 5 times as many teeth
   b. ring gear has about 15 times as many teeth
   c. drive pinion has about 15 times as many teeth
   d. two have the same number of teeth

6. The drive pinion is moved into mesh for cranking action by
   a. a shift lever
   b. pinion inertia
   c. sleeve turning in pinion
   d. an idler gear

7. The overrunning clutch
   a. protects the armature from damage after the engine starts
   b. is a one-way drive
   c. has a shell and rollers
   d. all of the above

8. The solenoid has
   a. one winding
   b. two windings
   c. three windings
   d. four windings

CHAPTER 21
CHARGING SYSTEMS

After studying this chapter, you should be able to:

1. Explain why a charging system is needed
2. Describe the construction and operation of an alternator
3. Explain the purpose and operation of alternator regulators
4. Discuss the possible causes of a defective charging system

To prevent the battery from going dead, the car must have a charging system. It keeps the battery charged by forcing current back into the battery while the engine is running. To control the alternator, a voltage regulator is always used with it. Wiring and switches connect the charging-system components. Fuses and fusible links act as circuit protection devices. They prevent further damage to the car electrical system if shorts or grounds occur in the charging system.

☐ 21-1 PURPOSE OF THE CHARGING SYSTEM

Figure 21-1 shows the basic components of the charging system. When current is taken out of the battery, the current must be put back in or a

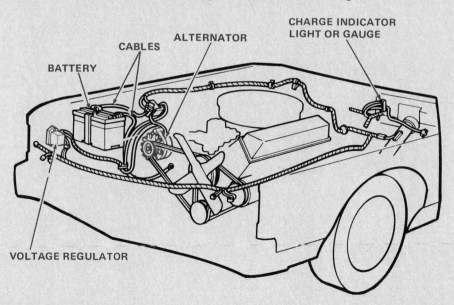

Fig. 21-1 Components of the charging system. *(Chrysler Corporation)*

run-down battery will result. The alternator does this job. It converts mechanical energy taken from the engine into electrical energy. The battery stores energy in chemical form which can be released as electricity. But the capacity of the battery is limited (Chap. 19).

The battery is part of every electric circuit on the car. Therefore the battery must have the capacity to supply current for all those additional electric loads. When the engine is running fast enough, the alternator takes over. Then it becomes the source of electric current for everything that is turned on. Now the alternator begins to put back into the battery the current taken out for starting. This is how the battery is kept charged. The alternator, along with the regulator and wiring, is called the *charging system* (Fig. 21-1).

CHARGING-SYSTEM OPERATION

□ 21-2 GENERATORS AND ALTERNATORS

A *generator* is a mechanical device that converts mechanical energy into electrical energy. There are two basic types: the direct-current (dc) generator and the alternating-current (ac) generator. These are shown in Fig. 21-2. Most mechanics refer to the dc generator as a "generator." The ac generator is called an "alternator."

For many years, cars used the dc generator. You won't see it today except on old cars and on some small-engine applications and farm tractors. The generator produces electricity when an armature is rotated in a stationary magnetic field.

The alternator is shorter than a generator and larger in diameter. In the alternator, the magnetic field rotates. The current is induced in stationary windings. The alternator is lighter in weight and simpler in construction. It has fewer parts to wear. Therefore the charging system today

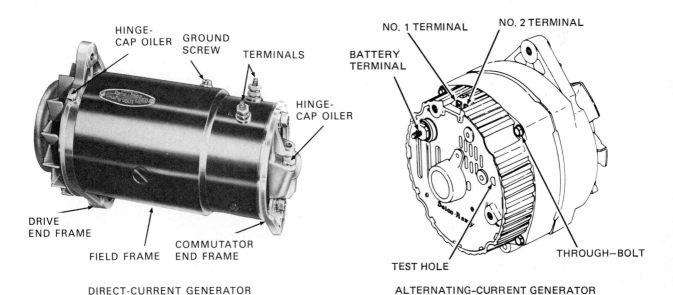

DIRECT-CURRENT GENERATOR
(GENERATOR)

ALTERNATING-CURRENT GENERATOR
(ALTERNATOR)

Fig. 21-2 Two types of generators are the direct-current generator and the alternating-current generator, which is usually called an "alternator."

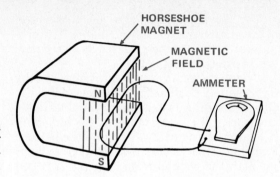

HORSESHOE MAGNET

MAGNETIC FIELD

AMMETER

N

S

Fig. 21-3 Inducing current in a conductor. Moving the conductor back and forth between the magnetic poles induces current in it.

requires much less service than the generator and regulator used years ago.

□ 21-3 GENERATING ELECTRICITY

Current flowing in a wire held in a magnetic field causes the wire to move. The reverse of this is also true. If you move a wire in a magnetic field, you will cause, or *induce,* current to flow in the wire. This process is called *electromagnetic induction* because electricity is induced by magnetism.

You can demonstrate this effect with a strong horseshoe magnet, a wire, and a sensitive ammeter (Fig. 21-3). Move the wire back and forth through the magnetic field. The meter needle moves first in one direction and then in the other. The same thing would happen if you held the wire stationary and moved the magnet. Either way, current flows through the wire.

Relative motion between the magnetic field and the wire is the key. The wire must cut across the magnetic field. When the wire cuts the magnetic lines of force, current flows in the wire. When the wire moves one way, the current flows in one direction. When the wire is moved in the opposite direction, the current flows in the other direction. This is how the alternator produces alternating current. The wires are moved back and forth, or the magnetic field is moved back and forth.

Actually, the "back-and-forth" movement in the alternator is rotary motion. The magnetic field rotates. This is the basic difference between a generator (dc) and an alternator (ac). In the generator, the magnetic field is stationary and the armature (conductors) rotates. In the alternator, the magnetic field rotates and the conductors (stator) are stationary.

Fig. 21-4 Alternator principles. The magnet rotates inside the stationary wire loop. As the magnet moves through the position shown at the top, current is induced in one direction in the loop. Then, as the magnet moves through the position shown at the bottom, current is induced in the opposite direction. Lines of force and directions of current flow in the top of the loop are shown in the small drawings to the right. The dot means the current is flowing toward you. The cross means it is flowing away from you.

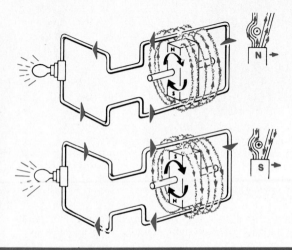

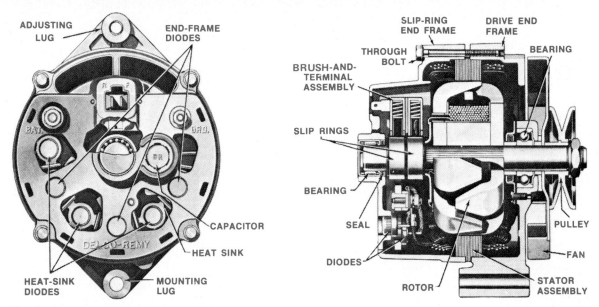

Fig. 21-5 End and side sectional views of an alternator. The manufacturer calls this unit a "Delcotron." *(Delco-Remy Division of General Motors Corporation)*

□ 21-4 ALTERNATOR PRINCIPLES

Figure 21-4 shows a simplified alternator. A stationary loop is held around a rotating magnet. As the magnetic field from the magnet cuts through the loop, current is induced in the loop. The current flows first in one direction as the north pole of the magnet passes the upper side of the loop. Then the current reverses direction as the north pole passes the lower side of the loop. As a result, the current that flows in the loop alternates. This makes it alternating current (ac).

The battery and most other electrical devices in the automobile cannot use ac. It must be converted into direct current (dc). Diodes do this job. They are described in □ 18-17.

□ 21-5 ALTERNATOR CONSTRUCTION

Figure 21-5 shows end and side sectional views of an alternator. In the alternator the rotating part is called the *rotor* (Fig. 21-6). It has a winding placed between two pole pieces, as shown in Fig. 21-7. When current is fed to the winding through the two brushes and slip rings, as shown in Fig. 21-6, magnetism is produced. The magnetism in the winding turns the points on the pole pieces into north and south poles. Magnetic lines of force go between the north and south poles, as shown in Fig. 21-6.

In the assembled alternator, the rotor is inside the stationary conductors, which are grouped together and called the *stator* (Fig. 21-8). When the rotor is rotated, the magnetic field it produces passes through the conductors in the stator. Current is induced in these conductors. The current is ac because north and south poles alternately pass the conductors. But the ac must be converted to dc. Diodes do this job (□ 21-6).

□ 21-6 DIODE OPERATION

A diode is a one-way electrical check valve (□ 18-17). It lets current flow through in one direction, but not in the other. For example, if you connect

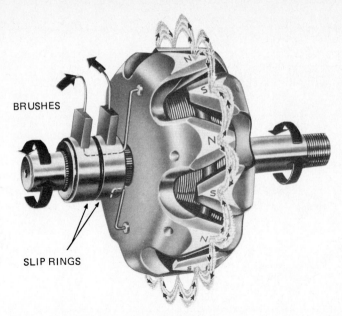

BRUSHES

SLIP RINGS

Fig. 21-6 The rotor of an alternator, showing the brushes in place on the slip rings. *(Delco-Remy Division of General Motors Corporation)*

a battery in one direction to a light bulb and a diode, the light will come on. But if you reverse the connections to the battery terminals, the light will not come on. The diode will not allow current to flow through it in the reverse direction.

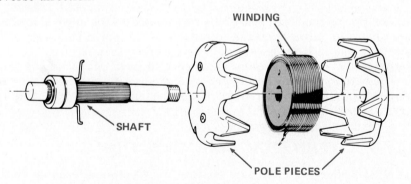

WINDING

SHAFT

POLE PIECES

Fig. 21-7 The rotor of an alternator, partly disassembled. *(Delco-Remy Division of General Motors Corporation)*

Fig. 21-8 The stator of an alternator. *(Delco-Remy Division of General Motors Corporation)*

Inside the alternator, alternating current is generated. If a simple alternator is connected through a diode to a battery, the diode will act as a *rectifier*. This is a device that changes alternating current to direct current. In the alternator, the rectifier allows only direct current (actually, pulsating dc) to flow through it to charge the battery.

□ 21-7 RECTIFYING ALTERNATING CURRENT

The diode is a *solid-state device*. It has no moving parts. The way the diode works in the alternator is a little more complicated than shown in Fig. 21-9. There are three sets of conductors in the alternator stator. Therefore, there are three different alternating currents, one in each set of conductors. This is why the automotive alternator is a "three-phase alternator."

The reason for having three phases in an alternator is the same as the reason for adding more cylinders to an automobile engine. More cylinders in an engine provide more power strokes and a smoother flow of power. Three phases in an alternator provide more current and a smoother flow of current.

The circuit for the diodes and the stator in a three-phase alternator is shown in Fig. 21-10. There are six diodes which make up the *diode rectifier,* or *rectifier bridge* (Figs. 21-11 and 21-12). The diodes usually are mounted in the slip-ring end frame. They work together to change the ac flowing in the stator windings into dc.

The three sets of conductors in the stator are all connected at the center. The current from each set of conductors makes up the total alternator output. In Fig. 21-10, 8 volts is generated in each stator winding. As the rotor revolves, its magnetic field cuts through windings A and B. The windings are connected so that the two voltages (8 + 8) add together to provide an internal alternator voltage of 16 volts. (The numbers in Fig. 21-10 show the voltages in each part of the circuit.)

Notice in Fig. 21-10 that only two diodes (the colored diodes) will conduct current. They are the only diodes in which current can flow in the forward direction. The other diodes will not conduct because they are *reverse-biased*. This means that the voltage is applied to them in the wrong direction. Current flow is blocked. Figure 21-10 shows that only 15 volts is available to charge the battery. This is because it takes from 0.5 to 0.7 volts to turn on each diode so that they will conduct, giving a total voltage drop of 1 to 1.4 volts.

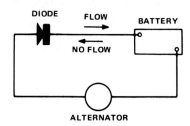

Fig. 21-9 Alternating current from an alternator can be changed to direct current by a diode. The diode allows current to flow in one direction only.

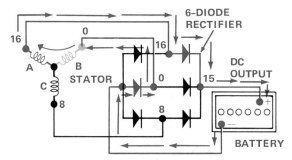

Fig. 21-10 In most automotive alternators, six diodes form a rectifier that changes the alternating current induced in the stator windings into direct current for charging the battery. *(Delco-Remy Division of General Motors Corporation)*

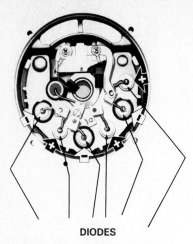

Fig. 21-11 Location of the six diodes in the end frame of an alternator. *(Delco-Remy Division of General Motors Corporation)*

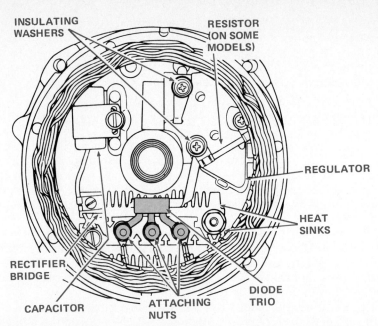

Fig. 21-12 In some alternators, the diodes are located in heat sinks to prevent their failure from overheating. *(Pontiac Motor Division of General Motors Corporation)*

□ 21-8 ALTERNATOR REGULATORS

The alternator must have a *regulator* to prevent damage to the car electrical system. An unregulated alternator will produce an excessively high voltage. This could cause damage by overcharging the battery, by burning out light bulbs and motors, and by shortening the life of the alternator. The regulator prevents these problems by limiting alternator voltage.

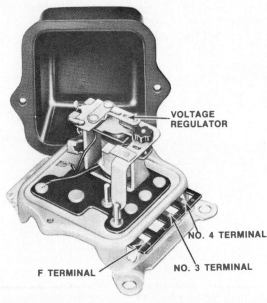

Fig. 21-13 An electromechanical type of alternator regulator with the cover removed. *(Pontiac Motor Division of General Motors Corporation)*

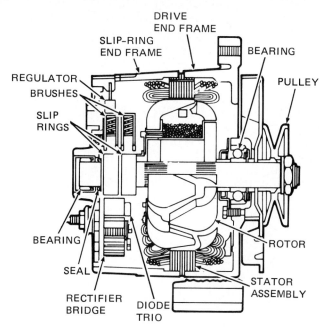

Fig. 21-14 An alternator with an integral, or built-in, solid-state voltage regulator. *(Pontiac Motor Division of General Motors Corporation)*

Earlier alternators used a separately mounted, or external, type of *electromechanical regulator* (Fig. 21-13). It uses vibrating contact points to limit current flow through the field windings. Late-model alternators have a solid-state regulator. Some are mounted internally in the alternator (Figs. 21-12 and 21-14). This type of regulator, which has no moving parts, is very small and compact (Fig. 21-15). It uses miniature transistors, diodes, resistors, and other electronic devices. When the regulator fits inside the alternator, this is called an *integral charging system*.

Both types of regulators control alternator voltage the same way. They limit the amount of current flowing through the field windings in the rotor. When the voltage goes too high, the voltage regulator cuts down the amount of current flowing to the field windings. This lowers the voltage by reducing the strength of the magnetic field. As a result, less current is induced in the stator windings.

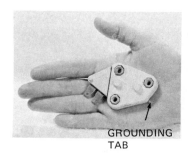

Fig. 21-15 A solid-state voltage regulator that fits inside an alternator. *(Delco-Remy Division of General Motors Corporation)*

CHARGING-SYSTEM SERVICE

□ *21-9 ALTERNATOR TROUBLE DIAGNOSIS*

Two conditions that occur with the alternator are:

1. Charged battery and a high charging rate
2. Discharged battery and a low charging rate

There could be other problems such as a noisy alternator or faulty ammeter or indicator-light operation. Noise is due to a loose mounting, a bad drive belt, or trouble inside the alternator. If the problem is inside the alternator, the alternator must be removed for bench checking. Bad bearings and some types of diode failure make noise. Faulty indicator-light or ammeter action is caused by a burned-out light, by defective wiring, or by trouble in the separately mounted regulator. If the problem is a bad regulator, it has to be removed and replaced with a new one.

☐ 21-10 CHARGED BATTERY AND A HIGH CHARGING RATE

If the alternator continues to force a high charging current into a charged battery, something is wrong. The voltage in the car will be high, head-lights will burn out, and other electrical devices may be damaged. The battery will be overcharged and will have a very short life.

The most likely cause of a high charging rate with a charged battery is trouble in the regulator. If the regulator is an external unit, it can be checked and adjusted or replaced. Defective regulators inside the alternator are replaced by disassembling the alternator.

☐ 21-11 DISCHARGED BATTERY AND A LOW CHARGING RATE

With a low battery, the charging rate should be high. If the battery is run-down and the alternator is producing little or no current, it could be caused by a loose or defective alternator drive belt or by some defect in the alternator or regulator. Make sure the drive belt is in good condition and tightened to the proper tension. If it is, look at the wiring and connections. A loose connection in the charging circuit can prevent current flow to the battery. The other possibility is trouble in the alternator or regulator. This requires checking and servicing of the alternator or regulator.

One way to determine if the trouble is in the alternator or in the regulator is to make an *alternator output test*. In this test, the regulator is bypassed. This allows the alternator to produce its maximum output. Many alternators with an internal regulator have a test hole in the end frame (Fig. 21-16). Insert a screwdriver in the hole until the blade touches the grounding tab (Fig. 21-15) on the regulator. Then move the screwdriver so its shank touches the end frame around the hole. This grounds the alternator field winding, bypassing the regulator. Now the alternator should produce its maximum output.

> **NOTE** You need a tester to check alternator output. The meters tell you the voltage and current output from the alternator. Many cars have charge-indicator lights instead of an ammeter in the instrument panel. On these, the only way to tell alternator output is with a test meter.

☐ 21-12 ADJUSTING ALTERNATOR DRIVE BELT

The drive belt must be properly tightened. A loose belt slips, squeals, and soon wears out. It does not drive the alternator fast enough to keep the battery charged. An excessively tight belt causes rapid bearing wear. Figure 21-17 shows the use of a belt-tension gauge. This tool applies a measured amount of tension to the belt to check the amount of deflection.

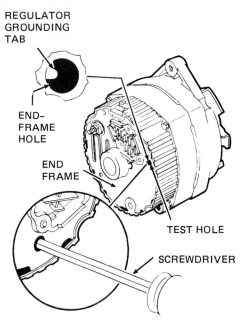

REGULATOR
GROUNDING
TAB

END–
FRAME
HOLE

END
FRAME

TEST HOLE

SCREWDRIVER

Fig. 21-16 To make an alternator output test, insert the screwdriver through the test hole in the alternator end frame until the screwdriver touches the grounding tab. Then ground the screwdriver against the end frame. *(Pontiac Motor Division of General Motors Corporation)*

If the deflection is too great, the belt tension is low and should be increased. To do this, loosen the alternator-mounting and adjusting-bracket bolts. Move the alternator outward to increase the tension. Tighten the bolts after adjustment is complete.

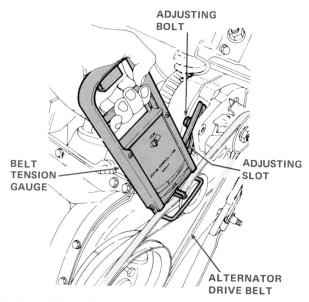

ADJUSTING
BOLT

BELT
TENSION
GAUGE

ADJUSTING
SLOT

ALTERNATOR
DRIVE BELT

Fig. 21-17 Using a belt-tension gauge to adjust the tension of the alternator drive belt. *(American Motors Corporation)*

□ 21-13 ALTERNATOR SERVICE

In some shops, a defective alternator is removed and replaced with a new or rebuilt alternator. However, an alternator can usually be taken apart easily. After the pulley nut and through bolts are removed, the alternator can be pulled apart and disassembled (Fig. 21-18).

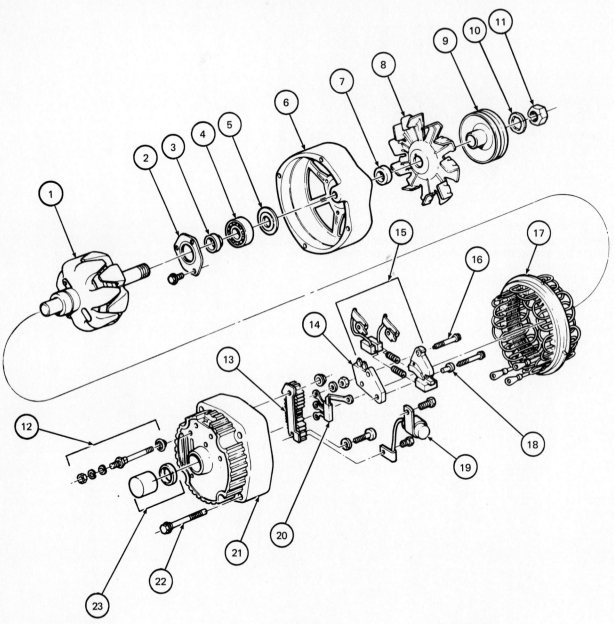

1. ROTOR	9. PULLEY	17. STATOR
2. FRONT-BEARING RETAINER PLATE	10. LOCKWASHER	18. INSULATING WASHER
3. COLLAR (INNER)	11. PULLEY NUT	19. CAPACITOR
4. BEARING	12. TERMINAL ASSEMBLY	20. DIODE TRIO
5. SLINGER	13. BRIDGE RECTIFIER	21. REAR HOUSING
6. FRONT HOUSING	14. REGULATOR	22. THROUGH-BOLT
7. COLLAR (OUTER)	15. BRUSH ASSEMBLY	23. BEARING-AND-
8. FAN	16. SCREW	SEAL ASSEMBLY

Fig. 21-18 A disassembled alternator. *(American Motors Corporation)*

Most alternator problems are caused by one of the three B's—defective belts (□ 21-12), bearings, or brushes and slip rings. If the slip rings on the rotor are slightly worn or pitted, they can be cleaned with 400-grain polishing cloth. Spin the rotor in a lathe while holding the polishing cloth against the slip rings. If they do not clean up, then replace the rotor. New slip rings can be installed on some rotors.

When you work in the shop, you will learn how to use the testers to check the parts of the alternator. Field windings and diodes should be checked with a test light or ohmmeter. If a diode tests defective, replace the diode rectifier or the heat sink with its three diodes.

□ 21-14 REGULATOR SERVICE

Many troubles that at first appear to be in the alternator can be traced to the regulator (□ 21-8). Suppose the charging-system indicator light comes on. You make an alternator output test (□ 21-11), and the alternator checks out good. Then the regulator is probably defective. However, before installing a new regulator, check out the wiring and connections. Try to find any condition that could have caused the problem or could have caused the regulator to fail.

Select the *one* correct, best, or most probable answer to each question. Then check your answers against the correct answers given at the end of the book.

1. In the alternator, the conductors in which current is induced
   a. are in the armature
   b. rotate
   c. are series connected
   d. are stationary

2. In most alternators, the magnetic field is produced by
   a. stationary field coils
   b. the stator windings
   c. field windings in the rotor
   d. alternator magnets

3. The typical automotive alternator is
   a. one-phase
   b. two-phase
   c. three-phase
   d. four-phase

4. The rectifier used with the alternator has
   a. six diodes
   b. five diodes
   c. four diodes
   d. two diodes

5. Most integral, or built-in, voltage regulators
   a. are adjustable
   b. are not adjustable
   c. are the electromechanical type
   d. do not use transistors

6. Trouble in the alternator could cause
   a. a charged battery and a high charging rate
   b. a discharged battery and a low charging rate
   c. noise in the alternator
   d. all of the above

7. The cause of a discharged battery and a low charging rate could be
   a. trouble in the alternator
   b. trouble in the regulator
   c. loose drive belt
   d. all of the above

8. When the alternator voltage goes too high,
   a. the regulator reduces current flow through the field windings
   b. the regulator reduces alternator speed
   c. the charge-indicator light comes on
   d. none of the above

CHAPTER 22
IGNITION SYSTEMS

After studying this chapter, you should be able to:
1. Explain the basic difference between the contact-point and electronic ignition systems.
2. Explain why spark-advance mechanisms are needed and how they work.
3. Discuss the advantages of electronic ignition systems.
4. Describe the difference between a Hall-effect distributor and other electronic distributors.
5. Explain the operation of the detonation-control system.
6. Describe the basic operation of an electronic spark-timing system.

In the typical running spark-ignition engine, less than 2 milliseconds—two one-thousandths (0.002) of a second—separate the spark at the plug and complete combustion. Therefore it is the crucial job of the ignition system to provide a spark at the right time. This spark must be hot enough to start the mixture burning. When the spark is weak (lacks enough heat) or occurs at the wrong time, maximum combustion pressure does not develop in the combustion chamber. Almost any change in engine operating conditions affects the voltage required to fire the plug and the best time for ignition to occur. The correct spark intensity and timing should produce maximum engine power, minimum fuel consumption and exhaust emissions, and no detonation. How contact-point and electronic ignition systems time and deliver the required spark is the subject of this chapter.

☐ 22-1 TYPES OF IGNITION SYSTEM

There are two general types of ignition system, contact point and electronic. Although they are slightly different in construction and operation, both do the same job. That job is to produce and distribute high-voltage surges to the spark plugs, at the correct instant. The contact-point ignition system is covered in the first part of the chapter. Then electronic ignition systems are described.

☐ 22-2 FUNCTION OF IGNITION SYSTEM

The ignition system (Figs. 22-1 and 22-2) supplies electric sparks that ignite, or set fire to, the compressed air-fuel mixture near the end of the

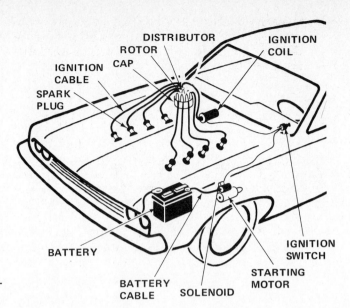

Fig. 22-1 Simplified contact-point ignition system.

compression stroke. The mixture burns and produces high pressure which pushes the piston down (□ 6-14).

The ignition system has mechanisms that vary the instant that the spark occurs. When the engine is idling, the spark occurs just before the piston reaches top dead center (TDC) on the compression stroke. But at higher speeds, the spark is advanced, or moved ahead, so that it occurs earlier. This gives the mixture enough time to start burning so that it will produce maximum pressure when the piston reaches TDC and starts down on the power stroke.

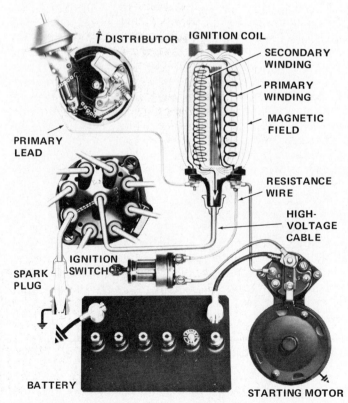

Fig. 22-2 Typical contact-point ignition system. It includes the battery, ignition switch, ignition coil (shown schematically), distributor (shown in top view with cap removed and placed below it), spark plugs (one is shown in sectional view), and wiring. *(Delco-Remy Division of General Motors Corporation)*

Also, when the throttle is only partly open, less mixture can get into the cylinder. There is less mixture to compress, and it will burn slower after it is ignited. Another mechanism in the ignition system advances the spark under these conditions so that the mixture has sufficient time to burn.

☐ 22-3 IGNITION-SYSTEM COMPONENTS

The ignition system includes the battery or alternator (source of electric power), ignition switch, ignition distributor, ignition coil, spark plugs, and wiring. Electronic ignition systems also have an electronic control unit. The ignition distributor and ignition coil, working together, take the low voltage from the battery or alternator and step it up to the high voltage required to jump the spark-plug gap in the combustion chamber. This high voltage may reach 47,000 volts or more. Figure 22-2 shows the components of a contact-point ignition system. It is the older system, used for many years, but now replaced in newer vehicles by the electronic ignition.

CONTACT-POINT IGNITION SYSTEM

☐ 22-4 PRIMARY AND SECONDARY CIRCUITS

The ignition system consists of two separate circuits—the *primary* circuit and the *secondary* circuit. The primary circuit includes the battery, ammeter, ignition switch, resistor or calibrated resistance wire, primary winding of the ignition coil, distributor contact points and condenser, vehicle frame, and primary wiring (Fig. 22-3). The secondary circuit includes the coil secondary wiring, distributor cap and rotor, spark-plug cables, spark plugs, and vehicle frame (Fig. 22-4).

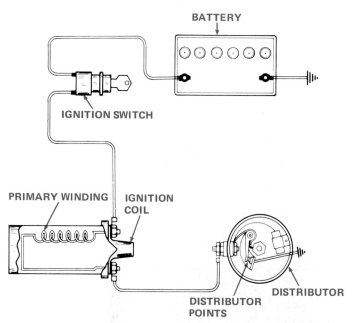

Fig. 22-3 Primary circuit in the contact-point ignition system.

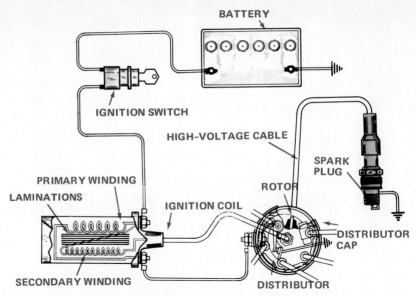

Fig. 22-4 Secondary circuit added to the primary circuit of the contact-point ignition system. Only one spark plug is shown.

With the ignition switch closed (in the ON position), primary-circuit current flows from the battery. The current flows through the primary winding of the coil and the closed distributor contact points to the ground (which is the return path), and then back to the battery. A cam mounted on the rotating distributor shaft causes the points to open and close at mechanically timed intervals. How long the points stay closed before they open again is called *dwell*. This is the number of degrees of distributor-cam rotation that the points stay closed. Figure 22-5 shows a typical contact-point distributor.

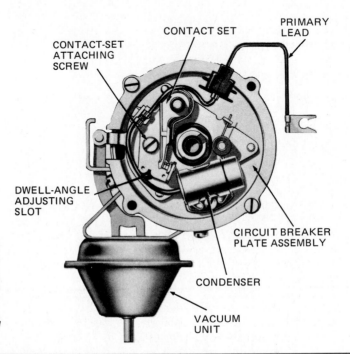

Fig. 22-5 Typical contact-point distributor. Note the cam in the center, which opens the points; the condenser, which controls arcing of the points; and the contact set, or breaker points. *(Delco-Remy Division of General Motors Corporation)*

☐ 22-5 IGNITION COIL

The ignition coil has two windings—a primary winding and a scondary winding. When the contact points are closed, current flows in the coil primary winding. The current flow through this winding causes a magnetic field to build up in the coil (Fig. 22-4). When the contact points open and break the circuit, the current flow stops and the magnetic field collapses. The collapsing field induces a very high voltage in the secondary winding. The distributor cap and rotor act as a rotary switch which sends the high voltage to the spark plug, causing a spark to jump the spark-plug gap. The spark must occur at the proper time to begin the power stroke.

☐ 22-6 CONTACT POINTS AND CONDENSER

The ignition spark occurs at the spark plug at almost the instant the contact points open. When the contact points begin to open, a voltage of up to 250 volts is induced in the primary circuit. This voltage is sometimes called the *ignition-system intermediate voltage*. It causes a small, momentary arc to form across the contact points. The arc forms when the current tries to flow across the points as they open to break the primary circuit. This arc could damage the points and shorten their useful life. To reduce the arc, a capacitor (or condenser) is connected across the contact points. The condenser has two purposes: (1) to bring the primary current to a quick stop, which helps collapse the magnetic field, and (2) to prevent or greatly reduce arcing across the points, thereby ensuring longer contact-point life.

☐ 22-7 HIGH VOLTAGE SURGE

The high-voltage surge flows from the coil secondary winding, across the distributor-rotor gap and spark-plug gap, to the spark-plug ground electrode (Fig 22-6). As the high-voltage surge jumps the spark-plug gap, it ignites the compressed air-fuel mixture in the cylinder to start the power stroke. Then the contact points close, and the ignition cycle repeats itself. This time it fires the next cylinder in the firing order. Because the rotor is keyed to the distributor shaft, when the points open again, the rotor has turned. Now it is aligned with the distributor-cap insert that is connected to the next spark plug to be fired.

> **NOTE** The distributor is driven from the engine camshaft and turns at the same speed as the camshaft. Therefore, the distributor shaft turns at one-half crankshaft speed. This means that 4000 engine rpm is 2000 distributor rpm.

☐ 22-8 PRIMARY RESISTANCE

To prevent excessive current flow in the primary circuit, some type of resistance is placed between the battery and the coil primary winding (Fig. 22-2). In many contact-point ignition systems, there is a resistor in the circuit between the ignition switch and the coil primary terminal. This resistor may be a calibrated resistance wire, an externally mounted resistor, or an internal resistance in the coil. The primary-circuit resistor prevents arcing and burning of the distributor contact points from excessive current flow. It does this by allowing full battery voltage to reach the coil primary winding only during cranking, for easier starting. During engine operation, the resistor reduces coil voltage to 5 to 8 volts.

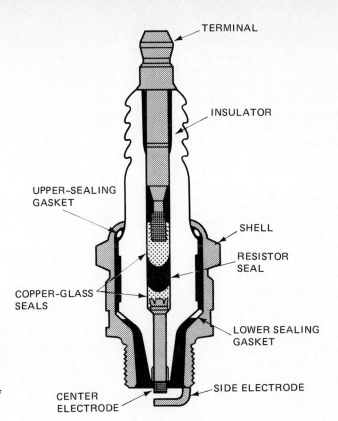

TERMINAL

INSULATOR

UPPER–SEALING
GASKET

SHELL

RESISTOR
SEAL

COPPER-GLASS
SEALS

LOWER SEALING
GASKET

CENTER
ELECTRODE

SIDE ELECTRODE

Fig. 22-6 Cutaway spark plug with a built-in resistor. High voltage from the coil causes a spark to jump from the center electrode to the side, or grounded, electrode. *(AC Spark Plug Division of General Motors Corporation)*

One system uses a temperature-sensitive external resistor to act as a current-compensating device. At low engine speeds, the primary current flows for longer periods of time. This heats up the resistor, thereby increasing its resistance and reducing the current flow. At high engine speeds, the current flows for shorter periods of time. This lets the resistor cool, increasing the current flow.

NOTE Most electronic ignition systems do not use a primary resistor.

☐ 22-9 ADVANCING THE SPARK

When the engine is idling, each spark is timed to occur at the spark-plug gap just as the piston approaches TDC on the compression stroke. This is shown in Fig. 22-7. At any speed faster than idle, the spark timing is *advanced,* so that the spark occurs earlier in the cycle. This gives the mixture more time to burn. Most distributors include a *centrifugal-advance,* or *mechanical-advance, mechanism.* It automatically advances the spark by pushing the breaker cam ahead as engine speed increases.

There is another condition during which spark advance should occur. This is when the engine operates at part throttle. At part throttle, less air-fuel mixture gets into the cylinders and combustion chambers. With less fuel in the combustion chambers, the mixture burns slower after it is ignited.

Since the mixture burns slower, the piston could be past TDC and moving down again before combustion produces a high pressure on the top of the piston. As a result, much of the energy in the fuel can be lost. The *vacuum-advance unit* is designed to prevent this loss by advancing the spark during part-throttle operation (Figs. 22-8 and 22-9). The unit

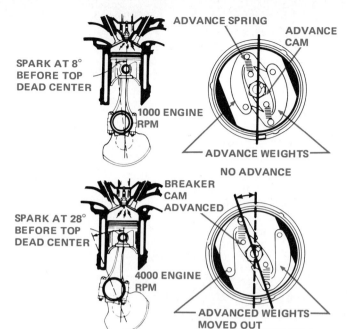

Fig. 22-7 Centrifugal-advance mechanism in the no-advance and full-advance positions. In the typical example shown, the ignition is timed at 8 degrees before top dead center on idle. There is no centrifugal advance at 1000 engine rpm, but there is 28 degrees of total advance (20 degrees centrifugal plus 8 degrees original timing) at 4000 engine rpm. *(Delco-Remy Division of General Motors Corporation)*

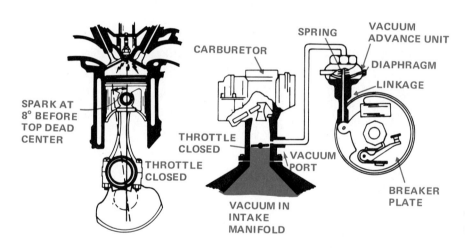

Fig. 22-8 When the throttle valve is closed, there is no vacuum advance.

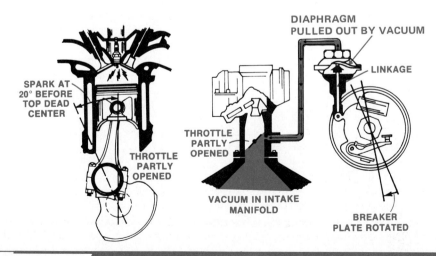

Fig. 22-9 When the throttle valve is partly open so that vacuum is applied to the vacuum-advance unit, the breaker plate is rotated, or moved ahead. The cam closes and opens the points earlier, to produce the vacuum advance.

moves the breaker plate so the primary circuit is opened earlier. The vacuum-advance mechanism, which is operated by intake-manifold vacuum, does improve part-throttle operation. However, under some conditions vacuum advance can increase the formation of nitrogen oxides (NO_x). The special controls that are used to prevent vacuum advance under conditions that could produce NO_x are described in Chap. 24.

NOTE *Ignition timing* usually refers to the adjustment of the distributor so that the primary current is stopped at the right time. When the primary current is stopped (either by the points opening or by the action of the transistor), a high-voltage surge is produced in the ignition-coil secondary winding. This high-voltage surge must reach the right spark plug at the right time. To change the time, the distributor is turned in its mounting. The adjustment shifts the position of the contact points, or the position of the pickup coil in the electronic system.

ELECTRONIC IGNITION SYSTEM

□ 22-10 ELECTRONIC IGNITION-SYSTEM COMPONENTS

The electronic ignition system has essentially the same components as the contact-point system (Fig. 22-10). Both include the battery or alternator, ignition switch, ignition distributor, ignition coil, wiring, and spark plugs. In addition, the electronic ignition system has an electronic control unit (ECU).

Instead of contact points, the electronic ignition distributor has a magnetic pulsing system which signals the electronic control unit. The electronic control unit then interrupts the primary current flow. Then the

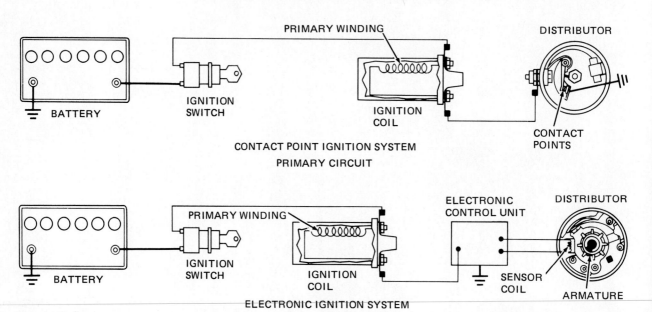

Fig. 22-10 Comparison of the primary circuits of a contact-point and an electronic ignition system.

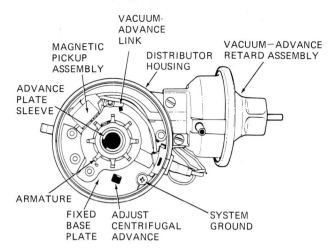

VACUUM-
ADVANCE
LINK

MAGNETIC
PICKUP
ASSEMBLY

DISTRIBUTOR
HOUSING

VACUUM—ADVANCE
RETARD ASSEMBLY

ADVANCE
PLATE
SLEEVE

ARMATURE

FIXED
BASE
PLATE

ADJUST
CENTRIFUGAL
ADVANCE

SYSTEM
GROUND

Fig. 22-11 Ignition distributor for an electronic ignition system. Note that Ford calls the rotating part an armature. Chrysler calls it a reluctor. *(Ford Motor Company)*

coil produces a high-voltage surge, which is led through the wiring, distributor cap, and rotor to the spark plug.

Figure 22-11 is a top view of an electronic ignition distributor for an eight-cylinder engine. Figure 22-12 shows this distributor partly disassembled. Instead of a cam and a set of contact points, it has a rotating member or "armature" with a series of tips and a magnetic pickup assembly. The voltage pulse is carried through wiring to the electronic control unit. The voltage pulse is a signal to the electronic control unit to turn off current flow to the primary circuit.

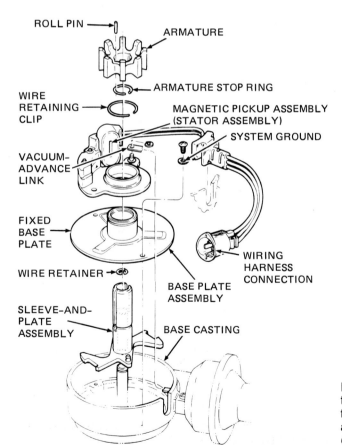

ROLL PIN

ARMATURE

ARMATURE STOP RING

WIRE
RETAINING
CLIP

MAGNETIC PICKUP ASSEMBLY
(STATOR ASSEMBLY)

SYSTEM GROUND

VACUUM-
ADVANCE
LINK

FIXED
BASE
PLATE

WIRE RETAINER

WIRING
HARNESS
CONNECTION

BASE PLATE
ASSEMBLY

SLEEVE–AND–
PLATE
ASSEMBLY

BASE CASTING

Fig. 22-12 Disassembled electronic ignition distributor, showing the magnetic pickup assembly and the armature. *(Ford Motor Company)*

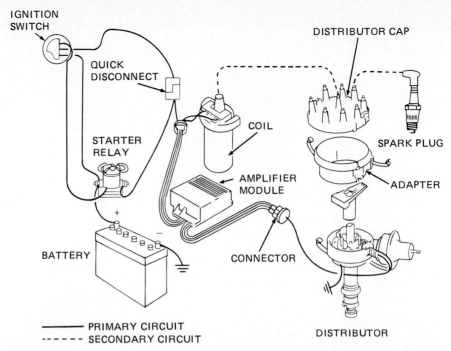

Fig. 22-13 Wiring circuit of a Ford electronic ignition system. *(Ford Motor Company)*

Figure 22-13 shows an electronic ignition system schematically. The secondary circuits are essentially the same in both types of ignition system, contact point and electronic. In the contact-point system, the contact points open to interrupt the flow of current to the ignition-coil primary winding. In the electronic system, the voltage pulse from the magnetic pickup coil causes a transistor in the electronic control unit to shut off the flow of current to the ignition-coil primary winding. The end effect is the same. The magnetic field in the ignition coil collapses, and a high voltage is produced in the ignition-coil secondary circuit. This high-voltage surge is carried through the wiring, distributor cap, and rotor to the spark plug.

Manufacturers have different names for some of the parts in the electronic ignition system. For example, Ford calls the rotating member an *armature* and Chrysler calls it a *reluctor*. Figure 22-14 is a chart showing the various names.

☐ 22-11 ADVANTAGES OF ELECTRONIC IGNITION

In the early 1970s, automotive manufacturers began to install electronic ignition systems in their cars and trucks. Electronic ignition systems have quicker response to voltage changes than contact-point systems and

Manufacturer	Part Name		
AMC	Trigger wheel	Sensor	Electronic control unit (ECU)
Chrysler	Reluctor	Pickup coil	Electronic control unit (ECU)
Ford	Armature	Magnetic pickup or stator	Ignition or amplifier module
General Motors	Timer core	Magnetic pickup	Electronic control module (ECM)

Fig. 22-14 Different names used by automobile manufacturers for the essential parts of the electronic ignition distributor.

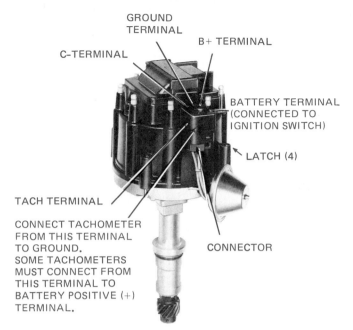

Fig. 22-15 Distributor for the HEI system which includes the ignition coil. *(Delco-Remy Division of General Motors Corporation)*

require less service. There are no contact points to wear and be replaced. Also, the electronic ignition system can produce higher secondary voltages than contact-point systems. This is important today because engines are run on leaner air-fuel mixtures. Leaner mixtures require higher voltages to ignite. The electronic systems supply these higher voltages.

Because of these higher voltages, electronic ignition systems have secondary cables that are larger in diameter (0.320 inch [8 mm]) than the wiring used in contact-point systems (0.276 inch [7 mm]). The insulation is made of silicone compounds, which provide better insulating properties to contain the higher voltages. Silicone insulation is softer than the insulation for contact-point wiring and must be handled with care.

□ 22-12 GENERAL MOTORS HIGH-ENERGY IGNITION (HEI)

This ignition system has a distributor which has the ignition coil mounted on top of it (Fig. 22-15). Some four- and six-cylinder engines have a separately mounted ignition coil. Both distributors have the electronic module mounted inside the distributor (Fig. 22-16). Mounting the module inside the distributor simplifies the wiring system (Fig. 22-17).

General Motors calls the distributor a *magnetic-pulse* distributor. It has a permanent magnet and pickup coil on top of which is mounted a pole piece. The pole piece has a series of teeth pointed inward. There are the same number of teeth as there are cylinders in the engine. The rotating trigger is called the *timer core*. It also has the same number of teeth, pointing outward, as there are engine cylinders.

Each time the teeth on the timer core and the teeth on the pole piece align and then move out of alignment, a magnetic field sweeps through the pickup coil. The pickup coil then sends a voltage pulse to the ignition-pulse amplifier, or electronic module. The amplifier shuts off the

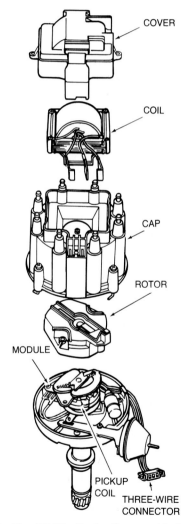

Fig. 22-16 Partly disassembled HEI distributor. *(Delco-Remy Division of General Motors Corporation)*

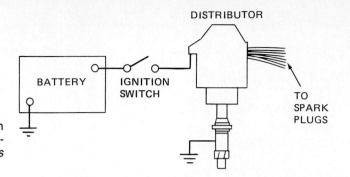

Fig. 22-17 Wiring diagram of an HEI ignition system. *(Delco-Remy Division of General Motors Corporation)*

flow of current to the ignition coil. The coil then produces a high-voltage surge which passes through the cables, cap, and rotor to the spark plug.

The name "high energy," comes from its ability to produce high voltages of more than 35,000 volts. This is considerably more than contact-point ignition systems can produce. The higher voltage permits the use of spark plugs with wide gaps—up to 0.080 inch [2 mm]. The higher voltage or "hotter" spark can more easily fire lean mixtures. Lean mixtures produce better fuel economy with less exhaust emissions.

□ 22-13 FORD ELECTRONIC IGNITION SYSTEMS

There are four variations of electronic ignition systems used by Ford. These are Dura-Spark models I, II, III, and IV. Basically all work the same. Figure 22-13 shows the basic system. Some have altitude and load compensation. In these, the electronic control module changes the spark advance as altitude and atmospheric pressure change. For example, as a car is driven up a mountain to higher altitudes, the system produces additional spark advance to compensate for the thinner mixture. It then retards the spark—to prevent detonation—as the car goes down to lower altitudes and higher atmospheric pressures.

The system also senses intake-manifold vacuum. This causes the module to change the spark advance as manifold vacuum changes. Therefore, when the throttle is open and the engine is under heavy load, the module retards the spark to prevent detonation. At lighter loads and part throttle, the module advances the spark.

Some Ford distributors have a bilevel rotor and cap with electrodes at upper and lower levels (Fig. 22-18). This is to provide more space between electrodes, which prevents arcing between electrodes and crossfiring. The wiring pattern of this distributor cap does not follow the firing order, as in other distributor caps, because of the two-level arrangement.

□ 22-14 CHRYSLER ELECTRONIC IGNITION SYSTEM

Figure 22-19 is the wiring diagram of the electronic ignition system used on Chrysler-built cars. Figure 22-20 is a top view, with the cap and rotor removed, of the distributor used with this system. The distributor is slightly different in design from the distributor used with other electronic ignition systems. Chrysler calls the trigger wheel a reluctor. The reluctor has the same number of tips as there are cylinders in the engine. However, the effect is the same. As each tip passes the pickup coil, the pickup coil sends a voltage pulse to the electronic control unit. The control unit

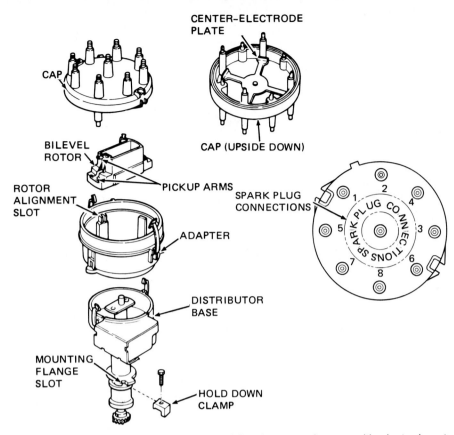

Fig. 22-18 Ford distributor which has a bilevel rotor and a cap with electrodes at upper and lower levels. *(Ford Motor Company)*

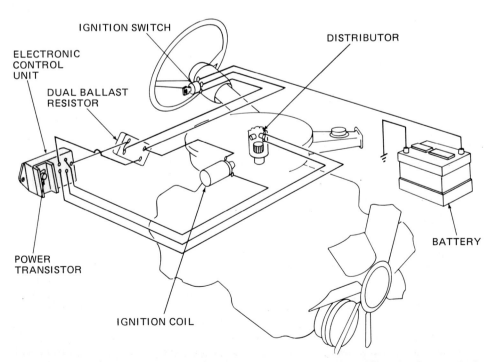

Fig. 22-19 Wiring circuit of a Chrysler electronic ignition system. *(Chrysler Corporation)*

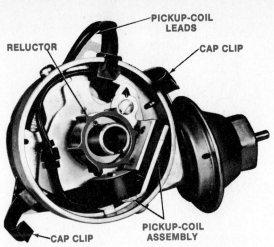

Fig. 22-20 Top view of the Chrysler electronic ignition distributor. The cap and rotor have been removed to show the reluctor and the pickup coil. *(Chrysler Corporation)*

then opens the primary circuit. As the magnetic field around the coil collapses, the coil produces a high-voltage surge. The distributor cap, rotor, and high-voltage cables send it to the spark plug that is ready to fire.

After the tip passes the pickup coil, the voltage pulse dies and the control unit closes the circuit. Then the cycle begins again as the next reluctor tip passes the pickup coil.

This distributor also has mechanical centrifugal- and vacuum-advance controls. The dual-ballast resistor (Fig. 22-19) maintains constant primary current even though engine speed varies. This provides a uniformly strong spark. The resistance is bypassed during starting so that full battery voltage is applied to the ignition coil. This assures a strong spark for starting.

□ 22-15 HALL-EFFECT DISTRIBUTOR

Some cars have an electronic distributor in which the pickup coil is replaced by a sensor that uses the *Hall effect* (Fig. 22-21). The Hall-effect principle is that when a thin slice of semiconductor material carrying an electric current is crossed at right angles by a magnetic field, a voltage appears at the edges of the conductor. This voltage is called the *sensor output voltage,* or *Hall voltage* (Fig. 22-21). It is proportional to both the current flowing through the conductor and the strength of the magnetic field. The voltage is unaffected by the speed at which the magnetic field cuts across the conductor.

The Hall-effect sensor is attached to the plate in the distributor (Fig. 22-22). A small permanent magnet is also mounted on the distributor plate facing the sensor, with a small air gap between the two. A distributor rotor with four metal shutters (for a four-cylinder engine) is attached to the distributor shaft. As the shaft turns, the shutters rotate through the air gap.

When no shutter is in the air gap, the sensor senses the presence of the small magnetic field from the permanent magnet. As long as this

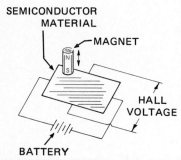

Fig. 22-21 Basic principle of a Hall-effect sensor. *(Chrysler Corporation)*

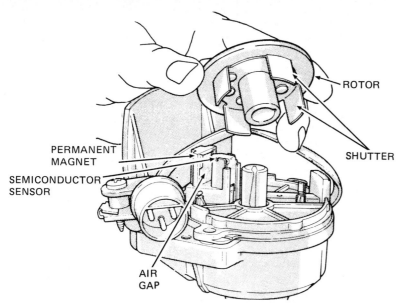

Fig. 22-22 Removing the rotor from a Hall-effect distributor. *(Chrysler Corporation)*

magnetic field acts on the sensor, it sends a small voltage signal to the ECU. The voltage signal causes the ECU to keep the primary circuit open. No current flows through the ignition-coil primary winding. However, the instant a shutter enters the air gap, the effect of the magnetic field on the sensor is cut off. As a result, the voltage signal from the sensor to the ECU drops to zero.

With no voltage signal from the sensor, the ECU closes the primary circuit. Now current flows through the ignition-coil primary winding. This builds up a strong magnetic field around the coil. Current continues to flow through the primary winding as long as the shutter is between the magnet and the sensor. The instant the shutter moves out of the air gap, the primary circuit is opened. This causes the magnetic field around the ignition coil to collapse. The resulting high-voltage surge is carried through the secondary circuit to the spark plug.

Operating characteristics of the Hall-effect distributor eliminate the need for distributor-mounted vacuum-advance and centrifugal-advance mechanisms. The length of each voltage signal or pulse and the frequency of the pulses are very accurate. Therefore they are used by the electronic control unit to provide a spark advance related to engine speed.

Vacuum advance is achieved by using a vacuum transducer in the electronic control unit (or spark-control computer). The electronic control unit receives signals from the Hall-effect sensor in the distributor, intake-manifold vacuum, engine coolant temperature, and carburetor which signal whether the engine is idling or running off idle. The electronic control unit computes the proper spark advance and opens the primary circuit accordingly.

☐ 22-16 DETONATION-CONTROL SYSTEM

This system was developed to provide a safeguard against detonation in engines using a turbocharger (☐ 14-15). The turbocharger is a device that forces more air-fuel mixture into the engine cylinders. However, if the

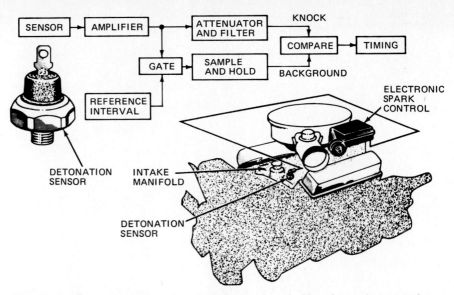

Fig. 22-23 Detonation sensor on an engine equipped with a detonation-control system. *(Chrysler Corporation)*

air-fuel mixture is compressed too much, it will detonate (□ 13-7). This occurs when the last part of the mixture ignites before the flame front reaches it (Fig. 13-1). For maximum power, it is desirable to pack as much air-fuel mixture as possible into the cylinder without causing detonation. To do this, and yet prevent detonation, the detonation-control system was developed (Fig. 22-23). A detonation sensor is mounted in the intake manifold, where it can sense the beginning of detonation. The instant it senses this, it signals the ESC controller, which immediately retards the spark. In this way, further detonation is prevented.

□ 22-17 ELECTRONIC SPARK TIMING (EST)

Many late-model electronic ignition systems have electronic control of the spark advance. These controls are used instead of separate centrifugal and vacuum-advance mechanisms attached to the distributor (□ 22-9). Various sensors feed information to the electronic control unit, or ignition computer, which then computes the proper spark advance for the operating conditions. Three variations of this system are described in following sections. These are the Chrysler electronic spark-control (ESC) system (□ 22-18), the Ford electronic engine-control (EEC) system (□ 22-19), and the General Motors electronic spark-timing (EST) system (□ 22-20).

□ 22-18 CHRYSLER ELECTRONIC SPARK CONTROL (ESC)

This system (Fig. 22-24) includes an electronic distributor without advance mechanisms, a spark-control computer, several engine sensors, and a specially calibrated carburetor or electronic fuel-injection (EFI) system. The purpose of electronic spark control is to provide voltage pulses at the right time. This causes the air-fuel mixture to burn with minimum exhaust emissions, improved fuel economy, and smoother idle. A similar earlier version of the system, called electronic lean burn (ELB), was used on some 1976 to 1978 Chrysler-built cars.

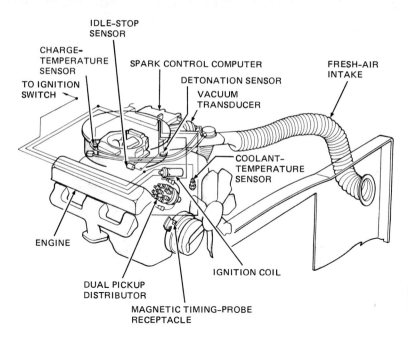

Fig. 22-24 Chrysler electronic spark-control (ESC) system. *(Chrysler Corporation)*

The Chrysler system electronically times the ignition to suit the operating conditions. It takes into consideration such factors as engine speed, engine temperature, intake-manifold vacuum, and the temperature of the air-fuel charge. To accomplish all this, the system uses a spark-control computer, an electronic distributor with one or two sensors (Fig. 22-25), and other sensors as described below.

1. SPARK-CONTROL COMPUTER

This device is mounted on the air cleaner (Fig. 22-26). The computer has two control modes, the START mode and the RUN mode. In the START mode, which is used for cranking and starting, the amount of advance is determined by the position of the distributor. Only static (or basic) timing is provided. When the engine starts and runs, the RUN mode takes over. It receives the signals from the sensors, allowing the computer to determine the correct spark advance for the operating conditions. The computer then advances or retards the spark. This system is more accurate and faster-acting than mechanical centrifugal-advance and vacuum-advance units (Fig. 22-11).

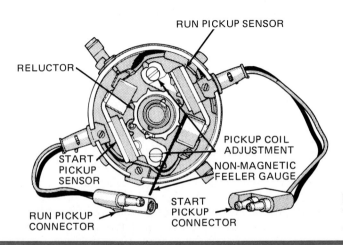

Fig. 22-25 Electronic distributor with two pickup sensors. *(Chrysler Corporation)*

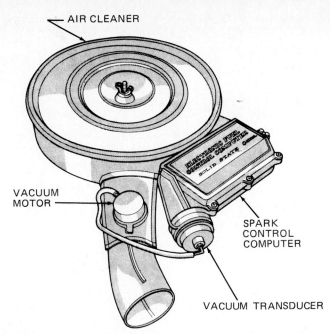

AIR CLEANER

VACUUM MOTOR

SPARK CONTROL COMPUTER

VACUUM TRANSDUCER

Fig. 22-26 Spark-control computer mounted on the air cleaner. *(Chrysler Corporation)*

2. IGNITION DISTRIBUTOR

The distributor used in carbureted engines has two pickup sensors (Fig. 22-25). The START pickup sensor operates during engine cranking to provide only the fixed spark advance for starting. When the engine starts, the RUN pickup sensor takes over. After analyzing the signals from all the sensors, the computer determines how much spark advance is needed. Then the computer retards the spark the amount necessary to deliver the required spark advance.

3. SENSORS

Seven or eight sensors are used in the Chrysler electronic spark-control system. Each sensor supplies the computer with information it needs to determine the correct instant to fire the spark plugs. These sensors are:

a. Coolant-temperature sensor
b. Air-fuel–charge temperature sensor
c. Idle-stop sensor
d. Intake-manifold vacuum sensor
e. Detonation sensor (☐ 22-16)
f. START and RUN pickup sensors in the distributor
g. Oxygen sensor (on cars with feedback carburetor)

☐ 22-19 FORD ELECTRONIC ENGINE CONTROL (EEC)

This system (Fig. 22-27) uses a microprocessor and is similar in many ways to the Chrysler electronic spark-control system (☐ 22-18). In addition to controlling spark advance, the Ford EEC system controls the exhaust-gas recirculation (EGR) valve and the air-injection system. These two emission control systems, which are described in Chap. 24, work to reduce HC, CO, and NO_x, in the engine exhaust gas.

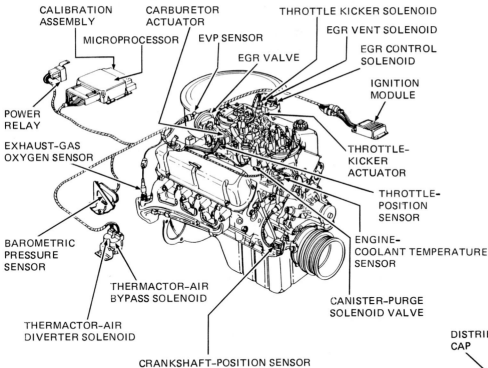

Fig. 22-27 Location of the components in the Ford electronic engine-control (EEC) III system. *(Ford Motor Company)*

The microprocessor in the EEC system is fed information from sensors that sense:

1. Inlet-air temperature.
2. Throttle position.
3. Coolant temperature.
4. Atmospheric pressure.
5. Intake-manifold vacuum.
6. Crankshaft and piston positions. This signal originates at a disk with four teeth 90 degrees apart on the crankshaft. When each tooth lines up with the sensor, it produces a signal that tells the microprocessor the crankshaft position. This system does not have any type of advance mechanism or signal generator in the distributor (Fig. 22-28). Therefore, ignition timing is *not* adjusted at the distributor. The *only* function of the distributor is to distribute the high-voltage pulses from the ignition-coil secondary winding to the correct spark plug.
7. Engine speed. The signal from the crankshaft disk and sensor also tells the microprocessor how fast the crankshaft is turning.

In a continuous process, the signals from each sensor are put together in the control computer. Then it produces the ideal spark advance for the engine operating condition.

The EEC system used on late-model cars has a feedback carburetor (□ 15-12). It automatically changes the amount of fuel so that the mixture is kept at the best air-fuel ratio for the operating condition. This version also controls the EGR and air-injection systems. In addition, during certain operating conditions, the later EEC system sends air from the air-injection pump to the catalytic converter to help burn any HC and CO left in the exhaust gas. The catalytic converter is described in Chap. 24.

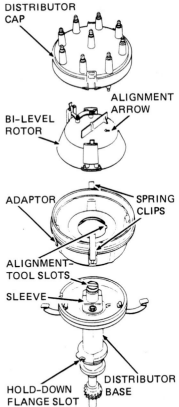

Fig. 22-28 Distributor in the Ford EEC system which has a bilevel rotor and serves only to distribute the sparks. There are no switches, sensors, or advance mechanisms in the distributor. *(Ford Motor Company)*

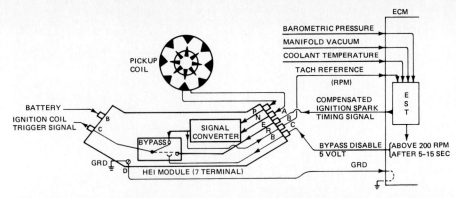

Fig. 22-29 Seven-terminal module used in the GM HEI distributor on engines with electronic spark timing (EST). *(Rochester Products Division of General Motors Corporation)*

☐ 22-20 GM ELECTRONIC SPARK TIMING (EST)

This system is similar to the Chrysler and Ford systems described in ☐ 22-18 and 22-19. It consists of the control circuits within the electronic control module (ECM) and an HEI distributor with a special seven-terminal module (Fig. 22-29). The distributor does not have mechanical advance mechanisms. Some earlier versions were called the *microprocessed sensing and automatic regulation* (MISAR) system. Now it is part of the widely used GM computer command control (CCC) system (Chap. 25). The electronic control module continuously monitors the signals from the sensors (Fig. 22-30). Based on this information, the module adjusts ignition timing for best fuel economy and driveability and minimum exhaust emissions. The sensors are:

1. Engine speed and piston position. In 1977 cars, this was a crankshaft sensor. In 1978 and later cars, the sensor is located inside the distributor.
2. Engine-coolant sensor.

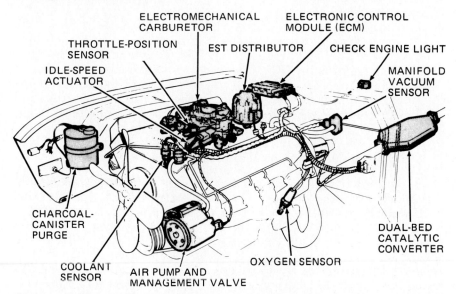

Fig. 22-30 Components and sensors in the GM computer command control (CCC) system. *(General Motors Corporation)*

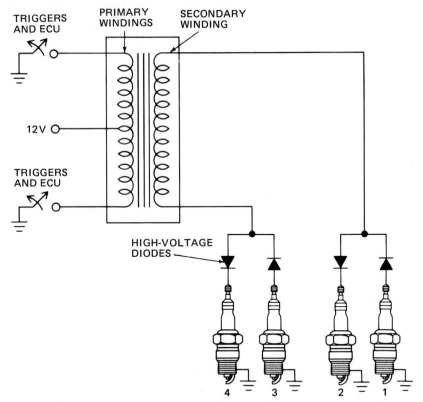

Fig. 22-31 Wiring diagram of a distributorless ignition system for a four-cylinder engine with a firing order of 1–3–4–2. *(Ford Motor Company)*

3. Manifold-vacuum sensor.
4. Atmospheric-pressure sensor.

In operation, the ECM receives the signals from the sensors, computes the proper spark advance, and then sends out a signal to the HEI module in the distributor. This signal causes the module to fire the spark plug at the proper time.

☐ 22-21 DISTRIBUTORLESS IGNITION SYSTEMS

Ford has developed an ignition system for a four-cylinder engine that has no distributor. Instead, the system fires two spark plugs at once, one in a cylinder during its exhaust stroke and the other in another cylinder near the end of the compression stroke. This system is shown schematically in Fig. 22-31. There are two primary windings and one secondary winding in the ignition coil. The action is controlled by a rotating sensor on the crankshaft (Fig. 22-27). The trigger has two triggering points, one for each primary winding in the coil. Each triggering point operates an ECU which stops the flow of current through one of the primary windings. When this happens, the magnetic field of the primary winding collapses and a high voltage is produced in the secondary winding.

The polarity of this high voltage, and the high-voltage diodes, determines which two plugs fire. For example, suppose that the upper end of the secondary winding (in Fig. 22-31) is negative. Then the electrons in the high-voltage pulse can flow to ground through plug 2. From ground the electrons flow through plug 3 and back to the other end of the secondary winding. Current cannot flow through plug 1 because the polarity of the high-voltage diode for plug 1 prevents it.

☐ 22-22 IGNITION SWITCH

In most cars, the ignition switch is mounted on the steering column, as shown in Fig. 22-32. This locks the steering shaft at the same time the ignition switch is turned off and the ignition key is removed. When this happens, a small gear on the end of the ignition switch rotates and releases a plunger. The plunger enters a notch in a disk on the steering shaft to lock the shaft. If a notch is not lined up with the plunger, the plunger rests on the disk. When the steering wheel, shaft, and disk are turned slightly, the plunger drops into a notch. When the ignition key is inserted and the ignition switch is turned on, the plunger is withdrawn from the disk to unlock the steering shaft.

The ignition switch has an extra set of contacts that are used when the switch is turned past ON to START. The contacts connect the starting-motor solenoid to the battery so that the starting motor can operate. As soon as the engine is started and the switch is released, it returns to ON and the starting motor is disconnected from the battery.

The alternator field circuit is connected to the battery through the ignition switch when it is turned to ON. When the ignition switch is turned to OFF, the alternator field circuit is disconnected so that the battery cannot discharge through the field circuit.

Another job of the ignition switch is to operate a buzzer or other audible signal if the key is left in the lock when the car door on the driver's side is open. This is a reminder to the driver to remove the key from the lock when leaving the car.

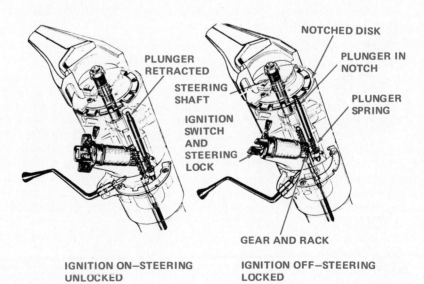

IGNITION ON—STEERING UNLOCKED

IGNITION OFF—STEERING LOCKED

Fig. 22-32 A combination ignition switch and steering-wheel lock, showing the two positions of the lock.

Accessories such as the radio and the heater blower motor are also connected to the battery through the ignition switch. This prevents the driver from leaving these units running when leaving the car.

□ 22-23 IGNITION-SYSTEM SERVICE

The ignition system is a basic part of the engine. Whatever happens in the ignition system affects engine operation. If the engine fails to start even though it cranks normally, or if the engine misses, lacks power, overheats, backfires, or pings, the trouble could be caused by a faulty ignition system. The chapters on engine service explain how to trouble-shoot an engine to locate problems and how to fix them. The troubles mentioned above could also be caused by problems in the fuel system, the cooling system, or the engine itself.

> **CAREFUL** When servicing Ford or GM high-energy ignition systems, never disconnect a spark-plug wire to create an open circuit with the engine running. This could cause arcing within the distributor, which would damage the cap, rotor, or magnetic pickup. Refer to the manufacturer's service manual for specific testing and servicing instructions.

CHAPTER 22
REVIEW QUESTIONS

Select the *one* correct, best, or most probable answer to each question. Then check your answers against the correct answers given at the end of the book.

1. The ignition coil has
   a. one winding
   b. two windings
   c. three windings
   d. four windings

2. The primary winding of the ignition coil is connected to the battery through the
   a. spark-plug wiring
   b. distributor cap and rotor
   c. distributor gearing
   d. distributor contact points

3. The distributor shaft is driven
   a. from the engine camshaft
   b. from the engine crankshaft
   c. by a belt and sprockets
   d. all of the above

4. The secondary circuit includes
   a. the ignition-coil secondary winding
   b. the contact points
   c. the battery
   d. none of the above

5. The purpose of the rotor in the distributor is to
   a. open and close the contact points
   b. switch the primary winding on and off
   c. act as a rotary switch
   d. none of the above

6. The purpose of the ignition condenser is to protect the contact points and to produce
   a. quick collapse of the magnetic field
   b. slow collapse of the magnetic field
   c. high voltage across the contact points
   d. minimum primary voltage

7. The device that pushes the breaker cam ahead as engine speed increases is the
   a. vacuum-advance mechanism
   b. centrifugal-advance mechanism
   c. full-advance mechanism
   d. vacuum-brake mechanism

8. The device in many distributors that shifts the position of the breaker plate to produce a change in spark timing is actuated by
   a. intake-manifold vacuum
   b. centrifugal advance
   c. engine speed
   d. throttle opening

9. With the throttle wide open, vacuum advance will be
   a. at a maximum
   b. at a minimum
   c. part to full
   d. more than centrifugal advance

10. In the electronic ignition system, the circuit between the battery and the ignition-coil primary winding is closed and opened by
    a. contact points
    b. a field relay
    c. a switch
    d. an electronic control unit

11. The timer core, reluctor, and armature are
    a. different components in different systems
    b. different names for the same component
    c. seldom used in electronic ignition systems
    d. distributor drive systems

12. Rotation of the timer core or reluctor
    a. carries magnetic lines of force through the sensor or pickup coil
    b. trips the contact points
    c. causes the spark to advance as engine speed increases
    d. provides vacuum and centrifugal advance

13. The timer core or reluctor rotates
    a. at half crankshaft speed
    b. at crankshaft speed
    c. at twice crankshaft speed
    d. at half camshaft speed

CHAPTER 23
LIGHTS, INSTRUMENTS, AND SIGNALING SYSTEMS

After studying this chapter, you should be able to:

1. Discuss the components of an automotive wiring circuit.
2. Explain the purpose of circuit protectors and describe how each type works.
3. Name the exterior lights on the car.
4. List the interior lights in the car.
5. Describe the purpose of the signaling and warning devices on the car.

There are many electrical and electronic devices on the modern car that have not been described in previous chapters. Many of these devices are lights, which act as signaling, warning, and safety devices. Other warning systems use buzzers and chimes, as well as visual displays such as the speedometer. Electronic instrument clusters and cathode-ray-tube displays, which look like small television sets, are coming into use. But because of the great variety of lighting systems and instrument-panel displays now in use, only those found on almost all cars are covered in this chapter.

☐ 23-1 WIRE AND CABLE

The wiring on an automobile connects the various electrical devices, such as the battery, alternator, starting motor, and ignition system. Most electrical devices are connected by a single wire. The return circuit is completed through the car frame. This return circuit is called *ground* and has the symbol ⏚ or ⌁.

When you study sketches of electric connections, you will often see a ground wire drawn in from the component to the car frame which is the common ground. Actually, the component is usually internally grounded. Installing the component on the metal parts of the car automatically makes the ground connection.

There are two types of automotive wiring—solid wires and stranded wires, or cables (Fig. 23-1). Both types are referred to as "wires." Solid wires carry low current. They should not be used when flexibility is re-

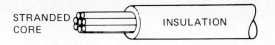

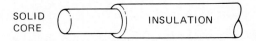

Fig. 23-1 Two types of automotive wiring. *(Chrysler Corporation)*

quired. Cables are used where current flow is high (for example, the battery cables) and when flexibility is required.

Regardless of the type of wiring used, the purpose of the conductor is to carry an electric current from one device (such as the battery) to another (such as a light). The purpose of the insulation around the conductor is to prevent its contact with any other conductor or with any part of the ground circuit.

When a group of wires are wrapped together, usually with a layer of insulating tape, the grouped wires are called a *wiring harness*. The wiring harness is easier to install and remove than are many separate wires. However, finding a problem in a wiring harness may be more difficult than checking only a single wire.

□ 23-2 WIRING CIRCUITS

An automotive wiring circuit contains eight basic components. These are:

1. A source of electric energy, such as the battery or alternator.
2. Conductors, which connect between the source and the other components in the circuit to provide a path for the electric current.
3. Terminals, at the ends of the conductors, which eliminate the need for soldering wires and components together (Fig. 23-2).
4. A circuit protector, such as a fuse, fusible link, or circuit breaker, to open the circuit and stop current flow when overheating caused by excessive current begins to occur.
5. Connectors, such as single connectors, which join together one pair of terminals (Fig. 23-2), and multiple connectors, which can conveniently connect and disconnect two or more pairs of terminals. Connectors usually have some type of locking tang to prevent separation unless the tang is released.

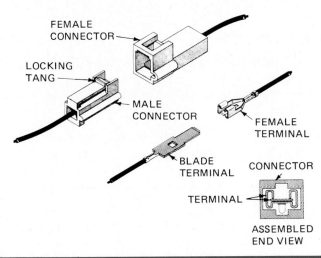

Fig. 23-2 Typical types of terminals and connectors used in automotive wiring systems. *(Chrysler Corporation)*

6. A switch, which opens and closes the circuit to stop and allow current flow.
7. A load, such as the starting motor, horn, or light, which is the device in an electric circuit that converts the electric energy from the source into work.
8. Ground, or the return path to the source for the electric current, which usually is the metal parts of the vehicle chassis.

The electrical units in the automobile are connected by wires of different sizes. The size of each wire depends on the amount of current the wire must carry. The greater the current, the larger the wire must be. The wires are gathered together to form wiring harnesses. Each wire is identified by the color of its insulation. For example, wires are light green, dark green, blue, red, black with a white tracer, and so on. The car manufacturers' shop manuals have special illustrations called *wiring diagrams* that show these various wires and their colors. If you have to trace a particular wire, refer to the shop manual to determine its color. Figure 23-3 shows the wiring to the instrument panel for one model car. Figure 23-4 shows the wiring to the fuse block.

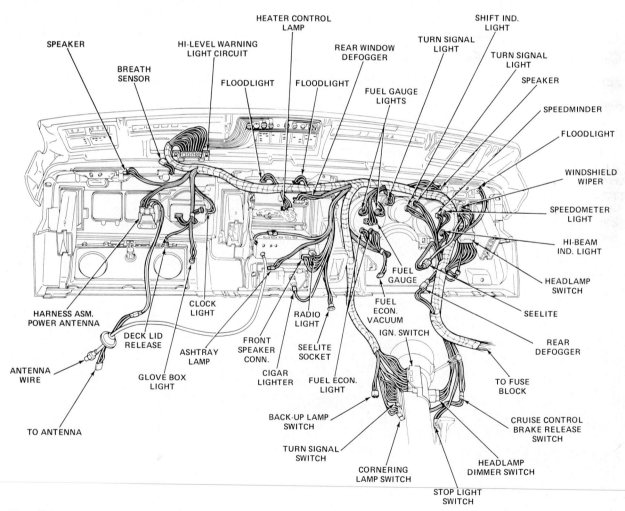

Fig. 23-3 Instrument-panel wiring for one model of car. *(Buick Motor Division of General Motors Corporation)*

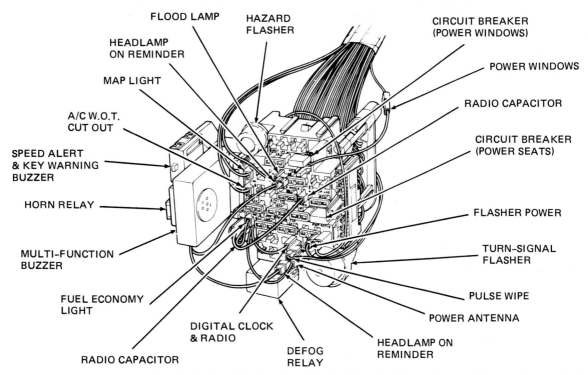

Fig. 23-4 Fuse-block wiring. *(Buick Motor Division of General Motors Corporation)*

☐ 23-3 PRINTED CIRCUITS

The instrument panel has a number of indicating devices, switches, and controls (Fig. 23-5). Because the instrument cluster is crowded, there can be problems in making connections between the instruments. One solution is the use of printed circuits.

A *printed circuit* is a flat piece of insulating material or board on which a series of conducting metallic strips are printed. Figure 23-6 shows part of a printed circuit. When a printed circuit is installed on the instrument cluster, the conducting strips carry current between the elec-

Fig. 23-5 Instrument panel on a late-model car. *(Mazda Motors of America, Inc.)*

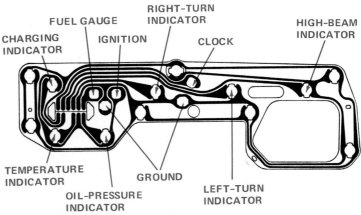

Fig. 23-6 A printed circuit. The black strips are the electrical conductors which form the printed circuit. *(Pontiac Division of General Motors Corporation)*

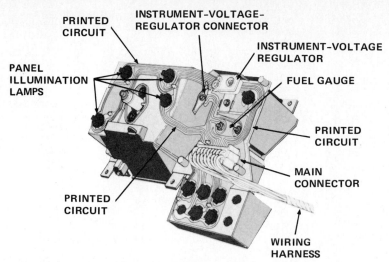

Fig. 23-7 View from the back of an instrument panel, showing how the printed circuit provides the conductors that connect the lights and other devices. *(Ford Motor Company)*

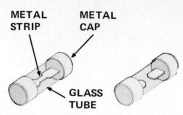

Fig. 23-8 A good and a blown cartridge-type fuse. *(Ford Motor Company)*

trical units. For example, when the indicator bulbs are installed, the contacts on the bulbs rest on the metallic strips to complete the circuit. Figure 23-7 shows how a printed circuit is installed behind the instrument panel.

CIRCUIT PROTECTORS

☐ 23-4 CIRCUIT-PROTECTION DEVICES

Fuses, fusible links, and circuit breakers are installed in various circuits to protect the electrical devices connected in the circuits. The purpose of these circuit-protection devices is to open the circuit if a short or ground develops and high current starts to flow. If this should happen, the fuse blows, the fusible link burns out, or the circuit breaker opens.

☐ 23-5 FUSES AND FUSE PANELS

A fuse is the device that is used most often to protect the components of an electric circuit from damage due to excessive current flow. A typical older-style cartridge fuse is shown in Fig. 23-8. It contains a soft metal strip, connected at the ends to the fuse caps. When too much current flows through the fuse, the current overheats the metal strip, and it melts, or blows. This opens the circuit and stops the current flow. Then the circuit should be checked to find out what caused the fuse to blow. After the trouble is fixed, a new fuse should be installed. Figure 23-9 shows a fuse panel that takes the round cartridge fuse.

Instead of the round fuse, many cars today use a U-shaped blade fuse (Fig. 23-10). This type of fuse can be plugged in and removed easily with your fingers. The fuse block, or fuse panel, in which these fuses are used is shown in Fig. 23-11. The number of amperes that the fuse will carry before it blows is marked on the fuse.

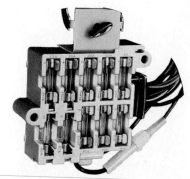

Fig. 23-9 A fuse block using round cartridge-type fuses. *(Chrysler Corporation)*

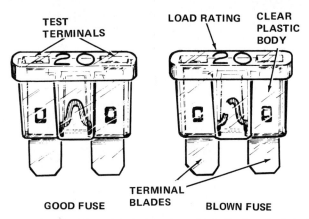

Fig. 23-10 A good and a blown blade-type fuse. Note the terminals to test the fuse. *(Buick Motor Division of General Motors Corporation)*

□ *23-6 FUSIBLE LINKS*

For added protection, many cars have fuse or fusible links in the insulated battery cable and in the larger high-current–carrying wires. Figure 23-12 shows how a fusible link is installed. It is a smaller wire than the wire it is protecting. If a short or ground occurs, the fusible link will melt and open the circuit. The other parts of the circuit will not be damaged. Figure 23-13 shows how to repair a burned-out fusible link.

□ *23-7 CIRCUIT BREAKERS*

Circuit breakers are used in headlight and windshield-wiper circuits. These circuits may have temporary overloads. But safe vehicle operation requires that normal circuit action be rapidly restored. In most circuit breakers, the current passes through a bimetallic strip (Fig. 23-14). There is a set of normally closed contacts at one end. When too much current flows, the heat causes the strip to bend, or warp. As the strip moves, the contacts separate. This opens the circuit and stops the current flow. However, with the contacts open, the bimetallic strip cools off and closes the contacts again. If the overload is still present, the circuit breaker will cycle by opening the contacts again. If the overload is no longer present, the circuit will resume normal operation.

Fig. 23-11 A fuse block using blade-type fuses. *(Ford Motor Company)*

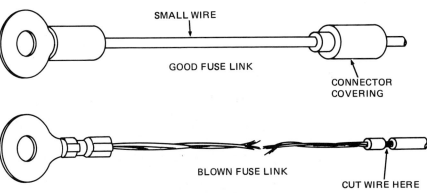

Fig. 23-12 A good and a blown, or burned-out, fusible link. *(ATW)*

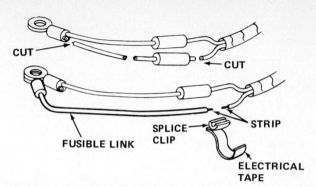

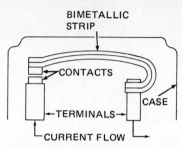

Fig. 23-13 Repairing a burned-out fusible link. Cut out the damaged section as shown in the top view. Strip back the insulation. Splice the wires with a splice clip, and then solder in the new fusible link. Tape the splice with a double layer of electrical tape. *(Buick Motor Division of General Motors Corporation)*

Fig. 23-14 Construction of a thermostatic type of circuit breaker which uses a bimetallic strip. *(Ford Motor Company)*

The type of circuit breaker that automatically reconnects the circuit is called *self-resetting*. Some circuit breakers must be *manually reset*. On this type, the contacts remain open after the circuit breaker is tripped. This forces a reset button to pop out on the case of the circuit breaker. To manually reset the circuit breaker, push in on the button.

LIGHTS

☐ 23-8 LIGHTING SYSTEMS

The lighting system in a typical automobile includes the headlights, parking lights, turn signals, side marker lights, stoplights, backup lights, taillights, and interior lights (Fig. 23-15). The interior lights include instrument-panel lights, various warning and indicator lights, and courtesy lights which turn on when a car door is opened. Most cars have an emergency flasher or hazard-warning system.

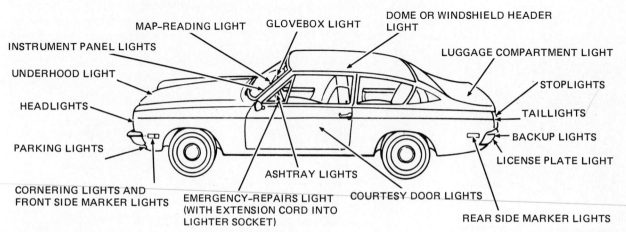

Fig. 23-15 Lights used on a typical car. *(Ford Motor Company)*

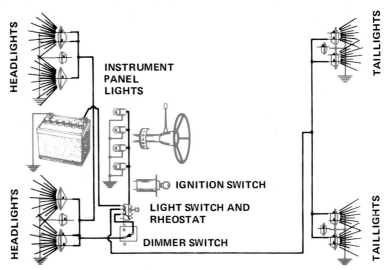

Fig. 23-16 Typical wiring system for headlights and taillights, showing headlights on high beam.

> **NOTE** The correct name for any light on an automotive vehicle is *lamp*. For example, we should say "headlamp" instead of "headlight" and "lamp bulb" instead of "light bulb." However, many people use either the term "light" or "lamp" to mean the unit that produces the light.

☐ *23-9 HEADLIGHTS*

A typical headlight wiring system for a car is shown in Fig. 23-16. Figure 23-17 shows a sealed-beam headlight. It has a reflector and a tungsten filament at the back and a lens at the front. When the filament is connected to the battery through the light switch, current flows through the filament and it glows white-hot. The light is concentrated by the reflector into a forward beam and is focused by the lens.

Headlights are made in two types and four sizes (two round and two rectangular). The round sizes are 5¾ inches [146 mm] in diameter and 7 inches [178 mm] in diameter. The rectangular headlights are 6½ by 4 inches [165 by 100 mm] and 7.9 by 5.6 inches [200 by 142 mm]. Round and rectangular headlights are shown in Fig. 23-18. The type of headlight is identified by the number 1 or 2 molded into the glass at the top of the lens. Type 1 has only one filament. Type 2 has two filaments: one for the high beam and the other for the low beam. The high beam is for

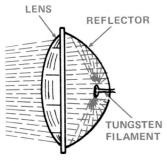

Fig. 23-17 Construction of a tungsten-filament sealed-beam headlamp.

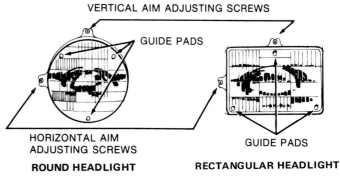

Fig. 23-18 Shapes of the round and rectangular headlights.

driving on the highway when there is no car approaching from the other direction. The low beam is for city driving and for passing a car coming in the opposite direction. The use of the low beam for passing prevents the oncoming driver from being temporarily blinded by the high beam.

Some cars have only one pair of headlights. These are type 2. Other cars have two pairs of headlights: one pair of type 1 and one pair of type 2.

The driver uses the dimmer switch to select the filament that will glow. For example, on a car having only one pair of headlights (type 2), the driver operates the dimmer switch to select either the high or low beam. On a car having two sets of headlights (one set of type 1 and one set of type 2), the arrangement is different. When the driver operates the dimmer switch for low-beam driving, one of the filaments in the type-2 lights comes on. When the driver changes the dimmer switch to high beam, the other filament in the type-2 lights comes on. At the same time, the single filament in the type-1 lights comes on.

☐ 23-10 HALOGEN HEADLAMPS

Since 1979, many cars have used halogen headlamps. These emit a much whiter and brighter light than other sealed-beam headlamps. This improves visibility on high beam by about 25 percent. Halogen headlamps require about 40 percent less power on low beam. This allows the car to have a smaller and lighter-weight alternator.

The halogen sealed beam has a small inner bulb filled with halogen which surrounds the tungsten filament (Fig. 23-19). The halogen bulb gets much hotter than other sealed-beam headlamps. This provides the brighter light. A halogen lamp can be identified by the word HALOGEN which is embossed in the face of the lamp.

> **CAUTION** To avoid accidently burning yourself, never touch a halogen lamp when it is on or shortly after it has been turned off.

☐ 23-11 AUTOMATIC HEADLIGHT DIMMER

This is a system that electronically selects the proper headlight beam for country driving. It holds the lights on upper, or high, beam until a car approaches from the other direction. Then, the headlights of the approaching car trigger the system so that it shifts the headlights to the lower beam. When the other car has passed, the system electronically shifts the headlights back to the upper beam.

The driver has a sensitivity control which allows adjustment of the system to the surrounding light. The dimmer switch is an override switch which allows the driver to manually control the system. This might be used, for example, if an oncoming car does not dim and the driver needs more light to see by. Operating the dimmer switch returns the headlights to the upper beam.

> **NOTE** The system may also be operated by the taillights of a vehicle that is being overtaken. Being close to the taillights of another car may cause the system to switch to low beam.

☐ 23-12 BACKUP LIGHTS

The backup lights come on when the driver shifts to reverse. The system has a switch assembled with the shift lever. Movement of the shift lever closes the switch so the backup lights come on.

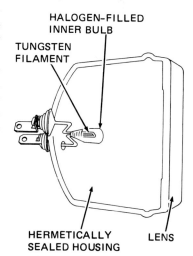

HALOGEN-FILLED INNER BULB

TUNGSTEN FILAMENT

HERMETICALLY SEALED HOUSING

LENS

Fig. 23-19 Construction of a halogen sealed-beam headlamp. *(Chrysler Corporation)*

☐ 23-13 HAZARD-WARNING SYSTEM

The emergency-flasher or hazard-warning system is designed to signal following cars that a car has stopped or stalled or has pulled to the side of the road. When the driver operates the flasher switch, it causes all four turn-signal lights to rapidly flash on and off. The system includes a flasher similar to the one used for turn signals (☐ 23-14). The system is operated by a switch usually located on the side of the steering column.

☐ 23-14 TURN SIGNALS

Turn signals permit the driver to signal an intention to make a left or right turn (Fig. 23-20). They are operated by a switch on the steering column. When the turn-signal lever is moved, the switch completes the circuits to the proper lights. The system has a flasher which closes and opens the circuits intermittently so that the lights flash on and off.

☐ 23-15 COURTESY LIGHTS

Courtesy lights come on when the car doors are opened so that passengers or driver can see to get in or out of the car. The courtesy lights are operated by switches in the door that close when a door is opened.

☐ 23-16 STOPLIGHT SWITCH

The stoplight switch operates lights at the rear of the car to warn the driver behind that the brakes are being applied. Years ago, the switch

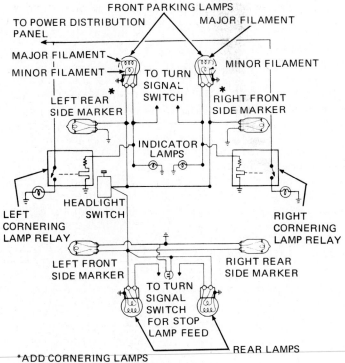

Fig. 23-20 Side-marker, cornering, and turn-signal circuits. *(Ford Motor Company)*

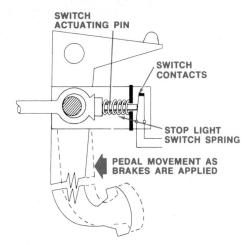

SWITCH
ACTUATING PIN

SWITCH
CONTACTS

STOP LIGHT
SWITCH SPRING

◀ PEDAL MOVEMENT AS
BRAKES ARE APPLIED

Fig. 23-21 A mechanical stop-light switch, closed, with the brakes applied.

was connected into the brake hydraulic system. When the brakes were applied, the pressure on the brake fluid operated the switch. The stop-light switch used on cars today is shown in Fig. 23-21. It is a mechanical switch that is operated by the brake pedal. When the brakes are applied, the switch contacts close and the stoplights come on.

☐ 23-17 FIBER-OPTIC MONITOR SYSTEMS

To get light to the various gauges and the speedometer, some cars use a fiber-optical device. This is a bundle, or rod, made of many flexible glass threads, or fibers. The fibers can conduct light around corners. Therefore, one light bulb can be used to illuminate several gauges. Several fiber-optic conductors are run from the one bulb.

Fiber optics can also be used as a *light-out* warning system. Fiber-optic conductors are run from the headlights to a headlight monitor mounted on top of a front fender (Fig. 23-22). When the headlights are on, the "lights" glow in the monitor. If a headlight burns out, the monitor also goes out. This warns the driver which headlight is not working.

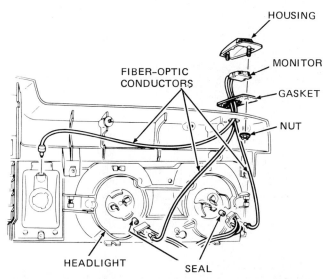

HOUSING

MONITOR

GASKET

NUT

FIBER–OPTIC
CONDUCTORS

HEADLIGHT   SEAL

Fig. 23-22 Fiber-optic monitoring system for headlights. *(Cadillac Motor Car Division of General Motors Corporation)*

□ 23-18 HORNS AND HORN RELAYS

The automobile horn is an electrically operated noisemaking device. It is used by the driver to provide an audible warning signal. Figure 23-23 is a sectional view of a typical horn. It has a field coil, a set of contact points, and a metal diaphragm. When the horn is operated by closing the horn button, current flows through the field coil. This produces a magnetic field that pulls the diaphragm down. The diaphragm movement produces a click. As the diaphragm moves down, the contacts are separated so no current can flow. The magnetic field in the field coil collapses, and the diaphragm is released. It moves up with another click. This vibrating action is so rapid that the separate clicks blend to form the horn sound you hear.

Most horn circuits have a relay connected between the battery and the horns (Fig. 23-24). When the horn button is pressed, current flows through the winding in the horn relay. This produces a magnetic field which pulls the armature down, closing the contact points in the relay. With the points closed, the horns are connected directly to the battery. Therefore the horns blow as long as the horn button is pressed.

Today, the horn relay also acts as a buzzer. If the driver leaves the ignition key in the ignition switch and then opens the car door, the horn relay buzzes. The circuit for this arrangement is shown in Fig. 23-25. When the ignition key is left in the ignition switch, the key closes a warning switch. The warning switch is located in the ignition switch and is connected to the door switch. When the door switch is closed as the door

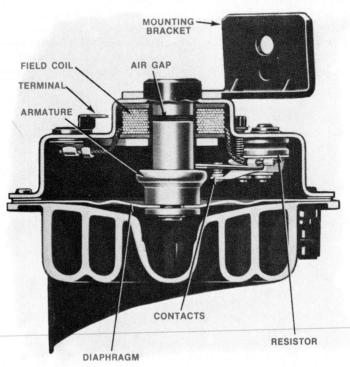

Fig. 23-23 Sectional view of a horn. (*Delco-Remy Division of General Motors Corporation*)

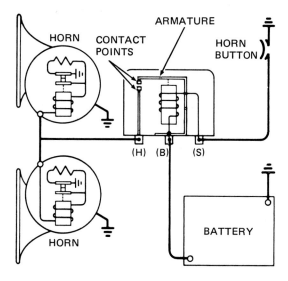

Fig. 23-24 A horn relay and horn wiring circuit. *(Delco-Remy Division of General Motors Corporation)*

is opened, the circuit is completed to the horn-relay winding. The circuit is completed through a second set of contact points that is above the armature. When the circuit to the winding is completed, the winding magnetism pulls the armature down. This opens the upper points to open the winding circuit. The magnetism dies, and the armature moves back up. The points close, and the action is repeated. This produces a buzzing sound that warns the driver to remove the ignition key.

□ 23-19 INDICATING DEVICES

In the car, the driver must be aware of certain engine and other operating conditions that could affect the car and its safety. Various *indicating devices* are used to make these conditions known to the driver. The most common are a warning light or a gauge with a dial and pointer in the instrument panel (Figs. 23-26 and 23-27). Other types of indicating devices provide an audible signal, such as a buzzer or chimes. Some cars

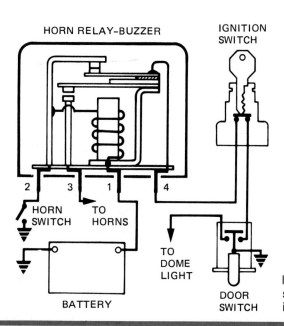

Fig. 23-25 Horn-relay wiring system which includes a "key-in-ignition" warning buzzer.

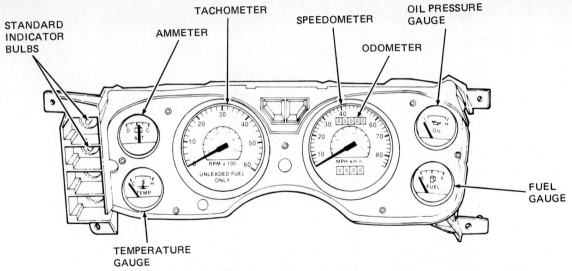

Fig. 23-26 An instrument panel that has gauges instead of charging, oil, and temperature indicator lights. *(Ford Motor Company)*

have a *voice alert system* which can speak several words or phrases to the driver. *Voice command systems* for cars are being developed and introduced. With this type of system, the driver can give the car certain commands such as "Close window." Then the car responds by performing the act, such as closing the window, or by providing the information desired.

Most cars have an ammeter or a charge indicator light, a fuel-level gauge, an oil-pressure gauge or light, and an engine-coolant temperature gauge or light. These indicators keep the driver informed of the operating condition of the engine. If the oil pressure drops too low or the temperature goes too high, the indicators alert the driver. Then the engine can be stopped before it is damaged. All cars have some type of *speedometer* and *odometer*. The speedometer tells the driver how fast the vehicle is moving. The odometer indicates the total distance a vehicle has traveled since it was new. Some instrument panels include a *tachometer* to indicate engine speed (Fig. 23-26).

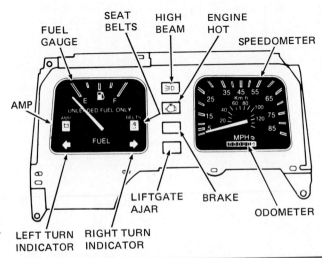

Fig. 23-27 An instrument panel that has charging and temperature indicator lights. *(Ford Motor Company)*

☐ 23-20 CHARGE INDICATORS

To ensure that the engine can be restarted after it is shut off, the battery must be kept charged. The instrument panel contains either an ammeter (Fig. 23-26) or an indicator light (marked AMP in Fig. 23-27) to provide this information to the driver. The operation of the ammeter in the charging system is described in ☐ 18-5. The ammeter tells the driver which way the current is flowing—to the battery or from the battery. The ammeter also tells how much current is flowing.

Many cars have an indicator light (Fig. 23-27) instead of an ammeter. When the alternator is not charging the battery, the light comes on. When the alternator is charging the battery, the light stays out. To check the indicator-light bulb, turn the ignition switch from OFF to ON. With current flowing from the battery to the ignition coil, the light should come on. It should go out when the engine starts.

☐ 23-21 FUEL, OIL, AND TEMPERATURE GAUGES

Two types of fuel, oil, and temperature gauges are used in cars. These are the *balancing-coil,* or *magnetic, gauge* and the *thermostatic,* or *thermal, gauge.* Each gauge has two main parts: a sending unit and a dial and pointer in the instrument panel. In most cars, the fuel, oil, and temperature gauges all operate on the same principle. The only difference is in the indicator-face markings.

☐ 23-22 FUEL GAUGES

Almost all cars have a fuel gauge (Figs. 23-26 and 23-27). This provides the driver with immediate information on the fuel level in the tank. The tank unit, or sending unit, contains a sliding contact that moves on a resistor as the float moves up and down in the tank. This changes the resistance to current flow through the tank unit.

In the magnetic fuel gauge, as the tank empties, the float drops. Now the sliding contact moves to reduce the resistance. The instrument-panel gauge contains two coils (Fig. 23-28). When the ignition switch is turned on, current from the battery flows through the two coils. This produces a magnetic field that acts on the armature to which the pointer is attached. When the resistance of the tank unit is high (tank filled and float up), most of the current flows through the F (full) coil to ground instead of through the tank unit. Therefore, the stronger magnetic field of the full

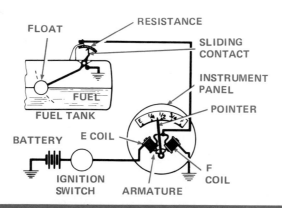

Fig. 23-28 Schematic wiring diagram of a magnetic fuel gauge using balancing coils.

coil pulls the armature to the right so that the pointer is on the full side of the dial.

When the tank begins to empty, the resistance of the tank unit decreases. This allows more current to flow from the empty coil and through the tank unit. As the current flow through the circuit increases, the magnetic field of the empty coil becomes stronger than that of the full coil. As a result, the empty coil pulls the armature toward it. The pointer swings toward the left, or E (empty), side of the dial.

Figure 23-29 is the wiring circuit of a thermostatic fuel gauge. It has a tank unit similar to that of the magnetic fuel gauge, with a float and a sliding contact that moves on a resistor. Current flows from the battery through a heater coil in the fuel-gauge instrument-panel unit and through the resistance in the tank unit. When the fuel level in the tank is low, most of the resistance is in the circuit. Very little current flows. When the tank is filled, the float moves up. Now the sliding contact cuts most of the resistance out of the circuit so more current flows. As it flows through the heater coil in the fuel gauge, the current heats the thermostat. The thermostat blade bends because of the heat. This moves the needle to the right, toward the F, or full, mark.

The thermostatic fuel gauge includes an *instrument voltage regulator* (IVR). The purpose of this thermostatic device (shown in Fig. 23-29) is to keep the voltage to the gauges at an average voltage of about 5 volts. In the IVR, current passes through a set of contact points and a bimetallic arm with a heating coil. As the arm warms up, it bends. This opens the contact points, allowing the arm to cool and close the contacts again. When input voltage is high, the contacts open and close rapidly. With a lower input voltage, the contacts vibrate at a slower rate.

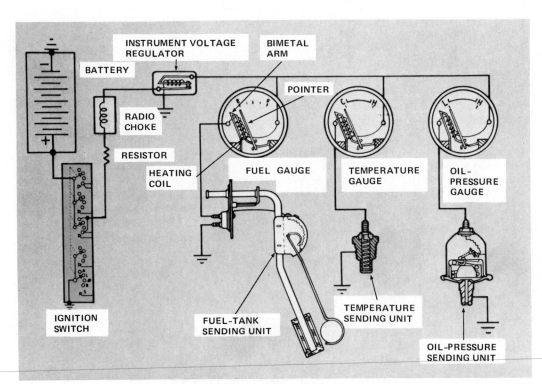

Fig. 23-29 A thermostatic, or thermal, gauge system, which includes an instrument voltage regulator and a radio choke. *(Ford Motor Company)*

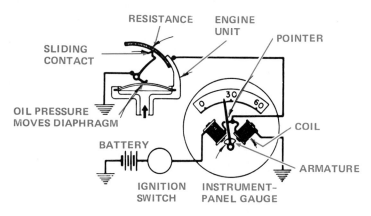

Fig. 23-30 A magnetic oil-pressure-gauge system.

To prevent static in the radio caused by the opening and closing of the IVR contacts, many thermostatic gauge systems include a *radio choke* (Fig. 23-29). The choke smoothes out the voltage and current surges caused by the action of the IVR.

☐ 23-23 OIL-PRESSURE INDICATORS

Most cars have some means of indicating to the driver that the engine oil pressure has dropped too low for continued operation. The indicator may be either a gauge or an indicator light on the instrument panel. Figure 23-30 shows the wiring circuit of a magnetic oil-pressure gauge. The sending unit is mounted on the engine so that engine oil pressure pushes up on the diaphragm. The upward movement causes the sliding contact to move, increasing the resistance in the circuit. More current now flows through the right coil. This pulls the armature and pointer around to indicate a higher oil pressure.

A thermostatic oil-pressure gauge is shown in Fig. 23-29. As oil pressure increases, the sending-unit diaphragm moves up. This reduces the resistance in the circuit, allowing more current to flow. With a higher current flow to the gauge, the pointer moves to the right, or high, side.

Most cars have an oil-pressure indicator light (Fig. 23-31). There are two parts to the oil-pressure light system, the switch and the light. The switch is a two-position switch mounted on the engine. With the engine off, or with low oil pressure, a small spring holds the contacts together. After the engine starts, the oil pressure overcomes the spring. This opens the contacts, turning off the light when the oil pressure gets high enough (usually 10 to 15 psi [69 to 102 kPa]).

☐ 23-24 ENGINE TEMPERATURE INDICATORS

A temperature-indicating gauge (Fig. 23-26) or light (Fig. 23-27) is installed in the instrument panel to warn the driver if the engine overheats. Overheating is a warning of abnormal conditions in the engine that could cause serious damage. The indicator warns the driver to stop the engine before serious damage is done. Figure 23-32 shows the wiring circuit of a magnetic temperature gauge. The engine unit is immersed in coolant so that the unit senses coolant temperature at all times. The unit is a thermistor, and its resistance decreases as it gets hot. This means that the right coil in the dash unit becomes stronger magnetically as the engine heats up. As a result, the armature and pointer are pulled around to show the increased temperature.

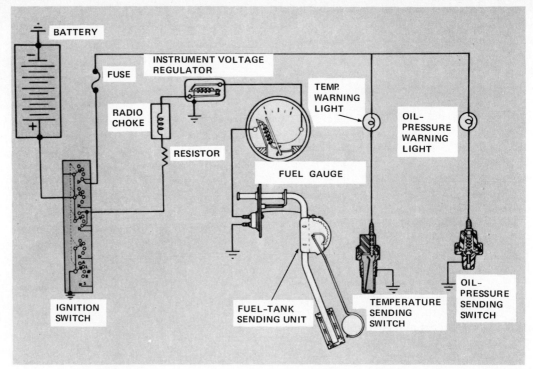

Fig. 23-31 An instrument system using a thermal fuel gauge, with warning lights to indicate improper oil pressure and engine temperature. *(Ford Motor Company)*

The thermostatic temperature gauge is shown in Fig. 23-29. Higher coolant temperature causes the temperature sending unit to allow a higher current flow. This causes the heating coil to get hotter. As a result, the bimetallic arm bends, swinging the pointer to the right. Now the temperature gauge indicates a higher temperature.

The temperature indicator-light system consists of two units. These are the light in the instrument cluster and the coolant temperature switch (Fig. 23-31). The indicator light comes on to indicate an overheating engine.

This system is designed to warn the driver of an overheating condition at approximately 5 to 10 degrees Fahrenheit (F) [2.8 to 5.6 degrees Celsius (C)] below the coolant boiling point. The use of plain water, without enough antifreeze to protect down to 0°F (−17°C), can keep the temperature indicator light from coming on, even though the water is boiling.

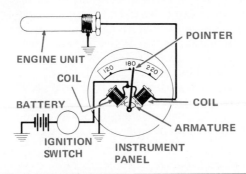

Fig. 23-32 A magnetic engine-temperature gauge system.

A "prove-out" circuit is provided through the ignition switch to check for a burned-out bulb. If the light stays off when the ignition switch is in the ON position, turn the ignition switch to the START position. The prove-out circuit should now light the bulb. If the bulb does not glow, the bulb or the prove-out circuit is defective.

□ 23-25 SPEEDOMETER AND ODOMETER

A *speedometer* (Figs. 23-26 and 23-27) is mounted in the instrument cluster to tell the driver how fast the car is moving. Most speedometers are driven from the transmission output shaft by a set of gears. The driven gear is fastened to a flexible shaft. It connects to the back of the speedometer head in the instrument panel.

Inside the speedometer, there is a small magnet mounted on a shaft which is turned by the cable (Fig. 23-33). The faster the car goes, the faster the magnet spins. This action produces a rotating magnetic field that drags on the metal ring surrounding the magnet. The faster the spinning, the more drag on the ring. The spinning action causes the ring to swing around against the drag of a spring. This, in turn, moves a pointer attached to the ring, which indicates the car speed.

The *odometer* is a meter that indicates the total distance a vehicle has traveled. It is usually located in the speedometer (Figs. 23-26 and 23-27). The odometer is operated by a pair of gears from the speedometer shaft (Fig. 23-33). The motion is carried through the gears to the mileage or kilometer rings on the odometer indicator. These numbered rings turn to show the distance the car has traveled.

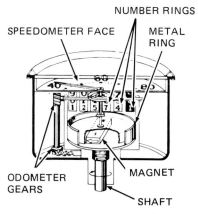

Fig. 23-33 A cutaway speedometer-odometer assembly.

SAFETY EQUIPMENT

□ 23-26 WINDSHIELD WIPERS AND WASHERS

Windshield wipers are driven by an electric motor. A typical system is shown in Fig. 23-34. The motor, through gearing and linkage, causes the wiper blades to move back and forth on the windshield. Most cars have a windshield washer as part of the windshield-wiper system. When the driver presses a button, a squirt of cleaning liquid covers the windshield. Now the blades can clean the windshield more effectively.

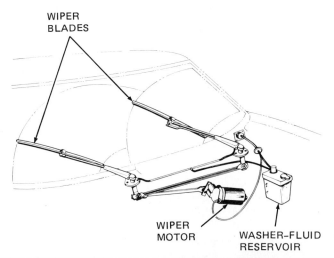

Fig. 23-34 A windshield-wiper and -washer system. *(Trico Products Corporation)*

Select the *one* correct, best, or most probable answer to each question. Then check your answers against the correct answers given at the end of the book.

1. A printed circuit is
   a. a wiring diagram in the service manual
   b. a board with conducting metallic strips printed on it
   c. a plate with wires soldered on it
   d. none of the above

2. The purpose of a fuse is to
   a. open the circuit if a short or ground occurs
   b. protect the system from excessive current flow
   c. blow out and open the circuit if high current flows
   d. all of the above

3. The two basic types of headlights are
   a. round and square
   b. one-filament and two-filament
   c. warning and stop
   d. upper-beam and lower-beam

4. The four sizes of headlights are
   a. two round and two rectangular
   b. three round and one rectangular
   c. one round and three rectangular
   d. four round

5. The purpose of the automatic headlight dimmer is to
   a. turn the headlights on when it gets dark
   b. select the proper headlight beam for city driving
   c. shift the headlights to the lower beam at night when another car approaches
   d. turn the headlights off after the driver leaves the car

6. A car with two sets of headlights has
   a. one pair of type 1 and one pair of type 2
   b. one round pair and one rectangular pair
   c. four headlights, each with two filaments
   d. four headlights, each with one filament

7. The stoplight switch is operated
   a. hydraulically
   b. electronically
   c. mechanically
   d. by brake-fluid pressure

8. The fuel-gauge system includes
   a. a tank unit and a dash unit
   b. an electronic sensor and a transistor
   c. a hydraulic plunger
   d. two tank units

PART 4

AUTOMOTIVE EMISSION CONTROLS

In recent years, there has been a great deal of attention focused on the automobile as an air polluter. In the spark-ignition engine, gasoline is mixed with air to produce a combustible mixture. However, when this mixture burns, complete combustion never occurs. Some polluting gases always come out of the tail pipe. These chemicals contribute to air pollution. They react to cause smog which is unhealthy to breathe and to live in. To help control this unhealthy condition, federal and state laws require car manufacturers to install pollution-control or "smog" devices on their cars. These devices reduce the amount of air pollutants given off by cars. There are two chapters in Part 4:

CHAPTER 24
AUTOMOTIVE EMISSION CONTROLS

After studying this chapter, you should be able to:
1. Describe the sources of each of the three major pollutants from the automobile.
2. Explain how the PCV system works.
3. Describe the operation of the evaporative control system.
4. Discuss each exhaust emission control device and system, explaining how it works and the pollutants that it controls.

Automobiles are blamed for about half of the air pollution in the United States. Smoke from power-plant and factory smokestacks, incinerators, and home heating also contributes to air pollution. Now federal and state laws require emission controls on all cars. Some emission controls were described in earlier chapters. This chapter covers the causes of air pollution and the most important automotive antipollution devices. They are called *automotive emission controls*.

AIR POLLUTION

□ 24-1 DANGERS FROM SMOG

When the smoke from factories and homes does not blow away and automobiles continue to operate in the same area, smog builds up. Smog makes your eyes sting. When smog is in the air, it is hard to breathe, and your throat and lungs may begin to feel sore. You may cough. People with breathing problems or heart trouble can become very ill, and some may die. Smog damages food and flower crops. Even house paint is affected by smog.

□ 24-2 POLLUTION FROM AUTOMOBILES

The automobile gives off pollutants from four places (Fig. 24-1). Pollutants can come from the fuel tank, the carburetor (on spark-ignition engines), the crankcase, and the tail pipe. Pollutants, or emissions, from the

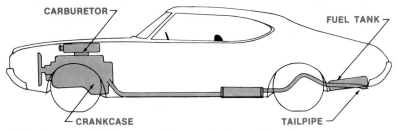

Fig. 24-1 Four possible sources of atmospheric pollution from the automobile.

fuel tank and carburetor consist of fuel vapors. Emissions from the crankcase consist of raw fuel and partly burned air-fuel mixture that has leaked past the pistons and rings into the crankcase. Emissions from the tail pipe consist of partly burned air-fuel mixture that did not complete combustion in the engine cylinders. In addition, there is a pollutant, called *oxides of nitrogen* (NO_x), that forms in any high-temperature combustion process.

☐ 24-3 COMBUSTION

Gasoline and diesel fuel are hydrocarbons (HC) made up mostly of hydrogen and carbon. When hydrocarbon burns completely, water (H_2O) and carbon dioxide (CO_2) are formed. Unfortunately, combustion is never complete. Therefore, some HC remains and some CO (carbon monoxide) is formed. Carbon monoxide is a poisonous gas.

There is another dangerous gas that the engine gives off: oxides of nitrogen. Actually, there are several oxides of nitrogen. Nitrogen makes up about 80 percent of our atmosphere. Oxygen forms almost 20 percent. Usually, nitrogen is an *inert* gas that will not unite with any other element. But in the high combustion temperatures in the engine cylinders, some nitrogen will unite with oxygen to form oxides of nitrogen. The chemical formula for these oxides of nitrogen is NO_x. The *"x"* stands for different amounts of oxygen. NO_x unites with atmospheric moisture in the presence of sunlight to form an acid. This acid contributes to the eye-irritating, cough-producing effects of smog. Oxides of nitrogen also are called *nitrogen oxides*.

The three basic pollutants coming from the engine are unburned gasoline (HC), carbon monoxide (CO), and oxides of nitrogen (NO_x). In addition, there is also loss of HC from the carburetor and fuel tank. The following sections describe how these pollutants are controlled.

EMISSION CONTROL SYSTEMS

☐ 24-4 CRANKCASE VENTILATION

Air must circulate through the crankcase when the engine is running. The reason is that water and liquid fuel appear in the crankcase when the engine is cold. Also, there is some blowby on the power strokes. *Blowby* is the name for the leakage of burned gases and unburned fuel vapor past the pistons and the rings and down into the crankcase. Water appears as a product of combustion. Water is also carried into the engine as moisture in the air that enters the engine. When the engine is cold, this water

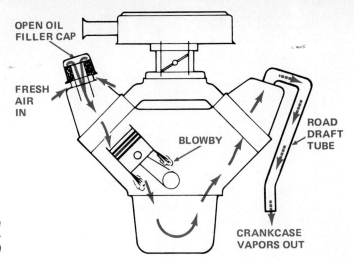

Fig. 24-2 An open crankcase ventilating system using a road-draft tube. *(Ford Motor Company)*

condenses on the cold engine parts and runs down into the crankcase. Fuel vapor also condenses on cold engine parts and runs down into the crankcase.

The water, liquid fuel, burned gases, and fuel vapor must be cleared from the crankcase. Otherwise, sludge and acids will form. Sludge is a gummy material that can clog oil lines and starve the engine lubricating system. This could ruin the engine. The acids corrode engine parts and also can damage the engine.

In older engines, the crankcase was ventilated by an opening at the front of the engine and a vent tube at the back. The forward movement of the car and the rotation of the crankshaft moved air through the crankcase (Fig. 24-2). The air passing through removed the water and fuel vapors, discharging them into the atmosphere. This caused air pollution.

To prevent this type of air pollution, engines have a positive crankcase ventilating (PCV) system. A typical system is shown in Fig. 24-3. Filtered air from the carburetor air cleaner is drawn through the crankcase. In the crankcase the air picks up the water and blowby gases. The air then flows back up to the intake manifold and enters the engine. There, the unburned fuel is burned.

Too much air flowing through the intake manifold during the idle period would upset the air-fuel–mixture ratio and cause poor idling. To

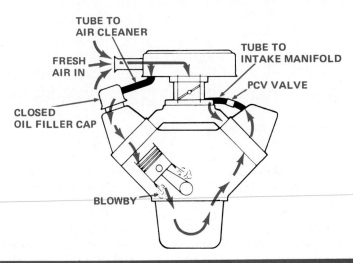

Fig. 24-3 A positive crankcase ventilating (PCV) system on a V-type engine. *(Ford Motor Company)*

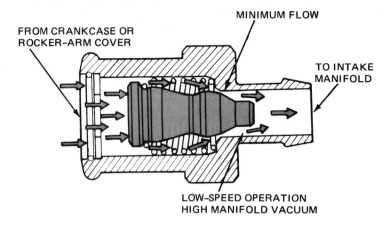

MINIMUM FLOW

FROM CRANKCASE OR
ROCKER–ARM COVER

TO INTAKE
MANIFOLD

LOW–SPEED OPERATION
HIGH MANIFOLD VACUUM

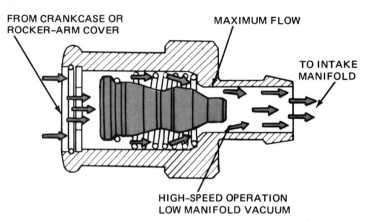

FROM CRANKCASE OR
ROCKER–ARM COVER

MAXIMUM FLOW

TO INTAKE
MANIFOLD

HIGH–SPEED OPERATION
LOW MANIFOLD VACUUM

Fig. 24-4   Operation of the PCV valve. *(Ford Motor Company)*

prevent this, a flow-control valve is used. The valve is called a *positive crankcase ventilation* (PCV) valve. The PCV valve allows only a small amount of air to flow during idle. But as engine speed increases, the valve opens to allow more air to flow. Figure 24-4 shows the valve in the two positions.

☐ 24-5 EVAPORATIVE CONTROL SYSTEMS

Gasoline vapor can escape from the fuel tank and carburetor. As temperatures change, the fuel tank "breathes." When the fuel tank heats up, the air inside expands. Some of it passes out through the vent in the tank cap (or the tank vent tube). When the tank cools, the air inside contracts and outside air enters. This breathing causes a loss of gasoline vapor, because any air leaving carries gasoline vapor with it. Gasoline vapor also is lost from the float bowl in the carburetor. When the engine is shut off, the float bowl is full. Heat from the engine vaporizes part or all of this gasoline. Then the gasoline vapor passes out through the carburetor vents.

To prevent the loss of gasoline vapor from the fuel tank and the carburetor, evaporative control systems are installed on all cars. The names for this type of system are evaporation control system (ECS), evaporation emission control (EEC), vehicle vapor recovery (VVR), and vapor saver system (VSS).

The systems shown in Figs. 24-5 and 24-6 are typical. They include a canister filled with activated charcoal. Hose and pipe connect the canister

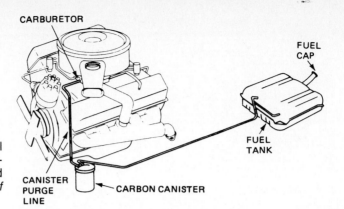

Fig. 24-5 Evaporative control system showing fuel-vapor recovery from the carburetor and fuel tank. *(Buick Motor Division of General Motors Corporation)*

to the fuel tank and the carburetor. Any vapor-filled air that leaves the fuel tank passes through the emission control pipe to the canister. The gasoline vapor is *adsorbed* by the activated charcoal. This means that the activated charcoal particles in the canister "grab" the molecules of HC in the air coming from the fuel tank. Then, when the engine is started, intake-manifold vacuum draws fresh outside air through an opening in the canister. This moving air pulls the HC out of the activated charcoal. These vapors are carried back to the carburetor and into the engine. In this way, the canister is purged, or cleaned, of gasoline. Now the canister is ready to do its job again.

When the engine is stopped, vapors form above the float bowl in the carburetor. The vapors pass through a float-bowl vent and line to the charcoal canister. Many evaporative control systems include roll-over and check valves. These shut off the lines if the car rolls over. This prevents leakage of fuel from the tank into the carburetor and canister, which could increase the danger of fire.

The fuel-return line (□ 14-6) parallels the main fuel line. This return line is shown in Fig. 24-6. It connects the pressure side of the fuel pump to the fuel tank. Any excess gasoline being pumped by the fuel pump is returned to the tank. This helps keep the fuel pump cool. It also returns to the fuel tank any vapor that might cause vapor lock.

Several arrangements are used at the fuel tank to separate fuel vapor from liquid fuel. An early arrangement was a standpipe assembly. It contains a series of pipes which connect to the canister tube. The tops of the pipes are above the fuel in the tank. Therefore, only vapor can enter them. Other vapor separator arrangements are shown in Figs. 24-6, 24-7,

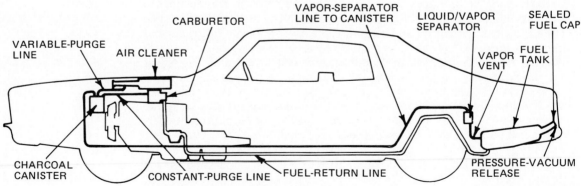

Fig. 24-6 Typical evaporative emission control system on a car. *(AC-Delco Division of General Motors Corporation)*

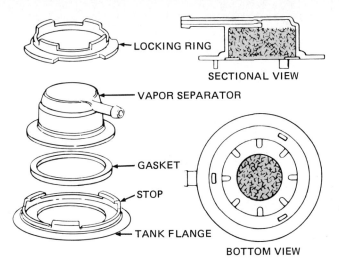

Fig. 24-7 Vapor separator using filter material. When assembling, rotate the locking ring fully against the tank-flange stops. *(Ford Motor Company)*

and 24-8. The types shown in Figs. 24-7 and 24-8 are mounted in the top of the fuel tank.

Figure 24-5 shows one type of charcoal canister. The fuel tank is sealed. It has a cap with two valves (Fig. 24-9) like the pressure-vacuum cap used on the radiator in a pressurized cooling system (□ 12-12). The cap will open if too much pressure develops in the tank. It will also open to admit air as fuel is withdrawn so that a vacuum does not develop in the tank. Pressure or vacuum in the tank could damage it.

Some cars use the crankcase instead of a canister as the storage place for gasoline vapor. When the engine is stopped, the gasoline vapors pass from the vapor separator at the fuel tank, through the fuel-tank vent line, and to the breather cap on the valve cover. From there, the vapors pass down into the crankcase. At the same time, fuel vapors from the carburetor float bowl also flow down into the crankcase. The vapors, being 2 to 4 times heavier than air, sink to the bottom of the crankcase. Then, when the engine is started, the PCV system clears the crankcase of

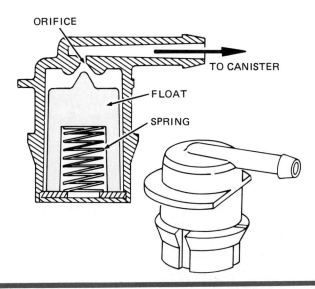

Fig. 24-8 Vapor separator using a float valve with an internal spring. *(Ford Motor Company)*

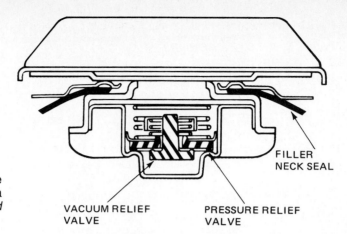

Fig. 24-9 Filler cap used on the tank of a car equipped with a vapor-recovery system. *(Ford Motor Company)*

FILLER NECK SEAL

VACUUM RELIEF VALVE

PRESSURE RELIEF VALVE

the vapors. The vapors are carried up to the intake manifold and then into the engine, where they are burned.

□ 24-6 CLEANING THE EXHAUST GASES

Complete combustion never occurs in the engine cylinders. So some HC and CO are contained in the exhaust gases. It is possible to increase the combustion temperature so that more of the HC will burn. But then, more NO_x is produced. So simply increasing combustion temperatures is not the answer.

Federal regulations require very low amounts of HC, CO, and NO_x in the exhaust gases. For example, the United States standards for cars made in 1983 are as follows:

- HC—0.41 gram (g) per vehicle mile (0.39 in California)
- CO—3.4 grams per vehicle mile (7.0 in California)
- NO_x—1.0 gram per vehicle mile (0.4 in California)

A gram is a very small amount. There are 454 g in 1 pound [0.45 kg], for example. In effect, these standards require almost the complete absence of pollutants in the exhaust gas. There are three ways to reduce pollutants in the exhaust gas.

1. CONTROLLING THE AIR-FUEL MIXTURE

First, gasoline has been changed to reduce lead pollution from the exhaust gas. Also, leaner carburetor settings and faster warm-up are used. Therefore more of the fuel is burned during start-up.

2. CONTROLLING COMBUSTION

Engineers have altered the combustion chambers of engines to improve combustion. They have lowered compression ratios, which also lowers engine power but helps the emission problem. They have modified ignition timing to prevent excessive emissions during certain operating conditions. And, they have recirculated part of the exhaust gases through the engine to modify the combustion process.

3. TREATING THE EXHAUST GASES

One procedure is to pump fresh air into the exhaust gases as they leave the engine. This supplies additional oxygen so that unburned HC and CO can burn. Another way to treat the exhaust gases is to use *catalysts* in the exhaust line. Catalysts are chemicals that cause a chemical reaction (such as combustion) without actually becoming part of the chemical process.

☐ 24-7 CONTROLLING THE AIR-FUEL MIXTURE

The octane rating of gasoline can be increased by adding a small amount of tetraethyl lead to it (Chap. 13). However, now lead is no longer added to most gasoline. Without lead, the catalytic converter works better to clean the exhaust gas. (Catalytic converters are described in ☐ 24-12 and 24-13.)

> **NOTE** From the standpoint of pollution, it is desirable to get the lead out of gasoline. Lead is a poisonous substance. In some cities the lead in the exhaust gases increases the lead in the air to almost the danger point. So lead is being removed from gasoline.

Carburetors have been modified to deliver leaner air-fuel mixtures, especially during idle. Many carburetors have an *idle limiter* (Fig. 24-10). This allows some idle-mixture adjustment, but prevents setting it richer than the legal limit. The latest carburetors have internal idle-mixture screws which are factory-set and sealed with a steel plug to prevent tampering. These cannot be adjusted, except by disassembling the carburetor and removing the steel plug.

Faster warm-up and quicker choke action are also important ways of reducing pollutants. During choking, a very rich mixture enters the cylinders. Some of the excess gasoline has no chance to burn. It exits in the exhaust gas as unburned HC. One way to reduce the amount of unburned gasoline in the exhaust is to preheat the mixture during warm-up. The thermostatic air cleaner (☐ 14-10) does this job (Fig. 24-11). It includes a

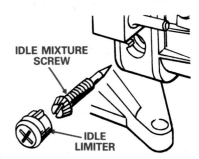

Fig. 24-10 Location of the idle limiter in one model of carburetor. *(Ford Motor Company)*

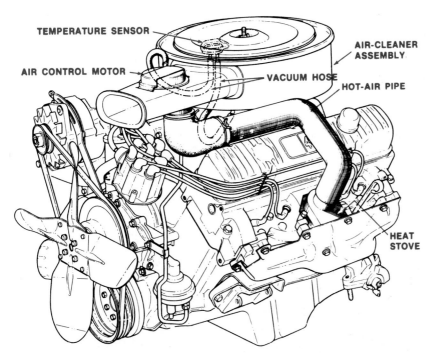

Fig. 24-11 Heated-air system using a thermostatic air cleaner installed on a V-type engine. *(Buick Motor Division of General Motors Corporation)*

heat stove on the exhaust manifold, a hot-air pipe, and a thermostatic door or damper in the snorkel tube of the air cleaner. The *snorkel tube* is the tube through which air enters the air cleaner.

Figure 24-12 shows the parts of the air cleaner. It has a thermostatic spring, called a *temperature-sensing spring,* shown in Fig. 24-12. When the entering air is cold, this spring holds the air-bleed valve closed. Now intake-manifold vacuum can work on the vacuum chamber in the snorkel tube. The vacuum chamber, called the motor in Fig. 24-12, has a diaphragm which is raised by the vacuum. This movement of the diaphragm tilts a damper so that the snorkel tube is blocked off. Now all air must come from the heat stove through the hot-air pipe. Figure 24-13 shows how the thermostatic air cleaner works.

As long as the choke is closed, a rich mixture is being fed to the engine, and the exhaust gas is loaded with unburned HC. To reduce the closed-choke time, some automatic chokes are equipped with an electric heating element (Fig. 15-21). This produces rapid opening of the choke.

□ 24-8 ELECTRONIC ENGINE CONTROL SYSTEMS

One way or another, an engine must be controlled. The primary control of a spark-ignition engine is the position of the throttle valve. As the driver's foot moves the accelerator pedal, the throttle valve opens and closes to allow more or less fuel into the engine.

With the need for improved driveability, exhaust emissions, and fuel economy, electronic control systems were introduced. These systems have different names, but all have some common characteristics. Sensors monitor engine-output factors such as exhaust-gas oxygen content, crankshaft speed, and others. Then a feedback system (□ 15-12) acts to adjust engine-input factors such as spark timing, air-fuel ratio, intake-air temperature, and exhaust-gas recirculation so that the desired engine output is obtained.

However, good driveability and minimum fuel consumption are not always compatible with minimum exhaust emissions. Therefore, the con-

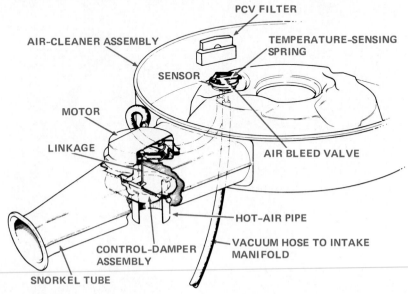

Fig. 24-12 A thermostatic air cleaner. *(Chevrolet Motor Division of General Motors Corporation)*

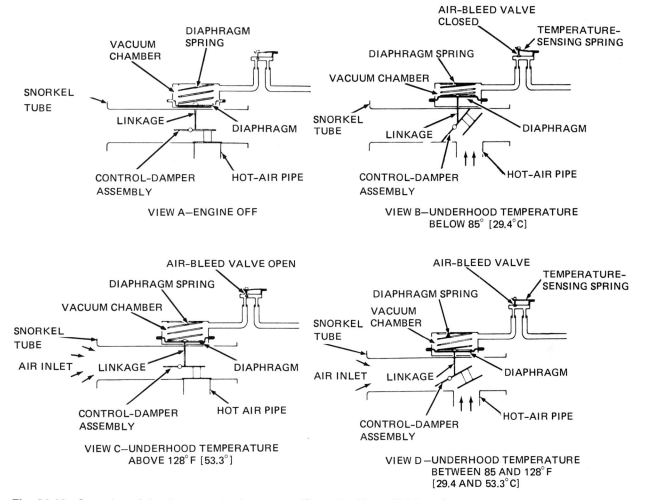

Fig. 24-13 Operation of the thermostatic air cleaner. *(Chevrolet Motor Division of General Motors Corporation)*

trol circuits in the electronic engine control system are programmed to automatically provide the input settings for the best possible engine output.

Electronic control of the carburetor air-fuel mixture is described in □ 15-12. Gasoline fuel-injection systems that electronically control the air-fuel mixture are described in Chap. 16. The purpose of these systems is to precisely control the air-fuel–mixture ratio. It must be kept within the "window" shown in Fig. 24-14 if the three-way catalytic converter is to work. Catalytic converters are described in later sections.

In the typical electronic engine control (EEC) system, an oxygen sensor is mounted in the exhaust pipe (Fig. 15-15). If there is too much oxygen, the fuel-delivery system (either a carburetor or fuel injection) is delivering too lean a mixture. Then the electronic control unit (ECU) signals the fuel-delivery system so that it enriches the mixture. If there is too little oxygen, the fuel-delivery system is delivering a mixture that is too rich. Then the ECU signals the fuel-delivery system so that it leans out the mixture. This precise control of the air-fuel mixture minimizes exhaust emissions. At the same time, the best possible fuel economy and driveability are obtained.

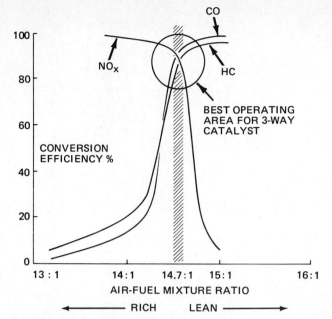

CO

NOₓ

HC

BEST OPERATING
AREA FOR 3-WAY
CATALYST

CONVERSION
EFFICIENCY %

13 : 1   14 : 1   14.7 : 1   15 : 1   16 : 1

AIR-FUEL MIXTURE RATIO

← RICH   LEAN →

Fig. 24-14 The air-fuel–mixture ratio "window" within which the ratio must remain if the three-way catalyst is to work. *(General Motors Corporation)*

☐ *24-9 CONTROLLING THE COMBUSTION PROCESS*

Late-model engines have been changed somewhat to improve the combustion process. During the 1960s, the compression ratios of engines went up a little each year. About 1969 the average was a little above $9.5 : 1$. Now the average is down around $8 : 1$ or a little higher. NO_x is formed during high-temperature combustion. Reducing the compression ratio reduces peak temperatures. This reduces the amount of NO_x that forms. However, reducing the compression ratio also reduces engine performance and efficiency.

Another method of controlling the formation of NO_x in the engine is to recirculate some of the exhaust gas back through the engine. Figure 24-15 shows this system. It is called the *exhaust-gas recirculation* (EGR) system. A part of the exhaust gas is picked up from the exhaust manifold and sent through the intake manifold and back through the engine. Usually, less than 10 percent of the exhaust gas is recirculated this way. The exhaust gas mixes with the air-fuel mixture. By absorbing some of the

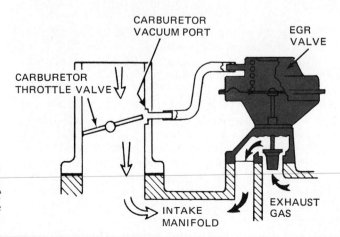

CARBURETOR
VACUUM PORT

EGR
VALVE

CARBURETOR
THROTTLE VALVE

INTAKE
MANIFOLD

EXHAUST
GAS

Fig. 24-15 Flow of exhaust gas through an exhaust-gas recirculation (EGR) system. *(Chevrolet Motor Division of General Motors Corporation)*

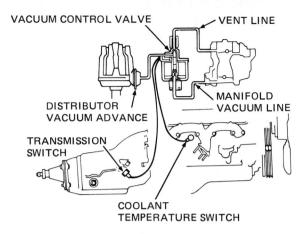

VACUUM CONTROL VALVE   VENT LINE

DISTRIBUTOR
VACUUM ADVANCE

MANIFOLD
VACUUM LINE

TRANSMISSION
SWITCH

COOLANT
TEMPERATURE SWITCH

Fig. 24-16 Transmission-controlled spark (TCS) system.

heat of combustion, the cooler exhaust gas lowers the combustion temperature. This reduces the amount of NO_x that forms.

Another way to mix some of the exhaust gases with the incoming air-fuel mixture is to leave part of the exhaust gases in the cylinders. The Chrysler NO_x control system does this by increasing the exhaust-valve and intake-valve overlap. The camshaft has been ground so that the cams provide this additional valve overlap (□ 10-7). If the overlap is increased, the exhaust gases have more time to mix with the incoming air-fuel mixture. The presence of the exhaust gases, as the mixture is compressed and ignited, lowers the combustion temperatures so that less NO_x is produced.

Figure 24-16 shows the *transmission-controlled spark* (TCS) system of NO_x control. It uses a TCS solenoid that is connected electrically to a switch in the transmission. The switch is open only when the transmission is in high gear. When the transmission is in a lower gear, the switch is closed, connecting the TCS solenoid to the battery. The solenoid therefore lifts its plunger. This shuts off the vacuum line from the carburetor to the vacuum-advance unit on the distributor.

The result is no vacuum advance. Then, when the transmission shifts into high gear, the transmission switch opens, and the solenoid is disconnected. Now the vacuum line from the carburetor to the vacuum unit on the distributor is open so that the vacuum advance results.

Operating without vacuum advance can cause engine overheating under some conditions. Therefore, the TCS system includes a safety circuit that shuts down the TCS system when the engine overheats (Fig 24-17). The safety circuit includes a thermostatic temperature override switch, which is mounted on the engine, and a relay. If the engine gets too hot, the thermostatic switch closes. This action opens the relay. With the

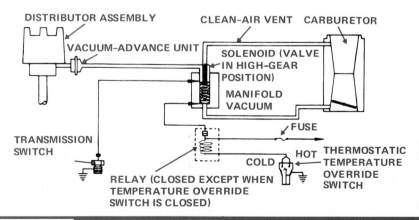

DISTRIBUTOR ASSEMBLY   CLEAN-AIR VENT   CARBURETOR

VACUUM-ADVANCE UNIT

SOLENOID (VALVE
IN HIGH-GEAR
POSITION)

MANIFOLD
VACUUM

TRANSMISSION
SWITCH

FUSE

RELAY (CLOSED EXCEPT WHEN
TEMPERATURE OVERRIDE
SWITCH IS CLOSED)

COLD   HOT

THERMOSTATIC
TEMPERATURE
OVERRIDE
SWITCH

Fig. 24-17 Schematic view of the transmission-controlled spark (TCS) system. *(Chevrolet Motor Division of General Motors Corporation)*

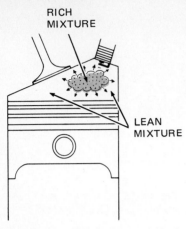

Fig. 24-18 Principle of stratified charging.

relay open, the solenoid circuit opens. The plunger moves to open the vacuum line to the vacuum-advance unit so that vacuum advance results. The system also restores vacuum advance when the engine is cold.

Vacuum advance is desirable when the engine starts and when the engine overheats. With vacuum advance, cold-engine operation is improved. Also, vacuum advance helps to prevent engine overheating, especially during long idling periods. Some engines have other vacuum-advance controls to prevent or allow vacuum advance under different operating conditions.

☐ 24-10 STRATIFIED CHARGE

Another way to improve combustion and reduce exhaust emissions is to use stratified charge. "Strata" means layers. Stratified charge means that the fuel and air are not mixed uniformly in the cylinder. They are in layers, some rich and some lean. The principle is shown in Fig. 24-18. The spark plug is surrounded by a small amount of rich mixture. A lean mixture fills the combustion chamber and surrounds the small pocket of rich mixture. Combustion starts in the rich mixture. Then, once started, the burning gases can ignite the lean mixture. The result is improved combustion. Fewer pollutants appear in the exhaust gas.

One way to achieve stratified charging is to give the mixture a swirling motion as it enters the cylinder. This can be done by careful placement of the intake port. Another method is the Honda CVCC (Compound Vortex Controlled Combustion) system (Fig. 24-19). Here, there is a separate small precombustion chamber. The precombustion chamber has its own intake valve and has the spark plug. Figure 24-20 shows how the system works. The carburetor delivers a rich mixture to the precombustion chamber and a lean mixture to the main cylinder. Ignition starts in

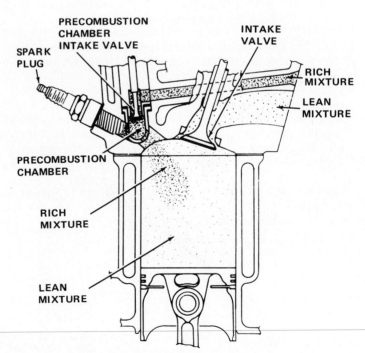

Fig. 24-19 Combustion chamber and valve arrangements of a Honda CVCC engine. *(Honda Motor Company, Inc.)*

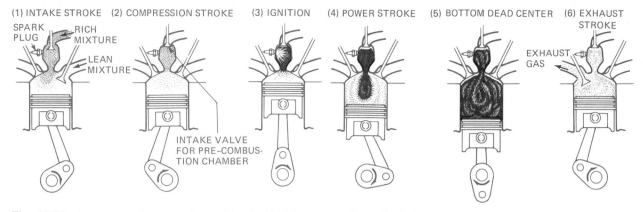

(1) INTAKE STROKE (2) COMPRESSION STROKE (3) IGNITION (4) POWER STROKE (5) BOTTOM DEAD CENTER (6) EXHAUST STROKE

SPARK PLUG
RICH MIXTURE
LEAN MIXTURE
INTAKE VALVE FOR PRE-COMBUS- TION CHAMBER
EXHAUST GAS

Fig. 24-20 Sequence of actions in the Honda CVCC system of stratified charge. *(Honda Motor Company, Inc.)*

the precombustion chamber. The rich mixture, as it burns, streams out into the lean mixture. There it mixes with the lean mixture, and combustion continues. The result is improved combustion and reduced exhaust emissions.

□ 24-11 TREATING THE EXHAUST GASES

After the exhaust gases leave the engine cylinders, the gases can be treated to reduce the HC, CO, and NO_x content. One method is to supply fresh air to the exhaust manifolds. This system, called the *air-injection system* (Fig. 24-21), provides additional oxygen to burn HC and CO coming out of the cylinders.

The air-injection pump pushes air through the air lines and the air manifold to a series of air-injection tubes, located near the exhaust

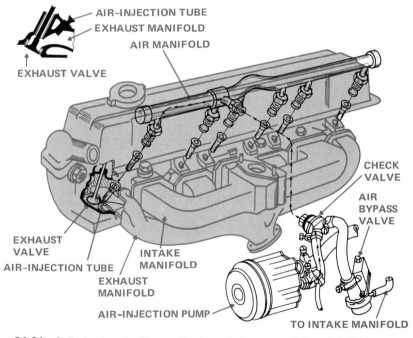

AIR-INJECTION TUBE
EXHAUST MANIFOLD
AIR MANIFOLD
EXHAUST VALVE
CHECK VALVE
AIR BYPASS VALVE
EXHAUST VALVE
AIR-INJECTION TUBE
INTAKE MANIFOLD
EXHAUST MANIFOLD
AIR-INJECTION PUMP
TO INTAKE MANIFOLD

Fig. 24-21 Cylinder head with manifolds and the parts of the air-injection system detached. *(Ford Motor Company)*

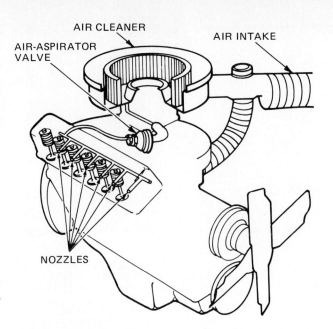

Fig. 24-22 Air-aspirator system, which is operated by pulses in the exhaust system. *(Chrysler Corporation)*

Labels in figure: AIR CLEANER, AIR-ASPIRATOR VALVE, AIR INTAKE, NOZZLES

valves. The oxygen in the air helps to burn any HC or CO in the exhaust gases. The check valve prevents any backflow of exhaust gases to the air pump in case of backfire. The air bypass valve operates during engine deceleration (when intake-manifold vacuum is high). Then it momentarily diverts air from the air pump to the air cleaner instead of to the exhaust manifold. This tends to prevent backfiring in the exhaust system.

Air injection also is used with certain types of catalytic converters (□ 24-13). Many electronic engine control systems also control the air-injection system (□ 15-12). For example, the Ford electronic engine control system using a feedback carburetor injects air into the exhaust manifold only part of the time. After the engine reaches normal operating temperature, air delivery is switched to the catalytic converter.

Some engines equipped with a catalytic converter use an *air-aspirator system* (Fig. 24-22) to deliver fresh air to the exhaust system. An *air-aspirator valve* is located in the tube between the air cleaner and the exhaust manifold or catalytic converter. The valve is opened and closed by the pulses in the exhaust system. At idle and slightly off idle, the negative-pressure pulses apply a slight vacuum at the ends of the nozzles. This vacuum causes the valve to open, admitting air from the clean-air side of the air cleaner into the exhaust system. The valve closes as soon as a pressure rise occurs in the exhaust system.

□ 24-12 CATALYTIC CONVERTERS

Catalytic converters provide another way to treat the exhaust gas (Fig. 24-23). These devices, located in the exhaust system, convert harmful pollutants into harmless gases. Inside the catalytic converter, the exhaust gases pass over a large surface area coated with a *catalyst* (Fig. 24-24). A catalyst is a material that causes a chemical reaction without actually becoming a part of the reaction process. For example, the metals platinum and palladium can act as *oxidizing catalysts*.

When exhaust gas and air are passed through a bed of platinum- or palladium-coated pellets, or through a coated honeycomb core, the HC and CO react with the oxygen in the air (O_2). Harmless water (H_2O) and

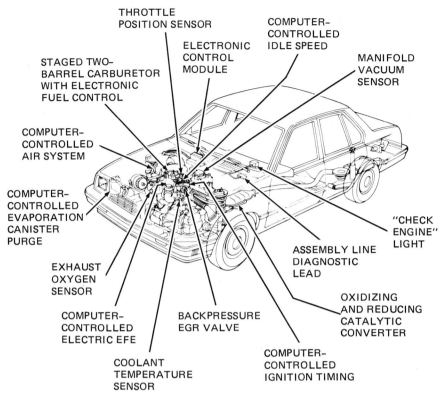

Fig. 24-23 Emission control systems on a late-model car. *(Chevrolet Motor Division of General Motors Corporation)*

carbon dioxide (CO_2) are formed. When the metal rhodium is used, the nitrogen oxides (NO_x) in the exhaust gas are reduced to harmless nitrogen (N_2) and oxygen (O). Therefore, rhodium is known as a *reducing catalyst*.

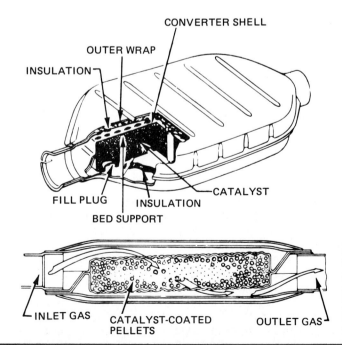

Fig. 24-24 Sectional view of a two-way pellet, or bead, type of oxidizing catalytic converter, showing (bottom) the flow of exhaust gas through it. *(Pontiac Motor Division of General Motors Corporation)*

Figure 24-24 shows a two-way *pellet-*, or *bead-*, *type catalytic converter*. It acts on the exhaust gas two ways, converting HC and CO to carbon dioxide and water. The converter is filled with coated pellets about the size of BB shot. As the exhaust gas flows through, the catalyst coating the pellets produces the chemical reaction. Another type of two-way catalytic-converter construction has a catalyst-coated honeycomb through which the exhaust gas must pass (Fig. 24-25). This is called a *monolith-type catalytic converter.*

Both types of two-way catalytic converters require additional air in the exhaust gas. The engines will be equipped with either the air-injection system (□ 24-11) or the air-aspirator system.

Cars equipped with catalytic converters must use nonleaded gasoline (□ 13-6). If the gasoline contains lead, the lead will coat the catalyst and the converter will stop working. If this happens to the pellet-type converter, the pellets can be replaced. On the honeycomb type, the complete catalytic converter must be replaced.

The catalytic converter gets hot. Therefore, the floor pan above it must be insulated to prevent this heat from flowing up into the passenger compartment.

Some engines have a miniconverter in addition to the main catalytic converter. The miniconverter is located close to the exhaust manifold. This enables the miniconverter to heat up quickly, thereby reducing HC and CO emissions during engine warm-up.

□ 24-13 DUAL-BED AND THREE-WAY CATALYTIC CONVERTERS

There are three general categories of catalytic converters. These are oxidizing, reducing, and three-way. The oxidizing converter (□ 24-12) handles HC and CO, using platinum or palladium as the catalyst. To control NO_x, rhodium is used as a reducing catalyst. It changes NO_x to harmless nitrogen (N_2) and oxygen (O). Instead of having two separate catalytic converters in the exhaust system, one for HC and CO and the other for NO_x, most manufacturers use either a *dual-bed catalytic converter* or a *three-way catalytic converter.*

The dual-bed converter (Fig. 24-26) is like two bead-type converters in one housing with an air chamber between them. The exhaust gas first passes through the upper bed, reducing the NO_x and oxidizing some of the

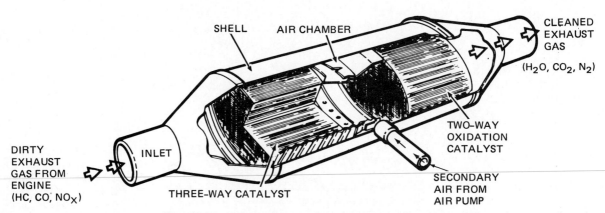

Fig. 24-25 A three-way catalytic converter using a monolithic, or honeycomb, substrate coated with catalyst. *(Ford Motor Company)*

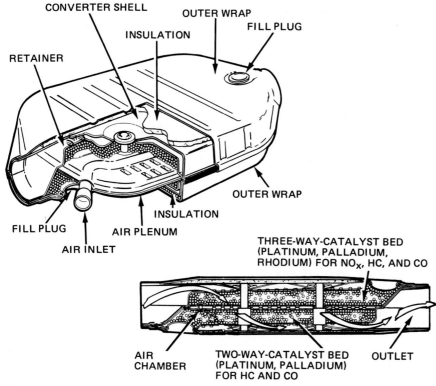

CONVERTER SHELL

OUTER WRAP

INSULATION

FILL PLUG

RETAINER

OUTER WRAP

FILL PLUG

INSULATION

AIR PLENUM

AIR INLET

THREE-WAY-CATALYST BED
(PLATINUM, PALLADIUM,
RHODIUM) FOR NO$_x$, HC, AND CO

AIR
CHAMBER

TWO-WAY-CATALYST BED
(PLATINUM, PALLADIUM)
FOR HC AND CO

OUTLET

Fig. 24-26 A dual-bed catalytic converter showing (top) the air chamber separating the two beds. *(Pontiac Motor Division of General Motors Corporation)*

HC and CO. Then the exhaust gas flows through the air chamber to the lower bed, where the air pump is adding sufficient air for final oxidizing of the HC and CO.

A three-way catalyst is a mixture of platinum and rhodium (sometimes mixed with palladium). It acts on all three of the regulated pollutants (HC, CO, and NO$_x$). However, this occurs only when the air-fuel–mixture ratio is precisely controlled (Fig. 24-14).

ANTIDIESELING DEVICES

☐ 24-14 PREVENTING RUN-ON

Some emission control devices tend to allow the spark-ignition engine to keep running after the ignition is turned off. This is sometimes called "dieseling," because the engine acts a little like a diesel engine. It runs without any spark from the ignition system. The high idle-speed setting leaves the throttle valve partly open. This allows enough air-fuel mixture to enter the cylinders to continue combustion. Hot spots in the combustion chamber provide ignition, so the engine continues to run.

Two methods are used to stop the engine once the ignition switch has been turned off. In one method there is an *idle-stop solenoid* on the carburetor (Fig. 24-27). When the ignition is on, the solenoid is connected to the battery. A plunger extends from the solenoid to keep the idle speed up

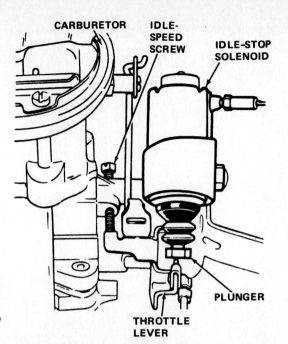

CARBURETOR IDLE-SPEED SCREW IDLE-STOP SOLENOID

PLUNGER

THROTTLE LEVER

Fig. 24-27 Idle-stop solenoid mounted on the carburetor to prevent engine dieseling when the ignition is turned off. *(Echlin Manufacturing Company)*

around 650 rpm. This means that the throttle valve is partly open. However, when the ignition switch is turned off, the solenoid is disconnected and the plunger retracts. This allows the throttle valve to fully close, stopping the engine.

In some air-conditioned cars, a higher idle speed is needed while the air conditioner is running. This is necessary to prevent engine stalling because of the extra load of the air-conditioner compressor. Some air-conditioned cars have a time-delay switch. It causes the air-conditioner clutch to engage for about 3 seconds after the ignition switch is turned off. The extra load on the engine causes it to stop without dieseling.

Select the *one* correct, best, or most probable answer to each question. Then check your answers against the correct answers given at the end of the book.

1. If perfect combustion takes place when gasoline is burned, then only
   a. HC and CO remain
   b. H_2O and SO_4 remain
   c. H_2O and CO_2 remain
   d. pure air results

2. The burned gases and air-fuel mixture that escape past the piston rings are called
   a. lost gas
   b. smoke
   c. blow up
   d. blowby

3. The purpose of the vapor-return line is to return to the fuel tank any vapor that
   a. escapes from the charcoal canister
   b. develops in the fuel pump
   c. leaks from the carburetor
   d. escapes from the fuel tank

4. In the PCV system, air flows from the air cleaner
   a. through the crankcase and into the exhaust manifold
   b. through the crankcase and into the intake manifold
   c. into the intake manifold and then into the crankcase
   d. into the cylinder head and then into the crankcase

5. The fuel tank is sealed and has
   a. a cap with two valves
   b. no cap
   c. two caps, one for pressure and the other for vacuum
   d. two outlets, one for pressure and the other for vacuum

6. EGR means
   a. extra gasoline required
   b. exhaust going rich
   c. exhaust-gas recirculation
   d. exhaust gas reduction

7. The purpose of the air-injection system is to inject air into
   a. the cylinders to improve combustion
   b. the intake manifold to increase combustion
   c. the carburetor to improve the air-fuel ratio
   d. the exhaust manifold to burn HC and CO

8. The purpose of the EGR system is to
   a. lower the NO_x in the exhaust gas
   b. increase the NO_x in the exhaust gas
   c. improve combustion
   d. increase engine efficiency

CHAPTER 25
SERVICING EMISSION CONTROLS

After studying this chapter, and with proper instruction and equipment, you should be able to:

1. Service the PCV system.
2. Service the evaporative control system.
3. Service the air-injection system.
4. Service the TCS and EGR systems.
5. Service the catalytic converter.
6. Service the thermostatic air cleaner.

Someday cars that give off excessive air pollutants may be banned from the streets. Laws limiting automotive air pollution are now in effect. The operation of the most widely used automotive emission control systems was covered in Chap. 24. The checks and service recommended for each of these systems are described in this chapter.

☐ 25-1 SERVICING THE PCV SYSTEM

The PCV valve must be replaced at regular intervals and whenever it clogs or sticks. When you install a new PCV valve (Fig. 25-1), inspect and clean the system thoroughly. This includes all hoses, grommets, and connectors. Clean the hoses with a brush, and wash the outsides. Thoroughly clean all connectors, especially the elbow connection. Wash the oil-filler cap, and shake it dry. Some types of oil-filler caps must not be dried with compressed air.

After all parts of the PCV system are clean, inspect them carefully. Replace any component that shows signs of damage, wear, or deterioration. The grommet into which the PCV valve fits must not be damaged or torn. Replace any cracked or brittle hose with a new hose. Replace any component, hose, or fitting that does not allow a free flow of air after cleaning.

Fresh air must be filtered before it enters the crankcase. Two different methods are used. In one method, the carburetor air-cleaner filter does the cleaning. In this system, the hose for the crankcase ventilation air is connected to the downstream, or clean-air, side of the carburetor air filter. No special service is required. The second method of cleaning the crankcase ventilation air is to use a separate filter, called a *PCV filter*. It mounts on the inside of the air-cleaner housing (Fig. 25-2). Ventilation air enters the air cleaner through the inlet or snorkel. Then the air passes through the PCV filter and into the crankcase.

Whenever the PCV system is serviced, the PCV filter must also be checked. To check the filter shown in Fig. 25-2, remove the retainer clip. Then remove the air-cleaner cover, and take out the PCV filter. Inspect it for damage, dirt buildup, and clogging. If the filter is clean, reinstall it in the air cleaner. A dirty or damaged PCV filter must be replaced.

☐ 25-2 SERVICING EVAPORATIVE CONTROL SYSTEMS

Evaporative control systems require little service. About the only periodic service required is to replace the filter, which is located in the bottom of the canister, at specified intervals. However, all canisters do not have a replaceable filter in them. No testers are needed to check evaporative control systems. Almost all problems can be found by visual inspection. Problems are also indicated by a strong odor of fuel. The infrared analyzer will quickly detect small vapor losses from around the fuel tank, canister, air cleaner, lines, or hose. Any loss will register on the HC meter of the analyzer.

The crankcase storage system requires an airtight crankcase to prevent the escape of HC vapor while it is stored there. Crankcase leaks also can be detected with an infrared exhaust analyzer.

Typical evaporative-control system defects are damaged lines, liquid-fuel and vapor leaks, and missing parts. The filler cap can be damaged or corroded so that its valves fail to work properly. A problem with the fuel-tank cap could deform the tank. This could also occur when the wrong cap is installed on the tank. Be sure that the fuel-tank filler cap is the proper cap specified by the manufacturer for the vehicle.

To service the evaporative control system, inspect the fuel-tank cap (Fig. 24-9). Inspect the condition of the sealing gasket around the cap. If the gasket is damaged, replace the cap. Inspect the filler neck and tank for stains resulting from fuel leakage. You can usually trace a stain back

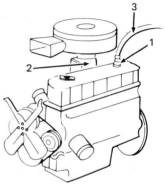

INLINE ENGINE
PCV VALVE LOCATIONS
1. ROCKER ARM COVER
2. CARBURETOR BASE
3. HOSE

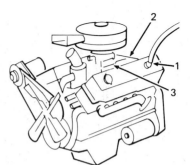

V-TYPE ENGINE
PCV VALVE LOCATION
1. ROCKER ARM COVER
2. REAR OF ENGINE
3. CARBURETOR BASE

Fig. 25-1 PCV-valve locations.

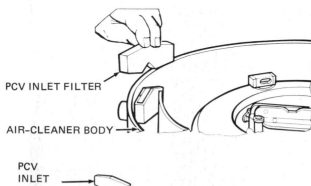

PCV INLET FILTER

AIR-CLEANER BODY

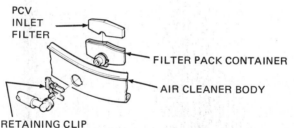

PCV INLET FILTER

FILTER PACK CONTAINER

AIR CLEANER BODY

RETAINING CLIP

Fig. 25-2 Replacing the PCV filter, located inside the air-cleaner body. *(Chrysler Corporation)*

to its origin. Then fix the cause of the leak. This may require replacing a gasket, clamp, or hose, or replacing the tank.

Inspect all lines and connections in the fuel and evaporative control systems for damage and leakage. Perform any necessary repairs. Test all clamps and connections for tightness.

> **NOTE** The hoses used in evaporative control systems are specially made to resist deterioration from contact with gasoline and gasoline vapor. When you replace a hose, make sure the new hose is specified by the manufacturer for use in evaporative control systems. Sometimes this type of hose is marked EVAP.

Inspect the charcoal-canister lines for liquid gasoline. If any is present, replace the liquid-vapor separator or the liquid check valve.

At scheduled intervals, some canisters require that you inspect and replace the filter in the bottom (Fig. 25-3). Servicing evaporative control systems requires no special tools. To replace the canister filter, remove the canister and turn it upside down (Fig. 25-3). Remove the bottom cover. Pull out the old filter with your fingers, and insert the new filter. If the canister itself is cracked or internally plugged, a new canister should be installed.

☐ 25-3 SERVICING THE AIR-INJECTION SYSTEM

In general, no routine service is required on the air-injection system. Hoses should be inspected and replaced, if required, whenever a tuneup is performed. Some systems use a separate filter to clean the air entering the pump. On these systems, the filter should be checked, cleaned, or replaced as recommended by the manufacturer. Most air pumps use a centrifugal filter. It is replaced only in case of mechanical damage.

The air-pump drive belt should be inspected periodically to make sure it is in good condition and has the proper tension (Fig. 25-4). The engine should be hot when the check is made. Inspect the belt for tension, wear, cracks, and brittleness. Install a new belt if necessary. Proper belt tension is important. A loose belt does not turn the air pump properly. This causes high exhaust-emission levels, and may result in noise. A tight belt overloads the rear bearing in the air pump. If the bearing be-

FIBER GLASS FILTER

BOTTOM OF CANISTER

Fig. 25-3 Replacing the air filter in the charcoal canister.

Fig. 25-4 Using a belt-tension gauge to check the adjustment of the air-pump drive belt. *(Chevrolet Motor Division of General Motors Corporation)*

comes noisy or fails, replacement of the air pump or bearing is necessary. When tightening the belt, do not pry against the pump housing. It is aluminum and will deform and break easily.

☐ 25-4 SERVICING THE TCS SYSTEM

The TCS system does not require regular service. However, every 12 months or 12,000 miles [19,300 km], or whenever a tuneup is performed, the operation of the system should be checked. Then the idle-stop solenoid should be adjusted (Fig. 24-27).

☐ 25-5 SERVICING THE EGR SYSTEM

There are differences in manufacturers' recommended service intervals for EGR systems. When the engine is operated with leaded gasoline, the EGR system should be checked for proper operation every 12 months or 12,000 miles [19,300 km]. For engines operated on unleaded gasoline, the EGR system is checked every 24 months or 24,000 miles [38,600 km]. Some cars have an EGR-maintenance reminder light on the instrument panel. The light comes on automatically to remind the driver to have the EGR system checked. Many late-model cars do not require regular EGR system service. Instead, if trouble develops in the EGR system, a diagnosis is performed.

A sticking EGR valve should be inspected for deposits. If there is more than a thin film of deposits, clean the EGR valve. Remove any deposits from the mounting surface and from around the valve and seat. The method of cleaning depends on the type of valve (Fig. 25-5). General Motors recommends cleaning an EGR valve from a V-type engine by holding the valve assembly in your hand and tapping the protruding stem lightly with a plastic hammer. Then lightly tap the sides of the valve. Shake out the loose particles. If you are not sure of how to clean a certain type of EGR valve, refer to the manufacturer's shop manual.

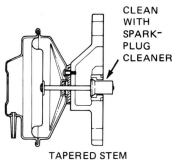

CLEAN WITH SPARK-PLUG CLEANER

TAPERED STEM

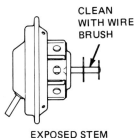

CLEAN WITH WIRE BRUSH

EXPOSED STEM

Fig. 25-5 Two different types of EGR valves and how to clean them. *(Ford Motor Company)*

CAREFUL Do not clamp the EGR valve in a vise or wash the EGR valve in solvent. Either may damage the valve and diaphragm.

□ 25-6 SERVICING THE CATALYTIC CONVERTER

The catalytic converter requires no service or maintenance in normal operation. By law, new-car manufacturers warrant catalytic converters to last for five years or 50,000 miles [80,500 km], whichever occurs first, in normal usage. Some converters have a drain hole in the front bottom of the converter for removing and replacing the pellets. Other types of defective catalytic converters require installation of a new converter.

No special tools are needed to replace a catalytic converter. Many converters can be removed by raising the vehicle on a lift and disconnecting the converter at the front and rear. When installing the new converter, use new nuts and bolts. Other converters have the exhaust pipe attached to the converter inlet. To replace the converter, cut the pipe.

If the bottom cover of a catalytic converter on a General Motors car is bulged, distorted, torn, or damaged, the cover can be replaced with the converter on the car (Fig. 25-6). A repair kit is available from General Motors dealers. However, if the inner shell of the converter is damaged, the converter must be replaced. When heat damage to the converter is indicated (bulging and distortion), inspect the remainder of the exhaust system for damage also. Unless the catalytic converter has a hole in it, or the converter pipe clamps are loose, exhaust-system noise is not the fault of the catalytic converter. Catalytic converters provide little noise control.

The use of fuel additives is not recommended on cars equipped with catalytic converters. The additive may harm the catalyst. Before using any fuel additive in the fuel tank or carburetor, check that the additive is

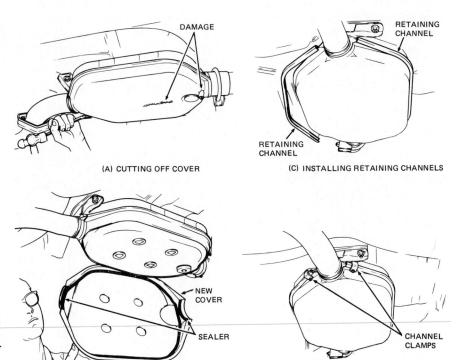

(A) CUTTING OFF COVER

(C) INSTALLING RETAINING CHANNELS

Fig. 25-6 Replacing a damaged bottom cover on a bead-type catalytic converter. *(Chevrolet Motor Division of General Motors Corporation)*

(B) PLACE SEALER BEAD AROUND NEW COVER

(D) INSTALLING CHANNEL CLAMPS

approved for use in cars with catalytic converters. Reasonable use of starting fluid will not harm the catalyst, according to General Motors.

During the chemical reaction in the catalytic converter, when the exhaust gas passes over the catalyst, the exhaust-gas temperature may rise to 1600 degrees Fahrenheit (F) [870 degrees Celsius (C)]. Therefore, cars equipped with catalytic converters have heat shields and insulation pads to protect chassis components and the passenger-compartment floor from heat damage (Fig. 25-7).

If a shield is missing, torn, or ripped, it must be replaced. Remove the damaged shield by carefully chiseling the shield loose at its welds. Whenever the vehicle has been operated on gravel roads, in off-road use, or under severe road-load conditions, Ford recommends a shield inspection at 5000-mile [8000-km] intervals.

□ 25-7 SERVICING THE THERMOSTATIC AIR CLEANER

To check the thermostatically controlled air cleaner, first make sure the hoses are tightly connected. The hot-air tube from the heat stove to the snorkel of the air cleaner should be in good condition. Inspect the system to ensure that there are no leaks. The system can be checked with a thermometer. Failure of the thermostatic system usually results in the damper door staying open. This means that the driver probably will not notice anything wrong in warm weather. But in cold weather the driver will notice hesitation, surge, and stalling. A typical checking procedure follows.

Remove the air-cleaner cover. Install a thermometer as close to the sensor as possible. Allow the engine to cool below 80°F [29°C] if it is hot. Reinstall the air-cleaner cover without the wing nut.

Start and idle the engine. When the damper begins to open, remove the air-cleaner cover and note the temperature reading. It should be between 85 and 115°F [29 and 46°C]. If it is difficult to see the damper, use a mirror. If the damper does not open at the correct temperature, check the vacuum motor and sensor.

With the engine off, the control damper should be in the "compartment," or cold-air-delivery, position (Fig. 24-13). To determine if the vacuum motor is operating, apply at least 9 inches Hg [229 mm] of vacuum to the fitting on the vacuum motor. The vacuum can be from the engine, from a distributor tester, or from a hand vacuum pump. With vacuum applied, the damper should move to the hot-air-delivery position (Fig. 24-13).

If the vacuum motor does not work properly, replace it. This can be done by drilling out the spot welds and unhooking the linkage. The new motor can be installed with a retaining strap and sheet-metal screws. Other types of vacuum motors have locking tabs which disengage and engage when the vacuum motor is rotated.

If the vacuum motor does work properly, the sensor should be replaced (Fig. 24-12). This is done by prying up the tabs on the retaining clip. The new sensor is then installed, and the tabs are bent down again.

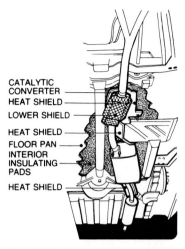

CATALYTIC
CONVERTER
HEAT SHIELD
LOWER SHIELD

HEAT SHIELD
FLOOR PAN
INTERIOR
INSULATING
PADS

HEAT SHIELD

Fig. 25-7 Heat shields and insulating pads surrounding the catalytic converter. *(Chrysler Corporation)*

Select the *one* correct, best, or most probable answer to each question. Then check your answers against the correct answers given at the end of the book.

1. The PCV filter is located in the
   a. charcoal canister
   b. air cleaner
   c. catalytic converter
   d. rocker-arm cover

2. In an evaporative control system using a canister without a filter in the bottom, the system requires
   a. no periodic service
   b. periodic replacement of the canister beads
   c. periodic replacement of the canister
   d. periodic replacement of the canister fresh-air filter

3. The drive belt should be checked periodically on the
   a. EGR system
   b. PCV system
   c. evaporative control system
   d. air-injection system

4. Prolonged fast idle after a cold start
   a. cleans the catalytic converter
   b. may damage the catalytic converter
   c. will warm the engine more rapidly
   d. conserves fuel

5. In the thermostatic air cleaner, the damper door in the snorkel does not open at the correct temperature. You should check the
   a. vacuum motor
   b. temperature sensor
   c. both *a* and *b*
   d. neither *a* nor *b*

PART 5

AUTOMOTIVE ENGINE SERVICE

Engine service includes *troubleshooting,* or *diagnosis,* to find the cause of trouble. Then you must correct the problem. This may require an adjustment, replacing a part, or rebuilding an assembly. You do whatever is necessary to eliminate the trouble and restore the engine to normal operating condition. This part of the book includes separate chapters on engine trouble diagnosis, testing instruments, and tuneup. Engine service is divided into separate chapters on valve-train service; connecting-rod, piston, and ring service; and crankshaft and cylinder service. There are six chapters in Part 5:

CHAPTER 26
ENGINE TROUBLE DIAGNOSIS

After studying this chapter, and with proper instruction and equipment, you should be able to:

1. List the basic engine troubles.
2. Describe the checks and corrections for at least six spark-ignition engine troubles.
3. Discuss how to make quick checks of the fuel and ignition systems.
4. Discuss how to identify the source of various types of engine noises.
5. Describe the causes of blue, black, and white exhaust smoke.
6. Diagnose the causes of troubles in several engines.

The person who works as an engine troubleshooter is called an engine *diagnostician,* a word that means diagnostic technician. The purpose of the diagnosis is to answer the question "*What* is wrong?" The diagnostician begins with the customer's complaints. The diagnostician listens to the engine and uses test instruments to find out exactly what is wrong. Then the diagnostician will tell the customer or write on the repair order what must be done to correct the engine trouble. The remedy might be something minor, like a spark plug. Or the remedy could be something major, like grinding valves or replacing piston rings. This chapter describes various engine troubles and what causes them.

□ 26-1 ENGINE TROUBLES

Various engine troubles are listed below. The process of pinpointing the possible causes of engine troubles to determine the problem is called *troubleshooting,* or *trouble diagnosis.* The troubles are listed below.

1. Engine does not crank when starting is attempted.
2. Engine cranks slowly but does not start.
3. Engine cranks at normal speed but does not start.
4. Engine runs but misses.
5. Engine lacks power, acceleration, or high-speed performance.
6. Engine overheats.

7. Engine idles roughly.
8. Engine stalls.
9. Engine backfires.
10. Engine has smoky exhaust—blue, black, or white.
11. Engine uses too much oil.
12. Engine has low oil pressure.
13. Engine uses too much fuel.
14. Exhaust gas has too much CO or HC.
15. Engine experiences run-on, or dieseling.
16. Engine is noisy (knocks, pings, clatters).
17. Special diesel-engine problems.

Each of the troubles is discussed in following sections. This includes the possible causes of each trouble and how to correct the conditions that are found. Some steps in trouble diagnosis require the use of engine testing instruments. These are described in Chap. 27. The trouble-diagnosis procedure covers both spark-ignition and diesel engines.

□ 26-2 ENGINE DOES NOT CRANK

The first thing you should think about if the engine does not crank when you try to start it is that the battery is dead. Often, the battery is the trouble. But you have to consider whether the driver ran down the battery while trying to start the car. If the driver did, the real cause of the trouble could be elsewhere. Make sure the gearshift lever is in neutral (N) or park (P). If nothing happens when you try to start, turn on the headlights and try to start the engine again. One of the following will happen:

- Lights stay bright with no cranking action.
- Lights dim a lot with no cranking action.
- Lights go out.
- Lights burn dimly or not at all when you turn them on.

Let's look at each of these in detail.

1. LIGHTS STAY BRIGHT
If the lights stay bright, there is an open circuit between the starting motor and the battery. The open circuit is probably in the wiring circuit, in the starting-motor solenoid, or in the motor itself. Also, the transmission may not be in neutral or park, or the neutral safety switch may need adjustment.

2. LIGHTS DIM A LOT
If the lights dim a lot, the battery may be run-down. It has enough power to light the lights, but when the load of the starting motor is added, the battery is too weak. Test the battery. If the battery is *not* run-down, remove the starting motor for further checks of it and of the engine. The trouble could be a jammed or shorted starting motor or a locked engine.

3. LIGHTS DIM A LITTLE
If the lights dim only a little when you try to start, the starting-motor solenoid may have burned or corroded contacts. The solenoid draws a little current. Therefore the lights dim from the added load on the battery. But the current for cranking cannot get to the starting motor because the corroded contacts are an open circuit in the solenoid. Listen for cranking action. If you hear the buzz of an electric motor running, the overrunning clutch in the starting motor is slipping.

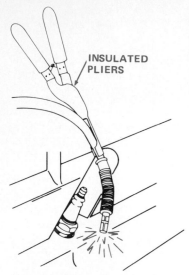

Fig. 26-1 To make a spark test, disconnect a spark-plug cable and crank the engine.

4. LIGHTS GO OUT

If the lights go out when you try to start, it is probably due to a bad connection at one of the battery terminals. The connection is good enough to let through the few amperes needed for the lights. But when the starting-motor load of several hundred amperes is added, the connection breaks down. Try wiggling the cable connections at the battery terminals. If that helps, then the terminals should be cleaned (Chap. 19).

5. LIGHTS BURN DIMLY OR NOT AT ALL

If the lights burn dimly or not at all when you first turn them on, the battery is probably run-down. Test the battery. If it is run-down, you should try to find out what caused it. Maybe the driver ran down the battery trying to start. Then the trouble is in the fuel system, in the ignition system, or in the engine itself. Maybe the alternator output is low, or maybe a short in the electrical system caused a slow drain on the battery. Also, the battery may no longer be able to hold a charge.

□ 26-3 ENGINE CRANKS SLOWLY BUT DOES NOT START

If the engine cranks slowly but does not start, the battery may be run-down. In cold weather, the engine is much harder to crank. If it is very cold, the engine won't turn over very fast. The driver may have run down the battery trying to start. Other possible causes include a bad battery, a defect in the charging system that prevents the alternator from charging the battery, a defective starting motor, and mechanical trouble in the engine.

□ 26-4 ENGINE CRANKS AT NORMAL SPEED BUT DOES NOT START

If the engine cranks at normal speed but does not start, the battery and starting motor are in good condition. The cause probably is in the ignition system or the fuel system. One of the following situations probably exists:

■ The fuel-delivery system is not delivering normal amounts of air-fuel mixture.
■ The ignition system is not delivering sparks properly.
■ In the diesel engine, the fuel-injection system is faulty, or the driver used the incorrect starting procedure.

To check the spark-ignition system, disconnect the lead from one spark plug. Use insulated pliers and hold the plug end about ¼ inch (6 mm) from the engine block (Fig. 26-1). On engines with high-energy ignition (HEI), attach the spark-plug lead to a spark tester (Fig. 26-2). The spark tester should be grounded to the engine. Then crank the engine. A good spark should jump the gap. If no spark occurs, the trouble is in the ignition system. If a spark does occur, the trouble probably is in the fuel system.

Failure to start could be due to overchoking. Try cranking with the throttle wide open. If this doesn't work, take off the air cleaner and open and close the throttle valve several times. If the accelerator pump delivers fuel each time you open the throttle valve (Fig. 26-3), the carburetor is getting fuel. Two other possible causes remain:

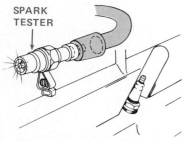

Fig. 26-2 To make a spark test using a spark tester, attach the spark-plug cable to the tester, and clamp the tester to a good ground. Then crank the engine. *(ATW)*

■ The ignition or valve timing is incorrect.
■ There are problems in the engine, such as fouled spark plugs or defective valves.

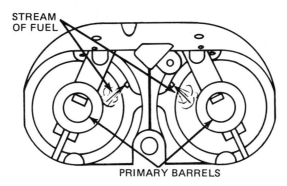

STREAM OF FUEL

PRIMARY BARRELS

Fig. 26-3 To find out if the accelerator pump is delivering fuel, shut off the engine and remove the air cleaner. Look into the carburetor and quickly open the throttle valves. You should see a stream of fuel discharging into each venturi. *(Ford Motor Company)*

Also, a plugged or collapsed exhaust system can build up back pressure (Fig. 26-4). This could prevent normal exhaust and intake so that the engine will not start.

NOTE The choke should be open when the engine is warm and closed when the engine is completely cold and the ignition switch is first turned on. If the choke does not work properly, the engine will be hard to start. If the choke is open, a cold engine will be hard to start. If the choke is closed, a hot engine will be hard to start.

The diesel engine may crank normally but not start if:

- The proper starting procedure has not been followed.
- The fuel system is not delivering the correct amount of fuel at the correct time. The pump timing could be off or the injection pump or injection valve inoperative.
- The glow plugs may be inoperative.

☐ 26-5 ENGINE RUNS BUT MISSES (SPARK IGNITION)

A missing engine is a rough engine. If one or more cylinders fail to fire, the power strokes are delivered unevenly. The result is roughness and loss of power. It is sometimes hard to track down a miss. The miss might occur at some speeds and not others. Also, the miss may skip around. To check out one or more misfiring cylinders, use an oscilloscope and a dynamometer. (The oscilloscope and dynamometer are discussed in Chap. 27.) If these testing instruments are not available, then the test can be made as follows.

Use insulated pliers to disconnect each spark-plug cable in turn to locate the missing cylinder. (Disconnecting the cable prevents the spark from reaching the spark plug, and the spark plug will not fire.) If disconnecting the cable changes the engine speed, then the cylinder was delivering power before you disconnected the cable. But if there is no change in engine speed, then that cylinder was missing before you disconnected the cable.

NOTE This test may not be recommended for use on engines equipped with certain types of electronic ignition systems. Consult the manufacturer's service manual for ignition-testing procedures.

A cylinder-balance test using a tachometer and a vacuum gauge can be used to check that a cylinder is delivering power. With most engine analyzers that include an oscilloscope, you can make a cylinder-balance test that will quickly pinpoint the missing cylinder. When the analyzer is

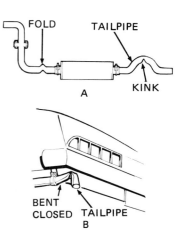

FOLD   TAILPIPE

KINK

A

BENT CLOSED   TAILPIPE

B

Fig. 26-4 A clogged or restricted exhaust system may cause the engine, hot or cold, to lack power. *(Ford Motor Company)*

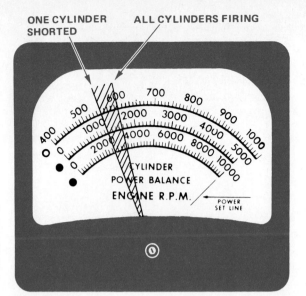

ONE CYLINDER SHORTED   ALL CYLINDERS FIRING

Fig. 26-5 To check for a misfiring cylinder, remove each spark-plug cable, one at a time. With the cable disconnected, if the cylinder is good, engine speed should drop about 50 rpm. *(Sun Electric Corporation)*

connected to the running engine, you turn a knob or push a button and the cylinders are shorted out, one by one, in the firing order. The scope then shows which cylinder is shorted out. If shorting out a cylinder causes the manifold vacuum or the engine speed to drop by 50 rpm or more (Fig. 26-5), the cylinder was delivering power. But if little or no change in rpm or vacuum takes place, then you know that the cylinder was not delivering power.

> **NOTE** In the diesel engine, a miss usually is caused by failure of the fuel system to deliver an adequate amount of fuel to the cylinder. This could be due to a clogged nozzle, air in the line, or injection-pump problems.

☐ 26-6 ENGINE STARTS BUT STALLS AT IDLE (DIESEL)

This could be caused by an incorrect low-idle setting, the fast-idle solenoid not working, or the fuel system not operating properly. Stalling at idle could also be due to mechanical problems in the engine.

☐ 26-7 ENGINE RUNS BUT IDLES ROUGHLY (DIESEL)

First, determine if the engine idles roughly without abnormal noise or smoke. If so, the slow-idle setting is incorrect or there is trouble in the fuel system. The possibilities include restrictions, improper pump timing, or dirty or wrong fuel. If the engine idles roughly with noise and smoke, the pump timing is off or the injection nozzles are not working properly.

☐ 26-8 ENGINE LACKS POWER, ACCELERATION, OR HIGH-SPEED PERFORMANCE (SPARK-IGNITION)

A complaint about lack of power, acceleration, or high-speed performance is hard to analyze. Almost any part of the car, from the engine to the tires, could be the cause. Try to find out if the engine lacks power, only cold, only hot, or both. An oscilloscope or dynamometer, along with other test instruments, may be needed to pinpoint the exact cause of this kind of trouble.

1. ENGINE LACKS POWER COLD OR HOT

If the engine lacks power hot or cold, the cause could be a miss (□ 26-5). The cause could also be carburetor or fuel-injection trouble (not delivering normal air-fuel mixture). A clogged exhaust system could restrict normal intake and exhaust action. This could be caused either by a bent or collapsed exhaust or tail pipe or by a clogged muffler (Fig. 26-4) or catalytic converter. There are many other possible causes outside the engine:

■ PCV valve stuck open
■ Clogged air cleaner
■ Incorrectly adjusted throttle linkage
■ Incorrect fuel for the engine
■ Weak ignition coil
■ Incorrect ignition timing

The above are most of the possible "outside" causes. Inside the engine, lack of power could be caused by the following:

■ Loss of compression from worn cylinder walls, pistons, or rings
■ Defective valves
■ Oil too heavy for the engine
■ Carbon buildup in the combustion chambers
■ Worn camshaft lobes
■ Excessive parts wear or mechanical friction

Also, dragging brakes, underinflated tires, and incorrect wheel alignment can rob power from the drive wheels.

2. ENGINE LACKS POWER ONLY WHEN COLD

If the engine lacks power only when it is cold, the cause is probably an incorrect air-fuel mixture reaching the cylinders or a failure of the warm-up systems. For example, if the choke is not working properly, the mixture will be too lean for good cold-engine operation. The manifold heat-control valve or the thermostatic air cleaner may not be operating properly. This means the mixture is not getting the heat it should have. If the thermostat in the cooling system is sticking open, the engine will take a long time to warm up and develop good hot-engine performance. Also, engine valves may stick partly open when cold and cause poor cold-engine performance.

3. ENGINE LACKS POWER ONLY WHEN HOT

To start normally when hot, the engine must have good compression and no intake-manifold leaks. However, the engine that lacks power only when hot probably is overheating. The causes of engine overheating are discussed in the following section. There are other possible causes of poor hot-engine performance. For example, an automatic choke sticking closed will deliver an air-fuel mixture that is too rich. This can reduce engine power. In addition, a rich mixture can foul spark plugs and piston rings with carbon, causing serious engine trouble. You can check the choke by removing the air cleaner and noting choke action as the engine warms up. If the choke does not open, you have located the trouble.

If the manifold heat-control valve and the thermostatic air cleaner do not work properly, they can overheat air-fuel mixture. This prevents adequate amounts of mixture from reaching the cylinders. Engine performance will be poor. If there is vapor lock in the fuel line or fuel pump, not enough fuel or no fuel will reach the carburetor. The engine will perform poorly or stall.

☐ 26-9 ENGINE MISSES, ONE CYLINDER (DIESEL)

This is due to a defective injection nozzle or to air in the tubing to that nozzle. Also, there could be a defect in the pump which keeps it from delivering fuel to the missing cylinder.

☐ 26-10 ENGINE MISSES ABOVE IDLE (DIESEL)

This is due to a plugged fuel filter, wrong or dirty fuel, or incorrect timing of the fuel pump.

☐ 26-11 LOSS OF POWER (DIESEL)

This could be due to a restriction in the air intake or exhaust, plugged fuel filter or vacuum vent in the fuel tank, or restriction in the fuel-return or fuel-injection system. It could also be caused by wrong or dirty fuel or compression leaks around the glow plugs or fuel nozzles.

☐ 26-12 ENGINE OVERHEATS

Most engine overheating is caused by loss of coolant through leaks in the cooling system. How to check the cooling system is described in Chap. 29. There are other possible causes of engine overheating. For example, high altitudes and hot climates make engines overheat more easily. Overloading the engine will cause it to overheat. Not enough lubricating oil may cause the engine to overheat and possibly fail! Improperly timed ignition or valves will cause engine overheating. A loose or slipping engine fan belt will result in poor water-pump and fan action and engine overheating. Idling the engine and driving at low speed for long periods can overheat the engine. If the emission control TCS system is bad, it may prevent vacuum advance even though the engine is getting hot. Therefore, the engine will get even hotter. So the TCS system also needs checking as a cause of engine overheating.

The following conditions in the cooling system are possible causes of engine overheating:

- Thermostat stuck closed
- Clogged cooling-system hoses
- Scale or rust buildup in the engine water jackets or radiator
- Defective water pump
- Not enough coolant in the system
- Thermostatic fan not working

☐ 26-13 ENGINE IDLES ROUGHLY (SPARK IGNITION)

A rough idle can be caused by improper carburetor or fuel-injection-system operation. Rough idle can also be caused by vacuum leaks and by any of the reasons for lack of power (☐ 26-8).

☐ 26-14 ENGINE STALLS (SPARK IGNITION)

If the engine starts and then stalls, note when the stalling takes place. Does the engine stall:

- Before the engine warms up?
- As the engine warms up?
- After slow-speed driving or idling?
- After high-speed or full-load driving?

The operating condition will give you a clue to the cause.

1. ENGINE STALLS BEFORE IT WARMS UP

If the engine stalls before it warms up, the cause is probably fuel-system trouble. Any one of the troubles listed below can cause stalling before the engine warms up:

- Idle mixture or idle speed out of adjustment
- Low float level in the carburetor
- Icing in the carburetor
- Open choke

With a low float level, not enough fuel can get to the engine. Icing is caused by cool, moist air entering the cold carburetor. Under some conditions the moisture condenses and turns to ice. This clogs the carburetor throttle valve and air horn, and the engine stalls.

Ignition-system troubles can cause engine stalling before warm-up. If the ignition system is bad enough to cause stalling, it probably would prevent starting. However, there might be an open primary resistance wire. When the engine is cranked, this wire is bypassed. Full battery voltage is applied to the ignition coil (☐ 22-8). Then, when the engine starts, the wire goes back into the circuit. If this wire is open, the engine stalls.

2. ENGINE STALLS AS IT WARMS UP

If the engine stalls as it warms up, the problem is probably in the fuel system. If the choke does not open, the mixture will become too rich for a warm engine. Then the engine will stall. Also, the manifold heat-control valve or the thermostat in the air cleaner may be sticking. This means the ingoing air-fuel mixture will be overheated. Not enough of the mixture will get to the cylinders for proper combustion. When this happens, the engine stalls.

Another possible cause of stalling is a low hot-idle speed. As the engine warms up, it could stall because the hot-idle speed is too low. Engine overheating (☐ 26-12) could cause vapor lock and stalling.

3. ENGINE STALLS AFTER LOW-SPEED DRIVING OR IDLING

The fuel system is a likely cause of this condition. A weak fuel pump may not deliver enough fuel at idle. The fuel pump could be weak at low speed and do a satisfactory job during intermediate- and high-speed driving. The float level in the carburetor may be too high, or the idle mixture may be too rich. These conditions can cause the engine to "load up" with an overrich mixture and stall. Engine overheating also can cause stalling after prolonged low-speed driving or idling. Even an engine in good condition can overheat under these conditions. The reason is that not enough air passes through the radiator to ensure adequate cooling (☐ 26-12).

4. ENGINE STALLS AFTER HIGH-SPEED DRIVING

If the engine stalls after high-speed driving, the problem is usually in the fuel system. High-speed driving builds up heat in the engine. Then, when the car stops—at a stop sign, for example—the heat causes a vapor lock. Stalling can also be caused by engine overheating (□ 26-12).

□ 26-15 ENGINE BACKFIRES

Backfiring is caused by early ignition. Combustion flashes back through the still-open intake valve. After-firing, which is another type of combustion outside the cylinder, occurs in the exhaust system in the manifold or the muffler. Backfiring or after-firing can result from the following:

■ Defective exhaust emission control air-bypass valve
■ Incorrect ignition or valve timing
■ Defective high-voltage wiring or distributor cap, which permits cross-firing
■ Spark plugs of the wrong heat range that overheat and cause preignition
■ Carbon in the engine, which develops hot spots that preignite the mixture
■ Hot or sticking valves

Valves will overheat if they do not seat properly or if they have been ground too much. Air-fuel mixtures that are too rich or too lean can also cause backfiring.

□ 26-16 ENGINE HAS SMOKY EXHAUST (SPARK IGNITION)

Smoky exhaust indicates that the engine is burning oil, the air-fuel mixture is too rich, or water has leaked into the combustion chamber. The color of the exhaust can tell you which condition exists. If the exhaust gas has a bluish tinge, the engine is burning oil. The problem of the engine using too much oil is described in □ 26-17. If the exhaust gas is more black than blue, the air-fuel mixture probably is too rich. Not all the fuel is burning in the engine. Black exhaust gas can also be caused by misfiring cylinders (□ 26-5). The causes of excessive fuel consumption are described in □ 26-19. Whitish exhaust smoke while the engine is cold may be considered normal. But after warm-up, it may indicate water in the combustion chamber. This condition may be caused by a cracked cylinder head or a blown cylinder-head gasket.

□ 26-17 ENGINE USES TOO MUCH OIL (SPARK IGNITION)

The engine can lose oil in three ways. These are by burning it in the combustion chamber, by leaking it in liquid form, and by passing it out of the crankcase through the PCV system as mist or vapor.

External leaks often can be seen by inspecting the seals around the oil pan, the valve cover, the timing cover, and at the oil-line and oil-filter connections. Oil and dirt around the leaky spot will locate the leak.

You can check the actual amount of oil the engine uses. Fill the crankcase to the correct level and drive several hundred miles. Then measure the additional amount of oil necessary to bring the oil level back up to the correct level. However, if the car is being driven around town in start-and-stop operation, the engine may never get warmed up. This means that the crankcase oil will be diluted with water and unburned fuel. For a proper check on the oil level, the car should be taken out on the highway and driven long enough for the engine to reach normal operating temperature. Then the water and unburned fuel will be evaporated from the oil.

If oil is being burned in the combustion chambers, the exhaust gas will have a bluish tinge. Oil can enter the combustion chambers past the valve guides and valve stems and past the piston rings.

If the valve guides are worn, there will be too much clearance around the valve stems. Oil will be drawn into the combustion chamber on each intake stroke. If the valve guides are worn, the underside of the valves usually will be covered with carbon. This condition requires replacement of the valve seals or installation of new valve guides and possibly new valves.

A common cause of excessive oil consumption is the failure of the piston rings to keep the oil out of the combustion chambers. Oil gets into the combustion chambers because of worn cylinder walls and worn or stuck piston rings. Another possible cause is worn engine bearings that throw off excessive amounts of oil onto the cylinder walls. There is more oil than the piston rings can control. Then some of the oil gets up into the combustion chambers.

Even with a good engine, oil consumption goes up with engine speed. More oil is pumped at high speed, so more oil gets on the cylinder walls. The piston rings have less time to control the oil. Also, at high speed, the oil gets hotter and thinner. Therefore it is more difficult for the piston rings to control.

□ 26-18 ENGINE HAS LOW OIL PRESSURE

Low oil pressure is often a warning of a worn oil pump or worn engine bearings. Worn bearings can pass so much oil that the oil pump cannot maintain pressure. This can be serious because the center bearings could get most of the oil. The end bearings could be oil-starved and fail from lack of oil. Other causes of low oil pressure include the following:

- Weak oil-pump pressure relief-valve spring
- Worn oil pump
- Oil-line leaks
- Clogged oil line

If the oil is diluted, foaming, or loaded with too much sludge, the oil pump cannot feed enough oil to the engine to keep the pressure up. An overheating engine may cause the oil to thin out because of the high temperature. This could prevent normal oil pressure.

□ 26-19 ENGINE USES EXCESSIVE FUEL

This means poor fuel economy, or few miles per gallon. The cause of this trouble may be underinflated tires or dragging brakes. Or the trouble may be in the fuel system, the ignition system, or the engine. It could be due to the way the car is driven. A fuel-mileage tester can be used to accurately check fuel consumption. You may need other test instruments to find the cause.

NOTE Before making tests, find out the answers to these questions: Is the car operated around town in start-and-stop driving? Does the driver pump the accelerator pedal when idling and try to be the first to get away when the traffic light changes? If so, fuel mileage will be poor.

Here are the conditions to check in the fuel system:

■ Failure of the choke to open, which means the engine is getting a rich mixture
■ Clogged air cleaner, which can act like a closed choke
■ High float level, which causes too much fuel to be delivered to the carburetor fuel nozzles
■ Idle-mixture screw set too rich
■ Accelerator-pump check valve in the carburetor not closing, which allows fuel to leak past the valve and into the carburetor
■ Metering rod stuck in the high-speed position, which allows the engine to be fed a mixture that is too rich
■ Worn carburetor jets, which allow too much fuel to flow
■ Power-valve diaphragm leaking or receiving low vacuum

Here are the conditions in the ignition system to consider:

■ Weak coil or condenser, which could cause missing, particularly at high engine speeds
■ Incorrect timing or faulty advance-mechanism action, either of which could prevent full use of the power in the air-fuel mixture
■ Dirty or worn spark plugs or contact points or defective wiring, which could cause missing and high fuel consumption

Here are the conditions in the engine to consider:

■ Worn or stuck piston rings
■ Worn cylinder walls
■ Worn or stuck valves
■ Leaking cylinder-head gasket

Any of these conditions cause loss of power, which means that more fuel must be burned to get the same engine speed.

□ 26-20 EXCESSIVE HC AND CO IN THE EXHAUST GAS (SPARK IGNITION)

Today, automobile-testing procedures include using the exhaust-gas analyzer (Chap. 27). The purpose of exhaust-gas testing is to identify cars with excessive pollutants in the exhaust gas. Some states require exhaust-gas testing of all cars during state inspection. Cars that do not pass give off too much HC or CO and must be repaired before they can be licensed. Excessive HC and CO appear in the exhaust gas because all the fuel does not burn completely during combustion. Possible causes are:

1. Missing because of ignition problems, such as faulty spark plugs, high-voltage wiring, distributor cap, ignition coil, condenser, or contact points
2. Improper ignition timing
3. Choke sticking closed, worn jets, high float level, and other conditions listed in □ 26-19 which cause excessive fuel consumption.
4. Faulty air-injection system, which does not supply enough air into the exhaust system to completely burn the HC and CO
5. Defective TCS (transmission-controlled spark) system, which permits vacuum advance in all gear positions instead of only in high
6. Defective catalytic converter, which must be replaced or recharged to restore exhaust-gas cleaning

☐ 26-21 ENGINE RUN-ON, OR DIESELING

Some engines have a tendency to continue running after the ignition switch has been turned off (☐ 24-14). If an engine does this, the following could be the trouble:

- Incorrect idle-stop solenoid adjustment or defective solenoid
- Engine overheating
- Hot spots in cylinders
- Advanced ignition timing
- On diesel engines, the cause is failure of the solenoid fuel valve to return to the OFF position when the ignition switch is turned off.

☐ 26-22 ENGINE NOISES

A skilled technician can often pinpoint the causes of engine troubles by listening to the engine operating under different conditions. The technician may use a listening rod or a stethoscope to locate the source of a noise. To do this, the pickup end of the rod or stethoscope is moved around on various places on the engine to find where the noise is loudest (Fig. 26-6). This enables the technician to find out which cylinder has the broken ring or which main bearing is knocking.

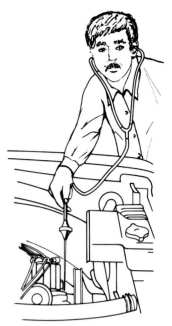

Fig. 26-6 A mechanic's stethoscope being used to locate engine noise.

CAUTION Keep away from the moving fan belt and fan when using a listening rod or stethoscope!

Here are descriptions of various noises and what they mean.

1. VALVE AND TAPPET NOISE

Valve and tappet noise is a regular clicking that increases with engine speed. The noise is caused by too much clearance in the valve train. If the valve train has mechanical lifters, the valves can be adjusted to minimize the noise. If the valve train has hydraulic valve lifters, the problem may be caused by a sticking plunger in the lifters. This requires servicing or replacement of the lifters.

Other causes of the valve and tappet noise include the following:

- Weak valve springs
- Worn valve-lifter faces
- Lifters loose in the block
- Rough camshaft lobes
- Rough or worn faces on the lifter adjustment screws
- Worn rocker arms

Any of these conditions could cause a clicking noise that synchronizes with valve action.

2. DETONATION

This is a pinging or chattering sound. It is most noticeable when the car is climbing a hill or accelerating. It can be caused by any of the following:

- Use of a low-octane gasoline
- Carbon deposits in the combustion chamber, which increase the compression ratio and the tendency of the engine to detonate
- Excessively advanced ignition timing

3. CONNECTING-ROD NOISE

Connecting-rod noise is usually a light knocking or pounding. The sound is most noticeable when the engine is "floating" (neither accelerating nor decelerating). The sound becomes more noticeable as the driver eases up on the accelerator pedal with the car running at medium speed. To find out which connecting rod is causing the trouble, short out each spark plug in turn. Rod noise will drop off when the cylinder that is responsible is not delivering power. Rod noise can be caused by a worn big-end bearing or crankpin, a bent rod, or insufficient oil.

4. PISTON-PIN NOISE

Piston-pin noise is somewhat like valve and tappet noise, but it has more of a metallic, double-knock sound. It can usually be heard most easily during idle with the spark advanced. It may also be noticeable at car speeds of about 30 mph [48 km/h]. Piston-pin noise is checked by idling the engine and then shorting out spark plugs one at a time. The noise will be reduced when the plug in a noisy cylinder is shorted out. Causes of piston-pin noise include a worn piston or bushing and lack of oil.

5. PISTON-RING NOISE

Piston-ring noise is similar to the valve and tappet noise. It is a click, a snap, or a rattle. It is most evident on acceleration. Low ring tension, broken or worn rings, or worn cylinder walls can produce this noise. Make the following test: Remove all spark plugs and add 1 to 2 fluid ounces [30 to 60 cc] of heavy engine oil to each cylinder. Replace the plugs. Crank the engine for several revolutions to work the oil down past the rings. Then start the engine. If the noise has been reduced, the rings are probably at fault.

6. PISTON SLAP

Piston slap is a hollow, muffled, bell-like sound. It is caused by the piston rocking back and forth in the cylinder and "slapping" the cylinder wall. Piston slap can be caused by worn cylinder walls or pistons, collapsed piston skirts, or misaligned connecting rods.

7. CRANKSHAFT KNOCK

Crankshaft knock is a heavy and dull metallic knock. It is most noticeable when the engine is under a heavy load or accelerating, especially if the engine is cold. If the noise is regular, it is probably caused by worn main bearings. If the noise is irregular and sharp, it is probably caused by a worn thrust bearing.

8. MISCELLANEOUS NOISES

Other noises coming from the engine compartment can be caused by loose accessories. These include the alternator, starting motor, horn, manifolds, flywheel, crankshaft pulley, and oil pan. Also, noise that seems to come from the engine may be coming from the clutch, transmission, or drive line.

> **NOTE** A noise like a rod-bearing knock in a diesel engine can be caused by air in the fuel system or by a nozzle or nozzles sticking open or opening at low pressure.

Select the *one* correct, best, or most probable answer to each question. Then check your answers against the correct answers given at the end of the book.

1. An engine is using too much oil. Mechanic A says that worn valve guides could be the cause. Mechanic B says that tapered cylinder walls could be the cause. Who could be right?
   a. A only
   b. B only
   c. either A or B
   d. neither A nor B

2. An engine will crank slowly because of
   a. a defective water pump
   b. vapor lock
   c. an undersized battery cable
   d. excessive fuel-pump pressure

3. Failure of an engine to start even though it cranks at normal speed could be due to a
   a. run-down battery
   b. defective starting motor
   c. sticking engine valve
   d. defective ignition

4. Missing in one cylinder is likely to result from
   a. a clogged exhaust
   b. an overheated engine
   c. vapor lock
   d. a defective spark plug

5. Irregular missing in different cylinders may result from
   a. a defective starting motor
   b. a defective carburetor
   c. an open cranking circuit
   d. an overcharged battery

6. Loss of engine power as the engine warms up is most likely caused by
   a. vapor lock
   b. excessive rolling resistance
   c. the throttle valve not closing fully
   d. heavy oil

7. An engine will lose power (hot or cold) if it has
   a. incorrect idle speed
   b. an automatic choke valve that is stuck open
   c. worn rings and cylinder walls
   d. none of the above

8. An engine may stall as it warms up if the
   a. ignition timing is off
   b. choke valve sticks closed
   c. battery is run-down
   d. throttle valve does not open fully

9. An engine will overheat if the
   a. automatic choke sticks
   b. fan belt breaks
   c. fuel pump is defective
   d. battery is run-down

10. The most probable cause of an engine stalling after idling or slow-speed driving is
    a. loss of compression
    b. a defective fuel pump
    c. sticking engine valve
    d. all of the above

11. Stalling of an engine after high-speed driving is probably caused by
    a. vapor lock
    b. incorrect ignition timing
    c. worn carburetor jets
    d. all of the above

12. Engine backfiring may result from
    a. spark plugs of wrong heat range
    b. vapor lock
    c. a run-down battery
    d. worn piston rings

13. A smoky blue exhaust may be due to
    a. an excessively rich mixture
    b. burning of oil in the combustion chamber
    c. a stuck choke valve
    d. incorrect valve adjustment

14. A smoky black exhaust may be due to
    a. worn piston rings
    b. worn carburetor jets
    c. spark plugs of wrong heat range
    d. none of the above

15. A light knock or pound with engine floating can result from worn
    a. main bearings
    b. connecting-rod bearings
    c. rings
    d. none of the above

16. A light double knock during idle can result from
    a. piston slap
    b. spark knock
    c. incorrect ignition timing
    d. loose or worn piston pin

17. A rattling or chattering sound during acceleration may be due to
    a. worn or collapsed pistons
    b. worn main bearings
    c. loose oil pan
    d. sticking engine valves

18. A hollow, muffled, bell-like sound, with the engine cold, is probably due to
    a. worn or collapsed pistons
    b. worn main bearings
    c. loose oil pan
    d. sticking engine valves

CHAPTER 27
ENGINE TESTING INSTRUMENTS

After studying this chapter, you should be able to:
1. Connect the tachometer and measure engine speed.
2. Make a cylinder-compression test on a gasoline engine.
3. Make a cylinder-compression test on a diesel engine.
4. Make a cylinder-leakage test.
5. Connect a vacuum gauge and interpret its readings.
6. Connect the exhaust-gas analyzer and measure engine emissions.
7. Connect the ignition-timing light and check ignition timing and advance.
8. Connect the oscilliscope and interpret its patterns.
9. Use the dynamometer to measure engine performance.

The chapter on engine trouble diagnosis (Chap. 26) described how to locate the causes of many engine troubles, usually without using testing instruments. Many trouble-diagnosis checks are almost second nature to experienced automotive technicians. They listen to the engine and perform the quick checks they decide are necessary. But to pinpoint the exact cause of other troubles, test instruments must be used. This chapter describes the most commonly used engine testing instruments.

☐ 27-1 ENGINE TESTING INSTRUMENTS

Quick and accurate diagnosis and service of the car engine requires the use of various engine testing instruments. This chapter covers some of the most frequently used testers. These include:

1. Tachometer, which measures engine speed in revolutions per minute (rpm)
2. Cylinder-compression tester, which measures the ability of the cylinders to hold compression pressure
3. Cylinder-leakage tester, which finds any points where compression-pressure leakage is occurring
4. Vacuum gauge, which measures intake-manifold vacuum
5. Exhaust-gas analyzer, which measures the amount of pollutants in the exhaust gas

6. Ignition-timing light, which is used to set the ignition timing and check the spark advance
7. Oscilloscope, which shows the overall operating condition of the ignition-system circuits
8. Chassis dynamometer, which checks the engine and vehicle components under actual operating conditions.

There are also instruments to test the battery, starting motor, charging system, and cooling system. There are other instruments to test ignition coils, condensers, spark plugs, distributor contact-point dwell, and distributor-advance mechanisms.

□ 27-2 TACHOMETER

The tachometer measures engine speed in revolutions per minute (rpm). It is a necessary instrument because the idle speed must be adjusted to a specified rpm. The tachometer is usually connected to the ignition system and operates electrically (Fig. 27-1). Diesel engines do not have an electric ignition system. They require a different type of tachometer. Some are triggered by a magnet on the crankshaft which is sensed by a magnetic probe (Fig. 27-2).

On spark-ignition engines, the tachometer measures the number of times the primary circuit is interrupted and translates this into engine rpm. The tachometer has a selector knob that can be turned to the number of cylinders in the engine being tested.

Some cars have a tachometer mounted on the instrument panel (Fig. 27-3). The purpose is to keep the driver informed about how fast the engine is turning. Knowing this, the driver can keep the rpm within the range at which the engine develops maximum torque or produces the best fuel economy. This enables the driver to get the best performance from the engine. Many of these tachometers have a red line at the top rpm on the dial. The red line marks the danger point for engine speed. This enables the driver to keep the engine below this speed.

Some car tachometers are mechanical instead of electrical. They are driven off a gear on the ignition distributor shaft. They operate somewhat like the speedometer (□ 23-25).

BLACK CLIP

YELLOW CLIP

IGNITION RESISTOR

Fig. 27-1 Tachometer connected to engine. *(Snap-on Tools Corporation)*

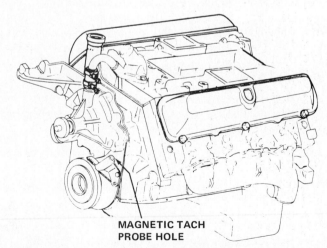

MAGNETIC TACH PROBE HOLE

Fig. 27-2 Probe hole into which the magnetic tachometer is inserted to check diesel-engine rpm. *(Oldsmobile Division of General Motors Corporation)*

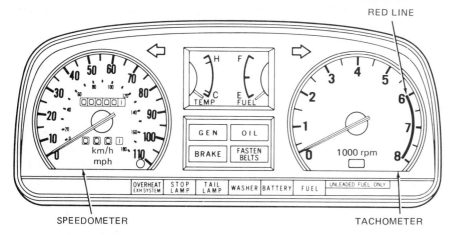

Fig. 27-3 Engine tachometer mounted in car instrument panel. *(Mazda Motors of America, Inc.)*

SPEEDOMETER   TACHOMETER

☐ 27-3 CYLINDER-COMPRESSION TESTER (SPARK IGNITION)

The cylinder-compression tester (Fig. 27-4) measures the ability of the cylinders to hold compression. Pressure, operating on a diaphragm in the tester, causes the needle on the face of this tester to move around to indicate the pressure being applied. To use the tester, first remove all the spark plugs. A recommended way to do this is to disconnect the wires, loosen the plugs one turn, reconnect the wires, and start the engine. Then run the engine for a few seconds at 1000 rpm. The combustion gases will blow out of the plug well any dirt that could fall into the cylinder when the spark plugs are removed. The gases also blow out of the combustion chamber any loosened carbon that was caked around the exposed threaded end of the plug. This procedure prevents carbon and dirt particles from lodging under a valve and holding the valve open during the compression test. Now, remove the spark plugs.

Next, screw the compression-tester fitting into the spark-plug hole of number 1 cylinder, as shown in Fig. 27-4. Disconnect the distributor lead from the negative terminal of the coil. This protects the coil, and other electronic units, from damaging high voltage. On electronic ignition systems, disconnect the positive lead to the control unit. Then hold the throttle wide open and operate the starting motor to crank the engine. The needle on the compression tester will move around to show the maximum compression pressure the cylinder is developing. Write down this figure. Test the other cylinders in the same way.

☐ 27-4 DIESEL-ENGINE COMPRESSION TEST

The compression test is different for diesel engines. The procedure for one engine is as follows. First, remove the air cleaner and install a manifold cover to keep dirt out of the engine. Disconnect the wire from the fuel shutoff solenoid terminal of the injection pump (Fig. 27-5). This prevents delivery of fuel during the test. Disconnect the glow-plug wires and remove the glow plugs. Screw the compression-tester fitting into the glow-plug hole of the cylinder to be checked. Then crank the engine for at least 12 crankshaft revolutions (six "puffs").

Check all cylinders the same way. The lowest compression reading should be not less than 70 percent of the highest. No cylinder should read less than the minimum specified by the engine manufacturer.

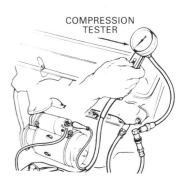

Fig. 27-4 Using a cylinder-compression tester. *(Sun Electric Corporation)*

403

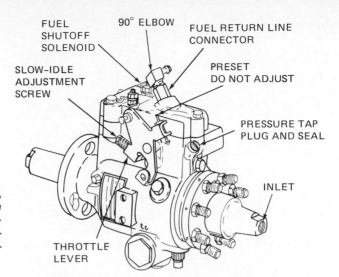

Fig. 27-5 Injection pump, showing locations of the slow-idle adjustment screw and the pressure tap plug. *(Oldsmobile Division of General Motors Corporation)*

Labels in figure:
FUEL SHUTOFF SOLENOID
90° ELBOW
FUEL RETURN LINE CONNECTOR
SLOW–IDLE ADJUSTMENT SCREW
PRESET DO NOT ADJUST
PRESSURE TAP PLUG AND SEAL
INLET
THROTTLE LEVER

In addition to the pressure reached, note the following. If everything is normal, the compression builds up quickly and evenly. If there is leakage past the piston rings, the compression is low on the first strokes but will tend to build up toward normal with later strokes. However, it does not reach normal and the pressure is rapidly lost after cranking stops.

□ 27-5 RESULTS OF THE COMPRESSION TEST

The manufacturer's specifications tell you what the compression pressure of the cylinders should be. If the results of the test show that the compression is low, there is leakage past the piston rings, valves, or cylinder-head gasket. To correct the trouble, you must remove the cylinder head and inspect the engine parts.

Before you do this, you can make one further test to pinpoint the trouble. Squirt a small quantity of engine oil through the spark-plug or glow-plug hole into the cylinder. Then retest the compression. If the pressure increases to a more normal figure, the low compression is due to leakage past the piston rings. Adding the oil helps seal the rings temporarily so that they can hold the compression pressure better. The trouble is caused by worn piston rings, a worn cylinder wall, or a worn piston. The trouble could also be caused by rings that are broken or stuck in the piston-ring grooves.

If the addition of oil does not increase the compression pressure, the leakage is probably past the valves. This could be caused by:

■ Broken valve springs
■ Incorrect valve adjustment
■ Sticking valves
■ Worn or burned valves
■ Worn or burned valve seats
■ Worn camshaft lobes
■ Dished or worn valve lifters

There is also the possibility that the cylinder-head gasket is "blown." This means that the gasket has burned away so that compression pressure is leaking between the cylinder head and the cylinder block. Low compression between two adjacent cylinders is probably caused by the head gasket having blown between the cylinders.

Whatever the cause—rings, pistons, cylinder walls, valves, or gasket—the cylinder head has to be removed so that the trouble can be fixed. Engine service is covered in later chapters.

☐ 27-6 CYLINDER-LEAKAGE TESTER

The cylinder-leakage tester (Fig. 27-6) does about the same job as the compression tester, but in a different way. It applies air pressure to the cylinder with the piston at TDC on the compression stroke. In this position, both valves are closed. Very little air should escape from the combustion chamber. Figure 27-7 shows the tester connected to an engine cylinder and how it pinpoints places where leaks occur.

To use the tester, first remove all spark plugs. Then remove the air cleaner, the crankcase filler cap or dipstick, and the radiator cap. Set the throttle wide open and fill the radiator to the proper level.

Connect the adapter, with the whistle, to the spark-plug or glow-plug hole of number 1 cylinder. Slowly crank the engine until the whistle sounds. This signals that the piston is moving up the cylinder on the compression stroke. Continue to crank the engine until the TDC timing marks on the engine align. Now the piston is at top dead center. Disconnect the whistle from the adapter hose and connect the tester, as shown in Figs. 27-6 and 27-7. Connect a shop air line to the tester and apply air pressure. The gauge reading will show the percentage of air leaking from the cylinder. Specifications vary, but if the reading is above 20 percent, there is excessive leakage.

When air leakage from the cylinder is excessive, listen at the air intake, tailpipe, and crankcase filler pipe. The sound of air escaping will pinpoint the source (Fig. 27-7). If air bubbles up through the radiator coolant, the trouble is a blown cylinder-head gasket or a cracked cylinder head.

Check the other cylinders in the same manner. A special TDC indicator supplied with the tester enables you to quickly find TDC on the other cylinders in a spark-ignition engine. When you use the tester, follow the instructions that explain how to use the TDC indicator.

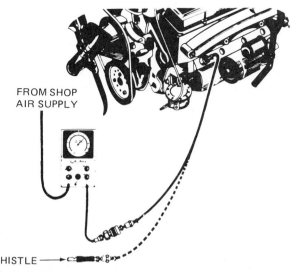

FROM SHOP AIR SUPPLY

WHISTLE →

Fig. 27-6 Cylinder-leakage tester. The whistle is used to locate TDC in number 1 cylinder. *(Sun Electric Corporation)*

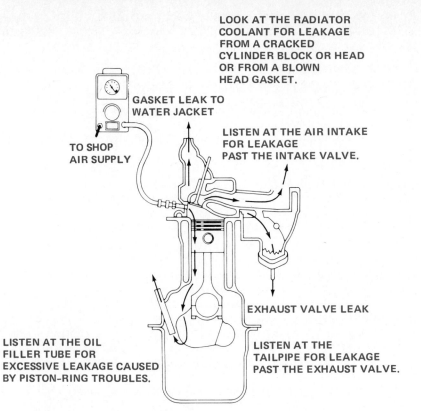

LOOK AT THE RADIATOR COOLANT FOR LEAKAGE FROM A CRACKED CYLINDER BLOCK OR HEAD OR FROM A BLOWN HEAD GASKET.

GASKET LEAK TO WATER JACKET

TO SHOP AIR SUPPLY

LISTEN AT THE AIR INTAKE FOR LEAKAGE PAST THE INTAKE VALVE.

EXHAUST VALVE LEAK

LISTEN AT THE OIL FILLER TUBE FOR EXCESSIVE LEAKAGE CAUSED BY PISTON-RING TROUBLES.

LISTEN AT THE TAILPIPE FOR LEAKAGE PAST THE EXHAUST VALVE.

Fig. 27-7 The cylinder-leakage tester applies air pressure to the cylinder through the spark-plug hole with the piston at TDC and both valves closed. Places where air is leaking pinpoint the problem. *(Sun Electric Corporation)*

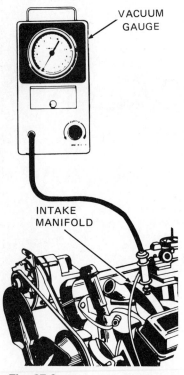

VACUUM GAUGE

INTAKE MANIFOLD

Fig. 27-8 Vacuum gauge connected to the intake manifold to check intake-manifold vacuum. *(Sun Electric Corporation)*

□ 27-7 ENGINE-VACUUM GAUGE (SPARK IGNITION)

The engine-vacuum gauge (Fig. 27-8) is an important tester for diagnosing troubles in an engine that runs but does not perform as well as it should. This gauge measures intake-manifold vacuum. The intake-manifold vacuum changes with different operating conditions and different engine defects. The way in which the vacuum varies from normal indicates what is wrong inside the engine.

Figure 27-8 shows the vacuum gauge connected to the intake manifold. With the gauge connected, start the engine and operate it as explained below. The test must be made with the engine at normal operating temperature. The meanings of various readings are explained below and in Fig. 27-9.

■ A steady and fairly high reading at idle indicates normal performance. Specifications vary with different engines, but a reading of 17 to 22 inches [432 to 599 mm] of mercury indicates the engine is OK. The reading will be lower at higher altitudes because of the lower atmospheric pressure. For every 1000 feet [305 m] above sea level, the reading will be reduced about 1 inch [25 mm].

   NOTE "Inches of mercury" refers to the way the scale is marked on the vacuum gauge. There is no mercury in the gauge.

■ A steady and low reading indicates late ignition or valve timing or possibly leakage around the pistons. Leakage around pistons (excessive blowby) could be due to worn or stuck piston rings, worn cylinder walls, or worn pistons. Each of these conditions reduces engine power. With reduced power, the engine does not "pull" as much vacuum.

■ A very low reading indicates a leaky intake manifold or throttle-body gasket or possibly leaks around the throttle-valve shaft. Air leaks into the manifold reduce the vacuum and engine power.

NOTE Some engines with high-lift cams and more valve overlap may have a lower and more uneven intake-manifold vacuum.

■ Back-and-forth movement of the needle that increases with engine speed indicates weak valve springs.
■ Gradual falling back of the needle toward zero with the engine idling indicates a clogged exhaust line.
■ Regular dropping back of the needle indicates a valve sticking open or a spark plug not firing.
■ Irregular dropping back of the needle indicates that valves are sticking only part of the time.
■ Floating motion or slow back-and-forth movement of the needle indicates an air-fuel mixture that is too rich.

A test can be made for loss of compression due to leakage around the pistons as a result of stuck or worn piston rings, worn cylinder walls, or worn pistons. Race the engine for a moment and then quickly release the throttle. The needle should swing around to 23 to 25 inches [584 to 635 mm] as the throttle closes. This indicates good compression. If the needle fails to swing around this far, there is loss of compression. Further checks should be made.

READING	DIAGNOSIS	READING	DIAGNOSIS
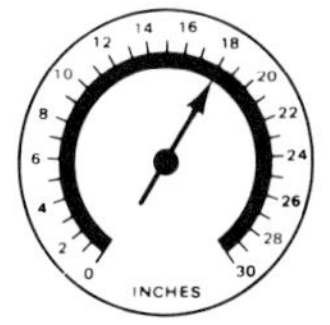 1	Average and steady at 17–21.	Everything is normal.	6	Needle drops to low reading, returns to normal, drops back, etc., at a regular interval.	Burned or leaking valve.
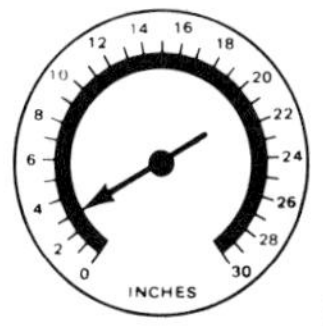 2	Extremely low reading—needle holds steady.	Air leak at the intake manifold or throttle body; incorrect timing.	7	Needle drops to zero as engine RPM is increased.	Restricted exhaust system.
 3	Needle fluctuates between high and low reading.	Blown head gasket between two side-by-side cylinders. (Check with compression test.)			
4	Needle fluctuates very slowly, ranging 4 or 5 points	Carburetor needs adjustment, sparkplug gap too narrow, sticking valves.	8	Needle holds steady at 12 to 16—drops to 0 and back to about 21 as you engage and release the throttle.	Leaking piston rings. (Check with compression test.)
5	Needle fluctuates rapidly at idle—steadies as RPM is increased.	Worn valves guides.			

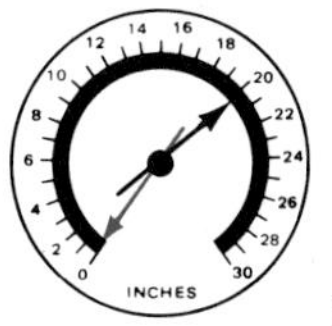

Fig. 27-9 Vacuum-gauge readings and their meanings.

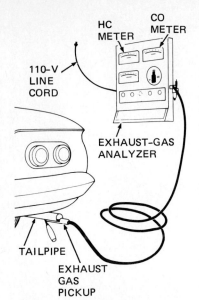

Fig. 27-10 Exhaust-gas analyzer connected for an exhaust-gas test.

NOTE This test does not apply to engines equipped with a deceleration valve as part of the emission control system.

☐ 27-8 EXHAUST-GAS ANALYZER

At one time the major use of the early type of exhaust-gas analyzer (sometimes called a *combustion-efficiency meter*) was to adjust the carburetor. It is still used for that purpose. Today, the newer type of infrared exhaust-gas analyzer (Figs. 27-10 and 27-11) has the added job of checking the emission controls. It is used by inserting a pickup tube or probe into the tail pipe of the car (Fig. 27-10). The probe draws out some of the exhaust gas and carries it through the analyzer. Two meters on the analyzer show how much HC and CO are in the exhaust gas (Fig. 27-11). The HC meter reads in parts per million (ppm). The CO meter shows the percentage of carbon monoxide in the exhaust gas.

Federal and state laws set the maximum legal limits on the amount of HC and CO permitted in the exhaust gas. The specifications for each engine are given on the decal in the engine compartment. Figure 27-12 is a chart showing the normal range of HC and CO emissions that can be expected from various cars.

Figure 27-13 shows one of the many other tests that can be made with the exhaust-gas analyzer. If fuel vapor is leaking out through a defective fuel-tank filler cap, there will be a reading on the HC meter.

A different kind of tester is required for NO_x, but it works in the same general way. It draws exhaust gas from the tail pipe and runs the gas through the analyzer. Generally, NO_x testers are available only in testing laboratories. They are not used today in the automotive service shop.

☐ 27-9 IGNITION-TIMING LIGHT (SPARK IGNITION)

The sparks must reach the spark plugs in the cylinders at exactly the right time. They must arrive a specific number of degrees before TDC on the compression stroke. Adjusting the distributor or other components in the ignition system to make the sparks arrive at the right time is called *ignition timing*. On most ignition systems, you adjust the timing by first disconnecting and plugging the vacuum lines to the distributor (Fig. 27-14). Then turn the distributor in its mounting. If you rotate the distribu-

Fig. 27-11 An infrared exhaust-gas analyzer includes meters that show the amounts of HC and CO in the exhaust gas. *(Chrysler Corporation)*

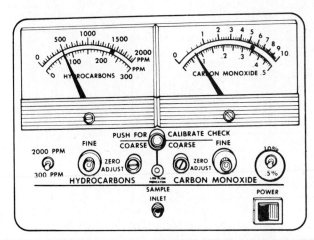

Vehicle Year	HC	CO
1967 and earlier	300–500 ppm	2.5–3.0%
1968–1969	200–300 ppm	2.0–2.5%
1970–1972	150–250 ppm	1.5–2.0%
1973–1974	100–200 ppm	1.0–1.5%
1975–1978	50–100 ppm	0.5–1.0%
1979–1983	50 ppm	0.0–0.5%

Fig. 27-12 Normal HC and CO limits at idle for various model years. *(Hamilton Test Systems)*

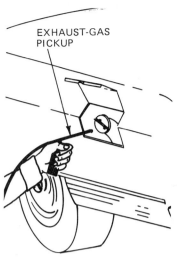

Fig. 27-13 Using the exhaust-gas analyzer to check the fuel-tank cap. *(Sun Electric Corporation)*

tor in the direction opposite to normal shaft rotation, you move the contact points or trigger wheel ahead. The primary circuit will open earlier. This advances the spark timing, so the sparks appear at the spark plugs earlier. Turning the distributor in the direction of normal shaft rotation retards the timing. The sparks appear at the plugs later.

To time the ignition, check the markings on the crankshaft pulley with the engine running. Since the pulley turns rapidly, you cannot see the markings in normal light. But by using a stroboscopic timing light, you can make the pulley appear to stand still. You use the timing light by clamping an inductive pickup around the cable to the number 1 spark plug (Fig. 27-15). The inductive pickup senses the voltage pulse and triggers the timing light. Therefore, every time the plug fires, the timing light gives off a flash of light (Fig. 27-16). The light lasts only a fraction of a second. However, the repeated flashes of light make the pulley appear to stand still.

To set the ignition timing, loosen the clamp screw that holds the distributor in its mounting. Then turn the distributor one way or the other. As you turn the distributor, the specified degree marking on the pulley will move ahead or back. When the timing is correct, the markings will align with a stationary timing pointer or timing mark on the engine (Fig. 27-16). Then tighten the distributor clamp.

> **NOTE** In the Ford EEC system and the GM MISAR system (1977 only), timing is not adjusted by moving the distributor. Instead, timing is adjusted by changing the position of the crankshaft sensor (Fig. 27-17).

☐ *27-10 OSCILLOSCOPE*

The oscilloscope, or "scope," is a high-speed voltmeter that uses a televisionlike picture tube to show ignition voltages. Figure 27-18 shows an electronic engine analyzer which includes an oscilloscope on the left. The oscilloscope traces a picture of the ignition-system voltages, and the length of time they occur, on the face of the tube. This is called the scope *pattern*. The pattern shows what is happening in the ignition system, in terms of changes in voltage. If something is wrong, the pattern will show it (to the trained technician). A review of ignition-system operation is helpful in interpreting the patterns.

When the primary current stops flowing, the collapsing magnetic field produces a high-voltage surge in the secondary circuit. The voltage can go up to 47,000 volts (or even higher). This high-voltage surge is delivered to the spark plug. There, the current jumps the gap between the insulated and grounded electrodes of the spark plug. The spark ignites the air-fuel mixture, and combustion begins. It takes a high voltage to start the spark arcing across the spark-plug gap. But once started, much

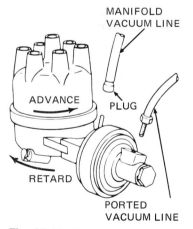

Fig. 27-14 Turning the distributor in the direction of distributor-shaft rotation retards ignition timing. Turning the distributor in the opposite direction advances ignition timing. *(Champion Spark Plug Company)*

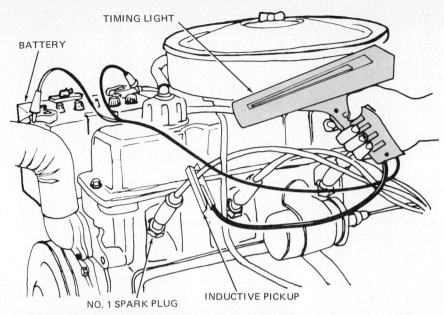

Fig. 27-15 Timing light used to check ignition timing.

less voltage is required to sustain the spark. A scope pattern of the secondary circuit shows how and when the plug voltage changes.

The pattern is drawn on the face of the tube by a stream of electrons. However, in the scope, the stream of electrons draws a picture of just one thing—the voltages in the system that the scope is attached to. Figure 27-18 shows the face of the picture tube and the secondary voltage for each spark plug. By changing the selector-switch on the scope, the igni-

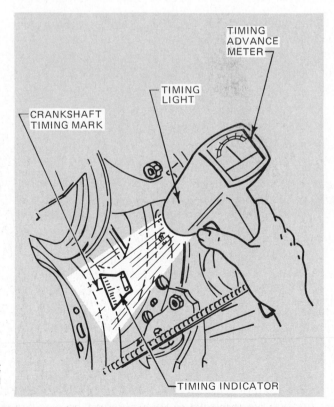

Fig. 27-16 The timing light flashes every time the spark-plug fires in number 1 cylinder.

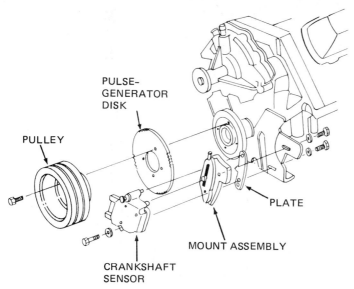

PULSE-
GENERATOR
DISK

PULLEY

PLATE

MOUNT ASSEMBLY

CRANKSHAFT
SENSOR

Fig. 27-17 Relationship of crankshaft sensor to pulse generator disk on the engine crankshaft. *(Oldsmobile Division of General Motors Corporation)*

tion primary-circuit voltages can be shown. This also allows the scope to be used for such things as checking alternator operation and injection valve opening in electronic fuel-injection systems.

When a voltage is detected by the scope, a "spike," or vertical line, appears on the face of the tube, as shown at the left in Fig. 27-19. The higher the spike, the higher the voltage. If the spike points down, it indicates that the ignition coil or the battery is connected backward.

To see how the scope picks up the voltages, and what the patterns mean, let us first study the *basic pattern* for the contact-point ignition system (Fig. 27-19). The basic pattern is what the scope would show if it were tracing the voltage changes for one spark plug. First, the current stops flowing in the coil primary winding. Then the high-voltage pulse

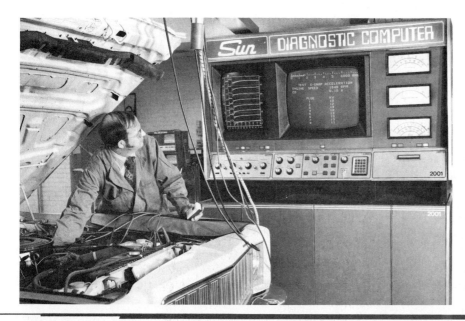

Fig. 27-18 A diagnostic engine analyzer. This tester includes an oscilloscope (top left) and other meters to check engine vacuum, fuel-pump pressure, dwell, and engine rpm. *(Sun Electric Corporation)*

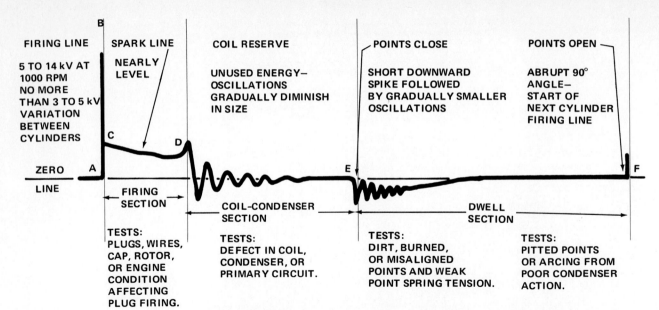

FIRING LINE

5 TO 14 kV AT
1000 RPM
NO MORE
THAN 3 TO 5 kV
VARIATION
BETWEEN
CYLINDERS

SPARK LINE

NEARLY
LEVEL

COIL RESERVE

UNUSED ENERGY—
OSCILLATIONS
GRADUALLY DIMINISH
IN SIZE

POINTS CLOSE

SHORT DOWNWARD
SPIKE FOLLOWED
BY GRADUALLY SMALLER
OSCILLATIONS

POINTS OPEN

ABRUPT 90°
ANGLE—
START OF
NEXT CYLINDER
FIRING LINE

ZERO
LINE

FIRING
SECTION

COIL-CONDENSER
SECTION

DWELL
SECTION

TESTS:
PLUGS, WIRES,
CAP, ROTOR,
OR ENGINE
CONDITION
AFFECTING
PLUG FIRING.

TESTS:
DEFECT IN COIL,
CONDENSER, OR
PRIMARY CIRCUIT.

TESTS:
DIRT, BURNED,
OR MISALIGNED
POINTS AND WEAK
POINT SPRING TENSION.

TESTS:
PITTED POINTS
OR ARCING FROM
POOR CONDENSER
ACTION.

Fig. 27-19 The basic oscilloscope pattern of the secondary circuit in a contact-point ignition system, showing one complete spark-plug firing cycle. *(American Motors Corporation)*

from the coil arrives at the spark plug. The voltage goes up, from A to B, as shown in Fig. 27-19. This is called the *firing line*. After the spark is established, the voltage drops off and holds fairly steady, from C to D. This is called the spark line. This is a very short time, measured in hundred-thousandths of a second. But the spark lasts for about 20 degrees of crankshaft rotation. This is long enough to ignite the compressed air-fuel mixture in the cylinder.

After most of the magnetic energy in the coil has been converted into electricity to make the spark, the spark across the spark-plug gap dies. However, there is still some energy left in the coil, and this produces a wavy line, from D to E. This line is called the *coil-condenser oscillation line*. It shows how the remaining energy is pushing electricity back and forth in the ignition secondary circuit. The voltage alternates, but it is no longer high enough to produce a spark at the plug gap. After a very short time, the voltage dies out. Then, at E, the points close, and current again starts to flow in the primary winding of the ignition coil. Now an alternating voltage is produced in the secondary circuit. This is the result of the buildup of current in the coil primary winding (shown by the oscillations that usually follow E). The section from E to F is called the *dwell* section. This is the time during which the contact points are closed or the electronic control unit keeps current flowing to the coil. During this time, the magnetic field is building up around the ignition-coil primary winding. Then at F, the points open (or the electronic control unit turns the coil off) and the cycle begins again at A as the spark occurs at the spark plug.

☐ *27-11 OSCILLOSCOPE PATTERNS*

The traces that the scope draws on the picture-tube face are called *patterns*. The patterns can be drawn in different ways. For example, the scope can be adjusted to draw a *display,* or *parade, pattern* (Fig. 27-20). The traces follow from left to right across the screen in normal firing

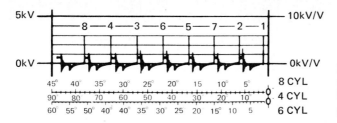

Fig. 27-20 Parade, or display, pattern of the ignition secondary voltages in an eight-cylinder engine. *(Sun Electric Corporation)*

order. However, the firing line for No. 1 cylinder, which triggers the retrace, appears on the far right of the screen (Fig. 27-20). The firing order for this engine is 1–8–4–3–6–5–7–2.

The scope can be adjusted in a different way so that the traces are stacked one above the other (Fig. 27-21). This is called a *raster pattern*. It lets you compare the traces so that you can see if something is wrong in a cylinder. The raster pattern is read from the bottom up in the firing order, with the No. 1 cylinder at the bottom. The firing order for the engine shown in Fig. 27-21 is 1–5–3–6–2–4.

A third way to display the traces is to superimpose them by placing one on top of the other (Fig. 27-22). This gives a quick comparison and shows whether the voltage pattern from any one cylinder differs from the others. This is because all the traces appear on top of one another.

☐ 27-12 USING THE SCOPE

There are several makes of oscilloscopes. Many of them are combined in consoles with other test instruments for testing separate ignition components, engine rpm, intake-manifold vacuum, and so on. Figure 27-18 shows a complete engine analyzer of this type.

Scopes have pickup sensors that can be clamped onto the ignition wires (Fig. 27-23). It is not necessary to disconnect and reconnect the ignition wiring. The *pattern pickup sensor* is clamped onto the wire that goes from the ignition coil to the distributor-cap center terminal. The sensor senses the high-voltage surges going to all the spark plugs. The *trigger pickup sensor* is clamped onto the wire that goes to the spark plug in number 1 cylinder. The trigger pickup senses when the spark plug fires. This is the signal to the scope to start another round of traces.

Figure 27-23 shows the scope connections for in-line and V-type engines that use the General Motors high-energy ignition (HEI) system. A

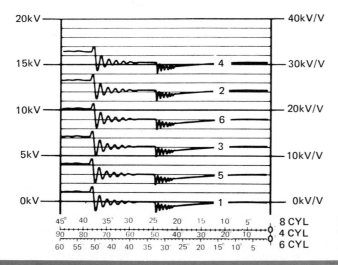

Fig. 27-21 Stacked, or raster, pattern of the ignition secondary voltages in a six-cylinder engine. *(Sun Electric Corporation)*

413

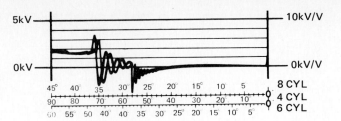

Fig. 27-22 Superimposed pattern of the ignition secondary voltages in a six-cylinder engine. *(Sun Electric Corporation)*

special HEI adapter is needed for the pattern pickup on distributors that have the coil built into the top of the cap.

□ 27-13 READING SCOPE PATTERNS

The patterns in Fig. 27-24 show the different troubles that occur in the ignition system. The pattern that the scope draws of any cylinder's ignition-circuit voltage shows the voltages that are occurring in the circuit. The way that the voltage varies from normal indicates where the electrical problem exists. For example, the scope can detect wide or narrow spark-plug gaps, open spark-plug wires, shorted coils or condensers, arcing contact points, and improper contact-point dwell.

Many abnormal engine conditions change the voltage needed to fire the spark plug, and this shows up on the scope. Other abnormal engine conditions can also be identified on the scope because they change the length or the slope of the spark line. When you work in a shop that has an oscilloscope, you will be given detailed instructions on how to use it.

□ 27-14 DYNAMOMETER

The chassis dynamometer can test engine power output under various operating conditions. Some dynamometers can duplicate any kind of road test at any load or speed desired by the dynamometer operator. The part of the dynamometer that you can see consists of two heavy rollers mounted at or a little above floor level. The car is driven onto these roll-

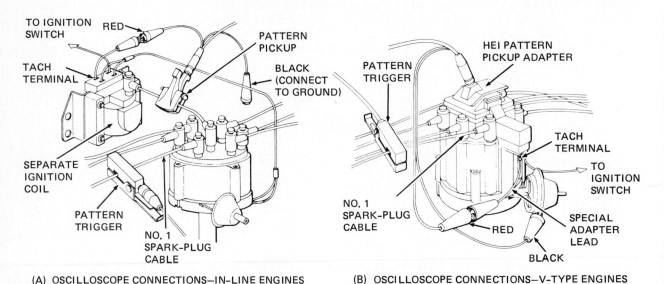

(A) OSCILLOSCOPE CONNECTIONS—IN-LINE ENGINES   (B) OSCILLOSCOPE CONNECTIONS—V-TYPE ENGINES

Fig. 27-23 Oscilloscope connections for testing the General Motors high-energy ignition (HEI) system. *(Sun Electric Corporation)*

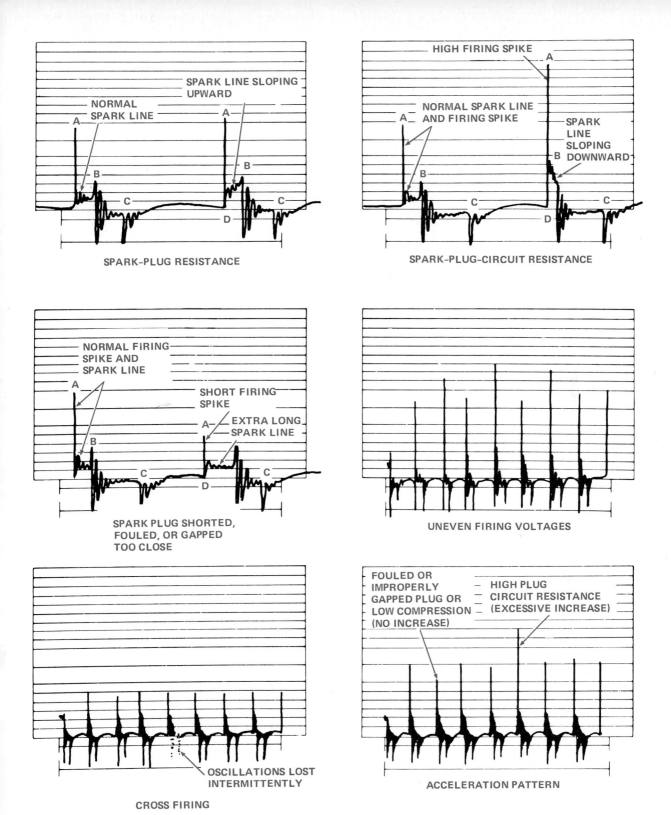

Fig. 27-24 Various abnormal scope traces and their causes. *(Ford Motor Company)*

Fig. 27-25 Car in place on a chassis dynamometer. The drive wheels turn the dynamometer rollers. At the same time, instruments on the test panel measure car speed, brake horsepower, and intake-manifold vacuum. When cars with front-wheel drive are being tested, the front wheels are placed on the rollers. *(Sun Electric Corporation)*

FLOAT-TYPE
HYDROMETER

RADIATOR

BALL-TYPE
HYDROMETER

RADIATOR

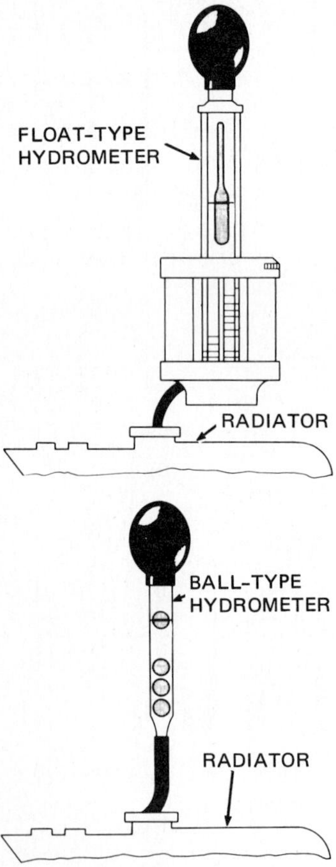

Fig. 27-26 Two types of hydrometer used to check the strength of the antifreeze in the coolant.

ers, so that the car wheels can drive the rollers (Fig. 27-25). Next, the engine is started, and the car is then operated as though it were out on an actual road test.

Under the floor there is a *power absorber* that can place various loads on the rollers. This allows the technician to operate the engine under various conditions. The technician can find out how the engine performs during acceleration, cruising, idling, and deceleration. The test instruments, such as the scope, tachometer, and vacuum gauge, are hooked into the engine. These instruments then show the actual state of the engine during various operating conditions.

The dynamometer can also be used to check the transmission and the differential. For example, the shift points and other operating conditions of an automatic transmission can be checked on the dynamometer. Diagnostic dynamometers have sensitive motored rollers that permit testing of wheel alignment, suspension, brakes, and steering.

☐ *27-15 COOLING-SYSTEM TESTERS*

There are three basic testers for the cooling system: the hydrometer, the pressure tester, and the belt-tension gauge. The hydrometer checks the concentration of antifreeze in the coolant. The pressure tester checks the ability of the cooling system to hold pressure. The pressure tester is also used to check the radiator pressure cap. The third tester checks the drive-belt tension.

The percentage of antifreeze in the coolant determines how well the car is protected against freezing. The more antifreeze—up to a point— the lower the temperature can go before the coolant freezes. If the coolant freezes in the engine, the engine can be seriously damaged. Water expands as it freezes. The expansive force is great enough to crack the cylinder head and the cylinder block. A hydrometer is used to test the coolant freezing point (Fig. 27-26).

The pressure tester is a small air pump with a pressure gauge (Fig. 27-27). It is attached to the radiator filler neck. The pump is operated to apply pressure. If the pressure holds steady and there are no signs of leaks, the cooling system is tight.

One type of belt-tension tester is shown in Fig. 21-17. If there is not enough tension, the belt will slip. The fan and water pump will not be driven fast enough, and the engine will overheat. Also, the belt will wear out rapidly. To adjust, move the alternator out slightly.

☐ 27-16 PCV-SYSTEM TESTER

In an engine with a PCV system (Chaps. 24 and 25), there should be a slight vacuum in the crankcase at idle. Figure 27-28 shows one type of PCV tester used to check crankcase vacuum. This tester is sometimes called an *inclined-ramp-and-ball tester*. Inside the tester there is a circular ramp which has a vacuum-sensitive ball rolling on it.

With the engine idling at normal operating temperature, remove the oil-filler cap. Place the PCV tester over the opening (Fig. 27-28). Note the position of the ball. If the ball settles in the GOOD (green) area, crankcase vacuum is adequate and the system in functioning properly. If the ball settles in the REPAIR (red) area, there is pressure in the crankcase. The system needs to be serviced. Clean the hoses, install a new PCV valve, and retest.

☐ 27-17 FUEL-SYSTEM TESTERS

Various testers check fuel-system performance. The exhaust-gas analyzer, engine-vacuum gauge, oscilloscope, and other instruments are used to check engine performance. An important part of the engine is the fuel system, and these test instruments also report on the fuel system. There are also fuel-pump pressure and capacity testers (Fig. 27-29) that check on how well the fuel pump is doing its job.

☐ 27-18 ELECTRICAL-SYSTEM TESTERS

A variety of testers are required to test the electrical equipment on the car. These include the distributor, coil, and condenser testers for the ignition-system components. Ammeters and voltmeters are required to check the charging system. Any of several instruments can be used to check the battery (Chap. 19).

Some cars have a special *diagnostic connector* under the hood. By plugging in the proper diagnostic tester, the car electrical system and air conditioning can be quickly checked.

☐ 27-19 SELF-DIAGNOSTIC SYSTEMS

The car has always carried indicating devices that warn the driver if some action is necessary (Chap. 23). For example, most cars have fuel gauges; speedometers; and charging-system, engine-temperature, and oil-pressure indicators. Some cars have additional indicators, such as a *sensor panel,* to alert the driver when other things need attention. For example, if the engine needs more oil, a special ENGINE OIL light comes on.

Many cars now have an electronic engine control (EEC) system to limit exhaust emissions while providing good fuel economy and driveability from the engine (☐ 24-8). A *self-diagnostic* capability is built into many EEC systems. This allows the system to alert the driver when something is wrong. The system then stores a trouble code which can be

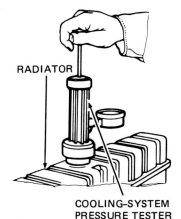

COOLING-SYSTEM
PRESSURE TESTER

Fig. 27-27 Pressure-testing the cooling system. *(Chrysler Corporation)*

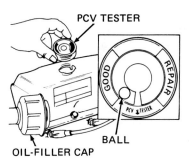

Fig. 27-28 Checking crankcase vacuum with a PCV tester. *(ATW)*

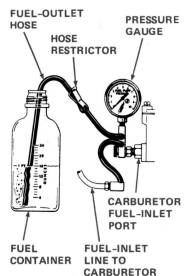

Fig. 27-29 Fuel-pump pressure and capacity tests. *(Ford Motor Company)*

read out by the technician. This means that the car can tell the technician many things that are wrong. Fewer shop instruments are needed to pinpoint exactly what is wrong.

CHAPTER 27
REVIEW QUESTIONS

Select the *one* correct, best, or most probable answer to each question. Then check your answers against the correct answers given at the end of the book.

1. The purpose of the tachometer is to
   a. measure engine intake-manifold vacuum
   b. measure engine rpm
   c. check engine compression
   d. check venturi vacuum

2. If pouring a small amount of oil into the cylinder increases the compression pressure, the loss of compression is probably due to leakage past the
   a. valves
   b. head gasket
   c. piston rings
   d. oil seals

3. The cylinder-compression tester measures the compression pressure on the
   a. exhaust stroke
   b. power stroke
   c. intake stroke
   d. compression stroke

4. The compression readings on a four-cylinder engine are 140, 135, 5, and 140. Mechanic X says that a burned valve could cause the readings. Mechanic Y says that broken piston rings could cause the readings. Who is right?
   a. X only
   b. Y only
   c. both X and Y
   d. neither X nor Y

5. If the vacuum-gauge needle swings around to 23 to 25 inches (584 to 635 mm) of mercury (Hg) as the throttle is quickly closed after racing the engine, it indicates
   a. stuck valves
   b. low compression
   c. normal compression
   d. worn piston rings

CHAPTER 28
ENGINE TUNEUP AND CAR CARE

After studying this chapter, and with proper instructions and equipment, you should be able to:

1. Define *tuneup*.
2. List and perform the major steps in an engine tuneup.
3. Remove, install, and time the ignition distributor.
4. Change the engine oil and filter.
5. Perform a chassis lubrication

An engine in the best mechanical condition will run poorly if it needs a tuneup. To tune an engine, a procedure must be followed. This chapter lists the steps in the complete engine tuneup procedure. Other parts of the car also need care. These are *car care* items. In addition, many moving parts in the steering and suspension systems may require periodic lubrication. These are also covered in this chapter.

☐ 28-1 ENGINE TUNEUP

Engine tuneup means different things to different people. To some, it means a quick, once-over check of the engine, which takes in only the more obvious trouble spots. To others, engine tuneup means using the proper test instruments to carry out a careful, complete analysis of all engine components. In addition, it means adjusting everything to specifications and repairing or replacing defective or worn parts.

This chapter combines two procedures. These are *engine tuneup* and *car care*. Engine tuneup includes checking and servicing the engine and its systems. Car care includes checking other components on the car, such as brakes, steering, suspension, and tires. Together, engine tuneup and car care cover most things in and on the car that could cause trouble.

☐ 28-2 TUNEUP AND CAR CARE

The tuneup procedure restores driveability, power, performance, and economy that have been lost through wear, corrosion, and deterioration of engine parts. These changes take place gradually in many parts during normal car operation. Because of federal and state laws limiting automotive emissions, the tuneup procedure should include checks of all emission controls. Here is the procedure.

1. Service and test the battery and starting motor (Chaps. 19 and 20). If the battery is low or the customer complains that the battery keeps running down, check the charging system (Chap. 21). If the battery is defective, a new battery is required.
2. Inspect the drive belts. Replace any that are in poor condition. Replace both belts of a two-belt set. Tighten the belts to the correct tension, using a belt-tension gauge (Fig. 21-17).
3. If the engine is cold, operate it for at least 20 minutes at 1500 rpm or until it reaches operating temperature. Note any operational problems during this warm-up time.
4. Connect the oscilloscope and perform an electronic diagnosis. Check for any abnormal ignition-system conditions that appear on the pattern. Make a note of any abnormality and the cylinder(s) in which it appears.
5. Perform a compression test as explained in □ 27-3 to 27-5. The cylinder-leakage test (27-6) and intake-manifold-vacuum test (□ 27-7) will give additional information on the condition of the engine.

   NOTE If engine mechanical problems are found, tell the owner the engine cannot be tuned without overhaul or repair.

6. Clean, inspect, file, gap, and test the spark plugs. The procedure is covered in □ 28-3.
7. On spark-ignition engines, inspect the ignition system (□ 28-4). Check the condition of the distributor rotor, cap, and primary and secondary wiring. Replace any defective parts. On the contact-point system, clean and adjust (or replace) the contact points. Lubricate the breaker cam. Check the centrifugal and vacuum advances. Adjust the ignition timing (□ 27-9).
8. Recheck the ignition system with the oscilloscope. Abnormal conditions first noted should now be eliminated.
9. Check the manifold heat-control valve, if used (□ 14-13). Lubricate it with heat-valve lubricant. Make sure it is working freely.
10. Test the fuel-pump operation with a fuel-pump tester (□ 27-17).
11. Clean or replace the air-cleaner filter. If the engine has a thermostatically controlled air cleaner, check its operation (□ 25-7).
12. Check the action of the throttle valves. Make sure they open fully when the accelerator pedal is pressed to the floor. Check the action of the choke and fast-idle system. Clean the external linkage to the carburetor or fuel-injection system.
13. Inspect all engine-vacuum fittings, hoses, and connections. Replace any brittle or cracked hose. Also, check for correct routing.
14. Clean the engine oil-filler cap if it has a filter in it.
15. Check the cooling system (□ 27-15).
16. Check and replace the PCV valve, filter, and hose as necessary (□ 25-1).
17. If the engine has an air pump, replace the pump-inlet air filter, if used. Inspect the system hoses and connections. Replace any brittle or cracked hose.
18. If the evaporative control system uses an air filter in the charcoal canister, replace the filter.
19. Check the transmission-controlled spark system if the vehicle is so equipped.

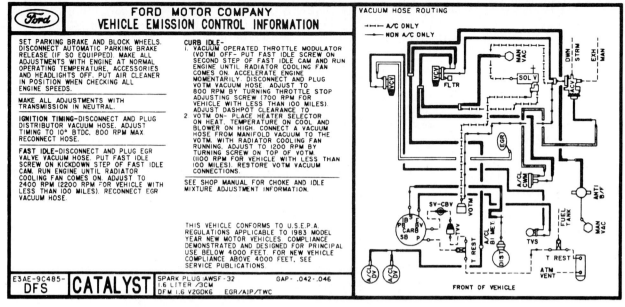

Fig. 28-1 A vehicle emission control information label, or decal, that is under the hood or on the engine of new cars. *(Ford Motor Company)*

20. On engines with exhaust-gas recirculation, inspect and clean the EGR valve and discharge port (□ 25-5).

21. Adjust the engine valves if necessary.

22. Adjust the engine idle speed (Fig. 28-1). Check the amount of HC and CO in the exhaust gas (□ 27-8). If required, adjust the idle-mixture screw (Fig. 28-2). Follow the procedure outlined on the vehicle emission control information decal in the engine compartment (Fig. 28-1).

23. Check the doorjamb sticker to see if an oil and oil-filter change is due. Car manufacturers recommend changing the oil filter every other time the oil is changed (□ 28-7).

24. While the car is on the lift, check the exhaust system for leaks which could admit CO into the car. Also look for loose bolts, rust spots, and other under-the-car damage.

25. Road-test the car on a dynamometer or on the road. Check for driveability, power, and idling. Any problem now found may require additional checking and service of other parts.

   NOTE The following items are not actually a part of the engine tuneup. However, they are important steps in vehicle maintenance and car care. Each of them can be quickly checked during a road test.

26. Check the brakes for even and adequate braking.

27. Check the steering system for ease and smoothness of operation. Check for excessive play in the system. Record any abnormal conditions.

28. Check the tires for inflation and for abnormal wear. Abnormal wear can mean suspension trouble, and wheel alignment should be recommended. These steps are covered later in the book.

29. Check the suspension system for looseness, excessive play, and wear. This is covered later in the book.

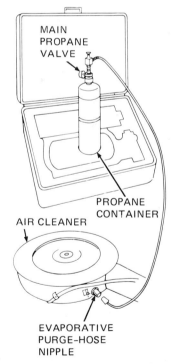

Fig. 28-2 Setup for adjusting idle mixture with propane. *(Ford Motor Company)*

NORMAL

Brown to grayish tan color and slight electrode wear. Correct heat range for engine and operating conditions.

RECOMMENDATION: Service and reinstall. Replace if over recommended mileage.

WORN

Center electrode worn away too much to be filed flat.

RECOMMENDATION: Replace with new spark plugs of proper heat range.

PREIGNITION

Improper heat range, incorrect ignition timing, lean air-fuel mixture, or hot spots in combustion chamber has caused melted electrodes. Center electrode generally melts first and ground electrode follows. Normally, insulators are white, but may be dirty due to misfiring or flying debris in combustion chamber.

RECOMMENDATION: Check for correct plug heat range, over-advanced ignition timing, lean air-fuel mixture, clogged cooling system, leaking intake manifold, and lack of lubrication.

DETONATION

Insulator has cracked and broken away as a result of the shock waves created by detonation.

RECOMMENDATION: Cause of detonation must be found and corrected. Check for use of low-octane fuel, improper air-fuel mixture, incorrect ignition timing, overheating, and increased octane requirement in the engine.

MECHANICAL DAMAGE

Something such as a foreign object in cylinder, or the piston, has struck the ground electrode. It has been forced into the center electrode, which has bent, and broken off the insulator.

RECOMMENDATION: Check that plug has the correct reach for the engine, that the gap was set properly, and that no foreign object remains in cylinder.

GAP BRIDGED

Deposits in the fuel have formed a bridge between the electrodes, eliminating the air gap and grounding the plug.

RECOMMENDATION: Sometimes plug can be serviced and reinstalled. Check for excess additives in fuel.

CARBON DEPOSITS

Dry soot, frequently caused by use of spark plug with incorrect heat range.

RECOMMENDATION: Carbon deposits indicate rich mixture or weak ignition. Check for clogged air cleaner, high float level, sticky choke or worn contact points. Hotter plugs will provide additional fouling protection.

OIL DEPOSITS

Oily coating.

RECOMMENDATION: Caused by poor oil control. Oil is leaking past worn valve guides or piston rings into the combustion chamber. Hotter spark plug may temporarily relieve problem, but correct the cause with necessary repairs.

SPLASHED DEPOSITS

Spotted deposits. Occurs shortly after long-delayed tuneup. After a long period of misfiring, deposits may be loosened when normal combustion temperatures are restored by tuneup. During a high-speed run, these materials shed off the piston and head and are thrown against the hot insulator.

RECOMMENDATION: Clean and service the plugs properly and reinstall.

ASH DEPOSITS

Poor oil control, use of improper oil, or use of improper additives in fuel or oil has caused an accumulation of ash which completely covers the electrodes.

RECOMMENDATION: Eliminate source of ash. Install new spark plugs.

OVERHEATED

Blistered, white insulator, eroded electrodes and absence of deposits.

RECOMMENDATION: Check for correct plug heat range, over-advanced ignition timing, low coolant level or restricted flow, lean air-fuel mixture, leaking intake manifold, sticking valves, and if car is driven at high speeds most of the time.

HIGH-TEMPERATURE GLAZING

Insulator has yellowish, varnish-like color. Indicates combustion chamber temperatures have risen suddenly during hard, fast acceleration. Normal deposits do not get a chance to blow off. Instead, they melt to form a conductive coating.

RECOMMENDATION: If condition recurs, use plug type one step colder.

Fig. 28-3 Appearance of spark plugs related to causes. *(Champion Spark Plug Company)*

30. Check the headlights and horns to make sure they work. Check all other lights. Replace any burned-out light bulbs. Adjust headlight aim if necessary.

□ 28-3 CLEANING OR REPLACING SPARK PLUGS

Spark plugs should be removed for examination and cleaned or filed and regapped as necessary.

NOTE The cost of labor is relatively high compared to the cost of spark plugs. Today, many technicians recommend installing new spark plugs instead of cleaning and regapping the old plugs.

The appearance of the spark plugs tells you a lot about the condition of the engine (Fig. 28-3). If the plug runs too hot or too cold, it should be

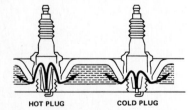

HOT PLUG   COLD PLUG

Fig. 28-4 Heat range of spark plugs. The longer the heat path (indicated by the arrows), the hotter the plug runs. *(AC Spark Plug Division of General Motors Corporation)*

replaced with a plug of a different heat range. The temperature that a plug will reach depends on the distance the heat must travel from the center electrode to reach the outer shell of the plug and enter the cylinder head. A plug that has a long heat path from the center electrode to the plug shell will run hot. The electrodes will be at a higher temperature (Fig. 28-4). A plug that has a short heat path from the center electrode to the plug shell will run cold. If the old plug is fouled from carbon deposits, the plug may be running too cold. A plug with a higher heat range should be installed.

A spark-plug cleaner is shown in Fig. 28-5. When the spark plug is placed in the cleaner, the cleaner sends a blast of grit against the electrodes and insulator. The grit cleans the electrodes and insulator. After the cleaning is done, the spark-plug electrodes are filed flat with an ignition file. Then a spark-plug gauge is used to adjust the electrode gap (Fig. 28-6).

□ 28-4 CHECKING THE IGNITION SYSTEM

There are several parts in the contact-point ignition system that can be checked with an oscilloscope and timing light while performing a tuneup. These are:

■ Cap and rotor
■ Wiring
■ Coil and condenser
■ Advance mechanisms
■ Points
■ Timing

First, remove the cap from the distributor (Figs. 28-7 and 28-8). Then clean and inspect the cap and rotor, as shown in Fig 28-9. If the cap is defective, install a new cap, as shown at the upper right in Fig. 28-9. Remove the leads, one at a time, and install them in the proper tower in the new cap.

Check the secondary wiring. If it has cracked insulation, replace it. Cracks can allow the high voltage to drain off so that the plug will not fire. The engine will miss.

The coil and condenser should be tested on a coil-condenser tester to find if they are in good condition. This test should be made anytime the scope indicates the possibility that they are defective.

The action of the centrifugal and vacuum-advance mechanisms can be checked with a timing light (□ 27-9). Check the amount of advance at various engine speeds and throttle openings to determine whether the advance mechanisms are working properly. An accurate test can be made if the distributor is removed from the engine and checked on a distributor tester.

If the points are worn or burned, they should be replaced. Points should be adjusted by loosening the locking screw and shifting the stationary point (Figs. 28-10 and 28-11). On General Motors window-type distributors, adjust the points by lifting the window and inserting a 1/8-inch Allen wrench in the point-adjusting screw. The point opening on new points can be measured with a thickness gauge. A thickness gauge should not be used on rough points. With rough points, the opening will be greater than the thickness of the gauge (Fig. 28-12).

One way to measure and adjust point opening is with a dwell meter. This meter measures the number of degrees of cam rotation that the points are closed. As the point opening is increased, the dwell angle is decreased. The dwell meter must be used while the engine is running. A

Fig. 28-5 Spark-plug cleaner and tester. *(Champion Spark Plug Company)*

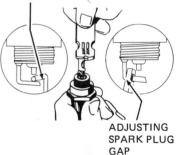

ROUND WIRE GAUGE

ADJUSTING SPARK PLUG GAP

Fig. 28-6 Using a spark-plug gauge to check and adjust the spark-plug gap.

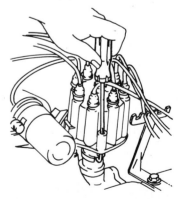

Fig. 28-7 Removing a distributor cap that has spring-loaded clamps. *(Delco-Remy Division of General Motors Corporation)*

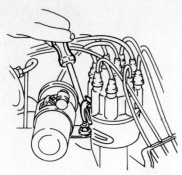

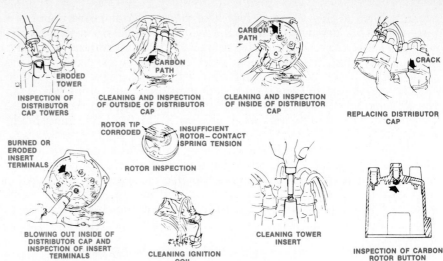

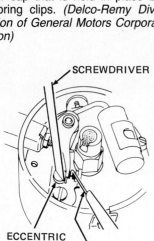

Fig. 28-8 Removing a distributor cap that is held in place by spring clips. *(Delco-Remy Division of General Motors Corporation)*

INSPECTION OF DISTRIBUTOR CAP TOWERS

ERODED TOWER

CLEANING AND INSPECTION OF OUTSIDE OF DISTRIBUTOR CAP

CARBON PATH

CLEANING AND INSPECTION OF INSIDE OF DISTRIBUTOR CAP

CARBON PATH

REPLACING DISTRIBUTOR CAP

CRACK

BURNED OR ERODED INSERT TERMINALS

ROTOR TIP CORRODED

INSUFFICIENT ROTOR—CONTACT SPRING TENSION

ROTOR INSPECTION

BLOWING OUT INSIDE OF DISTRIBUTOR CAP AND INSPECTION OF INSERT TERMINALS

CLEANING IGNITION COIL

CLEANING TOWER INSERT

INSPECTION OF CARBON ROTOR BUTTON

Fig. 28-9 Checking and servicing a distributor cap and rotor. *(Delco-Remy Division of General Motors Corporation)*

SCREWDRIVER

ECCENTRIC

WIRE THICKNESS GAUGE

Fig. 28-10 On some distributors, the point opening is adjusted by loosening the lock screw and turning the eccentric with a screwdriver. *(Delco-Remy Division of General Motors Corporation)*

distributor tester can also be used to measure point opening. The distributor must be removed from the engine and placed in the tester (Fig. 28-13).

□ 28-5 INSTALLING AND TIMING THE IGNITION DISTRIBUTOR

Timing the ignition should be done after the various mechanical checks listed above have been completed. Ignition timing is covered in □ 27-9. If the distributor has been removed, ignition timing must be reset when the distributor is reinstalled in the engine.

Follow the steps listed below to remove the distributor.

1. Disconnect the distributor-to-coil primary wire. Remove the cap and crank the engine so that the rotor is in position to fire number 1 cylinder. The timing mark on the engine pulley should be aligned with the tab or pointer on the engine front cover or timing-gear cover. Make a slight mark on the distributor housing directly beneath the center of the rotor blade (Fig. 28-14). Now make another slight mark on the block to align with the mark on the distributor housing.
2. Disconnect the vacuum hose from the distributor. Note the position of the distributor in its mounting. Remove the distributor clamping nut and clamp. Remove the distributor. Note the position of the rotor on the distributor housing after removal. The rotor may rotate a little as the distributor is removed. This is due to the movement of the spiral-driven gear as it is pulled out of the drive gear on the camshaft.

Follow the steps listed below to install the distributor.

1. Make sure that the timing mark on the pulley aligns with the stationary timing mark and that number 1 piston is at TDC on the compression stroke.
2. Check that the distributor-to-block gasket or seal is in place on the distributor. Turn the distributor rotor to the same position you noted when you removed the distributor.
3. Install the distributor. If you have positioned the rotor correctly, the

gear should slide down into the camshaft drive gear or oil pump without trouble. Using the marks that you made during distributor removal, check the rotor to make sure it is aligned with the mark on the housing. Then check that the housing is aligned with the mark on the block.

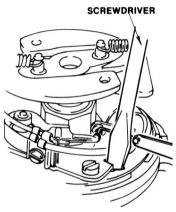

> **NOTE** If the distributor housing does not seat flush against the block, hold the distributor housing down lightly. Then bump the engine slightly with the starting motor until the distributor drops into place.

4. Install the distributor clamp. However, leave the nut loose enough to allow the distributor to be rotated for final ignition timing.
5. Attach the distributor-to-coil wire.
6. Install the distributor cap and adjust the ignition timing (□ 27-9). Then tighten the clamp nut and reconnect the vacuum hose to the distributor.

Fig. 28-11 On some distributors, the stationary-point base is moved back and forth with a screwdriver to adjust the point opening. *(Delco-Remy Division of General Motors Corporation)*

□ 28-6 CHECKING THE COOLING SYSTEM

Check the radiator and heater hoses for wear and tightness. A quick check is to squeeze the hose (Fig. 28-15). Note any cracks that appear as well as the hardness of the hose. Note the level and condition of the coolant. Find out how long the car has been driven with the old antifreeze. If the coolant looks dirty and rusty, suggest flushing the cooling system to the customer. This involves flushing out the radiator and replacing the old antifreeze with a new solution. Many manufacturers recommend draining the old coolant and putting in a new solution every two years. Check the coolant with a hydrometer to determine its freezing point (Fig. 27-26). If there is not enough antifreeze to protect the engine from freezing, add more antifreeze.

Test the cooling system with the pressure tester (Fig. 27-27). Pressure-test the radiator cap. Inspect the engine, radiator, and hoses for signs of leakage. Use a belt-tension tester to check the tension of the drive belts (Fig. 21-17). Adjust the belts if necessary.

> **CAUTION** Always keep your hands away from the engine fan. Even with the engine off, an electric fan could start at any time. Also, never remove the radiator cap from a hot engine. Always wait until the engine is cool.

□ 28-7 CHANGING THE OIL AND OIL FILTER

You should check the lubrication sticker on the car doorjamb to see if the engine oil should be changed. The car owner will often want the oil changed during a tuneup. If the sticker shows the filter needs changing, it should be changed too. A typical factory recommendation is that the oil filter should be changed the first time the oil is changed and then every other oil change after that. When the oil is changed, you should also determine if steering and suspension parts need lubrication (□ 28-8).

To change the oil, drive the car over a lift. Make sure the car is placed so that lift arms contact the specified lift points on the car frame. This will properly support the car and will avoid crushing the fuel line, brake line, catalytic converter, muffler, or tail pipe. Then raise the lift with the car on it so that you can drain the old oil.

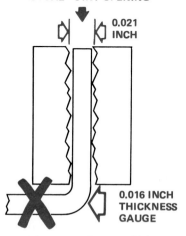

Fig. 28-12 Why a thickness gauge will not accurately measure the opening between used and rough contact points.

Fig. 28-13 Checking a contact-point distributor on an ignition-distributor tester. *(Sun Electric Corporation)*

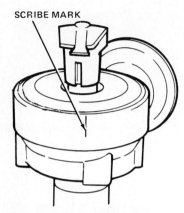

Fig. 28-14 Location of the reference marks made on the distributor housing to indicate rotor position. *(American Motors Corporation)*

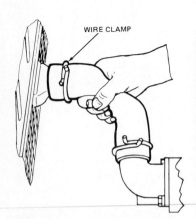

Fig. 28-15 To check the condition of the radiator hose, squeeze the hose. *(Chrysler Corporation)*

CAUTION Always make sure the lift lock or safety pin is in place before going under the car. The lock or safety pin keeps the lift from accidentally releasing and allowing the car to settle to the floor.

When the car is up on the lift, position the container under the drain plug. Then remove the plug and allow the oil to drain. Give the oil enough time to drain completely. Then install the plug.

CAUTION If the engine is hot, the oil will be hot enough to burn your hand. Be careful to avoid getting hot oil on your hand.

Install a new oil filter if needed (Fig. 28-16). If possible, fill the filter with fresh oil before installation. Lower the car and put in the proper amount and grade of oil. Be sure the oil is the grade called for by the car manufacturer and the viscosity needed for the temperature in which the car will be driven.

While the car is up on the lift, check the catalytic converter, the muffler, exhaust pipe, and tail pipe. A leak can be deadly. It can leak exhaust gas, which contains carbon monoxide, into the car. Carbon monoxide is a deadly gas. It can make the driver drowsy and lead to an accident.

□ *28-8 LUBRICATING THE CHASSIS*

Although lubrication of the chassis is not part of an engine tuneup, *chassis lubrication* is often performed with the oil change (□ 28-7). Special fluids and lubricants are needed, plus grease guns and dispensers. To guide the technician, car manufacturers publish lubrication charts, or "lube charts."

Figure 28-17 shows a manufacturer's chart for one model of car. Oil companies and others produce lube charts for all cars. When you work in the shop, you will learn chassis lubrication and servicing procedures.

There are many items that should *not* be lubricated. Some are permanently lubricated. On others, lubricant will be detrimental to their operation. In addition, some lubricants will cause the component to fail. For example, rubber bushings should not be lubricated. The lubricant will cause them to fail and will destroy their necessary frictional characteristics.

Listed below are the parts that Chrysler recommends should not be lubricated:

- Air pump
- Alternator bearings
- Brake-booster cylinder
- Clutch-release bearing
- Distributor
- Drive belts
- Fan-belt-idler-pulley bearings
- Front spring-shackle bolts and fixed eyebolts
- Propeller-shaft (drive-shaft) center bearings
- Rear spring-shackle bolts and fixed eyebolts
- Rear-wheel bearings in semifloating axles
- Rubber bushings
- Starting motor
- Throttle cable
- Throttle-linkage ball joints
- Water pump

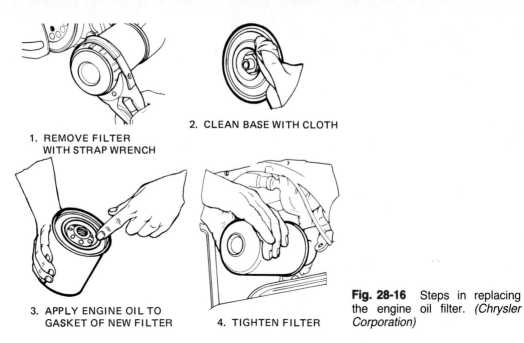

1. REMOVE FILTER
   WITH STRAP WRENCH

2. CLEAN BASE WITH CLOTH

3. APPLY ENGINE OIL TO
   GASKET OF NEW FILTER

4. TIGHTEN FILTER

Fig. 28-16 Steps in replacing the engine oil filter. *(Chrysler Corporation)*

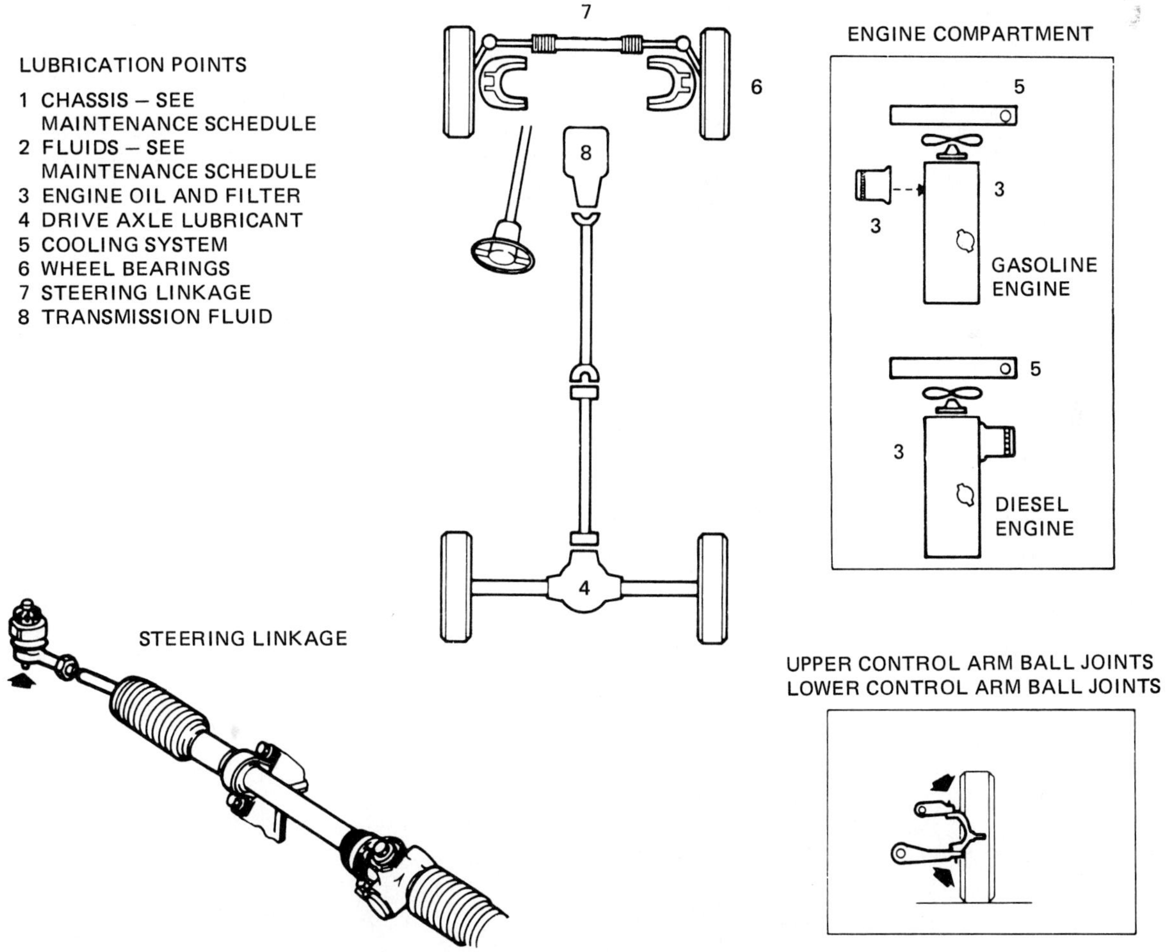

LUBRICATION POINTS

1 CHASSIS — SEE
  MAINTENANCE SCHEDULE
2 FLUIDS — SEE
  MAINTENANCE SCHEDULE
3 ENGINE OIL AND FILTER
4 DRIVE AXLE LUBRICANT
5 COOLING SYSTEM
6 WHEEL BEARINGS
7 STEERING LINKAGE
8 TRANSMISSION FLUID

ENGINE COMPARTMENT

GASOLINE ENGINE

DIESEL ENGINE

STEERING LINKAGE

UPPER CONTROL ARM BALL JOINTS
LOWER CONTROL ARM BALL JOINTS

Fig. 28-17 Lubrication points for a late-model car. *(Chevrolet Motor Division of General Motors Corporation)*

Select the *one* correct, best, or most probable answer to each question. Then check your answers against the correct answers given at the end of the book.

1. You determine when the engine oil was last changed by
   a. asking the driver
   b. inspecting the oil
   c. looking at the lube sticker
   d. measuring the amount of oil in the crankcase

2. If you have to replace one belt of a two-belt drive,
   a. tighten belts based on tension of new belt
   b. replace both belts
   c. check pulleys to see what is wrong
   d. replace defective pulley

3. When the car is up on the lift, check the exhaust system for leaks that could result in
   a. carbon monoxide leaking into the car
   b. water leaking into the car
   c. excessive noise
   d. excessive exhaust smoke

4. If the battery keeps running down,
   a. check the battery
   b. check the charging system
   c. check the drive belt
   d. all of the above

5. If the compression or other test shows that the engine has internal mechanical problems,
   a. tune it the best you can
   b. tell the driver that the engine needs repair or overhaul
   c. turn the job over to someone else
   d. install new spark plugs and return the car to the customer

6. If the spark-plug insulator is blistered, without deposits, and the electrodes are eroded, probably
   a. the plug is running too hot
   b. the plug is running too cold
   c. the valve guides are worn
   d. the piston rings are passing oil

7. To see how much the tuneup has reduced pollutants in the exhaust gas, you should check the HC and CO readings
   a. after the tuneup is completed
   b. before the tuneup is started
   c. both *a* and *b*
   d. neither *a* nor *b*

8. When checking the cooling system,
   a. keep your hands away from the engine fan
   b. never remove the radiator cap from a hot engine
   c. both *a* and *b*
   d. neither *a* nor *b*

CHAPTER 29
CYLINDER-HEAD AND VALVE-TRAIN SERVICE

After studying this chapter, and with proper instruction and equipment, you should be able to:

1. Discuss the causes of various valve troubles.
2. Adjust valve clearance on various engines.
3. List the steps and perform a valve job.
4. Discuss cylinder-head problems.
5. Diagnose valve-train problems.

Valve troubles cause many complaints about poor engine performance and excessive exhaust emissions. The valves must open, close, and seat properly if further engine troubles are to be avoided. This chapter covers various troubles with the cylinder head and valve train, their possible causes, and checks or corrections to be made.

☐ 29-1 CLEANLINESS

The major enemy of good engine-service work is dirt. A trace of dirt or abrasive in a bearing, on cylinder walls, or in other working parts in the engine can ruin an otherwise good service job. Some engine parts are precision finished to tolerances of less than 0.0001 inch [0.003 mm]. This means that pieces of dirt or abrasive only 0.001 inch [0.03 mm] in diameter can cause damage. Such fine pieces of dirt or abrasive are so small that normally you cannot see or feel them.

Dirt or abrasives can cause rapid wear and quick failure of engine parts. For example, if a main-bearing insert is installed with dirt under it, the bearing half will not fit snugly into the cylinder block or cap bore. The bearing will distort, and high spots may develop. This condition would probably cause quick bearing failure. Similarly, if abrasive is left on cylinder walls after honing a cylinder, pistons, rings, and other engine parts may wear rapidly and fail early. Be careful to remove all dirt and abrasives produced by any service work. Keep all engine parts clean. Then check that they are clean as they go back into the engine.

Before any major service work begins on an engine that has grease, dirt, and mud caked on the outside, the engine should be cleaned. This will prevent dirt from getting into the engine as it is disassembled. If

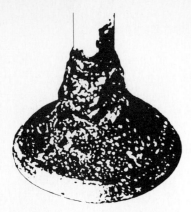

Fig. 29-1 An intake valve with gum and carbon deposits under the valve head.

steam cleaning is used, electrical parts should be covered or removed. This prevents moisture or cleaner from getting into them.

☐ 29-2 VALVE TROUBLES

The engine valves must open and close with definite timing in relation to the piston positions (☐ 10-4). They must seat tightly against the valve seats and open and close promptly. The clearance between the valve stems and valve guides must be correct. Failure of the valves to meet any of these requirements means valve trouble.

Valve troubles include valve sticking, valve burning, valve and seat breakage, valve-face and seat wear, and valve deposits. Each of these troubles is described in the following sections.

☐ 29-3 VALVE STICKING

Valves will stick open or partly open because of the following conditions:

■ Gum or carbon deposits on the valve stems (Fig. 29-1). This is usually due to worn valve guides that allow oil to work past them or to failure of the oil seal or shield on the valve stems.
■ Warped valve stems. This can result from the valve hitting the piston or a foreign object in the combustion chamber, overheating, an off-center valve seat, or a cocked valve spring.
■ Lack of oil.
■ Cold engine. However, when the engine warms up, the valves may work free.

If deposits such as gum or carbon are causing valves and piston rings to stick, the engine may have to be disassembled and cleaned. However, special additives can be put in the oil or fuel that help to free valves and rings. One type of liquid additive comes in a pressure can and is sprayed into the running engine through the air intake.

> **CAREFUL** Certain cleaners, which are sprayed directly into the intake air or added to the fuel, must not be used in cars equipped with a catalytic converter. These additives may damage the catalytic converter. Always read the label on the container before using it.

☐ 29-4 VALVE BURNING

Valve burning (Fig. 29-2) is often due to poor seating. The valve does not make contact with the valve seat all around the valve face. In a running engine the exhaust valve can get red-hot. Heat passes to the valve seat to help cool the valve. But when the valve-face-to-seat contact is not good, the valve cannot pass enough heat. It gets too hot and burns. Here are possible causes of poor valve seating:

■ Valve sticking
■ Valve clearance too small, so valve cannot close completely
■ Cocked or weak valve spring
■ Distorted valve seat
■ Dirt on valve seat

In addition to poor valve seating, other causes of valve burning include:

Fig. 29-2 Valve burning resulting from seat distortion. The valve failed to seat in one area. This allowed hot exhaust-gas leakage and burning of the valve. *(TRW, Inc.)*

430

- Overheated engine due to faulty engine cooling system or engine overload. For example, an engine can be overloaded by pulling a trailer or going up a long hill with wide-open throttle.
- Lean air-fuel mixture.
- Detonation due to engine deposits, low-octane fuel, or improper ignition timing.

☐ 29-5 VALVE BREAKAGE

A valve can break due to engine overheating or detonation (Fig. 29-3). Valve breakage also is caused by an off-center valve seat. This tends to bend the valve every time it closes. Too much valve clearance is another cause of valve breakage. Excessive clearance increases the impact load on the valve when it closes.

☐ 29-6 VALVE-FACE WEAR

In addition to the conditions listed in ☐ 29-4, excessive valve clearance, defective hydraulic lifters, or dirt on the valve face or seat can cause valve-face wear. Excessive valve clearance or a defective hydraulic lifter causes heavy impact seating. This wears the valve face and seat and may cause valve breakage (☐ 29-5).

Dirt may cause valve-face wear if the engine operates in dusty conditions or if the air cleaner is not functioning properly. Dirt enters the engine with the intake air. Some dirt deposits on the valve seat. Dirt in the engine also causes bearing, cylinder-wall, and piston and ring wear.

☐ 29-7 VALVE DEPOSITS

Too much gum in the fuel will cause gum deposits to form on the intake valves (Fig. 29-1). Carbon deposits may form from an air-fuel mixture that is too rich or from oil passing through a worn intake-valve guide (Fig. 29-4). Incomplete combustion can result in carbon deposits on the exhaust valves. Dirt or th   ng oil can also cause deposits to form on valves.

☐ 29-8 VALVE SERVICES

Many valve-train parts may require service. These include the valves, valve seats, valve guides, valve springs and retainers, pushrods, rocker arms, valve tappets, camshaft and drive, and camshaft bearings. The service jobs for these parts include:

- Adjusting valve clearance
- Replacing ball studs
- Removing cylinder head
- Removing valves
- Checking valve springs
- Servicing rocker arms and rocker-arm shafts
- Cleaning the cylinder head
- Cleaning, checking, and refacing valves
- Servicing valve guides
- Reconditioning valve seats
- Installing valves
- Checking pushrods
- Servicing hydraulic valve lifters

Fig. 29-3 Head of an exhaust valve broken off and embedded in the top of the piston. *(TRW, Inc.)*

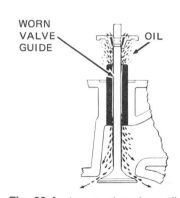

Fig. 29-4 Arrows show how oil runs down between a worn valve guide and valve stem to enter the combustion chamber. *(Dana Corporation)*

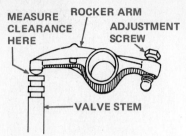

Fig. 29-5 Valve clearance is measured between the rocker arm and the tip end of the valve stem.

■ Servicing the camshaft and camshaft bearings
■ Installing the cylinder head
■ Checking valve-timing gears, or sprockets and belt or chain

Each of these services is described briefly in following sections. The *Auto Shop Workbook* provides step-by-step instructions, explaining how the job is done in the shop.

☐ 29-9 ADJUSTING VALVE CLEARANCE

Many engines with hydraulic valve lifters do not normally require adjustment of the valve clearance. However, if the valves and seats are refinished, then some adjustment may be necessary. This procedure is covered in ☐ 29-12.

A variety of adjustment procedures are required for mechanical valve lifters. Adjustments on engines with the camshaft in the cylinder block are covered in ☐ 29-10. Adjustments on engines with the camshaft in the cylinder head are described in ☐ 29-11.

☐ 29-10 ADJUSTING MECHANICAL VALVE-LIFTER CLEARANCE (CAMSHAFT IN CYLINDER BLOCK)

Here is a typical procedure for adjusting valve clearance on engines with the camshaft in the cylinder block, using mechanical valve lifters.

1. Remove the valve cover. Turn the crankshaft until the valves to be adjusted are fully closed. The valve lifters are on the base circle of the cams.
2. On the type of engine that has the rocker arms mounted on a shaft (Fig. 29-5), adjust the valve clearance by turning the self-locking adjustment screw. Get the proper clearance between the end of the valve stem and the rocker arm. Use a box wrench, as shown in Fig. 29-6. An open-end wrench could damage the screw head. Measure the clearance with a thickness gauge. Check the vehicle emission control informa-

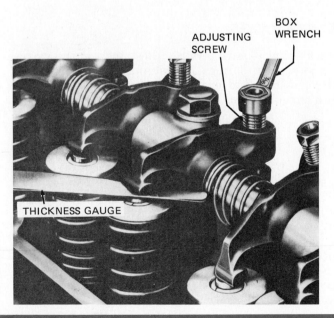

Fig. 29-6 Adjusting valve clearance on an engine with the rocker arms mounted on a shaft and the camshaft in the cylinder block. (Ford Motor Company)

tion decal under the hood, or a shop manual, for the correct specifications. Two settings may be given, one for the intake valve and a different clearance for the exhaust valve.

3. Turn the crankshaft to close the other valves. Then check and adjust them the same way.

4. On the type of engine that has the rocker arms mounted on ball studs (Fig. 29-7), turn the stud nuts up or down. Set the specified clearance between the valve stem and the rocker arm. Turning the stud nut up increases the clearance. Turning it down reduces the clearance.

□ 29-11 ADJUSTING MECHANICAL VALVE-LIFTER CLEARANCE (CAMSHAFT IN CYLINDER HEAD)

Various valve-train arrangements in overhead-valve engines were covered in Chap. 10. Valve-clearance adjustments for some of these engines are described below.

1. CHEVROLET VEGA

The valve train in a Chevrolet Vega engine is shown in Fig. 29-8. The valve-clearance adjustment is made by turning the adjustment screw located in the valve tappet. The adjustment screw has a tapered flat on one side. Therefore, adjustment must be made by turning the screw *full turns only*.

Turn the camshaft so the valve tappet is on the base circle of the cam. Then measure the clearance between the cam and the valve tappet with a thickness gauge (Fig. 29-8). Use the special tappet adjusting wrench to turn the adjustment screw. The screw must be turned complete revolutions so that the flat on the screw ends up directly above the valve stem. Turning the screw in, or clockwise, decreases clearance. Each full turn of the screw changes the clearance 0.003 inch [0.076 mm].

2. CHEVROLET LUV ENGINE

The Chevrolet LUV engine has rocker arms which are held in place by springs (Fig. 29-9). The rocker arms have dome-shaped ends which fit over ball studs in the cylinder head. The valve ends of the rocker arms fit into a depression in the valve-spring retainer and rest on the valve stems.

Fig. 29-7 Adjusting valve clearance on an engine with the rocker arms mounted on ball studs and the camshaft in the cylinder block. *(Chevrolet Motor Division of General Motors Corporation)*

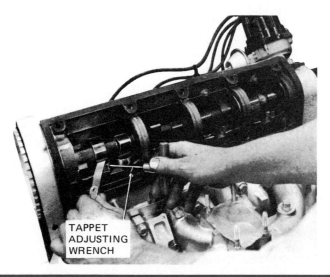

TAPPET ADJUSTING WRENCH

Fig. 29-8 Adjusting valve clearance on an engine with the camshaft in the cylinder head. *(Chevrolet Motor Division of General Motors Corporation)*

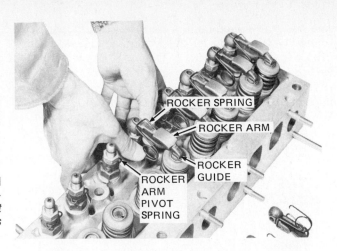

Fig. 29-9 Rocker arm and spring arrangement in the Chevrolet LUV engine. *(Chevrolet Motor Division of General Motors Corporation)*

To check the valve clearance, measure the clearance between the cam surface of the rocker arm and the base circle of the cam (Fig. 29-10). Use a flat thickness gauge. Adjust with a Phillips-head screwdriver inserted through the hole in the rocker-arm dome.

3. FORD 2000-cc FOUR-CYLINDER ENGINE

This Ford engine has rocker arms which float between a stationary stud on one side and the valve stem on the other. The center of the rocker arm rests on the cam. (This is similar to the arrangement in the Chevrolet LUV engine.) Figure 29-11 shows the use of a thickness gauge to check the clearance between the base circle of the cam and the rocker arm. Adjustment is made by loosening the locknut. Use a 15-mm open-end wrench to turn the adjustment screw in or out. Turning the screw in increases the clearance. Tighten the locknut securely after making the adjustment. Then recheck the clearance.

☐ 29-12 ADJUSTING VALVE TRAINS WITH HYDRAULIC VALVE LIFTERS

In valve trains with hydraulic valve lifters, no adjustment is usually needed. However, after valves and valve seats are refinished in engines with hydraulic lifters, then some adjustment may be required. Here are typical procedures for this type of adjustment.

1. FORD

First, bleed down the hydraulic valve lifter by forcing the oil out and the valve-lifter plunger down. Figure 29-12 shows a valve-lifter bleeding tool being used to do this job. Turn the crankshaft so that the lifter is on the base circle of the cam. The piston in number 1 cylinder should be at TDC on the compression stroke. Check the valves that are closed. Then turn the crankshaft to close another set of valves and check them. You can usually check all valves with only two or three positions of the crankshaft.

To check the valve-lifter adjustment, apply force against the lifter (Fig. 29-12). When the plunger bottoms, measure the clearance between the valve stem and the rocker arm. If the clearance is too small, then a shorter pushrod must be installed. If the clearance is excessive, then a longer pushrod should be installed.

Fig. 29-10 Adjusting valve clearance on the engine shown in Fig. 29-9. It has the camshaft in the cylinder head and rocker arms held in place by springs. *(Chevrolet Motor Division of General Motors Corporation)*

434

2. PLYMOUTH

The checking procedure for hydraulic valve lifters on Plymouth engines is necessary only when valves have been ground. A special tool is used with a scale to measure the increased height of the valve stem above the cylinder head (Fig. 29-13). This is done before the head is assembled and installed on the engine. If the height is too great, the end of the valve stem should be ground off.

3. CHEVROLET

This procedure is typical of the General Motors engines using the ball-pivot rocker arm (Fig. 29-14). With the valve lifter on the base circle of the cam, back off the adjustment nut until the pushrod is loose. Then slowly turn the adjustment nut down until all side play and clearance are gone. Turn the adjustment nut down one additional turn or the amount specified in the shop manual.

☐ 29-13 REPLACING BALL STUDS

Ball studs, if damaged, can be replaced. Some screw into tapped holes in the head. Others are a press fit and must be pulled with a special puller.

☐ 29-14 REMOVING THE CYLINDER HEAD

To remove the valves, you must first remove the cylinder head. This means draining the cooling system and removing the manifolds and any other parts that are in the way. Then remove the cylinder-head bolts and take off the head.

☐ 29-15 REMOVING VALVES

The cylinder head should be placed in a head stand. A valve-spring compressor is used to compress the valve springs (Fig. 29-15). Then the retainer locks, retainers, oil seals, and springs can be removed. Now the valve can be removed. If the stem end is peened over, or mushroomed, do not drive out the valve. This could break the valve guide or cylinder head. Instead, use a small grinding stone to grind off the mushroom.

> **NOTE** Do not interchange valves and other parts. Each valve, spring, lock, retainer, and pushrod should be reinstalled in the same place in the same cylinder from which it was taken. As you remove each valve, place it in a numbered valve rack (Fig. 29-16). This will prevent mixup during reassembly.

☐ 29-16 CHECKING VALVE SPRINGS

The valve springs should be checked for distortion, tension, and color change (Fig. 29-17). If discolored, the spring has been overheated and should be discarded. A bent or weak spring should also be discarded.

☐ 29-17 SERVICING ROCKER ARMS AND ROCKER-ARM SHAFT

Rocker arms with worn bearing surfaces should be replaced. On some rocker arms, worn or pitted valve ends can be resurfaced in the valve refacer.

Fig. 29-11   Checking valve clearance on the Ford 2000-cc engine. *(Ford Motor Company)*

LIFTER-
BLEEDING
TOOL

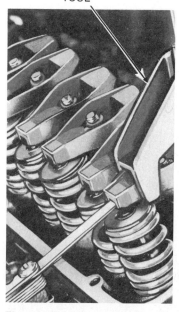

Fig. 29-12 Checking valve-train clearance on a ball-stud-mounted rocker arm. The hydraulic valve lifter has been bled down by force applied using the special tool. *(Ford Motor Company)*

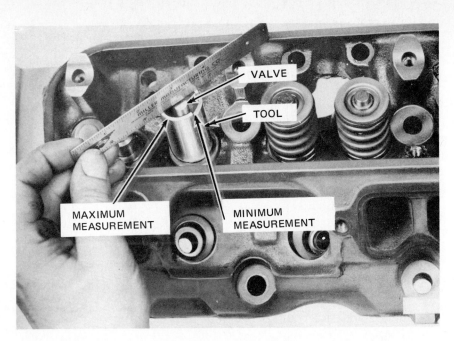

Fig. 29-13 Measuring the valve-stem length with a special tool after installing the valve in the cylinder head. *(Chrysler Corporation)*

☐ 29-18 CLEANING THE CYLINDER HEAD

The head should be cleaned of carbon, gasket material, and other deposits with a carbon scraper. A wire brush driven by a drill motor can be used to clean the combustion chambers and ports. Check and clean out water jackets.

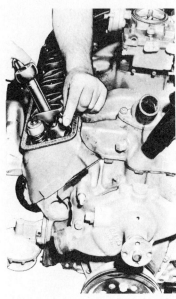

Fig. 29-14 Adjusting the rocker-arm stud nut to properly position the plunger in the hydraulic valve lifter. *(Chevrolet Motor Division of General Motors Corporation)*

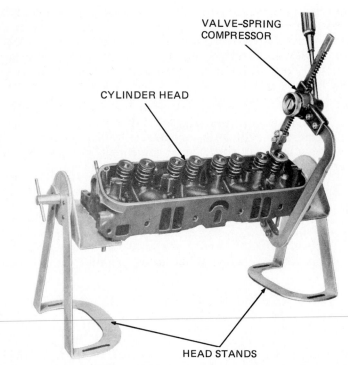

Fig. 29-15 Cylinder head mounted in head stands. *(Chrysler Corporation)*

CAUTION Always wear goggles when using a wire brush or compressed air. The goggles protect your eyes from flying particles that could injure your eyes. Be sure you do not blow particles toward anyone working near you when you use compressed air.

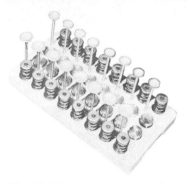

Fig. 29-16 Valve rack for holding valves and valve-train parts. *(Chevrolet Motor Division of General Motors Corporation)*

☐ 29-19 CLEANING, CHECKING, AND GRINDING VALVES

The various parts of each valve should be checked as shown in Fig. 29-18. If the valve faces are rough or pitted, they should be ground in a valve refacer and then checked for proper margin.

☐ 29-20 SERVICING VALVE GUIDES

Valve guides must be serviced before valve seats are ground. The stone holder for the valve-seat grinder is centered by a pilot inserted in the guide. If the guide is not in good condition, the seat will not be ground square and evenly. To service a valve guide, first clean it (Fig. 29-19) and then check it for wear. If worn, it must be replaced (if it is the replaceable type) or reamed to a larger size. Then valves with oversize stems are used. Knurling the valve guides is another method of restoring the guides to proper size.

☐ 29-21 REFINISHING VALVE SEATS

Whenever valves are ground, the valve seats also must be refinished. A valve-seat grinding stone, driven by an air or electric motor, is used to grind valve seats (Fig. 29-20). As the stone rotates on the seat, it removes pits and restores the seat to a smooth, round surface with the proper angle. Valve-seat cutters can be used instead of stones to refinish the valve seat.

On some engines, such as in the Plymouth Horizon and Dodge Omni, the exhaust valves should not be refaced on a machine. Instead, if the valve needs service, the seat should first be ground and then the valve lapped in by hand, using lapping compound. All trace of the lapping compound, which is a cutting abrasive, must be removed after lapping the valve.

In general, the lapping of valves in automotive engines is not recom-

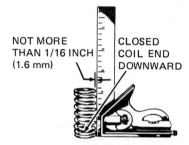

NOT MORE THAN 1/16 INCH (1.6 mm)   CLOSED COIL END DOWNWARD

Fig. 29-17 Checking valve-spring squareness. *(Ford Motor Company)*

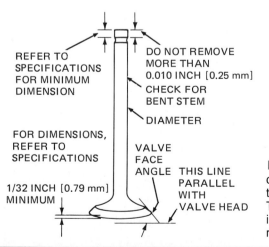

REFER TO SPECIFICATIONS FOR MINIMUM DIMENSION

DO NOT REMOVE MORE THAN 0.010 INCH [0.25 mm]

CHECK FOR BENT STEM

DIAMETER

FOR DIMENSIONS, REFER TO SPECIFICATIONS

VALVE FACE ANGLE

THIS LINE PARALLEL WITH VALVE HEAD

1/32 INCH [0.79 mm] MINIMUM

Fig. 29-18 Valve parts to be checked. On the valve shown, the stem is hardened at the end. Therefore, not more than 0.010 inch [0.25 mm] should be removed. *(Ford Motor Company)*

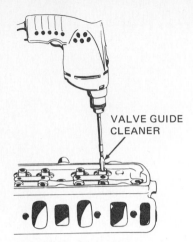

Fig. 29-19 Cleaning the valve guide with a valve-guide cleaner. *(Oldsmobile Division of General Motors Corporation)*

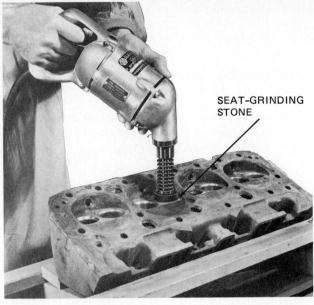

SEAT–GRINDING STONE

Fig. 29-20 Using the valve-seat grinder. The stone rotates at high speed. About once every revolution, it lifts off the seat to throw off loose grit and grindings. *(The Black and Decker Manufacturing Company)*

mended. The grinding process using the valve-refacing machine produces a precision finish which can be damaged by lapping.

NOTE If new valves are required, they should not need to be refaced. However, seating should be checked, as explained earlier. *Never reface or lap coated valves!*

☐ 29-22 INSTALLING VALVES

After the cylinder head, valve seats, and valves have been serviced and cleaned, the valves are reinstalled in the cylinder head. Valves and related parts should always go back into the same valve guide and seat

Fig. 29-21 Using a valve-spring compressor on the valve assemblies in the cylinder head. *(Chevrolet Motor Division of General Motors Corporation)*

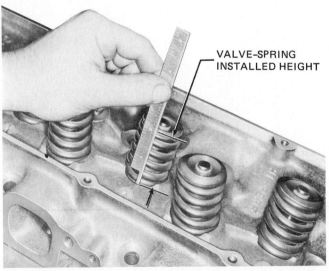

VALVE-SPRING INSTALLED HEIGHT

Fig. 29-22 Measuring valve-spring installed height. *(Chevrolet Motor Division of General Motors Corporation)*

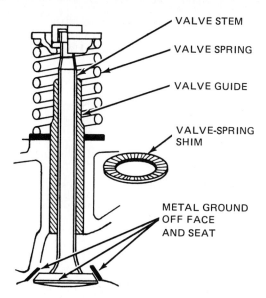

Fig. 29-23 A shim under the valve spring may be needed to obtain the proper installed height. (Silver Seal Products Company, Inc.)

Labels in figure:
VALVE STEM
VALVE SPRING
VALVE GUIDE
VALVE-SPRING SHIM
METAL GROUND OFF FACE AND SEAT

from which they were removed. Coat valves with engine oil. Use a spring compressor (Fig. 29-21) to compress the spring. Then install the oil seal, spring, retainer, and locks.

Measure the valve-spring installed height (Fig. 29-22). Add a shim if necessary to reduce the spring height to specifications (Fig. 29-23).

□ 29-23 CHECKING PUSHRODS

Pushrods should be checked for wear and distortion. If any defects are found, install a new pushrod.

□ 29-24 SERVICING HYDRAULIC VALVE LIFTERS

Manufacturers' shop manuals carry detailed servicing procedures for hydraulic valve lifters. However, many shops replace defective lifters with new ones instead of servicing used lifters. Labor costs to service a lifter can be greater than the price of a new one.

□ 29-25 SERVICING THE CAMSHAFT AND BEARINGS

Removing a camshaft from an engine is a major job. It is done when the camshaft needs regrinding or replacement, or if the camshaft bearings need replacement.

□ 29-26 INSTALLING THE CYLINDER HEAD

After the head has been assembled, it is installed on the cylinder block. Always use a new head gasket. Make sure the mating surfaces between the head and block are clean and smooth. The cylinder-head bolts should be tightened in the proper sequence and to the proper torque (Fig. 29-24).

All boltholes should be cleaned of dirt or coolant. Threads should be clean and straight. Dirty or battered threads will not allow normal bolt tightening. Then the head could come loose. It requires a torque above

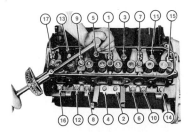

Fig. 29-24 Bolt-tightening sequence for the cylinder-head bolts on one model of V-8 engine. (Chrysler Corporation)

normal to overcome the excessive friction of dirty or battered threads. Dirt or water in a bolthole can result in a broken block. Bolts that do not seat properly leave the cylinder head loose. This will cause a blown gasket.

CHAPTER 29
REVIEW QUESTIONS

Select the *one* correct, best, or most probable answer to each question. Then check your answers against the correct answers given at the end of the book.

1. A possible cause of a valve sticking open or partly open could be
   a. gum deposit on valve stem
   b. warped valve stem
   c. lack of oil
   d. all of the above

2. A possible cause of valve burning could be
   a. valve sticking
   b. insufficient tappet clearance
   c. dirt on valve seat
   d. all of the above

3. To adjust valve clearance on engines with the rocker arms mounted on a shaft,
   a. turn the stud nut
   b. turn the adjusting screw in the cylinder head
   c. turn the adjusting screw in the rocker arm
   d. none of the above

4. To adjust the valve clearance on engines with the rocker arms mounted on ball studs,
   a. turn the stud nut
   b. turn the adjusting screw in the cylinder head
   c. turn the adjusting screw in the rocker arm
   d. grind the valve seat

5. On the General Motors pushrod engine using hydraulic valve lifters and ball-pivot rocker arms,
   a. pushrod looseness is checked during the adjustment procedure
   b. adjustment is made by turning the screw in the valve lifter
   c. no valve-clearance adjustment is necessary
   d. adjustment is made by turning the screw in the rocker arm

6. On Ford pushrod engines with hydraulic valve lifters, insufficient clearance after bleeding down the lifter requires correction by
   a. turning the adjustment screw
   b. installing shorter pushrods
   c. grinding the valves
   d. grinding the camshaft

CHAPTER 30
CONNECTING-ROD, PISTON, AND PISTON-RING SERVICE

After studying this chapter, and with proper instruction and equipment, you should be able to:

1. Remove the cylinder ring ridge.
2. Replace piston rings.
3. Replace connecting-rod bearings.
4. Install piston pins.
5. Diagnose the cause of bearing failure.
6. Diagnose the cause of piston failure.
7. Measure bearing clearance with Plastigage.
8. Check for bent or twisted connecting rods.

As pistons, rings, and cylinder walls wear, power is lost and oil is burned in the combustion chambers. There comes a time when the engine is losing so much power and burning so much oil that repair is required. This means that the cylinder head must be removed so that the cylinder bores can be checked to determine their condition. If the engine is badly worn, then the piston-and-connecting-rod assemblies must be removed and serviced.

☐ 30-1 PREPARING TO REMOVE PISTON-AND-ROD ASSEMBLIES

Before the piston-and-rod assembly (Fig. 30-1) can be removed, the engine oil must be drained and the oil pan removed. Then the cylinder head must be taken off. Next, the cylinders should be examined for wear. If a cylinder is worn, there will be a *ring ridge* at the top of it. This ridge marks the upper limit of top-ring travel. You can feel the ridge with your fingernail (Fig. 30-2). If a piston is forced out past this ridge, the piston-ring lands may be broken (Fig. 30-3).

If you find ridges, use a *ring-ridge remover* (Fig. 30-4). The ring ridge must be removed before you force the pistons out of the cylinders. The

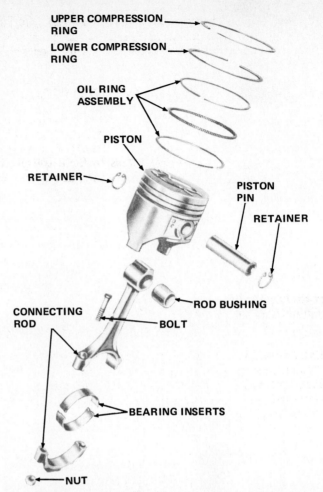

Fig. 30-1 A piston-and-connecting-rod assembly using a full-floating piston pin retained by snap rings. *(Ford Motor Company)*

ring-ridge remover has a cutting blade that will cut off the ridge as the tool is rotated. Then the pistons can be removed without damage.

□ 30-2 REMOVING PISTON-AND-ROD ASSEMBLIES

After you have removed the cylinder head and the oil pan, turn the crankshaft so that the number 1 piston is near BDC. Check the connecting rod and the cap for identifying marks. If there are no marks, use a small watercolor brush and white metal paint to mark a "1" on the rod cap and the rod. Then you can return the cap to the rod from which it came, and return rod and cap to the number 1 cylinder.

Next, remove the rod nuts and take off the rod cap. Then use rod guides to cover the rod bolts (Fig. 30-5). The guides protect the crankpins from the rod-bolt threads. If exposed, these threads could scratch or nick the crankpins. Short pieces of rubber hose, split and slipped over the bolts, serve the same purpose. With the guides or the hoses in place, slide the piston-and-rod assembly up in the cylinder. Take the assembly out from the top.

As you go from one cylinder to the next to remove the remaining piston-and-rod assemblies, turn the crankshaft to get at the rod nuts.

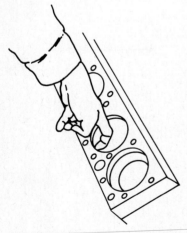

Fig. 30-2 If you can catch your fingernail under the ring ridge, it must be cut out before the pistons are removed.

Mark all rods and caps with the number of the cylinder from which they were removed. As you remove the piston-and-rod assemblies, set them in a piston rack in the same order the pistons are numbered.

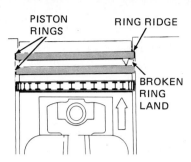

☐ 30-3 SEPARATING PISTONS AND RODS

To separate the pistons from the rods, remove the piston pins. The procedure varies, depending on how the rod and piston are attached to the pin. With a free-floating pin, remove the retainers and push the pin out (Fig. 30-1). With a press-fit pin, use a *pin press* to force the pin out of the connecting rod (Fig. 30-6). Never try to drive the pin out with a hammer. This will break the piston.

Fig. 30-3 When the ring ridge is not removed, trying to force the piston out of the cylinder will usually break the piston-ring lands. *(ATW)*

> **CAREFUL** Make sure the pistons have identifying marks so that each piston can be reattached to its matching connecting rod in the correct position. If the piston is installed on a rod backward, piston slap and early piston failure can result. Each piston-and-rod assembly should be reinstalled in the same cylinder from which it was removed.

☐ 30-4 CHECKING CONNECTING RODS

The rods should be cleaned and checked for nicks on the bearing surfaces and sides of the big-end bore. Look for cracks around the piston-pin hole and the cap-bolt holes. Check the rods for alignment. A bent rod can cause trouble with the bearing, piston, and cylinder wall. If any rod has defects, it should be replaced.

☐ 30-5 CHECKING PISTON-PIN BUSHINGS

If the rod is used with a free-floating piston pin, there is a bushing in the small end of the rod. If this bushing is worn, it can be replaced. Then the new bushing is reamed or honed to size.

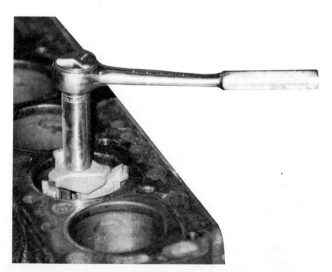

Fig. 30-4 Ring-ridge remover in place in the top of a cylinder. As the tool is turned in the cylinder, cutting blades remove the ring ridge. *(ATW)*

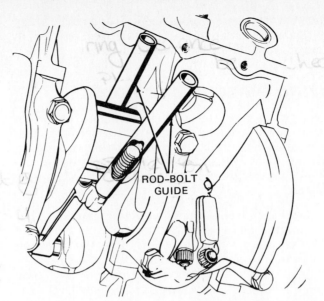

ROD–BOLT
GUIDE

Fig. 30-5 Using short pieces of rubber hose as rod-bolt guides to protect the connecting-rod journals from damage. *(Oldsmobile Division of General Motors Corporation)*

☐ 30-6 INSPECTING CONNECTING-ROD BEARINGS

Connecting-rod bearings are split insert-type bearings. They are serviced by replacement. As you remove the rod caps, examine upper and lower bearing halves for wear and other trouble. Figure 30-7 shows various kinds of trouble and their causes. Each type of bearing failure is described further below.

1. LACK OF OIL

If the oil supply fails, bearing material will be wiped off the shell. The friction heat can become so high that the rod will actually weld to the crankpin. When this happens, the engine "throws a rod." The rod freezes to the crankpin and breaks. Part of the rod may go through the cylinder wall. Failure of the oil supply can result from worn bearings, which pass all the oil the pump can supply. This oil-starves the bearings farthest

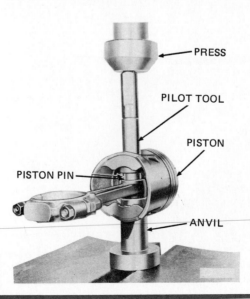

PRESS

PILOT TOOL

PISTON

PISTON PIN

ANVIL

Fig. 30-6 A piston-pin press is used to remove and install the piston pin. *(Chrysler Corporation)*

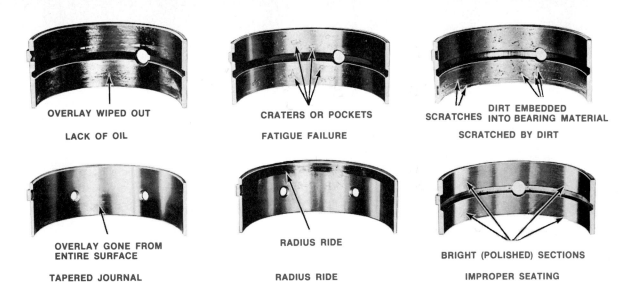

Fig. 30-7 Types of engine-bearing failures. The appearance of a bearing usually indicates the cause of its failure. *(Ford Motor Company)*

from the pump. Oil starvation also can result from low oil level in the oil pan, clogged lines, or a defective oil pump.

2. FATIGUE FAILURE

Fatigue failure of bearings normally is not a problem. However, unusual operating conditions or out-of-round bearing journals can cause this trouble. For example, if an engine is operated under heavy load with wide-open throttle, the upper bearing half may "fatigue out." This type of operation repeatedly overloads the upper bearing half. The hammering effect causes the metal to fatigue and flake out. A similar effect could be caused by an out-of-round journal. The out-of-round section of a journal overloads the bearing each revolution.

3. SCRATCHED BY DIRT

If the oil is dirty, particles of dirt will gouge out the soft bearing material and may also scratch the crankpin. The oil can become dirty if the oil and the oil filter are not changed at the proper intervals. If the bearing becomes overloaded with particles, bearing failure will soon occur.

4. TAPERED JOURNAL

A tapered journal is larger at one end than at the other. The bigger end puts more load on the bearing. This overload wipes out the bearing material at that end.

5. RADIUS RIDE

If the radius of the journal, where it curves up to the crank cheeks, is not cut away enough, the journal will ride on the edge of the bearing. This action will push the bearing to one side, overheat it, and cause it to fail. Radius ride usually occurs only after a crankshaft has been reground in an automotive machine shop.

6. IMPROPER SEATING

If the bearing is not properly seated in the bearing cap or rod, there will be high spots in the bearing. Figure 30-8 shows what happens if particles

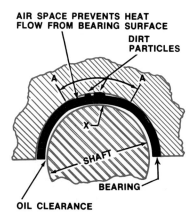

Fig. 30-8 Effect of dirt particles under the bearing insert, caused by improper installation. *(Federal-Mogul Corporation)*

445

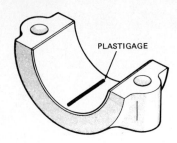

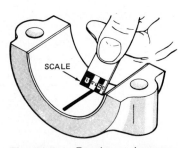

Fig. 30-9 Bearing clearance being checked with Plastigage. Top, Plastigage in place before tightening the cap. Bottom, measuring the amount of flattening (which is the bearing clearance) with the scale on the Plastigage package. *(Chrysler Corporation)*

of dirt are left in the cap or rod when the bearing is installed. The bearing is damaged in two ways. The shell is pushed up at the spot where the dirt particles occur, leaving the bearing with insufficient oil clearance (as at X). This condition causes frictional heating and rapid bearing wear. Also, air space is left between the bearing and rod or cap. This prevents normal heat flow away from the bearing. The condition makes the heating problem worse, so the bearing soon fails.

☐ 30-7 CHECKING CONNECTING-ROD-BEARING CLEARANCE

There are three ways of checking the clearance between the connecting-rod bearing and the crankpin journal. These are with Plastigage, with shim stock, or with micrometer and telescope gauge.

1. PLASTIGAGE

Plastigage is the most popular way to check bearing fit. It is a plastic material that comes in strips. To use Plastigage, first wipe the oil from the bearing and the journal. Then lay a strip of Plastigage on the bearing in the cap (Fig. 30-9). Next, put the cap into place and tighten the cap nuts to the specified torque. Then remove the cap and measure the amount that the Plastigage has flattened. Check the clearance with the chart on the Plastigage package (Fig. 30-9). The smaller the clearance, the flatter the Plastigage.

> **NOTE** Do not move the rod on the crankpin while the cap nuts are tight. Moving the rod will flatten the Plastigage too much and cause incorrect measurements.

2. SHIM STOCK

Shim stock is a sheet of thin metal that can be purchased in various thicknesses. To measure clearance with shim stock, first lubricate a strip of stock. Lay it lengthwise in the center of the bearing cap. Then install the cap and lightly tighten the cap nuts. Next, check the ease with which the rod can be moved on the crankpin. If the rod moves easily, there is too much clearance. Remove the cap. Put another strip of shim stock on top of the first strip, and repeat the procedure. Continue adding shim stock, until the rod is hard to move. The thickness of the shims is the clearance.

3. MICROMETER AND TELESCOPE GAUGE

This method requires a micrometer to measure the diameter of the crankpin. It also requires a telescope gauge or an inside micrometer to measure the inside diameter of the rod bearing with the cap in place. Bearing clearance is the difference between the bearing diameter and the crankpin diameter.

☐ 30-8 REPLACING CONNECTING-ROD BEARINGS

New connecting-rod bearings are required if the old ones are defective or worn. They are also required if the crankshaft is reground. Crankshaft grinding is described in Chap. 31.

> **NOTE** Engine rebuilders usually install new bearings, even though the old bearings seem to be in good condition. With the engine disassembled, it costs only a little more to install new bearings.

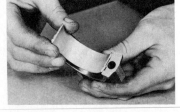

Fig. 30-10 Installing a new bearing insert in the connecting-rod cap. *(Service Parts Division of Dana Corporation)*

1. CHECKING THE CRANKPINS

Before installing the bearings, check the crankpins with a micrometer. This check will detect taper or an out-of-round condition. If crankpins are out of round or tapered more than 0.0015 inch [0.038 mm], the crankshaft must be replaced or the crankpins reground. Out-of-round or tapered crankpins can cause early bearing failure.

2. INSTALLING NEW BEARINGS

When installing new bearings, make sure your hands, the workbench, your tools, and all engine parts are clean. It takes only a little dirt to ruin a bearing. Be sure that the bores in the cap and the rod are clean. Keep the bearings wrapped up until you are ready to install them. Then handle them carefully. Wipe each bearing with a clean, lint-free cloth just before installing it.

Put the bearing shells into place in the cap and the rod (Fig. 30-10). If the shells have locking tangs, make sure the tangs enter the notches provided in the cap and the rod. The tangs in the rod and the tangs in the cap face one another when the cap is properly installed. Then coat each bearing with clean engine oil.

3. BEARING SPREAD

Bearing inserts have "spread." The ends are spread out a little beyond the diameter of the rod bore into which the shell fits (Fig. 30-10). This ensures a snug fit when the insert is pushed into place.

4. BEARING CRUSH

Bearing inserts also have a little additional height over a full half (Fig. 30-11). This additional height is crushed down as the cap bolts are tightened to provide a firm seat in the bearing bore. Firm seating is necessary for adequate heat transfer from the bearing to the cap or the rod.

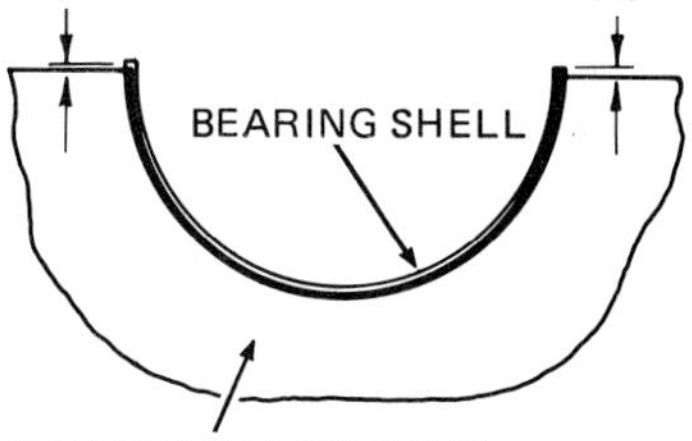

☐ 30-9 SERVICING PISTONS

As the pistons are removed from the engine and separated from the connecting rods, the pistons should be examined carefully. If they are in good condition, remove the rings (Fig. 30-12) and set aside the pistons for further inspection.

Examine damaged pistons to determine the cause of damage (Figs. 30-13 to 30-15). Make sure to correct the condition that caused the damage. Otherwise, the new pistons will also be damaged. Scrape the piston heads clean. Then soak them in a parts-cleaning solution, such as carburetor cleaner, which is safe to use on aluminum. Clean the piston inside and out.

> **CAREFUL** Do not clean the piston in caustic, or corrosive, solution or use a wire brush on the piston skirt. These could damage the finish, causing rapid piston failure.

Clean out the ring grooves with a ring-groove cleaner or with a piece of an old ring (Fig. 30-16). Clean out the oilholes or slots in the back of the ring grooves with a drill or a small, thin screwdriver.

☐ 30-10 INSPECTING PISTONS

Each piston should be examined for wear, scuffs, cracks, or scratches. Check the fit of the rings in the grooves and the condition of the piston-pin bosses or bushings. These checks are described in later sections.

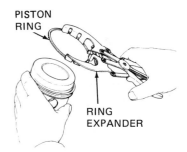

Fig. 30-11 Bearing crush.

THIS MAY BE AS LITTLE AS 0.00025 INCH [0.0063 mm]

ADDITIONAL HEIGHT OVER FULL HALF GIVES CRUSH ON ASSEMBLY

BEARING SHELL

BEARING CAP OR BORE IN ROD OR BLOCK

Fig. 30-12 A piston-ring expander is used to remove and install the piston ring. *(Chrysler Corporation)*

PISTON RING

RING EXPANDER

Fig. 30-13 A piston that has failed from scuffing. Note the scratch or scuff marks that run up and down the piston skirt. *(TRW, Inc.)*

Fig. 30-14 A piston that has failed due to detonation. The top-ring land has been shattered by the shock wave. *(TRW, Inc.)*

Measure the diameter of the piston with a micrometer. Compare this diameter with the diameter of the cylinder in which the piston is to be installed. If there is too much clearance, a new piston will be required. A typical piston clearance is 0.0005 to 0.0015 inch [0.013 to 0.038 mm] on a new or rebored engine. Most engines can be rebuilt without reboring if the cylinder taper does not exceed 0.005 inch [0.13 mm] or if the cylinder out-of-round does not exceed 0.003 inch [0.08 mm].

☐ *30-11 SELECTING NEW PISTONS*

New pistons are available in the original size and in various oversizes. When oversize pistons are selected, the cylinders are bored and honed to provide the correct piston clearance. (Cylinder service is described in Chap. 31.)

Engine manufacturers supply oversize pistons of the same weight as the original pistons. There is no engine-balance problem if all pistons are of the same weight, even if some are of different size. Aluminum pistons usually are supplied with the pin already fitted. This ensures factory specifications for piston-pin clearance.

> **CAREFUL** New pistons have a special finish. They must not be buffed with a wire wheel or finished to a smaller size. This would remove the finish and cause rapid piston wear after installation.

Fig. 30-15 A piston that has failed due to preignition. The excessive heat has melted a hole through the top of the piston. *(TRW, Inc.)*

☐ *30-12 PISTON-PIN SERVICE*

If there is excessive clearance between the piston and pin, most manufacturers recommend discarding both. Some pistons have piston-pin bushings. If these are worn, they should be reamed or honed oversize. Then new oversize pins are installed. This work usually is done in an automotive machine shop.

☐ *30-13 ALIGNING PISTON AND ROD*

After the piston and rod have been assembled, rod alignment should be checked. A diagonal wear pattern on a used piston indicates a bent rod (Fig. 30-17). The piston-and-rod alignment should be checked before the piston rings are installed.

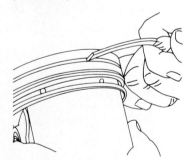

Fig. 30-16 Using a part of a broken compression ring, which has been sharpened on one end, to clean out the ring grooves. *(Service Parts Division of Dana Corporation)*

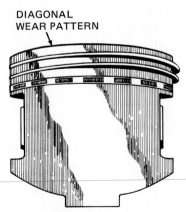

DIAGONAL
WEAR PATTERN

Fig. 30-17 A diagonal wear pattern across the face of a piston indicates a bent connecting rod. *(ATW)*

☐ 30-14 SERVICING PISTON RINGS

During an engine overhaul, new piston rings should be installed. Examine the old rings to see if they indicate any engine troubles. For example, scuffed rings may mean that not enough oil is getting to the cylinder walls. When cylinders are rebored, a new oversize ring set should be selected. Oversize rings often have special springs in back of them to provide more tension. The result is that the rings can do a better job of oil control.

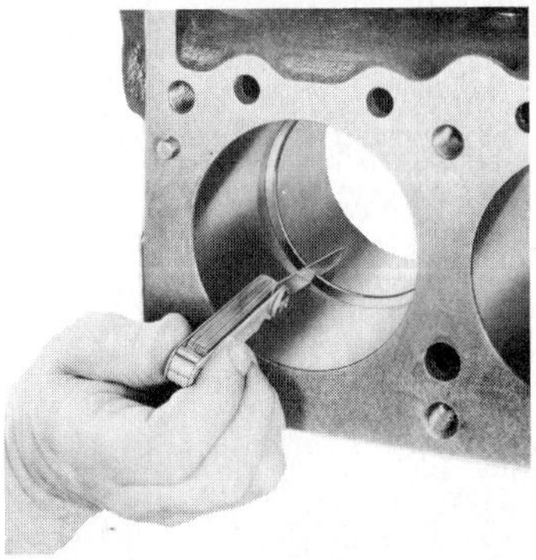

☐ 30-15 INSTALLING PISTON RINGS

The piston rings must be fitted to the cylinder and also to the ring grooves in the piston. First, push the ring down to the bottom of ring travel in the cylinder with a piston. Then check the piston-ring end gap with a thickness gauge (Fig. 30-18). If the ring gap is too small, make sure you have the right size ring set for the engine. A smaller ring set will have a larger end gap.

> **NOTE** If you are fitting rings to a tapered cylinder, be sure to fit the ring at the lower limit of ring travel. If you fit the ring to the upper part of the cylinder, the gap will be too small. When the ring moves down into the smaller diameter, the gap will close up and the ring can break. Make sure the ring has a gap at the point of minimum diameter. The point of minimum diameter is at the lower limit of ring travel.

After checking the ring gap, test the fit of the ring in the piston groove. Insert the outside of the ring into the groove, and roll the ring all the way around the piston (Fig. 30-19). If the fit is too tight, the groove probably is dirty and needs cleaning. An additional test should be made after the ring is installed in the groove. Insert a thickness gauge between the ring and the side of the groove to measure ring side clearance (Fig. 30-20). Clearance should be at least 0.001 inch [0.025 mm] and not more than 0.004 inch [0.10 mm] for most engines. Check the shop manual for the specifications on the engine you are servicing.

☐ 30-16 INSTALLING PISTON-AND-ROD ASSEMBLIES

After the rings have been installed in the piston grooves, the piston-and-rod assembly is ready for installation. Dip the piston assembly in oil until the pin is covered (Fig. 30-21). Pour out the excess oil. Now the rings

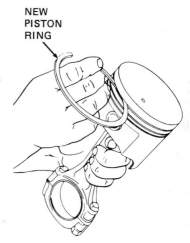

Fig. 30-18 The end gap of the piston ring is measured with the ring at the lower limit of its travel in the cylinder. *(Oldsmobile Division of General Motors Corporation)*

NEW PISTON RING

Fig. 30-19 Checking the fit of the piston ring in its groove in the piston. *(Chevrolet Motor Division of General Motors Corporation)*

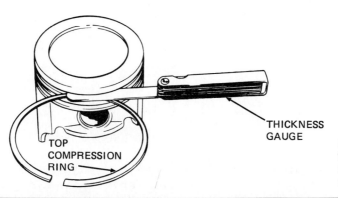

TOP COMPRESSION RING

THICKNESS GAUGE

Fig. 30-20 Checking the piston-ring side clearance. *(Oldsmobile Division of General Motors Corporation)*

must be compressed into the ring grooves so that they will enter the cylinder. Use a *loading sleeve* or a ring compressor for this job (Fig. 30-22). Clamp the compressor around the rings, compressing them into the piston grooves. Then push the piston down into the cylinder.

NOTE Use guide sleeves or rubber tubing to protect the crankpins from the threads on the rod bolts (Fig. 30-5). Also make sure the pistons and the rods are facing in the proper direction. Many pistons are notched toward the front of the engine (Fig. 30-22).

Fig. 30-21 Dip the piston assembly in engine oil deep enough to cover the piston rings and piston pin. *(ATW)*

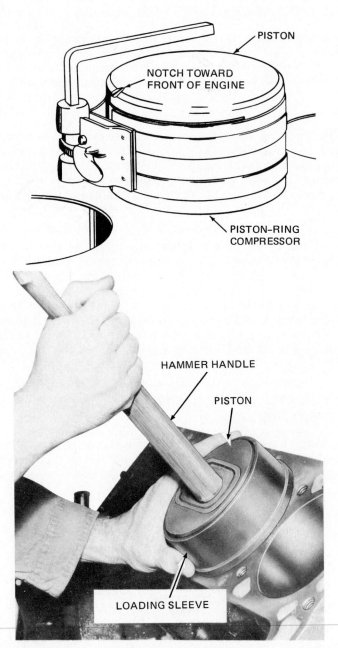

Fig. 30-22 Top, using an adjustable piston-ring compressor to install a piston with rings. Bottom, using a loading-sleeve type of piston-ring compressor. *(Oldsmobile Division and Cadillac Motor Car Division of General Motors Corporation)*

Select the *one* correct, best, or most probable answer to each question. Then check your answers against the correct answers given at the end of the book.

1. The ring ridge is
   a. in the cylinder head
   b. at the top of the cylinder
   c. at the bottom of the cylinder
   d. at the midpoint of piston travel

2. The ring ridge must be removed before taking the piston out of the cylinder to avoid
   a. damaging the piston pin
   b. scratching the cylinder wall
   c. breaking the connecting rod
   d. breaking the piston-ring lands

3. To separate the pistons from the rods,
   a. remove the piston pins
   b. remove the piston rings
   c. press the rod out of the piston
   d. none of the above

4. If the overlay is wiped out of the connecting-rod bearing, the cause is
   a. lack of oil
   b. dirt in the oil
   c. radius ride
   d. all of the above

5. Bearing crush is
   a. the additional spread of the bearing shell
   b. what happens when a bearing fails from lack of oil
   c. the amount the Plastigage is flattened
   d. the amount of additional height over a full half

6. To check piston-ring end gap with a thickness gauge, install the ring at the
   a. top of the cylinder
   b. piston-pin holes in the cylinder
   c. bottom of the cylinder
   d. center of the cylinder

7. The more the Plastigage is flattened,
   a. the greater the clearance
   b. the less the clearance
   c. the tighter the cap nuts should be torqued
   d. none of the above

8. Connecting-rod-bearing clearance can be checked with
   a. shim stock
   b. micrometer and telescope gauge
   c. Plastigage
   d. all of the above

CHAPTER 31
CRANKSHAFT AND CYLINDER SERVICE

After studying this chapter, and with proper instruction and equipment, you should be able to:

1. Replace the crankshaft and main bearings.
2. Measure a cylinder block for wear, taper, and out-of-round.
3. Recondition a cylinder block.
4. Install cylinder sleeves.
5. Replace an expansion-core plug.

Almost everything wears out. The car engine is no exception. Through normal use metal is worn away from bearings, cylinder walls, and other machined surfaces. Then the clearances are too large, and other problems, such as oil consumption and various noises, begin to be noticed. Rebuilding an engine includes checking and servicing the crankshaft and cylinder block. When these jobs are performed properly and with great attention to cleanliness, then the rate of wear is reduced. This restores engine performance. It also reduces fuel and oil consumption and prolongs the useful life of the car.

☐ 31-1 THE SHORT BLOCK

A worn engine may require major service work, such as boring the cylinders and grinding the crankshaft. Then it may be cheaper to install an engine *short block* (Fig. 31-1) than to rebuild the old engine. The short

Fig. 31-1 A rebuilt or remanufactured engine *short block.* (*Ford Motor Company*)

block is a remanufactured engine that includes all internal parts—pistons, piston pins, piston rings, connecting rods, bearings, and crankshaft. The bearings and rings are new. The other parts are new or are reconditioned. Serviceable used parts may also be used. All other parts, such as cylinder head, manifolds, and oil pan, are removed from the old engine. Then they are serviced as necessary and installed on the short block. The result is a rebuilt engine in less time, and with less parts and labor cost, than if you completely rebuilt the old engine.

□ 31-2 CHECKING CRANKSHAFT AND BEARINGS IN THE CAR

In some engines the crankshaft main bearings and journals can be checked without removing the crankshaft. The service manual for the engine you are servicing will tell whether the check can be made in this way. Checking connecting-rod-bearing clearance is described in □ 30-7.

The first step in checking the crankshaft bearings and journals is to drain the engine oil and remove the oil pan. Then, starting at the front of the engine, remove one main-bearing cap at a time to check the bearing and journal. Make sure the caps are numbered and that you know which side of the caps faces the front. Main-bearing caps must be replaced on the same journals and in the same position from which they were removed.

Some main-bearing-cap nuts or bolts are locked in place with lock washers or locking tangs. The locking tangs must be bent back before the nuts or bolts can be removed. If a bearing cap sticks, loosen it carefully to avoid damage. Light taps from a plastic hammer will usually loosen the cap.

CAREFUL Heavy hammering or prying can bend or break a cap. A bent or different cap can cause a bad bearing fit. It could require line boring of the block to fit a new main-bearing cap to the engine.

1. EXAMINING MAIN BEARINGS

Examine the main bearings in the bearing caps for wear or unusual damage (Fig. 30-7). Both main bearings and connecting-rod bearings can have the same sort of troubles.

CAREFUL If one main bearing has to be replaced, then all the main bearings should be replaced. Replacing only one main bearing could throw the crankshaft out of alignment so that the crankshaft would break or the bearings would fail.

If you find that some bearings are more worn than others, check the crankshaft for misalignment.

2. CHECKING CRANKSHAFT JOURNALS

There are two ways to measure the main journals with the crankshaft still in the engine. One way is to use a special crankshaft gauge (Fig. 31-2). The other way to measure the main journals with the crankshaft in the engine is with a special micrometer. Before using the micrometer, remove the upper bearing shell from the cylinder block.

If the journals are worn, tapered, or rough, the crankshaft must be removed for service.

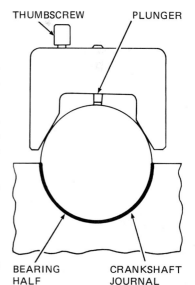

Fig. 31-2 Using a crankshaft gauge to check a main-bearing journal with the crankshaft in the engine. *(Federal-Mogul Corporation)*

453

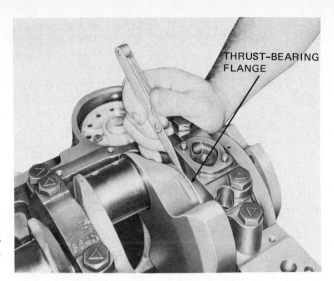

THRUST-BEARING FLANGE

Fig. 31-3 Measuring crankshaft end play at the thrust bearing with a thickness gauge. *(Chevrolet Motor Division of General Motors Corporation)*

□ 31-3 CHECKING MAIN-BEARING CLEARANCE

Main-bearing clearance can be checked with either Plastigage or shim stock. The procedure is the same as that for checking connecting-rod bearings. This is covered in □ 30-7 and in the *Auto Shop Workbook*.

□ 31-4 CHECKING CRANKSHAFT END PLAY

Crankshaft end play becomes excessive if the crankshaft thrust bearing is worn. The thrust bearing (□ 9-14) prevents excessive end play, or back and forth movement, of the crankshaft. End play can cause a knock that occurs every time the clutch is operated (on manual-transmission cars). End play is measured by forcing the crankshaft in one direction as far as it will go. Then the clearance at the thrust bearing is measured with a thickness gauge (Fig. 31-3).

□ 31-5 REPLACING MAIN BEARINGS

If there is too much clearance between the main bearings and the journals, and the journals are in good condition, the bearings should be replaced. Other conditions besides worn bearings also require replacement of bearings (Fig. 30-7). You will have no problem removing and replacing the bearing half in the cap. But you will have to use the crankshaft to help you remove and replace the upper bearing half.

To remove the upper bearing half, first remove the bearing cap. Loosen the other bearing-cap bolts about half a turn so that the crankshaft can rotate easily. Then use the special bearing-removal tool, called a *roll-out tool*. Insert the round section of the tool into the oilhole in the journal (Fig. 31-4). Then turn the crankshaft to apply force against the end of the bearing. The force will slide the bearing up and out. Turn the crankshaft so that the roll-out tool presses against the plain end of the bearing. Do not press against the end that has the bearing tang.

To install a new bearing upper half, coat the inside of the bearing with engine oil. Leave the outside of the bearing dry. Make sure the crankshaft journal and the bearing bore in the cylinder block are clean.

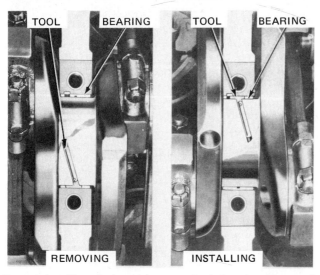

REMOVING   INSTALLING

Fig. 31-4 Removal and installation of the upper main bearing. The crankshaft journal is shown partly cut away so that the tool can be seen inserted into the oilhole in the journal. *(Chrysler Corporation)*

Use the roll-out tool to slide the insert into place (Fig. 31-4). Then install the bearing cap. Tap the cap with a plastic hammer to make sure the cap is seated. Then tighten the cap bolts. Check the bearing clearance with Plastigage (□ 30-7).

> **NOTE** Some technicians do not install bearings without removing the crankshaft. They say that you may not get the bearing upper half seated properly in the bore. The best way to install bearings is to remove the crankshaft so that you can be sure the bores into which the upper bearings fit are clean. Installing main bearings with the crankshaft in the engine sometimes is difficult. It may not be done successfully on all engines.

□ 31-6 REPLACING THRUST BEARING

Some crankshaft main journals do not have oilholes. For example, the rear main journals of many in-line engines do not have oilholes. The rear main oil seal and, in some engines, the thrust bearing are located there. To remove the upper half of this kind of bearing, first start to move the bearing out with a small punch and hammer. Then use pliers with taped jaws to hold the bearing half against the oil slinger (Fig. 31-5). Turn the crankshaft so that the bearing will rise up out of the bore. Install the new bearing in the same way. Lightly tap the bearing down the final distance with a punch and hammer.

□ 31-7 REPLACING MAIN-BEARING OIL SEAL

The main-bearing oil seal prevents engine oil from leaking out the rear of the engine, past the rear main bearing. The method of replacing the oil seal varies with different engines. On some engines the crankshaft must be removed to install a new seal. On others, the old seal can be pulled out with pliers or a special removing tool. Then the new seal can be pushed or pulled into place. Refer to the manufacturer's shop manual for the proper procedure.

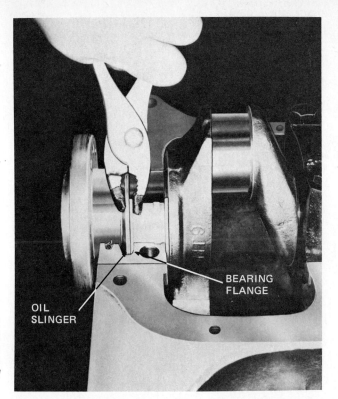

Fig. 31-5 Replacing a rear main-bearing half with pliers. On this engine, the crankshaft has no oilhole in the rear journal. *(Chevrolet Motor Division of General Motors Corporation)*

OIL
SLINGER

BEARING
FLANGE

☐ 31-8 REMOVING CRANKSHAFT

If the main journals or the crankpin journals are rough or worn, or if misalignment is suspected, the crankshaft must be removed from the engine. This operation requires removal of the oil pan and the oil pump. In addition, the connecting rods must be detached. Then the crankshaft gear, or the sprocket and chain or belt, must be removed from the front of the engine.

> **NOTE** For a complete engine overhaul, the cylinder head and piston-and-rod assemblies must be removed. However, if only the crankshaft is coming out, the piston-and-rod assemblies need not be removed. Instead, they can be detached from the crankpins and pushed up out of the way. Don't push them up too far or the top ring might be pushed up above the top of the cylinder. Then the ring will catch on the edge of the cylinder. You will have to remove the cylinder head to compress the ring and push it back down into the cylinder.

☐ 31-9 CHECKING CRANKSHAFT JOURNALS

After the crankshaft is removed, it should be checked for alignment and for journal wear or damage. Check the alignment by placing the crankshaft in V blocks. As the crankshaft is rotated, a dial indicator will show any out-of-roundness or misalignment of the main journals (Fig. 31-6). If the crankshaft is out of line, a new or reground crankshaft is usually installed. It is difficult to straighten a bent crankshaft.

Next examine the main journals and crankpin journals for wear, scratches, or other damage. Use a micrometer to measure the journals for wear, taper, and out-of-round. Worn journals can be ground in a special

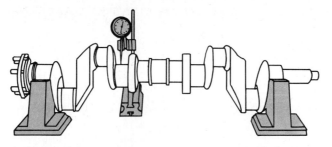

crankshaft lathe to return them to a usable condition. (This job is done in an automotive machine shop that specializes in crankshaft regrinding.) Then undersize bearings are used when the engine is reassembled.

Measurements should be taken at several places along the journal to check for taper. Then the crankshaft should be rotated by one-quarter or one-eighth turn to check for out-of-round. If the journals are ridged, or if they are tapered or out-of-round by more than 0.001 inch [0.025 mm], they should be reground. Any out-of-round or taper shortens the life of the bearings.

☐ 31-10 CLEANING CRANKSHAFT

Anytime the crankshaft is removed from the engine, the crankshaft should be cleaned in solvent. Use a valve-guide cleaning brush to clean out the oil passages. Then blow out all the passages with compressed air. Any trace of abrasive left in the oil passages will work out and get on the bearings. The abrasive could cause rapid bearing wear and engine damage. Coat all journals with oil after you have cleaned the crankshaft.

☐ 31-11 CYLINDER WEAR

Engine cylinders do not wear uniformly. They wear more at the top of the ring travel than at the bottom (Fig. 31-7). When the piston is at TDC at the start of the power stroke, pressures are the greatest. The compression rings apply the greatest pressure against the cylinder walls. Then, as the piston moves down on the power stroke, the pressure decreases. Therefore the cylinder walls wear more at the top of the ring travel than at the bottom.

Cylinders also tend to wear oval-shaped. This kind of wear is due to the side thrust of the pistons against the cylinder walls on the power stroke. The pistons are pushing down on the connecting rods at an angle, which produces the side thrust.

The washing action of gasoline droplets entering the combustion chamber can also cause cylinder-wall wear. This wear is most likely to occur in an area opposite the intake valve. The ingoing air-fuel mixture, especially when cold, usually contains droplets of liquid gasoline. These droplets hit the cylinder walls and wash off the oil. The result is wear in the area in which the oil has been washed away.

All these kinds of wear must be considered when checking the cylinders to decide how to service them.

☐ 31-12 CLEANING AND INSPECTING CYLINDER BLOCK

Before deciding whether to rebuild or discard the cylinder block, you should clean and inspect it. There are several cleaning methods. One method is steam cleaning with a spray of steam and soap.

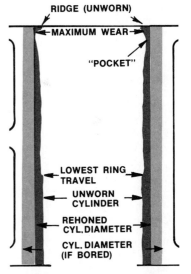

Fig. 31-7 Taper of an engine cylinder. Maximum wear is at the top, just under the ring ridge. Honing the cylinder usually requires removal of less metal than boring, as indicated. Metal to be removed by honing is shown solid. Metal to be removed by boring is shown both solid and shaded. *(Sunnen Products Company)*

Fig. 31-8   Checking the cylinder block for warpage with a precision straightedge.

Fig. 31-9   Honing a cylinder. (Sunnen Products Company)

Another cleaning method is to boil the block in a hot, caustic soda solution or similar chemical. Make sure all gasket material is removed from the gasket surfaces. Remove the pipe and expansion plugs so that the oil passages and the water jackets can be boiled out. After removing the block from the boil tank, rinse the block with water. Use compressed air to blow out the oil and water passages. You can also use long rods to clean out any loose deposits in the passages.

Blow out all threaded holes with compressed air. If the threads are not in good condition, use a tap to clean them. Or if they are badly damaged, you may have to use a thread insert to repair them (□ 4-18).

Check the block for cracks and for scratches in the cylinders and in the main-bearing and cam-bearing bores. Check the head end of the block for warpage by using a long precision straightedge (Fig. 31-8).

□ 31-13 SERVICING CYLINDERS

New piston rings can be installed in a cylinder with some taper and wear. But the more taper there is, the more blowby, the more oil burning, and the more exhaust emissions there will be. A cylinder with a large amount of taper should be reconditioned by *honing* or *boring* (□ 31-14). Honing may remove most of the taper (Fig. 31-7). However, boring may be required to remove it all.

Cylinder wear, taper, and out-of-round can be measured with:

■ An inside micrometer (□ 3-12)
■ A telescope gauge and an outside micrometer (□ 3-9)
■ A cylinder-bore gauge (Fig. 3-23)

□ 31-14 HONING OR BORING CYLINDERS

There are two methods of taking metal off the cylinder wall. These are honing and boring. The hone has a series of abrasive stones that are revolved in the cylinder to grind off metal (Fig. 31-9). Boring requires a boring bar, which rotates a cutting tool in the cylinder to shave off metal.

Usually, the hone is used to take off small amounts of metal. If cylinder wear is too great to be cleaned up by honing, the cylinder must be bored. Regardless of which method is used, the cylinder is finished to the proper oversize to fit the oversize piston and rings selected for it.

The cylinders must be reconditioned if they have scores or wear spots, or excessive wear, taper, or out-of-roundness. The amount of damage determines whether the cylinder should be honed or bored. It also determines if satisfactory performance can be achieved by installing new piston rings. One engine manufacturer states the cylinders may be honed if they are not more than 0.005 inch [0.13 mm] tapered or not more than 0.003 inch [0.076 mm] out-of-round. If worn more than this, then the cylinders should be bored.

☐ 31-15 CLEANING CYLINDERS

After honing or boring, the cylinder must be cleaned thoroughly. Even slight traces of grit left on the cylinder walls can cause rapid ring and piston wear. One way to clean the cylinder is to wipe the cylinder walls with fine crocus cloth. This loosens embedded grit and knocks off any metal fuzz left by the hone or the boring bar. Next, wash the cylinder walls with soapy water and a stiff brush or mop. Then wipe them with a cloth dampened with engine oil. The job is finished when the cloth comes away from the cylinder walls with no trace of dirt on it.

Clean out the oil and water passages to make sure all dirt and grit are removed.

> **NOTE** Do not try to clean the cylinder walls with gasoline or kerosene. Neither of these will remove all the grit from the cylinder walls.

☐ 31-16 INSTALLING CYLINDER SLEEVES

There are two types of cylinder sleeves: wet and dry (☐ 9-3). The wet sleeve is sealed to the block at the top and bottom. It is in direct contact with the coolant. The dry sleeve is pressed into the cylinder. This type is in contact with the cylinder wall from top to bottom.

Cracked blocks, scored cylinders, cylinders worn so badly that they must be rebored to an excessively large oversize—all these can often be repaired by the installation of a cylinder sleeve (Fig. 31-10). As a first step, the cylinders are bored oversize to take the sleeves. Then the sleeves are pressed into place. The sleeves are then finished to the proper size to take a standard piston and ring set.

☐ 31-17 REPLACING EXPANSION-CORE PLUGS

You may have to remove an expansion plug from the block (because of coolant leakage, for example). To do this, you can use a "freeze-plug puller." If this tool is not available, put the pointed end of a pry bar against the center of the plug. Tap the end of the bar with a hammer until the point goes through the plug. Then press the pry bar to one side to pop the plug out. Another method is to drill a small hole in the center of the plug and then pry the plug out.

One of two types of tool should be used to install an expansion-core plug (Fig. 31-11). One type is used for the cup-type plug. Another type is used for the expansion-type plug.

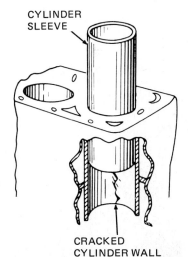

CYLINDER SLEEVE

CRACKED CYLINDER WALL

Fig. 31-10 Cracked blocks and badly scored or worn cylinder bores can sometimes be repaired by installing cylinder sleeves. *(Sealed Power Corporation)*

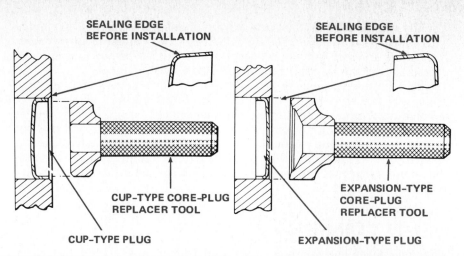

SEALING EDGE BEFORE INSTALLATION

SEALING EDGE BEFORE INSTALLATION

CUP–TYPE CORE–PLUG REPLACER TOOL

EXPANSION–TYPE CORE–PLUG REPLACER TOOL

CUP–TYPE PLUG

EXPANSION–TYPE PLUG

Fig. 31-11 Expansion-core plugs and installation tools. *(Ford Motor Company)*

CHAPTER 31
REVIEW QUESTIONS

Select the *one* correct, best, or most probable answer to each question. Then check your answers against the correct answers given at the end of the book.

1. Mechanic X says that main-bearing clearance can be checked with Plastigage. Mechanic Y says that main-bearing clearance can be checked with a thickness gauge. Who is right?
   a. X only
   b. Y only
   c. both X and Y
   d. neither X nor Y

2. Most cylinder wear occurs
   a. at the bottom of piston-ring travel
   b. at the midpoint of piston-ring travel
   c. at the top of piston-ring travel
   d. evenly up and down the cylinder

3. If a crankshaft main-bearing journal is tapered,
   a. a new tapered bearing must be installed
   b. an oversize bearing must be installed
   c. the crankshaft should be reground or replaced
   d. an undersize bearing must be installed

4. Before installing new main bearings, the mechanic should always
   a. check the crankshaft journals
   b. check the connecting-rod journals
   c. grind the crankshaft journals
   d. install a new crankshaft

5. If some main bearings are worn more than others,
   a. check the cylinder block alignment
   b. check the crankshaft for misalignment
   c. replace only the excessively worn bearings
   d. check that the connecting rods are properly torqued

PART 6

AUTOMOTIVE TRANSMISSIONS AND POWER TRAINS

This part of the book covers clutches, manual transmissions, transaxles, transfer cases, automatic transmissions, drive lines, and drive axles and differentials. These are the mechanisms that carry engine power to the driving wheels. For many years, most cars had the engine at the front and the driving wheels at the rear. However, many cars are now made with the engine at the front and with front-wheel drive. On many of these cars, the engines are installed transversely. The transmission-and-differential assembly, called a *transaxle,* is mounted on the engine. Also, some vehicles have four-wheel drive. This arrangement requires a *transfer case.* It transfers engine power to both the front and the rear axles. Clutches are used with *manual transmissions*. These transmissions are shifted by hand. Automatic transmissions required no separate clutch. There are six chapters in Part 6:

CHAPTER 32
CLUTCHES

After studying this chapter, you should be able to:
1. Explain the purpose of the clutch.
2. Describe the differences in construction and operation of coil-spring and diaphragm-spring clutches.
3. List three types of clutch linkage.
4. Describe the operation of hydraulic clutch linkage.
5. Explain the purpose of the clutch safety switch.
6. Describe the construction and operation of the self-adjusting clutch.
7. Discuss clutch troubles and their possible causes.

The *clutch* is the device that the driver operates to disconnect the engine from the transmission. When the clutch pedal is depressed, engine power is disconnected from the transmission. Then the engine no longer affects the rest of the power train, and the power train no longer affects the engine. This condition is needed for starting and stopping the car, and for changing gear ratios in the manual transmission. At one time, almost all cars had clutches. Now most cars are made with automatic transmissions. They do not need this type of clutch in the power train.

☐ 32-1 THE POWER TRAIN

The power train carries power from the engine crankshaft to the car wheels so the wheels rotate and the car moves. For many years, on most cars the engine had been mounted in the front and the rear wheels were driven (Fig. 32-1). This arrangement includes:

1. The engine, which produces the power
2. The clutch on vehicles with manual transmissions
3. The transmission, either manual or automatic
4. The drive shaft, which carries the power from the transmission to the differential
5. The differential, which sends the power to the two rear wheels through the wheel axles.

In recent years, cars have been downsized to make them more fuel efficient and to reduce air pollution from engines. The engines used in

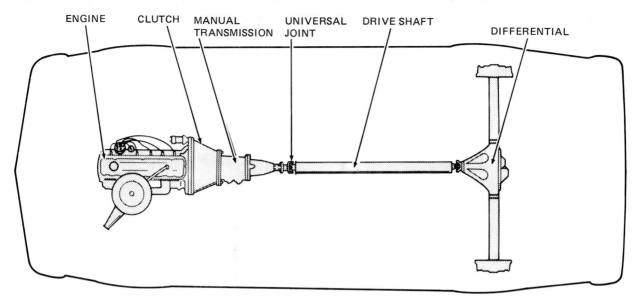

Fig. 32-1 Arrangement of the power train in a car with front-engine and rear-wheel drive.

these smaller cars are often mounted transversely and drive the front wheels (Fig. 32-2). The transmission and differential are combined into an assembly called the *transaxle*. Drive shafts from the transaxle drive the front wheels. In both arrangements, the clutch is attached to the engine flywheel (Fig. 32-3).

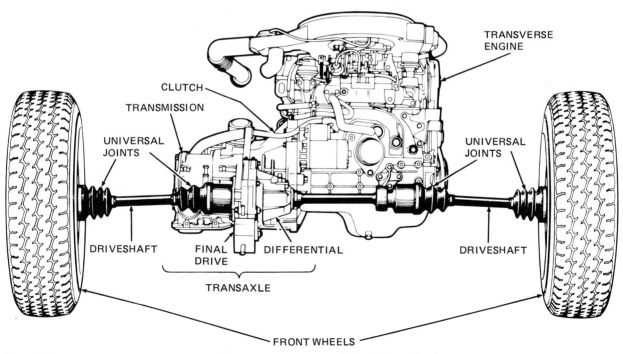

Fig. 32-2 Arrangement of the power train for a car with front-engine and front-wheel drive. *(Mazda Motors of America, Inc.)*

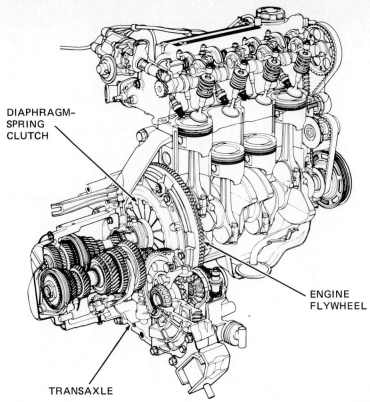

DIAPHRAGM–
SPRING
CLUTCH

ENGINE
FLYWHEEL

TRANSAXLE

Fig. 32-3 Location of the clutch between the engine and the transaxle. *(Mazda Motors of America, Inc.)*

CLUTCH CONSTRUCTION AND OPERATION

☐ 32-2 PURPOSES OF THE CLUTCH

The clutch is used on cars with transmissions that are shifted by hand, or *manually*. Its purpose is to allow the driver to couple the engine to or uncouple the engine from the transmission. The driver operates the clutch by foot. When the clutch is engaged (in the normal running position), the power from the engine can flow through the clutch and enter the transmission. When the clutch is disengaged, the engine is uncoupled from the transmission. Now, no power can flow through. It is necessary to interrupt the flow of power (to uncouple the engine) to shift gears.

☐ 32-3 LOCATION OF THE CLUTCH

The clutch is located just behind the engine, between the engine and the transmission. Figure 32-4 shows the parts of one type of clutch, detached from the engine. When the parts are assembled, the flywheel is bolted to the crankshaft. The friction disk (or *driven plate*) is installed next. It slides onto the end of the transmission shaft, which sticks through the clutch housing. The pressure-plate-and-cover assembly (usually called the *pressure plate*) is bolted to the flywheel. Then the other parts are installed.

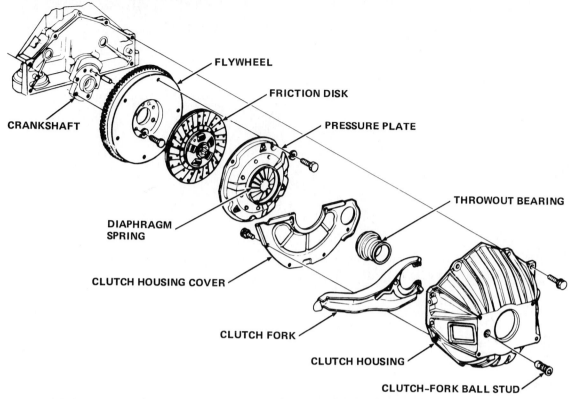

FLYWHEEL

FRICTION DISK

PRESSURE PLATE

CRANKSHAFT

THROWOUT BEARING

DIAPHRAGM SPRING

CLUTCH HOUSING COVER

CLUTCH FORK

CLUTCH HOUSING

CLUTCH-FORK BALL STUD

Fig. 32-4 Disassembled clutch and related parts. *(Chevrolet Motor Division of General Motors Corporation)*

☐ *32-4 TYPES OF CLUTCHES*

Automotive clutches may be classified in several ways. One classification is by the manufacturer's basic design, for example, Borg and Beck, Long, or Belleville-spring (diaphragm) clutch. The major difference is in how spring force is applied against the pressure plate. Both coil springs and diaphragm springs are used in automotive clutches. They both use spring force against the pressure plate to clamp the friction disk to the flywheel.

Clutches used in automobiles are known as *dry clutches*. They spin in air. Some clutches operate in oil. These are called *wet clutches*. Wet clutches are used in motorcycles and in some heavy trucks and industrial equipment. Also, some clutches have more than one friction disk. These are described in a later section.

☐ *32-5 CONSTRUCTION OF THE CLUTCH*

Figure 32-3 shows a diaphragm-spring clutch. Another type is the coil-spring clutch (Figs. 32-5 and 32-6). It has a series of coil springs set in a circle. The friction disk is about 11 inches [275 mm] in diameter. It is mounted on the transmission input shaft. The disk has splines in its hub that match splines on the input shaft. These splines consist of two sets of teeth. The internal teeth in the hub of the friction disk match the external teeth on the shaft. When the friction disk is driven, it turns the transmission input shaft.

The clutch also has a pressure plate, which includes a series of coil springs. The pressure plate is bolted to the engine flywheel (Fig. 32-3). The springs provide the force to hold the friction disk against the fly-

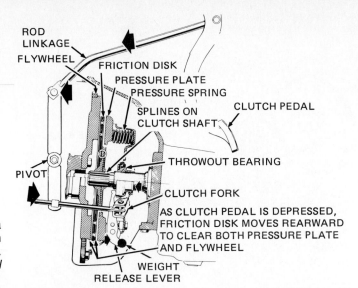

ROD LINKAGE
FLYWHEEL
FRICTION DISK
PRESSURE PLATE
PRESSURE SPRING
SPLINES ON CLUTCH SHAFT
CLUTCH PEDAL
THROWOUT BEARING
PIVOT
CLUTCH FORK
AS CLUTCH PEDAL IS DEPRESSED, FRICTION DISK MOVES REARWARD TO CLEAR BOTH PRESSURE PLATE AND FLYWHEEL
WEIGHT
RELEASE LEVER

Fig. 32-5 Sectional view of a clutch, showing the linkage from the foot pedal to the clutch fork. *(Buick Motor Division of General Motors Corporation)*

wheel. Then, when the flywheel turns, the pressure plate and the friction disk also turn. However, when the clutch is disengaged, the spring force is relieved. The friction disk and the flywheel can rotate separately.

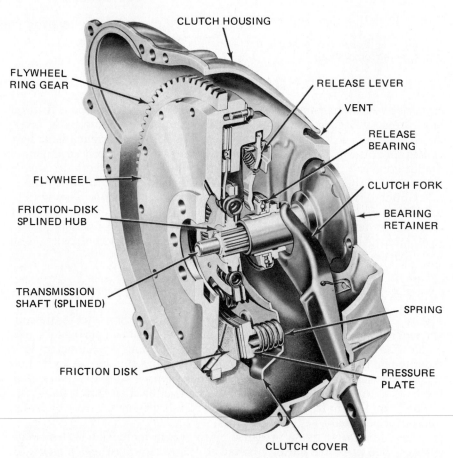

CLUTCH HOUSING
FLYWHEEL RING GEAR
RELEASE LEVER
VENT
RELEASE BEARING
FLYWHEEL
CLUTCH FORK
FRICTION-DISK SPLINED HUB
BEARING RETAINER
TRANSMISSION SHAFT (SPLINED)
SPRING
FRICTION DISK
PRESSURE PLATE
CLUTCH COVER

Fig. 32-6 Coil-spring clutch assembly, partially cut away. *(Ford Motor Company)*

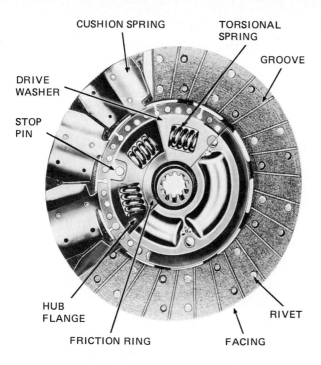

CUSHION SPRING TORSIONAL SPRING GROOVE DRIVE WASHER STOP PIN HUB FLANGE FRICTION RING FACING RIVET

Fig. 32-7 Typical friction disk, or driven plate. Facings and drive washer are partly cut away to show springs. *(Buick Motor Division of General Motors Corporation)*

□ 32-6 FRICTION DISK

The friction disk, or driven plate, is shown partly cut away in Fig. 32-7. It consists of a hub and a plate, with facings attached to the plate. The friction disk has cushion springs and dampening springs. The cushion springs are waved, or curled, slightly. The cushion springs are attached to the plate, and the friction facings are attached to the springs. When the clutch is engaged, the springs compress slightly to take up the shock of engagement. The dampening springs are spiral springs set in a circle around the hub. The hub is driven through these springs. They help to smooth out the power pulses from the engine and absorb the shocks of sudden engagement.

□ 32-7 OPERATION OF THE COIL-SPRING CLUTCH

Figure 32-8 shows, at the left, a sectional view of the coil-spring clutch. The major parts are shown disassembled at the right. In this clutch, nine springs are used, although only three are shown. The springs are held between the clutch cover and the pressure plate. With the clutch engaged, the springs clamp the friction disk tightly between the flywheel and the pressure plate (Fig. 32-9). This forces the friction disk to rotate with the flywheel.

When the driver depresses the clutch pedal to disengage the clutch, the linkage from the pedal forces the release bearing inward (to the left in Fig. 32-8). The release bearing is also called the *throwout bearing*.

As the release bearing moves left, it pushes against the inner ends of three release levers. The release levers are pivoted on eyebolts, as shown in Figs. 32-8 and 32-10. When the inner ends of the release levers are pushed in by the release bearing, the outer ends are moved to the right. This motion is carried by struts to the pressure plate (Fig. 32-11). The pressure plate moves to the right (in Fig. 32-10), and the springs are compressed. With the spring force off the friction disk, space appears on

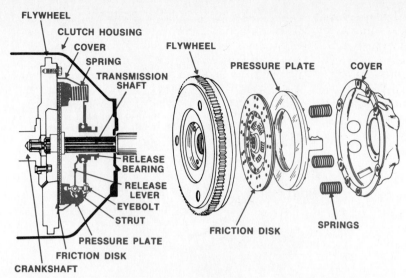

Fig. 32-8 Coil-spring clutch in the engaged position. Major parts are shown to the right.

both sides of the disk. Now the clutch is disengaged. The flywheel can rotate without sending power through the friction disk.

Releasing the clutch pedal takes the force off the release bearing. The springs push the pressure plate to the left (in Fig. 32-8). The friction disk is again clamped tightly between the flywheel and the pressure plate. The friction disk must again rotate with the flywheel. In this position, the clutch is engaged.

☐ 32-8 DIAPHRAGM-SPRING CLUTCH

A diaphragm-spring clutch (Figs. 32-3 and 32-4) is widely used on cars with small- to medium-size engines. It has a diaphragm spring that supplies the force to hold the friction disk against the flywheel. The diaphragm spring also acts as the release lever to take up the spring force when the clutch is disengaged.

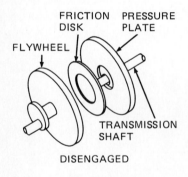

DISENGAGED

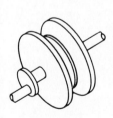

ENGAGED

Fig. 32-9 Basic clutch elements, showing clutch action. Top, clutch disengaged. The pressure plate and friction disk have moved away from the flywheel. Bottom, clutch engaged. The pressure plate clamps the friction disk to the flywheel so that all parts must rotate together.

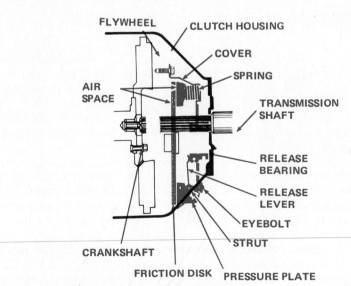

Fig. 32-10 Coil-spring clutch in the disengaged position.

The diaphragm spring is actually a Belleville spring that has a solid ring on the outer diameter. It has a series of tapering fingers pointing inward toward the center of the clutch (Fig. 32-4). The action of the clutch diaphragm is like the action that takes place when the bottom of an oil can is depressed. It "dishes" inward. When the throwout bearing moves in against the ends of the fingers, the entire diaphragm is forced against a pivot ring, causing the diaphragm to dish inward. This moves the pressure plate away from the friction disk. Figure 32-12 illustrates the two positions of the diaphragm-spring and clutch parts.

☐ 32-9 DOUBLE-DISK CLUTCHES

Sometimes a clutch with greater holding power is required. More power must go through the clutch, but size is limited so that a clutch with a larger diameter cannot be used. Then a clutch with two friction disks is installed by the manufacturer. Use of a second friction disk greatly increases the holding power of the clutch. Double-disk clutches are widely used in medium and heavy trucks.

Figure 32-13 shows a double-disk clutch. The two friction disks require the use of two pressure plates. The front pressure plate separates the two disks.

TYPES OF CLUTCH LINKAGE

☐ 32-10 CLUTCH LINKAGE

The clutch is controlled by the driver through the foot-operated clutch pedal and suitable linkage. The linkage carries the movement of the clutch pedal to the throwout bearing. There are three types of clutch linkages used in cars. These are rod, cable, and hydraulic. They all convert a light force applied to the clutch pedal into a greatly increased force that moves the pressure plate.

A rod-type clutch linkage is shown in Fig. 32-5. When the clutch pedal is depressed, the attached linkage forces the clutch fork to pivot. This pushes the throwout bearing (which is attached to the fork) to the left (Fig. 32-5). The clutch fork passes through a dust seal (Fig. 32-6). This prevents dirt, dust, and water from entering the clutch through the fork opening in the clutch housing.

A cable-operated linkage is shown in Fig. 32-14. On many cars, it is simpler for the manufacturer to install a cable system than to develop a workable rod-type linkage.

☐ 32-11 HYDRAULIC CLUTCH LINKAGE

A hydraulically operated clutch linkage (Fig. 32-15) is used where it would be difficult to run rods or cable from the foot pedal to the clutch fork. Hydraulic linkage is also used on high-output engines which require heavy pressure-plate springs. To reduce the force required to operate the clutch pedal, a hydraulic system is used.

Figure 32-15 shows a hydraulically operated clutch. The clutch pedal does not work the release lever directly through rods or cable. Instead, when the driver pushes down on the clutch pedal, a pushrod is forced into the *master cylinder*. This forces hydraulic fluid out of the master cylinder,

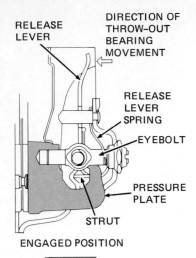

RELEASE LEVER

DIRECTION OF THROW-OUT BEARING MOVEMENT

RELEASE LEVER SPRING

EYEBOLT

PRESSURE PLATE

STRUT

ENGAGED POSITION

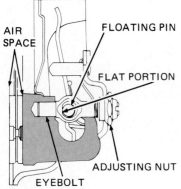

AIR SPACE

FLOATING PIN

FLAT PORTION

ADJUSTING NUT

EYEBOLT

RELEASED POSITION

Fig. 32-11 The two limiting positions of the pressure plate and release lever. *(Oldsmobile Division of General Motors Corporation)*

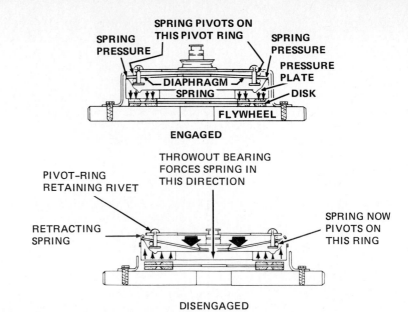

SPRING PIVOTS ON THIS PIVOT RING

SPRING PRESSURE

SPRING PRESSURE

PRESSURE PLATE

DIAPHRAGM SPRING

DISK

FLYWHEEL

ENGAGED

PIVOT-RING RETAINING RIVET

THROWOUT BEARING FORCES SPRING IN THIS DIRECTION

RETRACTING SPRING

SPRING NOW PIVOTS ON THIS RING

DISENGAGED

Fig. 32-12 Engaged and disengaged positions of the diaphragm-spring clutch. *(Chevrolet Motor Division of General Motors Corporation)*

through a tube, and into a servo, or "slave," cylinder. [This is similar to the action in a hydraulic brake system (Chap. 38) when the brakes are applied.]

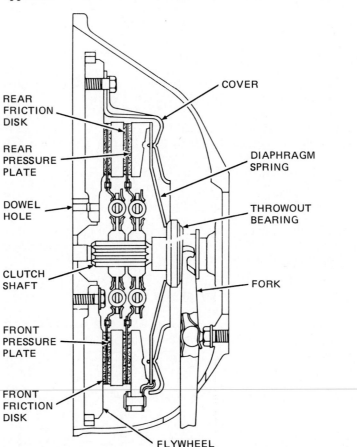

COVER

REAR FRICTION DISK

REAR PRESSURE PLATE

DIAPHRAGM SPRING

DOWEL HOLE

THROWOUT BEARING

CLUTCH SHAFT

FORK

FRONT PRESSURE PLATE

FRONT FRICTION DISK

FLYWHEEL

Fig. 32-13 A diaphragm-spring clutch using two pressure plates separated by an intermediate pressure plate. *(Chevrolet Motor Division of General Motors Corporation)*

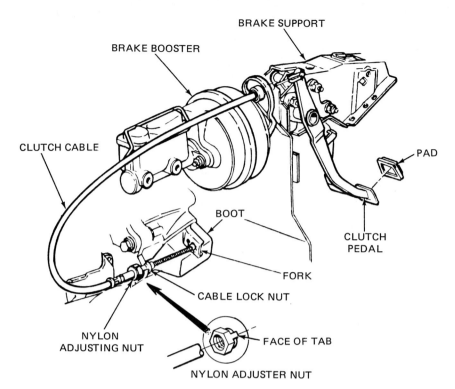

Fig. 32-14 A clutch fork operated by a cable from the foot pedal. The cable route should follow a smooth arc and maintain adequate clearance from all other parts. *(Ford Motor Company)*

As fluid is forced into the servo cylinder, the pressure forces a piston and pushrod out of the cylinder. The pushrod rests against the clutch fork, which pivots as the pushrod moves. As a result, the clutch fork forces the throwout bearing against the release levers on the pressure plate. This disengages the clutch.

□ 32-12 CLUTCH SAFETY SWITCH

Late-model cars using clutches have a clutch safety switch (Fig. 32-16) that prevents starting if the clutch is engaged. The clutch pedal must be

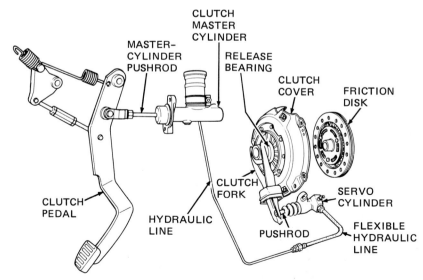

Fig. 32-15 A hydraulically operated clutch linkage. *(Nissan Motor Company, Ltd.)*

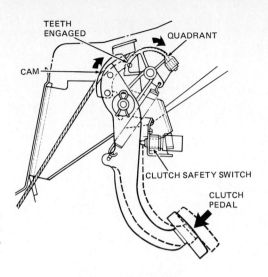

Fig. 32-16 Action of a self-adjusting clutch as the pedal is depressed. *(American Motors Corporation)*

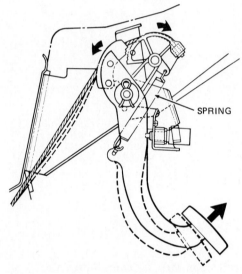

Fig. 32-17 Action in the self-adjusting clutch as the clutch pedal is released. *(American Motors Corporation)*

depressed at the same time that the ignition switch is turned to START. The movement of the clutch pedal closes the safety switch so that the circuit to the starting motor can be completed.

The purpose of the clutch safety switch is to prevent starting with the transmission in gear and the clutch engaged. If this happened, the car might move before the driver is ready. This could lead to an accident.

□ 32-13 SELF-ADJUSTING CLUTCH

In normal operation, clutch parts wear and require periodic adjustment. However, a self-adjusting clutch is used on many late-model cars. It eliminates the need for routine clutch adjustment. The two main parts in the self-adjusting clutch are a notched *cam* and a self-adjusting *quadrant gear* (Fig. 32-16). When the clutch pedal is depressed (Fig. 32-16), the notched cam on the pedal engages the teeth in the self-adjusting quadrant. This allows the pedal to pivot and the cable to tighten.

When the clutch pedal is released (Fig. 32-17), it returns to its stop. The quadrant, pulled by a spring, automatically tightens the cable by moving up one tooth. This compensates for clutch-disk wear.

☐ 32-14 CLUTCH TROUBLE DIAGNOSIS

When you work in the shop, you will see various kinds of clutch trouble and learn how to fix them. Usually, the kind of trouble you find tells you the cause. Clutch troubles include:

1. Clutch slips while engaged.
2. Clutch chatters or grabs when engaging.
3. Clutch spins or drags when disengaged.
4. Clutch is noisy when engaged.
5. Clutch is noisy when disengaged.
6. Clutch pedal pulsates.
7. Friction-disk facings wear rapidly.
8. Clutch pedal is stiff.

If the trouble is in the clutch itself, most manufacturers recommend replacing at least the pressure plate and friction disk. In past years, shop manuals carried instructions for disassembly and repair of the clutch. The different clutch troubles are described below.

☐ 32-15 CLUTCH SLIPS WHILE ENGAGED

Slippage while the clutch is engaged could be caused by an incorrect linkage adjustment. That could prevent full spring force on the pressure plate and the friction disk. The remedy is readjustment of the linkage. Slippage while the clutch is engaged could also be caused by worn friction-disk facings or weakening of the springs in the pressure plate.

☐ 32-16 CLUTCH CHATTERS OR GRABS WHEN ENGAGING

Chattering and grabbing of the clutch are usually due to oil on the facings of the friction disk. Loose facings on the friction disk, heat cracks in the face of the flywheel or pressure plate, broken clutch parts, or binding of the linkage could also cause chattering and grabbing of the clutch.

☐ 32-17 CLUTCH SPINS OR DRAGS WHEN DISENGAGED

If the clutch spins or drags when disengaged, the linkage may be out of adjustment. Or, the trouble could be due to internal clutch trouble, such as lining torn or loose from the friction disk, a warped friction disk or pressure plate, improper clutch adjustment, or binding of the friction-disk hub on the transmission input shaft.

☐ 32-18 CLUTCH NOISY WHEN ENGAGED

If the clutch is noisy when engaged, the friction disk has broken dampener springs, the disk hub is loose on the transmission input shaft, or there are broken parts in the pressure plate. Also, the transmission might be out of line with the engine.

☐ 32-19 CLUTCH NOISY WHEN DISENGAGED

If the clutch is noisy when disengaged, the cause probably is a worn or dry throwout bearing. It makes a grinding or squealing noise as it spins. The pilot bushing in the end of the crankshaft could be worn or in need of lubricant. Also, the release levers could be out of adjustment. In the diaphragm-spring clutch, worn retracting springs can produce noise.

☐ 32-20 CLUTCH PEDAL PULSATES

Clutch-pedal pulsations can be felt when light force is applied to the clutch pedal. There are several possible causes. The engine and transmission may be misaligned, the pressure plate or friction disk may be warped or misaligned, or the release levers may be out of adjustment.

☐ 32-21 FRICTION-DISK FACINGS WEAR RAPIDLY

Rapid wear of the friction-disk facings will result if the driver "rides" the clutch pedal, by resting a foot on the pedal. This partly releases the clutch, causing clutch slippage and rapid friction-disk wear. Incorrect linkage adjustment or misalignment of internal parts also produces excessive wear of the friction-disk facings.

☐ 32-22 CLUTCH PEDAL STIFF

A stiff clutch pedal, or a pedal that is hard to press down, probably is due to a misaligned or binding clutch linkage. A stiff clutch pedal can also be caused by a lack of lubricant in the clutch linkage.

☐ 32-23 CLUTCH SERVICE

Major clutch services include clutch-linkage adjustment, clutch replacement, and clutch overhaul. If a clutch defect develops, you must do more than just replace a worn part. You must determine what caused the part to wear and fix the trouble so that the new part will not wear rapidly.

One of the most common causes of rapid disk-lining wear and clutch failure is improper pedal free play. If pedal free travel is not sufficient, the clutch will not engage completely. It will slip and wear rapidly. In addition, the throwout bearing will be operating continuously and will soon wear out.

> **CAUTION** Asbestos is used in the facings of many friction disks because it can stand up under the high pressures and temperatures inside the clutch. However, authorities claim that breathing asbestos dust can cause lung cancer. For this reason, do not blow the dust out of the clutch housing with compressed air. This dust may contain powdered asbestos. The compressed air could send the dust up into the air around you and you could inhale it. Instead, use damp cloths to wipe out the clutch housing. After working on a clutch, always wash your hands thoroughly to remove any trace of asbestos dust.

☐ 32-24 CLUTCH ADJUSTMENT

Clutch adjustment should be checked regularly and adjusted as needed to make up for clutch-facing wear. To check, press on the pedal by hand until resistance is felt. Free travel of the pedal should be about one inch [25 mm]. If there is very little or no free travel, the clutch should be adjusted. The procedure is given in the manufacturer's service manual.

Select the *one* correct, best, or most probable answer to each question. Then check your answers against the correct answers given at the end of the book.

1. The friction disk is splined to a shaft which extends into the
   a. transmission
   b. drive shaft
   c. differential
   d. engine

2. The friction disk is positioned between the flywheel and the
   a. engine
   b. crankshaft
   c. pressure plate
   d. differential

3. When the clutch is engaged, spring force clamps the friction disk between the pressure plate and the
   a. flywheel
   b. differential
   c. reaction plate
   d. clutch pedal

4. When the clutch pedal is depressed, the throwout bearing moves in and causes the pressure plate to release its force on the
   a. throwin bearing
   b. pressure springs
   c. friction disk
   d. flywheel

5. The clutch cover is bolted to the
   a. friction disk
   b. flywheel
   c. car frame
   d. engine block

6. To make engagement as smooth as possible, the friction disk has a series of waved
   a. cushion pads
   b. cushion bolts
   c. cushion springs
   d. disks

7. The release levers in the typical clutch pivot on
   a. springs
   b. levers
   c. threaded bolts
   d. pins

CHAPTER 33
MANUAL TRANSMISSIONS AND TRANSAXLES

After studying this chapter, you should be able to:

1. Discuss the purpose of the manual transmission.

2. Explain the difference between three-speed, four-speed, and five-speed transmissions.

3. Describe how gear ratios are selected by the driver.

4. Explain the purpose of overdrive and how it is achieved.

5. Explain the purpose and operation of the manual transaxle.

Manual transmissions are transmissions that are shifted by hand. A car needs some sort of transmission. The engine should be turning fairly fast and producing considerable power to start the car moving. The engine must be turning fast while the car wheels are turning slowly. Later, when the car is out on the highway, the engine is turning fast and the wheels also are turning fast. The transmission makes these speed-and-torque changes possible. In a manual transmission, the driver selects the gear ratio by hand. Most cars with a front-mounted engine and front-wheel drive or a rear engine with rear-wheel drive use a transaxle. Like transmissions, transaxles may be either manually operated or automatic. This chapter describes the construction and operation of manual transmissions and transaxles. Chapter 34 covers automatic transmissions and transaxles.

☐ 33-1 GEARS

Various types of power-transmission devices are used to transfer power from the engine to the wheels. Most of these devices use *gears* (Fig. 33-1). All gears are basically similar. They are wheels with teeth that transmit power between shafts. The teeth may be on the edge, inside or outside, or at an angle. Usually, a gear is attached to a shaft. The gear teeth are *meshed* with the teeth of another gear fastened to a different shaft. "Meshed" means that the teeth of one gear are fitted into the teeth of the other gear. When one gear rotates, the other gear also rotates. If two gears are not the same size, the smaller gear is often called the *pinion gear*.

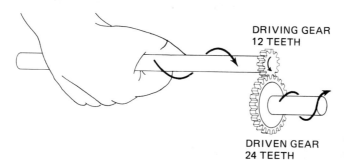

Fig. 33-1 Two meshing spur gears. Two revolutions of the small gear are required to turn the large gear once. This is a gear ratio of 2:1.

DRIVING GEAR
12 TEETH

DRIVEN GEAR
24 TEETH

The simplest gear is the spur gear. Two spur gears are shown meshed in Fig. 33-1. The sizes of the two gears determine the relative speed with which they turn. The big gear turns more slowly than the small gear. But the smaller gear has the greater turning force. This turning force is called *torque*. Torque is explained in ☐ 7-6. When speed is reduced through gears, torque is increased. When speed is increased through gears, torque is decreased.

For example, suppose the car is in first gear and the engine is turning 10 times to make the car wheels turn once. This gear reduction is achieved in both the transmission and in the *drive axle*. (Drive axles and differentials are described in Chap. 36). With a 10:1 gear reduction, there is a great increase in torque. The driven gear turns at one-tenth the speed of the driving gear. However, the driven gear now delivers 10 times more torque. This increase in torque gives the car the ability to accelerate rapidly.

Figure 33-1 shows two meshing spur gears, one with 12 teeth and the other with 24. The larger gear turns only half as fast as the smaller gear. While the large gear is making one complete revolution, the smaller gear is making two revolutions. If the larger gear is driving the smaller gear, there is a speed increase. There is also a torque reduction. The smaller gear turns faster, but it has less torque. If the smaller gear is driving the larger gear, there is a speed reduction but a torque increase.

NOTE Gears used in transmissions are not plain spur gears with straight teeth. Transmission gears have teeth that are twisted, as shown in Fig. 33-2. These are called *helical* gears. They run more quietly than spur gears and distribute the torque load over a larger area of each tooth.

MANUAL TRANSMISSIONS

☐ 33-2 THE MANUAL TRANSMISSION

A *manual transmission* is shown in Fig. 33-2. It is an assembly of gears and shafts that transmits power from the engine to the final drive, or drive axle. The manual transmission provides at least three forward-gear ratios (a "three-speed" transmission) and reverse. In addition, there is a *neutral* position. This permits disengaging the gears inside the transmission so that no power can flow through.

Today most manual transmissions in cars have four forward speeds. These positions, or "gears," are identified as first, second, third, and fourth. However, *first* sometimes is called "low," and *third* (in a three-speed transmission) or *fourth* (in a four-speed transmission) may be referred to as "high" by various manufacturers.

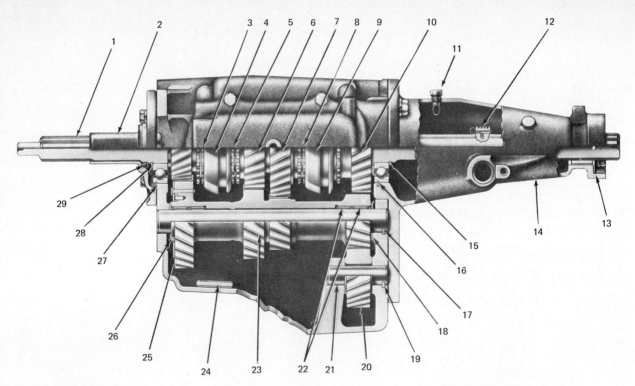

1. CLUTCH GEAR
2. CLUTCH GEAR BEARING RETAINER
3. 3RD SPEED SYNCHRONIZER RING
4. 2ND-3RD SPEED CLUTCH ASSY.
5. 2ND SPEED SYNCHRONIZER RING
6. 2ND SPEED GEAR
7. 1ST SPEED GEAR
8. 1ST SPEED SYNCHRONIZER RING
9. 1ST–REVERSE CLUTCH ASSY.
10. REVERSE GEAR
11. VENT
12. SPEEDOMETER GEAR AND CLIP
13. REAR EXTENSION SEAL
14. REAR EXTENSION
15. REAR BEARING-TO-SHAFT SNAP RING
16. REAR BEARING-TO-EXTENSION SNAP RING
17. COUNTERGEAR WOODRUFF KEY
18. THRUST WASHER
19. REVERSE IDLER SHAFT WOODRUFF KEY
20. REVERSE IDLER GEAR
21. REVERSE IDLER SHAFT
22. COUNTERGEAR BEARINGS
23. COUNTERGEAR
24. CASE MAGNET
25. ANTI-LASH PLATE ASSY.
26. THRUST WASHER
27. CLUTCH GEAR BEARING
28. SNAP RING
29. CLUTCH GEAR RETAINER LIP SEAL

Fig. 33-2 A three-speed transmission with parts named. *(Chevrolet Motor Division of General Motors Corporation)*

Different gear ratios are necessary because the internal combustion engine develops relatively little power at low engine speeds. The engine must be turning at a fairly high speed before it can deliver enough power to get the car moving. To help overcome this problem, the transmission has several forward-gear ratios. Through selection of the proper gear ratio, the engine torque, or twisting force, is increased. This permits putting the car into motion without stalling the engine or slipping the clutch excessively.

In an automatic transmission, the various ratios between the engine crankshaft and wheels are selected and changed automatically. The driver does not manually "shift" gears. The automatic controls inside the automatic transmission supply the proper ratio for the driving conditions. Chapter 34 describes the construction and operation of automatic transmissions.

□ 33-3 FUNCTION OF MANUAL TRANSMISSIONS

The simplest manual transmission used on cars has three forward-gear ratios between the engine and the car wheels. The crankshaft must revolve about 12, 8, or 4 times to turn the drive wheels once.

In first gear the crankshaft turns about 12 times for each car-wheel rotation. This ratio increases the engine torque enough to get the car moving. Then, in second gear, the crankshaft turns about 8 times to turn the car wheels once. After the car is moving, less torque is needed for acceleration. In second gear the engine turns fast enough to produce a car speed of up to about 30 mph [48 km/h].

In third, or high, gear the engine crankshaft turns about 4 times to turn the car wheels once. While the car is in motion and in third gear, normally it is not necessary to shift to lower gears. However, if additional torque is required, as when climbing a steep hill, the transmission can be shifted to a lower gear to get the higher torque.

□ 33-4 TYPES OF MANUAL TRANSMISSIONS

About 84 percent of all cars now made in the United States have automatic transmissions. Four-speed manual transmissions are installed in almost 15 percent. The remaining cars have either three-speed or five-speed manual transmissions. In some four-speed and all five-speed transmissions, the final forward-gear ratio is an *overdrive* ratio. These are described in later sections.

A *manual transaxle* is another kind of manual transmission. Most front-wheel-drive cars have a transaxle attached directly to the engine. The transaxle combines the transmission and the drive axle into a single assembly. However, the basic purpose, construction, and operation of the transmission section of a manual transaxle is the same as for the manual transmission. Manual transaxles are described further in later sections.

□ 33-5 SIMPLIFIED THREE-SPEED TRANSMISSION

A three-speed manual transmission is shown in Fig. 33-2. The simplified version of this transmission is shown in Fig. 33-3. It has three shafts and eight spur gears of varying sizes. The transmission housing and bearings are not shown. Four of the gears are rigidly connected to form the countershaft. These are the driven gear, second gear, first gear, and reverse gear. When the clutch is engaged and the engine is running, the clutch-shaft gear drives the countergear. The countergear rotates in a direction opposite, or counter, to the rotation of the clutch-shaft gear. With the

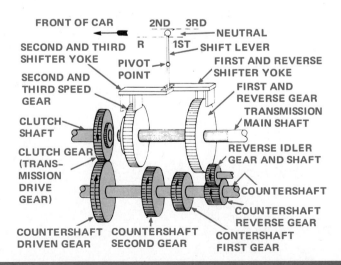

Fig. 33-3 Basic construction of a three-speed sliding-gear transmission. The gears are in neutral.

gears in neutral, as shown in Fig. 33-3, and the car stationary, the transmission main shaft is not turning.

The transmission main shaft is mechanically connected by shafts and gears in the drive axle to the car wheels. The two gears on the transmission main shaft may be shifted back and forth along the splines on the shaft. This is done by operating the gearshift lever in the driving compartment. The splines are matching internal and external teeth that permit endwise (axial) movement of the gears but cause the gears and shaft to rotate together. A floor-type shift lever is shown in Fig. 33-3. This type of lever illustrates more clearly the lever action in shifting gears. However, the transmission action is the same, regardless of whether a floor shift lever or a steering-column shift lever is used.

> **NOTE** The description below outlines the basic operation of all transmissions. However, more complex transmissions are used on modern cars. These include helical gears and synchromesh devices that synchronize the rotation of gears that are about to be meshed. This eliminates clashing of the gears and makes gear-shifting easier. Shifts are made with the clutch disengaged so that no power is flowing into the transmission.

☐ 33-6 SHIFTING INTO FIRST

When the gearshift lever is operated to place the gears in *first* (Fig. 33-4), the large gear on the transmission main shaft is moved along the shaft until it meshes with the first gear on the countergear. The clutch is disengaged for this operation so that the clutch shaft and the countergear stop rotating. When the clutch is again engaged, the transmission main shaft rotates, as the driving gear on the clutch shaft drives it through the countergear. The countergear is turning more slowly than the clutch shaft, and the small countergear is engaged with the large transmission main-shaft gear. A gear reduction of approximately 3 : 1 is achieved. The clutch shaft turns three times for each revolution of the transmission main shaft. There is further gear reduction in the drive axle. This produces a still higher gear ratio (approximately 12 : 1) between the engine crankshaft and the wheels.

> **NOTE** The actual gear ratio varies in different transmission. A typical gear ratio in first gear for a transmission used in some General Motors cars is 2.58 : 1. The clutch gear (and engine crankshaft) turns 2.58 times to turn the main shaft of the transmission once.

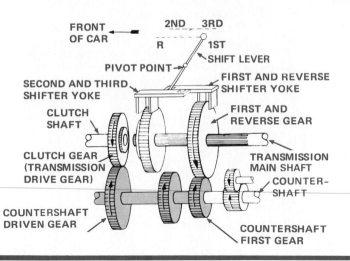

Fig. 33-4 Transmission with gears in first.

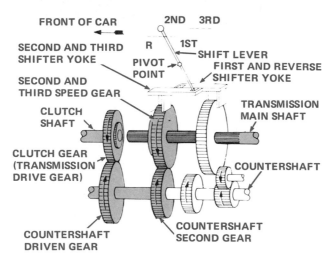

Fig. 33-5 Transmission with gears in second.

□ 33-7 SHIFTING INTO SECOND

Now suppose the clutch is operated and the gearshift lever is moved to *second* (Fig 33-5). The large gear on the transmission main shaft demeshes from the small first-speed countergear. The smaller transmission main-shaft gear is slid into mesh with the large second-speed countergear. This provides a somewhat reduced gear ratio. Now the engine crankshaft turns only about twice when the transmission main shaft turns once. The differential gear reduction increases this gear ratio to approximately 8 : 1.

□ 33-8 SHIFTING INTO THIRD

When the gears are shifted into *third* (Fig. 33-6), the two gears on the transmission main shaft are demeshed from the countergear. Also, the second-and-third-speed gear is forced axially against the clutch-shaft gear. External teeth on the clutch-shaft gear mesh with internal teeth in the second-and-third-speed gear. Then the transmission main shaft turns with the clutch shaft. A ratio of 1 : 1 is obtained. The differential reduction produces a gear ratio of about 4 : 1 between the engine crankshaft and the wheels.

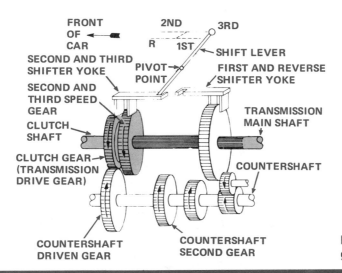

Fig. 33-6 Transmission with gears in third.

☐ 33-9 SHIFTING INTO REVERSE

When the gears are placed in *reverse* (Fig. 33-7), the larger of the transmission main-shaft gears is meshed with the reverse idler gear. This reverse idler gear is always in mesh with the small reverse gear on the end of the countergear. Putting the idler gear between the countergear reverse gear on the countergear and the transmission main-shaft gear causes the transmission shaft to rotate in the opposite direction. Now it rotates in the same direction as the countergear. This reverses the rotation of the wheels, so the car moves backward.

☐ 33-10 SYNCHROMESH TRANSMISSIONS

The type of transmission discussed above and illustrated in Figs. 33-3 to 33-7 is a *sliding-gear* transmission. Its operation is easy to illustrate and to understand. However, in cars this type of transmission is noisy and difficult to operate. Some transmissions use sliding gears for first and reverse. No recent automotive transmission shifts gears by actually moving the gears. In most transmissions, the gears are in constant mesh. Shifting is accomplished by locking the gears to each other or to shafts.

Modern automotive transmissions have helical gears with the teeth twisted at an angle to the main shaft (Fig. 33-2). Gears with helical teeth run more smoothly and make less noise than spur gears with straight-cut teeth. Automotive transmissions also include devices that cause the teeth of gears about to mesh to move at the same speed. This allows the teeth or locking devices to mesh without clashing. These devices are called *synchronizers* (Fig. 33-8). A transmission with synchonizers on the gears is called a *synchromesh transmission*. Some transmissions have synchronizers on only second gear and high gear. Other transmissions have synchronizers on all gears (Fig. 33-2).

Whenever the car is moving and in gear, the clutch gear is spinning and the main shaft is turning. When the clutch is disengaged, the clutch gear continues to spin until friction slows it to a stop. When shifting into second or third, the driver is meshing gears that may be moving at different speeds. Synchronizers are used in the manual transmission to avoid broken or damaged teeth and to make shifting easier (Fig. 33-8).

One type of synchronizer, shown in sectional view in Fig. 33-9, has a pair of synchronizing cones. One is an outside cone on the gear, and the other is an inside cone on the sliding sleeve. The sliding sleeve has splines that engage the splines on the gear to produce meshing. The illus-

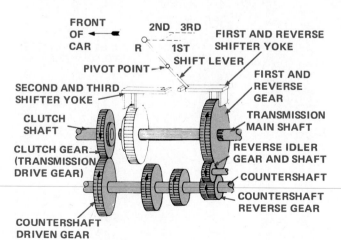

Fig. 33-7 Transmission with gears in reverse.

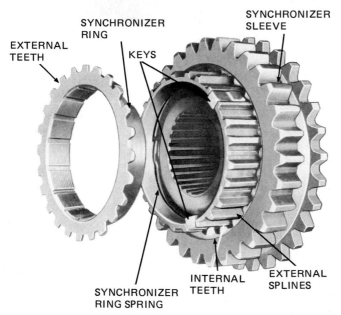

Fig. 33-8 A synchronizer assembly, used in synchromesh transmissions. *(Chevrolet Motor Division of General Motors Corporation)*

tration at the left (in Fig. 33-9), labeled "neutral position," shows the general construction of the synchronizing device. The illustration at the upper right shows the conditions as the drum, or sliding clutch sleeve, touches the gear. That is the instant that the two cones contact.

When contact is made, the gear and the drum are brought into synchronization. This means that they revolve at the same speed. Further movement of the shift lever moves the sliding sleeve into mesh with the gear. The splines on the sliding sleeve and the splines on the gear engage (lower right in Fig. 33-9). Lockup is completed. When the clutch is engaged, power can flow through the sliding sleeve and the gear.

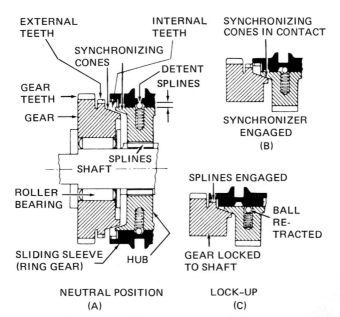

Fig. 33-9 Operation of a transmission synchronizer that uses cones.

□ 33-11 THREE-SPEED FULLY SYNCHRONIZED TRANSMISSION

A three-speed fully synchronized transmission is shown in Fig. 33-2. It has synchromesh in all the forward gears and in reverse. Figure 33-10 shows the transmission in each position of the shift lever. An additional sliding clutch sleeve is used for the first-and-reverse gear positions. The power flow through the transmission in each gear position is shown in Fig. 33-10. The sliding clutch sleeve is called a *synchronizer assembly* in the illustration.

□ 33-12 FOUR-SPEED TRANSMISSION

The additional forward speed in the four-speed transmission gives the car more flexibility. This is especially needed to get acceptable performance from small cars with small engines. A popular arrangement is a four-speed transmission with a floor-mounted shift lever. The combination is called "four on the floor." Figures 33-11 and 33-12 show the gears in a four-speed transmission in neutral. Each forward gear is selected by moving a synchronizer.

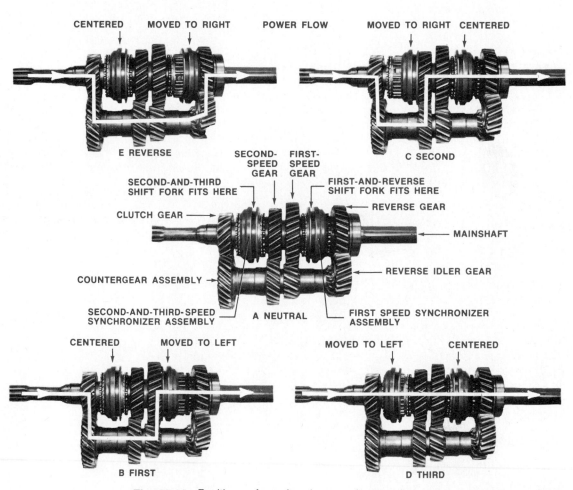

Fig. 33-10 Positions of synchronizers and power flow through a three-speed fully synchronized transmission.

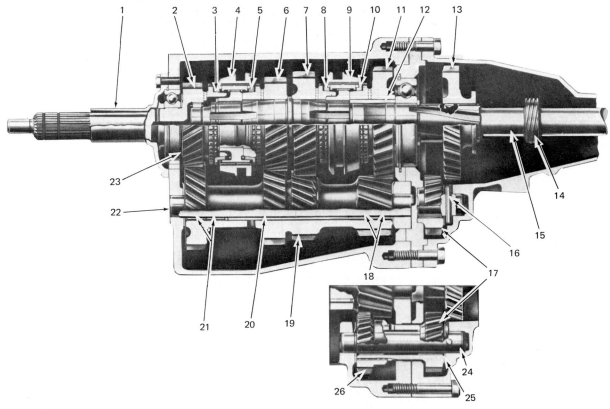

1. BEARING RETAINER
2. MAIN DRIVE GEAR
3. FOURTH-SPEED SYNCHRONIZING RING
4. THIRD-AND-FOURTH-SPEED CLUTCH ASSEMBLY
5. THIRD-SPEED SYNCHRONIZING RING
6. THIRD-SPEED GEAR
7. SECOND-SPEED GEAR
8. SECOND-SPEED SYNCHRONIZING RING
9. FIRST-AND-SECOND-SPEED CLUTCH ASSEMBLY
10. FIRST-SPEED SYNCHRONIZING RING
11. FIRST-SPEED GEAR
12. FIRST-SPEED GEAR SLEEVE
13. REVERSE GEAR
14. SPEEDOMETER DRIVE GEAR
15. MAINSHAFT
16. REVERSE IDLER SHAFT ROLL PIN
17. REVERSE IDLER GEAR (REAR)
18. COUNTERGEAR BEARING ROLLER
19. COUNTERGEAR
20. COUNTERSHAFT BEARING ROLLER SPACER
21. COUNTERSHAFT BEARING ROLLER
22. COUNTERGEAR SHAFT
23. OIL SLINGER
24. REVERSE IDLER SHAFT
25. THRUST WASHER
26. REVERSE IDLER GEAR (FRONT)

Fig. 33-11 A four-speed transmission with all parts named. *(Chevrolet Motor Division of General Motors Corporation)*

☐ 33-13 FOUR-SPEED TRANSMISSION WITH OVERDRIVE

This transmission is shown cut away in Fig. 33-13. Figure 33-14 shows the gears and shafts. In third gear, the ratio through the transmission is 1 : 1. This means the input and output shafts turn at the same speed. However, in fourth, the output shaft turns faster than the input shaft. It "overdrives" the output shaft. By shifting into overdrive, engine speed is reduced while car speed is maintained. This means less engine wear and fuel consumption.

☐ 33-14 FIVE-SPEED OVERDRIVE TRANSMISSION

Several five-speed transmissions with overdrive are used in cars today. Some of these transmissions are built as either a four speed or a five

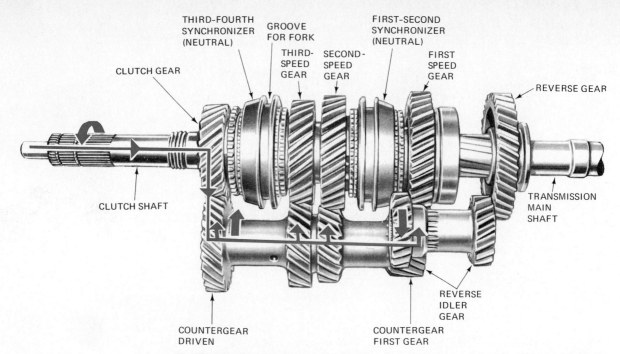

Fig. 33-12 Gear train and shafts of a four-speed transmission. *(Chevrolet Motor Division of General Motors Corporation)*

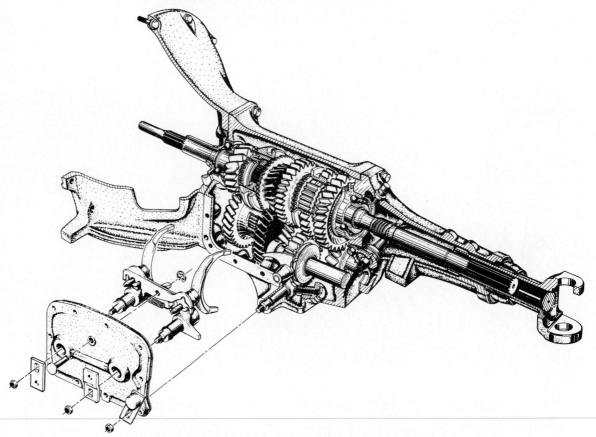

Fig. 33-13 A four-speed transmission which provides overdrive in fourth gear, cut away to show the gear train. *(Chrysler Corporation)*

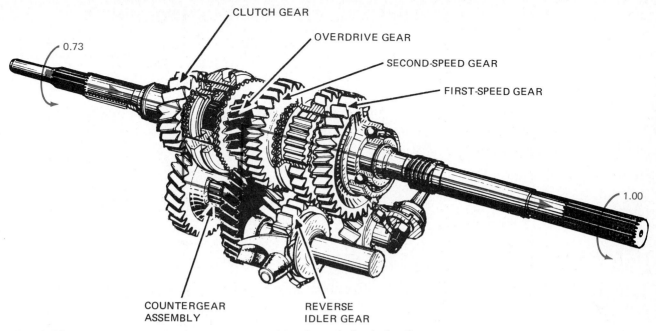

CLUTCH GEAR

OVERDRIVE GEAR

SECOND-SPEED GEAR

FIRST-SPEED GEAR

0.73

1.00

COUNTERGEAR
ASSEMBLY

REVERSE
IDLER GEAR

Fig. 33-14 Power flow through a four-speed overdrive transmission in fourth gear
(overdrive).

speed with overdrive. The basic gear arrangement is the same for both.
Extra gearing is then added to the transmission as it is built to obtain
fifth speed, or overdrive.

Figure 33-15 shows a five-speed overdrive transmission. The additional gearing is contained in an extension housing. This is bolted to the
back of the four-speed-transmission housing. Then the counter gear, or
cluster gear, is extended and the overdrive gear is added to the transmission output shaft. A single selector lever is used by the driver to shift the
transmission.

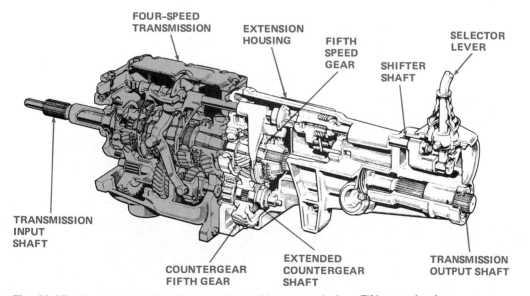

FOUR-SPEED
TRANSMISSION

EXTENSION
HOUSING

FIFTH
SPEED
GEAR

SHIFTER
SHAFT

SELECTOR
LEVER

TRANSMISSION
INPUT
SHAFT

COUNTERGEAR
FIFTH GEAR

EXTENDED
COUNTERGEAR
SHAFT

TRANSMISSION
OUTPUT SHAFT

Fig. 33-15 Construction of a five-speed overdrive transmission. Fifth gear is obtained by bolting the additional gearing to the back of the four-speed transmission.
(Ford Motor Company)

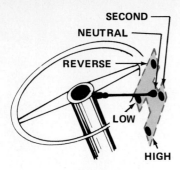

SECOND
NEUTRAL
REVERSE
LOW
HIGH

COLUMN SHIFT

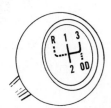

REVERSE   LOW

LOW   NEUTRAL   HIGH

FLOOR SHIFT

Fig. 33-16 Gearshift patterns for steering-column and floor-mounted shift levers.

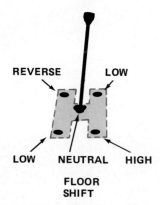

Fig. 33-17 Shift pattern for a four-speed overdrive transmission.

☐ 33-15 SELECTOR LEVERS AND LINKAGES

Transmission selector levers are located either on the steering column or on the floor (Fig. 33-16). Figure 33-17 shows the shift pattern for a floor-mounted four-speed transmission with overdrive. To shift a column-mounted selector lever into first, the driver pushes down on the clutch pedal to disconnect the transmission momentarily from the engine. Then the driver lifts the selector lever and pulls it back for first gear. When the lever is lifted, it pivots on its mounting pin and pushes down on the linkage rod in the steering column. This downward movement pushes the crossover blade at the bottom of the steering column (Fig. 33-18). When the crossover blade is pushed down, a slot in the blade engages a pin in the first-and-reverse shift lever (Fig. 33-18). Now, when the selector lever is moved into first, the first-and-reverse lever is rotated.

Figure 33-19 shows how movement of the first-and-reverse lever on the steering column is carried to the transmission by a linkage rod. The first-and-reverse lever on the transmission is rotated. This moves the first-and-reverse shift fork inside the transmission so that the first-and-reverse gear, or synchronizing drum, is moved. Figure 33-20 shows the first-and-reverse shift fork and the second-and-third shift fork.

If the shift is being made into second or third, the second-and-third shift lever at the bottom of the steering column is moved. This motion moves the second-and-third lever on the transmission. The second-and-third shift fork then moves the sliding clutch sleeve, or synchronizing drum, to shift into second or third.

There are various kinds and arrangements of transmission linkages in different cars. Some transmissions do not use linkage rods between the selector lever and the transmission. Instead, they use a single rail, or shifter shaft (Fig. 33-15). The lower end of the selector lever moves into the bracket on the end of the shifter shaft when a gear is selected. Then further movement of the selector lever causes the shifter shaft to move. This moves the fork that has been selected. The fork and the synchronizer sleeve it surrounds then move in the proper direction to produce the desired gear position. Construction and operation of the synchronizer is covered in ☐ 33-10.

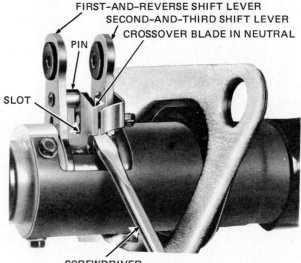

FIRST-AND-REVERSE SHIFT LEVER
SECOND-AND-THIRD SHIFT LEVER
CROSSOVER BLADE IN NEUTRAL
PIN
SLOT
SCREWDRIVER

Fig. 33-18 Shift levers and crossover blade at the bottom of the steering column. The screwdriver holds the crossover blade in neutral for an adjustment check. (*Chrysler Corporation*)

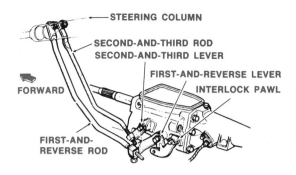

Fig. 33-19 Gearshift linkage between the shift levers at the bottom of the steering column and the transmission levers on the side of the transmission. *(Chrysler Corporation)*

STEERING COLUMN

SECOND-AND-THIRD ROD
SECOND-AND-THIRD LEVER

FIRST-AND-REVERSE LEVER
INTERLOCK PAWL

FORWARD

FIRST-AND-
REVERSE ROD

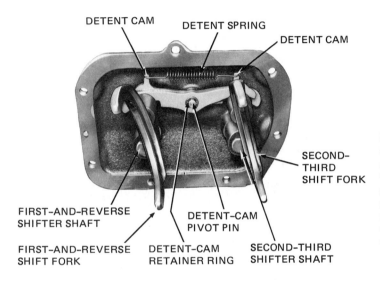

DETENT CAM   DETENT SPRING

DETENT CAM

SECOND-
THIRD
SHIFT FORK

FIRST-AND-REVERSE
SHIFTER SHAFT

DETENT-CAM
PIVOT PIN

FIRST-AND-REVERSE
SHIFT FORK

DETENT-CAM
RETAINER RING

SECOND-THIRD
SHIFTER SHAFT

Fig. 33-20 Transmission side cover, showing how shift forks are mounted on the ends of levers attached to shafts. The shafts can rotate in the side cover. Detent cams and springs prevent more than one of the shift forks from moving at the same time. *(Chevrolet Motor Division of General Motors Corporation)*

MANUAL TRANSAXLES

□ 33-16 PURPOSE OF THE TRANSAXLE

Many modern cars have the engine at the front, driving the front wheels. The most common arrangement has the engine mounted crossways, or in a transverse position (Fig. 32-2). The clutch, transmission, final drive, and differential are in a single assembly called the *transaxle*. The transaxle is attached to the engine, as shown in Figs. 32-2 and 32-3.

Figure 33-21 is a sectional view of a manual transaxle. It differs in design and construction from the manual transmissions described and illustrated earlier. However, the purpose is the same. The driver depresses the clutch pedal to uncouple the transmission from the engine. Then the driver can move the selector lever to any forward-gear position, neutral, or reverse.

A four-speed transaxle is shown in Fig. 33-21. Two synchronizers provide clashless shifting. The synchronizers work the same way as in other manual transmissions (□ 33-10). The differential, final drive (ring-and-pinion gears), and drive shafts are described later.

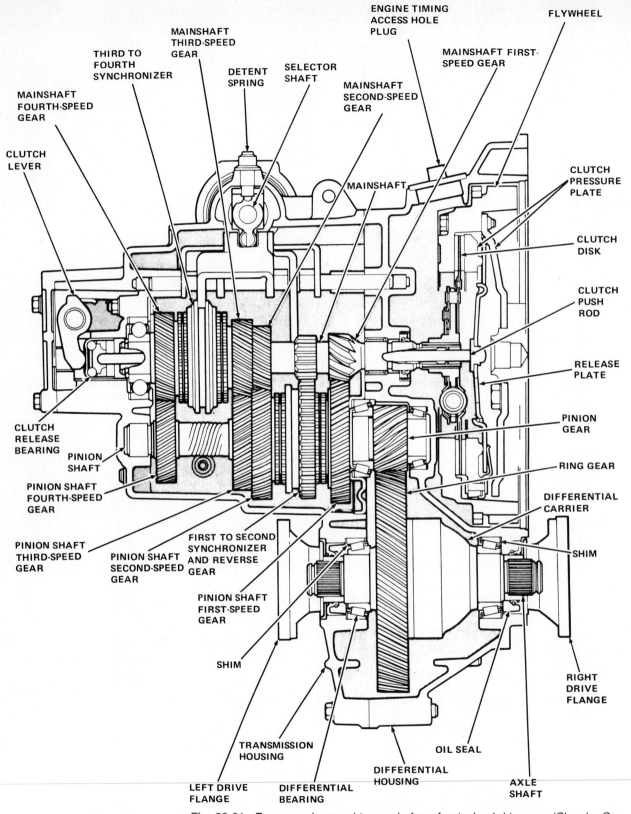

ENGINE TIMING ACCESS HOLE PLUG

FLYWHEEL

MAINSHAFT THIRD-SPEED GEAR

THIRD TO FOURTH SYNCHRONIZER

MAINSHAFT FIRST-SPEED GEAR

DETENT SPRING

SELECTOR SHAFT

MAINSHAFT FOURTH-SPEED GEAR

MAINSHAFT SECOND-SPEED GEAR

CLUTCH PRESSURE PLATE

MAINSHAFT

CLUTCH LEVER

CLUTCH DISK

CLUTCH PUSH ROD

RELEASE PLATE

CLUTCH RELEASE BEARING

PINION SHAFT

PINION GEAR

PINION SHAFT FOURTH-SPEED GEAR

RING GEAR

DIFFERENTIAL CARRIER

PINION SHAFT THIRD-SPEED GEAR

PINION SHAFT SECOND-SPEED GEAR

FIRST TO SECOND SYNCHRONIZER AND REVERSE GEAR

SHIM

PINION SHAFT FIRST-SPEED GEAR

SHIM

RIGHT DRIVE FLANGE

TRANSMISSION HOUSING

OIL SEAL

LEFT DRIVE FLANGE

DIFFERENTIAL BEARING

DIFFERENTIAL HOUSING

AXLE SHAFT

Fig. 33-21 Four-speed manual transaxle for a front-wheel-drive car. *(Chrysler Corporation)*

490

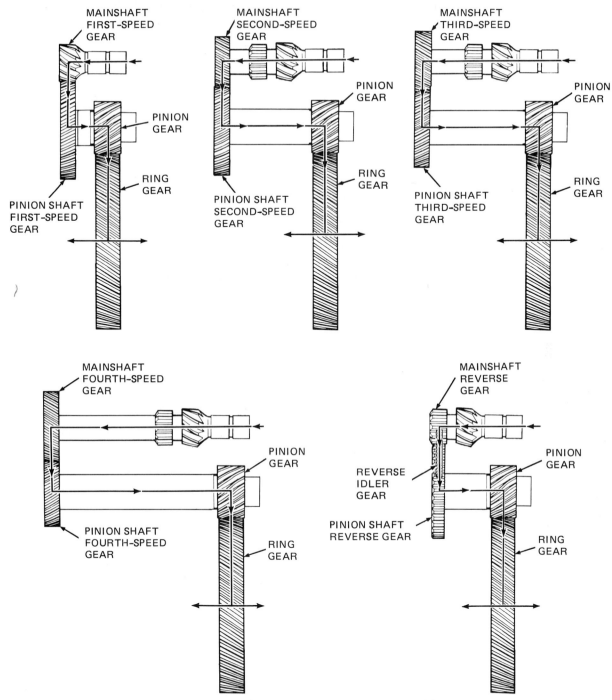

Fig. 33-22 Power flow through each gear position in a four-speed transaxle. The complete gear train is shown in neutral in Fig. 33-21.

□ *33-17 OPERATION OF THE TRANSAXLE*

Figure 33-22 shows the power flow through the transaxle shown in Fig. 33-21 for first, second, third, fourth, and reverse. The synchronizers are moved in one direction or the other to lock the different gears (Fig. 33-21).

The gears are locked to either the main shaft or the output shaft (in first, second, third, and fourth). In reverse, the reverse idler gear is brought into the gear train. This causes the output shaft to rotate in the reverse direction. Therefore the wheels turn backward so the car backs up.

Figure 33-23 shows a similar transaxle that is made as a four-speed and as a five-speed overdrive. (This is similar to the five-speed overdrive transmission described in □ 33-14). Extra gearing is added during manufacture to provide the fifth speed.

□ 33-18 TRANSAXLE SHIFT LINKAGE

In the transaxle shown in Fig. 33-21 and in other transaxles, shifting is done in the same way as in most manual transmissions. When the driver moves the selector lever, it engages a lever which moves a shift rod. The shift rod moves a lever on the transmission. This movement causes a fork in the transmission to shift a synchronizer one way or the other on a shaft. The synchronizer movement locks a gear to a shaft or to another gear so the desired gear ratio through the transmission is achieved.

□ 33-19 TRANSAXLE WITH DUAL-SPEED RANGE

A dual-range transaxle (Fig. 33-24) is used in some cars with front-wheel drive. It has four forward speeds plus reverse, as in other transaxles. In

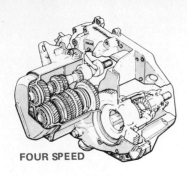

FOUR SPEED

FIFTH-SPEED GEARING

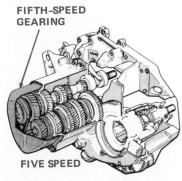

FIVE SPEED

Fig. 33-23 Top, a four-speed manual transaxle. Bottom, additional gearing is added to the back of the four-speed transaxle to make it into a five speed. *(American Motors Corporation)*

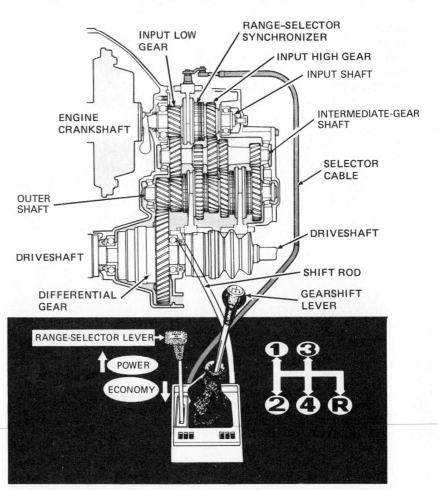

Fig. 33-24 Control levers and linkage for the "Twin Stick" dual-range transaxle. *(Chrysler Corporation)*

492

addition, the dual-range transaxle has an extra set of gears that provide overdrive in each gear position. This provides two speed ranges which the manufacturer calls the *economy range* and the *power range*. With four forward speeds in each range, the dual-range transaxle provides a total of eight forward speeds.

The gear ratios for both the single-range transaxle and the dual-range transaxle are shown in Fig. 33-25. In fourth gear, the power range of the two-speed transaxle provides a gear ratio of 1.105 : 1. The crankshaft turns 1.105 times to turn the output shaft once. When shifted into the economy range, fourth gear has a gear ratio of 0.885 : 1, which is overdrive. For each complete revolution of the output shaft, the crankshaft turns only 0.885 of one revolution.

□ 33-20 GEAR LUBRICANTS

Manual transmissions and transaxles are two types of gearboxes. There are others, such as transfer cases (Chap. 37). In the gearbox, the moving metal parts must not touch each other. They must be continuously separated by a thin film of lubricant to prevent excessive wear and premature failure. As gear teeth mesh, there is a sliding, or wiping, action between the contact faces. This action produces friction and heat. Without lubrication, the gears would wear quickly and fail. However, lubrication provides a fluid film between the contact faces. This prevents metal-to-metal contact. So all gearboxes in the car have some type of lubricant or *gear oil* in them.

Most gear oil is a straight mineral oil (refined from crude oil) with the required additives in it. Other gear oil is made from synthetic oil. Regardless of type, gear oil for use in most cars and light trucks has a classification of SAE75W, 75W-80, 80W-90, 85W-90, 90, or 140. The higher the number, the thicker the oil.

Gear oil is *not* recommended for use in all gearboxes. Gears that are lightly loaded, such as the planet-pinion gears in a planetary gearset, do not require gear oil. Instead, they are lubricated with SAE10W-30 engine oil, or automatic-transmission fluid (ATF). Some manual transaxles also are filled with automatic-transmission fluid.

To prevent the lubricant from leaking out, the gearbox has an oil-tight case. Seals are used around each cover and shaft (Figs. 33-2 and 33-21). In addition, seals are provided around the input shafts and the output shafts. The input shaft on many transmissions does not have a separate seal. Instead, an oil slinger is used to throw back any oil that

Gear Ratios	Standard Single-Range Transaxle	Dual-Range Transaxle	
		Power Range	Economy Range
1st	4.226	4.226	3.272
2nd	2.365	2.365	1.831
3rd	1.467	1.467	1.136
4th	1.105	1.105	0.855
Reverse	4.109	4.109	3.181

Fig. 33-25 Gear ratios of a standard single-range transaxle compared with gear ratios in each range of a dual-range transaxle. *(Chrysler Corporation)*

reaches it. Other designs have a passage in the front-bearing retainer that returns to the case any oil passing through the bearing.

☐ 33-21 SPEEDOMETER DRIVE

On many cars, the speedometer is driven by a pair of gears in the transmission-extension housing (Fig. 33-2). One of these gears is mounted on the transmission main shaft. The other gear is mounted on the end of the flexible shaft connecting the speedometer to the transmission gear.

MANUAL-TRANSMISSION TROUBLES

☐ 33-22 TRANSMISSION TROUBLE DIAGNOSIS

The type of trouble a transmission has is often a clue to the cause of the trouble. The first step in any transmission service job is to find the cause of trouble. Various troubles are listed below. Then, in following sections, possible causes of the various troubles are described. Internal transmission troubles are fixed by disassembling the transmission. Or the old transmission can be replaced by a new or rebuilt unit. Many shops handle transmission service by replacing the complete unit. Possible transmission troubles include:

1. Hard shifting into gear.
2. Transmission sticks in gear.
3. Transmission slips out of first or reverse.
4. Transmission slips out of second.
5. Transmission slips out of third.
6. No power through the transmission.
7. Transmission is noisy in neutral.
8. Transmission is noisy in gear.
9. Gears clash in shifting.
10. Oil leaks.

If the trouble is in the linkage, then the linkage should be lubricated and adjusted, as explained in the manufacturer's service manual. If the trouble is internal, then either disassemble the transmission for service or replace it with a new or rebuilt unit.

☐ 33-23 HARD SHIFTING INTO GEAR

If shifting into gear is hard, the reason may be that the clutch is not releasing. The clutch may need adjustment. Another possible cause is a gearshift linkage that is out of adjustment or in need of lubrication. The shifter fork inside the transmission might be bent. If so, the fork should be replaced. Also, the sliding gear or drum might be tight on the shaft splines, or the synchronizing unit might be damaged.

☐ 33-24 TRANSMISSION STICKS IN GEAR

If the transmission sticks in gear, the clutch may not be releasing and may need adjustment. The gearshift linkage may need adjustment or lubrication. Internal trouble, such as the gear or drum frozen on the shaft, may also be the cause.

☐ 33-25 TRANSMISSION SLIPS OUT OF FIRST OR REVERSE

If the transmission slips out of first or reverse, the gearshift linkage may be out of adjustment. Other possible causes of this trouble are gear or drum loose on the shaft, worn gear teeth, too much end play of the gears, and worn bearings.

☐ 33-26 TRANSMISSION SLIPS OUT OF SECOND

The transmission may slip out of second if the gearshift linkage is out of adjustment. This trouble may also be caused by a loose gear or drum on the main shaft or by too much shaft end play. The gear teeth may be worn.

☐ 33-27 TRANSMISSION SLIPS OUT OF THIRD

The transmission may slip out of third if the gearshift linkage is out of adjustment. The engine and transmission may be misaligned. Other causes of this trouble are too much main-shaft end play, worn gear teeth, and worn bearings or synchronizing unit.

☐ 33-28 NO POWER FLOW THROUGH TRANSMISSION

There may be no power flow through the transmission if the clutch is slipping. The clutch may require adjustment. If it has internal defects, it may need replacement. If there is damage such as broken gear teeth, shifter fork, gear, or shaft, there may be no power flow through the transmission.

☐ 33-29 TRANSMISSION NOISY IN NEUTRAL

Noise from a transmission in neutral is probably caused by a worn or dry clutch-shaft bearing, worn or dry countershaft bearings, worn gears, or too much shaft end play.

☐ 33-30 TRANSMISSION NOISY IN GEAR

Clutch defects, which require clutch replacement, may cause noise that seems to come from the transmission. Causes of noise in the transmission when it is in gear are worn, chipped, or broken gears and synchronizers; worn bearings; and lack of lubricant. The trouble also may be caused by some of the same conditions that make the transmission noisy in neutral.

☐ 33-31 GEAR CLASH DURING SHIFTING

If the gears clash during shifting, the probable cause is a synchronizer defect. The trouble could also be due to gears sticking or failure of the clutch to release.

☐ 33-32 OIL LEAKS FROM TRANSMISSION

Oil will leak from the transmission when the drain plug is loose, the cover gasket is damaged or loose, the cover bolts are loose, or the shift-lever seals are damaged. Leakage at the rear of the transmission is caused by wear of the transmission rear seal or the drive-line yoke. Oil will leak from the transmission because of foaming resulting from the use of improper lubricant or overfilling. Loose front-bearing retainer bolts and a cracked transmission case are other causes.

☐ 33-33 SERVICING MANUAL TRANSMISSIONS

Transmission troubles can be repaired in two ways. These are disassembling the transmission and replacing defective parts or replacing the old transmission with a new or rebuilt unit. If the problem is in the linkages between the shift lever and the transmission, it can usually be fixed with a linkage adjustment. Follow the procedures in the manufacturer's service manual. Different adjustment procedures are required for different cars.

CHAPTER 33
REVIEW QUESTIONS

Select the *one* correct, best, or most probable answer to each question. Then check your answers against the correct answers given at the end of the book.

1. Engines that are mounted transversely at the front of the car
   a. drive the rear wheels
   b. drive the front wheels through a transaxle
   c. drive either the front or rear wheels
   d. none of the above

2. A foot-operated clutch is used with the
   a. manual transmission
   b. automatic transmission
   c. differential
   d. all of the above

3. The purpose of the transmission is to change the gear ratio between the
   a. crankshaft and flywheel
   b. crankshaft and camshaft
   c. crankshaft and transmission input shaft
   d. crankshaft and transmission output shaft

4. In overdrive
   a. the crankshaft turns faster than the transmission output shaft
   b. the transmission output shaft turns faster than the crankshaft
   c. the crankshaft turns faster than the clutch
   d. the transmission output shaft turns faster than the drive shaft

5. In the manual transaxle, the
   a. transmission and drive axle are combined
   b. differential and transfer case are combined
   c. clutch is not required
   d. front and rear wheels are driven

CHAPTER 34
AUTOMATIC TRANSMISSIONS AND TRANSAXLES

After studying this chapter, you should be able to:

1. Describe the construction and operation of a torque converter.

2. Explain the construction and operation of a planetary gearset.

3. Explain how bands and clutches are used to control the planetary gearset.

4. Describe the difference between an automatic transmission and an automatic transaxle.

5. Describe the characteristics of automatic-transmission fluid (ATF).

Automatic transmission and transaxles do the job of shifting gears without any help from the driver. They start out in first as the car pulls away from a stop. Then the automatic transmission shifts from first into second and then into third gear as the car picks up speed. The shifting is done hydraulically with oil pressure.

There are three basic parts to the automatic transmission (Fig. 34-1). These are the torque converter, the planetary-gear system, and the hydraulic control systems. The torque converter passes the power from the engine to the gear train. Shifting action takes place in the gear train.

☐ 34-1 INTRODUCTION TO AUTOMATIC TRANSMISSIONS

In an automatic transmission, gear ratios are changed automatically. This eliminates the need for the driver to operate the clutch and manually "shift gears." The typical automatic transmission combines a fluid *torque converter,* a planetary-gear system, and a hydraulic control system in a single unit (Fig. 34-1). As car speed changes, various gear ratios between the crankshaft and the wheels are selected and then changed automatically. Automatic controls inside the transmission supply the proper ratio for the driving conditions. In addition to the forward-gear

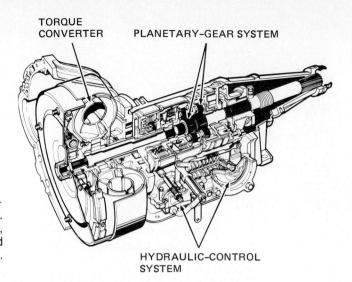

TORQUE
CONVERTER   PLANETARY–GEAR SYSTEM

HYDRAULIC–CONTROL
SYSTEM

Fig. 34-1 The automatic transmission has three basic parts. They are the torque converter, the planetary-gear system, and the hydraulic control system. *(Ford Motor Company)*

ratios, neutral, and reverse, the automatic transmission has a PARK position. This locks the transmission to prevent the car from moving or rolling away while parked.

Both manual and automatic transmissions use various gear sets to change the speed and direction of rotation of the transmission output shaft. Figure 34-2 shows the power flow from the engine crankshaft to the wheels on a car with front-wheel drive. The illustration includes other major components of a typical three-speed automatic transmission. In a car using the power train shown in Fig. 34-2, the automatic transmission and differential are combined into an *automatic transaxle*. Operation of the automatic transmission usually is similar in both front- and rear-wheel-drive cars. The biggest difference is in the locations of some components. Automatic transaxles are described in later sections.

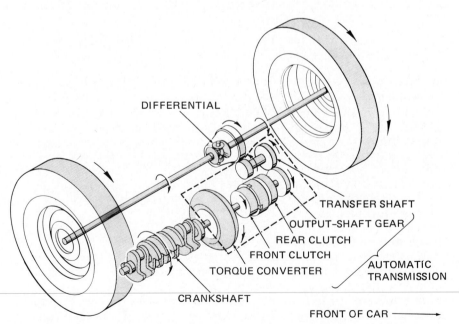

DIFFERENTIAL

TRANSFER SHAFT
OUTPUT–SHAFT GEAR
REAR CLUTCH
FRONT CLUTCH   AUTOMATIC
TORQUE CONVERTER   TRANSMISSION

CRANKSHAFT

FRONT OF CAR ⟶

Fig. 34-2 Power flow from the engine crankshaft to the drive wheels for a car with front-wheel drive. *(Chrysler Corporation)*

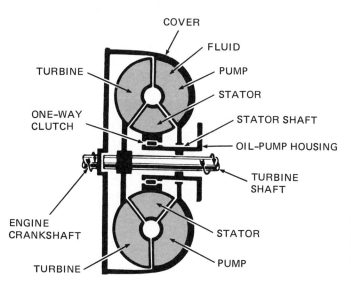

Fig. 34-3 A simplified torque converter, showing locations of the turbine, stator, pump, cover, and one-way clutch. *(Ford Motor Company)*

☐ 34-2 THE TORQUE CONVERTER

The clutch used with manual transmissions is a mechanical coupling (Chap. 32). When engaged, it couples the engine to the transmission. In automatic transmissions, a *fluid coupling* called a *torque converter* is used instead of a mechanical connection. It is always "engaged." But because the coupling is produced by a fluid, or oil, the driven member can slip and turn more slowly than the driving member. (*Member* is the name given to any essential part such as the pump, the turbine, or the stator.)

A torque converter has a driving member (the *pump*) and a driven member (the *turbine*). These are shown in Fig. 34-3. They have curved vanes between which oil passes to transmit torque (Fig. 34-4).

☐ 34-3 THE STATOR

To make the torque converter more effective, a third member is required. This member is called the *reaction member,* or *stator*. Its purpose is to change the direction of the oil coming off the turbine vanes (Fig. 34-5). When oil leaves the pump, the oil hits the turbine vanes. This causes the turbine to spin. As the oil leaves the turbine, the oil hits the stator vanes. They redirect the oil into the pump so that the oil is thrown into the turbine with even greater force. Each time the oil enters the pump, the oil gives the vanes another push. This effect is called *torque multiplication.*

In many torque converters, the torque is more than doubled. However, torque multiplication takes place only when the pump is turning considerably faster than the turbine. For example, this happens during acceleration after stopping for a stop sign.

The stator is mounted on a one-way clutch (Fig. 34-6) called a *freewheeling clutch, overrunning clutch,* or *sprag clutch.* This device permits the stator to run free when both the pump and turbine are turning at about the same speed. However, when torque increase and speed reduction take place, the stator stops. Then it acts as a reaction member, or reactor. This action is possible because the stator is mounted, through the overrunning clutch, on a tube or hollow stationary shaft called the *stator*

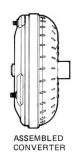

ASSEMBLED CONVERTER

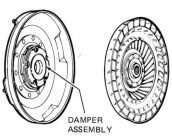

CONVERTER COVER   TURBINE

DAMPER ASSEMBLY

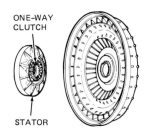

ONE-WAY CLUTCH

STATOR

IMPELLER

Fig. 34-4 Assembled and disassembled torque converter. *(Ford Motor Company)*

shaft (Fig. 34-3). The shaft is stationary because it is connected to the oil pump, which is bolted to the transmission case.

As turbine speed approaches pump speed, the torque increase gradually drops off until it becomes 1 : 1. This occurs when the turbine and pump speeds reach a ratio of approximately 9 : 10. This ratio is called the *coupling point* (Fig. 34-5D). Now the oil begins to strike the back faces of the stator vanes so that the stator begins to turn. In effect, the oil pushes the stator ahead so that it no longer enters into the torque-converter

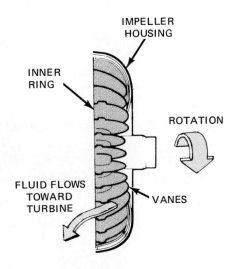

(A) IMPELLER OPERATION

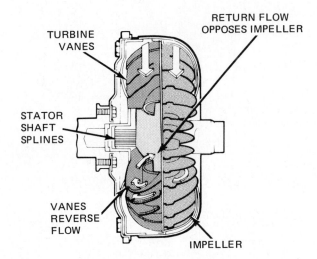

(B) DRIVING THE TURBINE

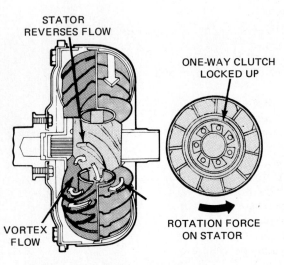

(C) TORQUE MULTIPLICATION

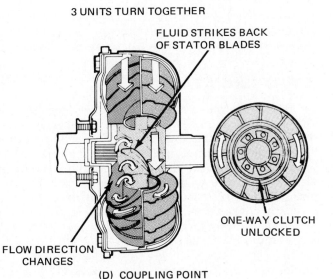

(D) COUPLING POINT

Fig. 34-5 Torque-converter action. (A) The impeller, or pump, sends a flow of oil, or fluid, against the turbine. (B) The turbine vanes receive the flow and spin the turbine. The vanes reverse the direction of fluid flow and send it back toward the impeller. (C) The stator reverses the flow of fluid into a helping direction and this multiplies the torque. (D) When the turbine speed nears the impeller speed, the fluid strikes the backs of the stator vanes, causing the stator to spin forward. This prevents the stator vanes from interfering with the fluid flow. *(Ford Motor Company)*

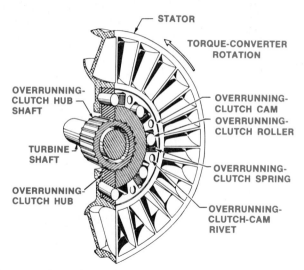

STATOR

TORQUE-CONVERTER
ROTATION

OVERRUNNING-
CLUTCH HUB
SHAFT

OVERRUNNING-
CLUTCH CAM

OVERRUNNING-
CLUTCH ROLLER

TURBINE
SHAFT

OVERRUNNING-
CLUTCH SPRING

OVERRUNNING-
CLUTCH HUB

OVERRUNNING-
CLUTCH-CAM
RIVET

Fig. 34-6 A one-way clutch used to support and control the stator in the torque converter. *(Chrysler Corporation)*

action. The torque converter acts as a simple fluid coupling under these conditions.

□ 34-4 ONE-WAY-CLUTCH OPERATION

A one-way clutch is completely mechanical in operation and requires no other control mechanism. It locks and unlocks, or *freewheels,* automatically as the result of the forces acting on it. The construction of a typical one-way clutch is shown in Fig. 34-6. It contains a series of rollers placed between the stator and the hub. The rollers permit the stator to overrun or freewheel when the oil strikes the back faces of the stator vanes.

However, when the oil strikes the front faces of the vanes, the oil attempts to turn the stator in the opposite direction. This action causes the rollers to lock the one-way clutch, so the stator is held stationary. Now it acts as a reaction member, changing the direction of the oil as it passes between the turbine and pump vanes.

Some one-way clutches use *sprags* instead of rollers. Sprags are shaped like slightly flattened rollers. A series of sprags is placed between the inner and outer races (Fig. 34-7). The sprags are held in place by two cages and small springs. During overrunning, when stator action is not needed, the outer race is unlocked (Fig. 34-7A). It is attached to the stator, so the stator can spin freely. The inner cage is attached to the stator shaft (Figs. 34-3 and 34-6). When stator action is needed, the oil is directed into the stator vanes. This attempts to spin the stator backward (Fig. 34-7B). When this happens, the sprags jam between the outer and inner races to lock the stator to the stator shaft (Fig. 34-5C).

□ 34-5 LOCKING THE TORQUE CONVERTER

There is always some slippage in the torque converter. The turbine can never turn at exactly pump speed, as long as the turbine is being driven by oil thrown from the pump. This slippage through the fluid represents a loss of fuel economy and increased fluid temperature.

To eliminate this loss, many torque converters now have a clutch. It is similar to the clutch used with a manual transmission (Chap. 32). The

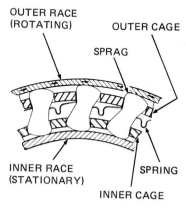

OUTER RACE
(ROTATING)

OUTER CAGE

SPRAG

INNER RACE
(STATIONARY)

SPRING

INNER CAGE

(A) FREE-WHEELING

OUTER RACE
(STATIONARY)

BACK FORCE

INNER RACE
(STATIONARY)

(B) LOCKED

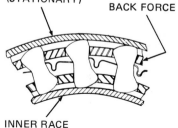

(C) ASSEMBLED

Fig. 34-7 Operation of a sprag type of one-way clutch. The complete sprag clutch is shown in view C.

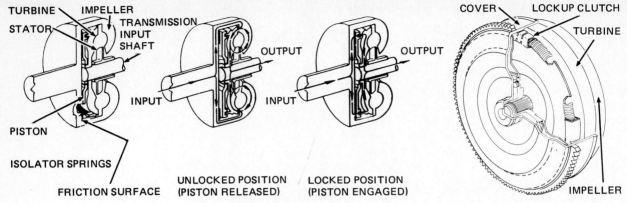

Fig. 34-8 Power flow through a hydraulically operated type of lockup torque converter. *(Chrysler Corporation)*

clutch engages automatically, locking the pump (or impeller) and turbine together (Fig. 34-8). Two types of locking mechanism are used, centrifugal and hydraulic (Fig. 34-8). A centrifugal converter clutch is shown on the transmission in Fig. 34-1. It has ten shoes made of friction material similar to that used in automatic-transmission bands (□ 34-7). The shoes are thrown outward against the converter cover by centrifugal force. This locks up the torque converter by forming a direct mechanical link between the pump and the turbine.

In the hydraulic-lockup torque converter, the converter cover is attached to and turns with the pump (Fig. 34-8). A pressure plate (called the *piston* in Fig. 34-8) is splined to the turbine input shaft, so they turn together. To lock up the torque converter, at the desired time the control system forces oil in back of the piston. As the oil pressure increases, the piston is moved against the converter cover (to the left in Fig. 34-8, top). This locks the pump and turbine together, locking up the torque converter.

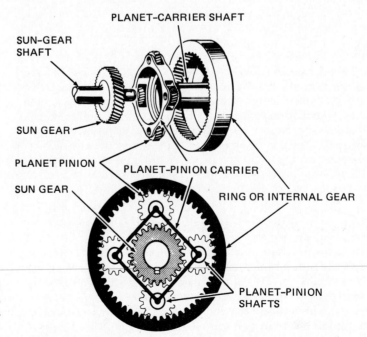

Fig. 34-9 A single planetary gearset. *(Chevrolet Motor Division of General Motors Corporation)*

502

□ 34-6 PLANETARY GEARS

Automatic transmissions have two or more *planetary-gear sets* (Fig. 34-9). In the automatic transmission, the job of the planetary gearset is to change speed and torque ratios, to reverse direction, and to act as a solid shaft. The planetary gearset consists of an internal gear (also called a *ring gear*), a sun gear, and two or more planet pinions on a carrier and shaft.

> **NOTE** Different manufacturers give different names to the parts of the planetary gearset. For example, the sun gear is also called a *center gear*. The internal gear is also called the *ring gear* or *annulus gear*. The planet-pinion carrier is also called the *planet-pinion cage*, and sometimes the *spider*. The planet pinions are also called *planet gears*. Planetary-gear systems are often called *planetary gearsets*. These different names are used throughout this book and in various manufacturers' service manuals.

When two gears are in mesh, they turn in opposite directions (Fig. 33-1). But if another gear is placed in the gear train (Fig. 34-10), the two outside gears turn in the same direction. The middle gear is called an *idler gear*. It does not do any work—it only idles. To get a combination of two gears to rotate in the same direction, use an internal gear (Fig. 34-11). The internal gear, also called an *annulus gear* or *ring gear,* has teeth on the inside. When the pinion gear and the internal gear rotate, they both rotate in the same direction.

When another gear is added in the center, meshed with the pinion gear, the combination is a single planetary gearset (Fig. 34-11). The center gear is called the "sun gear" because the other gears revolve around it. This is similar to the way planets in our solar system revolve around the sun. The gears between the sun gear and the internal gear are the planet pinions. They revolve around the sun gear, just as planets revolve around the sun.

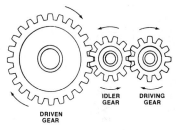

Fig. 34-10 The idler gear causes the driven gear to turn in the same direction as the driving gear.

□ 34-7 PLANETARY-GEARSET OPERATION

In Fig. 34-11, the two planet pinions rotate on shafts that are part of the planet-pinion carrier. Each of the two gears and the planet-pinion carrier are called members. The internal gear, the sun gear, and the planet-pinion-and-carrier assembly are all members. When one member is held stationary and another turns, there will be a speed increase, a speed reduction, or a direction reversal. The result depends on which member is stationary and which turns.

1. SPEED INCREASE #1

Suppose the sun gear is held stationary and the planet-pinion carrier turns. Then the internal gear will increase in speed. When the carrier revolves, it carries the planet pinions around with it. This movement makes the planet pinions rotate on their shafts. As the pinions rotate, they cause the internal gear to rotate also (Fig. 34-12). Note the conditions. The sun gear is stationary. The planet-pinion carrier is moving, carrying the pinions around with it. The planet pinions "walk around" the sun gear, which means they rotate on their shafts. As the planet pinions turn, they drive the internal gear ahead of them. This provides a

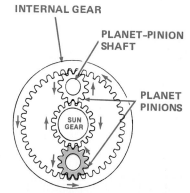

Fig. 34-11 A complete single planetary gearset using two planet-pinion gears. Two or more pinion gears are used to balance the forces so that the system will run smoothly.

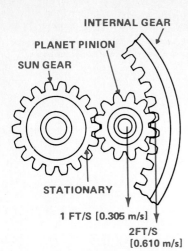

INTERNAL GEAR

PLANET PINION

SUN GEAR

STATIONARY

1 FT/S [0.305 m/s]

2 FT/S [0.610 m/s]

Fig. 34-12 If the sun gear is held stationary and the planet-pinion carrier is turned, the ring gear will turn faster than the carrier. The pinion pivots about the stationary teeth. If the center of the pinion shaft moves at 1 foot per second [0.3 m/s], the tooth opposite the stationary tooth will move at 2 feet per second [0.6 m/s] since it is twice as far away from the stationary tooth as the center of the shaft.

	Condition					
	1	**2**	**3**	**4**	**5**	**6**
Internal gear	D	H	T	H	T	D
Carrier	T	T	D	D	H	H
Sun gear	H	D	H	T	D	T
Speed	I	I	L	L	IR	LR

D—driven   L—decrease speed
H—held   R—reverse
I—increase speed   T—turning or driving

Fig. 34-13 Various conditions that are possible in the planetary gearset if one member is held and another member is turned.

speed increase through the planetary gearset when the internal gear is connected to the output shaft. Automatic transmissions can use this condition to provide an "overdrive" fourth gear.

2. SPEED INCREASE #2

Another combination is to hold the internal gear stationary and turn the planet-pinion carrier. This forces the sun gear to rotate faster than the planet-pinion carrier. There is a greater speed increase than in #1 above. This condition usually is not used in automatic transmissions.

3. SPEED REDUCTION #1

If the internal gear turns while the sun gear is held stationary, the planet-pinion carrier turns slower than the internal gear. With the internal gear turning the planet-pinion carrier, the planetary gearset provides speed reduction and a torque increase. This is the way second gear is obtained in many automatic transmissions.

4. SPEED REDUCTION #2

If the internal gear is held stationary and the sun gear turns, there is speed reduction. The planet pinions must rotate on their shafts. They also must walk around the internal gear, since they are in mesh with it. As the pinions rotate, the planet carrier rotates. But it rotates at a slower speed than the sun gear. This condition provides the greatest increase in torque. It is used for first gear in automatic transmissions.

Fig. 34-14 The planetary gears in an automatic transmission are controlled by bands, multiple-disk clutches, and overrunning clutches. This transmission uses a simple, or Simpson-type, planetary gearset. *(Ford Motor Company)*

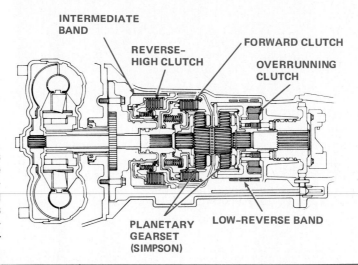

INTERMEDIATE BAND

REVERSE-HIGH CLUTCH

FORWARD CLUTCH

OVERRUNNING CLUTCH

PLANETARY GEARSET (SIMPSON)

LOW-REVERSE BAND

5. REVERSE #1

To get reverse, hold the planet-pinion carrier stationary and turn the internal gear. Then the planet pinions act as idlers that cause the sun gear to be driven in the reverse direction. Here, the planetary gearset acts as a direction-reversing system, with the sun gear turning faster than the internal gear. However, there is no need for a "high-speed" reverse gear in an automatic transmission. Therefore, this condition is not used to obtain reverse in passenger cars.

6. REVERSE #2

A second way to get reverse is to hold the planet-pinion carrier stationary and turn the sun gear. The internal gear turns in a reverse direction, but slower than the sun gear. This is the condition used to provide reverse gear in an automatic transmission.

7. DIRECT DRIVE

If any two of the three members—sun gear, planet-pinion carrier, or ring gear—are driven at the same speed, or locked together, then the planetary gearset is locked up. Now the input and output shafts turn at the same speed. There is no change of speed or direction through the system, so the gear ratio is 1 : 1. This condition is used for third gear in automatic transmissions.

8. NEUTRAL

When no *clutches* are engaged (□ 34-9) and no bands are applied (□ 34-10), all members in the planetary gearset can turn freely. No power can be transmitted through it. This condition provides the transmission with a neutral position for starting the engine without load.

The planetary-gear-system operating conditions are shown in Fig. 34-13. Look at condition 1. The letter T in this column indicates the driving member, which is the pinion carrier. H indicates that the sun gear is held stationary. D indicates that the ring gear is being driven. I designates an increase of speed between the pinion carrier and the ring gear. The three conditions used most frequently in automatic transmissions are listed in columns 3, 4, and 6.

> **NOTE** The description above covers the operation of a simple single planetary gearset, such as shown in Fig. 34-9. However, to obtain all the conditions required from the automatic transmission, two different types of planetary-gear trains are used. Both are sometimes referred to by the name of their designers. The *simple,* or *Simpson, planetary gear train* has two separate sets of planet gears (Figs. 34-1 and 34-14). They revolve around one common sun gear. The *compound,* or *Ravigneaux, planetary-gear train* (Fig. 34-15) is a different design. It has one ring gear, two sets of planet gears (long and short), two sun gears (forward and reverse), and a planet carrier.

HYDRAULIC CONTROLS

□ 34-8 PLANETARY-GEARSET CONTROLS

The planetary gears used in automatic transmissions are controlled by *bands, multiple-disk clutches,* and *overrunning,* or *one-way, clutches* (Fig.

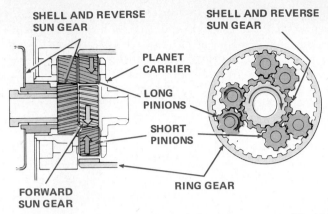

Fig. 34-15 A compound, or Ravigneaux-type, planetary gearset. *(Ford Motor Company)*

34-14). Many automatic transmissions have a one-way clutch to hold the rear planet carrier stationary in first gear (Fig. 34-14). This clutch operates automatically in the same way as the stator clutch (□ 34-4). Bands (□ 34-9) and multiple-disk clutches (□ 34-10) are operated by oil pressure ("hydraulic pressure") and springs.

□ 34-9 BANDS AND SERVOS

Figure 34-16 shows a planetary gearset with two control devices. These are the band and the multiple-disk clutch. The band is a brake band that wraps around the clutch drum (Fig. 34-17). When the band is applied, or tightened on the drum, the drum is held stationary. One end of the band is anchored to the transmission case. The other end is linked to a *servo* (Fig. 34-18), which is a hydraulically applied piston. The servo converts hydraulic pressure to mechanical movement, as the oil pushes against the piston in the servo.

The band is lined with friction material (Fig. 34-17). When oil pressure is directed to the *apply side* of the servo, the piston moves to the left (in Fig. 34-18). This applies the band. The friction material grips the

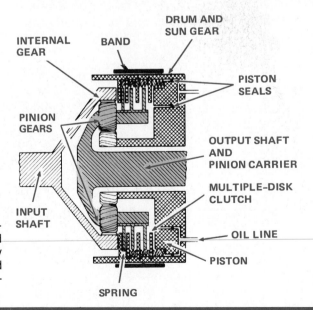

Fig. 34-16 Sectional view showing the two hydraulically operated control devices for the planetary gearset. One device is the band and drum. The other is the multiple-disk clutch.

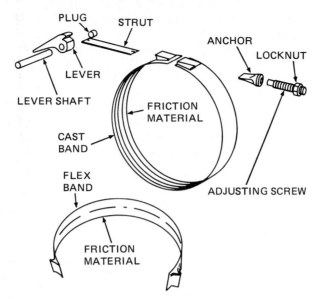

Fig. 34-17 Band with related linkages for an automatic transmission. *(Chrysler Corporation)*

surface of the drum and stops its rotation. This also stops the sun gear, which is attached to the drum.

When the band is applied, the sun gear (in Fig. 34-17) is held stationary. Now the planetary gearset acts as a speed reducer. The internal gear is turning because it is attached to the input shaft. This arrangement forces the pinion gears to rotate. They walk around the stationary sun gear, carrying the pinion carrier around with them. The carrier and output shaft rotate at a slower speed than the internal gear.

To release the band, the oil pressure is removed from in back of the piston. This allows a spring to force the piston back into its bore. In most transmissions, the spring is assisted by redirecting the oil pressure from the apply side to the *release side* of the servo piston (Fig. 34-18).

□ 34-10 CLUTCHES

To obtain direct drive through the planetary gearset, the band must be released and the clutch engaged. The multiple-disk clutch is located in-

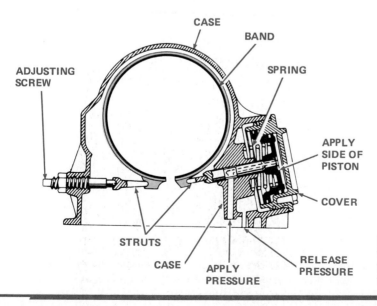

Fig. 34-18 Band shown in position in the transmission case, with the servo that operates to apply the band. *(Ford Motor Company)*

507

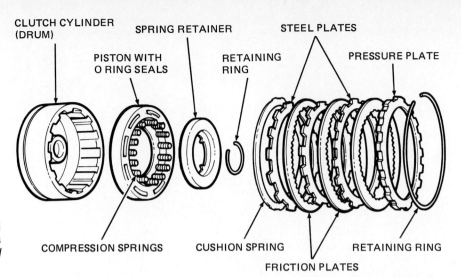

Fig. 34-19 A disassembled clutch, showing the steel plates and the friction plates. *(Ford Motor Company)*

CLUTCH CYLINDER (DRUM)

PISTON WITH O RING SEALS

SPRING RETAINER

RETAINING RING

STEEL PLATES

PRESSURE PLATE

COMPRESSION SPRINGS

CUSHION SPRING

RETAINING RING

FRICTION PLATES

side the drum (Fig. 34-16). Half of the disks, or *plates,* are splined to one member of the planetary gearset. The other half are splined to one of the other members. To engage the clutch, oil is directed into it through the oil line. This produces pressure behind the piston, pushing it to the left (in Fig. 34-16). The two sets of clutch plates are forced together by oil pressure. Now the pinion carrier (splined to one set of clutch plates) and the sun gear (splined to the other set) are locked together. The planetary gearset is in direct drive.

NOTE When the clutch is engaged, power flows *through* the clutch. However, power does *not* flow through the band when it is applied (☐ 34-9). The applied band only holds one member to prevent its rotation. Power flows through the other two members that are turning.

Figure 34-19 shows a disassembled clutch. The clutch plates are alternately splined to the drum and to the clutch hub. Compression springs prevent the clutch from engaging too quickly. When the oil pressure is released, the springs push the piston away from the clutch plates. This allows the two sets of plates to rotate independently of each other. Now the clutch is disengaged. Weak clutch springs cause the clutch to engage quickly and disengage slowly.

NOTE The arrangement shown in Fig. 34-16 and described above is only one of several arrangements used in automatic transmissions. In other transmissions, when the band is applied, it holds the internal gear or the pinion carrier stationary. Many transmissions lock different members together when the clutch is engaged. However, the principle is the same in all transmissions. In the planetary gearset (in a three-speed automatic transmission), there is speed reduction when the band is applied. There is direct drive when the clutch is engaged.

☐ 34-11 ACCUMULATORS

Sudden application of a band or engagement of a clutch would cause a rough shift. To prevent this, an *accumulator* is used in automatic trans-

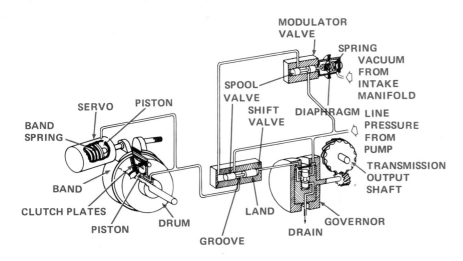

MODULATOR VALVE

SPRING

VACUUM FROM INTAKE MANIFOLD

SPOOL VALVE

SHIFT VALVE

DIAPHRAGM

LINE PRESSURE FROM PUMP

SERVO

PISTON

BAND SPRING

TRANSMISSION OUTPUT SHAFT

BAND

CLUTCH PLATES

PISTON

DRUM

LAND

GROOVE

DRAIN

GOVERNOR

Fig. 34-20 Schematic diagram showing one type of hydraulic control system that has been used to operate the band and clutch.

missions. The accumulator cushions the shock of clutch and servo operation. The result is a smooth but rapid clutch engagement or band application.

□ 34-12 HYDRAULIC CIRCUITS

Figure 34-20 is a simplified diagram of a hydraulic control circuit for a single planetary gearset in an automatic transmission. The major purpose of the hydraulic circuit is to apply and release a band, or to engage and disengage a clutch. By this action, the hydraulic circuit controls the shift from speed reduction to direct drive. The shift must take place at the right time. This depends on car speed and throttle opening, or engine load. These two factors produce two varying oil pressures that work against the two ends of the *shift valve*.

The shift valve (Fig. 34-20) is a *spool valve* inside a bore or hole in the valve body. A spool valve is a rod with indented or cutaway sections. It is used to control oil flow in automatic transmissions. The smaller diameter is called the *valve groove*. The larger diameters are called *valve lands*.

Pressure at one end of the shift valve comes from the *governor* (□ 34-13). This is known as *governor pressure*. Pressure at the other end of the shift valve changes as vacuum in the intake manifold changes. This is called *throttle pressure*.

□ 34-13 GOVERNOR ACTION

In the automatic transmission, the governor is a device that controls, or *governs*, gear shifting in relation to car speed. Governor pressure changes with car speed. This is because the governor is driven by the output shaft in the transmission (Fig. 34-21). As output-shaft speed and car speed go up, the governor pressure increases. This pressure works against one end of the shift valve, as shown in Fig. 34-20.

Governor pressure is a modified line pressure. An oil pump in the front of the transmission (Fig. 34-21) produces the line pressure. (Lugs on the converter hub engage the pump and drive it.) The oil then passes to the governor. As car speed increases, the governor spins faster. Centrifugal force acts on the governor valve. This causes the valve to open, allowing more pressure to pass through. The result is a modified pressure that changes with car speed pushing against the right end of the shift valve (in Fig. 34-20).

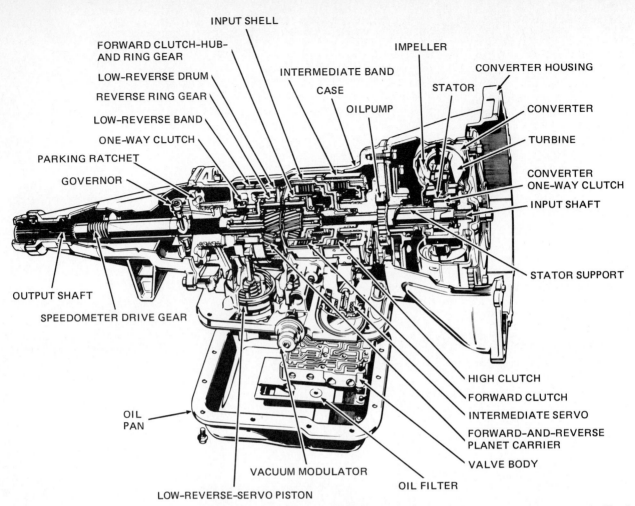

INPUT SHELL

FORWARD CLUTCH-HUB-
AND RING GEAR

LOW-REVERSE DRUM

REVERSE RING GEAR

LOW-REVERSE BAND

ONE-WAY CLUTCH

PARKING RATCHET

GOVERNOR

OUTPUT SHAFT

SPEEDOMETER DRIVE GEAR

INTERMEDIATE BAND

CASE

OILPUMP

IMPELLER

STATOR

CONVERTER HOUSING

CONVERTER

TURBINE

CONVERTER
ONE-WAY CLUTCH

INPUT SHAFT

STATOR SUPPORT

HIGH CLUTCH

FORWARD CLUTCH

INTERMEDIATE SERVO

FORWARD-AND-REVERSE
PLANET CARRIER

VALVE BODY

OIL
PAN

VACUUM MODULATOR

OIL FILTER

LOW-REVERSE-SERVO PISTON

Fig. 34-21 A complete automatic transmission with the major parts named. *(Ford Motor Company)*

□ *34-14 THROTTLE PRESSURE*

Working on the other end of the shift valve is a pressure that changes as intake-manifold vacuum changes. Line pressure enters the *modulator valve* at the upper right in Fig. 34-20. The modulator valve has a spool valve attached to a spring-loaded diaphragm. Vacuum increases in the intake manifold when the throttle valve is partly closed or when engine load decreases. This vacuum pulls the diaphragm and modulator valve to the right (in Fig. 34-20).

As the modulator valve moves to the right (in Fig. 34-20), it closes off the line-pressure passage from the pump. This reduces the oil pressure on the left end of the shift valve. Now governor pressure pushes the shift valve to the left. Line pressure passes through the shift valve to the servo and clutch for the planetary gearset. As the pressure acts on the servo and clutch, the band releases and the clutch engages. This upshifts the planetary gearset from speed reduction to direct drive.

□ *34-15 SHIFT ACTION*

When the planetary gearset changes from a lower-speed ratio to a higher-speed ratio, such as from speed reduction to direct drive, this is called an *upshift*. When the speed ratio through the planetary gearset is changed from a higher-speed to a lower-speed ratio, a *downshift* has taken place. In an automatic transmission, the hydraulic control system must control both the upshifts and the downshifts.

The reason for varying the pressure at the left end of the shift valve (in Fig. 34-20) is to change the upshift according to driving conditions. When the car is accelerating, high torque is needed. The gears should stay in low. Then, when cruising speed is reached, less torque is needed. As engine load is reduced, intake-manifold vacuum increases so that the upshift occurs.

If the driver again wants fast acceleration, the throttle is pushed to the floor. This reduces intake-manifold vacuum. The planetary gearset downshifts into speed reduction. This increases torque to the drive wheels.

□ 34-16 HYDRAULIC VALVES

The sections above provide a simplified description of how upshifts and downshifts are controlled in an automatic transmission. The actual valves are more complicated. For example, they have springs for proper positioning when oil pressure is not acting on them. There are other valves in the hydraulic control system, including valves to ease the shifts, regulate pressures, and time downshifts. There is also a *manual valve*. It moves as the driver moves the transmission selector lever to the desired driving range.

In the automatic transmission, the hydraulic valves are contained in a main-control assembly called the *valve body* (Fig. 34-21). It directs fluid under pressure to the torque converter, band servos, clutches, and governor to control transmission operation. The valve body is a complicated casting. It contains a complex pattern of fluid passages and several bores containing multiple-land spool valves. Each passage, bore, and valve forms a specific oil circuit with a specific function.

□ 34-17 AUTOMATIC-TRANSMISSION FLUID (ATF)

The automatic transmission must be filled to the proper level with automatic-transmission fluid (ATF). The fluid used in an automatic transmission is a special oil. The oil has had several additives added to it, such as viscosity-index improvers, oxidation and corrosion inhibitors, extreme-pressure and antifoam agents, detergents, dispersants, friction modifiers, pour-point depressants, and fluidity modifiers. The oil usually is dyed red. If leakage occurs, you can easily tell whether it is engine oil or transmission fluid.

There are several types of automatic-transmission fluid. This is because various models of automatic transmission have different requirements for the lubricating oil. Most automotive automatic transmissions require either type F or Dexron II automatic-transmission fluid.

□ 34-18 FORD C6 AUTOMATIC TRANSMISSION

Most automatic transmissions provide three forward speeds, one reverse, neutral, and park. All have torque converters. The Ford C6 transmission has been used in many models of cars for many years. This transmission is shown cut away in Fig. 34-22. The complete hydraulic system for the Ford C6 is shown in Fig. 34-23. The operation of the Ford C6 transmission is described below.

1. THE MANUAL SHIFT VALVE

The action starts at the manual shift valve, shown at the bottom in Fig. 36-22. After starting the engine, the driver moves the selector lever on the steering column or console to the driving range desired. The driver can put the selector lever in R, or reverse, to back up the car. Or the driver can put it in D, or drive, for normal operation. In D the transmission will automatically upshift from first to second to third. If the driver does not want the transmission to shift up to third, the driver can move the selector lever to 2 or 1. In 2 the transmission will remain in second. In 1 the transmission will remain in first. The driver may need 1 or 2 for slowing down while descending a long hill.

2. UPSHIFTING

Let's assume the driver selects D. Starting out, the transmission is in first. Then, as car speed increases, the shifts are made from low to second and from second to third. Shift points are determined by car speed and manifold vacuum.

3. FIRST GEAR

In first gear, the forward clutch is engaged. This locks the front planetary ring gear to the input shaft, so they turn together. As the ring gear rotates, it drives the planet pinions. They, in turn, drive the sun gear. This

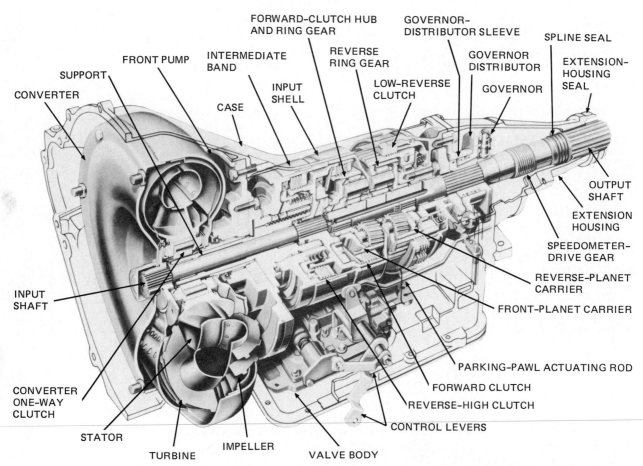

Fig. 34-22 A Ford C6 automatic transmission. *(Ford Motor Company)*

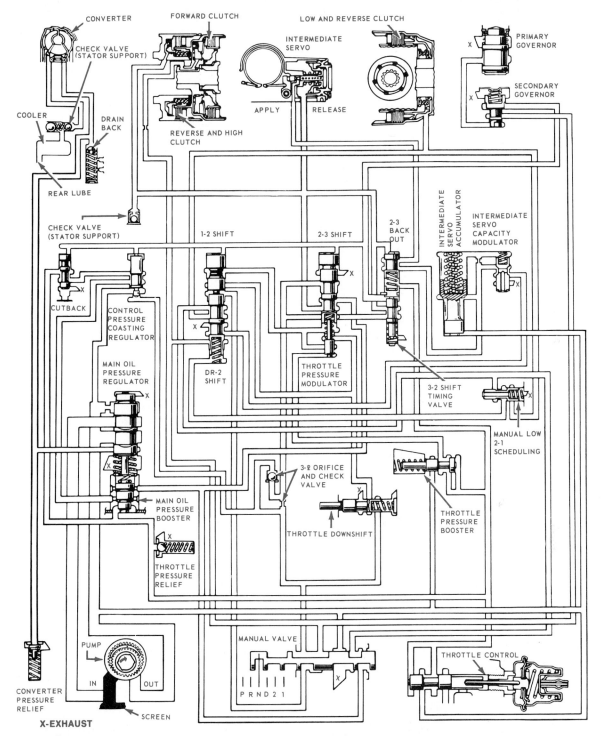

Fig. 34-23 The complete hydraulic system of the Ford C6 automatic transmission. *(Ford Motor Company)*

produces a gear reduction through the front planetary gearset. As the sun gear turns, it drives the rear planet pinions. They drive the ring gear of the rear planetary gearset. The ring gear is splined to the output shaft, so it turns. There also is gear reduction in the rear planetary gearset. With gear reduction in both sets, the transmission is in low, or first, gear.

4. SECOND GEAR

When the upshift to second gear takes place, the hydraulic system applies the intermediate band. It holds the sun gear and the reverse-and-third clutch drum stationary. Now there is gear reduction in the front gear set only. The transmission is in second.

5. THIRD GEAR, OR DIRECT DRIVE

When the hydraulic system produces the shift into third, both the forward clutch and the reverse-and-third clutch are engaged. This locks the planetary gearsets so that there is direct drive through both. The transmission is in third gear.

6. REVERSE

In reverse, the reverse-and-third clutch and the low-and-reverse clutch are both engaged. This condition causes gear reduction through both planetary gearsets. Also, the direction of rotation is reversed in the rear set.

☐ 34-19 OTHER AUTOMATIC TRANSMISSIONS

A variety of automatic transmissions is used in automobiles. However, they all work in about the same way. All have planetary gearsets that are controlled by bands and clutches.

AUTOMATIC TRANSAXLES

☐ 34-20 PURPOSE OF AUTOMATIC TRANSAXLES

The transaxle is used with engines mounted transversely at the front of the car (Fig. 1-7). The transaxle is also used in rear-engine cars with rear-wheel drive. Figure 34-2 shows the major components of an automatic transaxle with the engine crankshaft and drive train. The major difference between an automatic transaxle and a manual transaxle (Chap. 33) is that the automatic transaxle uses an automatic transmission instead of a manual transmission converter. However, the automatic transmission works the same, as described earlier in this chapter.

☐ 34-21 CHRYSLER AUTOMATIC TRANSAXLE

Figure 34-24 shows the automatic transaxle and drive train for a front-wheel-drive car built by Chrysler. The transmission section of the transaxle uses the Chrysler TorqueFlite automatic transmission. The complete Chrysler TorqueFlite transaxle is shown in sectional view in Fig. 34-25. Construction and operation of the differential is described in Chap. 36.

The Chrysler TorqueFlite transaxle includes a differential and two couplings for the drive shafts to the two front wheels. It also includes the TorqueFlite automatic transmission, adapted to fit into the transaxle case.

The automatic transmission in the transaxle has two multiple-disk clutches, two bands with servos, an overrunning clutch, and a Simpson type of planetary gearset. These units, and their operation, were described earlier in this chapter. A gear on the end of the output shaft is meshed with a gear on the end of the transfer shaft. The transfer shaft carries the governor. The other end of the transfer shaft, next to the torque converter, has a pinion gear that meshes with the ring gear of the differential. The differential takes care of any difference in rotational speed of the two front wheels when the car makes a turn (Chap. 36).

☐ 34-22 TORQUEFLITE TRANSAXLE OPERATION

The driver moves the selector lever to the desired operating range. This moves the manual valve, through linkage, to the proper operating position. Then car speed and throttle-valve position take over to produce the shift pattern that has been selected. The governor and throttle position control the hydraulic system so that upshifts or downshifts are made according to operating conditions.

AUTOMATIC TRANSMISSION AND TRANSAXLE SERVICE

☐ 34-23 SERVICING THE AUTOMATIC TRANSMISSION

Special training and special tools are needed to diagnose and correct all automatic-transmission troubles successfully. Essential tools you need

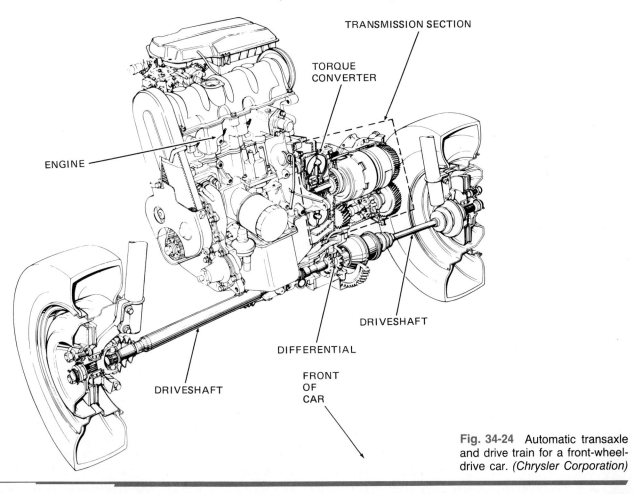

Fig. 34-24 Automatic transaxle and drive train for a front-wheel-drive car. (Chrysler Corporation)

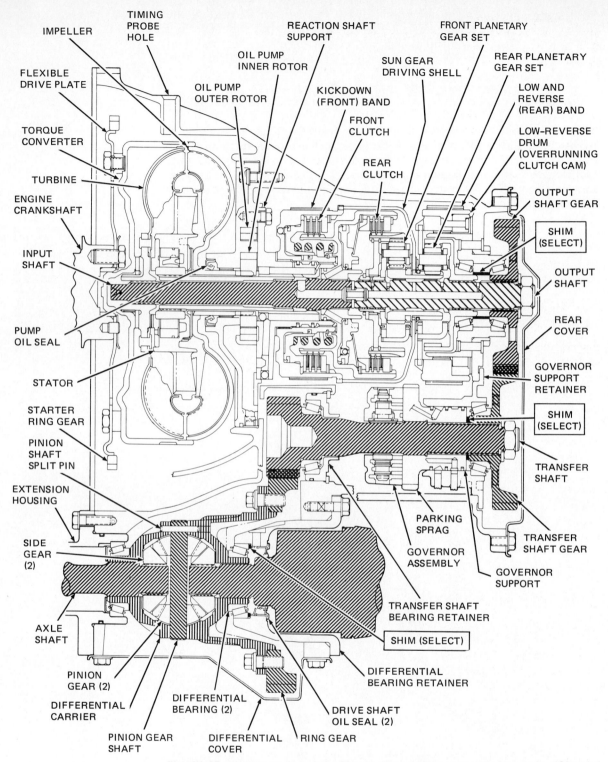

Fig. 34-25 Sectional view of the Chrysler TorqueFlite automatic transaxle. *(Chrysler Corporation)*

are a tachometer, a vacuum gauge, and an oil-pressure gauge (Chap. 27).

However, there are many services that you can perform on automatic transmissions. These services include:

- Linkage adjustment
- Checking and adjusting fluid level in the transmission
- Draining old fluid
- Cleaning screens and filters
- Adjusting bands

Bands are adjusted by tightening and then loosening the adjusting screw (Fig. 34-18) a specified number of turns. However, procedures vary from one transmission to another.

Some manufacturers recommend draining the fluid and putting in fresh fluid at periodic intervals. Other manufacturers do not recommend this service. Before attempting any of the above services on an automatic transmission, refer to the manufacturer's service manual that covers the transmission you are servicing.

CHAPTER 34
REVIEW QUESTIONS

Select the *one* correct, best, or most probable answer to each question. Then check your answers against the correct answers given at the end of the book.

1. In the automatic transmission, a band is applied by
   a. an accumulator
   b. a clutch
   c. a servo
   d. a governor

2. The device in an automatic transmission that is used most often to obtain direct drive is
   a. an accumulator
   b. a clutch
   c. a servo
   d. a governor

3. The governor is driven by the
   a. stator clutch
   b. transmission input shaft
   c. engine crankshaft
   d. transmission output shaft

4. A car will not move in any selector lever position. The probable cause is
   a. a converter clutch that will not disengage
   b. a stator clutch that will not disengage
   c. low fluid level
   d. an overfilled transmission

5. When the torque converter is installed, lugs on the converter hub must engage the
   a. oil pump
   b. stator
   c. impeller
   d. one-way clutch

CHAPTER 35
DRIVE LINES

After studying this chapter, you should be able to:

1. Explain the function of drive lines.

2. Name the two types of joints in a drive line and explain the purpose, construction, and operation of each.

3. Describe the differences between the drive lines for rear-drive cars and those for front-drive cars.

4. Identify and name the parts of disassembled drive lines.

5. List the three jobs that the inner universal joint on a drive shaft for a front-drive car must perform.

Drive lines are also called *drive shafts* and, sometimes, *propeller shafts.* They carry the engine power from the transmission to the car wheels. The two most widely used arrangements are:

- Engine mounted at the front of the car with a long shaft to the rear to drive the rear wheels
- Engine mounted at the front of the car with two short shafts, usually called the *drive axles,* to drive the front wheels

This chapter describes the drive mechanisms used with these two basic arrangements. There are other arrangements such as four-wheel drive using a transfer case (Chap. 37) and rear-wheel drive with a rear-mounted engine.

FRONT-MOUNTED ENGINE WITH REAR WHEELS DRIVEN

☐ 35-1 CONSTRUCTION OF DRIVE SHAFTS

The drive shaft connects the transmission output shaft to the differential at the wheel axles (Fig. 35-1). The transmission and the engine are more or less rigidly attached to the car frame. The rear wheels are attached to the car frame by springs. They allow the rear wheels to move up and down. As a result, the following conditions occur:

- The drive line must change length as the wheels move up and down.
- The angle of drive must change as the wheels move up and down.

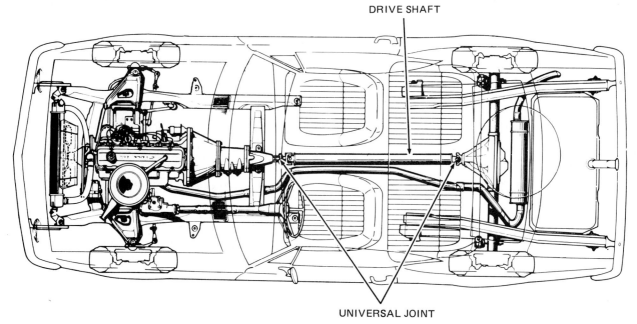

DRIVE SHAFT

UNIVERSAL JOINT

Fig. 35-1 Location of the drive line in the power train of a car with a front-mounted engine and rear-wheel drive.

Figure 35-2 shows how the length of the drive line and the angle of drive change as the wheels move up and down. In the top illustration, the wheels and differential are in the up position. The drive angle is small. Also, the drive line is at its maximum length. In the bottom illustration, the differential and wheels are in the down position. This is their position when the wheels drop into a depression in the road. In this position, the drive angle is increased. Also, the drive-line length is reduced, because as the rear wheels and differential swing down, they also move forward. The rear wheels and differential must move this way because they are attached to the springs.

Most drive shafts are hollow tubes, with two or more *universal joints* and a *slip joint*. (These are described in following sections.) Figure 35-3 shows a one-piece drive shaft. Some drive shafts are the two-piece type with a support bearing at the center (Fig. 35-4).

☐ 35-2 UNIVERSAL JOINTS

The universal joint allows driving power to be carried through two shafts that are at an angle to each other. Figure 35-5 shows a simple universal joint. It is a double-hinged joint, consisting of two Y-shaped yokes and a

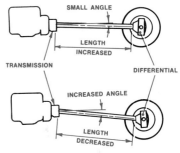

SMALL ANGLE

LENGTH INCREASED

TRANSMISSION   DIFFERENTIAL

INCREASED ANGLE

LENGTH DECREASED

Fig. 35-2 As the rear-axle housing, with differential and wheels, moves up and down, the angle and the distance between the axle housing and the transmission changes. The reason the drive shaft shortens as the angle increases is that the axle housing and differential move in a shorter arc than the drive shaft.

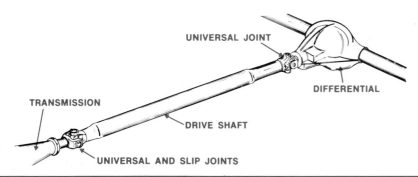

UNIVERSAL JOINT

DIFFERENTIAL

TRANSMISSION

DRIVE SHAFT

UNIVERSAL AND SLIP JOINTS

Fig. 35-3 The drive shaft connects the transmission with the differential. This is a one-piece drive shaft with two universal joints and one slip joint.

519

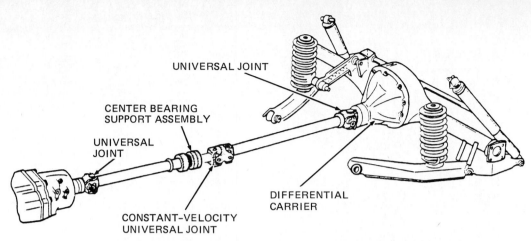

UNIVERSAL JOINT

CENTER BEARING
SUPPORT ASSEMBLY

UNIVERSAL
JOINT

CONSTANT-VELOCITY
UNIVERSAL JOINT

DIFFERENTIAL
CARRIER

Fig. 35-4 Two-piece drive shaft that uses three universal joints. The front-shaft section is supported at its rear by a bearing. A constant-velocity universal joint is located in back of the bearing. (*Buick Motor Division of General Motors Corporation*)

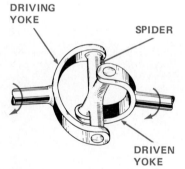

DRIVING
YOKE

SPIDER

DRIVEN
YOKE

Fig. 35-5 A simple universal joint.

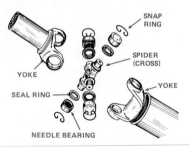

SNAP
RING

SPIDER
(CROSS)

YOKE

YOKE

SEAL RING

NEEDLE BEARING

Fig. 35-6 A disassembled cross-and-two-yoke universal joint.

cross-shaped member. The cross-shaped member is called the "spider." The four arms of the spider are assembled into bearings in the ends of the two yokes.

In operation, the driving shaft causes one of the yokes to rotate. This causes the spider to rotate. The spider then causes the driven yoke and shaft to rotate. When the driving and driven shafts are at an angle, the yokes swing around in the bearings on the ends of the spider arms.

A cross-and-two-yoke universal joint is shown in Fig. 35-6. It is almost the same as the simple universal joint shown in Fig. 35-5. However, the four bearings on the ends of the spider arms are needle bearings.

With the cross-and-two-yoke universal joint, there is a change in speed when the drive shaft and the driven shaft are at an angle to each other. The change in speed occurs because the driven yoke and driven shaft speed up and then slow down twice with every revolution of the drive line. The greater the angle between the drive and driven shafts, the greater the speed-up-and-slow-down action. This type of action causes increased wear of the universal joint. To eliminate the speed-up-and-slow-down action, *constant-velocity universal joints* are used on many cars.

☐ 35-3 CONSTANT-VELOCITY UNIVERSAL JOINTS

A constant-velocity (CV) universal joint is shown in Figs. 35-4 and 35-7. It consists of two universal joints linked by a ball and socket. The ball and socket splits the angle of the drive and driven shafts between the two universal joints of the constant-velocity unit. Because the two universal joints operate at the same angle, the speed-up-and-slow-down action is canceled out. The speedup resulting at any instant from the action of one universal joint is canceled out by the slowdown of the other. Therefore no speed change occurs between the two shafts connected to a constant-velocity universal joint.

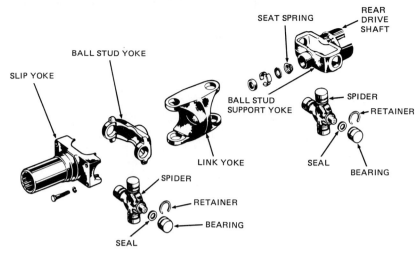

Fig. 35-7   A constant-velocity universal joint.

□ 35-4 SLIP JOINTS

Any change in drive-line length is taken care of by a slip joint (Fig. 35-8). It consists of external splines on the end of one shaft and matching internal splines on the mating hollow shaft. The splines cause the two shafts to rotate together but permit the two to slip back and forth inside the hollow shaft. This movement allows the effective length of the drive shaft to change as the wheels move up and down.

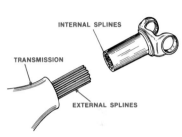

Fig. 35-8   The slip joint uses matching internal and external splines.

FRONT-MOUNTED ENGINE WITH FRONT WHEELS DRIVEN

□ 35-5 DRIVE SHAFTS FOR FRONT-WHEEL DRIVE

Front-wheel drive is becoming more popular. With it, the long drive shaft to the rear axle is eliminated. This also eliminates the tunnel in the floor of the car required for the drive shaft. Front-wheel drive is widely used on smaller cars. Figure 35-9 shows the drive train layout used in most small front-drive cars. Some large cars also have front drive.

Driving the front wheels makes the front suspension more complicated (Chap. 40). The front wheels must swing from side to side so that the car can be steered. Also, they must be supported in such a way that they can be driven. This requires universal joints in both front-wheel drive shafts. These are constant-velocity universal joints designed to drive the wheels even though they are turned many degrees from straight ahead.

Figure 35-9 shows the drive shafts and universal joints in a front-drive car. The inner ends of the two drive shafts are connected to the transaxle. Figure 35-10 shows a similar front-wheel-drive car raised on a lift to show the layout and construction. Each drive shaft has universal joints and slip joints covered by boots. Figure 35-11 shows how the drive-

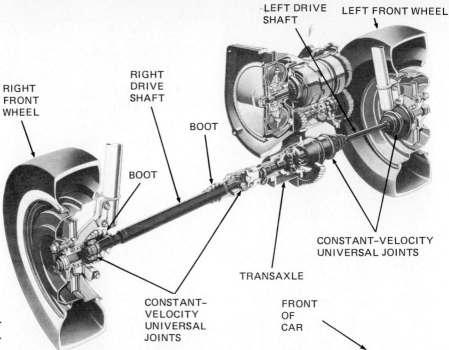

RIGHT
FRONT
WHEEL

RIGHT
DRIVE
SHAFT

LEFT DRIVE
SHAFT

LEFT FRONT WHEEL

BOOT

BOOT

CONSTANT-VELOCITY
UNIVERSAL JOINTS

TRANSAXLE

CONSTANT-
VELOCITY
UNIVERSAL
JOINTS

FRONT
OF
CAR

Fig. 35-9 Drive shafts and universal joints in a front-drive car. (*Chrysler Corporation*)

shafts are connected to the transaxle. Figure 35-12 shows the construction of a drive shaft for a front-wheel-drive car. Figure 35-13 shows how splines on the outer-housing shaft mesh with splines in the hub to drive the wheel.

Typically, two different types of universal joints are used on each driveshaft. They carry engine power from the transaxle through the

Fig. 35-10 Front-wheel-drive car raised on a lift so that the driveshafts can be seen. (*Chrysler Corporation*)

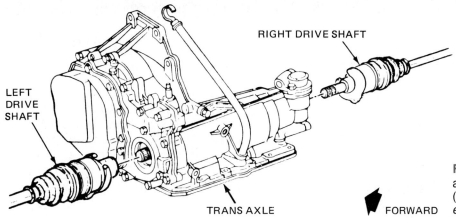

RIGHT DRIVE SHAFT

LEFT DRIVE SHAFT

TRANS AXLE

FORWARD

Fig. 35-11 How the drive shafts are connected to the transaxle. (*Chevrolet Motor Division of General Motors Corporation*)

driveshafts to the wheel hubs. The universal joints also permit the length of each driveshaft assembly to change. The construction of the inboard universal joint serves as a slip joint (□ 35-7).

□ 35-6 OUTBOARD CV UNIVERSAL JOINT

Figure 35-12 shows the type of constant-velocity universal joint used at the outboard, or wheel, position on many front-wheel-drive cars. It includes an outer race, cage, inner race, and balls. The outer race has a splined shaft that enters the wheel hub (Fig. 35-13). The balls roll in curved grooves in the outer race. The inner race has grooves that match the grooves in the outer race. When the universal joint is transmitting torque at an angle, the balls roll in their grooves to accommodate the drive angle.

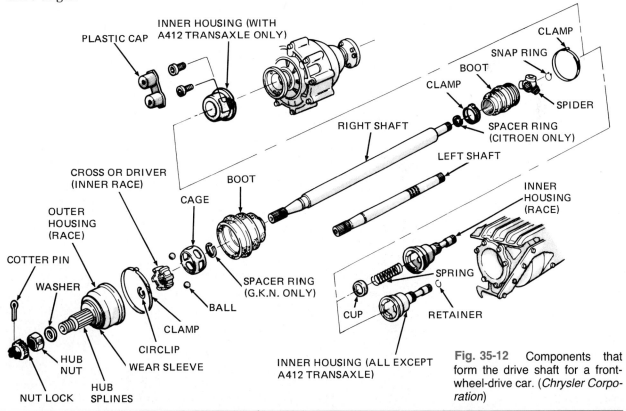

PLASTIC CAP
INNER HOUSING (WITH A412 TRANSAXLE ONLY)
CLAMP
SNAP RING
BOOT
CLAMP
SPIDER
RIGHT SHAFT
SPACER RING (CITROEN ONLY)
LEFT SHAFT
CROSS OR DRIVER (INNER RACE)
BOOT
CAGE
INNER HOUSING (RACE)
OUTER HOUSING (RACE)
COTTER PIN
WASHER
SPACER RING (G.K.N. ONLY)
BALL
SPRING
HUB NUT
CLAMP
CUP
RETAINER
CIRCLIP
NUT LOCK
WEAR SLEEVE
HUB SPLINES
INNER HOUSING (ALL EXCEPT A412 TRANSAXLE)

Fig. 35-12 Components that form the drive shaft for a front-wheel-drive car. (*Chrysler Corporation*)

☐ 35-7 INBOARD CV UNIVERSAL JOINTS

Several types of universal joints are used on the inner ends of the driveshafts in front-wheel-drive cars. Tri-pot, double-offset, and cross-groove are used as inboard joints. A tri-pot type of constant-velocity universal joint is shown in Fig. 35-9. It is shown disassembled at the right, or inner, end of the drive shaft in Fig. 35-12. A spider, or *trunnion,* is splined to the inboard end of the drive shaft. The spider has three balls, or rollers, spaced equally around it. These fit into grooves in the inner housing, which is splined to the transaxle assembly. The balls on the spider roll in and out to change the effective length of the drive shaft. At the same time, the design of the joint allows the drive angle to change.

OTHER DRIVE LINES

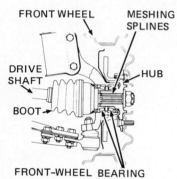

Fig. 35-13 Splines on the outer-housing shaft mesh with splines in the hub to drive the wheel. (*Chrysler Corporation*)

☐ 35-8 REAR DRIVE WITH REAR-MOUNTED ENGINE

Some cars have the engine mounted at the rear. In these cars, short drive shafts carry the engine power to the rear wheels. Each drive shaft has universal joints and slip joints. Some models of Volkswagen use this type of rear drive (Fig. 35-14).

☐ 35-9 FOUR-WHEEL DRIVE

Some vehicles, especially those that are used off the road, can drive all four wheels. The driver may select two-wheel or four-wheel drive. In some four-wheel-drive vehicles, engagement and disengagement of the front axles are automatic. This is called "full-time" four-wheel drive. Each drive shaft to the front and rear axles has universal joints and slip joints. Chapter 37 covers this arrangement.

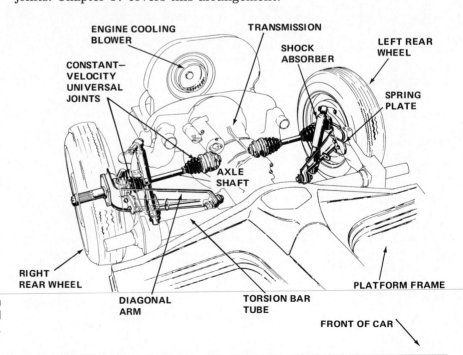

Fig. 35-14 Some Volkswagen models have a rear-mounted engine and rear-wheel drive. (*Volkswagen of America, Inc.*)

□ 35-10 SERVICING THE UNIVERSAL JOINT AND DRIVE SHAFT

Universal joints and drive shafts usually require no service. Most universal joints are prelubricated and do not need additional lubrication. However, in case of wear or damage, the universal joints may be replaced. Refer to the manufacturer's shop manual to determine the proper servicing and replacement procedures.

CHAPTER 35
REVIEW QUESTIONS

Select the *one* correct, best, or most probable answer to each question. Then check your answers against the correct answers given at the end of the book.

1. How many universal joints are used in the drive shafts for a car with a transaxle?
   a. two
   b. three
   c. four
   d. five

2. The drive shaft must have two types of joints. These joints are
   a. U and universal
   b. transmission and differential
   c. slip and spline
   d. universal and slip

3. In a car with front-wheel drive, the inner universal joint must
   a. accommodate a change of drive angle
   b. change effective length of the drive shaft
   c. act as a constant-velocity joint
   d. all of the above

4. In a slip joint, the slipping may occur between
   a. splines
   b. balls and trunnion
   c. balls and grooves
   d. all of the above

5. Universal joints and drive shafts usually require
   a. servicing every 6 months or 6000 miles [10,000 km]
   b. no service
   c. annual service
   d. none of the above

CHAPTER 36
DIFFERENTIALS

After studying this chapter, you should be able to:
1. Explain the construction and operation of a differential.
2. Identify the parts of a disassembled differential.
3. Describe the operation of a limited-slip differential.
4. Discuss differential troubles and their possible causes.

The differential is placed between the drive-wheel axles. Its purpose is to allow the driven wheels to turn at different speeds. If the two wheels were rigidly connected to the same shaft, the wheels would have to skid during a turn. This would greatly shorten the life of the tires. The differential allows each wheel to turn at a different speed while continuing to deliver power to both wheels.

□ 36-1 DIFFERENTIAL APPLICATIONS

Differentials are used at the rear of vehicles with rear-wheel drive. They are used at the front in the transaxles of vehicles with front-wheel drive. In addition, they are used in transfer cases (Chap. 37). The basic differential described in this chapter is located between the two drive wheels (Fig. 36-1). It is connected to the transmission through the drive shaft. All differentials operate in the same way.

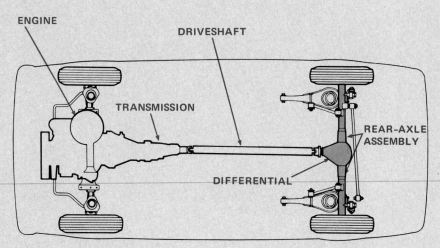

Fig. 36-1 Location of the differential in the power train of a front-wheel-drive car. (*Mazda Motors of America, Inc.*)

NOTE Manufacturers' service manuals usually refer to the differential located in the rear as the *rear axle,* or *rear-axle assembly.* By this, they mean the rear-axle housing, the wheel axles, and the differential. In this book, the term *differential* is used to designate the differential assembly itself.

□ 36-2 PURPOSE OF THE DIFFERENTIAL

When the car rounds a turn, the outer wheel must travel farther than the inner wheel. For example, suppose a rear-drive car makes a left turn, as shown in Fig. 36-2. The inner rear wheel, turning on a 20-foot [6.1-m] radius, travels 31 feet [9.4 m] during the 90 degree turn. The outer rear wheel, being nearly 5 feet [1.5 m] from the inner wheel, turns on a 24⅔-foot [7.5-m] radius (in the car shown), and it travels 39 feet [11.9 m].

If the drive shaft were geared rigidly to both rear wheels, each wheel would have to skid an average of 4 feet [1.2 m] to make the turn. Doing this, the tires would not last very long. Also, what is worse is that the car would be difficult to control during turns. The job of the differential is to avoid these problems. The differential allows one drive wheel to turn faster than the other when the car goes around a curve.

The differential performs the same job in a front-wheel-drive car (Fig. 36-3). When rounding a curve, the outer front wheel must travel farther than the inner front wheel.

Also, in some four-wheel-drive vehicles (Chap. 37), the transfer case has a differential. This differential compensates for any difference in front-wheel and rear-wheel travel in some operating modes. These vehicles also have a differential in the front-drive axle and in the rear-drive axle.

□ 36-3 CONSTRUCTION OF THE DIFFERENTIAL

Figure 36-4 shows the construction of a rear-axle-and-differential assembly. The two drive wheels are mounted on axles. On the inner ends of the axles are bevel gears, which are called *differential side gears,* or *axle*

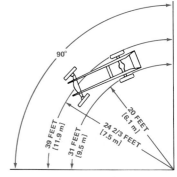

Fig. 36-2 The difference in rear-wheel travel as the car makes a 90 degree turn with the inner wheel turning on a 20-foot [6.1-m] radius.

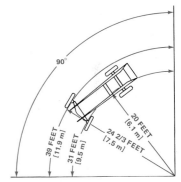

Fig. 36-3 The difference in front-wheel travel with the inner wheel turning on a 20-foot [6.1-m] radius. (*ATW*)

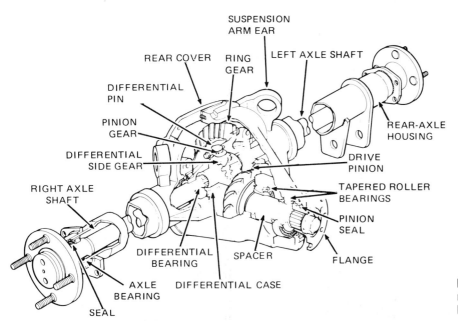

Fig. 36-4 Construction of a rear-axle-and-differential assembly. (*Ford Motor Company*)

527

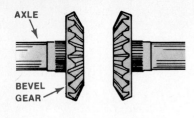

Fig. 36-5 Inner ends of the axle shafts with bevel gears (differential side gears) installed on them.

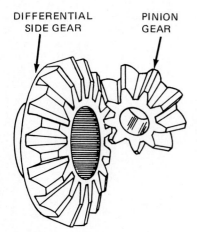

Fig. 36-6 Two meshing bevel gears.

gears (Fig. 36-5). The teeth on bevel gears are cut at an angle. When two bevel gears are put together so that their teeth mesh, one shaft can be driven by the shaft that is at a 90 degree angle (Fig. 36-6).

Figure 36-7 shows the main parts of a differential in exploded view. To build up a differential, the differential case is added to the two wheel axles and differential side gears shown in Fig. 36-8. The differential case has bearings that permit it to rotate on the two axles. Next, the two pinion gears and the supporting pinion shaft are added (Fig. 36-9). The shaft fits into the differential case. The two pinion gears are meshed with the differential side gears.

NOTE *Pinion gear* is the name given to the smallest gear in a gear set.

Now the ring gear (Fig. 36-10) is added by bolting it to the flange on the differential case. Finally, the drive pinion (Fig. 36-11) is added, which is meshed with the ring gear and attached to the end of the drive shaft. When the drive shaft rotates (Fig. 36-12), the drive pinion turns. This rotates the ring gear.

☐ *36-4 OPERATION OF THE DIFFERENTIAL*

When the car is on a straight road, the ring gear, differential case, differential pinion gears, and two differential side gears all turn as a unit without any relative motion. The two differential pinion gears do not rotate on the pinion shaft. This is because they exert equal force on the two side gears. As a result, the side gears turn at the same speed as the ring gear, which causes both drive wheels to turn at the same speed also.

However, when the car begins to round a curve, the differential pinion gears rotate on the pinion shaft. This permits the outer wheel to turn

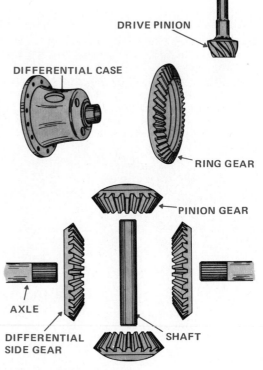

Fig. 36-7 Basic parts of a differential.

faster than the inner wheel (Fig. 36-2). Suppose one wheel turns slower than the other as the car rounds a curve. As the differential case rotates, the pinion gears must rotate on their shaft. The reason for this is that the pinion gear must "walk around" the slower-turning differential side gear. Therefore, the pinion gears carry additional rotary motion to the faster-turning outer wheel on the turn. The action is shown in Fig. 36-13. The differential-case speed is considered to be 100 percent. The rotating action of the pinion gears carries 90 percent of this speed to the slower-rotating inner wheel. They send 110 percent of the speed to the faster-rotating outer wheel. This is how the differential allows one drive wheel to turn faster than the other. Whenever the car goes around a turn, the outer drive wheel travels a greater distance than the inner drive wheel. Then the two pinion gears rotate on their shaft and drive the outer wheel faster.

□ 36-5 FINAL DRIVE, OR AXLE RATIO

The ring gear and pinion form the *final drive*, or drive *axle ratio*, through the power train. The ring gear usually has about 3 to 4 times as many teeth as the pinion. Therefore, three or four revolutions of the pinion will be required to turn the ring gear (and car wheels) once. This provides a 3 : 1 or 4 : 1 final drive or axle ratio.

□ 36-6 HYPOID GEARS

In cars with a front-mounted engine and rear-wheel drive, the ring gear and drive pinion are *hypoid gears*. This is a type of gear that is cut in a spiral form (Fig. 36-12). Then the pinion can be set below the center line of the ring gear so that the car floor can be lower.

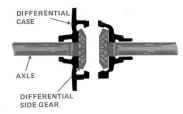

Fig. 36-8 Adding the differential case to the inner ends of the axle shafts.

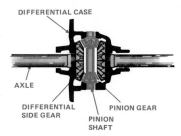

Fig. 36-9 Adding the two pinion gears and pinion shaft to the differential case.

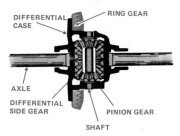

Fig. 36-10 Adding the ring gear to the differential case.

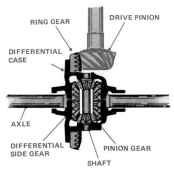

Fig. 36-11 Adding the drive pinion completes the basic differential. The drive pinion, or pinion gear, is meshed with the ring gear.

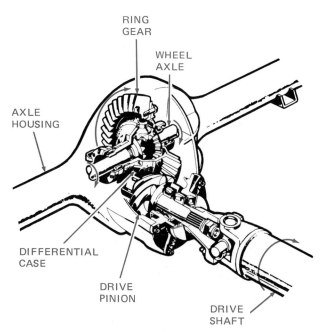

Fig. 36-12 The pinion gear is connected to the end of the drive shaft. When the drive shaft rotates, it turns the ring gear which turns the wheel axles. (*Ford Motor Company*)

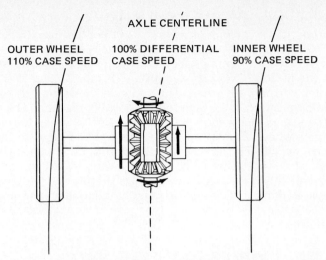

OUTER WHEEL
110% CASE SPEED

AXLE CENTERLINE

100% DIFFERENTIAL
CASE SPEED

INNER WHEEL
90% CASE SPEED

Fig. 36-13 Differential action on turns. (*Chevrolet Motor Division of General Motors Corporation*)

☐ *36-7 DIFFERENTIALS IN TRANSAXLES*

Together with the transmission, the differential assembly is an integral part of the transaxle (Fig. 36-14). The differential performs the same job in the transaxle as in the rear axle described earlier. The differential transfers power from the transmission to the drive wheels through axle

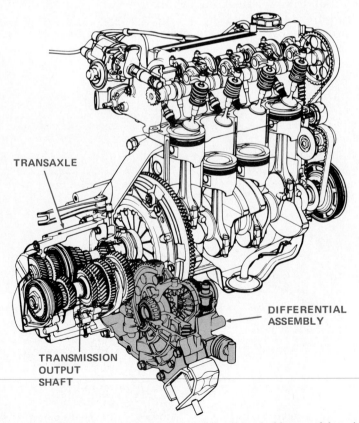

TRANSAXLE

DIFFERENTIAL
ASSEMBLY

TRANSMISSION
OUTPUT
SHAFT

Fig. 36-14 The differential is part of the transaxle. (*Mazda Motors of America, Inc.*)

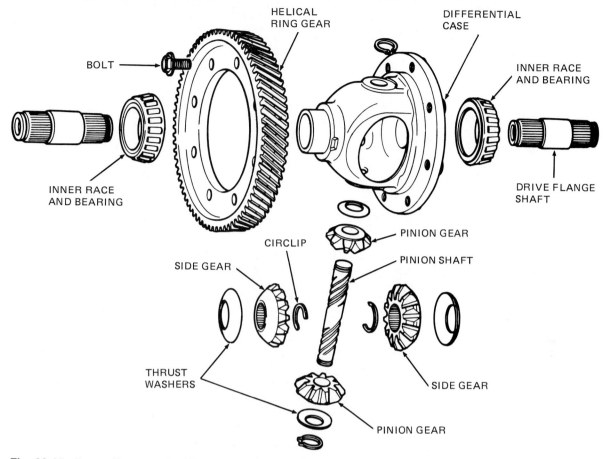

Fig. 36-15 Parts of a transaxle differential assembly. The ring gear has helical-cut teeth. (*Chrysler Corporation*)

shafts. The major difference is in the gear set through which power is transferred. The ring gear and drive pinion are usually *helical-cut gears* (Fig. 36-15).

The construction of the differential is basically the same as described in □ 36-3. The differential has two pinion gears meshing with side gears. Power is transmitted to the differential through a transfer gear on the transmission output shaft (Fig. 36-14). The transfer gear performs the same job as the drive pinion, or pinion gear, in the rear-axle differential.

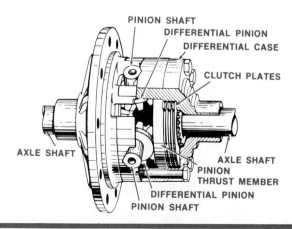

Fig. 36-16 A limited-slip differential. (*Chrysler Corporation*)

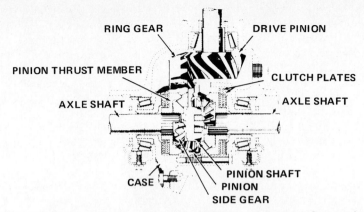

Fig. 36-17 Sectional view of a limited-slip differential. (*Chrysler Corporation*)

□ 36-8 LIMITED-SLIP DIFFERENTIALS

In operation, the differential delivers the same amount of torque to each drive wheel when both wheels have equal traction (□ 36-4). When one wheel has less traction than the other—for example, when one wheel is spinning on ice—the other wheel cannot deliver torque. All the turning effort goes to the spinning wheel. To provide traction to both drive wheels, many cars have a *limited-slip differential*. This type of differential delivers maximum torque to the wheel with maximum traction. In the standard differential, maximum torque is delivered to the wheel with minimum traction.

One type of limited-slip differential is shown in Fig. 36-16. It has two sets of clutch plates. Also, the ends of the pinion-gear shafts lie rather loosely in notches in the two halves of the differential case. Figure 36-17 is a sectional view of the limited-slip differential. During normal straight-ahead driving, the power flow is as shown in Fig. 36-18.

The rotating differential case carries the pinion-gear shafts around with it. Since there is considerable side thrust, the pinion shafts tend to

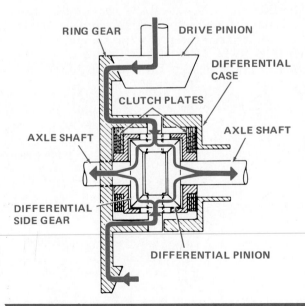

Fig. 36-18 Power flow through a limited-slip differential on a straightaway. (*Chrysler Corporation*)

slide up the sides of the notches in the two halves of the differential case. As the pinion shafts slide up, they are forced outward. This force is carried through the pinion thrust members to the two sets of clutch plates. The clutch plates lock the axle shafts to the differential case. Therefore both wheels turn.

If one wheel spins on ice or tends to slip, the force is released on the clutch plates feeding power to that wheel. The torque is sent to the other wheel. This prevents the wheel on the ice from slipping.

During normal driving, if the car rounds a curve, force is released on the clutch for the inner wheel just enough to permit some slipping (Fig. 36-19). This release of force permits the outer wheel to turn faster than the inner wheel.

Two types of limited-slip differentials are used in late-model cars. Figure 36-20 shows one type that has spring-loaded clutch plates. Figure 36-21 shows a limited-slip differential using spring-loaded clutch cones. The action is the same as in the limited-slip differential described above. The difference is that the plates or cones are preloaded with springs to give a more positive action.

☐ 36-9 DIFFERENTIAL TROUBLE DIAGNOSIS

The first indication of differential trouble is noise. The kind of noise you hear can help you determine what is causing the trouble. However, be sure that the noise actually is coming from the differential. It is sometimes possible to be fooled by universal-joint, wheel-bearing, or tire noise. Note whether the noise is a hum, a growl, or a knock. Note whether the noise is produced when the car is operating on a straight road or only on turns. Note whether the noise is more noticeable when the engine is driving the car or when the car is coasting. Usually, a meaningful test for differential noise cannot be made by running the car with the drive wheels raised off the ground.

1. HUMMING

A humming noise if often caused by incorrect internal adjustment of the drive pinion or the ring gear (Fig. 36-22). Incorrect adjustment prevents normal tooth contact and can cause rapid tooth wear and early failure of

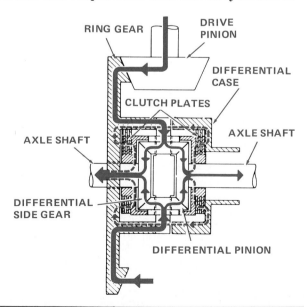

Fig. 36-19 Power flow through a limited-slip differential when rounding a turn. Heavy arrows show greater torque to the left axle shaft. (*Chrysler Corporation*)

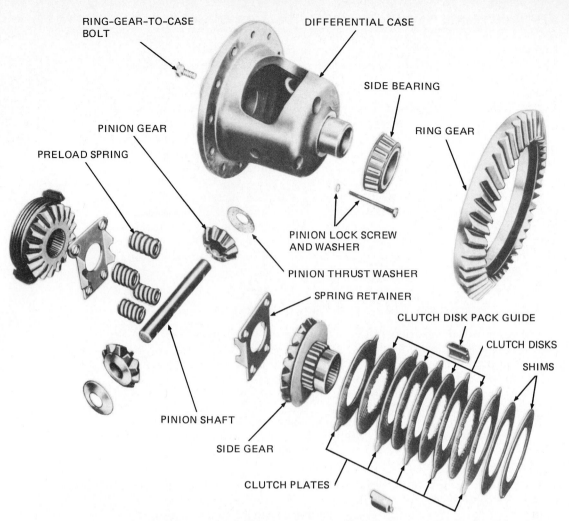

RING-GEAR-TO-CASE BOLT

DIFFERENTIAL CASE

SIDE BEARING

PINION GEAR

RING GEAR

PRELOAD SPRING

PINION LOCK SCREW AND WASHER

PINION THRUST WASHER

SPRING RETAINER

CLUTCH DISK PACK GUIDE

CLUTCH DISKS

SHIMS

PINION SHAFT

SIDE GEAR

CLUTCH PLATES

Fig. 36-20 A disassembled limited-slip differential using clutch plates. (*Chevrolet Motor Division of General Motors Corporation*)

the differential. The humming noise will take on a growling sound as wear progresses. Refer to the shop manual covering the car you are servicing when you make differential adjustments.

2. NOISE ON ACCELERATION

If the noise is louder when the car is accelerating, there probably is heavy contact on the heel ends of the gear teeth. If the noise is louder when the car is coasting, there probably is heavy toe contact. Both these conditions must be corrected. Refer to the manufacturer's shop manual for servicing procedures.

3. NOISE ON CURVES

If the noise is present only when the car is going around a curve, the trouble is inside the differential case. Pinion gears tight on the pinion shaft, damaged gears or pinions, too much backlash between gears, or worn differential-case bearings can cause this trouble. When the car rounds a curve, these parts inside the differential case are moving relative to one another.

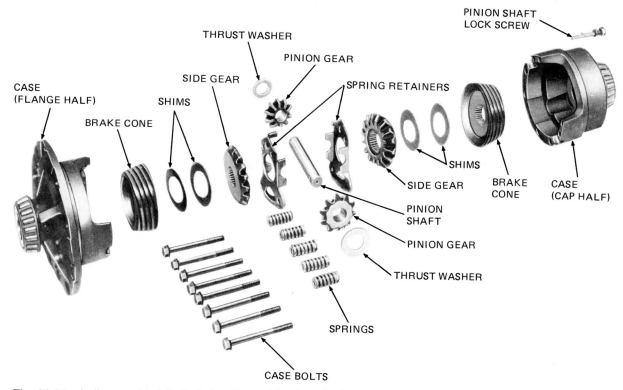

Fig. 36-21 A disassembled limited-slip differential using clutch cones. (*Chevrolet Motor Division of General Motors Corporation*)

☐ 36-10 SERVICING THE DIFFERENTIAL

Repair and overhaul procedures on drive axles and differentials vary from one car model to another. Always refer to the manufacturer's service manual for the car you are working on when you begin to repair a differential.

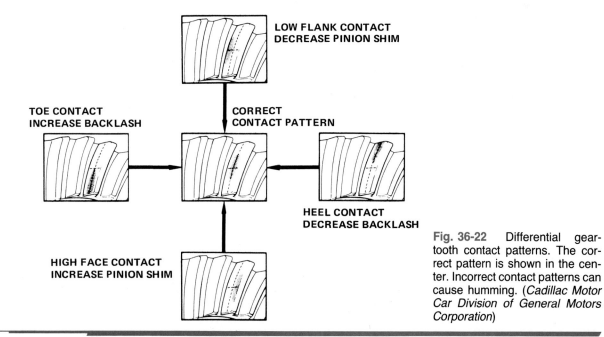

Fig. 36-22 Differential gear-tooth contact patterns. The correct pattern is shown in the center. Incorrect contact patterns can cause humming. (*Cadillac Motor Car Division of General Motors Corporation*)

Select the *one* correct, best, or most probable answer to each question. Then check your answers against the correct answers given at the end of the book.

1. The purpose of the differential is to
   a. allow the inner wheel to turn faster than the outer wheel
   b. allow both wheels to turn together on a curve
   c. allow the outer wheel to turn faster on a curve
   d. none of the above

2. In the differential, the ring gear is bolted to the
   a. differential housing
   b. differential case
   c. drive pinion
   d. axle shaft

3. When the car is moving in a straight line, the
   a. pinion gears are spinning on their shaft
   b. pinion gears are holding the side gears stationary
   c. ring gear is driving the drive pinion
   d. pinion gears are not turning on their shaft

4. The limited-slip differential
   a. delivers maximum torque to the wheel with maximum traction
   b. delivers maximum torque to the wheel that has minimum traction
   c. allows both driving wheels to slip freely
   d. allows the spinning wheel to gain speed

5. The limited-slip differential transfers power to the wheel with the most traction by using
   a. bands
   b. clutches
   c. servos
   d. all of the above

CHAPTER 37
TRANSFER CASES AND LOCKING HUBS

After studying this chapter, you should be able to:

1. Explain the purpose and operation of the transfer case.
2. Describe the various types of transfer cases.
3. Describe the construction and operation of the transfer case with a differential.
4. Explain the construction and operation of the transfer case with planetary gears.
5. List three types of locking hubs used on the front wheels of front-wheel-drive vehicles and describe the operation of each.

Some vehicles have power trains that can drive all four wheels. In these vehicles, the power from the engine, after passing through the transmission, enters a *transfer case*. The transfer case has gearing that sends the power to the rear wheels and (if required) to the front wheels. The driver can select two-wheel or four-wheel drive. In some four-wheel-drive vehicles, engagement and disengagement of the front wheels is automatic. This is called *full-time* four-wheel drive.

TRANSFER CASES

☐ 37-1 PURPOSE OF THE TRANSFER CASE

The purpose of the transfer case is to give the vehicle the ability to drive only two wheels or to drive all four wheels. The advantage of four-wheel drive (4WD) is that with all four wheels driving, the vehicle is able to travel over roads or terrain in which a car with two-wheel drive would get stuck. A vehicle with four-wheel drive can go across fields, ford shallow streams, climb steep hills, and travel over muddy or snow-covered roads.

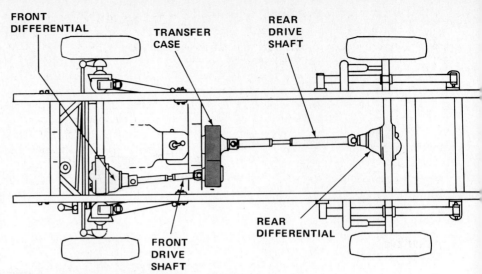

Fig. 37-1 Suspension and drive-train parts for a typical four-wheel-drive vehicle. The transfer case allows the driver to select rear-wheel drive or four-wheel drive. (*Ford Motor Company*)

☐ 37-2 FOUR-WHEEL DRIVE AND THE TRANSFER CASE

Many utility vehicles, some trucks, and a few cars have four-wheel drive (Figs. 37-1 and 37-2). Engine power can flow to all four wheels. With all four wheels driving, the vehicle can travel over rugged terrain and up steep grades. It can go through rough or muddy ground where two-wheel-drive cars would get stuck. A transfer case is required on vehicles with four-wheel drive.

The transfer case (Fig. 37-2) is an auxiliary transmission mounted in back of the main transmission. By shifting gears in the transfer case, engine power is divided and transferred to both the front and rear differentials. Transfer cases in automotive vehicles are classed as *full-time* or *part-time*. With a full-time transfer case, the front axle is engaged automatically as soon as the rear wheels begin to spin. With part-time four-wheel drive, the transfer-case shift lever must be moved to engage or disengage the front differential.

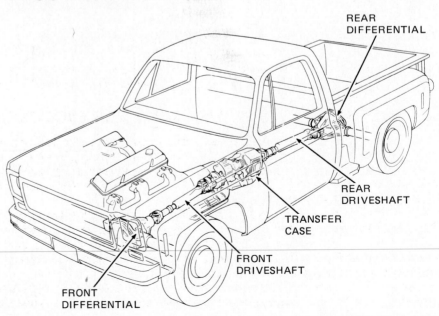

Fig. 37-2 Pickup truck with four-wheel drive. (*Chevrolet Motor Division of General Motors Corporation*)

Figures 37-1 and 37-2 show how the design of the transfer case allows the front drive shaft to be placed to one side of the engine crankcase. Because the front driveshaft is not run under the crankcase, the vehicle ground clearance is increased.

The typical transfer case may be operated in either of two modes. In one, both the front and the rear wheels are driven. In the other, only the rear wheels are driven. In most vehicles, a transfer case also provides the driver with a selection of either of two drive speeds, or *ranges,* high or low. The change from the high-speed range to the low-speed range is made when the driver moves the transfer-case shift lever. As the shift lever is moved, it moves a gear on the main drive shaft in the transfer case from engagement with the high-speed drive gear to engagement with the low-speed drive gear. High gear in the transfer case provides direct drive, or a gear ratio of $1:1$. Low speed usually produces a gear ratio of about $2:1$.

The front axle is engaged by shifting a sliding gear or a "dog" clutch into engagement with a driven gear on the front-wheel drive shaft inside the transfer case. The sliding gears and clutches are positively driven by splines on the shafts.

Figure 37-3 shows the simplified power flow through one type of transfer case. Two parts are moved by the transfer-case shift lever to provide the various gear combinations. A sliding gear on the main shaft locks either the low-speed gear or the high-speed gear to the main shaft. In many transfer cases, this shift cannot be made unless the transmission is in neutral (or in park in an automatic transmission). Otherwise, the transfer-case main shaft and the sliding gear, which is splined to it, will be turning. Gear clash will result.

To engage and disengage the front axle, another sliding gear or a clutch is used to lock the front-axle drive gear to the front-axle drive shaft. In most transfer cases, the front axle can be engaged or disengaged while the vehicle is moving. All the driver must do is release the accelerator pedal to remove the torque load through the gears. Then the shift lever can be moved as desired. However, both the front and rear wheels must be turning at the same speed. If the rear wheels have lost traction and are spinning, or if the brakes are applied and either the front or rear wheels are locked and sliding, gear clashing will occur when engagement of the front axle is attempted.

Various types of transfer cases are installed in automotive vehicles. Some have all gears, as described above. Others are full-time units which have a chain that drives the front drive-shaft, instead of gears. This reduces the weight of the transfer case, improving fuel economy. In addition, some full-time transfer cases used in cars have no low range.

□ 37-3 TYPES OF TRANSFER CASES

Transfer cases have been used with a variety of manual and automatic transmissions. They provide full-time or part-time four-wheel drive, a low range which doubles the number of gear ratios in the transmission, and a power-takeoff point to operate auxiliary equipment, such as a winch.

The transfer case is used in all vehicles with four-wheel drive. Figure 37-1 shows its location in a vehicle. Figure 37-2 shows its location in a pickup truck. The main purpose of the transfer case is to provide a means of sending engine power to both the front and rear wheels. There are two general types, part-time or full-time.

In the full-time transfer case, power is available to all four wheels at any time. The transfer case has a gearshift which provides for either

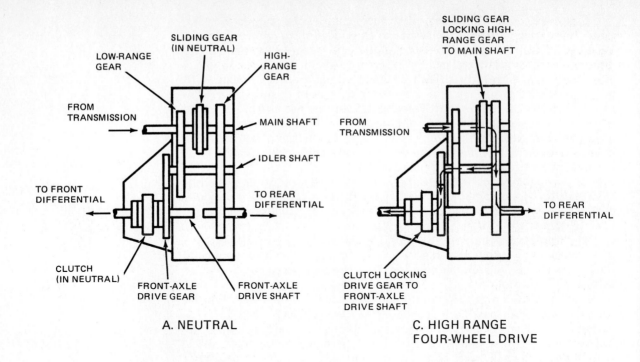

SLIDING GEAR
(IN NEUTRAL)

LOW-RANGE
GEAR

HIGH-
RANGE
GEAR

FROM
TRANSMISSION

MAIN SHAFT

IDLER SHAFT

TO FRONT
DIFFERENTIAL

TO REAR
DIFFERENTIAL

CLUTCH
(IN NEUTRAL)

FRONT-AXLE
DRIVE GEAR

FRONT-AXLE
DRIVE SHAFT

A. NEUTRAL

SLIDING GEAR
LOCKING HIGH-
RANGE GEAR
TO MAIN SHAFT

FROM
TRANSMISSION

TO REAR
DIFFERENTIAL

CLUTCH LOCKING
DRIVE GEAR TO
FRONT-AXLE
DRIVE SHAFT

C. HIGH RANGE
FOUR-WHEEL DRIVE

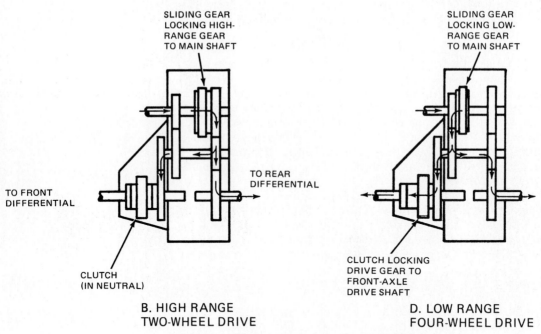

SLIDING GEAR
LOCKING HIGH-
RANGE GEAR
TO MAIN SHAFT

TO REAR
DIFFERENTIAL

TO FRONT
DIFFERENTIAL

CLUTCH
(IN NEUTRAL)

B. HIGH RANGE
TWO-WHEEL DRIVE

SLIDING GEAR
LOCKING LOW-
RANGE GEAR
TO MAIN SHAFT

CLUTCH LOCKING
DRIVE GEAR TO
FRONT-AXLE
DRIVE SHAFT

D. LOW RANGE
FOUR-WHEEL DRIVE

Fig. 37-3 Basic operation of a transfer case. (*ATW*)

direct drive through the transfer case (high range) or gear reduction (low range). Gear reduction means torque increase at the wheels. The transfer case is shifted into low range by the driver when additional torque is needed, such as for climbing steep hills.

The part-time transfer case can be shifted into gear reduction, just as the full-time unit. In addition, the part-time unit also has a gearshift that sends power to only the rear wheels or to both the front and rear wheels.

The gear positions in a typical transfer case for the various transfer-case shift-lever positions are shown in Figs. 37-4 to 37-7. The transfer-case shift lever is located on the floor of the passenger compartment. Figure 37-8 shows two different shift patterns, which vary according to the design of the transfer case.

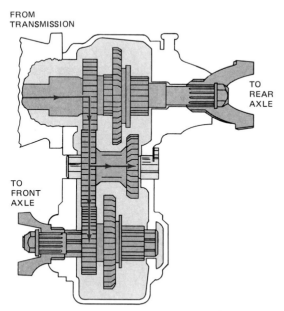

Fig. 37-4 Gearing in the transfer case with the gears in neutral. (*American Motors Corporation*)

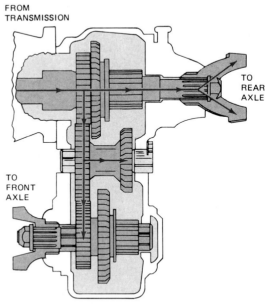

Fig. 37-5 Gearing with the transfer case in two-wheel drive, high range. Only the rear wheels are being driven. (*American Motors Corporation*)

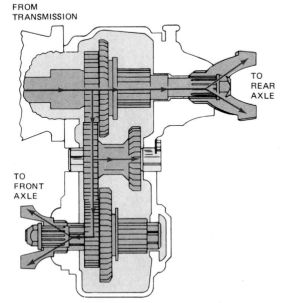

Fig. 37-6 Gearing with the transfer case in four-wheel drive, high range. All four wheels are being driven. (*American Motors Corporation*)

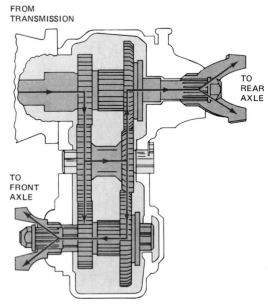

Fig. 37-7 Gearing with the transfer case in four-wheel drive, low range. (*American Motors Corporation*)

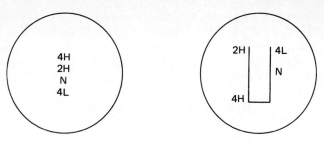

Fig. 37-8 Shift patterns for transfer cases. (*American Motors Corporation*)

□ 37-4 FULL-TIME TRANSFER CASE WITH DIFFERENTIAL

If a vehicle has full-time four-wheel drive, a controllable differential is built into the transfer case (Fig. 37-9). The purpose of this interaxle differential is to compensate for any difference in front-wheel and rear-wheel travel while the transfer case is in high range and four-wheel drive. The differential allows the front and rear axles to operate at their own speeds, without forcing wheel slippage in normal dry-road driving.

When differential action is not wanted, such as for maximum engine braking or maximum wheel torque, the driver moves the transfer-case shift lever either to low range or to the LOCK position. This locks together the output shafts in the transfer case for the front and rear axles. Now differential action cannot occur. Equal torque is delivered to both the front and rear axles.

During turns, the front wheels travel a greater distance than the rear wheels. This is because the front wheels move through a wider arc than the rear wheels (Fig. 36-2). With full-time four-wheel drive, it is the differential in the transfer case (Fig. 37-9) that allows the front wheels to travel farther or turn faster than the rear wheels without slipping. As a result, power-train and tire wear are reduced while the advantages of full-time four-wheel drive are retained.

This differs from the operation of a part-time transfer case. It delivers equal power to each axle while in four-wheel drive. During turns made on a dry surface, one of the axles must slip. Therefore, the driver must shift the part-time transfer case out of four-wheel drive on returning to a dry surface.

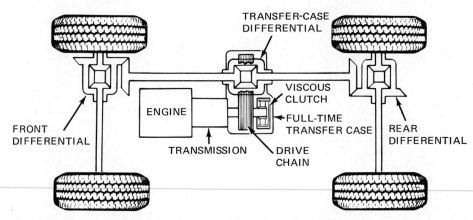

Fig. 37-9 Location of the *interaxle differential* in the transfer case. This vehicle has three separate differentials. (*American Motors Corporation*)

There is a disadvantage to a transfer case with a simple differential in it. If the wheels on either axle lose traction and begin to spin, the transfer-case differential continues to deliver maximum torque to the axle with the minimum traction. As a result, insufficient torque to move the vehicle may be provided to the wheels that still have traction.

To overcome this problem, most full-time transfer cases have some type of limited-slip differential in them. The slip-limiting device may be a viscous coupling (Fig. 37-9), brake cones, or clutch plates. Regardless of type, its job is to divert torque from the spinning axle. This causes more torque to be supplied to the wheels with the most traction. A widely used transfer case of this type is the Quadra-Trac. It is built by the Warner Gear Division of the Borg-Warner Corporation. The operation of limited-slip differentials is covered in Chap. 36.

☐ 37-5 PART-TIME TRANSFER CASE WITH PLANETARY GEARS

In 1980, a new design of the part-time transfer case for automotive vehicles was introduced by the New Process Gear Division of Chrysler Corporation (Fig. 37-10). This transfer case has an aluminum case, chain drive, and a planetary gearset for reduced weight and increased mechanical efficiency. The internal parts of the transfer case do not rotate in two-wheel drive. This leaves most of the lubricant undisturbed and reduces the power loss caused by dragging parts through it.

An internal oil pump turns with the rear output shaft to maintain lubrication to critical bearings and bushings whenever the rear drive shaft is turning. This provides improved lubrication during normal operation. In addition, the oil pump allows towing of the vehicle with the transfer case in neutral at any safe speed up to 55 mph [89 km/h] and for any distance. It is not necessary to disconnect the drive shafts. However, the front-wheel locking hubs should be in UNLOCK or AUTO (depending

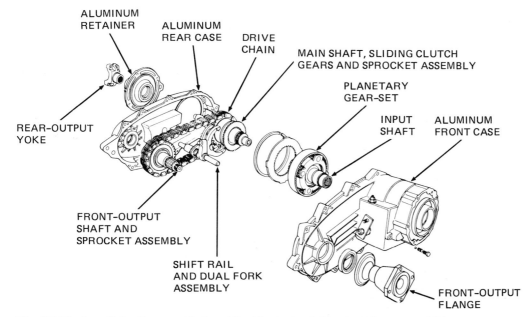

Fig. 37-10 A partially disassembled part-time four-wheel-drive transfer case, which uses a planetary gearset to achieve gear reduction. (*Chrysler Corporation*)

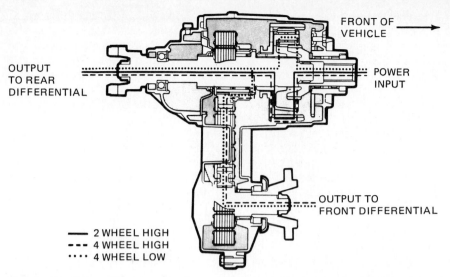

FRONT OF VEHICLE →

OUTPUT TO REAR DIFFERENTIAL

POWER INPUT

OUTPUT TO FRONT DIFFERENTIAL

— 2 WHEEL HIGH
--- 4 WHEEL HIGH
··· 4 WHEEL LOW

Fig. 37-11 Power flow through the part-time transfer case with planetary gears. (*Chrysler Corporation*)

upon the hub type) to prevent unnecessary rotation of the drive-train components. Locking hubs are described in later sections.

Figure 37-11 shows the power flow through the transfer case for each drive condition. In neutral, rotation of the input shaft spins only the planetary gears and the ring gear around them. With both the planetary gears and the ring gear spinning freely, no power is transmitted through the planetary gearset. Planetary gears are described in Chap. 34.

FRONT-DRIVE AXLES

□ *37-6 FOUR-WHEEL-DRIVE DRIVE AXLES*

The most widely used application of four-wheel drive is in multipurpose utility vehicles, such as the American Motors Jeep, Chevrolet Blazer, and Ford Bronco. These vehicles, along with most other four-wheel-drive cars and trucks normally drive the rear axle. But when four-wheel-drive is engaged through the transfer case, power is also delivered to the front axle.

The front axle on most four-wheel-drive vehicles is very similar to the rear axle on vehicles with rear-wheel drive. As in the rear axle, the differential and front-axle shafts are carried inside a rigid tube, or axle housing (Fig. 37-12). However, the front axle is the steering axle. Therefore universal joints are located in the right and left axle shafts so that the outer ends can swing with the steering knuckle. Steering systems are described in Chap. 41.

In 1980, Ford introduced full-size 4×4 trucks with independent front suspension (Fig. 37-13). This system utilizes two steel axle carriers and an additional universal joint in the right axle shaft next to the differential. These permit each front wheel to move up and down independently of the other. Instead of a one-piece tube to serve as the axle housing, the tube is split into two shorter sections and joined together at a pivot point.

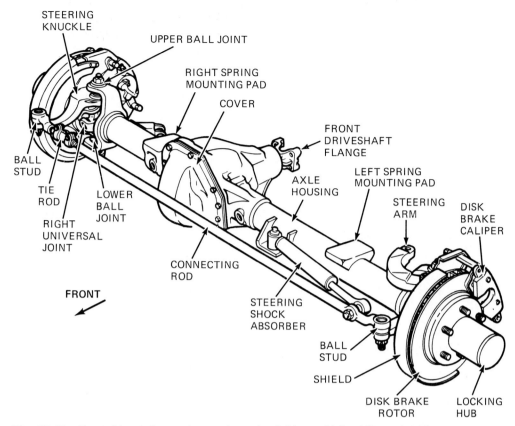

Fig. 37-12 Front-drive axle used on a four-wheel-drive vehicle. (*Chevrolet Motor Division of General Motors Corporation*)

The axle shaft can flex near the pivot because of the centrally located third universal joint. Off road, this provides greater wheel control and traction than a solid axle does, according to Ford.

With independent front suspension, each wheel is able to react to the road conditions individually. Bumps are absorbed by each front wheel instead of some of the shock being transmitted through the solid front

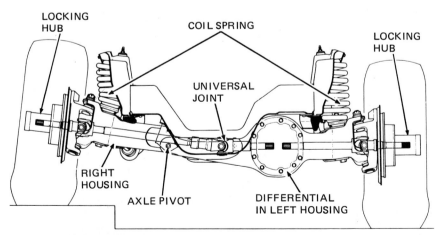

Fig. 37-13 A front axle for a four-wheel-drive vehicle with independent front suspension. (*Ford Motor Company*)

axle to the other wheel. Front coil springs are used on Ford F-150 models (Fig. 37-13). For heavier loads and handling requirements of F-250 and F-350 models, tapered leaf springs are used. Figure 37-12 shows the spring mounting pads for leaf springs on the axle housing.

NOTE A designation such as *4×4* is used with vehicles to indicate the number of wheels on the ground and the number of wheels that can be driven. For example, the typical car has four wheels on the ground and two-wheel drive. Therefore, it is designated *4×2*. A four-wheel-drive vehicle is a *4×4*. There are four wheels on the ground and all four can be driven.

LOCKING HUBS

□ 37-7 LOCKING HUBS

Three different types of hubs are used on front-drive axles. These are the manual locking hub (Fig. 37-14), the automatic locking hub with manual overide (Fig. 37-15), and the full-automatic automatic locking hub used with full-time four-wheel drive (Fig. 37-16). Locking hubs are also called *freewheeling hubs*. This is because their purpose is to disengage the front axle, allowing it to freewheel while the vehicle is in two-wheel drive. As a result, fuel economy and tire life are increased, and engine and transfer-case wear is decreased.

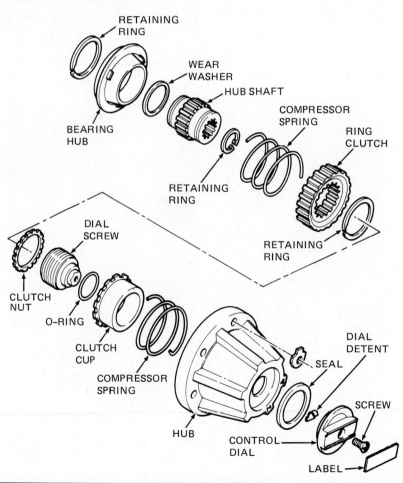

Fig. 37-14 One type of manual locking hub. (*American Motors Corporation*)

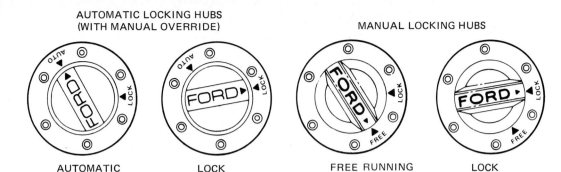

AUTOMATIC
POSITION

LOCK
POSITION

FREE RUNNING
POSITION

LOCK
POSITION

Fig. 37-15 Positions of the control knob on manual locking hubs, and on automatic locking hubs with manual override. (*Ford Motor Company*)

A locking hub is a type of clutch that disengages the outer ends of the axle shafts from the wheel hub. Then the axle shafts do not turn, or *back-drive,* the differential. Therefore the differential does not turn the driveshaft from the transfer case to the front differential. The engine power saved by not having to turn these parts has been reported to increase fuel economy by as much as two miles per gallon.

Many vehicles with part-time four-wheel drive are equipped with manual locking hubs (Fig. 37-14). These hubs are locked or unlocked by the driver, who must turn a knob or lever at each wheel (Fig. 37-15). Another type of hub is the automatic locking hub (Fig. 37-16). It engages when the transfer-case shift lever is moved to four-wheel drive. When the lever is in two-wheel drive, the front axle and drive shaft are not engaged

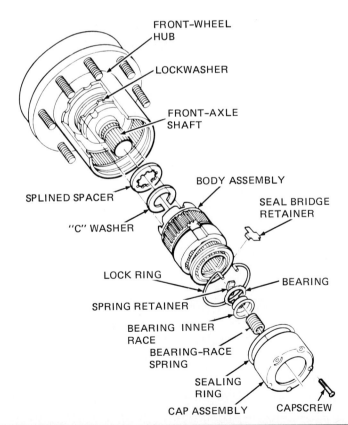

FRONT-WHEEL HUB

LOCKWASHER

FRONT-AXLE SHAFT

BODY ASSEMBLY

SEAL BRIDGE RETAINER

SPLINED SPACER

"C" WASHER

LOCK RING

BEARING

SPRING RETAINER

BEARING INNER RACE

BEARING-RACE SPRING

SEALING RING

CAP ASSEMBLY

CAPSCREW

Fig. 37-16 A fully automatic locking hub. (*Ford Motor Company*)

and do not rotate. Some automatic locking hubs can be manually locked by turning the control knob at each wheel (Fig. 37-15).

Locking hubs are not used in some vehicles with full-time four-wheel drive. Instead, the hubs are always engaged with the front-axle shafts. The interaxle differential in the transfer case (Fig. 37-9) prevents damage and undue wear of power-train parts.

CHAPTER 37
REVIEW QUESTIONS

Select the *one* correct, best, or most probable answer to each question. Then check your answers against the correct answers given at the end of the book.

1. Transfer cases are classified as
   a. half-time and part-time
   b. half-time and four-wheel
   c. part-time and full-time
   d. full-time and extended

2. With a part-time transfer case, the
   a. rear axle is engaged when the shift lever is moved
   b. rear axle engages automatically when the front wheels slip
   c. front axle is engaged when the shift lever is moved
   d. front axle engages automatically when the rear wheels slip

3. With a full-time transfer case, the
   a. rear axle is engaged when the shift lever is moved
   b. rear axle engages automatically when the front wheels slip
   c. front axle is engaged when the shift lever is moved
   d. front axle engages automatically when the rear wheels slip

4. The use of locking hubs on a four-wheel-drive vehicle improves
   a. ride quality
   b. traction
   c. fuel economy
   d. all of the above

5. The purpose of having a limited-slip differential in the full-time transfer case is to
   a. improve traction by sending more torque to the wheels with the most traction
   b. improve fuel economy by disengaging the front axle on turns
   c. improve traction by sending less torque to the wheels with the most traction
   d. improve fuel economy by overdriving the rear axle

PART 7
AUTOMOTIVE BRAKES, SUSPENSION, AND STEERING

Earlier chapters describe how the engine operates to produce power and how this power is carried through the transmission and drive line to the car wheels. However, there is much more to the basic car. The car body is suspended on springs for a smooth ride. In addition, the car has systems and devices to provide brakes and steering. All this is supported by wheels and the tires, which provide the only contact between the car and the road.

There are six chapters in part 7. They are:

CHAPTER 38
AUTOMOTIVE BRAKES

After studying this chapter, you should be able to:

1. Explain the purpose, construction, and operation of automotive brakes.
2. Describe the difference between drum and disk brakes.
3. Explain how power brakes work.
4. Discuss the purpose of antilock devices and how they work.

A *brake* is an energy-conversion device that is used to slow, stop, and hold the car. In operation, the brake uses friction to change the kinetic energy of motion into heat energy. When the driver presses the brake pedal, the car slows and stops. The brake that we operate with our foot during normal driving is called the *foot brake,* or *service brake.* Cars also have a parking brake. This chapter describes how automotive brakes work.

☐ 38-1 AUTOMOTIVE BRAKING SYSTEMS

Two completely independent braking systems are used on the car (Fig. 38-1). They are the *service brake* and the *parking brake.*

1. Service brake. The service brakes act to slow, stop, or hold the vehicle during normal driving. They are foot-operated by the driver depressing and releasing the brake pedal.
2. Parking brake. The primary purpose of the parking brake is to hold the vehicle stationary while it is unattended. The parking brake is mechanically operated by the driver when a separate parking-brake foot pedal or hand lever is set.

Basically, all car brakes are friction brakes (Fig. 38-2). When the driver applies the brake, the control device forces brake shoes, or pads, against the rotating brake drums or disks at the wheels. Friction between the shoes or pads and the drums or disks then slows or stops the wheels so that the car is braked.

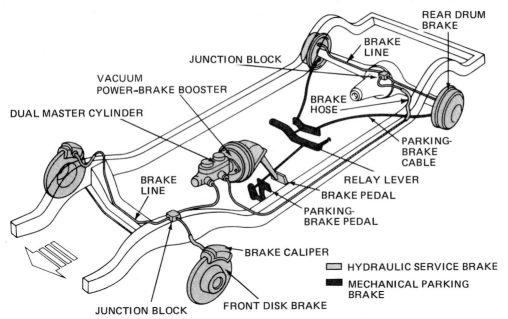

Fig. 38-1 Layout of the complete braking system on an automobile chassis. (*Texaco, Inc.*)

□ 38-2 BRAKE OPERATION

Braking action starts at the brake pedal. When the pedal is pushed down, brake fluid is sent from the master cylinder to the wheels. At the wheels, the fluid pushes brake shoes, or pads, against revolving drums or disks. The friction between the stationary shoes, or pads, and the revolving drums or disks slows and stops them. This slows or stops the revolving wheels, which, in turn, slow or stop the car.

Figure 38-3 shows the brake lines, or tubes, through which the fluid flows. There are two chambers and two pistons in the master cylinder. One chamber is connected to the front-wheel brakes. The other chamber is connected to the rear-wheel brakes. This is called a *dual-braking system*. There is a reason for splitting the system into two sections. If one section should fail, the other can still work. It will provide braking until the failed section can be fixed.

In earlier braking systems, there was only one chamber in the master cylinder, which was connected to all four wheel brakes. If that one section failed, the whole system failed. The dual-braking system provides added safety because the rear and front sections seldom fail at the same time.

□ 38-3 DUAL-BRAKING SYSTEM

A schematic layout of a dual-braking system is shown in Fig. 38-4. Some brake lines connect the master cylinder to the rear wheels. Other brake lines go from the pressure-differential valve to each of the front wheels. The brake fluid must first pass through the pressure-differential valve. This valve turns on a red brake warning light on the instrument panel if either of the brake systems fails (□ 38-17). In many brake systems, one section of the master cylinder is connected to the front wheels. The other section is connected to the two rear wheels. This is called a *front/rear split*

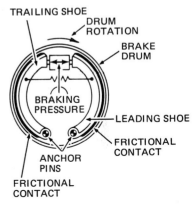

DRUM BRAKE

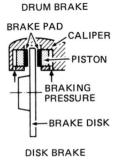

DISK BRAKE

Fig. 38-2 The two basic types of wheel-brake mechanisms. (*Robert Bosch Corporation*)

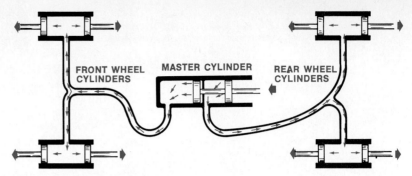

Fig. 38-3 The flow of brake fluid to the four wheel cylinders when the two pistons are pushed into the master cylinder.

(Fig. 38-1). Figure 38-4 shows a *diagonal split system*. One section of the master cylinder is connected to the left-front- and right-rear-wheel brakes. The other section is connected to the right front and left rear.

There are two different types of brakes used at the wheels. They are drum brakes and disk brakes. Figure 38-4 shows a system using front disk brakes and rear drum brakes. Both the drum brake and the disk brake do the same job. However, the brakes are constructed differently.

□ 38-4 MASTER CYLINDER

Figure 38-5 shows a master cylinder in cutaway view. This master cylinder has two main parts. The top part is a plastic fluid reservoir. The lower

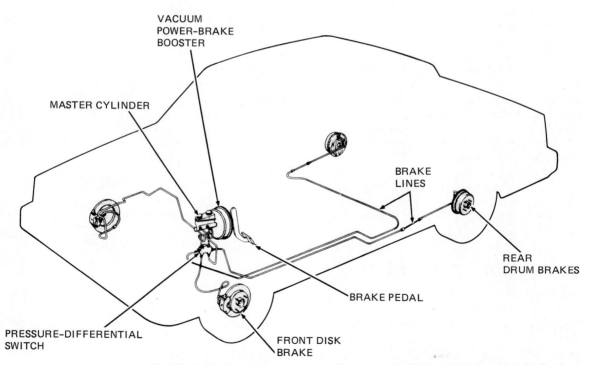

Fig. 38-4 Braking system on a car. The system is diagonally balanced, with floating-caliper front disk brakes and rear drum brakes. A vacuum-operated power-brake booster reduces driver brake-pedal effort. (*Chrysler Corporation*)

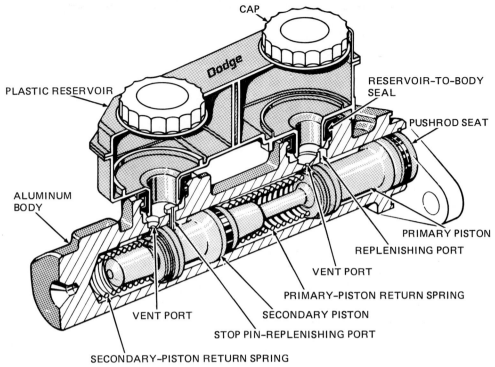

Fig. 38-5 A "composite" master cylinder which has separate plastic fluid reservoirs attached to an aluminum body. (*Chrysler Corporation*)

part is an aluminum body with a highly polished bore. It contains the pistons, springs, and seals.

In the car, a pushrod connects the brake pedal to the primary piston in the master cylinder. When the brake pedal is pushed down, the pushrod pushes the primary piston in the master cylinder. The fluid trapped ahead of the piston is pushed out of the master cylinder and into the brake line connected to two wheels. The fluid flows through the brake line to the wheel cylinders or calipers.

When the pushrod moves the primary piston, the secondary piston also is pushed to the left (in Fig. 38-5). Movement of the secondary piston sends brake fluid to the brakes at the other wheels.

Not all master cylinders are constructed like the one shown in Fig. 38-5. Figure 38-6 shows a typical master cylinder with a one-piece body in exploded view. However, all master cylinders have the same basic parts and work in the same general way.

□ 38-5 BRAKE LINES

The brake fluid is carried by steel pipes called brake lines from the master cylinder to the various valves and then to the brakes at the wheels. You can see the brake lines and how they are connected in Fig. 38-4. Brake lines usually pass under the floor pan, where they are exposed to stones and other damage. Because of this, brake lines often are wrapped with a wire "armor" to protect them against damage.

A short, flexible brake hose (or "flex hose") is used to connect the stationary brake lines to the brake assemblies that move up and down

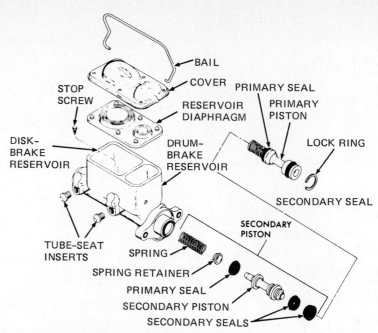

Fig. 38-6 Exploded view of a master cylinder that has a single-piece body. (*Chevrolet Motor Division of General Motors Corporation*)

and swing with each front wheel for steering. Steel tubing will crack if it vibrates or is flexed too much. Only a single flexible hose is needed at the rear axle to take care of the up-and-down movement of the housing. This line is shown in Fig. 38-1.

□ 38-6 BRAKE FLUID

Brake fluid is a very special fluid that is little affected by high or low temperatures. It is *not* a type of engine oil. Brake fluid does not damage the metal or rubber parts in the brake system. Engine oil will damage the brake system. For this reason, only the brake fluid recommended by the manufacturer should be put into the brake system.

> **CAREFUL** Never put engine oil in a brake system. Engine oil will cause rubber parts in the system, such as the piston cups, to swell and break apart. This could cause complete brake failure. Use only the brake fluid recommended by the car manufacturer!

□ 38-7 DRUM BRAKES

The drum brake has an iron, steel, or aluminum drum to which the wheel is bolted. The drum and wheel rotate together. Inside the drum and attached to the steering knuckle or axle housing is the brake assembly (Fig. 38-7). At the front wheels, the brake is attached to the steering knuckle. In Fig. 38-7 (center) you can see the boltholes by which the front-wheel brake is attached. At the rear wheels, the brake is attached to the axle housing. You can see the boltholes in the axle housing in Fig. 38-7 (left).

There are two brake shoes at each wheel. The bottoms of the shoes are held apart by an adjusting screw—also known as a *star wheel*. The tops of the shoes are held apart by a wheel cylinder. The shoes are made of metal. Glued (called *bonded*) or riveted to each shoe is a facing of

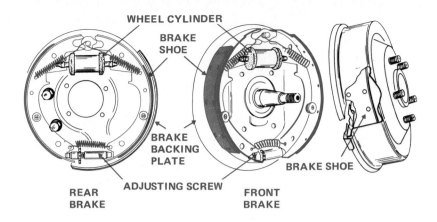

Fig. 38-7 Basic construction of the drum brake. Right, the brake drum has been partly cut away to show the shoe inside.

friction material. The facing is called the *brake lining*. These brake linings are made of a tough material such as asbestos. It can hold up under the rubbing pressure and heat produced during braking.

The brake backing plate is bolted to the axle housing at the rear wheels, or to the steering knuckle at the front wheels. At the right in Fig. 38-7, you can see the brake drum in place over the brake shoes. The drum has been partly cut away to show one of the shoes. Each shoe is attached at one point to the brake backing plate. The attachment is loose so that the shoe can move slightly.

□ 38-8 OPERATION OF THE DRUM BRAKE

When brake fluid is forced from the master cylinder, it flows through the brake lines into the wheel cylinder (Fig. 38-8). A wheel cylinder is shown disassembled at the top and in sectional view at the bottom of Fig. 38-9. There are two pistons, with piston cups, inside the wheel cylinder. When the brake fluid is forced into the wheel cylinder, the brake fluid pushes the pistons apart. This action pushes the brake-shoe actuating pins out. Therefore the brake shoes are forced tightly against the rotating brake drum. Then friction between the brake linings and the drum slows or stops the rotation of the drum and the wheel.

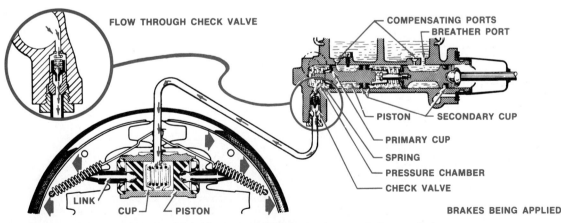

Fig. 38-8 Conditions in the drum-brake system while the brakes are being applied. Brake fluid flows from the master cylinder to the wheel cylinder, as shown by the arrows. The fluid forces the wheel-cylinder pistons outward, applying the brakes.

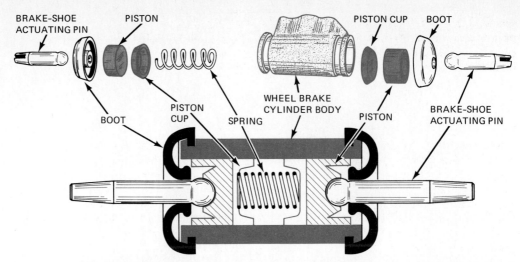

Fig. 38-9 Wheel cylinder for a drum brake, disassembled at the top and in sectional view at the bottom.

☐ 38-9 SELF-ADJUSTING DRUM BRAKES

Drum brakes have self-adjusters that automatically adjust the brakes as the brake lining wears. Repeated use of the brakes gradually wears the brake lining off the shoes. As the lining wears, the distance between the lining and the drum increases. Then the brake pedal has to be pushed down farther to move the shoes the additional distance to contact the drum.

Brakes on older cars without self-adjusters have to be adjusted periodically. To adjust the brakes, turn the adjusting screw, or star wheel. As the adjusting screw is turned, the lower ends of the shoes are moved out. This eliminates the excessive distance between the shoes and the drum.

Figure 38-10 shows one type of self-adjusting drum brake. It includes an adjuster lever and spring. The self-adjusting action takes place only when the brakes are applied while the car is moving in reverse. Then every time the brakes are applied, the brake shoes move outward. The cable guide of the self-adjuster moves outward with the secondary shoe. This outward movement causes the adjuster lever to pivot slightly upward in a hole in the secondary shoe. If the brake linings have worn enough, the lever will now be in back of the next tooth on the adjuster

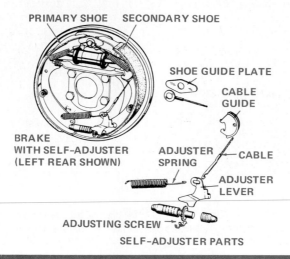

Fig. 38-10 A drum brake with the self-adjuster in place. Right, the self-adjuster disassembled. (*Bendix Corporation*)

screw. Then when the brake pedal is released, the adjuster spring will pull the adjuster lever down. As the adjuster lever moves down, it will turn the adjuster screw a full tooth. This is enough to spread the lower ends of the shoes slightly, moving them closer to the drum.

☐ 38-10 PISTON RETURN STROKE

When the brakes are released, the spring tension on the brake shoes pulls the shoes away from the brake drum. Also, the return springs in the master cylinder push the pistons back toward the released position. All these actions force the brake fluid out of the wheel cylinders and back into the master cylinder. The brake-fluid flow is shown by the white arrows in Fig. 38-11. However, in some drum-brake systems pressure is trapped in the brake line and wheel cylinder when the check valve closes in the master cylinder. This is called *residual line pressure*. It causes the piston cups in the wheel cylinder to be held tight against the wheel-cylinder wall, as shown by the colored arrows in Fig. 38-11. Therefore, no air can leak into the line, and no brake fluid can leak out of the wheel cylinders.

☐ 38-11 DISK BRAKES

The disk brake has a metal disk (also called a *rotor*) instead of a drum. Figure 38-12 shows a wheel partly cut away so that the positions of the caliper and disk can be seen. A flat shoe, or disk-brake pad, is located on each side of the disk. In operation these two flat shoes are forced tightly against the rotating disk. The shoes squeeze the rotating disk to stop the car. Figure 38-13 shows how the disk brake works. Fluid from the master cylinder forces the pistons to move in, toward the disk. This action pushes the friction pads tightly against the disk. The friction between the shoes and the disk slows and stops it. This provides the braking action. Pistons are made of either plastic or steel.

There are three general types of disk brakes. They are the floating-caliper type, the fixed-caliper type, and the sliding-caliper type. Floating-caliper and sliding-caliper disk brakes use a single piston. Fixed-caliper disk brakes have either two or four pistons. Each type of disk brake is described in a following section.

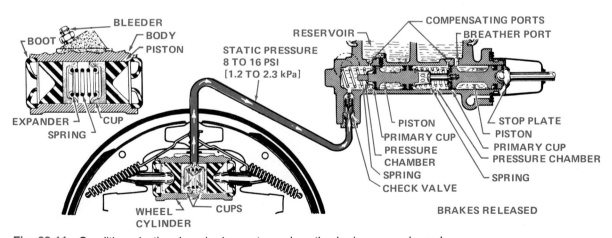

Fig. 38-11 Conditions in the drum-brake system when the brakes are released. Then brake fluid flows back to the master cylinder, as shown by the arrows. (*Buick Motor Division of General Motors Corporation*)

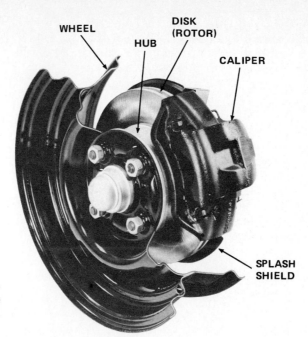

WHEEL

HUB

DISK (ROTOR)

CALIPER

SPLASH SHIELD

Fig. 38-12 A disk-brake assembly, showing the location of the caliper assembly on the disk. (*Ford Motor Company*)

□ *38-12 FLOATING-CALIPER DISK BRAKE*

Figure 38-14 shows a floating-caliper (also called a pin-caliper) disk brake at a front wheel. The caliper is the part that holds the two brake shoes on each side of the disk. In the floating-caliper brake, two steel guide pins thread into the steering-knuckle adapter (Fig. 38-15). The caliper floats on four rubber bushings which fit on the inner and outer ends of the guide pins. The rubber bushings allow the caliper to move in or out slightly when the brakes are applied. Figure 38-16 shows a floating caliper. In this type of brake, the guide pins locate and retain the shoes.

When the brakes are applied, the brake fluid flows to the cylinder in the caliper and pushes the piston out. The piston forces the inner shoe against the disk. At the same time, the hydraulic pressure in the cylinder causes the whole caliper to move inward. This pulls the outer shoe against the disk. As a result, the two shoes squeeze the disk tightly. This action causes the caliper to move forward slightly in the direction that the disk is turning. The slight movement of the caliper brings together the machined abutments on the caliper and on the adapter (Fig. 38-15).

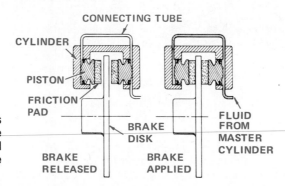

CONNECTING TUBE

CYLINDER

PISTON

FRICTION PAD

BRAKE DISK

FLUID FROM MASTER CYLINDER

BRAKE RELEASED

BRAKE APPLIED

Fig. 38-13 Sectional views showing how hydraulic pressure forces the friction pads inward against the brake disk to produce braking action.

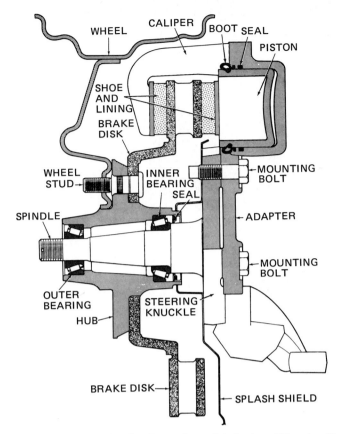

Fig. 38-14 Sectional view of a floating-caliper disk brake. (*Chrysler Corporation*)

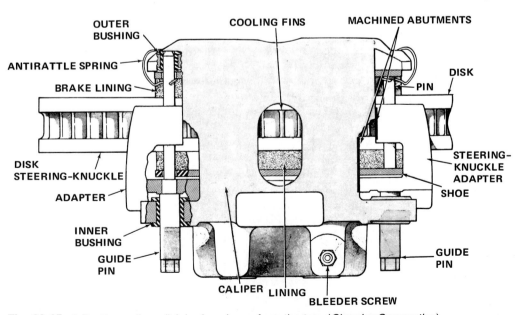

Fig. 38-15 A floating-caliper disk brake, shown from the top. (*Chrysler Corporation*)

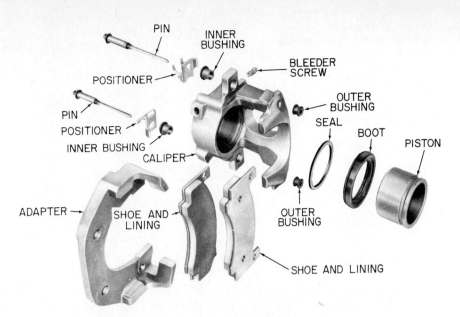

Fig. 38-16 A disassembled floating-caliper disk brake using one piston. (*Chrysler Corporation*)

□ 38-13 FIXED-CALIPER DISK BRAKE

This brake has four pistons, two on each side of the disk (Fig. 38-17). The reason for the name "fixed caliper" is that the caliper is bolted solidly to the steering knuckle. When the brakes are applied, the caliper cannot move because it attaches solidly to the steering knuckle (Fig. 38-18). When the brakes are applied, the four pistons push the inner and outer brake shoes in against the disk. Some brakes of this type have used only two pistons, one on each side of the disk.

□ 38-14 SLIDING-CALIPER DISK BRAKE

The sliding-caliper (Fig. 38-19) is similar to the floating-caliper disk brake. Both types use a single piston. Machined abutments on the

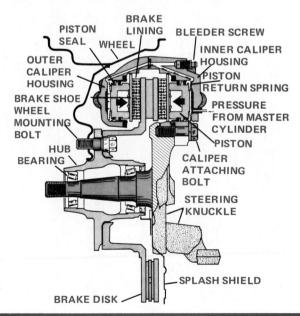

Fig. 38-17 A fixed-caliper disk brake.

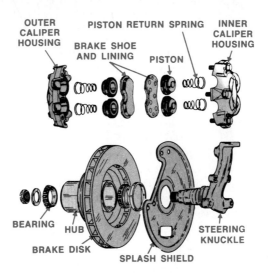

Fig. 38-18 A disassembled fixed-caliper disk brake.

adapter position and align the caliper. A support key (or retainer clip) on each end of the caliper keeps it in position on the adapter. However, the support key allows the caliper to slide in and out slightly. The outer brake shoe is flanged to fit machined fingers on the caliper. The inner shoe is held in position by the adapter.

□ 38-15 SELF-ADJUSTMENT OF DISK BRAKES

Disk brakes are self-adjusting. Each piston has a square-cut seal on it to prevent fluid leakage (Fig. 38-20). When the brakes are applied, the piston moves toward the disk. This distorts the piston seal, as shown in the center illustration in Fig. 38-20. When the brakes are released, the seal relaxes and returns to its original position. This pulls the piston away from the disk. As the brake linings wear, the piston "overtravels" and takes a new position in relation to the seal. This action provides self-adjustment of disk brakes.

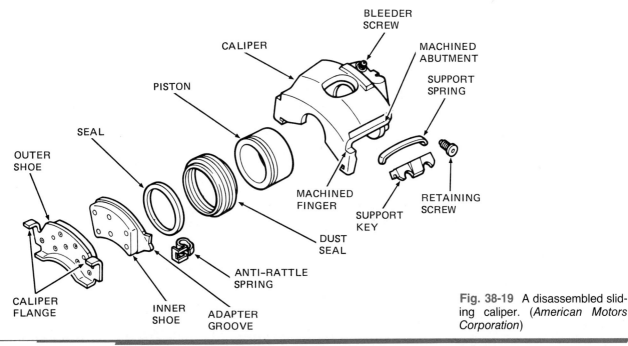

Fig. 38-19 A disassembled sliding caliper. (*American Motors Corporation*)

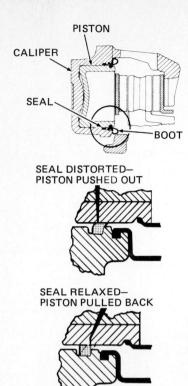

Many disk-brake shoes have a wear indicator (Fig. 38-21). The purpose of the wear indicator is to make a noise. This warns the driver that the brake linings are thin and new linings are required. When the brake linings are worn, the tab touches the disk when the brakes are applied. This gives off a scraping noise.

□ 38-16 METERING VALVE

Figure 38-22 shows the valves which may be used in brake systems that include disk brakes. Some disk-brake systems have a metering valve. This valve keeps the front disk brakes from applying until after the rear drum brakes apply. If the front brakes are applied first, the rear tires might skid as the weight shifts to the front end. Also, by delaying the front brake action at low speeds, disk-brake lining life is increased.

□ 38-17 WARNING LIGHT

The dual-brake system uses a pressure-differential valve (Fig. 38-22) to operate a warning light. This light warns the driver if one-half of the braking system has failed. The valve has a piston that is centered when both front and rear brakes are operating normally (Fig. 38-22). However, if one section should fail, there is low pressure on one side of the piston. The high pressure from the side with normal pressure will push the piston to the low-pressure side. This pushes up the plunger of the brake warning-light switch. The plunger is mounted in the top center of the pressure-differential valve. Contacts inside the switch are closed. This connects a warning light on the instrument panel to the battery. The light warns the driver that there is brake trouble.

Fig. 38-20 Seal action, which provides the self-adjusting of disk brakes. (*Ford Motor Company*)

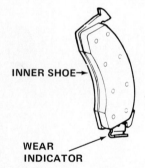

Fig. 38-21 An inner shoe ("disk-brake pad") with a wear indicator on it for a sliding-caliper disk brake. (*Cadillac Motor Car Division of General Motors Corporation*)

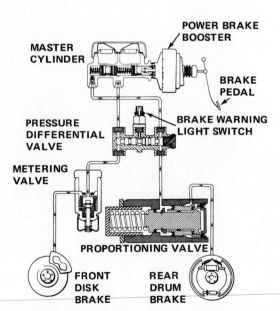

Fig. 38-22 Valves used in the hydraulic system of a car with front disk brakes and rear drum brakes. (*Ford Motor Company*)

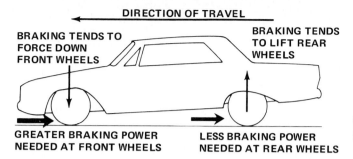

DIRECTION OF TRAVEL

BRAKING TENDS TO FORCE DOWN FRONT WHEELS

BRAKING TENDS TO LIFT REAR WHEELS

GREATER BRAKING POWER NEEDED AT FRONT WHEELS

LESS BRAKING POWER NEEDED AT REAR WHEELS

Fig. 38-23 During braking, the front wheels are forced down and the rear wheels up. (*Ammco Tools, Inc.*)

□ 38-18 PROPORTIONING VALVE

The proportioning valve (Fig. 38-22) provides balanced braking on cars with front disk brakes and rear drum brakes. During hard braking, more of the car weight is transferred to the front wheels (Fig. 38-23). As a result, more braking is needed at the front wheels and less at the rear wheels. If equal brake pressure were applied, the rear wheels could lock up. The proportioning valve reduces maximum pressure to the rear brakes.

□ 38-19 COMBINATION VALVE

In many cars the pressure-differential valve, the metering valve, and the proportioning valve are combined in a single unit. Figure 38-24 is a sectional view of this combination valve.

□ 38-20 ANTILOCK BRAKE SYSTEMS

About 40 percent of all car accidents involve skidding. The most efficient braking takes place when the wheels are still revolving. Once the brakes lock the wheels and the tires begin to skid, braking and steering are much less effective. Antilock brake systems use devices that relieve the hydraulic pressure at the wheels which are about to skid. This action reduces braking force that would cause a skid.

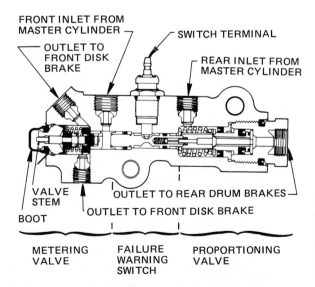

FRONT INLET FROM MASTER CYLINDER

OUTLET TO FRONT DISK BRAKE

SWITCH TERMINAL

REAR INLET FROM MASTER CYLINDER

VALVE STEM

BOOT

OUTLET TO REAR DRUM BRAKES

OUTLET TO FRONT DISK BRAKE

METERING VALVE

FAILURE WARNING SWITCH

PROPORTIONING VALVE

Fig. 38-24 Combination valve with warning-light switch, metering valve, and proportioning valve all in the same assembly. (*Delco Moraine Division of General Motors Corporation*)

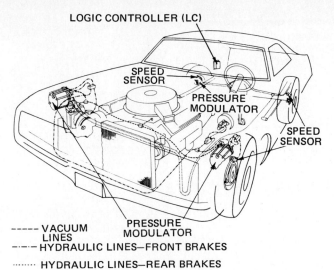

LOGIC CONTROLLER (LC)

SPEED SENSOR

PRESSURE MODULATOR

SPEED SENSOR

PRESSURE MODULATOR

----- VACUUM LINES
—··— HYDRAULIC LINES—FRONT BRAKES
·········· HYDRAULIC LINES—REAR BRAKES

Fig. 38-25 Antilock brake system used by Chrysler, showing the locations of the components and their connections to the vacuum and hydraulic lines. (*Chrysler Corporation*)

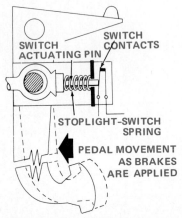

SWITCH ACTUATING PIN

SWITCH CONTACTS

STOPLIGHT-SWITCH SPRING

PEDAL MOVEMENT AS BRAKES ARE APPLIED

Fig. 38-26 A mechanical stoplight switch shown closed, with the brakes applied. (*Ford Motor Company*)

ATMOSPHERIC PRESSURE

VACUUM

DIAPHRAGM

PISTON

MASTER CYLINDER

Fig. 38-27 When there is a vacuum on one side of the diaphragm and atmospheric pressure on the other side, the diaphragm will move toward the vacuum side.

Figure 38-25 shows the antilock system used by one manufacturer. A magnetic wheel is attached to the brake disk. The sensor is a coil of wire, or a winding, that bolts to the brake splash shield and does not move. As the car wheels and brake disk revolve, the magnetic wheel produces an alternating current in the sensor. A similar action takes place at the other wheels. The signals from the car wheels are fed into a logic control unit.

When the brakes are applied, the logic control unit compares the ac signals from the wheels. The frequency of the ac increases with the speed of the wheel. If the frequency of the ac from all wheels is about the same, normal braking is indicated. However, if the signal from any wheel shows a rapid decrease in frequency, it means that the wheel is slowing down too fast. It is beginning to skid.

When the logic control unit senses a rapid drop in the frequency of the signal, it immediately signals the modulator to reduce the hydraulic pressure to the brake for that wheel. When the pressure is reduced, the braking force at that wheel is reduced and it continues to turn. This prevents the skid.

☐ *38-21 STOPLIGHT SWITCH*

Figure 38-26 shows a mechanical stoplight switch. When the brake pedal is pushed down for braking, it causes the contacts in the stoplight switch to close. This connects the stoplights to the battery so that the stoplights come on. Figure 38-26 shows the action during braking with the contacts closed.

☐ *38-22 POWER BRAKES*

About 85 percent of all American-built cars have power brakes. With power brakes, only a light pedal force is required to slow or stop the car. When the brake pedal is pushed down, a vacuum or hydraulic booster takes over and does most of the work of pushing the pistons into the master cylinder. The vacuum comes from the engine intake manifold. Figure 38-27 is a simplified drawing that shows how the vacuum power-brake unit works. When vacuum is applied to one side of the diaphragm, atmospheric pressure causes the diaphragm to move to the right. This

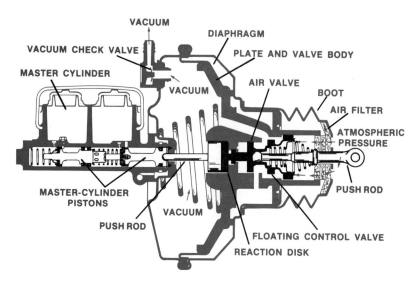

Fig. 38-28 A vacuum-operated power-brake booster shown with the brakes released.

movement pushes the piston into the master cylinder (☐ 38-8).

In the vacuum power-brake system, the brake pedal does not directly work on the master cylinder. Instead, the brake pedal works a vacuum valve, which then admits vacuum to the power cylinder. Figure 38-22 shows a power-brake system using a vacuum booster.

Figure 38-28 shows the vacuum power-brake assembly when the brakes are released. The floating control valve is preventing any atmospheric pressure from entering the power brake. When the brake pedal is pushed down to apply the brakes, the pushrod moves the air valve away from the floating control valve (Fig. 38-29). Now, atmospheric pressure passes the valves and enters the space to the right of the diaphragm. The atmospheric pressure forces the diaphragm to the left. The pushrod pushes the master-cylinder pistons into the master cylinder. This action causes braking to take place.

The reaction disk (Fig. 38-29), next to the air valve, gives the driver some braking "feel." A small proportion of the braking force being applied by the power-brake unit feeds back through the reaction disk. This feedback is felt by the driver through the pushrod and linkage to the brake pedal.

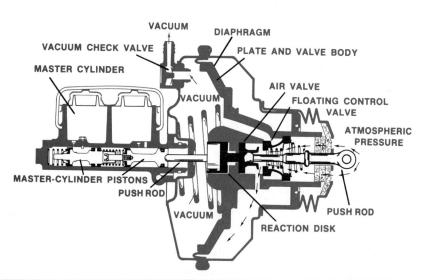

Fig. 38-29 The position of the internal parts in the vacuum power-brake booster when the brakes are applied.

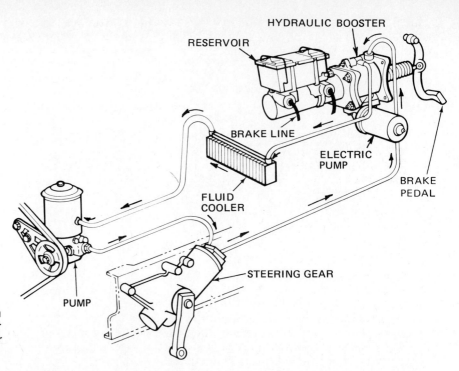

When the brake pedal is released, the air valve moves back to contact the floating control valve. This contact reseals the power-brake unit from atmospheric pressure. Now the conditions shown in Fig. 38-28 are restored.

Some cars are equipped with a hydraulic brake booster (Fig. 38-30). It uses hydraulic pressure supplied by the power-steering pump to assist in applying the brakes (Fig. 38-30). The hydraulic booster is smaller than the vacuum booster. Also, the hydraulic booster can supply about twice the assist power of a vacuum booster.

☐ 38-23 PARKING BRAKES

The parking brake is operated by a separate foot pedal or handbrake lever. Operation of the parking brake causes the rear brakes to be applied mechanically for parking. The pedal or lever is connected to the rear-wheel brake shoes or pads by cables or linkage. One system is shown in Fig. 38-31. When the lever is operated, the cable forces the brake shoes to move into contact with the brake drums.

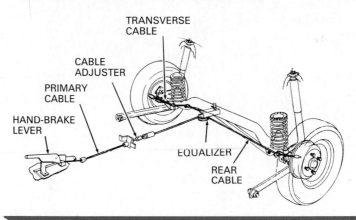

Fig. 38-31 Typical parking-brake system operated by a hand lever. (*Ford Motor Company*)

In some cars the parking brake is released by a vacuum cylinder. This happens when the engine is started and the transmission selector lever is moved out of park.

Select the *one* correct, best, or most probable answer to each question. Then check your answers against the correct answers given at the end of the book.

1. Brake action starts at the
   a. wheels
   b. master cylinder
   c. wheel cylinders
   d. brake pedal

2. The two basic types of wheel-brake mechanisms are
   a. drum and self-adjusting
   b. drum and disk
   c. disk and floating caliper
   d. floating caliper and fixed caliper

3. Self-adjustment of disk brakes is due to
   a. adjusting lever and spring
   b. caliper action
   c. piston-seal action
   d. brake-pad action

4. Disk-brake action results from the
   a. disk being locked to the caliper
   b. disk being clamped between two brake shoes
   c. curved shoes pressing against the inside of the drum
   d. disk rotating

5. The floating-caliper disk brake usually has
   a. one piston
   b. two pistons
   c. three pistons
   d. four pistons

6. The fixed-caliper disk brake usually has
   a. one piston
   b. two pistons
   c. three pistons
   d. four pistons

7. The sliding-caliper disk brake has
   a. one shoe
   b. two shoes
   c. three shoes
   d. four shoes

CHAPTER 39
BRAKE SERVICE

After studying this chapter, and with proper instruction and equipment, you should be able to:

1. Diagnose drum-brake troubles.
2. Diagnose disk-brake troubles.
3. Adjust brakes.
4. Bleed brakes.
5. Perform brake-service jobs.

Many conditions require you to make a visual inspection and then check the operation of the brakes. Any complaint of faulty braking should be diagnosed to determine its cause. Sometimes the condition is corrected by a simple adjustment. Other conditions may require that you perform major brake service. This chapter provides an introduction to brake trouble diagnosis and service. When you work in the shop, you will learn more about the procedures and how to use the special brake tools.

CAUTION Brake lining usually is made of asbestos. Breathing asbestos dust could cause lung cancer. For this reason, do not use the air hose to blow away dust from the brakes. Instead, wipe away dust with a damp cloth or use a brake-assembly washer (Fig. 39-1). Avoid breathing any brake dust. Wash your hands after handling dusty brake parts and brake lining.

DRUM-BRAKE TROUBLE DIAGNOSIS

☐ 39-1 DRUM-BRAKE TROUBLES

Various types of drum-brake troubles require you to quickly and accurately diagnose the cause of the trouble. These conditions include:

1. Brake pedal goes to floorboard.
2. One brake drags.

Fig. 39-1 Using a brake-assembly washer to clean the dust and dirt from a drum brake. *(Ammco Tools, Inc.)*

3. All brakes drag.
4. Car pulls to one side during braking.
5. Soft, or spongy, pedal.
6. Poor braking requiring excessive pedal pressure.
7. Brakes too sensitive or brakes grab.
8. Noisy brakes (brake squeal).
9. Air in system.
10. Loss of brake fluid.
11. Brakes do not self-adjust.
12. Brake warning light comes on.

The causes of these various conditions and the ways of finding them are described in the following sections.

☐ 39-2 BRAKE PEDAL GOES TO FLOORBOARD

This condition seldom occurs with a dual-braking system. One section might fail, but it would be rare for both to fail at the same time. When the brake pedal goes to the floorboard, braking action does not take place. This trouble means that either there is not enough brake fluid in the master cylinder or the brake shoes are worn or out of adjustment. Loss of brake fluid could be due to leaks. Also, air trapped in the hydraulic system could cause the trouble.

☐ 39-3 ONE BRAKE DRAGS

When one brake drags, the brake shoes are not moving away from the drum when the brakes are released. This problem could be caused by any of the following:

■ Incorrect parking-brake adjustment
■ Weak or broken shoe return springs

- Shoes out of adjustment
- Sticking piston in wheel cylinder
- Restricted brake line that will not release pressure
- Loose wheel bearing that allows the wheel to wobble so that the drum hits the brake shoes

□ 39-4 ALL BRAKES DRAG

If all the brakes drag, the probable cause is that the master-cylinder pistons are not returning completely. The pushrod linkage needs adjustment or the master cylinder should be rebuilt or replaced. If the linkage is out of adjustment, the piston cups in the master cylinder are prevented from clearing the compensating ports. Therefore, pressure is not relieved as it should be. Instead, pressure continues to be applied to the brake fluid so that the brake shoes do not retract properly. A similar condition could result from the use of engine oil in the hydraulic system. Engine oil causes the rubber parts, such as the piston cups, to swell. *Engine oil must never be put into the brake system!*

□ 39-5 CAR PULLS TO ONE SIDE DURING BRAKING

This trouble means that more braking friction is being applied to one drum or disk than the other. This problem could be caused by any of the following:

- Grease or brake fluid on lining
- Broken self-adjuster
- Restricted brake line or hose
- Sticking wheel-cylinder piston
- Brake backing plate loose
- Mismatched brake linings
- Incorrect tire pressures
- Unmatched tires on same axle
- Front wheels out of line

Brake linings with grease or brake fluid on them must be replaced. A leaky wheel cylinder could cause brake fluid to get onto the brake linings. At the rear, a defective axle seal or high lubricant level in the differential could allow oil to leak past the seal onto the brake linings (Fig. 39-2).

□ 39-6 SOFT OR SPONGY PEDAL

This trouble probably is caused by air in the brake system. Sometimes it can be caused by incorrect brake-shoe adjustments. Causes of air leaking into the system are described in □ 39-10.

□ 39-7 POOR BRAKING REQUIRING EXCESSIVE PEDAL FORCE

Poor braking requiring excessive pedal force could be caused by any of the following:

- Power-booster failure
- Piston stuck in wheel cylinder
- Brake linings soaked with water
- Brake linings hot

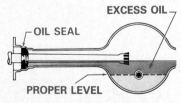

Fig. 39-2 A high lubricant level in the differential and axle housing may cause leakage past the oil seal. This would result in oil-soaked brake linings. *(Pontiac Motor Division of General Motors Corporation)*

- Brake drums glazed
- Shoes out of adjustment
- Failure of one section of the dual-brake system

When brake linings become soaked with water, they may lose braking ability. Usually, good braking will be restored as soon as the linings dry out.

If brakes are used continuously for a period of time, such as when coming down a long hill, they may overheat and "fade." The linings and drums become so hot that they are ineffective. To prevent excessive braking when coming down a long hill, the driver should shift to a lower gear so that the engine is allowed to do part of the braking. The excessive heating may also glaze the brake drum so that it becomes too smooth for effective braking. The remedy here is to refinish the drums to remove the glaze. Also, if the brake linings are charred or burned, they should be replaced.

If the system is a power-brake system, failure of the power booster will require a high pedal force. Causes of power-brake failures are described in □ 39-25.

□ 39-8 BRAKES TOO SENSITIVE OR BRAKES GRAB

When the brakes are too sensitive, slight force on the brake pedal may cause the brakes to grab. The causes of these problems could be any of the causes listed in □ 39-5 and any of the following conditions:

- Binding linkage.
- Defective power brake.
- Defective metering or combination valve.
- Backing plates loose.
- Brake shoes out of adjustment.
- Brake drums scored.
- Wrong type of brake lining for car.
- Brake linings have grease on them.

□ 39-9 NOISY BRAKES (BRAKE SQUEAL)

If the linings wear down so much that the rivets touch the brake drum, the brakes may squeal when applied. Noise also could result from warped brake shoes or a rough or worn brake drum. Figure 39-3 shows various types of brake-drum defects. Loose parts can cause rattles. Some cars have brake squeal caused by vibration between the shoes and the drums.

□ 39-10 AIR IN SYSTEM

If air gets into the hydraulic system, the brakes will be spongy. The result will be poor braking action. This trouble could be due to a plugged filler vent in the master cylinder. If the vent becomes plugged, air could be drawn into the system on the return stroke of the piston (Fig. 39-4). This is not likely to happen on a dual master cylinder with a rubber reservoir diaphragm (Fig. 38-6). Loose connections or damaged brake lines could also allow air to get into the system. However, the most common cause of air in the system is low brake fluid in the master cylinder. This condition results from loss of brake fluid (□ 39-11).

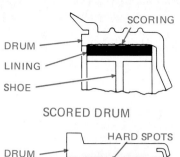

SCORED DRUM

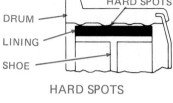

HARD SPOTS

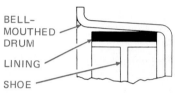

BELL-MOUTHED DRUM

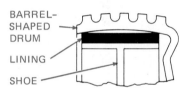

BARREL-SHAPED DRUM

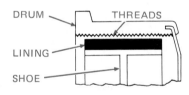

THREADED DRUM

Fig. 39-3 Various types of brake-drum defects that require drum service. (Bear Manufacturing Company)

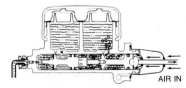

Fig. 39-4 If the air vent in the master-cylinder cover becomes clogged, air may be drawn into the system. The air gets past the low-pressure seal on the primary piston during its return stroke. (Pontiac Motor Division of General Motors Corporation)

Fig. 39-5 Incorrect installation of the pin in the wheel cylinder will cause a side thrust on the piston. This permits brake fluid to leak out past the cup. The pin must align with the notch in the brake shoe. *(Pontiac Motor Division of General Motors Corporation)*

☐ 39-11 LOSS OF BRAKE FLUID

Loss of brake fluid is due to a leak. The leak could be in the master cylinder, a wheel cylinder, a connection, or a brake line. Usually, the point of leakage is easy to find because it will be covered with dirt that stuck to the fluid as it leaked out. If the leak occurs after a brake job, the brake-shoe actuating pin in a wheel cylinder may not be properly installed. If the pin is installed in a cocked position (Fig. 39-5), the piston will not set straight and a leak may result.

☐ 39-12 BRAKES DO NOT SELF-ADJUST

Failure of the brakes to self-adjust could be caused by defects in the adjuster mechanism. For example, the self-adjuster cable may be broken, the lever might not engage the star wheel, or the self-adjuster might be put together incorrectly.

☐ 39-13 BRAKE WARNING LIGHT COMES ON

The warning light on the instrument panel comes on if one section of the dual-braking system fails. Both sections of the dual-braking system should be checked so that the trouble can be found and fixed. It is dangerous to drive a car with only one brake section working. Only half of the wheels are bring braked.

DISK-BRAKE TROUBLE DIAGNOSIS

☐ 39-14 DISK-BRAKE TROUBLES

Many of the troubles with drum brakes can also occur with disk brakes. However, there are some problems that occur only with disk brakes. These include:

1. Excessive pedal travel.
2. Brake roughness or chatter (pedal pulsations).
3. Excessive pedal force.
4. Pull.
5. Noises.
6. Brakes heat up during driving and fail to release.
7. Leaky caliper cylinder.
8. Grabbing or uneven brake action.
9. Brake pedal can be depressed without braking action.
10. Brake warning light comes on (☐ 39-13).

☐ 39-15 EXCESSIVE PEDAL TRAVEL

Excessive pedal travel could be caused by any of the following:

■ Excessive disk runout. This means that the disk wobbles as it rotates. When this happens, the pistons are pushed farther into the caliper. Therefore, additional pedal movement is required to push the pistons out. The runout of the disk is checked with a dial indicator (Fig. 39-6). If runout is excessive, the disk should be refinished or a new disk installed.

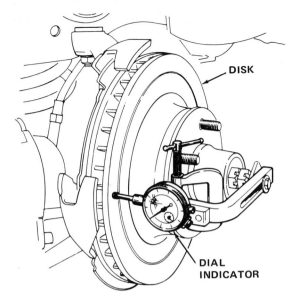

Fig. 39-6 Checking a disk for runout with a dial indicator. *(Chevrolet Motor Division of General Motors Corporation)*

- Air in the system or insufficient brake fluid in the master cylinder.
- Warped or tapered shoes.
- Loose wheel bearing.
- Damaged piston seal.
- Trouble in the power-brake booster.
- Failure of one section of the dual-braking system.

☐ 39-16 BRAKE ROUGHNESS OR CHATTER (PEDAL PULSATIONS)

Brake roughness or chatter could be caused by a disk with too much runout (☐ 39-15). Brake roughness or chatter could also be caused by a disk whose two sides are not parallel (the disk is thicker in one part than in another). A loose wheel bearing could also cause the trouble.

☐ 39-17 EXCESSIVE PEDAL FORCE

The most common cause of excessive pedal force is trouble in the power-brake unit. If this is not the cause, other possible causes are:

- Failure of one section of the dual-braking system
- Brake fluid or grease on the brake linings
- Worn linings
- Incorrect linings
- Sticking piston in caliper

☐ 39-18 PULL

If the car pulls to one side when the brakes are applied, it means there is more braking action on that side. Possible causes could be any of the following:

- Brake fluid or grease on brake linings
- Sticking piston in caliper
- Damaged or bent brake shoe
- Uneven tire pressure

573

- Unmatched tires on same axle
- Caliper loose on steering-knuckle adapter
- Front end out of alignment
- Unmatched brake linings
- Broken spring or loose suspension parts
- Restriction in brake hose or brake line

☐ 39-19 NOISES

Some noises occur with disk brakes. For example, a groan will sometimes result when the brakes are slowly released. Rattles could be caused by loose parts or excessive clearance between the shoe and the caliper. Scraping noises could be caused by the following:

- Long mounting bolts
- Disk rubbing the caliper, which could be caused by loose mounting bolts
- Loose wheel bearings
- Worn brake linings, which allow the wear indicator to scrape the disk

☐ 39-20 BRAKES HEAT UP DURING DRIVING AND FAIL TO RELEASE

This trouble occurs when the shoes maintain contact with the disk. The trouble could be caused by the driver "riding" the brake pedal. Another possible cause is the failure of the power-brake booster to release properly. Also, the pedal linkage could be stuck, or a piston could be stuck in the caliper.

☐ 39-21 LEAKY CALIPER CYLINDER

A leaky caliper cylinder probably is caused by a damaged or worn piston seal. The leak may also be caused by scores or corrosion on the piston or in the cylinder.

☐ 39-22 GRABBING OR UNEVEN BRAKE ACTION

This trouble could be due to trouble in the power-brake booster or to any of the conditions listed in ☐ 39-18.

☐ 39-23 BRAKE PEDAL CAN BE DEPRESSED WITHOUT BRAKING ACTION

When this trouble occurs, it means that the pistons are not pushing the brake shoes out into contact with the disk. This trouble may happen if the brakes have just been serviced. Pumping the brake pedal several times may force the pistons out enough to produce normal braking. If this action does not produce normal braking, then the trouble may be due to the following:

- Leaks in the system
- Damaged piston seals
- Air in the system
- Leaks past the primary cups in the master cylinder

☐ 39-24 SERVICING BRAKES

When you work in the shop, you will learn the various brake jobs. They are listed below.

1. ADJUSTMENTS

On earlier drum brakes without self-adjusters, adjustments were required periodically to compensate for lining wear. With the self-adjusting drum brakes and with disk brakes, no adjustments are required.

2. REPLACING BRAKE LININGS

When linings wear, the shoes must be replaced. On drum brakes, replacement of the shoes requires removal of the wheel and brake drum to get at the shoes (Fig. 39-7). On most disk brakes, the shoes are replaced after removing the wheel and the caliper (Fig. 39-8).

3. DRUM AND DISK SERVICE

Some manufacturers recommend installing new disks if the old ones are worn or scored. Other manufacturers recommend refinishing the disks. Drums can be ground or turned to remove irregularities or scores. However, too much metal must not be removed. This leaves the drum too thin for effective braking action. Also, it may be too thin for safe use.

4. MASTER CYLINDERS

Master cylinders may require disassembly for replacement of internal parts. Honing of the cylinder may also be required. Some technicians prefer to install a new or rebuilt master cylinder.

5. WHEEL CYLINDERS

Wheel cylinders may require disassembly for replacement of the pistons or cups. Honing of the cylinder may also be required. If the bore does not clean properly, a new or rebuilt wheel cylinder should be installed.

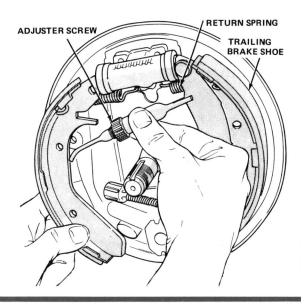

Fig. 39-7 Replacing the brake shoes on a rear drum brake of a front-wheel-drive car. *(Chrysler Corporation)*

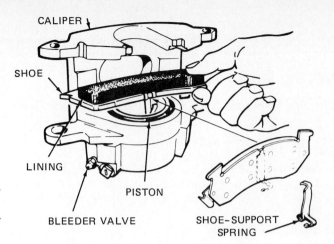

Fig. 39-8 Installing the inner shoe in the disk-brake caliper. *(Chevrolet Motor Division of General Motors Corporation)*

6. CALIPERS

New seals are required if the old seals are worn. Cylinders should be cleaned if they are corroded or rough.

7. INSTALLING BRAKE LINES

Brake lines are made of special steel and rubber tubing. Only tubing recommended by the manufacturer must be used.

8. FLUSHING THE HYDRAULIC SYSTEM

If dirt, engine oil, or other damaging material has gotten into the system, the system must be flushed. Clean brake fluid or flushing compound must be forced through the system to wash it out.

9. FILLING AND BLEEDING THE HYDRAULIC SYSTEM

After flushing, or at any time that brake fluid must be added, the hydraulic system must be bled (Fig. 39-9). All air must be removed from the system. Air is removed by applying pressure at the master cylinder and then opening each bleeder valve in turn at each wheel. This bleeds off any air in any of the lines going to the wheel cylinders or calipers. Refer to the service manual for the proper procedure.

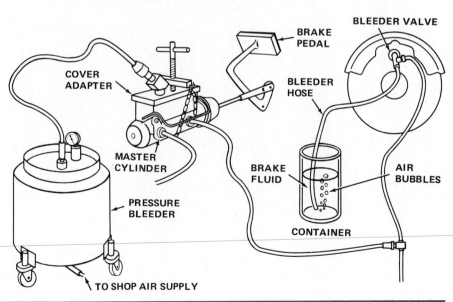

Fig. 39-9 Bleeding the hydraulic system with a pressure bleeder. *(Pontiac Motor Division of General Motors Corporation)*

576

☐ 39-25 POWER-BRAKE TROUBLES

The power-brake booster is an assist unit that helps apply the brakes. A quick check for normal operation is to start the engine while your foot is pressing against the brake pedal. As the engine starts, you should feel the brake pedal fall away or sink slightly. Troubles that power-brake units can have are listed below and their possible causes follow:

1. Excessive pedal force required.
2. Brakes grab.
3. Pedal goes to floor.
4. Brakes fail to release.

☐ 39-26 EXCESSIVE PEDAL FORCE REQUIRED

When excessive pedal force is required, it usually means that there is trouble inside the power booster. The trouble can be caused by any of the following:

■ Defective vacuum-check valve
■ Collapsed hose
■ Plugged vacuum fitting
■ Clogged air inlet
■ Faulty diaphragm
■ Any of the causes listed in ☐ 39-7 and 39-17.

☐ 39-27 BRAKES GRAB

In the vacuum power-brake booster, when the brakes grab, the trouble could be caused by a damaged reaction disk or by a sticking air or vacuum valve. Conditions listed in ☐ 39-8 and 39-22 can also cause brakes to grab.

☐ 39-28 PEDAL GOES TO FLOOR

This condition could be due to any of the troubles listed in ☐ 39-2 and 39-23. In some power-brake units, the trouble could also result from failure of the compensating valve to close or from a leaking hydraulic-plunger seal.

☐ 39-29 BRAKES FAIL TO RELEASE

If the brakes fail to release, the trouble could be due to a broken diaphragm return spring, faulty check-valve action, or a sticking hydraulic-plunger seal. The causes listed in ☐ 39-4 and 39-20 could also prevent the brakes from releasing.

Select the *one* correct, best, or most probable answer to each question. Then check your answers against the correct answers given at the end of the book.

1. Oil must not be put into the brake hydraulic system because the oil will
   a. cause the shoes to slip on the disk
   b. excessively reduce the force required to brake
   c. damage rubber parts in the system
   d. all of the above

2. Spongy brakes and poor braking action can be caused by
   a. air in the hydraulic system
   b. brake fluid in the hydraulic system
   c. failure of the brakes to self-adjust
   d. worn brake shoes

3. If all brakes drag, the cause could be
   a. master-cylinder pistons are not returning completely
   b. pushrod linkage needs adjustment
   c. master cylinder is defective
   d. all of the above

4. Brake linings with grease or brake fluid on them should be
   a. washed in solvent
   b. dried in a low-temperature oven
   c. discarded
   d. scraped to remove the grease or brake fluid

5. When excessive pedal force is required for braking, the most probable cause is
   a. worn drums or disks
   b. power-brake failure
   c. misadjusted linkage
   d. low fluid level in master cylinder

6. Bleeding the hydraulic system means
   a. removing excessive brake fluid from the system
   b. flushing the system
   c. removing air from the system
   d. closing the bleed valves

7. Drum brakes grabbing could be caused by
   a. binding linkage
   b. backing plates loose or shoes out of adjustment
   c. brake drums scored
   d. all of the above

8. If drum brakes heat up during driving and fail to release, the cause could be
   a. shoes fail to release from the drum
   b. low brake fluid
   c. air in hydraulic system
   d. shoes badly worn

CHAPTER 40
SPRINGS AND SUSPENSION SYSTEMS

After studying this chapter, you should be able to:
1. List the three basic types of springs used in cars and describe how they work.
2. Describe the construction and operation of each type of rear-suspension system.
3. Describe the construction and operation of each type of front-suspension system.
4. Explain the purpose and operation of shock absorbers.
5. Explain how automatic level control works.

Springs are part of the suspension system of the automobile. Their purpose is to absorb road shocks that result from the wheels hitting holes or bumps. There are three types. These are coil, leaf, and torsion bar (Fig. 40-1). The coil spring is the most widely used for both front- and rear-suspension systems.

□ 40-1 FUNCTION OF SPRINGS

The car frame supports the weight of the engine, the power train, the car body, and the passengers. The frame, in turn, is supported by the springs. There is a spring at each wheel. The weight of the car, applies an initial compression to the springs. The springs will further compress or expand as the car wheels hit bumps or holes in the road. However, springs alone cannot do the complete job of absorbing road shocks. The tires absorb the impact of many bumps and holes in the road. The springs in the car seats also help to absorb shock. As a result, very little shock from road bumps and holes gets to the passenger.

□ 40-2 TYPES OF SPRINGS

There are three basic types of automotive springs. They are leaf, coil, and

COIL

LEAF

TORSION BAR

Fig. 40-1 Three types of springs used in automotive suspension systems. *(Ford Motor Company)*

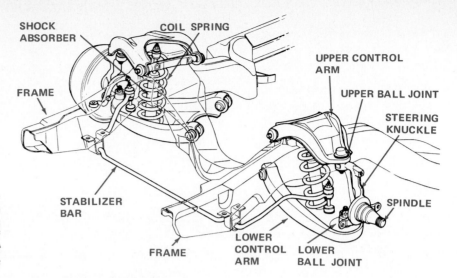

Fig. 40-2 Front-wheel suspension using coil springs on the lower control arms. The wheels mount on the tapered spindles of the steering knuckles. *(Chevrolet Motor Division of General Motors Corporation)*

torsion bar (Fig. 40-1). In addition, air suspension is used in some trucks and buses and in a few cars.

Most cars use either coil springs or torsion-bar springs at the front wheels (Figs. 40-2 and 40-3). Some cars use coil springs at the rear wheels. Others use leaf springs.

□ 40-3 LEAF SPRINGS

The leaf spring most commonly used in automobiles is made up of several long plates, or leaves. Figure 40-4 shows a typical leaf-spring installation at a rear wheel. Figure 40-5 shows how the spring at each rear wheel is mounted on the frame. The leaf spring acts like a flexible beam. A solid beam strong enough to support the car weight would not be very flexible. For example, if you tried to bend a solid beam (Fig. 40-6), the top edge would try to get longer while the bottom edge would try to push together. The result is that the top edge of the beam might pull apart and the beam might break.

Because the leaf spring consists of a series of thin leaves, one on top of another (Fig. 40-6), it does not break when bent. When the spring is bent, the individual leaves bend and slip over one another. This provides a spring with great flexibility and strength.

Some lightweight cars use single-leaf springs. Single-leaf springs are tapered from the center to the ends so that they work in the same way as multileaf springs. Figure 40-7 shows a rear-suspension system using two single-leaf springs. They are attached in the same way as multileaf springs.

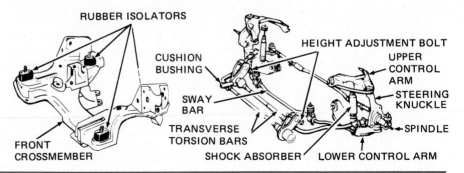

Fig. 40-3 A front-suspension system using transverse torsion bars. *(Chrysler Corporation)*

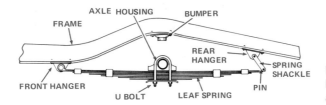

Fig. 40-4 A leaf spring, showing how it is attached to the frame and axle housing.

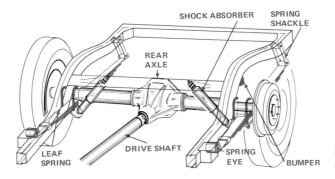

Fig. 40-5 A rear-suspension system using leaf springs.

□ 40-4 LEAF-SPRING INSTALLATION

Figures 40-4 and 40-5 show how leaf springs are installed in rear-suspension systems. The spring leaves are of graduated length. The front end of the longest leaf is bent into a circle to form a spring eye. The spring eye is attached to the spring hanger by a bolt. Rubber bushings insulate the bolt from the spring hanger (Fig. 40-8). The rubber bushings serve two purposes. They absorb vibration and prevent it from reaching the car frame. The bushings also allow the spring eye to twist back and forth as the leaf spring bends.

The rear end of the spring also is bent to form a spring eye. This spring eye is attached to the car frame through a spring shackle. The shackle is needed to take care of the changes in the length of the leaf spring as it bends. As the spring is pushed upward or downward by bumps or holes in the road, the length between the two spring eyes is changed. The shackle forms a swinging support that permits this change in length. The shackle includes rubber bushings to absorb vibration and prevent it from reaching the car frame.

The center of the spring is hung from the rear-axle housing by a pair of U-bolts. The rear of the car is, in effect, hung from the axle housing by two pairs of U-bolts. There are rubber bumpers on the car frame above the axles. The purpose of these bumpers is to absorb the shock that would result if the axle housing actually moved up far enough to hit the frame. The axle housing would move up this far only if the wheels hit a very large bump or if the rear of the car were carrying a very heavy load.

Two shock absorbers, one for each spring, are shown in Fig. 40-5. Shock absorbers are described in □ 40-13.

□ 40-5 COIL-SPRING REAR SUSPENSION

In the rear-suspension systems of many cars, coil springs are used instead of leaf springs. The coil spring is made from a length of steel rod wound into a coil (Fig. 40-2). The coil spring is very elastic and will compress when a weight is put on it. The heavier the weight, the more the spring will compress. Figure 40-9 shows a car using a coil spring at each wheel.

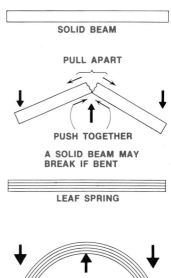

Fig. 40-6 Compare the effects of bending a solid beam and a leaf beam, or spring.

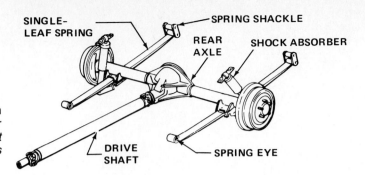

Fig. 40-7 A rear-suspension system using a tapered-plate, or single-leaf, spring. *(Chevrolet Motor Division of General Motors Corporation)*

A rear-suspension system using coil springs is shown in Fig. 40-10. Each spring is assembled between spring seats in the car frame or body and lower control arms, or pads, on the axle housing. When the rear wheels hit a hole or a bump in the road, the springs expand or compress to absorb the shock.

The coil-spring rear-suspension system shown in Fig. 40-10 has four control arms. Two of the arms are upper control arms, and two are lower control arms. The purpose of the arms is to keep the rear-axle housing in alignment with the frame. The two upper control arms are pivoted on the rear cross member and the differential carrier. The upper control arms prevent sideward movement of the axle housing. The two lower control arms are pivoted on the frame and the axle housing. The lower control arms prevent forward-and-backward movement of the housing. These arms permit the rear-axle housing to move up and down. But they prevent sideward or forward-and-backward movement. As in other suspension systems, a shock absorber is used at each wheel. Figure 40-9 shows a coil-spring rear-suspension system on a front-wheel-drive car. Additional control arms are not needed on this car.

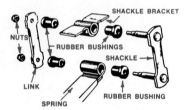

Fig. 40-8 A disassembled spring shackle for a leaf spring.

□ 40-6 COIL-SPRING FRONT SUSPENSION

The front-suspension system must allow the wheels to move up and down. It must also allow the wheels to pivot from side to side so that the car can be steered. Figure 40-11 shows two views of a front-suspension system using coil springs. Figure 40-2 shows a similar system.

In the system shown in Fig. 40-11, the coil spring is held between a spring seat in the car frame and a lower control arm. The inner ends of both the lower and upper control arms are pivoted on the car frame. The outer ends of the control arms are connected to the steering knuckle. The

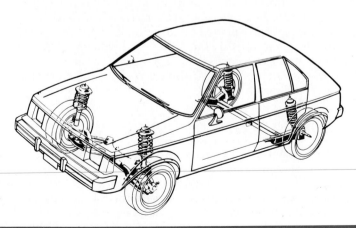

Fig. 40-9 Locations of the coil springs used at the front and rear of the car. This car has MacPherson-strut front- and rear-suspension systems. *(Chrysler Corporation)*

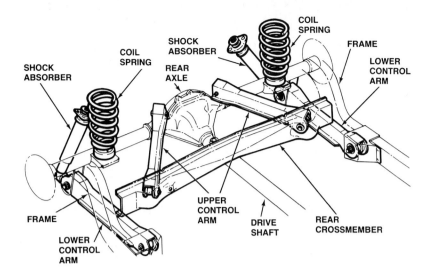

Fig. 40-10 A coil-spring rear-suspension system using four control arms. *(American Motors Corporation)*

steering knuckle is attached to the control arms through ball joints. These ball joints allow the steering knuckles to swing to the left or right for steering. In the assembled car, the wheels are mounted on the spindles of the steering knuckles. Swinging the knuckles from left to right pivots the front wheels so that the car can be steered. Steering systems are described in Chap. 41.

Figure 40-12 shows what happens when a front wheel hits a bump in the road. Figure 40-13 shows what happens when a front wheel drops into a hole in the road. When a front wheel hits a bump, the wheel moves up, as shown by the dashed lines in Fig. 40-12. As the wheel moves up, the two control arms pivot upward. This action compresses the spring between the lower control arm and the car frame. When a front wheel drops into a hole (Fig. 40-13), the control arms pivot downward. This allows the spring to expand.

In the coil-suspension system shown in Figs. 40-11, 40-12, and 40-13, the shock absorbers are centered in the springs. Shock absorbers are described in □ 40-13.

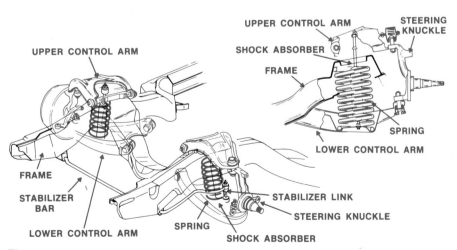

Fig. 40-11 Front-suspension system with the coil springs mounted on the lower control arms, which are each attached to the frame at a single point.

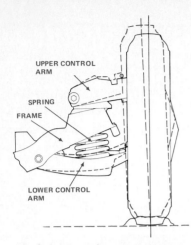

Fig. 40-12 Front suspension at one wheel, showing the action as the wheel meets a bump in the road. The upward movement of the wheel, shown in dashed lines, raises the lower control arm, causing the spring to compress.

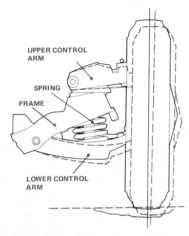

Fig. 40-13 Front suspension at one wheel, showing the action as the wheel meets a hole in the road. The downward movement of the wheel, shown in dashed lines, lowers the lower control arm, permitting the spring to expand.

Fig. 40-14 A coil-spring front-suspension system which has the spring mounted on the upper control arm.

□ 40-7 COIL SPRING ABOVE UPPER CONTROL ARM

Another type of front-suspension system has the coil springs mounted between the upper control arm and a spring tower that is part of the front-end sheet metal (Fig. 40-14). The action of this type of coil-spring front-suspension system is the same as the action of the system explained in □ 40-6. When the wheel meets a bump or a hole, the control arms pivot and compress or expand the spring. The system shown in Fig. 40-14 has a lower control arm with only one point of attachment to the frame. A *strut rod,* or *brake-reaction rod,* is used to prevent the outer end of the lower control arm from swinging forward or backward (□ 40-9).

□ 40-8 MacPHERSON FRONT SUSPENSION

The MacPherson front suspension (Fig. 40-9) is similar to the coil-spring suspension shown in Fig. 40-14. However, the top of the coil spring fits into a tower that is part of the body sheet metal. No upper control arm is needed. The shock absorber is built into a strut that connects the lower control arm to the mounting assembly in the tower. Figure 40-15 shows the system in a car. Figure 40-16 shows the MacPherson strut partly disassembled. Each MacPherson-strut assembly includes a strut, coil spring, stabilizer, and shock absorber. This system is widely used on small cars. A variation of it also is used for the rear suspension in some cars.

□ 40-9 STRUT ROD FOR LOWER CONTROL ARM

In many front-suspension systems, the lower control arm has only one point of attachment to the frame (Fig. 40-14). With this system an extra part is required. It is called a strut rod, or a brake-reaction rod. The strut rod is fastened between the outer end of the lower control arm and the car frame. The purpose of the strut rod is to prevent the outer end of the lower control arm from swinging forward or backward during braking or when the wheel hits holes or bumps in the road. In the front-suspension system shown in Fig. 40-11, no strut rod is needed because the lower control arm has two points of attachment to the frame. These two points of attachment provide enough forward-and-backward rigidity for the lower control arm.

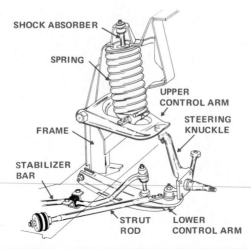

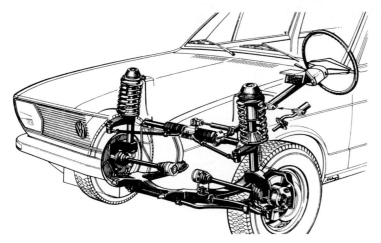

Fig. 40-15 A MacPherson-strut front suspension. *(Volkswagen of America, Inc.)*

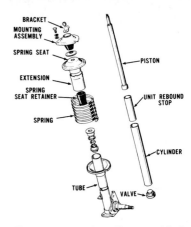

Fig. 40-16 A disassembled MacPherson strut. *(Ford Motor Company)*

□ 40-10 STABILIZER BAR

In Figs. 40-2 and 40-11 you can see a part labeled "stabilizer bar." This bar is a long steel rod formed to fasten at each end to the two lower control arms. The stabilizer bar is sometimes called a *sway bar*.

When the car goes around a curve, centrifugal force tends to keep the car moving in a straight line. Therefore the car "leans out" on the turn. This "lean out" is also called "body roll." With lean out, or body roll, additional weight is thrown on the outer spring. This weight puts additional compression on the outer spring, and the lower control arm pivots upward. As the lower control arm for the outer wheel pivots upward, it carries the end of the stabilizer bar up with it. At the inner wheel on the turn, there is less weight on the spring. Weight has shifted to the outer spring because of the centrifugal force. Therefore, the inner spring tends to expand. The expansion of the inner spring tends to pivot the lower control arm downward. As this happens, the lower control arm for the inner wheel carries the end of the stabilizer bar downward.

Now the outer end of the stabilizer bar is carried upward by the outer lower control arm. The inner end is carried downward by the inner lower control arm. This combined action twists the stabilizer bar. The resistance of the bar to twisting opposes the tendency of the frame to twist and untwist on turns. There is less body roll than there would be without the stabilizer bar.

□ 40-11 TORSION-BAR FRONT SUSPENSION

In the torsion-bar front-suspension system, two steel bars serve as the springs (Figs. 40-3 and 40-17). The ends of the bar are locked to a cross

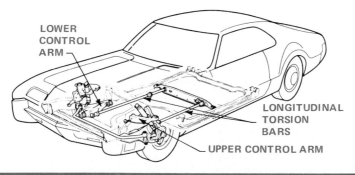

Fig. 40-17 Front-suspension system using longitudinal torsion bars. The bars twist varying amounts as the wheels move up and down. This provides the springing action. *(Oldsmobile Division of General Motors Corporation)*

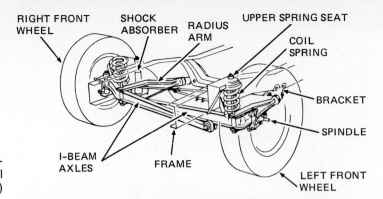

Fig. 40-18 A twin I-beam front-suspension system using coil springs. (Ford Motor Company)

member or to the body. The other end of the bars is attached to the lower control arms. In operation, the lower control arms pivot up and down, twisting the torsion bars. The effect is very similar to the actions of the coil and leaf springs. Torsion bars that run across the car (Fig. 40-3) are called *transverse torsion bars*. When the torsion bars are installed so that they run from front to rear on the car, they are called *longitudinal torsion bars* (Fig. 40-17).

☐ 40-12 LIGHT-TRUCK FRONT SUSPENSION

Two other types of front suspensions are used on light trucks. The twin I-beam front-suspension system (Fig. 40-18) uses two I beams. Each front wheel is supported at the outer end by an I beam. The opposite ends of the I beams are attached to the car frame by pivots. Coil springs are used at each wheel.

Another front-suspension system for trucks is shown in Fig. 40-19. This system uses a single I-beam front axle. A leaf spring and a shock absorber are used at each wheel.

☐ 40-13 PURPOSE OF SHOCK ABSORBERS

Shock absorbers are needed because springs do not "settle down" fast enough. After a spring has been compressed and released, it continues to shorten and lengthen, or oscillate, for a short time. You can demonstrate

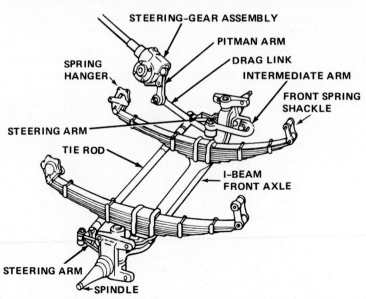

Fig. 40-19 A truck front-suspension system using a single I-beam front axle and two leaf springs. (Ford Motor Company)

to yourself the action of a spring by hanging a small weight on a spring (Fig. 40-20). Lift the weight and then let it drop. As the weight drops, it expands the spring. Then the spring pulls the weight up. The weight then drops again. The spring, as it lengthens and shortens, keeps the weight moving up and down for some time. These oscillations are shown by the wavy line at the right in Fig. 40-20.

If the car springs were not controlled, they would act the same way. For example, when a wheel hits a bump, the spring compresses. Then the spring expands after the wheel passes the bump. The expansion of the spring would cause the car to be thrown upward. Now, having overexpanded, the spring would shorten again. This action could cause the wheel to momentarily leave the road, and the car would drop down. The action would be repeated until the oscillations gradually died out.

Such spring action on a car would produce a very bumpy and uncomfortable ride. Also, this action could be dangerous, because a bouncing wheel makes the car difficult to control. So a device is needed to control the oscillating action of the spring. This device is the shock absorber.

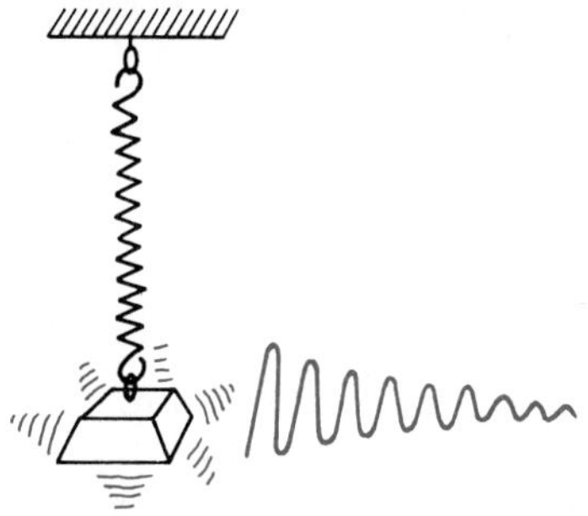

☐ 40-14 OPERATION OF THE SHOCK ABSORBER

The shock of the wheel meeting a bump or a hole is absorbed by the shock absorber. Because of the shock absorber, as soon as the wheel passes the hole or the bump, it returns to contact with the road and does not bounce. The most commonly used shock absorber is the direct-acting, or telescope, type (Fig. 40-21). Several illustrations in this chapter show the locations of the shock absorbers at the front and rear of the car. In operation, the shock absorbers lengthen and shorten as the wheels meet irregularities in the road. As they do this, a piston inside the shock absorber moves up and down in a chamber filled with fluid. Movement of the piston puts the fluid under high pressure and forces it to flow through the small openings. Since the fluid can pass through these openings only slowly, the fluid slows the motion of the piston. This, in turn, restrains the movement of the spring.

Figure 40-21 shows a shock absorber in cutaway view. During compression and rebound, the piston moves up and down. The fluid in the shock absorber is forced through small openings in the piston. You can see one of the fluid passages through the piston in Fig. 40-21. This action controls spring movement.

When the wheel receives a sudden severe shock, pressure in the shock absorber could go so high that it would rip open. To prevent this, a

Fig. 40-20 If a weight hanging from a coil spring is set into up-and-down motion, the weight will oscillate for some time. The distance it moves up and down will gradually shorten, as indicated by the curve. Finally, the motion will die out.

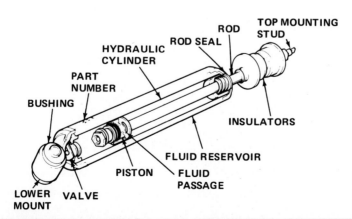

Fig. 40-21 A shock absorber, cut away to show the internal parts. *(Ford Motor Company)*

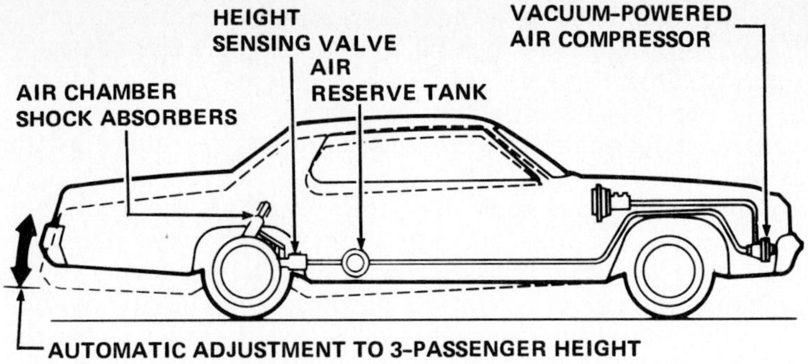

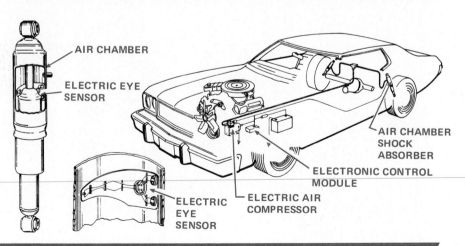

Fig. 40-22 Action of an automatic-level-control system. The dotted lines show the lower height of the car before the automatic level control restores the correct height. *(Chrysler Corporation)*

HEIGHT
SENSING VALVE

AIR
RESERVE TANK

VACUUM–POWERED
AIR COMPRESSOR

AIR CHAMBER
SHOCK ABSORBERS

AUTOMATIC ADJUSTMENT TO 3-PASSENGER HEIGHT

valve in the shock absorber opens when the internal pressure gets excessive. When the valve opens, it allows a slightly faster spring movement. However, some restraint is still imposed on the spring.

☐ 40-15 AUTOMATIC LEVEL CONTROL

The automatic-level-control system (Fig. 40-22) takes care of changes in the amount of load in the rear of the car. In a car without automatic level control, additional weight makes the rear end of the car lower. This changes the handling characteristics of the car. It also causes the headlights to point upward. The automatic level control prevents this by automatically raising the rear end of the car to level when a load is added. The system also automatically lowers the rear end of the car to level when the load is removed.

The automatic-level-control system includes a compressor, an air-reserve tank, a height-control valve, and two special shock absorbers with built-in air chambers (Fig. 40-22). The compressor is operated by engine intake-manifold vacuum. The vacuum operates a pump that builds up air pressure in the reserve tank. When a load is added to the rear of the car, additional air is passed through the height-control valve to the two rear shock absorbers. These shock absorbers have air chambers (Fig. 40-23). The air entering this chamber raises the upper shell of the shock absorber. As the upper shell of the shock absorber is raised, the rear of the car is returned to its normal level.

Figure 40-23 shows an electronic type of automatic-level-control system. The air is supplied by an electric air compressor, instead of a vacuum-powered air compressor. No separate height-control valve is needed. A photo-optic sensor (electric eye) is built into the left rear shock ab-

AIR CHAMBER

ELECTRIC EYE
SENSOR

AIR CHAMBER
SHOCK
ABSORBER

ELECTRONIC CONTROL
MODULE

ELECTRIC
EYE
SENSOR

ELECTRIC AIR
COMPRESSOR

Fig. 40-23 An electronic automatic-level-control system. It uses an electric eye to switch the electric air compressor on and off. *(Monroe Auto Equipment Company)*

sorber. The sensor signals the electronic control module when any change in height has occurred. If a load has been added to the car and additional height is needed, the electronic control module turns on the air compressor.

In both types of automatic level control, a time-delay device is used. It allows air to enter or leave the shock absorber only after a change in level has lasted about 15 seconds. This prevents fast valve action, which could raise or lower the car after each bump or hole in the road. The automatic-level-control system works only when loads are added to or removed from the rear of the car.

☐ 40-16 SERVICING SUSPENSION SYSTEMS

Suspension-system service is closely tied in with wheel alignment and steering service. Chapter 41 describes steering systems. Wheel alignment is covered in Chap. 42.

CHAPTER 40
REVIEW QUESTIONS

Select the *one* correct, best, or most probable answer to each question. Then check your answers against the correct answers given at the end of the book.

1. One end of the leaf spring is attached to the frame with a
   a. chain
   b. lever
   c. shackle
   d. brace

2. Three types of springs used in automotive suspension systems are
   a. coil, leaf, and torsion bar
   b. coil, torsion bar, and lever
   c. leaf, suspension, and shock
   d. lever, leaf, and coil

3. MacPherson struts are used in
   a. rear-suspension systems
   b. front-suspension systems
   c. both *a* and *b*
   d. neither *a* nor *b*

4. Which of the following statements is *true* about a MacPherson-strut front suspension?
   a. Upper and lower control arms are used.
   b. Two ball joints are used with each strut.
   c. Only an upper-control arm is used.
   d. The shock absorber is built into the strut.

5. The four control arms used on some rear-suspension systems
   a. prevent sideward movement of the axle housing
   b. prevent forward-and-backward movement of the axle housing
   c. both *a* and *b*
   d. neither *a* nor *b*

CHAPTER 41
STEERING SYSTEMS

After studying this chapter, you should be able to:

1. Explain the purpose, construction, and operation of manual steering systems.
2. Discuss front-end geometry and the various angles involved.
3. Describe the construction and operation of power-steering systems.
4. Discuss the construction and operation of tilt and telescoping steering wheels.
5. Explain the operation of the steering column lock.

The steering system allows the driver to guide the car down the road and turn right or left, as desired. The system includes the steering wheel, which the driver turns, linkages, and the front-wheel supports. Most steering systems were manual until a few years ago. Then power steering became popular. Now it is installed on more than 80 percent of the cars manufactured in the United States.

☐ 41-1 OPERATION OF THE STEERING SYSTEM

Figure 41-1 is a simplified view, from above, of a steering system. The method of supporting the front wheels on steering knuckles is described and illustrated in Chap. 40. The steering knuckles are attached to the upper and lower control arms by *ball joints* (Fig. 40-2). These ball joints permit the steering knuckles to swing from right to left. This movement turns the front wheels one way or the other so that the car can be steered.

The simplified steering system shown in Fig. 41-1 includes the steering wheel, steering gear, tie rods, steering arms, and wheels. When the steering wheel is turned, gears inside the steering gear cause the pitman arm to swing to the left or right. As the pitman arm swings, it pulls or pushes on the tie rods. This action pulls or pushes on the steering arms. The steering knuckles and wheels turn the amount desired by the driver to steer the car.

Before we describe the steering gears and linkages in detail, let's discuss the various angles in the front-suspension system.

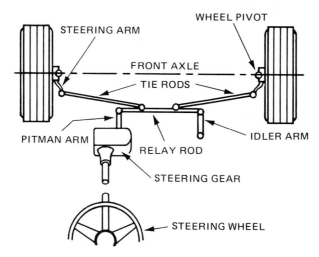

Fig. 41-1 Simplified drawing of a pitman-arm manual-steering system.

□ 41-2 FRONT-END GEOMETRY

The term "front-end geometry" or "steering geometry" refers to the various angles between the front wheels, the frame, and the attachment parts. The angles include:

1. Camber
2. Steering-axis inclination
3. Caster
4. Toe
5. Turning radius

Each of these angles is described in following sections. The technician checks these angles when doing a *wheel alignment* (Chap. 42). Each angle is important. If the angles are incorrect, the car will be harder to control and tires will wear rapidly.

□ 41-3 CAMBER

Camber is the tilting of the front wheels from the vertical (straight up and down). When the wheel tilts outward at the top, the camber is positive (Fig. 41-2). When the tilt is inward, the camber is negative. The amount of tilt is measured as the number of degrees from the vertical. This measurement is called the *camber angle*. On a moving car, an average running camber of zero provides the longest tire life.

The purpose of camber is to give the wheels a slight outward tilt to start with (on most cars). Then, when the car is loaded and moving, the load will bring the wheels to vertical again. When the wheels are set to zero camber, then loading the car could give the front wheels a negative camber. The tops of the wheels would tilt inward. When the car is rolling forward, the car will pull toward the wheel with the most positive camber.

Any amount of camber—positive or negative—will cause uneven tire wear. The tilt puts more of the load on one side of the tread rather than centering the load over the entire tread.

□ 41-4 STEERING-AXIS INCLINATION

Steering-axis inclination is the amount the ball joints are tilted inward from the vertical (Fig. 41-2). An actual cutaway front suspension at one wheel is shown in Fig. 41-3. Steering-axis inclination is measured by drawing a line through the centers of the two ball joints. Then you meas-

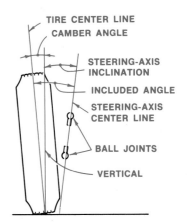

Fig. 41-2 Camber angle and steering-axis inclination. Positive camber is shown.

591

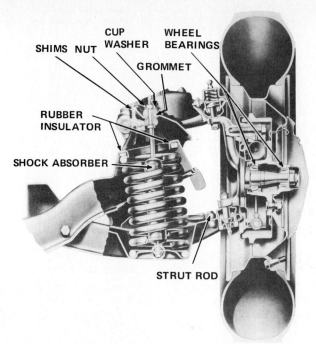

Fig. 41-3 A coil-spring front-suspension system, cut away to show how the ball joints allow the steering knuckle to pivot.

ure how many degrees this line is off from the vertical. There are three reasons for having steering-axis inclination:

- It helps provide steering stability.
- It reduces steering force.
- It permits a reduction in caster angle.

The inward tilt, or inclination, of the steering axis tends to keep the wheels pointed straight ahead. It also helps recovery, or the return of the wheels to the straight-ahead position, after a turn.

On the car, the tire is in contact with the ground. The wheel cannot move down. Therefore, when it is swung away from straight ahead, the end of the spindle moves down. This forces the ball joints to move up. The result is that the car body is actually lifted. The lift is not very much, only about 1 inch [25 mm] or less. But it is enough to help bring the wheels back to the straight-ahead position when the car completes a turn. This is one purpose of steering-axis inclination: When the front wheels are turned away from straight ahead, the front end of the car is raised slightly. Then the weight of the car helps to bring the wheels back to the straight-ahead position when the turn is completed. Steering-axis inclination provides steering stability and reduces the effort required to return the steering wheel to straight ahead. Steering-axis inclination cannot be adjusted, but it can be measured. Incorrect steering-axis inclination means that the steering knuckle or control arm is bent.

☐ 41-5 CASTER

In addition to being tilted inward toward the center of the car, the steering axis is also tilted forward or backward. Backward tilt from the vertical is called *positive caster* (Fig. 41-4). Caster provides steering stability. It does this because the wheel trails behind the point at which the forward push is applied. In the car, the push is at the center line of the steering axis (Fig. 41-4). This puts the push ahead of the wheel. Therefore, the wheel tends to point straight ahead. This helps steering stability. Positive caster helps to keep the wheels pointed straight ahead. It

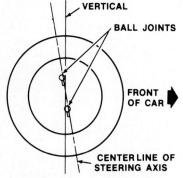

Fig. 41-4 The left front wheel as viewed from the driver's seat. The backward tilt of the steering axis from the vertical is positive caster.

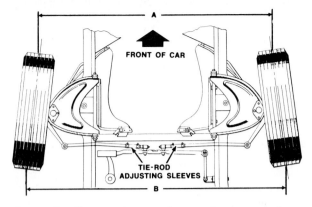

Fig. 41-5 Toe-in. The wheels are viewed from above, with the front of the car at the top of the illustration. Distance A is less than distance B. *(Bear Manufacturing Company)*

helps overcome any tendency for the car to wander or steer away from straight ahead.

Positive caster increases steering-wheel returnability. Because of this, cars with power steering often have slightly more positive caster than manual-steering cars. The additional positive caster helps overcome the tendency of the power steering to hold the wheels in a turn. But because of the power steering, the driver does not notice that the additional positive caster requires greater turning force. Cars with manual steering often have a small negative caster.

☐ 41-6 TOE

On a car with *toe-in,* the distance between the tires on the front wheels is less at the front than at the back (Fig. 41-5). The actual toe-in usually is less than 0.5 inch [13 mm]. But toe is very important. The purpose of toe is to ensure parallel rolling of the front wheels when the car moves forward. For example, to start with, there is toe-in. But when the car begins to move forward, the backward push of the road on the tires takes up the play in the steering linkage. This brings the tires into parallel, so they both roll straight ahead.

☐ 41-7 TURNING RADIUS

Turning radius, or *toe-out on turns,* is the difference in angles between the two front wheels when they are making a turn (Fig. 41-6). The inner wheel follows a smaller arc. Therefore the inner wheel must be turned more than the outer wheel. In Fig. 41-6, the inner wheel turns 23 degrees away from straight ahead, but the outer wheel turns in only 20 degrees. The angle of the steering arms from parallel produces this difference. In Fig. 41-7, the tie rod is pushing against the left steering-knuckle arm almost at a right angle. The right end of the tie rod not only moves to the left but also moves the right steering arm a greater distance. This is due to the obtuse angle between the arm and the tie rod. A "swing-down" effect of the tie rod also helps turn the right wheel more than the left.

☐ 41-8 STEERING LINKAGES

There are several types of steering linkages. All have the same job. They carry the movement of the steering wheel from the steering gear to the steering arms at the wheel. Figure 41-8 shows the parts of one type of steering linkage. It includes an intermediate rod, which is supported at one end by the pitman arm and at the other end by the idler arm. The outer ends of the intermediate rod are attached to the steering-knuckle arms by short tie rods. Notice that the tie rods have adjuster sleeves. The

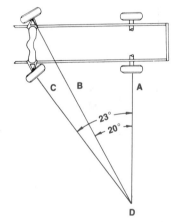

Fig. 41-6 Toe-out on turns, also called *turning radius.*

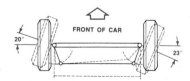

Fig. 41-7 The toe-out on turns, or turning radius, is obtained when the front wheels make a turn.

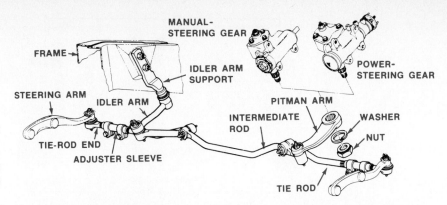

Fig. 41-8 Basic parts of the steering linkage for pitman-arm steering gears.

purpose of these sleeves is to adjust toe. When an adjuster sleeve is turned, it shortens or lengthens the effective length of the tie rod. This swings the front wheel slightly one way or the other.

□ 41-9 TILT AND TELESCOPING STEERING WHEELS

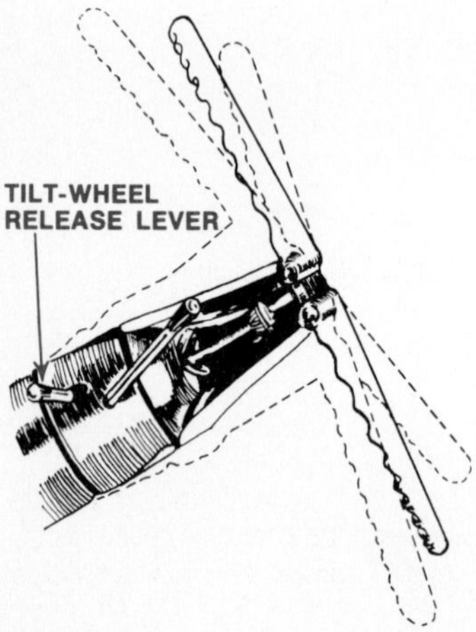

Many cars have steering wheels that can be tilted at various angles (Fig. 41-9). The purpose of the tilt steering wheel is to allow the driver to change the angle as desired. The driver can also change the position of the steering wheel during a long drive.

Some cars also have a telescoping steering wheel (Fig. 41-10). It can be extended or shortened to suit the driver. Another type of steering wheel and column can be swung to the right when the driver gets into or out of the car.

□ 41-10 COLLAPSIBLE STEERING COLUMN

The collapsible steering column is a safety device. It will collapse on impact. For example, in a front-end collision, the driver will be thrown forward and into the steering wheel. This will cause the steering column to collapse and thereby cushion the driver's impact.

NOTE A driver wearing a shoulder belt will not be thrown into the steering wheel.

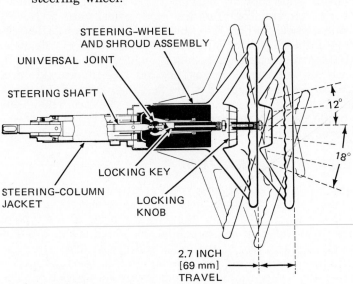

Fig. 41-9 A tilt steering wheel. Lifting the release lever permits the steering wheel to be tilted to various positions. *(Buick Motor Division of General Motors Corporation)*

Fig. 41-10 A tilting-and-telescoping steering wheel. *(Chrysler Corporation)*

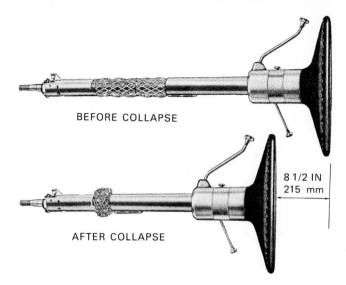

BEFORE COLLAPSE

AFTER COLLAPSE

8 1/2 IN
215 mm

Fig. 41-11 A "Japanese lantern" type of energy-absorbing steering column which can collapse during impact. *(Cadillac Motor Car Division of General Motors Corporation)*

There are several types of collapsible steering columns. These include the "Japanese-lantern" type, the tube-and-ball type, and the shear-capsule type. Figure 41-11 shows the Japanese-lantern type. It gets its name from the fact that on impact the column collapses like a Japanese lantern. The tube-and-ball type has two tubes with balls between them (Fig. 41-12). On impact, the balls must make grooves in the tubes to permit movement. This action absorbs the shock. On the shear-capsule type (Fig. 41-13), the impact cuts the capsule to permit the steering column to collapse. The shearing action absorbs the shock.

☐ 41-11 STEERING LOCK

The combination ignition switch and steering-wheel lock (Fig. 41-14) does several jobs. It locks the steering wheel when the ignition switch is turned off. When the ignition key is inserted and the ignition switch is turned to ON, the gear rotates. This pulls the rack and plunger out of the locking position. Then, when the switch is turned to OFF, the rotation of the gear moves the rack and plunger toward the locked position. If the plunger is lined up with a notch in the disk, the plunger moves in to lock the steering wheel. If it is not lined up, the plunger is spring-loaded against the disk. Then a slight turn of the steering wheel will bring a

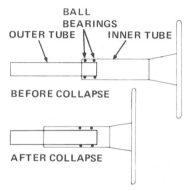

BALL
BEARINGS
OUTER TUBE   INNER TUBE

BEFORE COLLAPSE

AFTER COLLAPSE

Fig. 41-12 Tube-and-ball type of energy-absorbing steering column. *(General Motors Corporation)*

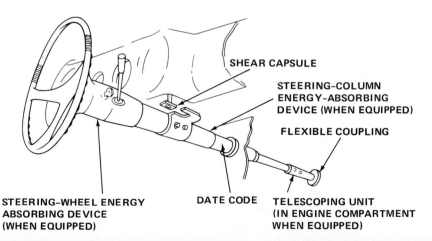

SHEAR CAPSULE

STEERING-COLUMN
ENERGY-ABSORBING
DEVICE (WHEN EQUIPPED)

FLEXIBLE COUPLING

STEERING-WHEEL ENERGY
ABSORBING DEVICE
(WHEN EQUIPPED)

DATE CODE

TELESCOPING UNIT
(IN ENGINE COMPARTMENT
WHEN EQUIPPED)

Fig. 41-13 Shear-capsule type of collapsible steering column.

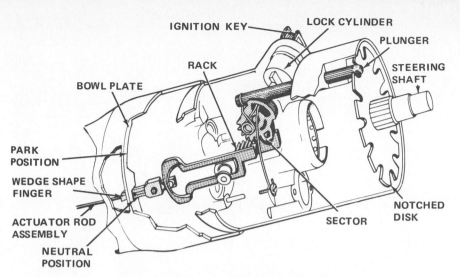

Fig. 41-14 A combination ignition switch and steering lock, showing the ignition switch at OFF and the plunger in the notched disk locking the steering. *(Buick Motor Division of General Motors Corporation)*

notch into line. The plunger will drop into the notch to lock the steering wheel.

NOTE The ignition switch also serves as a starting switch. When it is turned past ON to START, it connects the starting motor to the battery. This cranks the engine for starting.

□ 41-12 STEERING GEARS

The steering gear converts the rotary motion of the steering wheel into straight-line motion. This moves the linkage to the steering arms on the steering knuckles, swinging the front wheels left or right. There are two basic types of steering gears. One type has a pitman arm attached to a shaft from the steering box (Fig. 41-8). The second type is the *rack-and-pinion steering gear* (□ 41-13).

The pitman-arm steering gear has two essential parts. They are a worm gear on the end of the steering shaft and a matching sector gear or toothed roller attached to the sector shaft.

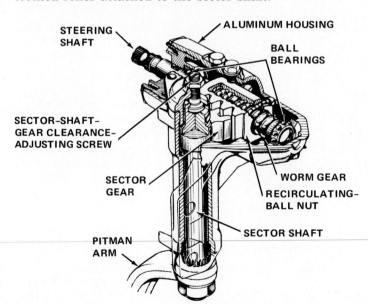

Fig. 41-15 A cutaway recirculating-ball manual-steering gear. *(Chrysler Corporation)*

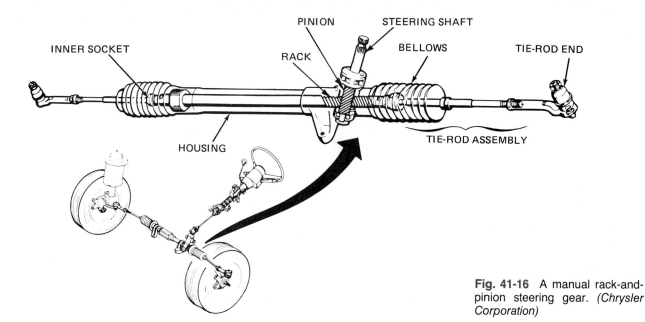

Fig. 41-16 A manual rack-and-pinion steering gear. *(Chrysler Corporation)*

Figure 41-15 shows a pitman-arm steering gear. As the steering shaft and worm gear rotate, the sector gear must follow the worm gear. The sector gear is moved toward one end of the worm or the other, as the ball nut moves up and down on it. The sector-gear movement causes the pitman arm to swing one way or the other.

Friction is kept low by using balls between the major moving parts. The balls roll between the worm teeth and the grooves cut in the hole in the ball nut. As the worm turns, the balls roll in the worm teeth. The balls must also roll in the grooves inside the ball nut. As the worm rotates, the balls cause the nut to move up or down along the worm. This motion is carried by the teeth on the outside of the ball nut to the teeth on the sector gear. The sector gear must move. This movement rotates the sector shaft which swings the pitman arm.

The steering gear in Fig. 41-15 is called a *recirculating-ball steering gear*. The balls move from one end of the worm gear to the other. When the balls reach the end, they enter ball-return guides, which take them back into the ball nut.

☐ 41-13 RACK-AND-PINION STEERING

The rack-and-pinion steering gear, used mostly on smaller cars, is shown in Fig. 41-16. This system has a pinion gear on the end of the lower steering shaft. The pinion is meshed with a rack of gear teeth cut on the underside of the major cross member of the steering linkage. When the steering wheel is turned, the pinion turns. This moves the rack to the left or right. The movement is carried through tie rods to the steering arms at the front wheels.

☐ 41-14 POWER STEERING

In the power-steering system, a pump sends fluid under pressure into the steering gear. This high-pressure fluid does about 80 percent of the work of steering. Figure 41-17 shows the power-steering system for a pitman-arm steering gear. The steering-gear assembly looks almost like the manual-steering gear, except that the steering-gear box is larger. The

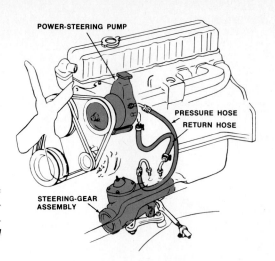

Fig. 41-17 An integral type of pitman-arm power-steering gear installed on the engine. *(Chevrolet Motor Division of General Motors Corporation)*

POWER-STEERING PUMP

PRESSURE HOSE

RETURN HOSE

STEERING-GEAR ASSEMBLY

pump is driven by a belt from the crankshaft pulley. In operation, the pump produces a high pressure on the power-steering fluid. This fluid is a special oil.

Figure 41-18 shows the working parts of a typical power-steering pump. The rotor rotates, and the vanes move in and out of the slots in the pump rotor. As the vanes move out of the slots, the space between the vanes increases. Fluid is drawn into the space. Then, with further rotation, the vanes are pushed back into the slots. This decreases the space between the vanes. The fluid is forced out under pressure. It goes through hoses to the steering-gear assembly. The pump has a flow-control or pressure-relief valve, which opens if the pressure goes too high.

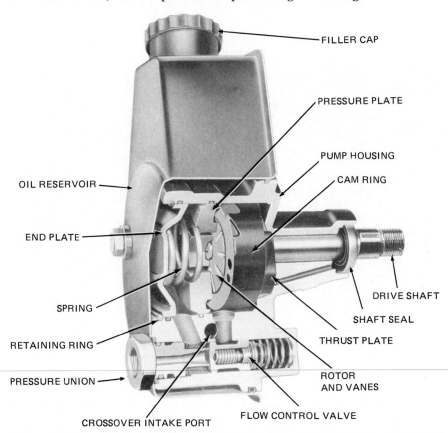

FILLER CAP

PRESSURE PLATE

PUMP HOUSING

CAM RING

OIL RESERVOIR

END PLATE

DRIVE SHAFT

SHAFT SEAL

SPRING

THRUST PLATE

RETAINING RING

ROTOR AND VANES

PRESSURE UNION

FLOW CONTROL VALVE

CROSSOVER INTAKE PORT

Fig. 41-18 A vane-type power-steering pump. *(Cadillac Motor Car Division of General Motors Corporation)*

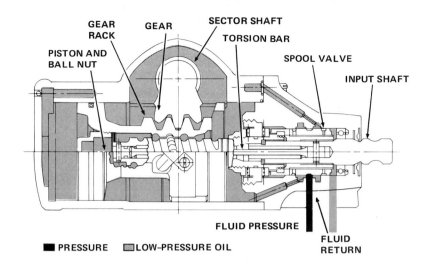

GEAR RACK · GEAR · SECTOR SHAFT · TORSION BAR · SPOOL VALVE · INPUT SHAFT · PISTON AND BALL NUT · FLUID PRESSURE · FLUID RETURN

■ PRESSURE ☐ LOW-PRESSURE OIL

Fig. 41-19 A cutaway pitman-arm power-steering gear shown in the straight-ahead position. *(Ford Motor Company)*

☐ 41-15 POWER-STEERING-GEAR OPERATION

Figure 41-8 shows a pitman-arm type of manual-steering gear and a similar power-steering gear. They look similar on the outside. However, the power-steering gearbox is slightly larger and has two hoses connected to it. Figure 41-19 shows the recirculating-ball power-steering gear in cutaway view. Basically, this is a manual recirculating-ball steering gear with a piston and spool valve added to it. The piston ball nut has a gear rack on it. The rack is meshed with the sector gear on the sector shaft. When the sector shaft moves, the attached pitman arm turns with it.

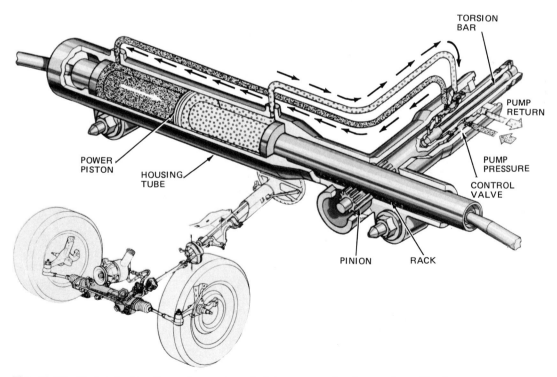

TORSION BAR · PUMP RETURN · PUMP PRESSURE · CONTROL VALVE · POWER PISTON · HOUSING TUBE · PINION · RACK

Fig. 41-20 Hydraulic flow through a rack-and-pinion power-steering system. *(Ford Motor Company)*

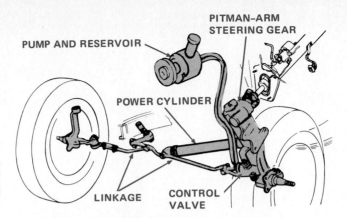

Figure 41-20 shows the rack-and-pinion type of power-steering gear. The rack acts as the power piston. The control valve is connected to the pinion gear.

Power-steering gears made by different manufacturers sometimes vary in appearance and construction. But they all work in the same general way. When the car is driven straight ahead, fluid pressure from the pump is equal to both sides of the piston (Fig. 41-19). However, when a turn is made, the twisting force on the input shaft causes a valve to operate. This valve moves to open passages that send fluid at high pressure to one side of the piston-and-ball nut. Most of the steering force required to make the turn is supplied by the high-pressure fluid.

☐ 41-16 LINKAGE-TYPE POWER STEERING

A linkage type of pitman-arm power steering is used on some cars and light trucks (Fig. 41-21). This type of power steering has a separate power cylinder and control valve. They are connected into the steering linkage as shown in Fig. 41-21. When a turn is made, the control valve operates to send high-pressure fluid to one or the other end of the piston in the power cylinder. One end of the power cylinder is fastened to the car frame. The other end connects to the steering linkage (Fig. 41-21). Figure 41-22 shows the action in the hydraulic system and power cylinder during a right turn.

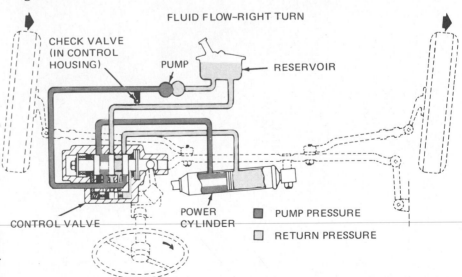

Fig. 41-22 Action in the linkage-type power-steering system during a right turn. *(Ford Motor Company)*

Select the *one* correct, best, or most probable answer to each question. Then check your answers against the correct answers given at the end of the book.

1. The tilting of the front wheel away from vertical is called
   a. caster
   b. camber
   c. toe
   d. turning radius

2. The inward tilt of the center line of the ball joints is called
   a. caster
   b. camber
   c. steering-axis inclination
   d. included angle

3. The backward tilt of the center line of the ball joints is called
   a. negative caster
   b. positive caster
   c. camber
   d. steering-axis inclination

4. Toe-out on turns, or turning radius, is
   a. the difference in angles between the front wheels during a turn
   b. the difference in camber during turns
   c. the amount the front wheels toe out during turns
   d. none of the above

5. Camber angle plus steering-axis inclination is called the
   a. caster
   b. toe
   c. turning radius
   d. included angle

6. In the rack-and-pinion steering gear
   a. the pinion is on the steering shaft
   b. the rack connects to the tie rods
   c. the tie rods connect to steering arms
   d. all of the above

7. The power-steering pump is driven by
   a. gears from the crankshaft
   b. a belt from the crankshaft pulley
   c. a chain and sprockets from the crankshaft
   d. the eccentric on the camshaft

8. In the rack-and-pinion power-steering gear, the rack functions as the
   a. control valve
   b. power piston
   c. pinion gear
   d. torsion bar

CHAPTER 42
STEERING AND SUSPENSION SERVICE

After studying this chapter, and with proper instruction and equipment, you should be able to:

1. Diagnose steering and suspension troubles.
2. Service steering linkages and suspension systems.
3. List and perform the basic steps in a wheel alignment.
4. Balance wheels.
5. Service steering gears.

Many conditions besides wheel alignment influence how a vehicle steers. Before caster, camber, toe, turning radius, and steering-axis inclination are checked, other factors should be checked and corrected, if necessary. These include tire pressure and condition, wheel-bearing condition and adjustment, wheel and tire balance and runout, ball-joint and steering-linkage looseness, rear leaf-spring condition, and front-suspension height. If any of these factors are off, you cannot accurately align the wheels. It is even possible that a "wheel alignment" could make the abnormal conditions worse.

☐ 42-1 STEERING AND SUSPENSION TROUBLE DIAGNOSIS

Many different conditions can cause steering difficulties. These problems may develop from defects within the steering system itself; from tire, spring, wheel, shock absorber, or frame trouble; or from improper wheel alignment. The various troubles that can occur because of conditions in the steering or suspension system include:

1. Excessive play in steering system.
2. Hard steering.
3. Car wander.
4. Car pulls to one side during normal driving.
5. Car pulls to one side during braking.
6. Front-wheel shimmy at low speed.
7. Front-wheel tramp (high-speed shimmy).

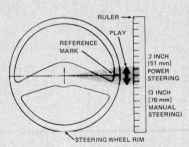

Fig. 42-1 Checking for play in the steering wheel. *(Motor Vehicle Manufacturers Association)*

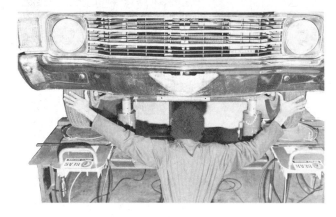

Fig. 42-2 Checking looseness in steering linkage and tie rods. *(ATW)*

8. Steering kickback.
9. Tire squeal on turns.
10. Incorrect tire wear.
11. Hard or rough ride.
12. Sway on turns.
13. Spring breakage.
14. Sagging springs.
15. Noises.

Each of these troubles is described in following sections.

□ 42-2 EXCESSIVE PLAY IN STEERING SYSTEM

Excessive play in the steering system shows up as free movement of the steering wheel without corresponding movement of the front wheels (Fig. 42-1). A small amount of free play is desirable because it makes steering easier. But when the play is excessive, it can make steering harder. With manual steering, the steering-wheel rim should move less than 3 inches [76 mm] before the front wheels begin to move. If the car has power steering, wheel-rim movement should be less than 2 inches [51 mm]. Excessive play can be due to the following causes:

■ Looseness in the steering gear or linkage
■ Worn steering-knuckle parts
■ Loose wheel bearings

The tie rods and linkage may be checked for looseness by raising the car. Grasp the front wheels and push out on both wheels at the same time (Fig. 42-2). Then pull in on both wheels at the same time. Excessive movement means worn linkage parts.

Worn steering-knuckle parts such as ball joints can be checked by raising the car. Then grasp the wheel at the top and bottom (Fig. 42-3). If you can wobble the wheel, there is looseness in the wheel bearings or ball joints. Have someone apply the brakes as you again try to rock the wheel. If applying the brakes eliminates the free play, the wheel bearing is loose.

Figures 42-4 and 42-5 show how to check for ball-joint wear. Axial play is checked by moving the wheel up and down. Radial play is checked by rocking the wheel back and forth. Some cars have wear-indicating ball joints. On these, a visual check may be all that is necessary (Fig. 42-6). When the grease-fitting nipple has receded into the ball-joint socket, replace the ball joint.

Fig. 42-3 Checking for wear in the steering knuckle and wheel bearing. *(ATW)*

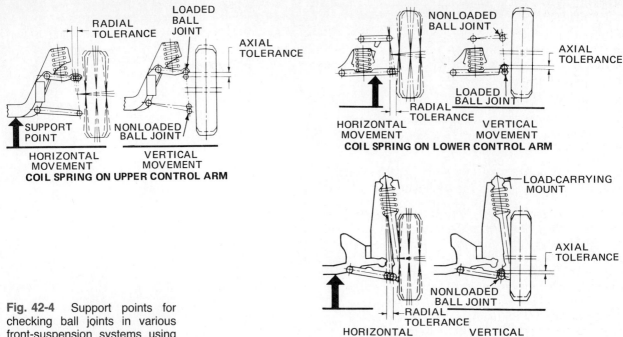

Fig. 42-4 Support points for checking ball joints in various front-suspension systems using coil springs. *(Motor Vehicle Manufacturers Association)*

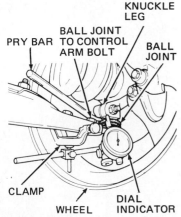

Fig. 42-5 Using a dial indicator to measure the amount of play in a ball joint. *(Motor Vehicle Manufacturers Association)*

A quick check for steering-gear wear or looseness can be made by watching the pitman arm while an assistant turns the steering wheel. The steering wheel should be turned one way and then the other with the front wheels on the floor. If the steering-wheel rim moves excessively after reversing wheel direction, there is looseness in the steering gear.

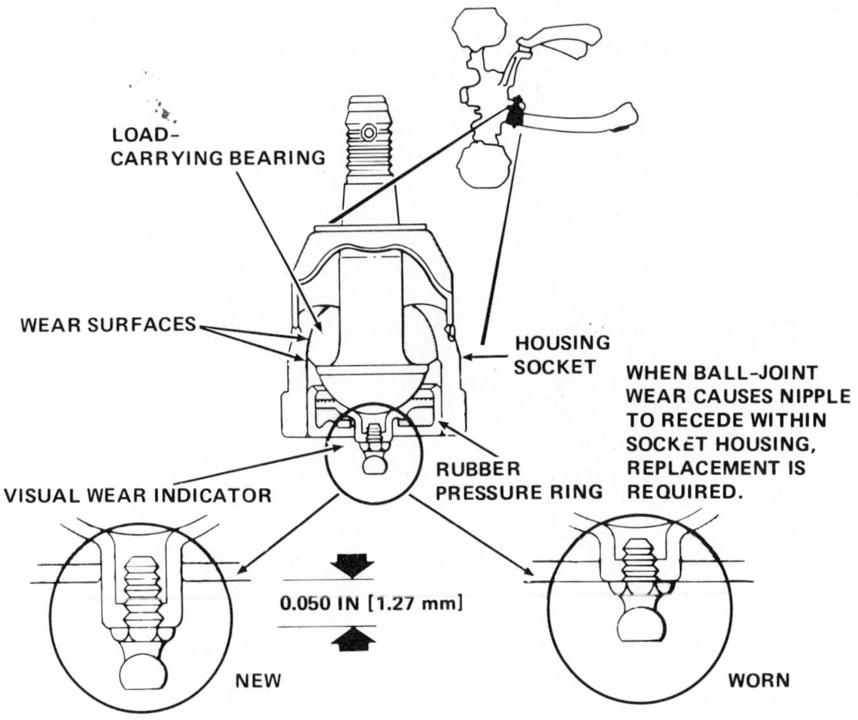

Fig. 42-6 How wear-indicating ball joints show that ball-joint replacement is necessary. In a worn ball joint, the grease-fitting nipple recedes into the socket.

☐ 42-3 HARD STEERING

If hard steering occurs just after the steering system has been worked on, the trouble probably is due to improper adjustments in the steering gear or linkages. If hard steering occurs at other times, it could be due to any one of the following problems:

- Inoperative power steering
- Low or uneven tire pressure
- Excessive friction in the steering gear or linkage or at the ball joints
- Improper front-wheel alignment—incorrect camber, caster, or steering-axis inclination
- Frame misalignment
- Sagging springs

On a car with power steering, failure of the power steering will cause the steering system to revert to mechanical steering. It will require greater steering effort to turn the steering wheel. When this happens, the power-steering system and the pump should be checked. First, check the fluid level in the pump fluid reservoir. If the problem is not low fluid level, install a pressure gauge in the system and check the pressures.

The steering linkage can be checked for binding by raising the front end of the car. Turn the steering wheel from left to right. If you feel any binding, disconnect the linkage from the pitman arm. If this relieves the hard steering, the trouble is in the linkage. If hard steering is still a problem, the trouble is in the steering gear itself.

☐ 42-4 CAR WANDER

Car wander shows up as trouble in keeping the car moving straight ahead. The steering wheel has to be kept moving to prevent the car from wandering from one side of the road to the other. Possible causes of car wander are the following:

- Low or uneven tire pressure
- Linkage or steering-gear binding
- Improper front-wheel alignment—incorrect camber, caster, or steering-axis inclination
- Loose rear springs
- Unevenly distributed load in the car
- Looseness in the steering-gear linkage or at the ball joints

Both binding and looseness in the steering gear or linkage can cause car wander. With binding, the wheels cannot resume their normal straight-ahead position. With looseness, the wheels are not under direct control of the driver.

☐ 42-5 CAR PULLS TO ONE SIDE DURING NORMAL DRIVING

Continual force must be applied to the steering wheel to keep the car moving straight ahead. When this condition occurs, the trouble could be due to any of the following:

- Uneven tire pressure
- Uneven camber or caster
- Tight wheel bearing on one side

- Uneven springs—sagging, loose, or broken
- Wheels not tracking because of a bent frame or other bent parts

Anything that tends to unbalance the forces acting on the wheels will make the car pull to one side.

☐ 42-6 CAR PULLS TO ONE SIDE DURING BRAKING

If the car pulls to one side during braking, there may be uneven braking at the two front wheels. Conditions that could cause the car to pull to one side during braking include:

- Loose strut rod
- Uneven braking action at the front wheels
- Uneven tire inflation
- Incorrect or uneven caster
- Causes listed in ☐ 42-5

☐ 42-7 FRONT-WHEEL SHIMMY AT LOW SPEED

With front-wheel shimmy at low speed, the front wheels oscillate on the ball joints. The wheels try to turn in and then turn out. This action causes the front end of the car to shake from side to side, or shimmy. Low-speed shimmy can result from any of the following:

- Uneven or low tire pressure
- Looseness in the steering gear or linkages
- Front springs too flexible or too weak
- Incorrect or unequal camber
- Irregular or unmatching tire treads

If tire treads are worn unevenly, the worn spots can cause a change in the road resistance to the tire. With each tire revolution, there is a tendency for the tire to toe more and then less.

☐ 42-8 FRONT-WHEEL TRAMP (HIGH-SPEED SHIMMY)

Front-wheel tramp, or high-speed shimmy, is often confused with low-speed shimmy. In front-wheel tramp, the tires tend to move up and down, or bounce, rather than turn in and out as they do with low-speed shimmy. Sometimes the tires bounce so high that they leave the road. The basic conditions that can cause this trouble are as follows:

- Wheels are out of balance.
- Wheels have too much runout.
- Shock absorbers are defective.
- Causes listed in ☐ 42-7.

Wheels that are out of balance have more weight on one side than on the other. As the wheel rotates, the heavy part causes the wheel to run off center. As the heavy part swings around the top, it tends to pull the tire up off the road. Wheels that have too much runout do not run true. They wobble as they rotate. This condition also tends to pull the tire off the road as the tire rotates.

If the shock absorbers are not working, they cannot stop the spring oscillations after bumps. The tires will tend to keep bouncing up and down.

☐ 42-9 STEERING KICKBACK

Steering kickback, or steering shock, is felt as sharp and rapid movements of the steering wheel when the front wheels meet obstructions on the road. It is normal to have some kickback. When the kickback becomes excessive, checks should be made. Excessive kickback could be caused by any of the following:

- Low tire pressure
- Sagging springs
- Defective shock absorbers
- Looseness in the steering gear or linkages

☐ 42-10 TIRE SQUEAL ON TURNS

If turns are taken too fast, some tire squeal can be expected. If tire squeal on turns is not due to excessive speed, then it is probably due to low or uneven tire pressure or to incorrect front-wheel alignment.

☐ 42-11 INCORRECT TIRE WEAR

If the tires wear abnormally, the type of wear is often a good indication of the cause. Figure 42-7 shows different types of tire wear and their causes and corrections. The causes include:

- Wear at tread sides from underinflation.
- Wear at tread center from overinflation.
- Wear at one tread side from excessive camber.
- Featheredge wear from excessive toe or toe-out on turns. Either of these drags the tire sideways to produce the featheredge wear.
- Cornering wear from excessive speed on turns.
- Uneven or spotty wear from mechanical problems such as unbalanced wheels, grabbing brakes, and so on.
- Rapid wear from high speed.

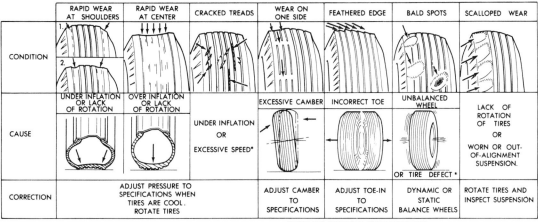

Fig. 42-7 Types of tire wear and their causes and corrections. *(Chrysler Corporation)*

☐ 42-12 HARD OR ROUGH RIDE

A hard or rough ride may be due to excessive tire pressure. The trouble also may be caused by defective shock absorbers or excessive friction in the spring suspension.

☐ 42-13 SWAY ON TURNS

If the car sways excessively on turns, this could be due to a faulty stabilizer bar. Weak or sagging springs and incorrect caster are other possible causes.

☐ 42-14 SPRING BREAKAGE

Spring breakage seldom occurs. The most common cause is overloading of the car. Another cause is defective shock absorbers that allow the springs to overwork. Leaf springs can break if the center or U-bolts are loose or if the spring shackle binds.

☐ 42-15 SAGGING SPRINGS

Sagging springs could be due to a broken leaf in a leaf spring or to a weak spring. Other possible causes of sagging springs are a defective shock absorber and installation of the wrong coil spring.

☐ 42-16 NOISES

Noises in the steering or suspension system could come from looseness in the system. Also, noises could be caused by a lack of lubrication.

☐ 42-17 SERVICING STEERING LINKAGE AND SUSPENSION

Steering and suspension service includes:

- ■ Removal, replacement, and adjustment of tie rods
- ■ Removal and replacement of other linkage parts, including idler arm, center link, stabilizer bar, and struts
- ■ Removal and replacement of upper and lower control arms and springs
- ■ Removal and replacement of shock absorbers
- ■ Removal and replacement of wheels
- ■ Checking front-end alignment and adjusting camber, caster, and toe
- ■ Checking rear-wheel alignment and adjusting as necessary

For specific details on any of these jobs, refer to the manufacturer's service manual covering the car you are working on.

☐ 42-18 WHEEL ALIGNMENT

There are many different types of wheel aligners. Some are mechanical types that attach to the wheel spindles (Fig. 42-8). Others have lights that display the measurements on a screen in front of the car (Fig. 42-9). In adjusting front alignment, you measure camber, caster, and toe-in. These are the three things you adjust. You also check steering-axis inclination and toe-out on turns. These are not adjustable. If they are out of specifications, parts are bent or damaged and must be replaced. However,

Fig. 42-8 A magnetic-gauge type of camber and caster tester. This gauge also measures steering-axis inclination (kingpin inclination). *(Snap-on Tools Corporation)*

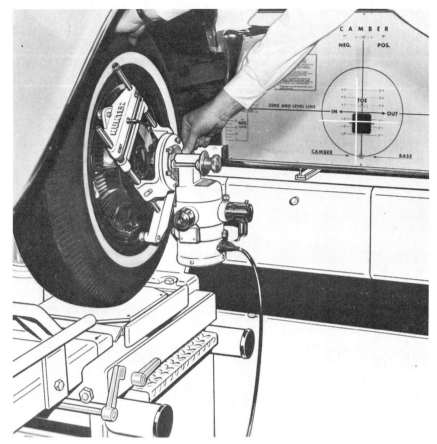

Fig. 42-9 Adjusting the wheel-mounted light projector on a light-beam type of wheel aligner. The projector shines horizontal and vertical lines on the screen in front of the car to show the wheel alignment. *(Hunter Engineering Company)*

before you make the alignment checks, here are the preliminary things you must do:

- Check and correct tire pressure.
- Check and adjust wheel bearings.
- Check ball joints. If they are too loose, replace them.
- Check steering linkages. Make any corrections necessary.
- Check rear leaf springs for cracks, broken leaves, and loose U-bolts. Make any corrections necessary.
- Check front-suspension height.

> **NOTE** Many vehicles, including those with front-engine and front-wheel drive, may require four-wheel alignment. On many of these vehicles, rear-wheel toe (and sometimes camber) can be checked and adjusted.

☐ 42-19 WHEEL BALANCE

The wheel may be checked for balance on or off the car. This job is done by two methods: static and dynamic balancing. To static-balance (or "bubble-balance") a wheel, it is taken off the car. The wheel is placed on a static balancer that detects any imbalance (Fig. 42-10). A wheel that is statically out of balance is heavier in one section. This will cause the bubble in the center of the balancer to move off center. To balance the wheel, weights are added until the bubble returns to center.

Fig. 42-10 Balancing an assembled tire and wheel on a static balancer, or bubble balancer. *(Ammco Tools, Inc.)*

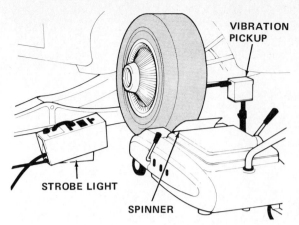

VIBRATION PICKUP

STROBE LIGHT

SPINNER

Fig. 42-11 An electronic-type of dynamic wheel balancer ("spin balancer") that balances the wheel on the car. A magnet is attached to the brake backing plate. Any movement of the magnet is sensed by a vibration pickup. This causes the strobe light to flash, indicating where to attach the wheel weight. *(Ford Motor Company)*

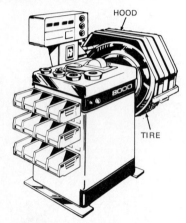

HOOD

TIRE

Fig. 42-12 An off-the-car wheel balancer, with a safety hood installed over the tire. *(Stewart-Warner Alemite)*

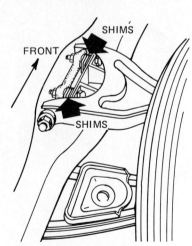

SHIMS

FRONT

SHIMS

Fig. 42-13 Location of caster and camber adjusting shims on many General Motors cars. The shims and upper-control-arm shaft are inside the frame bracket. *(Snap-on Tools Corporation)*

To dynamic-balance (or "spin-balance") a wheel, the wheel is run at road speeds either on or off the car. Figure 42-11 shows an electronic wheel balancer being used to balance a wheel on the car. Lack of balance shows up as a tendency of the wheel to move off center or out of line. In the shop you will learn more about wheel balancing.

If a wheel is out of balance, one or more weights are installed on the wheel rim, as shown in Fig. 42-10.

CAUTION To prevent injury from stones thrown out of the spinning tire, off-the-car wheel balancers should have a safety hood (Fig. 42-12). The hood fits around or over the tire while it is spinning to catch any stones that fly from the tire tread.

□ 42-20 ADJUSTING CAMBER AND CASTER

Several different ways to adjust camber and caster are used. Some of the methods include adjustment by removing or installing shims, by turning a cam, by shifting the inner shaft, and by shortening or lengthening the strut rod.

1. ADJUSTMENT BY INSTALLING OR REMOVING SHIMS

The shims are located at the upper-control-arm shafts. They are placed either inside or outside the frame bracket. Figure 42-13 shows the location of the shims in many General Motors cars. The shims are inside the frame bracket. Figure 42-14 shows the location of the shims in many Ford cars. The shims are outside the frame bracket. When the shims are inside the frame bracket (Fig. 42-13), adding shims moves the upper control arm inward. This reduces positive camber. When the shims and shaft are outside the frame bracket (Fig. 42-14), adding shims moves the upper control arm outward. This increases positive camber. If shims are added at one of the attachment bolts and removed from the other, the outer end of the upper control arm shifts one way or the other. This increases or decreases caster. Figure 42-15 shows these adjustments.

2. ADJUSTMENT BY TURNING A CAM

There have been several variations of this method. Figure 42-16 shows an arrangement used on some Chrysler-built cars. The two bushings at the inner end of the upper control arm are attached to the frame brackets by two attachment bolts and cam assemblies. When the cam bolts are turned, the camber and caster are changed. If both are turned the same amount and in the same direction, the camber is changed. If only one cam bolt is turned, or if the two are turned in opposite directions, the caster is changed.

3. ADJUSTMENT BY SHIFTING INNER SHAFT

This system uses slots in the frame at the two points where the inner shaft is attached (Fig. 42-17). When the attaching bolts are loosened, the inner shaft can be shifted in or out to change camber. Only one end is shifted to change caster.

4. ADJUSTMENT BY CHANGING LENGTH OF STRUT ROD

This arrangement allows changing the caster by changing the length of the strut rod (Fig. 42-18). Camber is changed by turning the cam at the inner end of the lower control arm.

5. MacPHERSON-STRUT CAMBER AND CASTER ADJUSTMENTS

Some cars with MacPherson struts do not have any adjustment for camber or caster. Other cars with this type of suspension have a camber adjustment only. On these cars, turn the cam bolt at the lower end of the strut to move the top of the wheel in or out to camber (Fig. 42-19).

Wrong alignment settings can cause excessive tire wear. Therefore, a caster-camber adjustment kit is available for installation on some cars with nonadjustable MacPherson struts (Fig. 42-20). After the kit is installed, caster and camber can be adjusted by moving the top of the strut.

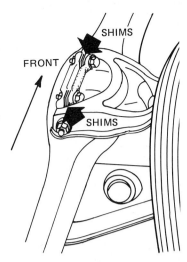

Fig. 42-14 Location of caster and camber adjusting shims on many Ford and other cars. The shims and upper-control-arm shaft are outside the frame bracket. *(Snap-on Tools Corporation)*

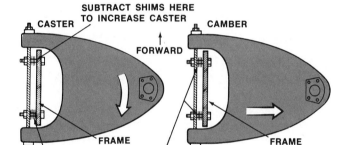

Fig. 42-15 Caster and camber adjustments on some cars using shims. *(Chevrolet Motor Division of General Motors Corporation)*

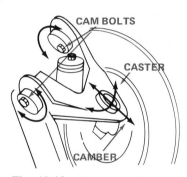

Fig. 42-16 Turning the cam bolts moves the upper control arm toward or away from the frame to adjust caster and camber. *(Ammco Tools, Inc.)*

Fig. 42-17 Adjusting caster and camber by shifting the position of the inner shaft using slots in the frame. *(Chrysler Corporation)*

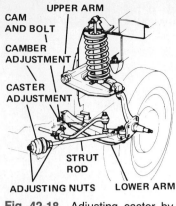

Fig. 42-18 Adjusting caster by changing the length of the strut rod. *(Ford Motor Company)*

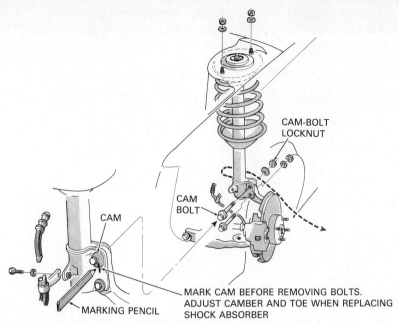

Fig. 42-19 On some cars with MacPherson struts, camber is adjusted by turning a cam bolt. *(Chrysler Corporation)*

The kit includes a slotted plate that is installed between the strut and the inner fender. Unless a kit of this type is installed, the top of the strut is fixed in position because it is bolted through the holes in the inner fender.

6. I-BEAM FRONT-AXLE CAMBER AND CASTER ADJUSTMENTS

Caster adjustment on an I-beam axle can be made by inserting tapered caster shims between the spring seat on the axle and the spring (Fig. 42-21) or by bending the axle. In general, when caster variation between wheels is 1 degree or less, a caster shim may be installed at only one wheel to correct it. If caster variation exceeds 1 degree, the caster should be adjusted by bending the axle or by replacing it.

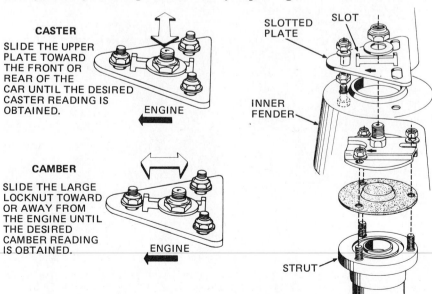

Fig. 42-20 A kit that can be installed on some cars with MacPherson struts to provide camber and caster adjustments. *(Moog Automotive, Inc.)*

The I-beam axle should be replaced if excessive bending is required. A severe bend in an axle may have caused invisible cracks and weakened the axle. As a result, the axle may later fail.

7. TWIN I-BEAM CAMBER AND CASTER ADJUSTMENTS

According to the manufacturer, camber and caster cannot be adjusted on the twin I-beam front-suspension system (Fig. 40-18). Only the toe can be adjusted. However, manufacturers of alignment equipment make available bending tools and attachments that can be used to bend the axles or the radius arms. Bending the axle for each wheel will correct improper camber and steering-axis inclination. The caster can be corrected by bending the radius arm.

INCREASING POSITIVE CASTER

INCREASING NEGATIVE CASTER

Fig. 42-21 Using tapered shims to adjust the caster on an I-beam front axle. (*Bear Manufacturing Company*)

☐ 42-21 ADJUSTING TOE

After adjusting caster and camber, toe is adjusted (Fig. 42-22). Place the front wheels in the straight-ahead position. Then check the position of the spokes in the steering wheel. If they are not aligned, they can be properly positioned while setting toe. Toe is adjusted by turning the adjuster sleeves in the linkage (Fig. 42-22).

☐ 42-22 SERVICING STEERING GEARS

The pitman-arm type of manual steering gears have two basic adjustments (Fig. 42-23). One of these takes up the worm-gear and steering-shaft end play. The other adjusts the backlash or free play between the worm and sector.

Other adjustments are required on power-steering gears. Refer to the manufacturer's shop manual covering the unit being serviced before attempting to adjust or repair a power-steering gear.

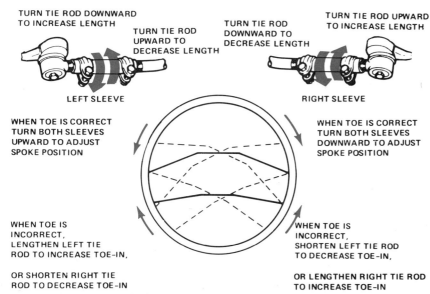

TURN TIE ROD DOWNWARD TO INCREASE LENGTH

TURN TIE ROD UPWARD TO DECREASE LENGTH

TURN TIE ROD DOWNWARD TO DECREASE LENGTH

TURN TIE ROD UPWARD TO INCREASE LENGTH

LEFT SLEEVE

RIGHT SLEEVE

WHEN TOE IS CORRECT TURN BOTH SLEEVES UPWARD TO ADJUST SPOKE POSITION

WHEN TOE IS CORRECT TURN BOTH SLEEVES DOWNWARD TO ADJUST SPOKE POSITION

WHEN TOE IS INCORRECT, LENGTHEN LEFT TIE ROD TO INCREASE TOE-IN,

OR SHORTEN RIGHT TIE ROD TO DECREASE TOE-IN

WHEN TOE IS INCORRECT, SHORTEN LEFT TIE ROD TO DECREASE TOE-IN,

OR LENGTHEN RIGHT TIE ROD TO INCREASE TOE-IN

Fig. 42-22 Adjusting toe and aligning the spokes in the steering wheel. If the steering wheel is in its proper position, adjust both tie rods equally to maintain the position of the spokes. (*Ford Motor Company*)

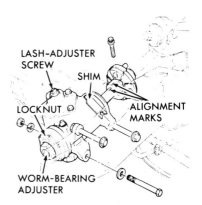

LASH-ADJUSTER SCREW

SHIM

LOCKNUT

ALIGNMENT MARKS

WORM-BEARING ADJUSTER

Fig. 42-23 Adjusting points on a pitman-arm type of manual steering gear. (*Chevrolet Motor Division of General Motors Corporation*)

Select the *one* correct, best, or most probable answer to each question. Then check your answers against the correct answers given at the end of the book.

1. Excessive play in the steering system can be due to
   a. looseness in the steering gear or linkage
   b. worn steering-knuckle parts
   c. loose wheel bearings
   d. all of the above

2. During the diagnosis of a complaint of hard steering, the steering is still hard after the front wheels are raised off the floor. Mechanic X says the next step is to disconnect the linkage from the pitman arm. Mechanic Y says the next step is to remove the steering gear for a bench check. Who is right?
   a. mechanic X
   b. mechanic Y
   c. both X and Y
   d. neither X nor Y

3. Mechanic X says that car wander can be caused by binding in the steering gear or linkage. Mechanic Y says car wander can be caused by looseness in the steering gear or linkage. Who is right?
   a. mechanic X
   b. mechanic Y
   c. both X and Y
   d. neither X nor Y

4. With front-wheel shimmy at low speed, the
   a. front wheels try to turn in and then out
   b. front wheels bounce up and down
   c. steering gear is jammed or tight
   d. none of the above

5. With front-wheel tramp the
   a. front wheels try to turn in and out
   b. front wheels bounce up and down
   c. steering gear is jammed
   d. none of the above

6. Rapid wear of the tread at the outer edges, or shoulders, of a tire is caused by
   a. over inflation
   b. underinflation
   c. lack of wheel balance
   d. excessive camber

7. Rapid wear of the tread at the center of a tire is caused by
   a. overinflation
   b. underinflation
   c. lack of wheel balance
   d. excessive camber

CHAPTER 43
TIRES AND WHEELS

After studying this chapter, you should be able to:
1. Discuss the design and construction of various types of tires, including bias tires and radials.
2. Discuss space-saving spare tires such as the collapsible and compact types.
3. Discuss tire wear and possible causes of abnormal wear.
4. Discuss the various kinds of tire service and how they are done.

Improved tire design and improved highways make tire problems much less common today. Yet there is still need for tire service. The automotive technician should know how tires are made and how they do their job. Also, you should know what various patterns of abnormal wear mean. Abnormal tire wear usually is a sign of trouble in the steering, suspension, or brake system.

☐ 43-1 PURPOSE OF TIRES

The tire does two jobs. First, the tire is an air-filled cushion that absorbs most shocks caused by road irregularities. The tire flexes, or gives, as it meets bumps and holes in the road. This absorbs the shock before it reaches the passengers. Second, the tire grips the road to provide good traction. Good traction enables the car to accelerate, brake, and take turns without skidding.

☐ 43-2 TIRE CONSTRUCTION

There are two general types of tires: those with inner tubes and those without tubes, called tubeless tires. On the tube type, both the tube and the tire are mounted on the wheel rim (Fig. 43-1). The *tube* is a hollow rubber doughnut that is inflated with air after it is installed inside the tire and the tire is put on the wheel rim. This inflation causes the tire to resist any change of shape.

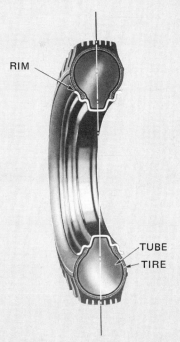

RIM

TUBE
TIRE

Fig. 43-1 Tire and tire rim cut away so that the tube can be seen.

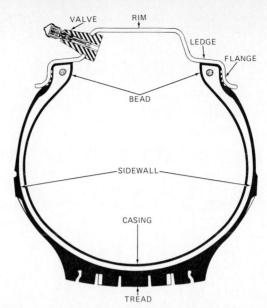

Fig. 43-2 Sectional view of a tubeless tire, showing how the tire bead rests between the ledges and flanges of the rim to produce an airtight seal. *(Pontiac Motor Division of General Motors Corporation)*

Tubes are used in some truck tires and in motorcycle tires. Today, tubes seldom are used in passenger car tires. Cars use tubeless tires. The tubeless tire does not use an inner tube. The tubeless tire is mounted on the rim so that the air is retained between the rim and the tire (Fig. 43-2).

The amount of air pressure used in the tire depends on the size and load it is to carry. Passenger car tires are usually inflated from about 22 to 30 psi [155 to 205 kPa]. Tires on heavy-duty trucks or buses may be inflated up to 100 psi [690 kPa].

Tubeless tires and tube tires are made in about the same way. Layers of cord, called plies, are shaped on a form and impregnated with rubber. The rubber sidewalls and treads are then applied and vulcanized into place to form the completed tire (Fig. 43-3). *Vulcanizing* is a process of

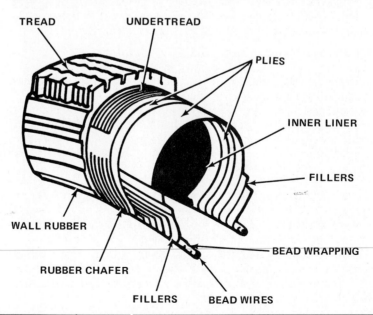

Fig. 43-3 Construction of a tubeless tire. *(Chevrolet Motor Division of General Motors Corporation)*

heating the rubber under pressure. This molds the rubber into the desired form and gives it the proper wear characteristics and flexibility. The number of layers of cord, or plies, varies according to the intended use of the tire. Passenger-car tires have 2, 4, or 6 plies. Heavy-duty truck and bus tires may have up to 14 plies. Tires for extremely heavy-duty service, such as earthmoving equipment, may have up to 32 plies.

□ 43-3 BIAS VERSUS RADIAL PLIES

There are two ways to apply the plies: on the bias (diagonally) and radially (Fig. 43-4). For many years most tires were of the bias type. These tires had the plies crisscrossed. One layer runs diagonally one way and the other layer runs diagonally the other way. This makes a carcass that is strong in all directions because of the overlapping plies. However, the plies tend to move against one another in bias tires. This generates heat, especially at high speed. Also, the tread tends to "squirm," or close up, as it meets the road (Fig. 43-5). This increases tire wear.

Tires with radial plies (Fig. 43-4) were introduced to remedy these problems. In a radial tire, all plies run parallel to one another and vertical to the tire bead. Belts are applied on top of the plies to provide strength parallel to the tire bead. Then the tread is vulcanized on top of the belts. The belts are made of rayon, nylon, fiberglass, and steel mesh.

Radial tires now are installed on about 97 percent of all new cars built in the United States. All radial tires work in the same way, regardless of the belt material. The belt provides added strength. Radial tires put more rubber on the road than a bias-ply tire. The radial is more flexible, so more of the tread stays on the pavement (Fig. 43-6). Also, the tread has less tendency to heel up when the car goes around a curve (Fig. 43-7). This keeps more rubber on the road and reduces the tendency of the tire to skid. Radial tires wear more slowly than bias-ply tires. This is because the radial-tire tread does not squirm as the tire meets the pavement. The bias-ply tire tends to squirm (Fig. 43-5). As the treads pinch together, they slide sideways. This causes tread wear. There is less heat buildup on the highway in the radial tire. This also slows radial-tire wear.

Bias-ply tires may also be belted, as shown in Fig. 43-4. These are called *belted-bias tires*. They cost less than radial tires. However, even some tire manufacturers who make belted-bias tires recommend the radial tire.

CAUTION Never mix radial and bias-ply tires, either belted or unbelted, on a car. Mixing the two types can cause poor car handling and increase the possibility of skidding. This precaution is very important for snow tires. Regular bias-ply snow tires on the rear and radials on the front can result in oversteer. This can cause spin-out on wet or icy roads.

□ 43-4 TIRE TREAD

The tread is the part of the tire that rests on the road. There are many different tread designs (Fig. 43-8). Snow tires have large rubber cleats molded into the tread for cutting through snow to improve traction.

Some tires have steel studs that stick out through the tread. Studs help the tire get better traction in ice and snow. However, some people claim studded tires shorten the life of the road surface. Because of this possibility, studded tires are banned in certain areas.

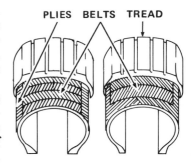

Fig. 43-4 The three types of tire construction, as determined by the way the plies are laid. *(Chevrolet Motor Division of General Motors Corporation)*

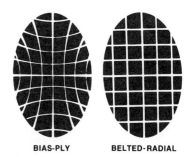

Fig. 43-5 Bias-ply tread tends to squirm as it meets the road. The radial-tire tread tends to remain apart.

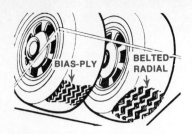

Fig. 43-6 Tread patterns ("footprints") of a bias-ply tire and a radial tire on a flat surface. The radial tire puts more rubber on the road.

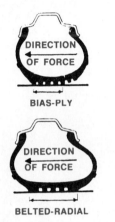

Fig. 43-7 Difference in the amount of tread a bias-ply tire and a radial tire apply to the surface during a turn.

☐ *43-5 TIRE VALVE*

Air is put into the tire, or into the inner tube, through a valve that opens when an air hose is applied to it (Fig. 43-2). Sometimes the valve is called a "Schrader valve." On a tubed tire, the valve is mounted in the inner tube and sticks out through a hole in the wheel. On the tubeless tire, the valve is mounted in the hole in the wheel rim (Fig. 43-2). When the valve is closed, spring force and air pressure inside the tire or tube hold the valve on its seat. Most valves carry a valve cap, which is screwed down over the valve end. The cap protects the valve from dirt and acts as an added safeguard against air leaks.

☐ *43-6 TIRE SIZE*

Tire size is marked on the sidewall of the tire. An older tire might be marked 7.75-14. This means that the tire fits on a wheel that is 14 inches [356 mm] in diameter at the rim where the tire bead rests. The 7.75 means that the tire itself is about 7.75 inches [197 mm] wide when it is properly inflated.

Figure 43-9 shows a tire with an explanation of each mark on it. Tires have several markings on the sidewall. The markings include a letter code to designate the type of car the tire is designed for. D means a lightweight car, F means intermediate, G means a standard car. H, J, and L are for large luxury cars and high-performance vehicles. For example, some cars use a G78-14 tire. The 14 means a rim 14 inches [356 mm] in diameter. The 78 indicates the ratio between the tire height and width (Fig. 43-10). This tire is 78 percent as high as it is wide. The ratio of the height to the width is called the *aspect ratio* or *profile ratio*. Four aspect ratios are 83, 78, 70, and 60. The lower the number, the wider the tire looks. For example, a 60 tire is only 60 percent as high as it is wide.

Fig. 43-8 Various types of tire tread. *(B. F. Goodrich Company; Goodyear Tire and Rubber Company)*

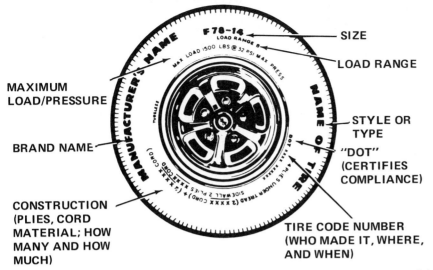

Fig. 43-9 Every marking on a tire is important information. Note the location of tire size, pressure, and load limit.

The addition of an R to the sidewall marking, such as in GR78-14, indicates that the tire is a radial. Also, if a tire is a radial, the word "radial" must be molded into the sidewall. Some radial tires are marked in the metric system. For example, a tire marked 175R13 is a radial tire which measures 175 mm [6.9 inches] wide. It mounts on a wheel with a diameter of 13 inches [330 mm].

Some cars use metric-size tires. The meaning of each letter and number of a metric tire size is shown in Fig. 43-11. This is the latest size designation for tires. Comparing the two tire-size labels, a tire formerly marked as an ER78-14 now is marked P195/75R14.

To identify the load that a tire can safely carry, each tire is classified into a load range. The load range indicates the allowable load for the tire as inflation pressure is increased. In Fig. 43-9, the tire is marked "Load Range B." Most passenger-car tires are in load range B. There are three load ranges for passenger-car tires: B, C, and D. Under the old system, "ply rating" was used to indicate load range. The load-range-B tire has the same load-carrying capacity as the tire with a 4-ply rating. Load range C equals a 6-ply-rating tire. Load range D equals an 8-ply rating tire.

□ 43-7 COLLAPSIBLE SPARE TIRE

This tire (Fig. 43-12) is designed to save space in the luggage compartment. It is installed on the wheel in a deflated condition. It barely protrudes beyond the rim. There is a pressure can of inflation propellant, called the "inflator," in the luggage compartment. Instructions on how to install and safely inflate the collapsible spare tire are printed on the inflator can. The procedure is described in □ 43-28.

CAUTION This tire must not be driven more than 150 miles [240 km] and at a speed of 50 mph [80 km/h] or less. The tire must not be inflated from the air hose in the shop or in a service station. This can cause the tire to explode.

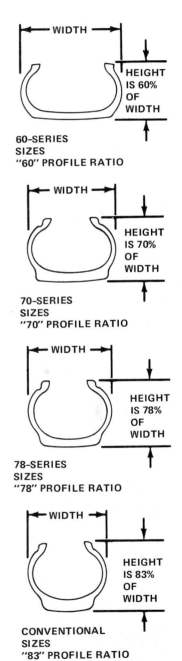

Fig. 43-10 Four aspect ratios of car tires. (*American Motors Corporation*)

619

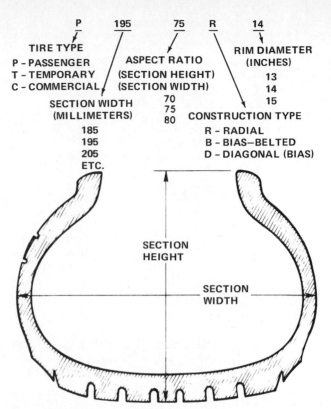

Fig. 43-11 Meanings of the size designations for a metric tire. *(Chevrolet Motor Division of General Motors Corporation)*

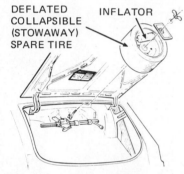

Fig. 43-12 A collapsible spare tire with inflator. *(Buick Motor Division of General Motors Corporation)*

Fig. 43-13 A compact spare tire. *(ATW)*

☐ 43-8 COMPACT SPARE TIRE

Another tire that saves space in the luggage compartment is the compact spare tire (Fig. 43-13). This spare is lighter and considerably smaller than the standard tire being used on the car. The compact spare tire can be driven for the 1000- to 3000-mile [1600- to 4800-km] life of the tread. It is mounted on a narrow 15 × 4 wheel. The tire must not be mounted on any other wheel. No other tire, wheel cover, or trim ring should be installed on the special wheel. Also, the compact spare tire should not be used on the rear of a car equipped with a limited-slip differential. The collapsible spare tire is smaller in diameter than the tire on the other side of the rear axle. Differential action must take place continuously. This may cause damage and failure of the limited-slip differential.

NOTE The compact spare tire is for emergency use only. As soon as the standard tire has been repaired, reinstall it on the car. The compact spare carries an inflation pressure of 69 psi [415 kPa]. It provides a rough and noisy ride.

☐ 43-9 WHEELS

Most cars use a pressed steel or disk wheel (Fig. 43-14). This type of wheel also is called a *safety-rim* wheel. The outer part, called the rim, is of one-piece construction and is welded to the disk. This forms the seamless and airtight wheel that is needed to mount a tubeless tire. The center of the rim is smaller in diameter than the rest. This gives the rim the name "drop center." The center well is necessary to permit removal and installation of the tire. The bead of the tire must be pushed off the bead seat

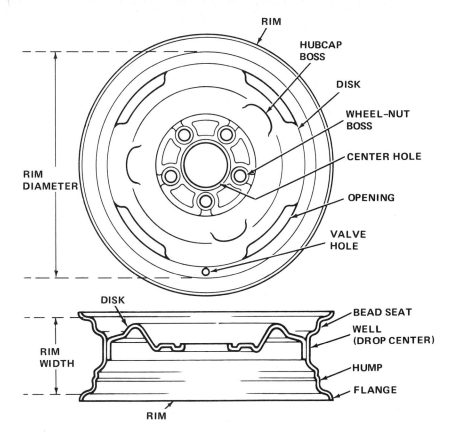

RIM

HUBCAP BOSS

DISK

WHEEL-NUT BOSS

CENTER HOLE

OPENING

VALVE HOLE

RIM DIAMETER

DISK

RIM WIDTH

BEAD SEAT

WELL (DROP CENTER)

HUMP

FLANGE

RIM

Fig. 43-14 Construction of a car wheel. *(American Motors Corporation)*

and into the smaller diameter. Only then can the tire beads be worked up over the rim flange. Tire service is described later in the chapter.

The 14-inch [356-mm] wheel is used on most cars today. However, some smaller cars have 12-inch [305-mm] and 13-inch [330-mm] wheels. For 14-inch [356-mm] wheels, three different rim widths often are used, depending on the tire specified for the car. The rim widths are 4.5 inches [114 mm], 5 inches [127 mm], and 6 inches [152 mm]. Optional larger tires usually require larger rim widths.

Most manufacturers recommend that a wheel be replaced if it is bent or leaks air. The new wheel must be exactly the same as the old wheel. Installation of the wrong wheel could cause the wheel bearing to fail, the brakes to overheat, the speedometer to read inaccurately, and the tire to rub the body and frame.

☐ 43-10 SPECIAL WHEELS

Plain steel wheels, decorated with hubcaps or wheel covers, are used on cars today. A large variety of special wheels are available for almost any vehicle. These wheels can be classified as styled steel wheels or styled aluminum wheels. A very popular wheel is the "mag" wheel, similar in appearance to the magnesium wheels used on some race cars (Fig. 43-15). However, for passenger cars, mag wheels are made of aluminum. The term "mag wheel" is used to mean almost any chromed, aluminum-offset, or wide-rim wheel.

Some aluminum wheels are lighter than the steel wheels they replace. Lighter wheels reduce unsprung weight. This improves handling and performance. Also, some aluminum wheels can improve brake and tire performance by allowing them to run cooler.

Fig. 43-15 A mag wheel. *(Shelby International, Inc.)*

□ 43-11 TIRE SERVICE

Tire service includes periodic checking of the air pressure and addition of air as needed. Failure to maintain correct air pressure can cause rapid tire wear, early tire failure, and poor fuel economy. Incorrect air pressure can also cause handling problems (□ 43-12). Tire service includes periodic inspection of the tire for abnormal wear, cuts, bruises, or other damage. In addition, tire service includes the repair and replacement of tires.

□ 43-12 TIRE INFLATION AND WEAR

The driver has more effect on tire life than any other factor. Good drivers usually get longer tire life than careless drivers. Rapid tire wear can be caused by rapid starting and stopping, severe braking, high-speed driving, and striking or rubbing curbs. Too little air in the tire can cause hard steering, front-wheel shimmy, steering kickback, and tire squeal on turns. Also, the tire with too little air will wear on the shoulders and not in the center of the tread as shown at the upper left in Fig. 43-16. The additional flexing that results from insufficient air pressure also can damage the sidewalls, even causing separation of plies.

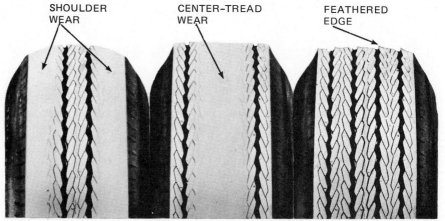

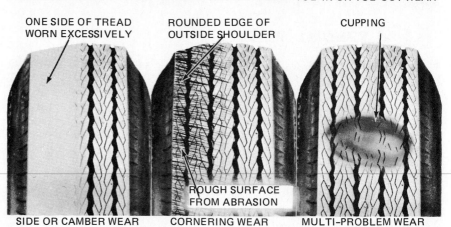

Fig. 43-16 Patterns of abnormal tire-tread wear. *(Buick Motor Division of General Motors Corporation)*

The underinflated tire is subject to rim bruises. If the tire should strike a rut or stone, or bump a curb too hard, the tire will flex so much that it will be pinched against the rim. Any of these different kinds of damage can lead to early tire failure.

With overinflation, the tire rides on the center of the tread so that only the center wears, as shown at the upper center in (Fig. 43-16). The overinflated tire will not flex normally, with the result that the tire cords can be weakened or even broken.

□ 43-13 TOE-IN OR TOE-OUT TIRE WEAR

Excessive toe-in or toe-out causes the tire to be dragged sideways as it is moving forward. For example, a tire on a front wheel that toes-in 1 inch [25 mm] from straight ahead will be dragged sideways about 150 feet [46 m] every mile [1.6 km]. This sideward drag scrapes off rubber, as shown at the upper right in Fig. 43-16. Then featheredges of rubber appear on one side of the tread. If both sides show this type of wear, the front end is misaligned. If only one tire shows this type of wear, the steering arm probably is bent. This condition causes one wheel to toe-in more than the other.

□ 43-14 CAMBER WEAR

If a wheel has excessive camber, the tire will not run more on one shoulder than on the other. The tread will wear excessively on that side, as shown at the lower left in Fig. 43-16.

□ 43-15 CORNERING WEAR

Cornering wear, shown at the lower center in Fig. 43-16, is caused by taking curves at excessive speeds. The tire not only skids, but also tends to roll, producing the diagonal type of wear shown. The remedy is to have the driver slow down around curves.

□ 43-16 UNEVEN TIRE WEAR

Uneven tire wear, with the tread unevenly or spottily worn, as shown at the lower right in Fig. 43-16, can result from several mechanical problems. These problems include misaligned wheels, unbalanced wheels, uneven or grabbing brakes, overinflated tires, or out-of-round brake drums.

□ 43-17 HIGH-SPEED WEAR

Tires wear more rapidly at high speed than at low speed. Tires driven consistently at 70 to 80 mph [112 to 129 km/h] will give less than half the mileage of tires driven at 30 mph [48 km/h].

□ 43-18 CHECKING TIRE PRESSURE AND INFLATING TIRES

To check tire pressure and inflate the tires, first determine the correct inflation pressure for the tire. You can find this specification printed on a tire placard on one of the doorjambs (or at some similar place) on the car. Specifications are for cold tires. Tires that are hot from being driven or from sitting in the sun will have an increased air pressure. Air expands when hot. Tires that have just come off the interstate highway may show as much as a 5- to 7-psi [35- to 48-kPa] increase.

As a hot tire cools, it loses pressure. Never bleed a hot tire to reduce its pressure. If you do this, then when the tire cools, its pressure could drop below the specified minimum.

There are times when the tire pressure should be on the high side. For example, one tire manufacturer recommends increasing the pressure by 4 psi [28 kPa] for high speed, trailer pulling, or extra-heavy loads. However, never exceed the maximum pressure specified on the tire sidewall.

If the tire valve has a cap, always install the cap after checking pressure or adding air.

□ 43-19 TIRE ROTATION

The amount of wear a tire gets depends on its location on the car. For example, the right rear tire wears about twice as fast as the left front tire. This is because some roads are slightly crowned (higher in the center) and also because the right rear tire is driving. The crown causes the car to lean out a little, so the right tires carry more weight. The combination of this and carrying power through the right rear tire causes it to wear faster. To equalize wear as much as possible, tires should be rotated any time wear is noticeable and at the mileage specified by the car manufacturer. One manufacturer recommends rotating radial tires after the first 7500 miles [12,000 km] and then every 15,000 miles [24,000 km]. Bias tires should be rotated every 7500 miles [12,000 km]. Figure 43-17 shows the recommended rotation pattern for bias, bias-belted, and radial tires. Bias and bias-belted tires can be switched from one side of the car to the other. To do this reverses their direction of rotation. This could cause handling and wear problems.

On cars with a collapsible spare tire or a compact spare tire, use the four-wheel rotation pattern shown in Fig. 43-17. Always mark the location (LR or RR) on the side of a studded tire before removing it from the wheel. Studded tires should never be rotated. A studded tire should be put back on the same wheel from which it was removed. Always mount the tire so that it rolls in the same direction.

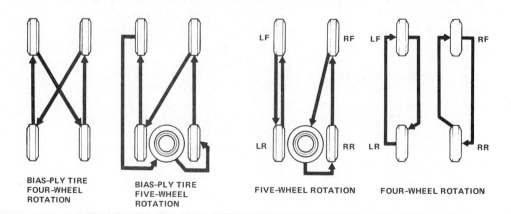

BIAS-PLY TIRE FOUR-WHEEL ROTATION

BIAS-PLY TIRE FIVE-WHEEL ROTATION

FIVE-WHEEL ROTATION

FOUR-WHEEL ROTATION

BIAS AND BIAS-BELTED TIRES

RADIAL TIRES

Fig. 43-17 Tire-rotation patterns for cars with and without a rotatable spare tire. *(Chevrolet Motor Division of General Motors Corporation)*

□ 43-20 TIRE INSPECTION

The purpose of inspecting the tires is to determine whether they are safe for further use. When an improper wear pattern is found, the technician must know the causes of abnormal tread wear (Fig. 43-16). The technician must correct the cause or notify the driver of what is wrong. When the tires are found to be serviceable, they can be rotated (Fig. 43-17). After the tires are cool, check and adjust the inflation pressures.

When inspecting a tire, check for bulges in the sidewalls. A bulge is a danger signal that can mean the plies are separated or broken and that the tire is likely to go flat. A tire with a bulge should be removed from the rim so that the tire can be checked inside and out. If the plies are broken or separated, the tire should be thrown away. To make a complete tire inspection, remove all stones from the tread. This is to make sure that no tire damage is hidden by the stones. Also, any time the tire is to be spin-balanced, remove all stones from the tread. This will ensure that no person is struck and injured by stones thrown from the tread as the tire rotates.

Many tires have tread-wear indicators, which are filled-in sections of the tread grooves. When the tread has worn down enough to show the indicators (Fig. 43-18), the tire should be replaced. There also are special tire-tread guages that can be inserted into the tread grooves to measure how much tread remains. A quick way to check tread wear is with a penny (Fig. 43-19). If at any point you can see all Lincoln's head, the tread is excessively worn. Some state laws require a tread depth of at least 1/32 inch [0.79 mm] in any two adjacent grooves at any location on the tire. A tire with little or no tread has poor traction on the road and will produce poor braking.

> **NOTE** A tire can look OK from the outside and still have internal damage. To completely inspect a tire, remove it from the rim. Then examine it closely, inside and out.

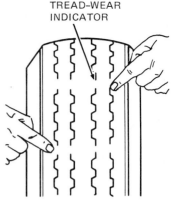

TREAD-WEAR INDICATOR

Fig. 43-18 A tire tread worn down so much that the tread-wear indicator shows.

Fig. 43-19 Using a penny to check tread wear.

□ 43-21 TUBE INSPECTION

Tubes usually give little trouble if correctly installed. However, careless installation can cause trouble. For example, if the wheel rim is rough or rusty or if the tire bead is rough, the tube may wear through. Dirt in the casing can cause the same trouble. Another condition that can cause trouble is installing a tube that is too large in the tire. Sometimes an old tube (which may have stretched) is put in a new tire. When a tube that is too large is put into a casing, the tube can overlap at some point. The overlap will rub and wear and possibly cause early tube failure.

A radial tire that is used with a tube must have a special radial-tire inner tube in it. If regular tubes are used in radial tires, the tube splice may come apart.

Always check carefully around the valve stem when inspecting a tube. If the tube has been run flat or at low pressure, the valve stem may be broken or tearing away from the tube. Valve-stem trouble requires installation of a new tube.

□ 43-22 REMOVING WHEEL FROM CAR

Radial tires must be removed from the car to be repaired (Fig. 43-20). Also, if the tire has been run flat, remove the tire for inspection. To repair a tire, first take off the hubcap or wheel cover. Then remove the wheel

Fig. 43-20 Using an impact wrench to remove the lug nuts. (ATW)

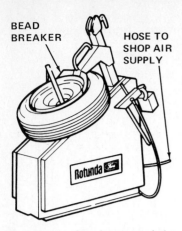

BEAD
BREAKER   HOSE TO
SHOP AIR
SUPPLY

Rotunda

Fig. 43-21 An air-powered tire changer is used to break the bead so that the tire can be removed from the wheel. *(Ford Motor Company)*

from the car. If you are using a lug wrench, loosen the lug nuts before raising the car. It is easier to loosen the lug nuts first, because the wheel will not turn if the car weight is on it. On some cars the lug nuts on the right side of the car have right-hand threads. The lug nuts on the left side have left-hand threads. The reason is that the forward rotation of the wheels tends to tighten the nuts, not loosen them.

☐ 43-23 DEMOUNTING TIRE FROM DROP-CENTER RIM

With the wheel off the car, make a chalk mark across the tire and rim so you can reinstall the tire in the same position. This preserves the balance of the wheel and tire. Next, release the air from the tire. This can be done by holding the tire valve open or removing the valve core. The tire should then be removed from the rim, using a shop tire changer.

☐ 43-24 USING SHOP TIRE CHANGERS

Today, many shops have an air-powered tire changer (Fig. 43-21). After the bead is pushed off the rim (this is called "breaking the bead"), a tool is used with the tire changer to lift the bead up over the rim (Fig. 43-22). The powered tire changer also has a tool to remount the tire on the rim.

☐ 43-25 REMOUNTING TIRE ON RIM

To mount the tire on the rim, use the tire changer. Coat the rim and beads with rubber lubricant or a soap-and-water mixture. This will make the mounting procedure easier. Do not use a nondrying lubricant, such as antifreeze, silicone, grease, or oil. They will allow the tire to "walk around" the rim so that the tire balance is lost. Oil or grease will damage the rubber. When you are remounting the same tire that was removed from the rim, make sure the chalk marks on the tire and rim align. After the tire is on the rim, reposition the beads against the bead set. Slowly inflate the tire (Fig. 43-23). If the beads do not hold air, use a tire-mounting band to spread the beads. You usually will hear a "pop" as the beads seat on the rim. Then install the valve core and inflate the tire to the recommended pressure.

   CAUTION Do not stand over the tire while inflating it. If the tire should explode, you could be injured.

☐ 43-26 CHECKING THE WHEEL

When the tire is off the wheel, check the rim for dents and roughness. Steel wool can be used to clean rust spots from standard steel wheels. Aluminum wheels can be cleaned only with mild soap and water. File off nicks or burrs. Then clean the rim to remove all filings and dirt. A wheel that has been bent should be discarded. A bent wheel may be weakened by heating, welding, or straightening so that it could fail on the highway.

   Some wheels now have decorative plastic inserts. The plastic can be cleaned by using a sponge and soap and water.

Fig. 43-22 Using the powered tire changer to lift the upper bead above the rim. The center post rotates, carrying the bead-lifting tool around with it.

☐ 43-27 TIRE VALVE

If the valve in the wheel requires replacement, remove the old valve and install a new one. There are two types: the snap-in type (Fig. 43-2) and the type that is secured with a nut. To remove the snap-in type, cut off the base of the old valve. Lubricate the new valve with rubber lubricant. Then attach a tire-valve installing tool to the valve and pull the new valve into place.

On the clamp-in type that is secured with a nut, remove the nut to take the old valve out. Be sure to tighten the nut sufficiently when installing the new valve.

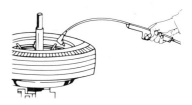

Fig. 43-23 Inflating the tire while seating the beads. Never exceed a pressure of 40 psi [276 kPa] in a passenger-car tire. *(Tire Industry Safety Council)*

☐ 43-28 SERVICING COLLAPSIBLE SPARE TIRE

The space-saving collapsible tire is described in ☐ 43-7. It is installed on the wheel deflated (Fig. 43-12). The wheel must be installed on the car before the tire is inflated.

> **CAUTION** Do not inflate the tire before the wheel is mounted on the car. Follow the safety cautions listed on the inflator can.

The inflator can has detailed instructions on how to install and inflate the tire. Briefly, here is the inflation procedure:

1. If the temperature is 10 degrees Fahrenheit (F) [−12 degrees Celsius (C)] or below, the inflator must be heated. Put the inflator over the defroster outlet of the car. Set the heater at "Defrost" at the highest temperature. Then run the blower at the fastest speed for 10 minutes.
2. Do not inflate the tire off the car. First bolt the wheel to the car with the air valve at the bottom. Remove the plastic cap from the inflator and the cap from the tire valve.
3. Push the inflator onto the valve stem until you hear the sound of gas entering the tire.

> **CAUTION** Keep your hands off the metal parts of the inflator. They become extremely cold during discharge. You could freeze your fingers!

4. When the sound stops, wait 1 minute. Then remove the inflator and install the valve cap. The gas in the inflator, when completely used up, will properly fill the tire.

> **NOTE** After you have inflated the tire and have removed the jack so that the tire rests on the pavement, the tire may look underinflated. This can happen especially in cold weather. Drive slowly for the first mile [1.6 km]. This will warm up the tire and increase the pressure.

5. If the inflator is the nonrefillable type, dispose of it in a safe waste receptacle. Do not burn or puncture the inflator. If it is the refillable type, it can be recharged with the proper equipment.
6. The collapsible spare tire must not be driven farther than necessary. The maximum distance is 150 miles [240 km]. As soon as the regular tire has been repaired and installed in place of the collapsible spare tire, remove the valve core from it. This will allow the gas to escape so that the tire collapses. It can then be stored, as before, in the luggage compartment.

> **CAUTION** This tire must not be used for more than 150 miles [240 km] and at speeds not to exceed 50 mph [80 km/h]. To exceed these limits is to risk a blowout of the collapsible spare tire. Also, do not inflate this tire from the usual air hoses in service stations or from the shop air hose. This can cause the tire to overinflate and explode.

☐ 43-29 TUBE REPAIR

If a tire tube has been punctured but has no other damage, it can be repaired with a patch. Remove the tube from the tire to find the leak. Inflate the tube and then submerge it in water. Bubbles will appear where there is a leak. Mark the spot. Then deflate the tube and dry it.

There are two ways to patch a tube leak. They are the cold-patch method and the hot-patch method. With the cold-patch method (also known as *chemical vulcanizing*), first make sure the rubber is clean, dry, and free of oil or grease. Buff, or roughen, the area around the leak. Then cover the area with vulcanizing cement. Let the cement dry until it is tacky. Press the patch into place. Roll it from the center out with a "stitching tool" or with the edge of a patch-kit can.

With the hot-patch method, prepare the tube in the same way as for the cold patch. Put the hot patch into place and clamp it. Then, with a match, light the fuel on the back of the patch. As the fuel burns, the heat vulcanizes the patch to the tube. After the patch has cooled, recheck the tube for leaks by submerging the tube in water.

Another kind of hot patch uses a vulcanizing hot plate. The hot plate supplies the heat required to bond the patch to the tube.

☐ 43-30 TIRE REPAIR

No attempt should be made to repair a tire that has been badly damaged. If the plies are torn or have holes in them, the tire should be thrown away. A puncture bigger than $\frac{1}{4}$ inch [6.36 mm] should not be patched. Instead, the tire should be replaced. Even though you might be able to patch the tire so that it will hold air, it would be dangerous to use. The tire might blow out on the highway.

To repair small holes in a tubeless tire, first make sure that the object that caused the hole has been removed. Check the tire for other puncturing objects. Sometimes a tubeless tire can carry a nail for a long distance without losing air.

A radial tire should be removed from the wheel for repair. The plug should be of the head type and applied from inside the tire (Fig. 43-24).

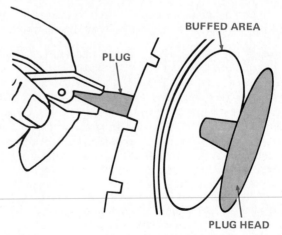

Fig. 43-24 Installing a head-type plug in a radial tubeless tire. *(Rubber Manufacturers Association)*

Figure 43-25 shows the area of a tire in which a puncture can be repaired. Punctures outside this area require replacement of the tire.

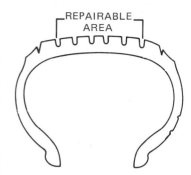

Fig. 43-25 The area of a tire in which a puncture can safely be patched. *(Chrysler Corporation)*

> **NOTE** Leaks from a tubeless tire are located in the same way as leaks from a tube. With the tire on the wheel and inflated, submerge the tire and wheel in water. Bubbles will show the location of any leaks. If a water tank is not available, coat the tire with soapy water. Bubbles will show the location of leaks.

If air leaks from around the spoke welds of the wheel, you can repair the leaks. Clean the area and apply two coats of cold-patch vulcanizing cement on the inside of the rim. Allow the first coat to dry before applying the second coat. Then cement a strip of rubber patching material over the area.

□ 43-31 REPAIRING PUNCTURE WITH RUBBER PLUG (TIRE ON RIM)

A temporary repair of a small puncture with the tire still mounted on the rim can be made (Fig. 43-26). However, this repair is only a temporary fix. As soon as possible, the tire must be removed from the rim and repaired from the inside (□ 43-32).

Remove the puncturing object and clean the hole. Apply vulcanizing cement to the outside and inside of the hole. There are different kinds of rubber plugs. The kind shown in Fig. 43-26 is installed with a plug needle. To use this plug, cover the hole with vulcanizing cement. Then select a plug of the right size for the hole. The plug should be at least twice the diameter of the hole. Roll the small end of the plug into the eye of the needle. Dip the plug into vulcanizing cement. Push the needle and plug through the hole. Then pull the needle out. Trim off the plug ⅛ inch [3.2 mm] above the tire surface. Check for leakage. If there is no leakage, the tire is ready to use after it is inflated. However, the tire should not be driven faster than 40 mph [64 km/h] or farther than 75 miles [120 km]. For continued use, the tire must be removed from the wheel and a permanent repair made.

□ 43-32 REPAIRING TIRE REMOVED FROM RIM

There are three methods of repairing holes in tires. These are the rubber-plug, the cold-patch, and the hot-patch method. Permanent repairs are made from inside the tire, with the tire off the rim.

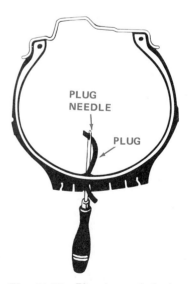

Fig. 43-26 Plugging a hole in the tire with a plug needle and plug.

- Rubber-plug method. Rubber plugs can be used in the same way as explained in □ 43-31. The basic difference is that the repair is made from inside the tire. The area inside the tire around the puncture is buffed and cleaned. Then the plug is installed from inside the tire.
- Cold-patch method. In the cold-patch method, first clean and buff the inside area around the puncture. Then coat the area around the puncture with vulcanizing cement. Allow it to dry for 5 minutes. Next, remove the backing from the patch. Place the patch over the puncture, stitching it down with the stitching tool. Start stitching at the center and work out, making sure to stitch down the edges of the patch.

> **NOTE** Make sure no dirt gets on the cement or patch during the repair. Dirt could allow leakage.

■ Hot-patch method. The hot-patch method is very similar to the cold-patch method. The difference is that after the patch has been put into place over the area, heat is applied. This is done by lighting the patch with a match or with an electric hot plate, according to the type of patch being used.

After the repair is done, mount the tire on the rim. Inflate and test it for leakage, as explained in □ 43-30.

□ 43-33 REPAIRING A TIRE THAT USES A TUBE

If a tire that uses a tube has a small hole, clean out the hole. Then repair the tube. No repair to the tire is necessary. The tube will hold the air. However, if the hole is large, up to ¼ inch [6 mm] in diameter, the tire should be repaired with a patch on the inside. This prevents dirt or water from working in between the tire and tube and causing tube failure.

CHAPTER 43
REVIEW QUESTIONS

Select the *one* correct, best, or most probable answer to each question. Then check your answers against the correct answers given at the end of the book.

1. One purpose of tires is to
   a. grip the road and provide good traction
   b. substitute for springs
   c. act as brakes
   d. none of the above

2. Two general types of tires are
   a. tube type and tubeless
   b. solid and tubeless
   c. air and pneumatic
   d. split-rim and drop-center

3. Typical passenger-car tire inflation pressures are from
   a. 12 to 22 psi
   b. 22 to 36 psi
   c. 40 to 100 psi
   d. none of the above

4. Vulcanizing means
   a. heating rubber under pressure
   b. spraying with a special paint
   c. melting rubber while stirring it
   d. none of the above

5. Bias-ply tires have
   a. all plies running parallel to one another
   b. belts of steel mesh in the tires
   c. one ply layer that runs diagonally one way and another layer that runs diagonally the other way
   d. all of the above

PART 8
AUTOMOTIVE AIR CONDITIONING

This part covers ventilating, heating, and air conditioning systems used in automotive vehicles. Many of these systems are manually controlled by knobs or levers on the dash which the driver moves to get the desired temperature. Other systems are automatic. The driver sets the temperature desired. Then the system automatically heats or cools as necessary to maintain that temperature in the car.

There are two chapters in Part 8: They are:

CHAPTER 44
VENTILATING, HEATING, AND AIR CONDITIONING

After studying this chapter, you should be able to:

1. Explain the need for ventilating the passenger compartment.
2. Describe the operation of the heater.
3. Name the basic parts and explain the operation of the refrigeration system.
4. Explain the difference between a thermostatic expansion valve and an orifice valve.
5. Describe the purpose and operation of the suction throttling valve.

Today all cars have heaters, and about 80 percent of all new cars have air conditioners. You adjust some systems manually. In other systems, you set the controls, and the system automatically maintains the temperature you selected. For example, if heat is needed inside the car, the heating system goes to work. Or, if the interior of the car needs cooling, the air-conditioning system automatically provides cooling.

☐ 44-1 PASSENGER-COMPARTMENT VENTILATION

For health and comfort, fresh air must be allowed to get into the passenger compartment to replace the stale and smoke-filled air inside the car. This process is called *ventilation*. There are two methods of ventilation available to the driver and passengers: uncontrolled and controlled.

Uncontrolled ventilation occurs when anyone opens a window so that air can enter. This method has been used for years. It has the advantage of providing almost any quantity of fresh air quickly. However, the disadvantage is that opening the window also allows wind, rain, dust, bugs, and other airborne particles to enter.

Two types of controlled ventilation systems are in use. One type is the ram-air system. Basically, this is a duct on each side of the car which can be opened to admit outside air (Fig. 44-1). However, most cars have a power-ventilating system. In this system, there is continuous low-speed operation of the heater and air-conditioner blower. This results in a steady flow of outside air into the car when the ignition switch is turned

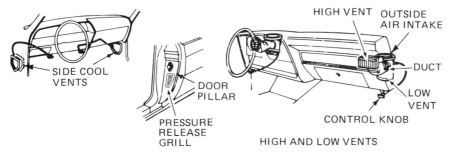

SIDE COOL VENTS

DOOR PILLAR

PRESSURE RELEASE GRILL

HIGH VENT

OUTSIDE AIR INTAKE

DUCT

LOW VENT

CONTROL KNOB

HIGH AND LOW VENTS

Fig. 44-1 Basic components in a ram-air ventilating system. *(Ford Motor Company)*

on. With the side windows closed, outside air flows into the air inlets, through the car, and out the air outlets (Fig. 44-2).

□ 44-2 CAR HEATER

Heat from the engine coolant is used by the car heating system to heat the car interior. The basic system is shown in Fig. 12-1. It consists of a small radiator or "heater core" that is connected by two hoses to the engine cooling system. Hot coolant flows through the hoses and the heater core. A small electric fan forces air through the heater core. The air absorbs heat from the heater core, and then flows into the passenger compartment to warm it.

A car heater installation is shown in Fig. 44-3. This system includes a *defroster*. The driver can operate controls that will direct the heated air into the passenger compartment. Or all or part of the heated air can be directed against the windshield. This will melt any ice or frost, and evaporate any mist, that has formed there.

The amount of heat that gets into the car interior is determined by the amount of air that is allowed to flow through the heater core. In most heaters, three doors are provided to adjust airflow. Figure 44-4 shows a schematic diagram of the system. The amount of air that enters is determined by the blower speed. The blower motor is connected to the battery through a switch. It can be turned to operate the blower slow or fast (and at an intermediate speed in many systems).

After the air enters the system, its direction of flow is determined by the position of the temperature door. In Fig. 44-4, three positions of this door are indicated, labeled A, B, and C. If the temperature door is open wide (position C), then most of the air entering has to pass through the heater core. Maximum heating is obtained. If the door is closed (position

AIR INLET

AIR OUTLET

Fig. 44-2 Airflow pattern as fresh air circulates through the passenger compartment. *(Buick Motor Division of General Motors Corporation)*

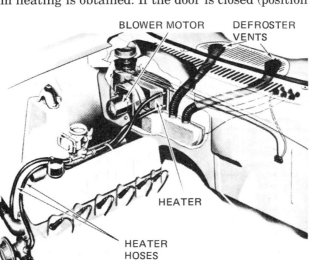

BLOWER MOTOR

DEFROSTER VENTS

HEATER

HEATER HOSES

Fig. 44-3 A car heater system. Hot coolant from the engine cooling system circulates through the heater core. A fan on the blower motor blows air through the heater core.

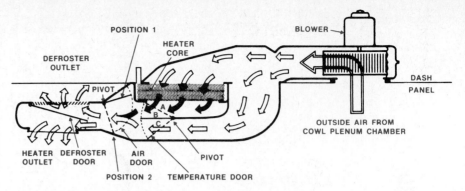

Fig. 44-4 Three doors that control the airflow through an automotive heater. *(Chevrolet Motor Division of General Motors Corporation)*

A), then no air can pass through the heater core. The air temperature is unchanged.

The air door determines the amount of air, either hot or cold, flowing through the system. It can be adjusted for full airflow (position 1) or for no airflow at all (position 2), or any place in between.

The defroster door can be adjusted so that the heated air is directed up through the defroster outlets to the inside of the windshield. Or the defroster door can be adjusted so that most of, or all, the heated air is directed into the car.

The doors to the system shown in Fig. 44-4 are operated by cables attached to heater controls on the instrument panel.

□ 44-3 VACUUM-OPERATED HEATER CONTROLS

Figure 44-5 shows a heater-control system that uses vacuum motors to control the system. The unit is mounted under the instrument panel. The control assembly is mounted in the instrument panel. It is attached to the main unit by various cables and hoses. Vacuum to operate the vacuum motors is obtained from the engine intake manifold when the engine is running.

Figure 44-6 is a schematic drawing of the heater system. Outside air is drawn into the system through the cool-air intake and flows into the blower housing. From the blower housing, the air flows through the heater case to the temperature-blend door (5 in Fig. 44-6). This door directs air through or around the heater core, depending on the position of the door. The door position is controlled by the temperature-control lever, which is a manual control on the instrument panel (at the top in Fig. 44-6). Setting the control lever at the COOL position causes the door to block off passage of the air through the heater core. The air passes through the system unchanged in temperature. Moving the lever to WARM causes the door to direct all the air through the heater core so that the air is heated. At various positions between COOL and WARM, part of the air goes through the heater core and part bypasses the heater core. The heated and unheated air blend and enter the car. Moving the temperature-control lever moves the temperature-blend door to give the desired amount of heat in the car.

In this system, air can be directed in the following three ways:

■ To the floor
■ Through registers into the car
■ To the defroster vents

The registers are the two louvered outlets mounted at the two extreme ends of the instrument panel. The louvers can be adjusted to aim

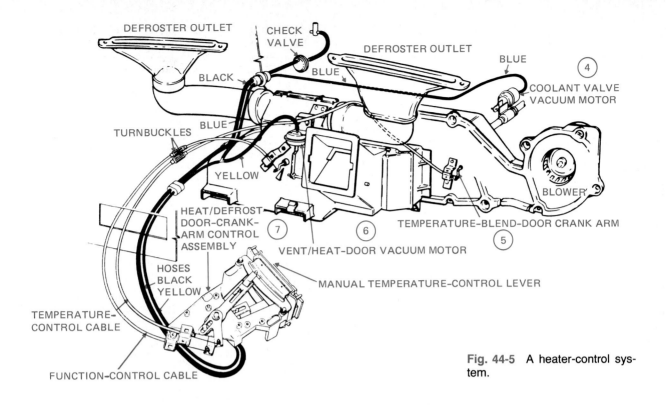

Fig. 44-5　A heater-control system.

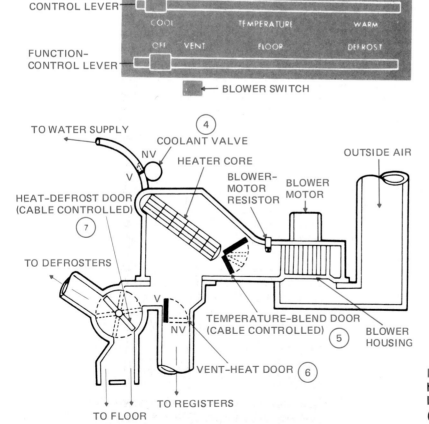

Fig. 44-6　Instrument-panel heater controls with a schematic layout of the car heater system. *(Ford Motor Company)*

the flow of air. Also, the heat can be shut off entirely so that untreated outside air flows into the car. When the function-control lever (top of Fig. 44-6) is set at VENT, a vacuum motor opens the vent-heat door (6 in Fig. 44-6). At the same time, another vacuum motor closes the coolant valve (4 in Fig. 44-6) so that the flow of hot coolant to the heater core is cut off.

REFRIGERATION

□ 44-4 REFRIGERATION

The automotive air conditioner uses a process of refrigeration to cool and dry the air.

Refrigeration works by the process of evaporation. *Evaporation* happens when a liquid turns into a gas, or vapor. Put a little water on your hand. Blow on your hand, or wave your hand in the air. Your hand feels cool because as the water evaporates, it takes heat from your hand.

The removal of heat by evaporation is the basic principle of refrigeration. For example, heat is removed from food put into the refrigerator by the evaporation of a liquid in the refrigeration system.

Figure 44-7 shows a refrigerator containing food, plus a jug of a liquid refrigerant called "Freon-12," "refrigerant-12," or "R-12." Freon-12 is a liquid at temperatures below −22 degrees Fahrenheit (F) [−30 degrees Celsius (C)]. At temperatures above −22°F [−30°C], Freon-12 evaporates. Since the temperature in the refrigerator shown in Fig. 44-7 is well above −22°F [−30°C], the Freon-12 evaporates. As Freon-12 evaporates, it takes heat from the food and therefore cools the refrigerator. The refrigerating action continues as long as there is any Freon-12 left in the jug to evaporate. Because the Freon-12 refrigerates, it is called a "refrigerant."

There are some drawbacks to the system shown in Fig. 44-7. It is wasteful to allow all the refrigerant to escape. Besides, having refrigerant vapor floating around could be dangerous. Also, since the refrigerant boils, or evaporates, at −22°F [−30°C], it tends to bring everything down to this temperature. Everything would be frozen.

Two things must be done to improve the system. First, the refrigerant must be recaptured and turned back into a liquid. Second, the refrigerant action must be controlled so that the proper temperature can be maintained.

□ 44-5 BASIC REFRIGERATION CYCLE

Figure 44-8 is a simplified diagram of an automotive air conditioner. The *evaporator* serves the same purpose as the Freon-12 in the jug in Fig. 44-7. As the refrigerant evaporates, it absorbs heat. The low-pressure vapor is then carried through a suction line to the *compressor*.

The compressor is a type of pump. It takes in the vaporized refrigerant and applies to it a high pressure—up to 200 psi [1379 kPa]. The high pressure causes the temperature of the vapor to go above 100°F [38°C]. Then the hot vapor, under high pressure, is sent to the *condenser*. The condenser is a long tube equipped with fins. As the hot vapor passes through the condenser, the hot vapor loses its heat and condenses into liquid again.

During this cycle, the refrigerant has carried heat out of the passenger compartment of the car. The refrigerant then gets rid of this heat in the condenser, which is mounted in front of the engine radiator. Now the liquid flows through an expansion valve and back into the evaporator.

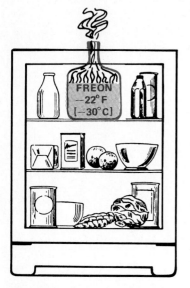

Fig. 44-7 A simple refrigerator. Evaporation of the refrigerant, Freon-12, removes heat from inside.

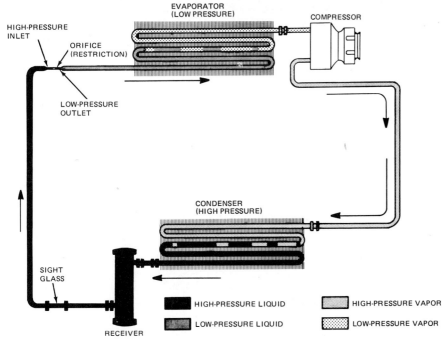

HIGH-PRESSURE INLET

EVAPORATOR (LOW PRESSURE)

COMPRESSOR

ORIFICE (RESTRICTION)

LOW-PRESSURE OUTLET

CONDENSER (HIGH PRESSURE)

SIGHT GLASS

RECEIVER

HIGH-PRESSURE LIQUID

LOW-PRESSURE LIQUID

HIGH-PRESSURE VAPOR

LOW-PRESSURE VAPOR

Fig. 44-8 Basic refrigeration system. Arrows show flow of refrigerant.

The expansion valve has a very small diameter hole, or *orifice,* that restricts the flow of the liquid. Refrigerant flow must be restricted. There must be a pressure differential between the condenser and the evaporator. The pressure must be high on the compressor side but low on the evaporator side. High pressure is necessary to condense the refrigerant. Low pressure is necessary to allow the refrigerant to evaporate.

AIR CONDITIONING

□ 44-6 AIR-CONDITIONER ACTION

The car heater puts heat into the car interior. The air conditioner does just the opposite. It takes heat out of the car interior. The blower that is used for heating is also used for air conditioning. For heating, the blower blows air through the heater core. For cooling, it blows air through the evaporator.

> **NOTE** In automotive shop manuals the term "air conditioner" often is shortened to "A/C."

In addition to cooling the air, the evaporator also takes moisture out of the air. This action is the same as the action of moisture condensing on a cold glass. What happens is that as the air flows through the cold evaporator, moisture condenses on the evaporator core. The moisture runs off the evaporator core and drops outside the car. The air conditioner cools the air and dries it. Dry air feels cooler than moist air. The air conditioner helps keep the car interior comfortable in two ways—by cooling the air and by drying it.

□ 44-7 AUTOMOTIVE AIR CONDITIONER

Figure 44-9 shows the installation of an air conditioner in a car. The system includes a compressor, a condenser, and an evaporator. You cannot see the evaporator in Fig. 44-9. It is in the assembly under the instrument panel. Figure 44-10 is a schematic layout of an air conditioner showing the locations of the heater core and evaporator core.

Notice that the assembly has several doors. These doors can be opened or closed to direct the flow of air through either the heater core or the evaporator core. Also, the doors can be operated so that the air flowing through the evaporator core can be taken from outside or picked up from inside the car. Air picked up from inside the car is called *recirculated* air. The heated air can also be directed to the defroster outlets or into the dash outlets by operation of other doors.

□ 44-8 AIR-CONDITIONER OPERATION

Figure 44-11 shows the basic air-conditioning system. The compressor takes in the vapor from the evaporator and puts the vapor under pressure. The high-pressure vapor, or gas, is sent to the condenser. In the condenser the vapor loses heat and returns to liquid form. The liquid then flows to the evaporator, where it evaporates. As the liquid turns to vapor, it takes in heat. The vapor then passes back into the compressor. This flow is continuous as long as the air conditioner is operating.

Following sections describe some of the important parts of the automotive air conditioner. These include the receiver, the expansion valve, the orifice tube, the suction throttling valve, and the magnetic clutch on the compressor.

□ 44-9 RECEIVER

The purpose of the receiver (Fig. 44-11) is to ensure a supply of liquid refrigerant to the evaporator. The liquid refrigerant flows through an outlet at the bottom of the receiver so that no vapor can mix with the liquid refrigerant. In some systems the outlet is at the top of the receiver, but it is connected to a pipe that goes to the bottom. The liquid refrigerant always settles at the bottom of the receiver so that the outlet always picks up liquid rather than vapor.

The receiver also contains a substance called a *desiccant* that absorbs water. Any moisture in the system is absorbed by the desiccant so that the moisture can do no harm. If moisture were not absorbed, it might freeze in a valve and prevent normal air-conditioner action.

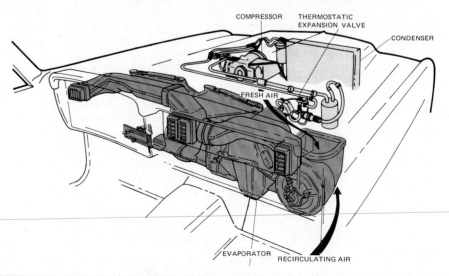

Fig. 44-9 The location of major components in a car air conditioner. *(Ford Motor Company)*

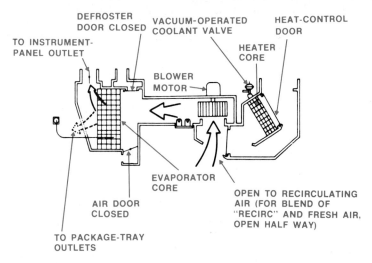

Fig. 44-10 A schematic diagram of a car air conditioner. (American Motors Corporation)

□ 44-10 EXPANSION VALVE

The *expansion valve* is located in the circuit between the condenser and the evaporator (Fig. 44-11). The purpose of the expansion valve is to regulate the flow of liquid refrigerant to the evaporator. Figure 44-12 is a sectional view of an expansion valve. A tube is connected to a temperature-sensing bulb located on the top of the evaporator. The bulb is filled with a gas that expands or contracts with changing temperatures. As the temperature in the evaporator goes up, the gas expands. The expansion of the gas exerts pressure on the diaphragm. It overcomes spring tension and forces the valve off its seat. With the valve off its seat, liquid refrigerant is able to flow into the evaporator. Cooling takes place.

As the temperature in the evaporator goes down, the gas in the bulb contracts. The pressure on the diaphragm drops, and the spring pushes the valve closed. This stops the flow of liquid refrigerant to the evaporator. Cooling stops. In operation, the valve takes the position needed to provide the right amount of cooling in the car. If cooling needs are low, the valve is almost closed, and only a little cooling is provided. If cooling needs are high, the valve is opened wider so that more liquid refrigerant flows and cooling is increased.

□ 44-11 ORIFICE TUBE

There must be a restriction in the refrigerant line between the condenser and the evaporator. Two types of restrictions are used. One is the expan-

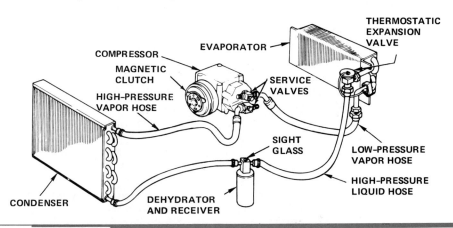

Fig. 44-11 A schematic layout of an air conditioner using a thermostatic expansion valve. (Ford Motor Company)

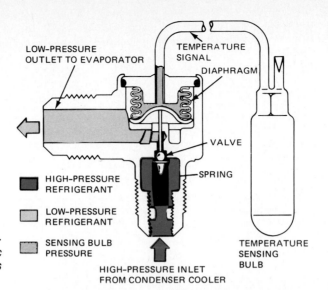

LOW-PRESSURE
OUTLET TO EVAPORATOR

TEMPERATURE
SIGNAL

DIAPHRAGM

VALVE

SPRING

HIGH-PRESSURE
REFRIGERANT

LOW-PRESSURE
REFRIGERANT

SENSING BULB
PRESSURE

HIGH-PRESSURE INLET
FROM CONDENSER COOLER

TEMPERATURE
SENSING
BULB

Fig. 44-12 A cutaway thermostatic expansion valve. *(Pontiac Motor Division of General Motors Corporation)*

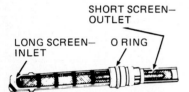

SHORT SCREEN—
OUTLET

LONG SCREEN—
INLET

O RING

Fig. 44-13 An orifice tube, or expansion tube. *(Oldsmobile Division of General Motors Corporation)*

sion valve (□ 44-10). The other type is a fixed orifice, or *orifice tube* (Fig. 44-8). Figure 44-13 shows a cutaway view of an orifice tube. The small diameter limits the amount of liquid refrigerant that can flow from the condenser to the evaporator. Because of the restriction, the high-pressure liquid refrigerant on the condenser side of the orifice comes out as low-pressure liquid refrigerant on the evaporator side (Fig. 44-8).

The expansion tube is protected at both ends from contamination by filter screens (Fig. 44-13). These screens prevent dirt particles that might be circulating with the refrigerant from getting into the orifice and blocking it. The typical diameter of the opening in the orifice tube is about 0.072 inch [1.83 mm]. This is much larger than the maximum opening of the thermostatic expansion valve. The size of the passage allows the orifice tube to be more tolerant of dirt particles in the system.

The orifice has no moving parts. It works automatically and requires no adjustments. For these reasons, many automotive manufacturers have switched to air conditioners using this type of restriction in the condenser-to-evaporator line. An air conditioner using an orifice tube is often identified as being a *CCOT system*. CCOT stands for "cycling-clutch orifice tube," a type of refrigeration-control system. The system controls the amount of cooling by turning the compressor on and off. This is done through the automatic cycling of the compressor clutch.

□ 44-12 SUCTION THROTTLING VALVE

The suction throttling valve is located between the evaporator and the compressor. Its main purpose is to prevent freezing of moisture on the evaporator. If the evaporator temperature goes below 32°F [0°C], any moisture in the air going through the evaporator will freeze. If the evaporator froze, cooling would be reduced. Figure 44-14 is a sectional view of a suction throttling valve. Spring force and atmospheric pressure on one side of the valve piston and evaporator pressure on the other side control the valve operation. When evaporator pressure exceeds the specific maximum, it pushes the piston back. This action opens the valve so that liquid refrigerant can now flow from the evaporator to the compressor.

The vacuum element comes into operation when the driver turns the control to full cooling. When the driver does this, vacuum from the engine is admitted to the end of the vacuum element. Now the assist spring is

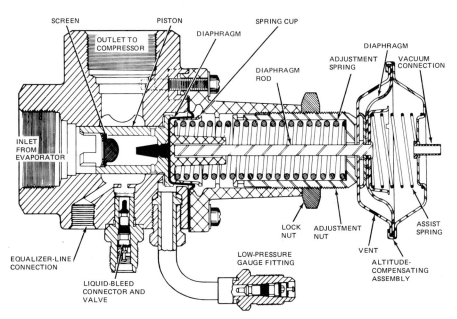

Fig. 44-14 A cutaway suction throttling valve. *(Pontiac Motor Division of General Motors Corporation)*

compressed. The compression of the assist spring allows the valve to move farther out so that more refrigerant can flow.

□ 44-13 CONTROL PANELS

The air-conditioning system is controlled by levers or buttons on the instrument panel. Some controls are vacuum-operated, just as in the vacuum-operated heater systems (□ 44-3). In one system, the levers are set manually and adjusted by the driver for different conditions. In a fully automatic system, the driver sets the temperature desired. Then the system takes over. The system will cool when cooling is needed to maintain the temperature set. The system will also heat when heating is needed to maintain the preset temperature.

□ 44-14 MAGNETIC CLUTCH

As part of the control system, the compressor has a magnetic clutch (Fig. 44-15). This clutch is located in the compressor pulley. The pulley is driven by a belt from the crankshaft pulley. When cooling is needed, the magnetic clutch is engaged. The compressor is then driven through the magnetic clutch so that cooling is obtained. The purpose of the magnetic clutch is to engage the compressor for cooling and to disengage it when cooling is not needed.

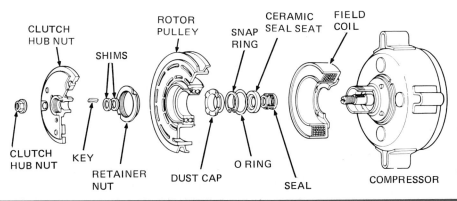

Fig. 44-15 A disassembled compressor clutch. *(Ford Motor Company)*

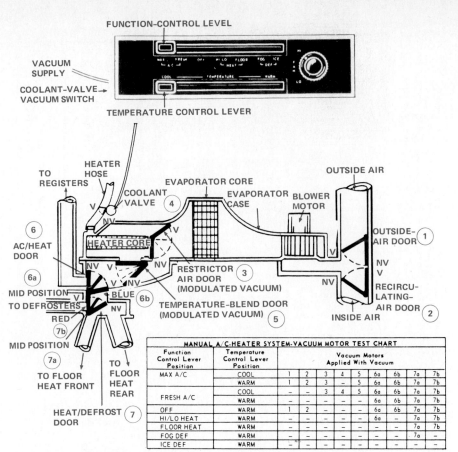

Fig. 44-16 A manually controlled air-conditioning-and-heating system. *(Ford Motor Company)*

Function Control Lever Position	Temperature Control Lever Position	Vacuum Motors Applied With Vacuum								
		1	2	3	4	5	6a	6b	7a	7b
MAX A/C	COOL	1	2	3	4	5	6a	6b	7a	7b
	WARM	1	2	3	–	5	6a	6b	7a	7b
FRESH A/C	COOL	–	–	3	4	5	6a	6b	7a	7b
	WARM	–	–	–	–	–	6a	6b	7a	7b
OFF	WARM	1	2	–	–	–	6a	6b	7a	7b
HI/LO HEAT	WARM	–	–	–	–	–	6a	–	7a	7b
FLOOR HEAT	WARM	–	–	–	–	–	–	–	7a	7b
FOG DEF	WARM	–	–	–	–	–	–	–	7a	–
ICE DEF	WARM	–	–	–	–	–	–	–	–	–

MANUAL A/C-HEATER SYSTEM-VACUUM MOTOR TEST CHART

□ 44-15 MANUAL TEMPERATURE-CONTROL SYSTEM

Figure 44-16 shows schematically the manual temperature-control system. Air enters from either outside or inside the car, depending on the positions of doors 1 and 2. These are the outside air door and the recirculating door. The position of these doors is controlled by the movement of the function-control lever (Fig. 44-16). When the lever is moved to the left—to MAX A/C—the outside air door is closed, and the recirculating air door is opened. If the lever is set at FRESH A/C, fresh air from outside will be brought into the system.

The speed with which the air moves is controlled by the speed of the blower. The setting of the FAN knob (Fig. 44-16) determines the speed of the blower and the speed with which air is brought into the system.

The air goes first through the evaporator core and may or may not be cooled, depending on the position of the temperature-control lever. If the lever is set at A/C, then the magnetic clutch on the compressor will be actuated. The compressor will operate, and cooling will result. If the lever is set at HEAT or DEF (for defrost), the magnetic clutch will not operate, and no compressor action will take place. There will be no cooling.

After passing through the evaporator core, the air meets the air-restrictor door (3 in Fig. 44-16). This door can be swung up to admit air to the heater core or swung down to prevent air from entering the heater core. The temperature-blend door (5) can be moved varying amounts to control the percentage of heater-core air and evaporator-core air that mix at this point. Next, the air meets the air-conditioner-heat door (6), which

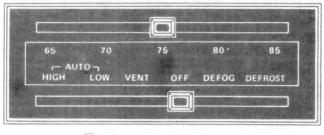

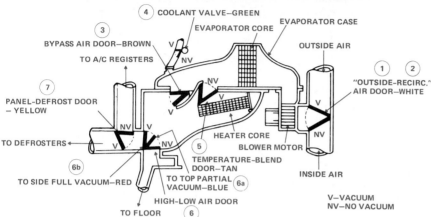

Fig. 44-17 Control panel and schematic diagram for an automatic heater-air-conditioner system. *(Ford Motor Company)*

can be moved one way or the other. In the up position, the passage to the registers is blocked, and the air moves down into the defroster-floor-heat position. Now the air, which has been warmed, can move to the defrosters or to the floor-heat outlets, depending on the position of the heat-defrost door (7).

The system also includes a coolant valve (4). It shuts off the flow of hot coolant from the engine cooling system when the air conditioner is running. Both the coolant valve and the air door are operated by vacuum motors.

□ 44-16 AUTOMATIC TEMPERATURE CONTROL

Figure 44-17 is a schematic layout of an automatic-temperature-control system. The control panel has two levers. The upper lever can be moved to select the desired temperature (65° to 85°F). The lower lever can be moved all the way to the left to get automatic action in HIGH. In this position, the blower will operate at the maximum speed until the desired temperature is reached. Then the blower will slow down and operate just fast enough to maintain the desired temperature. If slower action is desired, the driver can set the lever at LOW. If the driver wants only untreated outside air to enter, the driver sets the lever at VENT. At this setting the outside-recirculating door (1 and 2 in Fig. 44-17) is moved down so that outside air enters. If the driver wants to defog or defrost the windshield, the driver sets the lever at either of these positions.

The air passes through the evaporator core after it leaves the blower. Whether the air is cooled depends on whether the air conditioner is working. Next, the air either bypasses the heater core or passes through the heater core. If the system calls for heat, then the air conditioner will not be working but the heater core will be hot. This is because hot coolant from the engine cooling system will be circulating through the heater core. With this operating condition, the coolant valve (4) will be open. Also, the bypass air door (3) will be closed, and the temperature-blend door (5) will be open. The direction the heated air then takes depends on the positions of the high-low door (6) and the panel-defrost door (7).

If the system calls for cooling, the evaporator core is cold and the air-conditioning system is working. Air passing through the evaporator core is cooled. Then the air goes through the open bypass door and to the air-conditioning registers.

In this system there is a delay circuit in the heating section. This delay circuit prevents the blower from coming on until the coolant circulating in the heater core is warm. This prevents the circulation of cold air, which would be uncomfortable for the people in the car. Vacuum motors operate the coolant valve and the air doors.

CHAPTER 44
REVIEW QUESTIONS

Select the *one* correct, best, or most probable answer to each question. Then check your answers against the correct answers given at the end of the book.

1. The ram-air system of controlled ventilation uses
   a. no blower motor or fan
   b. one blower motor
   c. two blower motors
   d. the air-conditioner blower

2. The small radiator in the heater which warms cool air passing through it is the
   a. evaporator
   b. heater core
   c. condenser
   d. water pump

3. Heater operation is controlled by
   a. cables and vacuum motors
   b. links and levers
   c. pumps and plungers
   d. none of the above

4. The purpose of the defroster is to
   a. wash dirt off the windshield
   b. warm the passenger compartment
   c. clear the windshield
   d. none of the above

5. When the heater is operating, the amount of heat delivered to the passenger compartment depends on
   a. the position of the control lever on the instrument panel
   b. the position of the doors in the heater
   c. both *a* and *b*
   d. neither *a* nor *b*

CHAPTER 45

HEATER AND AIR-CONDITIONER SERVICE

After studying this chapter, and with proper instruction and equipment, you should be able to:

1. Service the car heater.

2. Describe the safety precautions for working around air conditioners.

3. Perform a sight-glass diagnosis.

4. Perform an air-conditioner performance test.

5. Evacuate and charge the refrigerant system.

A variety of heater and air-conditioner troubles may be reported by the driver. These include not enough heat, not enough cooling, improper circulation (heat coming out of the air-conditioner ducts, for example), and the system quitting when the car is accelerated. These troubles can be in either the control system or the air-conditioner-heater system. The heater is part of the engine cooling system. Manually operated heater systems require little servicing. Air-conditioning systems require more service. This chapter describes how to troubleshoot and service both car heaters and air conditioners.

□ 45-1 SERVICING HEATING SYSTEMS

Heater problems usually result in one of these three complaints: leaks, no heat, or failure of the blower to work.

Leaks usually can be seen and are easily found. They could be caused by leaky hoses or connections, leaks in the radiator core, or leaks in the control valve. No heat could be due to a bad control valve or to clogged hoses or heater core. Failure of the blower to work is probably an electrical problem requiring replacement of the blower, switch, or wiring.

If the system automatically adjusts heating according to the temperature-control setting, failure to heat could be due to several things. A vacuum motor may not be working, the coolant valve may be stuck, the thermostatic control may not be working, or conditions listed in the previous paragraph may be causing the trouble.

The shop manual for the car you are working on will tell you how to completely check and service the system.

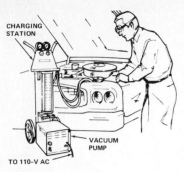

Fig. 45-1 Never work on an air conditioner unless you are wearing safety goggles. To be safe, you must have the proper tools and equipment and know how to use them. *(Ford Motor Company)*

□ 45-2 SERVICING AIR CONDITIONERS

Never work on air conditioners unless you have the proper equipment and know how to use it. This includes attempting to troubleshoot or service an air conditioner. The air-conditioning system contains the refrigerant, which is a high-pressure liquid and vapor. The liquid, if released, can turn to vapor almost instantly, freezing anything it touches. This includes skin and eyes! Here are cautions you *must* observe:

■ Undercoating. Never apply undercoating to any connections of the refrigerant lines or to the air-conditioning parts.
■ Steam cleaning and welding. Never apply any form of heat to any refrigerant line or to any component of the system. The refrigerant system is under pressure. Heating the refrigerant could increase the pressure excessively and cause an explosion.
■ Handling refrigerant. The refrigerant is about the safest refrigerant available, but you can be seriously hurt if you handle it carelessly.

Be sure to use only the refrigerant specified for automotive air-conditioning systems. The kind used in equipment such as boat air horns or fire-alarm signals is not pure and can ruin an air conditioner.

Refrigerant that escapes into the air can evaporate so quickly that it will freeze anything it touches, including skin and eyes. You could be blinded if you get refrigerant in your eyes!

CAUTION Always wear safety goggles (Fig. 45-1) when servicing any part of an air-conditioning system!

When discharging refrigerant from an air conditioner, discharge it into the shop exhaust system or into the open air. The refrigerant evaporates so quickly that it will displace all the air around the car. This could cause you to suffocate if the immediate area in which you are working is enclosed and without ventilation!

Do not discharge refrigerant in a room where there is an open flame. Refrigerant turns into a poisonous gas when it comes in contact with a flame. The gas is very dangerous if inhaled. This poisonous gas is also produced when you use a flame-type leak detector. But only a small amount of gas is produced; just don't inhale it.

Never heat a container of refrigerant when charging an air-conditioner system. The container could explode.

□ 45-3 TROUBLE DIAGNOSIS

Problems in the refrigerant system are indicated by the temperatures of the refrigerant lines and hoses. Once the system is normalized (after several minutes of operation), feel the temperature of each hose with your hand. The chart in Fig. 45-2 lists the lines and hose in the system and the normal temperature that you should feel for each. The temperatures of the lines and hose are used along with the sight-glass readings to determine if a problem exists in the refrigerant system.

A quick check of the system operation can be made by examining the sight glass with the air conditioner operating. The *sight glass* is a glass-covered peephole found in the top of some receivers (Fig. 45-3). All refrigerant leaving the receiver passes under the sight glass. The appearance of the refrigerant gives some indication of whether the system has the proper charge, or amount of refrigerant in it. With the engine running at about 1500 rpm and the controls set for maximum cooling, watch for bubbles in the sight glass. Here are the conditions that you may see and the procedure to follow for each condition.

Line	Should Feel
Evaporator inlet	Cold
Evaporator outlet	Cold
Low-pressure hose	Cold
High-pressure hose	Hot

Fig. 45-2 Normal temperature of air-conditioning lines, as they should feel to your hand. If any line is not as specified to the touch, the refrigerant system has a malfunction. *(Ford Motor Company)*

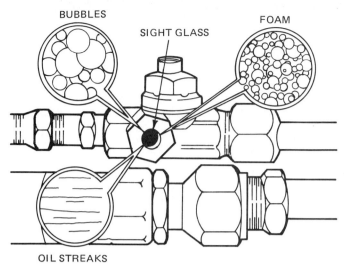

BUBBLES

SIGHT GLASS

FOAM

OIL STREAKS

Fig. 45-3 A typical sight glass showing different conditions that can be observed. *(Ford Motor Company)*

- Bubbles in the sight glass. This probably means the system is low on refrigerant. Check the system with a leak detector (Fig. 45-4). Correct the leak, if any. Then evacuate and charge the system. (The procedures on how to evacuate and charge the system are covered in □ 45-5.
- No bubbles, with the sight glass clear. This means the system is either fully-charged or empty. Feel the high- and low-pressure lines at the compressor. Keep your hands away from belts and the engine fan! The high-pressure line should feel warm or hot (Fig. 45-2). The low-pressure, or suction, line should be cold.
- Little or no difference in temperature between the lines at the compressor. The system is empty or nearly empty. Turn off the engine. Add about 0.5 pound [230 g] of refrigerant to the system. Check it with a leak detector. Correct the leak. Then evacuate and charge the system.
- Large difference in temperature between the lines at the compressor. The system probably has the proper charge of refrigerant in it. But the system could be overcharged. Too much refrigerant may have been added. This could result in poor cooling, especially at low speeds. Check for overcharging by temporarily disconnecting the compressor clutch while the system is operating. Watch the sight glass. If the refrigerant in the sight glass remains clear for more than 15 seconds (before foaming and then settling away), an overcharge is indicated. The excess refrigerant should be bled off. If the refrigerant in the sight glass foams and settles away from the sight glass in less than 45 seconds, the system probably has not been overcharged with refrigerant.

Some cars do not have a sight glass. On some systems, using the sight glass is not an accurate indicator of refrigerant-system condition. If there is no sight glass, install a gauge set to check the system pressure (Fig. 45-5).

□ 45-4 AIR-CONDITIONER PERFORMANCE TEST

To test the air conditioner for performance, you need a gauge set (Fig. 45-5). The gauge set is attached to the refrigerant system to measure the

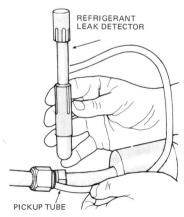

REFRIGERANT LEAK DETECTOR

PICKUP TUBE

Fig. 45-4 Using a small butane leak detector. *(Chrysler Corporation)*

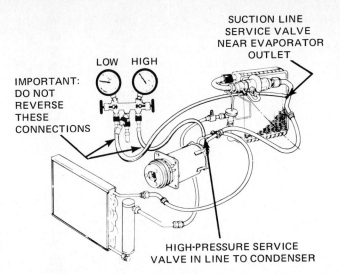

Fig. 45-5 Gauge-set connections for a performance test. *(Ford Motor Company)*

pressures. These pressures tell you where there is trouble. Refer to the car shop manual for details on how to use the gauge set and on what the various results mean.

□ 45-5 EVACUATING AND CHARGING THE SYSTEM

"Evacuating" means removing any air or moisture from the system after it has been opened for service or has leaked. If the system has been opened, air and moisture have entered. All this air and moisture must be removed by applying a vacuum to the system. The vacuum is produced by a special vacuum pump used for air-conditioning service work. Figure 45-1 shows a charging station that includes a vacuum pump.

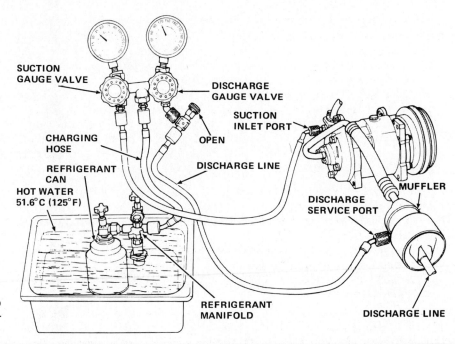

Fig. 45-6 Adding refrigerant to the air conditioner. *(Chrysler Corporation)*

"Charging" the system means to add refrigerant to it. To charge the system, connect a refrigerant container to the charging hose (center hose) of the gauge set. Then open the gauge valve to allow refrigerant to flow into the system (Fig. 45-6). This job is done with the engine running so that the compressor will be in operation.

CAUTION You must have a thorough understanding of air-conditioning service and safety before you attempt to do any work on an air-conditioning system. You should have the proper equipment and the shop manual covering the air conditioner that you are working on.

CHAPTER 45
REVIEW QUESTIONS

Select the *one* correct, best, or most probable answer to each question. Then check your answers against the correct answers given at the end of the book.

1. The most frequent complaint about the car heater is that it
   a. squeaks
   b. leaks
   c. gets too hot
   d. blows cold air

2. If an air-conditioner is equipped with a sight glass, you can check it to determine the
   a. temperature inside the car
   b. temperature under the hood
   c. condition of the engine cooling system
   d. condition of the refrigerant system

3. Slow-moving bubbles or a broken column of liquid under the sight glass indicates
   a. normal operation
   b. no refrigerant in the system
   c. an overcharge of refrigerant in the system
   d. the system is low on refrigerant

4. Under normal conditions, the hose which should feel hot to your hand is the
   a. evaporator inlet
   b. evaporator outlet
   c. high-pressure line
   d. low-pressure line

5. If there is little or no difference in temperature between the lines at the compressor,
   a. the system is empty or nearly empty
   b. the system is overcharged
   c. there is water in the system
   d. none of the above

GLOSSARY

Absolute pressure A method of measuring intake-manifold vacuum.

A/C See Air conditioning.

AC or ac Abbreviation for alternating current.

Accelerator A foot-operated pedal, linked to the throttle valve, used to control the flow of fuel to the engine.

Accelerator pump In the carburetor, a pump (linked to the accelerator) which momentarily enriches the air-fuel mixture when the accelerator is depressed at low speed.

Accessories Devices not considered essential to the operation of a vehicle, such as the radio, car heater, and electric window lifts.

Accumulator A device used in automatic transmissions to cushion the shock of clutch and servo actions.

Additive A substance added to fuel or oil to improve some property of the fuel or oil.

Adjust To bring the parts of a component or system to a specified relationship, dimension, or pressure.

Adjustments Necessary or desired changes in clearances, fit, or settings.

Advance The moving ahead of the ignition spark in relation to piston position; produced by centrifugal or vacuum devices in accordance with engine speed and intake-manifold vacuum, or electronically.

Aerobic gasket material A type of formed-in-place gasket, also known as self-curing, room-temperature-vulcanizing (RTV), and silicone rubber. A material that cures only in the presence of air, normally used on surfaces that flex or vibrate.

AIR Abbreviation for air-injection reactor, part of a system of exhaust emission control. See Air-injection system.

Air-aspirator system An air-injection system using a valve opened and closed by pulses in the exhaust system.

Air bleed An opening into a fuel passage through which air can pass, or bleed, into the fuel as it moves through the passage.

Air cleaner A device, mounted on or connected to the engine air intake, for filtering dirt and dust out of the air being drawn into the engine.

Air conditioning (A/C) An accessory system that conditions passenger-compartment air by cleaning, cooling, and drying it.

Air-cooled engine An engine that is cooled by the passage of air around the cylinders, not by the passage of a liquid through water jackets.

Air filter A filter that removes dirt and dust particles from air passing through it.

Air-fuel mixture The air and fuel traveling to the combustion chamber after being mixed by the carburetor.

Air-fuel ratio The proportions of air and fuel (by weight) supplied to the engine cylinders for combustion.

Air-injection system An exhaust emission control system that injects air at low pressure into the exhaust manifold to help complete the combustion of unburned hydrocarbons and carbon monoxide in the exhaust gas.

Air pollution Contamination of the air by natural and manufactured pollutants.

Air pressure Atmospheric pressure; also the pressure produced by an air pump or by compression of air in a cylinder.

Air pump Any device for compressing air. In the air-injection system of exhaust emission control, an engine-driven (belt-driven) pump incorporating a rotor and vanes.

Alignment The act of lining up, or the state of being in a true line.

Alternating current An electric current that flows first in one direction and then in the other.

Alternator In the vehicle electric system, a device that converts mechanical energy into electric energy for charging the battery and operating electrical accessories. Also known as an ac generator.

Ammeter A meter for measuring the amount of current (in amperes) flowing through an electric circuit.

Amperage The amount of current, in amperes.

Ampere A unit of measure for current. One ampere corresponds to a flow of 6.28×10^{18} electrons per second.

Anaerobic sealant A material that cures only when subjected to pressure and the absence of air; the material hardens when squeezed tightly between two surfaces.

Antibackfire valve A valve used in the air-injection system to prevent backfiring in the exhaust system during deceleration.

Antidieseling solenoid See Idle solenoid.

Antifreeze A chemical, usually ethylene glycol, that is added to the engine coolant to raise its boiling point and lower its freezing point.

Antilock brake system A system installed with the brakes to prevent wheel lockup during braking.

Antiseize compound A coating placed on some threaded fasteners to prevent corrosion, seizing, galling, and pitting.

Arcing Name given to the spark that jumps an air gap between two electrical conductors; for example, the arcing of the distributor contact points.

Armature A part moved by magnetism, or a part moved through a magnetic field to produce current.

Aspect ratio The ratio of tire height to width. For example, a G78 tire is 78 percent as high as it is wide. The lower the number, the wider the tire.

Atmospheric pressure The weight of the atmosphere per unit area. Atmospheric pressure at sea level is 14.7 psi absolute [101.35 kPa]; it decreases as altitude increases.

Automatic choke A device that positions the choke valve automatically in accordance with engine temperature or time.

Automatic level control A suspension system that compensates for variations in load in the rear of the car; positions the rear at a pre-designed level regardless of load.

Automatic transmission A transmission in which gear ratios are changed automatically, eliminating the necessity of hand-shifting gears.

Automatic-transmission fluid Any of several types of special oil used in automatic transmissions.

Auxiliary air inlet An extra hole in the air-cleaner housing that is opened and closed by a vacuum motor to allow additional air to enter if a partial vacuum develops in the air cleaner.

Axle A theoretical or actual crossbar

supporting a vehicle on which one or more wheels turn.

Axle ratio The ratio between the rotational speed (rpm) of the drive shaft and that of the driven wheel; gear reduction in the final drive, determined by dividing the number of teeth on the ring gear by the number of teeth on the pinion gear.

Backfire Noise made by the explosion of the air-fuel mixture in the intake or exhaust system, usually during cranking and deceleration.

Backlash In gearing, the clearance between the meshing teeth of two gears.

Backup lights White lights at the rear of the car that come on when the transmission is shifted into reverse.

Ball bearing An antifriction bearing with an inner race and an outer race, and one or more rows of balls between them.

Ball joint A flexible joint consisting of a ball within a socket, used in front-suspension systems and valve-train rocker arms.

Band In an automatic transmission, a hydraulically controlled brake band installed around a metal clutch drum; used to stop or permit drum rotation.

Barrel Term sometimes applied to the cylinders in an engine; used in referring to the number of throttle bores in a carburetor.

Battery An electrochemical device for storing energy in chemical form so that it can be released as electricity; a group of electric cells connected together.

Battery acid The electrolyte used in a battery; a mixture of sulfuric acid and water.

BDC See Bottom dead center.

Bead That part of the tire which is shaped to fit the rim; the bead is made of steel wires, wrapped and reinforced by the plies of the tire.

Bearing A part that transmits a load to a support and in so doing absorbs most of the friction and wear of the moving parts. A bearing is usually replaceable.

Bearing caps In the engine, caps held in place by bolts or nuts which, in turn, hold bearing halves in place.

Bearing clearance The space between the bearing and the shaft rotating within it.

Bearing crush The additional height (over a full half) which is manufactured into each bearing half to ensure complete contact of the bearing back with the housing bore when the engine is assembled.

Bearing spin A type of bearing failure in which a lack of lubrication overheats the bearing until it seizes on the shaft, shears its locking lip, and rotates in the housing or block.

Bearing spread A purposely manufactured small extra distance across the parting faces of the bearing half, in excess of the actual diameter of the housing bore.

Belt In a tire, a flat strip of material—fiberglass, rayon, or woven steel—which underlies the tread, all around the circumference of the tire.

Belted-bias tire A tire in which the plies are laid diagonally, crisscrossing one another, with a circumferential belt on top of them. The rubber tread is vulcanized on top of the belt and plies.

Belted-radial tire A tire in which the plies run parallel to one another and perpendicular to the tire bead. Belts running parallel to the tire tread are applied over this radial section.

Belt tension The tightness of a drive belt.

Bevel gear A gear shaped like the lower part of a cone; used to transmit motion through an angle.

Bias-ply tire A tire in which the plies are laid diagonally, crisscrossing one another at an angle of about 30 to 40 degrees.

Bleeding A process by which air is removed from a hydraulic system (brake or power steering) by draining part of the fluid or operating the system to work out the air.

Block See Cylinder block.

Blowby Leakage of compressed air-fuel mixture and burned gases (from combustion) past the piston rings into the crankcase.

Body On a vehicle, the assembly of sheet-metal sections, together with windows, doors, seats, and other parts, that provides enclosures for the passengers, engine, and luggage compartments.

Boiling Conversion from the liquid to the vapor state, taking place throughout the liquid. The conversion is accompanied by bubbling as vapor rises from below the surface.

Boost pressure The pressure in the intake manifold while the turbocharger is operating.

Bore An engine cylinder, or any cylindrical hole; also used to describe the process of enlarging or accurately refinishing a hole, as "to bore an engine cylinder." The bore size is the diameter of the hole.

Boring bar An electric-motor-powered cutting tool used to machine, or bore, an engine cylinder, thereby removing metal and enlarging the cylinder diameter.

Bottom dead center (BDC) The piston position at the lower limit of its travel in the cylinder, when the cylinder volume is at its maximum.

Brake An energy-conversion device used to slow, stop, or hold a vehicle or mechanism; a device that changes the kinetic energy of motion into useless and wasted heat energy.

Brake drum A metal drum mounted on a car wheel to form the outer shell of the brake; the brake shoes press against the drum to slow or stop drum-and-wheel rotation for braking.

Brake fluid A special fluid used in hydraulic brake systems to transmit force through a closed system of tubing known as the brake lines.

Brake horsepower Power available from the engine crankshaft to do work, such as moving the vehicle; bhp = torque × rpm/5252.

Brake lining A high-friction material, often a form of asbestos, attached to the brake shoe by rivets or a bonding process. The lining takes the wear when the shoe is pressed against the brake drum, or rotor.

Brake shoe In drum brakes, arc-shaped metal pieces lined with a high-friction material (the brake lining) which are forced against the revolving drums to produce braking action. In disk brakes, flat metal pieces lined with brake lining which are forced against the rotor face.

Brake system A combination of one or more brakes and their operating and control mechanism.

Brush A block of conducting substance, such as carbon, which rests against a rotating ring or commutator to form a continuous electric circuit.

BTDC Abbreviation for before top dead center; any position of the piston between bottom dead center and top dead center, on the upward stroke.

Bushing A one-piece sleeve placed in a bore to serve as a bearing surface.

Cables Stranded conductors, usually covered with insulating material, used for connections between electric devices.

Calibrate To check or correct the initial setting of a test instrument.

Caliper In a disk brake, a housing for pistons and brake shoes, connected to the hydraulic system; holds the brake shoes so that they straddle the disk.

Cam A rotating lobe or eccentric that can be used with a cam follower to change rotary motion to reciprocating motion.

Camber The tilt of the top of the wheels from the vertical; when the tilt is outward, the camber is positive. Also, the angle which a front-wheel spindle makes with the horizontal.

Cam follower See Valve lifter.

Camshaft The shaft in the engine which has a series of cams for operating the valve mechanisms. It is driven by gears, or by sprockets and a toothed belt or chain from the crankshaft.

Camshaft bearings Full-round sleeve bearings that support the camshaft.

Canister A special container in an evaporative control system that contains charcoal to trap vapors from the fuel system.

Capacity The ability to perform or to hold.

Carbon (C) A black deposit that is left on engine parts such as pistons, rings, and valves by the combustion of fuel and which inhibits their action.

Carbon dioxide (CO_2) A colorless, odorless gas that results from complete combustion; usually considered harmless. The gas absorbed from air by plants in photosynthesis; also used to carbonate beverages.

Carbon monoxide (CO) A colorless, odorless, tasteless, poisonous gas that results from incomplete combustion. A pollutant contained in engine exhaust gas.

Carburetion The actions that take place in the carburetor; converting liquid fuel to vapor and mixing it with air to form a combustible mixture.

Carburetor The device in an engine fuel system which mixes fuel with air and supplies the combustible mixture to the intake manifold.

Casing The outer part of the tire assembly, made of fabric or cord to which rubber is vulcanized.

Caster Tilting of the steering axis forward or backward to provide directional steering stability. Also, the angle which a front-wheel kingpin makes with the vertical.

Catalyst A substance that can speed or slow a chemical reaction between substances, without itself being consumed by the reaction.

Catalytic converter A mufflerlike device for use in an exhaust system. It converts harmful exhaust gases into harmless gases by promoting a chemical reaction between the catalysts and the pollutants.

Celsius A thermometer scale on which water boils at 100 degrees and freezes at 0 degrees. The formula $C = \frac{5}{9}(F - 32)$ converts Fahrenheit readings to Celsius readings.

Centimeter (cm) A unit of linear measure in the metric system; equal to approximately 0.390 inch.

Centrifugal advance A rotating-weight mechanism in the distributor that advances and retards ignition timing through the centrifugal force resulting from changes in the rotational speed of the distributor shaft.

Cetane number A measure of the ignition quality of diesel fuel, or how high a temperature is required to ignite it. The lower the cetane number, the higher the temperature required to ignite a diesel fuel.

Charcoal canister A container filled with activated charcoal; used to trap gasoline vapor from the fuel tank and carburetor while the engine is off.

Charge A specific amount of refrigerant or refrigerant oil.

Charging rate The amperage flowing from the alternator into the battery.

Chassis The assembly of mechanisms that make up the major operating part of the vehicle; usually assumed to include everything except the car body.

Chassis lubrication The procedure for lubricating the moving parts and wear points in the steering and suspension systems.

Check To verify that a component, system, or measurement complies with specifications.

Check valve A valve that opens to permit the passage of air or fluid in one direction only, or operates to prevent (check) some undesirable action.

Chemical reaction The formation of one or more new substances when two or more substances are brought together.

Chip One or more integrated circuits manufactured as a very small package capable of performing many functions.

Choke In the carburetor, a device used when starting a cold engine. It "chokes off" the airflow through the air horn, producing a partial vacuum in the air horn for greater fuel delivery and a richer mixture. It operates automatically on most cars.

CID See Cubic inch displacement.

Circuit The complete path of an electric current, including the current source. When the path is continuous, the circuit is closed and current flows. When the path is broken, the circuit is open and no current flows. Also used to refer to fluid paths, as in refrigerant and hydraulic systems.

Circuit breaker A resettable protective device that opens an electric circuit to prevent damage when the circuit is overheated by excess current flow.

Clearance The space between two moving parts, or between a moving and a stationary part, such as a journal and a bearing. The bearing clearance is filled with lubricating oil when the mechanism is running.

Closed crankcase ventilation system A system in which the crankcase vapors (blowby gases) are discharged into the engine intake system and pass through to the engine cylinders rather than being discharged into the air.

Clutch A coupling that connects and disconnects a shaft from its drive while the drive mechanism is running. In an automobile power train, the device which engages and disengages the transmission from the engine. In an air-conditioning system, the device that engages and disengages the compressor shaft from its continuously rotating drive-belt pulley.

Clutch disk See Friction disk.

Clutch fork In the clutch, a Y-shaped member into which the throwout bearing is assembled.

Clutch gear See Clutch shaft.

Clutch pedal A foot pedal used by the driver to operate the clutch.

Clutch shaft The shaft on which the clutch is assembled, with the gear that drives the countershaft in the transmission on one end. On the clutch-gear end, it has external splines that can be used by a synchronizer drum to lock the clutch shaft to the main shaft for direct drive.

Clutch solenoid In automotive air conditioners, a solenoid that operates a clutch on the compressor drive pulley. When the clutch is engaged, the compressor is driven and cooling takes place.

CNG Abbreviation for compressed natural gas, which can be used as an engine fuel.

CO See Carbon monoxide.

CO$_2$ See Carbon dioxide.

Coil In an automobile ignition system, a transformer used to step up the battery voltage (by induction) to the high voltage required to fire the spark plugs.

Coil spring A spring made of an elastic metal such as steel, formed into a wire and wound into a coil.

Coil-spring clutch A clutch using coil springs to hold the pressure plate against the friction disk.

Cold patching A method of repairing a punctured tire or tube by gluing a thin rubber patch over the hole.

Collapsible spare tire A wheel that mounts a special deflated tire. It is furnished with a can of tire-inflation propellant to use when the tire must be inflated and installed.

Collapsible steering column An energy-absorbing steering column designed to collapse if the driver is thrown into it.

Combination valve A brake-warning-lamp valve in combination with a proportioning and/or metering valve.

Combustion Burning; fire produced by the proper combination of fuel, heat, and oxygen. In the engine, the rapid burning of air and fuel in the combustion chamber.

Combustion chamber The space between the top of the piston and the cylinder head, in which the fuel is burned.

Commutator A series of copper bars at one end of a generator or starting-motor armature, electrically insulated from the armature shaft and insulated from one another by mica. The brushes rub against the bars of the commutator, which form a rotating connector between the armature windings and brushes.

Compact spare tire A special high-pressure spare tire, mounted on a narrow wheel, that can be used on cars without a limited-slip differential.

Compression Reduction in the volume of a gas by squeezing it into a smaller space. Increasing the pressure reduces the volume and increases the density and temperature of the gas.

Compression-ignition engine An engine operating on the diesel cycle, in which the fuel is injected into the cylinders, where the heat of compression ignites it.

Compression pressure The pressure in the combustion chamber at the end of the compression stroke.

Compression ratio The volume of the cylinder and combustion chamber when the piston is at BDC, divided by the volume when the piston is at TDC.

Compression ring The upper ring or rings on a piston, designed to hold the compression and combustion pressures in the combustion chamber, thereby preventing blowby.

Compression stroke The piston movement from BDC to TDC immediately following the intake stroke, during which both the intake and exhaust valves are closed while the air or air-fuel mixture in the cylinder is compressed.

Compression tester An instrument for testing the amount of pressure, or compression, developed in an engine cylinder during cranking.

Compressor The component of an air-conditioning system that compresses refrigerant vapor to increase its pressure and temperature.

Condensation A change of state during which a gas turns to liquid, usually because of temperature or pressure changes. Also, moisture from the air, deposited on a cool surface.

Condenser In the ignition system, a capacitor connected across the contact points to reduce arcing by providing a storage place for electricity (electrons) as the contact points open. In an air-conditioning system, the radiatorlike heat exchanger in which refrigerant vapor loses heat and returns to the liquid state.

Conductor Any material or substance that allows current or heat to flow easily.

Connecting rod In the engine, the rod that connects the crank on the crankshaft with the piston.

Connecting-rod bearing See Rod bearing.

Connecting-rod cap The part of the connecting-rod assembly that attaches the rod to the crankpin.

Connecting-rod journal See Crankpin.

Constant-velocity joint Two closely coupled universal joints arranged in such a way that their acceleration-deceleration effects cancel out. This results in an output drive-shaft speed that is always identical with the input drive-shaft speed, regardless of the angle of drive.

Contact points In the contact-point ignition system, the stationary and the movable points in the distributor which open and close the ignition primary circuit.

Contaminants Anything other than refrigerant and refrigerant oil in a refrigeration system; includes rust, dirt, moisture, and air.

Control arm A part of the suspension system designed to control wheel movement precisely.

Coolant The liquid mixture of about 50 percent antifreeze and 50 percent water used to carry heat out of the engine.

Cooling system The system that removes heat from the engine by the forced circulation of coolant and thereby prevents engine overheating. In a liquid-cooled engine, it includes the water jackets, water pump, radiator, and thermostat.

Corrosion Chemical action, usually by an acid, that eats away, or decomposes, a metal.

Countershaft The shaft in the transmission which is driven by the clutch gear; gears on the countershaft drive gears on the main shaft when the latter are engaged.

Crankcase The lower part of the engine in which the crankshaft rotates, including the lower section of the cylinder block and the oil pan.

Crankcase emissions Pollutants emitted into the atmosphere from any portion of the engine crankcase ventilation or lubrication system.

Crankcase ventilation The circulation of air through the crankcase of a running engine to remove water, blowby, and other vapors; prevents oil dilution, contamination, sludge formation, and pressure buildup.

Cranking motor See Starting motor.

Crankpin The part of a crankshaft to which a connecting rod is attached; also called the crank throw or connecting-rod journal.

Crankshaft The main rotating member or shaft of the engine, with cranks to which the connecting rods are attached; converts up-and-down (reciprocating) motion into circular (rotary) motion.

Crankshaft gear A gear, or sprocket, mounted on the front of the crankshaft; used to drive the camshaft gear, chain, or toothed belt.

Crank throw One crankpin with its two webs. See also Crankpin.

Cross-firing Jumping of the high-voltage surge in the ignition secondary circuit to the wrong high-voltage lead, so that the wrong spark plug fires. Usually caused by improper routing of the spark-plug cables, faulty insulation, or a defective distributor cap or rotor.

Cubic centimeter (cu cm or cc) A unit of volume in the metric system; equal to approximately 0.061 cubic inch.

Cubic inch displacement (CID) The cylinder volume swept out by the pistons of an engine as they move from BDC to TDC, measured in cubic inches.

Curb idle The normal hot-idle speed of an engine.

Current A flow of electrons, measured in amperes.

Cycle A series of events that repeat themselves. In the automotive engine, the four piston strokes that together produce the power.

Cycling-clutch orifice-tube system An air-conditioning system in which a small restriction (the orifice tube) in the refrigerant line acts as the flow-control valve and the compressor clutch is automatically engaged and disengaged (cycling

clutch) to prevent evaporator icing.

Cycling-clutch system An air conditioner in which the conditioned-air temperature is controlled by starting and stopping the compressor.

Cylinder A circular, tubelike opening in an engine cylinder block or casting in which a piston moves up and down.

Cylinder block The basic framework of the engine, in and on which the other engine parts are attached. It includes the engine cylinders and the upper part of the crankcase.

Cylinder-compression tester See Compression tester.

Cylinder head The part of the engine that covers and encloses the cylinders. It contains cooling fins or water jackets and the valves.

Cylinder liner See Cylinder sleeve.

Cylinder sleeve A replaceable sleeve, or liner, set into the cylinder block to form the cylinder bore.

Dashpot A device that controls the rate at which the throttle valve closes.

DC or dc See Direct current.

Deceleration A decrease in velocity or speed. Also, allowing the car or engine to coast to idle speed from a higher speed with the accelerator at or near the idle position.

Defroster The part of the car heater system designed to melt frost or ice on the inside or outside of the windshield; includes the required duct work.

Degree Part of a circle. One degree is $\frac{1}{360}$ of a complete circle.

Desiccant A drying agent. In a refrigeration system, desiccant is placed in the receiver-dehydrator to remove moisture from the system.

Detent A small depression in a shaft, rail, or rod into which a pawl or ball drops when the shaft, rail, or rod is moved; this provides a locking effect.

Detergent A chemical added to engine oil that helps keep internal parts of the engine clean by preventing the accumulation of deposits.

Detonation Commonly referred to as spark knock or ping. In the combustion chamber of a spark-ignition engine, an uncontrolled second explosion (after the spark occurs at the spark plug) with spontaneous

combustion of the remaining compressed air-fuel mixture, resulting in a pinging sound.

Device A mechanism, tool, or other piece of equipment designed to serve a special purpose or perform a special function.

Diagnosis A procedure followed in locating the cause of a malfunction; answers the question "What is wrong?"

Diagonal-brake system A dual-brake system with separate hydraulic circuits connecting diagonal wheels together (RF to LR and LF to RR).

Diaphragm A thin dividing sheet or partition that separates an area into compartments; used in fuel pumps, modulator valves, vacuum-advance units, and other control devices.

Diaphragm-spring clutch A clutch in which a single-piece diaphragm spring, rather than several small coil springs, applies force against the friction disk.

Diesel cycle An engine operating cycle in which air is compressed and then fuel oil is injected into the compressed air at the end of the compression stroke. The heat produced by the compression ignites the fuel oil, eliminating the need for an electric ignition system.

Diesel engine An engine operating on the diesel cycle and burning diesel fuel oil instead of gasoline.

Diesel fuel A light oil sprayed into the cylinders of a diesel engine near the end of the compression stroke.

Dieseling A condition in which a spark-ignition engine continues to run after the ignition is off; caused by carbon deposits or hot spots in the combustion chamber glowing sufficiently to furnish heat for combustion.

Differential A gear assembly between axles that permits one wheel to turn at a different speed from the other, while transmitting power from the drive shaft to the wheel axles.

Differential case The metal unit that encases the differential pinions and side gears, and to which the ring gear is attached.

Differential side gears The gears inside the differential case which are internally splined to the axle shafts, and which are driven by the differential pinion gears.

Dimmer switch A two-position switch operated by the driver to select the high or low headlight beam.

Diode A solid-state electronic device that allows the passage of an electric current in one direction only. Used in the alternator to change alternating current to direct current for charging the battery.

Dipstick See Oil-level indicator.

Direct current (DC or dc) Electric current that flows in one direction only.

Directional signals A system on the car that flashes lights to indicate the direction in which the driver intends to turn.

Disassemble To take apart.

Discharge To bleed some or all refrigerant from a system by opening a valve or connection and permitting the refrigerant to escape.

Discharge side In an air conditioner, the portion of the refrigerant system under high pressure; it extends from the compressor outlet to the expansion valve or orifice tube.

Disk In a disk brake, the rotor, or revolving metal disk, against which shoes are pressed to provide braking action.

Disk brake A brake in which brake shoes, on a viselike caliper, grip a revolving disk to stop it.

Dispersant A chemical added to oil to prevent dirt and impurities from clinging together in lumps that could clog the engine lubricating system.

Displacement In an engine, the total volume of air or air-fuel mixture an engine is theoretically capable of drawing into all cylinders during one operating cycle. Also, the volume swept out by the piston in moving from one end of a stroke to the other.

Distributor Any device that distributes. In the ignition system, the rotary switch that directs high-voltage surges to the engine cylinders in the proper sequence. See Ignition distributor.

Distributor advance See Centrifugal advance, Ignition advance, and Vacuum advance.

Distributor cam The cam on the top end of the distributor shaft which rotates to open and close the contact points.

Distributor timing See Ignition timing.

Diverter valve In the air-injection system, a valve that diverts air-pump output into the air cleaner or the atmosphere during deceleration; this prevents backfiring and popping in the exhaust system.

DIY Abbreviation for "do-it-yourself."

DOHC See Double-overhead-camshaft engine.

Double-overhead-camshaft engine An engine with two camshafts in each cylinder head; one camshaft operates the intake valves, the other operates the exhaust valves.

Drive line The driving connection between the transmission and the differential; made up of one or more drive shafts.

Drive pinion A rotating shaft with a small gear on one end that transmits torque to another gear; used in the differential. Also called the clutch shaft, in the manual transmission.

Drive shaft An assembly of one or two universal joints connected to a shaft or tube; used to transmit power from the transmission to the differential. Also called the propeller shaft.

Driveability The general operation of a vehicle, usually rated from good to poor; based on characteristics of concern to the average driver, such as smoothness of idle, even acceleration, ease of starting, quick warm-up, and no tendency to overheat at idle.

Driven disk The friction disk in a clutch.

Drum brake A brake in which curved brake shoes press against the inner circumference of a metal drum to produce the braking action.

Dual-brake system A brake system consisting of two separate hydraulic systems; usually, one operates the front brakes, and the other operates the rear brakes.

Dwell In a contact-point distributor, the number of degrees of distributor-cam rotation that the points stay closed before they open again.

Dwell meter A precision electrical instrument used to measure the dwell, or number of degrees the distributor points are closed before they open again.

Dynamic balance The balance of an object when it is in motion (for example, the dynamic balance of a rotating wheel).

Dynamometer A device for measuring the power available from an engine to do work. An engine dynamometer measures the power available at the flywheel; a chassis dynamometer measures the power available at the drive wheels.

Eccentric A disk or offset section (of a shaft, for example) used to convert rotary to reciprocating motion. Sometimes called a cam.

ECU See Electronic control unit.

EGR system See Exhaust-gas recirculation system.

Electric-assist choke A choke in which a small electric heating element warms the choke spring, causing it to release more quickly. This reduces exhaust emissions during the start-up of a cold engine.

Electric current A movement of electrons through a conductor such as a copper wire; measured in amperes.

Electric fuel pump A fuel pump that uses either an electric motor or a solenoid to draw fuel from the tank and deliver it to the carburetor or fuel-injection system.

Electric system In the automobile, the system that electrically cranks the engine for starting; furnishes high-voltage sparks to the engine cylinders to fire the compressed air-fuel charges; lights the lights; and powers the heater motor, radio, and other accessories. Consists, in part, of the starting motor, wiring, battery, alternator, regulator, ignition distributor, and ignition coil.

Electrode In a spark plug, the spark jumps between two electrodes. The wire passing through the insulator is the center electrode. The small piece of metal welded to the spark-plug shell (and to which the spark jumps) is the side, or ground, electrode.

Electrolyte The mixture of sulfuric acid and water used in lead-acid storage batteries. The acid enters into chemical reaction with active material in the plates to produce voltage and current.

Electromagnetic induction The characteristic of a magnetic field that causes an electric current to be created in a conductor if it passes through the field, or if the field builds and collapses around the conductor.

Electron A negatively charged particle that circles the nucleus of an atom. The movement of electrons is an electric current.

Electronic control unit (ECU) The system computer that receives information from sensors and is programmed to operate various circuits and systems based on that information.

Electronic fuel-injection system A system that injects fuel into the engine and includes an electronic control unit to time and meter the fuel flow.

Electronic ignition system An ignition system that uses transistors and other semiconductor devices as an electric switch to turn the primary current on and off.

Electronics Electrical assemblies, circuits, and systems that use electronic devices such as transistors and diodes.

Element A substance that cannot be further divided into a simpler substance. In a battery, the group of unlike positive and negative plates, separated by insulators, that make up each cell.

Emission control Any device or modification added onto or designed into a motor vehicle for the purpose of reducing air-polluting emissions.

Emission standards Allowable automobile emission levels, set by local, state, and federal legislation.

End play As applied to a crankshaft, the distance that the crankshaft can move forward and back in the cylinder block.

Energy The capacity or ability to do work. The most common forms are heat, mechanical, electrical, and chemical. Usually measured in work units of pound-feet [kilogram-meters], but also expressed in heat-energy units (Btus [joules]).

Engine A machine that converts heat energy into mechanical energy. A device that burns fuel to produce mechanical power; sometimes referred to as a power plant.

Engine efficiency The ratio of the power actually delivered to the power that could be delivered if the engine operated without any power loss.

Engine fan See Fan.

Engine mounts Flexible rubber insulators through which the engine is bolted to the car body or frame.

Engine power The power available from the crankshaft to do work.

Usually measured in units of horsepower and kilowatts.

Engine tuneup A procedure for inspecting, testing, and adjusting an engine, and replacing any worn parts, to restore the engine to its best performance.

Ethylene glycol Chemical name of a widely used type of permanent antifreeze.

Evacuate To use a vacuum pump to pump any air and moisture out of an air-conditioner refrigerant system; required whenever any component in the refrigerant system has been replaced.

Evaporation The transformation of a liquid to the gaseous state.

Evaporative control system A system that prevents the escape of fuel vapors from the fuel tank or air cleaner while the engine is off. The vapors are stored in a charcoal canister or in the engine crankcase until the engine is started.

Evaporator The heat exchanger in an air conditioner in which refrigerant changes from a liquid to a gas (evaporates), taking heat from the surrounding air as it does so.

Exhaust emissions Pollutants emitted into the atmosphere through any opening downstream of the exhaust ports of an engine.

Exhaust gas The burned and unburned gases that remain (from the air-fuel mixture) after combustion.

Exhaust-gas analyzer A device for sensing the amounts of air pollutants in the exhaust gas of a motor vehicle. The analyzers used in automotive shops check HC and CO; those used in testing laboratories can also check NO_x.

Exhaust-gas recirculation (EGR) system An NO_x control system that recycles a small part of the inert exhaust gas back through the intake manifold to lower the combustion temperature.

Exhaust manifold A device with several passages through which exhaust gases leave the engine combustion chambers and enter the exhaust piping system.

Exhaust pipe The pipe connecting the exhaust manifold to the next component in the exhaust system (usually the catalytic converter).

Exhaust stroke The piston stroke (from BDC to TDC) immediately following the power stroke, during which the exhaust valve opens so

that the exhaust gases can escape from the cylinder to the exhaust manifold.

Exhaust system The system that collects the exhaust gases and discharges them into the air. Consists of the exhaust manifold, exhaust pipe, muffler, tail pipe, and resonator (if used).

Exhaust valve The valve that opens during the exhaust stroke to allow burned gases to flow from the cylinder to the exhaust manifold.

Expansion plug A slightly dished plug that is used to seal core passages in the cylinder block and cylinder head. When driven into place, it is flattened and expanded to fit tightly.

Expansion tank A tank connected by a hose to the filler neck of an automobile radiator; the tank provides room for heated coolant to expand and to give off any air that may be trapped in the coolant. Also, a similar device used in some fuel tanks to prevent fuel from spilling out of the tank through expansion.

Expansion valve A flow-control valve located between the condenser and evaporator in an air conditioner; controls the amount of refrigerant sprayed into the evaporator.

Fan The bladed device in back of the radiator that rotates to draw cooling air through the radiator or around the engine cylinders; an air blower, such as the heater fan and the A/C blower.

Fastener Any device that holds or joins other parts together.

Fast-idle cam A mechanism on the carburetor, connected to the automatic choke, that holds the throttle valve slightly open when the engine is cold; causes the engine to idle at a higher rpm as long as the choke is applied.

Feedback carburetor A carburetor used with an oxygen sensor and a control system to automatically adjust the air-fuel ratio for minimum exhaust emissions.

Field coil A coil, or winding, in a generator or starting motor which produces a magnetic field as current passes through it.

Field relay A relay that is part of some alternator charging systems; connects the alternator field to the battery when the engine runs and

disconnects it when the engine stops.

Filter A device through which air, gases, or liquids are passed to remove impurities.

Filter separator A combination fuel filter and vapor separator located between the fuel pump and carburetor on some cars.

Fins On a radiator or heat exchanger, thin metal projections over which cooling air flows to remove heat from hot liquid flowing through internal passages. On an air-cooled engine, thin metal projections on the cylinder and head which greatly increase the area of the heat-dissipating surfaces and help cool the engine.

Firing line The high-voltage vertical spike, or line, that appears on the oscilloscope pattern of the ignition-system secondary circuit. The firing line shows when the spark plug begins to fire and the voltage required to fire it.

Firing order The order in which the engine cylinders fire, or deliver their power strokes, beginning with number 1 cylinder.

Fixed-caliper disk brake Disk brake using a caliper which is fixed in position and cannot move; the caliper usually has four pistons, two on each side of the disk.

Flasher An automatic-reset circuit breaker used in the directional-signal and hazard-warning circuits.

Flat rate Method of paying mechanics and technicians, by use of a manual which indicates the time normally required to do each service job.

Flex plate On a vehicle with automatic transmission, a light plate bolted to the crankshaft to which the transmission torque converter is attached.

Float bowl In a carburetor, the reservoir from which fuel is metered into the passing air.

Floating-caliper disk brake Disk brake using a caliper mounted through rubber bushings which permit the caliper to float, or move, when the brakes are applied; there is one large piston in the caliper.

Float level The float position at which the needle valve closes the fuel inlet to the carburetor, to prevent further delivery of fuel.

Float system In the carburetor, the system that controls the entry of fuel and the fuel level in the float bowl.

Flooded Term used to indicate that the engine cylinders received "raw" or liquid gasoline, or an air-fuel mixture too rich to burn.

Fluid Any liquid or gas.

Fluid coupling A device in the power train consisting of two rotating members; transmits power from the engine, through a fluid, to the transmission.

Flush In an air conditioner, to wash out the refrigerant passages with Refrigerant-12 to remove contaminants. In a brake system, to wash out the hydraulic system and the master and wheel cylinders, or calipers, with clean brake fluid to remove dirt or impurities that have gotten into the system.

Flywheel On a vehicle with manual transmission, a heavy metal wheel attached to the crankshaft which rotates with it; helps smooth out the power surges from the engine power strokes; also serves as part of the clutch and engine cranking system.

Flywheel ring gear A gear, fitted around the flywheel, that is engaged by teeth on the starting-motor drive to crank the engine.

Force Any push or pull exerted on an object; measured in pounds and ounces, or in newtons (N) in the metric system.

Formed-in-place gasket A gasket formed by a bead of plastic gasket material applied by a machine or squeezed from a tube.

Four-barrel carburetor A carburetor with four throttle valves. In effect, two 2-barrel carburetors in a single assembly.

Four-cycle See Four-stroke cycle.

Four-speed A manual transmission having four forward speed ratios.

Four-stroke cycle The four piston strokes—intake, compression, power, and exhaust—that make up the complete cycle of events in the four-stroke-cycle engine. Also called four-cycle and four-stroke.

Four-wheel drive A vehicle with drive axles at both front and rear, so that all four wheels can be driven.

Frame The assembly of metal structural parts and channel sections that supports the car engine and body and is supported by the wheels.

Franchise A locally owned business that carries a nationally known name. The local business has been granted authority or license to market a product, service, or method, often exclusively within a certain area.

Free-wheeling hubs See Locking hubs.

Freon-12 Refrigerant used in automobile air conditioners. Also known as Refrigerant-12 and R-12.

Friction The resistance to motion between two bodies in contact with each other.

Friction bearing Bearing in which there is sliding contact between the moving surfaces. Sleeve bearings, such as those used in connecting rods, are friction bearings.

Friction disk In the clutch, a flat disk, faced on both sides with friction material and splined to the clutch shaft. It is positioned between the clutch pressure plate and the engine flywheel. Also called the clutch disk or driven disk.

Friction horsepower The power that an engine uses to overcome its own internal friction.

Front-end geometry The angular relationship between the front wheels, wheel-attaching parts, and car frame. Includes camber, caster, steering-axis inclination, toe, and turning radius.

Front-wheel drive A vehicle having its drive wheels located on the front axle.

Fuel Any combustible substance. In a spark-ignition engine, the fuel (gasoline) is burned and the heat of combustion expands the resulting gases, which force the piston downward and rotate the crankshaft.

Fuel filter A device located in the fuel line that removes dirt and other contaminants from fuel passing through.

Fuel gauge A gauge that indicates the amount of fuel in the fuel tank.

Fuel-induction system In the spark-ignition engine, the system that supplies the air-fuel mixture to the cylinders; includes either a carburetor or a fuel-injection system.

Fuel-injection system A system that delivers fuel under pressure into the combustion chamber or into the intake airflow.

Fuel injector A nozzle or valve that sprays fuel into the passing intake air (spark ignition engine) or into the compressed air in the engine cylinders (diesel engine).

Fuel line The pipe or tubes through which fuel flows from the fuel tank to the carburetor or fuel-injection system.

Fuel pump The electrical or mechanical device in the fuel system which forces fuel from the fuel tank to the carburetor or fuel-injection system.

Fuel system In an automobile, the system that delivers the fuel and air to the engine cylinders. Consists of the fuel tank and lines, gauge, fuel pump, carburetor or fuel-injection system, and intake manifold.

Fuel tank The storage tank for fuel on the vehicle.

Full throttle Wide-open throttle position, with the accelerator pressed all the way down to the floorboard.

Fuse A device designed to open an electric circuit when the current is excessive, to protect equipment in the circuit.

Fuse block A boxlike unit that holds the fuses for the various electric circuits in an automobile.

Fusible link A type of circuit protector in which a special wire melts to open the circuit when the current is excessive.

Gap The air space between two electrodes, as the spark-plug gap or the contact-point gap.

Gas The state of matter in which the matter has neither a definite shape nor a definite volume; air is a mixture of several gases. In an automobile, the discharge from the tail pipe is called the exhaust gas. Also, gas is a slang expression for the liquid fuel gasoline.

Gas engine An engine that uses a gas (*not* a liquid) for fuel.

Gasket A thin layer of soft material, such as paper, cork, rubber, or copper, placed between two flat surfaces to make a tight seal.

Gasket-cement A liquid adhesive material, or sealer, used to install gaskets; in some applications, a layer of gasket cement is used as the gasket.

Gasohol An engine fuel made by mixing 10 percent ethyl alcohol with 90 percent unleaded gasoline.

Gasoline A liquid blend of hydrocarbons, obtained from crude oil; used as the fuel in most automobile engines.

Gassing Hydrogen gas escaping from a battery during charging.

Gas-turbine engine An engine in which the output shaft is spun by the force of combustion gases flowing against curved turbine blades located around the shaft.

Gauge set One or more instruments attached to a manifold (a pipe fitted with several outlets for connecting pipes) and used for measuring pressure.

Gear lubricant A type of grease or oil designed especially to lubricate gears.

Gear ratio The number of revolutions of a driving gear required to turn a driven gear through one complete revolution. For a pair of gears, the ratio is found by dividing the number of teeth on the driven gear by the number of teeth on the driving gear.

Gears Mechanical devices that transmit power or turning force from one shaft to another; gears contain teeth that mesh as the gears turn.

Gearshift A linkage-type mechanism by which the gears in an automobile transmission are engaged and disengaged.

Generator A device that converts mechanical energy into electrical energy; can produce either ac or dc electricity. In automotive usage, a dc generator (now seldom used).

Glaze The very smooth, mirrorlike finish that develops on engine cylinder walls.

Glow plug A small electric heater installed in the precombustion chamber of diesel engines to preheat the chamber for easier starting in cold weather.

Governor A device that controls, or governs, another device, usually on the basis of speed or load.

Governor pressure Pressure at one end of a shift valve, which is controlled by governor action. One of two signals that determine when an automatic transmission will shift.

Grease Lubricating oil to which thickening agents have been added.

Grommet A device, usually made of hard rubber or similar material, used to encircle or support a component. In emission systems, a grommet is located in the valve-cover assembly to support and help seal the PCV valve.

Ground The return path for current in an electric circuit.

Ground-return system System of vehicle wiring in which the chassis and frame are used as part of the electric return circuit to the battery or alternator; also known as the single-wire system.

Gulp valve In the air-injection system, a type of antibackfire valve which allows a sudden intake of fresh air through the intake manifold during deceleration; prevents backfiring and popping in the exhaust system.

Halogen headlamp A sealed-beam headlamp with a small inner bulb filled with halogen which surrounds the tungsten filament.

Harmonic balancer See Vibration damper.

HC See Hydrocarbon.

Head See Cylinder head.

Headlights Lights at the front of a vehicle, designed to illuminate the road ahead of the vehicle.

Heat of compression Increase of temperature brought about by the compression of air or air-fuel mixture; the source of ignition in a diesel engine.

Heat-control valve In the engine, a thermostatically operated valve in the exhaust manifold; diverts heat to the intake manifold to warm it before the engine reaches normal operating temperature.

Heated-air system See Thermostatic air cleaner.

Heater A small radiator, or heater core, mounted under the dash, through which hot coolant circulates; when heat is needed, a fan is turned on to circulate air through the hot core.

HEI See High-Energy Ignition (HEI) system.

Helical gear A gear in which the teeth are cut at an angle to the center line of the gear.

Heli-Coil See Thread insert.

Hemispherical combustion chamber A combustion chamber resembling a hemisphere, or half a round ball.

High compression Term used to refer to the increased compression ratios of modern automotive engines, as compared with engines built in the past.

High-Energy Ignition (HEI) system A General Motors electronic ignition system without contact points and with all ignition-system components contained in the distributor. Capable of producing 35,000 volts.

High-pressure lines Lines from the air-conditioner compressor outlet to the thermostatic-expansion-valve inlet that carry high-pressure refrigerant. The two longest high-pressure lines are the discharge and liquid lines.

High-speed system In the carburetor, the system that supplies fuel to the engine at speeds above about 25 mph [40km/h]. Also called the main-metering system.

High-voltage cables The secondary (or spark-plug) cables or wires that carry high voltage from the ignition coil to the spark plugs.

Hone A tool with abrasive stones that is rotated in a bore or bushing to remove material.

Horn An electrical noisemaking device on a vehicle, used for signaling.

Horn relay A relay connected between the battery and the horns. When the horn button is pressed, the relay is energized; it then connects the horns to the battery.

Horsepower A measure of mechanical power, or the rate at which work is done. One horsepower equals 33,000 ft-lb (foot-pounds) of work per minute, the power necessary to raise 33,000 pounds a distance of one foot in one minute.

Hot patching A method of repairing a tire or tube by using heat to vulcanize a patch onto the damaged surface.

Hub The center part of a wheel.

Hydraulic brakes A braking system that uses hydraulic pressure to force the brake shoes against the brake drums, or rotors, as the brake pedal is depressed.

Hydraulic pressure Pressure exerted through the medium of a liquid.

Hydraulics The use of a liquid under pressure to transfer force or motion, or to increase an applied force.

Hydraulic valve lifter A valve lifter that uses oil pressure from the engine lubricating system to keep the lifter in constant contact with the cam lobe and with the valve stem, push rod, or rocker arm.

Hydrocarbon (HC) A compound containing only carbon and hydrogen atoms, usually derived from fossil fuels such as petroleum, natural gas, and coal; an agent in the formation of photochemical smog. Gasoline is a blend of liquid hydrocarbons refined from crude oil.

Hydrogen (H) A colorless, odorless, highly flammable gas whose combustion produces water; the simplest and lightest element.

Hydrometer A device used to measure specific gravity. In automotive servicing, a device used to measure the specific gravity of battery electrolyte to determine the battery's state of charge; also a device used to measure the specific gravity of coolant to determine its freezing temperature.

Hypoid gear A type of gear used in the differential (drive pinion and ring gear) of most cars with a front engine and rear-wheel drive; cut in a spiral form to allow the pinion to be set below the center line of the ring gear, so that the car floor can be designed lower.

IC See Internal-combustion (IC) engine.

Idle Engine speed when the accelerator pedal is fully released and there is no load on the engine.

Idle limiter A device that controls the maximum richness of the idle air-fuel mixture in the carburetor; also aids in preventing overly rich idle adjustments. Limiters are of two types: the external plastic-cap type, installed on the head of the idle-mixture adjustment screw, and the internal needle type, located in the idle passages of the carburetor.

Idle mixture The air-fuel mixture supplied to the engine during idling.

Idle-mixture screw The adjustment screw (on some carburetors) that can be turned in or out to lean or enrich the idle mixture.

Idler arm In the steering system, a link that supports the tie rod and transmits steering motion to both wheels through the tie-rod ends.

Idle solenoid An electrically operated plunger used to provide a predetermined throttle setting at idle.

Idle speed The speed, or rpm, at which the engine runs without load when the accelerator pedal is released.

Idle system In the carburetor, the passages through which fuel is fed when the engine is idling.

Ignition The action of the spark in starting the burning of the compressed air-fuel mixture in the combustion chamber of a spark-ignition engine. In a diesel engine, the start of the burning of fuel after its temperature has been raised by the heat of compression.

Ignition advance The moving forward, in time, of the ignition spark relative to the piston position. TDC or 1 degree ATDC is considered advanced as compared with 2 degrees ATDC.

Ignition coil The ignition-system component that acts as a transformer to step up (increase) the battery voltage to many thousands of volts. The high-voltage surge from the coil is transmitted to the spark plug to ignite the compressed air-fuel mixture.

Ignition distributor The unit in the ignition system which usually contains the mechanical or electronic switch that closes and opens the primary circuit to the coil at the proper time and then distributes the resulting high-voltage surges to the spark plugs.

Ignition lag In a diesel engine, the delay in time between the injection of fuel and the start of combustion.

Ignition resistor A resistance connected into the ignition primary circuit to reduce the battery voltage to the coil during engine operation.

Ignition retard The moving back, in time, of the ignition spark relative to the piston position. TDC or 1 degree BTDC is considered retarded as compared with 2 degrees BTDC.

Ignition switch The switch in the ignition system (usually operated with a key) that opens and closes the ignition-coil primary circuit. May also be used to open and close other vehicle electric circuits.

Ignition system In the automobile, the system that furnishes high-voltage sparks to the engine cylinders to fire the compressed air-fuel mixture. Consists of the battery, ignition coil, ignition distributor, ignition switch, wiring, and spark plugs.

Ignition timing The delivery of the spark from the coil to the spark plug at the proper time for the power stroke, relative to the piston position.

I-head engine An overhead-valve (OHV) engine; an engine with the valves in the cylinder head.

Impeller A rotating finned disk; used in centrifugal pumps, such as water pumps, and in torque converters.

Included angle In the front-suspension system, camber angle plus steering-axis-inclination angle.

Independent front suspension A front-suspension system in which each front wheel is independently supported by a spring.

Indicator A device using a light or a dial and pointer to make some condition known; for example, the temperature indicator or oil-pressure indicator.

Induction The action of producing a voltage in a conductor or coil by moving the conductor or coil through a magnetic field, or by moving the field past the conductor or coil.

Inertia The property of an object that causes it to resist any change in its speed or direction of travel.

Infrared analyzer A test instrument used to measure very small quantities of pollutants in exhaust gas. See Exhaust-gas analyzer.

In-line engine An engine in which all the cylinders are located in a single row or line.

In-line steering gear A type of integral power steering; uses a recirculating-ball steering gear to which is added a control valve and an actuating piston.

Inner tube See Tire tube.

Inspect To examine a component or system for surface condition or function.

Install To set up for use on a vehicle any part, accessory, option, or kit.

Instrument voltage regulator A thermostatic device that keeps the voltage to the instrument-panel gauges at about 5 volts.

Insulation Material that stops the travel of electricity (electrical insulation) or heat (heat insulation).

Insulator A poor conductor of electricity or heat.

Intake manifold A casting with several passages through which air or air-fuel mixture flows from the air intake or carburetor to the ports in the cylinder head or cylinder block.

Intake stroke The piston stroke from TDC to BDC immediately following the exhaust stroke, during which the intake valve opens and the cyl-

inder fills with air or air-fuel mixture from the intake manifold.

Integral Built into, as part of the whole.

Integrated circuit Many very small solid-state devices capable of performing as a complete electronic circuit, with one or more integrated circuits manufactured as a "chip."

Interaxle differential A two-position differential located between two driving axles; used in the transfer case of some four-wheel-drive vehicles.

Internal-combustion (IC) engine An engine in which the fuel is burned inside the engine itself, rather than in a separate device (as in a steam engine).

Internal gear A gear with teeth pointing inward, toward the hollow center of the gear.

Jet A calibrated passage in the carburetor through which fuel flows.

Journal The part of a rotating shaft which turns in a bearing.

Jump-starting Starting a car that has a dead battery by connecting a charged battery to the starting system.

Kickdown In automatic transmissions, a system that produces a downshift when the accelerator is pushed down to the floorboard.

Kilogram (kg) In the metric system, a unit of weight and mass, approximately equal to 2.2 pounds.

Kilometer (km) In the metric system, a unit of linear measure, equal to 0.621 mile.

Kilowatt (kW) A unit of power, equal to about 1.34 hp.

Kinetic energy The energy of motion; the energy stored in a moving body through its momentum; for example, the kinetic energy stored in a rotating flywheel.

Kingpin In older cars and trucks, the steel pin on which the steering knuckle pivots; attaches the steering knuckle to the knuckle support or axle.

Kingpin inclination Inward tilt of the kingpin from the vertical. See Steering-axis inclination.

Knock A heavy metallic engine sound that varies with engine speed; usually caused by a loose or worn bearing; name also used for

detonation, pinging, and spark knock. See Detonation.

Knuckle A steering knuckle; a front-suspension part that acts as a hinge to support a front wheel and permit it to be turned to steer the car. The knuckle pivots on ball joints or, in older cars, on kingpins.

Laminated Made up of several thin sheets or layers.

Lash The amount of free motion in a gear train, between gears, or in a mechanical assembly, such as the lash in a valve train.

Lead (pronounced "leed") A cable or conductor that carries electric current.

Lead (pronounced "led") A heavy metal; used in lead-acid storage batteries.

Leaded gasoline Gasoline to which small amounts of tetraethyl lead are added to improve engine performance and reduce detonation.

Leaf spring A spring made up of a single flat steel plate, or several plates of graduated lengths assembled one on top of another, used on vehicles to absorb road shocks by bending, or flexing, in the middle.

Leak detector Any device used to locate an opening where refrigerant may escape. Common types are flame, electronic, dye, and soap bubbles.

Lean mixture An air-fuel mixture that has a relatively high proportion of air and a relatively low proportion of fuel. An air-fuel ratio of 16:1 is a lean mixture, compared with an air-fuel ratio of 13:1.

Light A gas-filled bulb enclosing a wire that glows brightly when an electric current passes through it; a lamp. Also, any visible radiant energy.

Limited-slip differential A differential designed so that when one wheel is slipping, the most torque is supplied to the wheel with the best traction; also called a nonslip differential.

Line boring Using a special boring machine, centered on the original center of the cylinder-block main-bearing bores, to rebore the crankcase into alignment.

Lines of force See Magnetic lines of force.

Lining See Brake lining.

Linkage A hydraulic system, or an

assembly of rods or links, used to transmit motion.

Linkage-type power steering A type of power steering in which the power-steering units (power cylinder and valve) are part of the steering linkage; frequently a bolt-on type of system.

Liquefied petroleum gas (LPG) An engine fuel obtained from petroleum and natural gas; stored as a liquid under pressure, it vaporizes at atmospheric pressure. Butane and propane are liquefied gases used as engine fuels.

Liquid-cooled engine An engine that is cooled by the circulation of liquid coolant around the cylinders.

Liquid line In an air conditioner, hose that connects the receiver-dehydrator outlet and the thermostatic-expansion-valve inlet. High-pressure liquid refrigerant flows through the line.

Liter (L) In the metric system, a measure of volume; approximately equal to 0.26 gallon (U.S.), or about 61 cubic inches. Used as a metric measure of engine-cylinder displacement.

Lobe A projecting part; for example, the rotor lobe or the cam lobe.

Locking hubs Hubs that can be disengaged so that the front axle can freewheel while the vehicle is in two-wheel drive.

Lower beam A headlight beam used to illuminate the road ahead of the vehicle when the car is meeting or following another vehicle.

Low-speed system The system in the carburetor that supplies fuel to the air passing through during low-speed, part-throttle operation.

LPG See Liquefied petroleum gas.

Lubricating system The system in the engine that supplies engine parts with lubricating oil to prevent contact between any two moving metal surfaces.

Machining The process of using a machine to remove metal from a metal part.

Magnetic Having the ability to attract iron. This ability may be permanent, or it may depend on a current flow, as in an electromagnet.

Magnetic clutch A magnetically operated clutch used to engage and disengage the air-conditioner compressor.

Magnetic field The space around a magnet which is filled by invisible lines of force.

Magnetic lines of force The imaginary lines by which a magnetic field may be visualized.

Magnetic switch A switch with a winding which, when energized by connection to a battery or alternator, causes the switch to open or close a circuit.

Magnetism The ability, either natural or produced by a flow of electric current, to attract iron.

Mag wheel A magnesium wheel assembly; also used to refer to many types of styled-chrome, aluminum-offset, or wide-rim wheel.

Main bearings In the engine, the bearings that support the crankshaft.

Main jet The fuel nozzle, or jet, in the carburetor that supplies the fuel when the throttle is partially to fully open.

Maintenance-free battery A battery without vent plugs so that water cannot be added.

Make A distinctive name applied to a group of vehicles produced by one manufacturer; may be further subdivided into car lines, body types, etc.

Malfunction Improper or incorrect operation.

Manifold A device with several inlet or outlet passageways through which a gas or liquid is gathered or distributed. See Exhaust manifold, Intake manifold, and Manifold gauge set.

Manifold gauge set A high-pressure and a low-pressure gauge mounted together as a set; used for checking pressures in the air-conditioning system.

Manifold heat-control valve See Heat-control valve.

Manifold pressure The pressure in the intake manifold while the turbocharger is operating.

Manifold vacuum The vacuum in the intake manifold that develops as a result of the vacuum in the cylinders on their intake strokes.

Manual low Position of the units in an automatic transmission when the driver moves the selector lever to the low- or first-gear position.

Manual transmission A transmis-

sion that the driver must shift by hand, or manually.

Manual valve A spool valve in the valve body of an automatic transmission that is manually positioned by the driver through linkage.

Manufacturer Any person, firm, or corporation engaged in the production or assembly of motor vehicles or other products.

Master cylinder The liquid-filled cylinder in the hydraulic braking system or clutch where hydraulic pressure is developed when the driver depresses a foot pedal.

Matter Anything that has weight and occupies space.

Measuring The act of determining the size, capacity, or quantity of an object.

Mechanism A system of interrelated parts that make up a working assembly.

Member Any essential part of a machine or assembly.

Meshing The mating, or engaging, of the teeth of two gears.

Meter (m) A unit of linear measure in the metric system, equal to 39.37 inches. Also, the name given to any test instrument that measures a property of a substance passing through it, as an ammeter measures electric current. Also, any device that measures and controls the flow of a substance passing through it, as a carburetor jet meters fuel flow.

Metering rod and jet A device consisting of a small, movable cone- or step-shaped rod and a jet; used to increase or decrease fuel flow according to engine throttle opening, engine load, or a combination of both.

Metering valve A valve in the disk-brake system that prevents hydraulic pressure to the front brakes until after the rear brakes are applied.

Microprocessor The small, on-board solid-state electronic device that acts as the central processing unit. Sensors provide input information which the microprocessor uses to determine the desired response (if any) as an output signal.

Misfire In the engine, a failure to ignite the air-fuel mixture in one or more cylinders. This condition may be intermittent or continuous in one or more cylinders.

Miss See Misfire.

Model year The production period for new motor vehicles or new engines, designated by the calendar year in which the period ends.

Modification An alteration; a change from the original.

Modulated-displacement engine See Multiple-displacement engine.

Modulator A pressure-regulated governing device; used, for example, in automatic transmissions.

Moisture Humidity, dampness, wetness, or very small drops of water.

Molecule The smallest particle into which a substance can be divided and still retain the properties of that substance.

Monolithic timing Making accurate spark-timing adjustments with an electronic timing device while the engine is running.

Motor A device that converts electric energy into mechanical energy; for example, the starting motor.

Motor vehicle A vehicle propelled by a means other than muscle power, usually mounted on rubber tires, which does not run on rails or tracks.

Mph Abbreviation for miles per hour, a measure of speed.

Muffler In the engine-exhaust system, a device through which the exhaust gases must pass and which reduces the exhaust noise. In an air-conditioning system, a device to minimize pumping sounds from the compressor.

Multiple-disk clutch A clutch with more than one friction disk; usually there are several driving disks and several driven disks, alternately placed.

Multiple-displacement engine An engine that can run either on all its cylinders or, for fuel economy, on various numbers of cylinders. For example, an eight-cylinder engine that can cut off the flow of air-fuel mixture to four cylinders during idle, and then operate on six or eight cylinders as load and power demands increase.

Multiple-viscosity oil An engine oil that has a low viscosity when cold (for easier cranking) and a higher viscosity when hot (to provide adequate engine lubrication).

Mutual induction The condition in which a voltage is induced in one coil by a changing magnetic field caused by a changing current in another coil. The magnitude of the induced voltage depends on the number of turns in the two coils.

Needle bearing An antifriction bearing of the roller type, in which the rollers are very small (needle size) in diameter.

Needle valve A small, tapered, needle-pointed valve that can move into or out of a seat to close or open the passage through it. Used to control the fuel level in the carburetor float bowl.

Negative One of the two poles of a magnet, or one of the two terminals of an electrical device.

Negative terminal The terminal from which electrons flow in a complete electric circuit. On a battery, the negative terminal can be identified as the battery post with the smaller diameter; the minus sign $(-)$ is often also used to identify the negative terminal.

Neutral In a transmission, the setting in which all gears are disengaged and the output shaft is disconnected from the drive wheels.

Neutral-start switch A switch wired into the ignition switch to prevent engine cranking unless the transmission selector lever is in NEUTRAL.

Nitrogen (N) A colorless, tasteless, odorless gas that constitutes 78 percent of the atmosphere by volume and is a part of all living tissues.

Nitrogen oxides (NO$_x$) Any chemical compound of nitrogen and oxygen; a basic air pollutant. Automotive exhaust-emission levels of nitrogen oxides are limited by law.

Nonconductor Same as insulator.

Normally aspirated engine An engine that does not use any type of supercharger or turbocharger.

North pole The pole from which the lines of force leave a magnet.

NO$_x$ See Nitrogen oxides.

NO$_x$ control system Any device or system used to reduce the amount of NO$_x$ produced by an engine.

Nozzle The opening, or jet, through which fuel or air passes as it is discharged.

Octane rating A measure of the antiknock properties of a gasoline. The higher the octane rating, the more resistant the gasoline is to spark knock or detonation.

Odometer The meter that indicates the total distance a vehicle has traveled, in miles or kilometers; usually located in the speedometer.

OHC See Overhead-camshaft (OHC) engine.

Ohm The unit of electrical resistance.

Ohmmeter An instrument used to measure electrical resistance.

OHV See Overhead-valve (OHV) engine.

Oil A liquid lubricant usually made from crude oil and used for lubrication between moving parts. In a diesel engine, oil is used for fuel.

Oil clearance The space between the bearing and the shaft rotating within it.

Oil cooler A small radiator that lowers the temperature of oil flowing through it.

Oil dilution Thinning of oil in the crankcase; caused by liquid fuel leaking past the piston rings from the combustion chamber.

Oil filter A filter that removes impurities from the engine oil passing through it.

Oil-level indicator The dipstick that is removed and inspected to check the level of oil in the crankcase of an engine or compressor.

Oil pan The detachable lower part of the engine which encloses the crankcase and acts as an oil reservoir.

Oil-pressure indicator A gauge that indicates (to the driver) the oil pressure in the engine lubricating system, or a light that comes on if the oil pressure drops too low.

Oil pump In the lubricating system, the device that forces oil from the oil pan to the moving engine parts.

Oil pumping Leakage of oil past the piston rings and into the combustion chamber, usually as a result of defective rings or worn cylinder walls.

Oil ring The lower ring or rings of a piston; designed to prevent excessive amounts of oil from working up the cylinder walls and into the combustion chamber. Also called an oil-control ring.

Oil seal A seal placed around a rotating shaft or other moving part to prevent leakage of oil.

Oil viscosity A rating of an oil's ability to flow. The higher the number, the higher the viscosity (the thicker the oil).

One-way clutch See Sprag clutch.

One-wire system On automobiles, use of the car body, engine, and frame as a path for the ground side of the electric circuits; eliminates the need for a second wire as a return path to the battery or alternator.

Open circuit In an electric circuit, a break or opening which prevents the passage of current.

Open system A crankcase emission control system that draws air through the oil-filler cap and does not include a tube from the crankcase to the air cleaner.

Orifice A small opening, or hole, into a cavity.

Orifice tube A restriction in the refrigerant line of an air conditioner that acts as a flow-control valve.

O ring A type of sealing ring made of a special rubberlike material; in use, the O ring is compressed into a groove to provide the sealing action.

Oscillating Moving back and forth, as a swinging pendulum.

Oscilloscope A high-speed voltmeter that visually displays voltage variations on a television-type picture tube. Used to check engine ignition systems; also used to check charging systems and electronic fuel-injection systems.

Output shaft The main shaft of the transmission; the shaft that delivers torque from the transmission to the drive shaft.

Overcharging Continued charging of a battery after it has reached the charged condition. This action damages the battery and shortens its life.

Overdrive Transmission gearing that causes the output shaft to overdrive, or turn faster than the input shaft.

Overhaul To completely disassemble a unit, clean and inspect all parts, reassemble it with the original or new parts, and make all adjustments necessary for proper operation.

Overhead-camshaft (OHC) engine An engine in which the camshaft is mounted over the cylinder head, instead of inside the cylinder block.

Overhead-valve (OHV) engine An engine in which the valves are mounted in the cylinder head above

the combustion chamber, instead of in the cylinder block. In this type of engine, the camshaft is mounted in the cylinder block, and the valves are actuated by pushrods.

Overrunning clutch A drive unit that transmits rotary motion in one direction only. In the other direction, the driving member overruns and does not pass the motion to the other member. Widely used as the drive mechanism for starting motors.

Oxides of nitrogen See Nitrogen oxides.

Oxygen (O) A colorless, tasteless, odorless, gaseous element that makes up about 21 percent of air. Capable of combining rapidly with all elements except the inert gases in the oxidation process called burning. Combines very slowly with many metals in the oxidation process called rusting.

Oxygen sensor A device in the exhaust pipe which measures the amount of oxygen in the exhaust gas and sends this information as a varying voltage signal to the electronic control unit.

Pan See Oil pan.

Parade pattern An oscilloscope pattern showing the ignition voltages on one line, from left to right across the scope screen in engine firing order.

Parallel The quality of objects being the same distance from each other at all points; usually applied to lines and, in automotive work, to machined surfaces.

Parallel circuit The electric circuit formed when two or more electrical devices have their terminals connected, positive to positive and negative to negative, so that each may operate independently of the others from the same power source.

Parking brake Mechanically operated brake that is independent of the foot-operated service brakes on the vehicle; set when the vehicle is parked.

Particle A very small piece of metal, dirt, or other impurity which may be contained in the air, fuel, or lubricating oil used in an engine.

Passage A small hole or gallery in an assembly or casting, through which air, coolant, fuel, or oil flows.

Passenger car Any four-wheeled motor vehicle manufactured primarily for use on streets and high-

ways and carrying 10 passengers or fewer.

Pawl An arm pivoted so that its free end can fit into a detent, slot, or groove at certain times to hold a part stationary.

PCV See Positive crankcase ventilation.

PCV valve The valve that controls the flow of crankcase vapors in accordance with ventilation requirements for different engine speeds and loads.

Petroleum The crude oil from which gasoline, lubricating oil, and other such products are refined.

Photochemical smog Smog caused by hydrocarbons and nitrogen oxides reacting photochemically in the atmosphere. The reactions take place under low wind velocity, bright sunlight, and an inversion layer in which the air mass is trapped (as between the ocean and mountains in Los Angeles). Can cause eye and lung irritation.

Pickup coil In an electronic ignition system, the coil in which voltage is induced by the reluctor.

Pilot bearing A small bearing, in the center of the flywheel end of the crankshaft, which carries the forward end of the clutch shaft.

Pilot shaft A shaft that is used to align parts, and which is removed before final installation of the parts; a dummy shaft.

Ping Engine spark knock or detonation that occurs usually during acceleration. Caused by excessive advance of ignition timing or low-octane fuel.

Pinion gear The smaller of two meshing gears.

Pin press A small press used to force the piston pin in and out of the piston.

Piston A movable part, fitted to a cylinder, which can receive or transmit motion as a result of pressure changes in a fluid. In the engine, the round plug that slides up and down in the cylinder and which, through the connecting rod, forces the crankshaft to rotate.

Piston clearance The space between the piston and the cylinder wall.

Piston displacement The cylinder volume displaced by the piston as it moves from the bottom to the top of the cylinder during one complete stroke.

Piston pin The cylindrical or tubular metal piece that attaches the piston to the connecting rod. Also called the wrist pin.

Piston rings Rings fitted into grooves in the piston. There are two types: compression rings for sealing the compression pressure in the combustion chamber, and oil rings to scrape excessive oil off the cylinder wall. See Compression ring and Oil ring.

Piston skirt The lower part of the piston, below the piston-pin hole.

Pitman arm In the steering system, the arm that is connected between the steering-gear sector shaft and the steering linkage, or tie rod. It swings back and forth for steering as the steering wheel is turned.

Pivot A pin or shaft upon which another part rests or turns.

Planetary-gear system A gear set consisting of a central sun gear surrounded by two or more planet pinions which are, in turn, meshed with a ring (or internal) gear; used in automatic transmissions and transfer cases.

Planet carrier In a planetary-gear system, the carrier or bracket that contains the shaft upon which the planet pinion turns.

Planet pinions In a planetary-gear system, the gears that mesh with, and revolve about, the sun gear; they also mesh with the ring (or internal) gear.

Plastigage A plastic material available in strips of various sizes; used to measure crankshaft main-bearing and connecting-rod-bearing clearances.

Plate In a battery, a rectangular sheet of spongy lead. Sulfuric acid in the electrolyte chemically reacts with the lead to produce an electric current.

Plies The layers of cord in a tire casing; each of these layers is a ply.

Pneumatic tools Tools using compressed air as the energy source.

Polarity The quality of an electric component or circuit that determines the direction of current flow.

Pollutant Any substance that adds to the pollution of the atmosphere. In a vehicle, any such substance in the exhaust gas from the engine or evaporating from the fuel tank or carburetor.

Pollution Any gas or substance, in the air, which makes the air less fit to breathe. Also, noise pollution is the name applied to excessive noise from machinery or vehicles.

Port In the engine, the passage to the cylinder opened and closed by a valve, and through which gases flow to enter and leave the cylinder.

Ported vacuum switch (PVS) A coolant-temperature-sensing vacuum-control valve used in distributor and EGR vacuum systems. Sometimes called the vacuum-control valve or coolant override valve.

Positive crankcase ventilation (PCV) A crankcase ventilation system; uses intake-manifold vacuum to return the crankcase vapors and blowby gases from the crankcase to the intake manifold to be burned, thereby preventing their escape into the atmosphere.

Positive terminal The terminal to which electrons flow in a complete electric circuit. On a battery, the positive terminal can be identified as the battery post with the larger diameter; the plus sign (+) is often also used to identify the positive terminal.

Post A point at which a cable is connected to the battery.

Potential energy Energy stored in a body because of its position. A weight raised to a height has potential energy because it can do work coming down. Likewise, a tensed or compressed spring contains potential energy.

Power The rate at which work is done. A common power unit is the horsepower, which is equal to 33,000 ft-lb/min (foot-pounds per minute).

Power brakes A brake system that uses hydraulic or vacuum and atmospheric pressure to provide most of the force required for braking.

Power piston In some carburetors, a vacuum-operated piston that allows additional fuel to flow at wide-open throttle; permits delivery of a richer air-fuel mixture to the engine.

Power plant The engine or power source of a vehicle.

Power steering A steering system that uses hydraulic pressure from a pump to multiply the driver's steering force.

Power stroke The piston stroke from TDC to BDC immediately following the compression stroke, during which both valves are closed and the fuel burns, expanding the compressed air, thereby forcing the piston down to transmit power to the crankshaft.

Power train The mechanisms that carry power from the engine crankshaft to the drive wheels; includes the clutch, transmission, drive shaft, differential, and axles.

ppm Abbreviation for parts per million; the unit used in measuring the level of hydrocarbons in exhaust gas with an exhaust-gas analyzer; 1 part per million is 1 drop in 16 gallons [60.8 L].

PR Abbreviation for ply rating; a measure of the strength of a tire, based on the strength of a single ply of designated construction.

Precombustion chamber In some engines, a separate small combustion chamber where combustion begins.

Preignition Ignition of the air-fuel mixture in the combustion chamber by some unwanted means, before the ignition spark occurs at the spark plug.

Preload In bearings, the amount of load placed on a bearing before actual operating loads are imposed. Proper preloading requires bearing adjustment and ensures alignment and minimum looseness in the system.

Pressure Force per unit area, or force divided by area. Usually measured in pounds per square inch (psi) and kilopascals (kPa).

Pressure bleeder A piece of shop equipment that uses air pressure to force brake fluid into the brake hydraulic system for bleeding.

Pressure cap A radiator cap with valves which causes the cooling system to operate under pressure at a higher and more efficient temperature.

Pressure-differential valve The valve in a dual-brake system that turns on a warning light if the pressure drops in one part of the system.

Pressure plate That part of the clutch which exerts force against the friction disk; it is mounted on and rotates with the flywheel.

Pressure regulator A device that operates to prevent excessive pressure from developing. In hydraulic systems, a valve that opens to release oil from a line when the oil pressure reaches a specified maximum.

Pressure-relief valve A valve in the oil line that opens to relieve excessive pressure.

Pressure tester An instrument that clamps in the radiator filler neck; used to pressure-test the cooling system for leaks.

Pressurize To apply more than atmospheric pressure to a gas or liquid.

Prevailing torque fasteners Nuts and bolts designed to have a continuous resistance to turning.

Primary The low-voltage circuit of the ignition system.

Primary winding The outer winding of relatively heavy wire in an ignition coil.

Printed circuit An electric circuit made by applying a conductive material to an insulating board in a pattern that provides current paths between components mounted on or connected to the board.

Propeller shaft See Drive shaft.

Proportioning valve A valve that reduces pressure to the rear wheels during braking.

Prussian blue A blue paste used to determine the contact area between two surfaces.

psi Abbreviation for pounds per square inch, a measure of pressure.

Pull The result of an unbalanced condition. For example, uneven braking at the front brakes or unequal front-wheel alignment will cause a car to swerve (pull) to one side when the brakes are applied.

Pulley A small wheel with a V-shaped groove around the rim; drives, or is driven by, a belt.

Pump A device that transfers gas or liquid from one place to another.

Purge To remove, evacuate, or empty trapped substances from a space. In an air conditioner, to remove moisture and air from the refrigerant system by flushing with nitrogen or Refrigerant-12.

Purge valve A valve used on some charcoal canisters in evaporative emission control systems; limits the flow of vapor and air to the carburetor during idling.

Pushrod In the overhead-valve engine, the rod between the valve lifter and the rocker arm; transmits cam-lobe lift.

PVS See Ported vacuum switch.

Quad carburetor A four-barrel carburetor.

Quick charger A battery charger that produces a high charging current which charges, or boosts, a battery in a short time.

Races The metal rings on which ball or roller bearings rotate.

Rack-and-pinion steering gear A steering gear in which a pinion on the end of the steering shaft meshes with a rack of gear teeth on the major cross member of the steering linkage.

Radial tire A tire in which the plies are placed radially, or perpendicular to the rim, with a circumferential belt on top of them. The rubber tread is vulcanized on top of the belt and plies.

Radiator In the cooling system, the device that removes heat from coolant passing through it; takes hot coolant from the engine and returns the coolant to the engine at a lower temperature.

Radiator pressure cap See Pressure cap.

Radio choke An electric coil used to prevent static in the radio caused by opening and closing of the contact points in the instrument-voltage regulator.

Raster pattern An oscilloscope pattern showing the ignition voltages one above the other, from the bottom to the top of the screen in the engine firing order.

Ratio Proportion; the relative amounts of two or more substances in a mixture. Usually expressed as a numerical relationship, as in 2:1.

Readout The visual delivery or display of information from an electronic device, circuit, or system.

Rear-end torque The reaction torque that acts on the rear-axle housing when torque is applied to the wheels; tends to turn the axle housing in a direction opposite to rotation.

Reassembly Putting back together of the parts of a device.

Rebore To increase the diameter of a cylinder.

Recapping A form of tire repair in which a cap of new tread material is placed on the old casing and vulcanized into place.

Receiver In a car air conditioner, a metal tank for holding excess refrigerant. Liquid refrigerant is delivered from the condenser to the receiver.

Receiver-dehydrator In a car air conditioner, a container for storing liquid refrigerant from the condenser. A sack of desiccant in this container removes small traces of moisture that may be left in the system after purging and evacuating.

Recharging The action of forcing electric current into a battery in the direction opposite to that in which current normally flows during use. Reverses the chemical reaction between the plates and electrolyte.

Reciprocating motion Motion of an object between two limiting positions; motion in a straight line, back and forth or up and down.

Recirculating-ball-and-nut steering gear A type of steering gear in which a nut, meshing with a gear sector, is assembled on a worm gear; balls circulate between the nut and worm threads.

Rectifier A device that changes alternating current to direct current; in the alternator, a diode.

Refrigerant A substance used to transfer heat in an air conditioner, through a cycle of evaporation and condensation.

Refrigerant-12 The refrigerant used in vehicle air-conditioning systems. It is sold under trademarks such as Freon-12.

Refrigeration Cooling of an object or a substance by removal of heat through mechanical means.

Regulator In the charging system, a device that controls alternator output to prevent excessive voltage.

Relay An electrical device that opens or closes a circuit or circuits in response to a voltage signal.

Release bearing See Throwout bearing.

Relief valve A valve that opens when a preset pressure is reached. This relieves or prevents excessive pressures.

Reluctor In an electronic ignition system, the metal rotor (with a series of tips) which replaces the cam used in a contact-point distributor.

Remove and reinstall (R and R) To perform a series of servicing procedures on an original part or assembly; includes removal, inspection, lubrication, all necessary adjustments, and reinstallation.

Replace To remove a used part or assembly and install a new part or assembly in its place; includes cleaning, lubricating, and adjusting as required.

Reserve capacity A battery rating; the number of minutes a battery can deliver a 25-ampere current before the cell voltages drop to 1.75 volts per cell.

Resistance The opposition to a flow of current through a circuit or electrical device; measured in ohms. A voltage of one volt will cause one ampere to flow through a resistance of one ohm. This is known as Ohm's law, which can be written in three ways: amperes = volts/ohms; ohms = volts/amperes; and volts = amperes × ohms.

Resonator A device in the exhaust system, similar to a muffler, that reduces exhaust noise.

Retard Usually associated with the engine spark-timing mechanisms; the opposite of spark advance. To delay the occurrence of the spark in the combustion chamber.

Return spring A pull-back spring, often used in brake systems.

Rich mixture An air-fuel mixture that has a relatively high proportion of fuel and a relatively low proportion of air. An air-fuel ratio of 13:1 indicates a rich mixture, compared with an air-fuel ratio of 16:1.

Ring See Compression ring and Oil ring.

Ring gap The gap between the ends of the piston ring when the ring is in place in the cylinder.

Ring gear A large gear carried by the differential case; meshes with and is driven by the drive pinion.

Ring grooves Grooves cut in a piston, into which the piston rings are assembled.

Ring ridge The ridge formed at the top of a cylinder as the cylinder wall below is worn away by piston-ring movement.

Road-draft tube A method of removing fumes and pressure from the engine crankcase; used prior to crankcase emission control systems. The tube, which was connected into the crankcase and suspended slightly above the ground, depended on venturi action to create a partial vacuum as the vehicle moved. The method was ineffective below about 20 mph [32 km/h].

Rocker arm In engines with the valves in the cylinder head, a device that rocks on a shaft (or pivots on a stud) as the cam moves the pushrod, causing a valve to open.

Rod bearing In an engine, the split insert-type bearing in the connecting rod in which a crankpin of the crankshaft rotates. Also called a connecting-rod bearing.

Roller tappet A valve lifter with a hardened steel roller on the end riding against the camshaft.

Room temperature 68 to 72°F [20 to 22°C].

Room-temperature-vulcanizing sealant See Aerobic gasket material.

Rotary The motion of a part that continually rotates or turns.

Rotary engine An engine, such as a gas turbine or a Wankel, in which the power is delivered to a spinning rotor (and *not* to a reciprocating piston as in the piston engine).

Rotary-valve steering gear A type of power-steering gear.

Rotor A revolving part of a machine, such as an alternator rotor, disk-brake rotor, distributor rotor, or Wankel-engine rotor.

rpm Abbreviation for revolutions per minute, a measure of rotational speed.

RTV sealant See Aerobic gasket material.

Run-on See Dieseling.

Runout Wobble.

SA Designation for lubricating oil that is acceptable for use in engines operated under the mildest conditions.

SAE Abbreviation for Society of Automotive Engineers. Used to indicate a grade or weight of oil measured according to Society of Automotive Engineers standards.

SB Designation for lubricating oil that is acceptable for minimum-duty engines operated under mild conditions.

SC Designation for lubricating oil that meets requirements for use in the gasoline engines in 1964 to 1967 passenger cars and trucks.

Schematic A pictorial representation, most often in the form of a line drawing. A systematic positioning of components and their relationship to one another or to the overall function.

Schrader valve A spring-loaded valve through which a connection can be made to a refrigeration system; also used in tires.

Scope Short for oscilloscope.

Scored Scratched or grooved, as a cylinder wall may be scored by abrasive particles moved up and down by the piston rings.

Screens Pieces of fine mesh used to prevent solid particles from circulating through any liquid or vapor system and damaging vital moving parts. In an air conditioner, screens are located in the receiver-dehydrator, expansion valve, orifice tube, and compressor.

Scuffing A type of wear in which there is a transfer of material between parts moving against each other; shows up as pits or grooves in the mating surfaces.

SD Designation for lubricating oil that meets requirements for use in the gasoline engines in 1968 to 1971 passenger cars and some trucks.

SE Designation for lubricating oil that meets requirements for use in the gasoline engines in 1972 and later cars and in certain 1971 passenger cars and trucks.

Seal A material, shaped around a shaft, used to close off the operating compartment of the shaft, preventing oil leakage.

Sealed-beam headlight A headlight that contains the filament, reflector, and lens in a single sealed unit.

Seat The surface upon which another part rests, as a valve seat. Also, to wear into a good fit.

Secondary circuit The high-voltage circuit of the ignition system; consists of the coil, rotor, distributor cap, spark-plug cables, and spark plugs.

Sector A gear that is not a complete circle; specifically, the gear sector on the pitman shaft in many steering systems.

Segments The copper bars of a commutator.

Self-adjuster A mechanism used on drum brakes; compensates for shoe wear by automatically adjusting the shoe-to-drum clearance.

Self-diagnostic system Indicating devices on the car that alert the driver when something is wrong in the system.

Self-discharge Chemical activity in the battery which causes the battery to discharge even though it is furnishing no current.

Self-induction The inducing of a voltage in a current-carrying coil of wire because the current in that wire is changing.

Semiconductor A material that acts as an insulator under some conditions and as a conductor under other conditions.

Sensor Any device that receives and reacts to a signal, such as a change in voltage, temperature, or pressure.

Series circuit An electric circuit in which the devices are connected end to end, positive terminal to negative terminal. The same current flows through all the devices in the circuit.

Service brake The foot-operated brake used for retarding, stopping, and controlling the vehicle during normal driving conditions.

Service manual A book published annually by each vehicle manufacturer, listing the specifications and service procedures for each make and model of vehicle. Also called a shop manual.

Service rating A designation that indicates the type of service for which an engine lubricating oil is best suited. See SA, SB, SC, SD, SE, and SF.

Servo A device in a hydraulic system that converts hydraulic pressure to mechanical movement. Consists of a piston that moves in a cylinder as hydraulic pressure acts on it.

SF Designation for lubricating oil that meets requirements for use in gasoline engines in 1981 and later passenger cars and trucks and in certain 1980 models.

Shackle The swinging support by which one end of a leaf spring is attached to the car frame.

Shift lever The lever used to change gears in a transmission. Also, the lever on the starting motor which moves the drive pinion into or out of mesh with the flywheel teeth.

Shift valve In an automatic transmission, a valve that moves to produce the shifts from one gear ratio to another.

Shim A slotted strip of metal used as a spacer to adjust the wheel alignment on many cars; also used to make small corrections in the position of body panels and other parts.

Shimmy Rapid oscillation. In wheel shimmy, for example, the front wheel turns in and out alternately and rapidly; this causes the front end of the car to oscillate or shimmy.

Shock absorber A device placed at each vehicle wheel to regulate spring rebound and compression.

Shoe In the brake system, a metal plate that supports the brake lining and absorbs and transmits braking forces.

Short circuit A defect in an electric circuit which permits current to take a short path, or circuit, instead of following the desired path.

Shroud A hood placed around an engine fan to improve fan action.

Side clearance The clearance between the sides of moving parts when the sides do not serve as load-carrying surfaces.

Sight glass In a car air conditioner, a viewing glass or window set in the refrigerant line, usually in the top of the receiver-dehydrator; the sight glass allows a visual check of the refrigerant passing from the receiver to the evaporator.

Silicone rubber See Aerobic gasket material.

Single-overhead-camshaft (SOHC) engine An engine in which a single camshaft is mounted over each cylinder head, instead of inside the cylinder block.

Slip joint In the power train, a variable-length connection that permits the drive shaft to change its effective length.

Slip rings In an alternator, the rings that form a rotating connection between the armature windings and the brushes.

Sludge An accumulation of water, dirt, and oil in the oil pan; sludge is very viscous and tends to reduce lubrication.

Smog A term coined from the words "smoke" and "fog." First applied to the foglike layer that hangs in the air under certain atmospheric conditions; now generally used to describe any condition of dirty air and/or fumes or smoke.

Smoke Small gas-borne or airborne particles, exclusive of water vapor, that result from combustion; such particles emitted by an engine into the atmosphere in sufficient quantity to be observable.

Smoke in exhaust A visible blue or black substance often present in the engine exhaust. A blue color indicates excessive oil in the combustion chamber; black indicates excessive fuel.

SOHC See Single-overhead-camshaft (SOHC) engine.

Solenoid An electromechanical device which, when connected to an electrical source such as a battery, produces a mechanical movement. This movement can be used to control a valve or to produce other movements.

Solenoid relay A relay that connects a solenoid to a current source when its contacts close; specifically, the starting-motor solenoid relay.

Solenoid switch A switch that is opened and closed electromagnetically, by the movement of a solenoid core. Usually, the core also causes a mechanical action, such as the movement of a drive pinion into mesh with flywheel teeth for cranking.

Solid-state device A device that has no moving parts except electrons. Diodes and transistors are examples.

Solvent A cold liquid cleaner used to wash away grease and dirt.

South pole The pole at which magnetic lines of force enter a magnet.

Spark advance See Advance.

Spark duration The length of time a spark is established across a spark gap, or the length of time current flows in a spark gap.

Spark-ignition engine An engine operating on the Otto cycle, in which the fuel is ignited by the heat from an electric spark as it jumps the gap at the end of the spark plug.

Spark knock See Detonation.

Spark line Part of the oscilloscope pattern of the ignition secondary circuit; the spark line shows the voltage required to sustain the spark at the spark plug, and the number of distributor degrees through which the spark exists.

Spark plug The assembly, which includes a pair of electrodes and an insulator, that provides a spark gap in the engine cylinder.

Spark-plug heat range The distance heat must travel from the center electrode to reach the outer shell of the spark plug and enter the cylinder head.

Spark test A quick check of the ignition system; made by holding the metal spark-plug end of a spark-plug cable about $\frac{1}{4}$ inch [6 mm] from the cylinder head, or block; cranking the engine; and checking for a spark.

Specifications Information provided by the manufacturer that describes each automotive system and its components, operation, and clearances. Also, the service procedures that must be followed for a system to operate properly.

Specific gravity The weight per unit volume of a substance as compared with the weight per unit volume of water.

Specs Short for specifications.

Speedometer An instrument that indicates vehicle speed; usually driven from the transmission.

Splayed crankpins The slight spreading apart of a crankpin in a V-type engine so that each rod has its own crankpin. This reduces vibration in some V-6 engines that have a 90 degree angle between the banks.

Splines Slots or grooves cut in a shaft or bore. Splines on a shaft are matched to splines in a bore, to ensure that the two parts turn together.

Spool valve A rod with indented sections; used to control oil flow in automatic transmissions.

Sprag clutch In an automatic transmission, a one-way clutch; a clutch that can transmit power in one direction but not in the other.

Spring A device that changes shape under stress or force but returns to its original shape when the stress or force is removed; the component of the automotive suspension system that absorbs road shocks by flexing and twisting.

Spring shackle See Shackle.

Sprung weight That part of the car which is supported on springs (includes the engine, frame, and body).

Spur gear A gear in which the teeth are parallel to the center line of the gear.

Stabilizer bar An interconnecting shaft between the two lower suspension arms; reduces body roll on turns.

Stacked pattern See Raster pattern.

Starter See Starting motor.

Starting motor The electric motor that cranks the engine, or turns the crankshaft, for starting.

Starting-motor drive The drive mechanism and gear on the end of the starting-motor armature shaft; used to couple the starting motor to, and disengage it from, the flywheel ring-gear teeth.

Static balance The balance of an object while it is not moving.

Stator The stationary member of a machine, such as an electric motor or generator, in or about which a rotor revolves; in an electronic ignition system, a small magnet embedded in plastic (or a light-emitting diode) which when used with a reluctor replaces contact points. Also, the third member, in addition to the turbine and pump, in a torque converter.

Steering-and-ignition lock A device that locks the ignition switch in the OFF position and locks the steering wheel so it cannot be turned.

Steering arm The arm attached to the steering knuckle that turns the knuckle and wheel for steering.

Steering axis The center line of the ball joints in a front-suspension system.

Steering-axis inclination The inward tilt of the steering axis from the vertical.

Steering gear That part of the steering system that is located at the lower end of the steering shaft; changes the rotary motion of the steering wheel into the linear motion of the front wheels for steering.

Steering kickback Sharp and rapid movements of the steering wheel as the front wheels encounter obstructions in the road; the shocks of these encounters "kick back" to the steering wheel.

Steering knuckle The front-wheel spindle that is supported by upper and lower ball joints and by the wheel; the part on which a front wheel is mounted and which is turned for steering.

Steering shaft The shaft extending from the steering gear to the steering wheel.

Steering system The mechanism that enables the driver to turn the wheels for changing the direction of vehicle movement.

Steering wheel The wheel at the top of the steering shaft that is used by the driver to guide or steer the car.

Stoichiometric ratio In a spark-ignition engine, the ideal air-fuel-mixture ratio of 14.7 : 1, which must be maintained on engines with dual-bed and three-way catalytic converters.

Stoplights Lights at the rear of the car which indicate that the brakes are applied.

Stoplight switch The switch that turns the stoplights on and off.

Stratified charge In a spark-ignition engine, an air-fuel charge with a small layer or pocket of rich air-fuel mixture. The rich mixture is ignited first; then ignition spreads to the leaner mixture filling the rest of the combustion chamber. The diesel engine is a stratified-charge engine.

Stroke In an engine cylinder, the distance that the piston moves in traveling from BDC to TDC or from TDC to BDC.

Strut A bar that connects the lower control arm to the car frame; used when the lower control arm is attached to the frame at only one point. Also called a brake-reaction rod.

Stud extractor Tool used to remove the part of a bolt or stud that has broken off in a hole.

Suction line In an air conditioner, the tube that connects the evaporator outlet and the compressor inlet. Low-pressure refrigerant vapor flows through this line.

Suction pressure The pressure at the air-conditioner compressor inlet; the compressor intake pressure, as indicated by a gauge set.

Suction-throttling valve In an air conditioner, a valve located between the evaporator and the compressor; controls the temperature of the air flowing from the evaporator, to prevent freezing of moisture on the evaporator.

Sulfation The lead sulfate that forms on battery plates as a result of the battery action that produces electric current.

Sulfuric acid See Electrolyte.

Sulfur oxides (SO$_x$) Acids that can form in small amounts as the result of a reaction between hot exhaust gas and the catalyst in a catalytic converter.

Sun gear In a planetary-gear system, the center gear that meshes with the planet pinions.

Supercharger In the intake system

of the engine, a pump that pressurizes the ingoing air or air-fuel mixture. This increases the amount of fuel that can be burned, increasing engine power. If the supercharger is driven by the engine exhaust gas, it is called a turbocharger.

Superimposed pattern On an oscilloscope, a pattern showing the ignition voltages one on top of the other, so that only a single trace, and variations from it, can be seen.

Suspension The system of springs and other parts which supports the upper part of a vehicle on its axles and wheels.

Suspension arm In the front suspension, one of the arms pivoted on the frame at one end and on the steering-knuckle support at the other end.

Sway bar See Stabilizer bar.

Swept volume See Piston displacement.

Switch A device that opens and closes an electric circuit.

Synchronize To make two or more events or operations occur at the same time or at the same speed.

Synchronizer A device in the transmission that synchronizes gears about to be meshed, so that no gear clash will occur.

Synthetic oil An artificial oil that is manufactured; not a natural mineral oil made from petroleum.

Tachometer A device for measuring engine speed, or rpm.

Taillights Steady-burning low-intensity lights used on the rear of a vehicle.

Tank unit The part of the fuel-level-indicating system that is mounted in the fuel tank.

Taper A gradual reduction in the width of a shaft or hole; in an engine cylinder, uneven wear, with more at the top than at the bottom.

Tappet See Valve lifter.

Tappet noise A regular clicking noise in the valve train that increases with engine speed.

Temperature The measure of heat intensity, in degrees. Temperature is *not* a measure of heat quantity.

Temperature gauge A gauge that indicates to the driver the temperature of the coolant in the engine cooling system.

Temperature indicator A gauge that indicates to the driver the temperature of the engine coolant, or a light that comes on if the coolant gets too hot.

Temperature-sending unit A device, in contact with the engine coolant, whose electrical resistance changes as the coolant temperature increases or decreases; these changes control the movement of the indicator needle in the temperature gauge.

Tetraethyl lead A chemical which, when added to engine fuel, increases its octane rating, or reduces its tendency to detonate.

Thermal Of or pertaining to heat.

Thermistor A heat-sensing device with a negative temperature coefficient of resistance; as its temperature increases, its electrical resistance decreases. Used as the sensing device for engine-temperature indicating devices.

Thermometer An instrument that measures heat intensity (temperature) by the thermal expansion of a liquid.

Thermostat A device for the automatic regulation of temperature; usually contains a temperature-sensitive element that expands or contracts to open or close off the flow of air, a gas, or a liquid.

Thermostatic air cleaner An air cleaner in which a thermostat controls the preheating of intake air.

Thermostatic expansion valve Component of a refrigeration system that controls the rate of refrigerant flow to the evaporator. Commonly called the expansion valve.

Thermostatic gauge An indicating device (for fuel quantity, oil pressure, engine temperature) that contains a thermostatic blade or blades.

Thermostatic vacuum switch A temperature-sensing device extending into the coolant; connects full manifold vacuum to the distributor when coolant overheats. The resultant spark advance causes an increase in engine rpm, which lowers the coolant temperature.

Thickness gauge Strips of metal made to an exact thickness, used to measure clearances between parts.

Thread insert A threaded coil that is used to restore the original thread size to a hole with damaged threads; the hole is drilled oversize and tapped; then the insert is threaded into the tapped hole.

Throttle-body injection On a spark-ignition engine, a type of fuel-injection system which sprays fuel into the intake air passing through the throttle body on the intake manifold.

Throttle pressure Pressure at one end of the shift valve, which changes as engine intake-manifold vacuum changes. One of the two signals that determine when an automatic transmission will shift.

Throttle-return check Same as dashpot.

Throttle valve A disk valve in the carburetor base that pivots in response to accelerator-pedal position; allows the driver to regulate the volume of air or air-fuel mixture entering the intake manifold, thereby controlling the engine speed. Also called the throttle plate.

Throwout bearing In the clutch, the bearing that can be moved in to the release levers by clutch-pedal action, to disengage the engine crankshaft from the transmission.

Thrust bearing In the engine, the main bearing that has thrust faces to prevent excessive end play, or forward and backward movement of the crankshaft.

Tie rods In the steering system, the rods that link the pitman arm to the steering-knuckle arms; small steel components that connect the front wheels to the steering mechanism.

Tilt steering wheel A type of steering wheel that can be tilted at various angles, through a flex joint in the steering shaft.

Timing In an engine, delivery of the ignition spark or operation of the valves (in relation to the piston position) for the power stroke. See Ignition timing and Valve timing.

Timing belt A toothed belt that is driven by a sprocket on the crankshaft and that drives the sprocket on the camshaft.

Timing chain A chain that is driven by a sprocket on the crankshaft and that drives the sprocket on the camshaft.

Timing gear A gear on the crankshaft. It drives the camshaft by meshing with a gear on its end.

Timing light A light that can be connected to the ignition system to flash each time the number 1 spark plug fires; used for adjusting the timing of the ignition spark.

Timing marks Marks on gears, sprockets, and other parts that must be properly aligned when the engine is assembled. Lines or numbers on the crankshaft vibration damper or other parts used to adjust ignition timing so that the spark plugs fire at the right time.

Tire The casing-and-tread assembly (with or without a tube) that is mounted on a car wheel to provide pneumatically cushioned contact and traction with the road.

Tire tread See Tread.

Tire tube An inflatable rubber device mounted inside some tires to contain air at sufficient pressure to inflate the casing and support the vehicle weight.

Tire-wear indicator Small strips of rubber molded into the bottom of the tire-tread grooves; they appear as narrow strips of smooth rubber across the tire when the tread depth decreases to $\frac{1}{16}$ inch [1.6 mm].

Toe-in The amount, in inches or millimeters, by which the front of a front wheel points inward.

Toe-out on turns The difference between the angles each of the front wheels makes with the car frame during turns. On a turn, the inner wheel turns, or toes out, more. Also called turning radius.

Top dead center The piston position when the piston has reached the upper limit of its travel in the cylinder and the center line of the connecting rod is parallel to the cylinder walls.

Torque Turning or twisting force, usually measured in pound-feet, kilogram-meters, or newton-meters.

Torque converter In an automatic transmission, a fluid coupling that incorporates a stator to permit a torque increase.

Torque wrench A special handle for a socket set that measures the torque or twisting force being applied to a nut or bolt while tightening it.

Torsional vibration Rotary vibration that causes a twist-untwist action on a rotating shaft, so that a part of the shaft repeatedly moves ahead of, or lags behind, the remainder of the shaft; for example, the action of a crankshaft responding to the cylinder firing impulses.

Torsion-bar spring A long, straight bar that is fastened to the frame at one end and to a control arm at the other. Spring action is produced by a twisting of the bar.

Tracking Rear wheels following directly behind (in the tracks of) the front wheels.

Transaxle A power-transmission device that combines the functions of the transmission and the drive axle (differential) into a single assembly.

Transfer case An auxiliary transmission mounted behind the main transmission. Used to divide engine power and transfer it to both front and rear differentials, either full time or part time.

Transistor A solid-state electronic device that can be used as an electric switch or as an amplifier.

Transmission An assembly of gears that provides the different gear ratios, as well as neutral and reverse, through which engine power is transmitted to the final drive to rotate the drive wheels.

Transmission-controlled spark (TCS) system An NO_x exhaust-emission control system; makes use of the transmission gear position to allow distributor vacuum advance in high gear only.

Transmission-oil cooler A small radiator, either mounted separately or as part of the engine radiator, which cools the transmission fluid.

Tread The part of the tire that contacts the road. It is the thickest part of the tire and is cut with grooves to provide traction for driving and stopping.

Trouble diagnosis The detective work necessary to find the cause of a trouble.

Tubeless tire A tire that holds air without the use of a tube.

Tuneup A procedure for inspecting, testing, and adjusting an engine, and replacing any worn parts, to restore engine performance.

Turbocharger A supercharger driven by the engine exhaust gas.

Turn signal See Directional signals.

Turning radius See Toe-out on turns.

Two-stroke cycle The two piston strokes during which fuel intake, compression, combustion, and exhaust take place in a two-stroke-cycle engine.

Unit An assembly or device that can perform its function only if it is not further divided into its components.

Universal joint In the power train, a jointed connection in the drive shaft that permits the driving angle to change.

Unleaded gasoline Gasoline to which no lead compounds have been intentionally added. Gasoline that contains 0.05 g or less of lead per gallon; required by law to be used in 1975 and later vehicles equipped with catalytic converters.

Unsprung weight The weight of that part of the car which is not supported on springs; for example, the wheels and tires.

Upper beam A headlight beam intended primarily for distant illumination, not for use when other vehicles are being met or followed.

Upshift To shift a transmission into a higher gear.

Vacuum Negative gauge pressure, or a pressure less than atmospheric pressure. Vacuum can be measured in pounds per square inch (psi) but is usually measured in inches or millimeters of mercury (Hg); a reading of 30 inches [762 mm] Hg would indicate a perfect vacuum.

Vacuum advance The advancing (or retarding) of ignition timing by changes in intake-manifold vacuum, reflecting throttle opening and engine load. Also, a mechanism on the ignition distributor that uses intake-manifold vacuum to advance the timing of the spark to the spark plugs.

Vacuum-advance control Any type of NO_x emission control system designed to allow vacuum advance only during certain modes of engine and vehicle operation.

Vacuum gauge In automotive-engine service, a device that measures intake-manifold vacuum and thereby indicates actions of engine components.

Vacuum modulator In automatic transmissions, a device that modulates, or changes, the main-line hydraulic pressure to meet changing engine loads.

Vacuum motor A small motor, powered by intake-manifold vacuum; used for jobs such as raising and lowering headlight doors.

Vacuum pump A mechanical device used to evacuate a system.

Vacuum switch A switch that closes

or opens its contacts in response to changing vacuum conditions.

Valve A device that can be opened or closed to allow or stop the flow of a liquid or gas.

Valve body A casting located in the oil pan, which contains most of the valves for the hydraulic control system of an automatic transmission.

Valve clearance The clearance between the rocker arm and the valve-stem tip in an overhead-valve engine; the clearance in the valve train when the valve is closed.

Valve float A condition in which the engine valves do not close completely or fail to close at the proper time.

Valve grinding Refacing a valve in a valve-refacing machine.

Valve guide A cylindrical part or hole in the head in which a valve is assembled and in which it moves up and down.

Valve lash Same as valve clearance.

Valve lifter A cylindrical part of the engine which rests on a cam of the camshaft and is lifted, by cam action, so that the valve is opened. Also called a lifter, tappet, valve tappet, or cam follower.

Valve overlap The number of degrees of crankshaft rotation during which the intake and exhaust valves are open together.

Valve refacer A machine for removing material from the seating face of a valve to true the face.

Valve rotator A device installed in place of the valve-spring retainer, which turns the valve slightly as it opens.

Valve seat The surface against which a valve comes to rest to provide a seal against leaking.

Valve-seat inserts Metal rings inserted in cylinder heads to act as valve seats (usually for exhaust valves).

Valve spool A spool-shaped valve such as in the power-steering unit.

Valve spring The spring in each valve assembly which has the job of closing the valve.

Valve stem The long, thin section of the valve that fits in the valve guide.

Valve-stem seal A device placed on or around the valve stem to reduce the amount of oil that can get on the stem and then work its way down into the combustion chamber.

Valve tappet See Valve lifter.

Valve timing The timing of the opening and closing of the valves in relation to the piston position.

Valve train The valve-operating mechanism of an engine; includes all components from the camshaft to the valve.

Vane A flat, extended surface that is moved around an axis by or in a fluid. Part of the internal revolving portion of an air-supply pump.

Vapor A gas; any substance in the gaseous state, as distinguished from the liquid or solid state.

Vaporization A change of state from liquid to vapor or gas, by evaporation or boiling; a general term including both evaporation and boiling.

Vapor lines Lines that carry refrigerant vapor. See Suction line.

Vapor-liquid separator A device in the evaporative emission control system; prevents liquid fuel from traveling to the engine through the charcoal-canister vapor line.

Vapor lock A condition in the fuel system in which gasoline vaporizes in the fuel line or fuel pump; bubbles of gasoline vapor restrict or prevent fuel delivery to the carburetor.

Vapor-recovery system An evaporative emission control system that recovers gasoline vapor escaping from the fuel tank and carburetor float bowl. See Evaporative control system.

Vapor-return line A line from the fuel pump to the fuel tank through which any vapor that has formed in the pump is returned to the tank.

Variable-venturi (VV) carburetor A carburetor in which the size of the venturi changes according to engine speed and load.

Vent An opening through which air can leave an enclosed chamber.

Venturi In the carburetor, a narrowed passageway or restriction that increases the velocity of air moving through it; produces the vacuum responsible for the discharge of fuel from the fuel nozzle.

Vibration A rapid back-and-forth motion; an oscillation.

Vibration damper A device attached to the crankshaft of an engine to oppose crankshaft torsional vibration (the twist-untwist actions of the crankshaft caused by the cylinder firing impulses). Also called a harmonic balancer.

Viscosity The resistance to flow exhibited by a liquid. A thick oil has greater viscosity than a thin oil.

Viscosity rating An indicator of the viscosity of engine oil. There are separate ratings for winter driving and for summer driving. The winter grades are SAE5W, SAE10W, and SAE20W. The summer grades are SAE20, SAE30, SAE40, and SAE50. Many oils have multiple viscosity ratings, as, for example, SAE20W-30.

Viscous Thick; tending to resist flowing.

Voice alert system A type of indicating device in the car which can speak several words or phrases to the driver.

Voice command system A type of interactive control system in which the driver can give the car certain spoken commands and the system responds by performing the act or by providing the information desired.

Volatile Evaporating readily. For example, Refrigerant-12 is volatile (evaporates quickly) at room temperature.

Volatility A measure of the ease with which a liquid vaporizes. Volatility has a direct relationship to the flammability of a fuel.

Voltage The force which causes electrons to flow in a conductor. The difference in electrical pressure (or potential) between two points in a circuit.

Voltage regulator A device that prevents excessive alternator or generator voltage by alternately inserting and removing a resistance in the field circuit.

Voltmeter A device for measuring the potential difference (voltage) between two points, such as the terminals of a battery or alternator or two points in an electric circuit.

Volumetric efficiency A measure of how completely the engine cylinder fills up on the intake stroke of a spark-ignition engine.

V-type engine An engine with two banks or rows of cylinders, set at an angle to form a V.

VV carburetor See Variable-venturi (VV) carburetor.

Wankel engine A rotary engine in which a three-lobe rotor turns eccentrically in an oval chamber to produce power.

Warranty work Repair work that the manufacturer agrees to pay for—if it is required—while the vehicle (or a certain part) is new.

Wastegate A control device on a turbocharger to limit boost pressure, thereby preventing engine and turbocharger damage.

Water jackets The spaces between the inner and outer shells of the cylinder block or head, through which coolant circulates.

Water pump In the cooling system, the device that circulates coolant between the engine water jackets and the radiator.

Wedge combustion chamber A combustion chamber resembling a wedge in shape.

Wheel A disk or spokes with a hub at the center (which revolves around an axle) and a rim around the outside for mounting of the tire.

Wheel alignment A series of tests and adjustments to ensure that wheels and tires are properly positioned on the vehicle.

Wheel balancer A device that checks a wheel-and-tire assembly (statically, dynamically, or both) for balance.

Wheelbase The distance between the center lines of the front and rear axles. For trucks with tandem rear axles, the rear center line is considered to be midway between the two rear axles.

Wheel cylinders In a hydraulic braking system, hydraulic cylinders located in the brake mechanisms at the wheels. Hydraulic pressure from the master cylinder causes the wheel cylinders to move the brake shoes into contact with the brake drums for braking.

Wheel tramp Tendency for a wheel to move up and down so it repeatedly bears down hard, or "tramps," on the road. Sometimes called high-speed shimmy.

Wiring harness A group of individually insulated wires, wrapped together to form a neat, easily installed bundle.

Work The moving of an object against an opposing force; measured in foot-pounds, meter-kilograms, or joules. The product of a force and the distance through which it acts.

Worm gear Type of gear in which the teeth resemble threads; used on the lower end of the steering shaft in a pitman-arm steering gear.

WOT Abbreviation for wide-open throttle.

INDEX

ANSWERS TO REVIEW QUESTIONS

CHAPTER 1
1. *c* 2. *d* 3. *b* 4. *c* 5. *a* 6. *c* 7. *d* 8. *d* 9. *b* 10. *a*
CHAPTER 2
1. *b* 2. *a* 3. *c* 4. *b* 5. *a* 6. *d* 7. *b* 8. *c*
CHAPTER 3
1. *b* 2. *d* 3. *d* 4. *b* 5. *c* 6. *c* 7. *a* 8. *b* 9. *a* 10. *d* 11. *c*
12. *c* 13. *b* 14. *d* 15. *c*
CHAPTER 4
1. *b* 2. *a* 3. *c* 4. *a* 5. *d* 6. *c* 7. *d* 8. *b* 9. *c* 10. *a* 11. *d*
12. *d* 13. *b* 14. *a* 15. *b*
CHAPTER 5
1. *c* 2. *a* 3. *d* 4. *b* 5. *c* 6. *b* 7. *a* 8. *b* 9. *d* 10. *a* 11. *a*
12. *a* 13. *d* 14. *c* 15. *d*
CHAPTER 6
1. *b* 2. *c* 3. *b* 4. *c* 5. *c* 6. *b* 7. *b* 8. *b*
CHAPTER 7
1. *b* 2. *a* 3. *b* 4. *c* 5. *b* 6. *c* 7. *d* 8. *c* 9. *a* 10. *c*
CHAPTER 8
1. *c* 2. *a* 3. *d* 4. *c* 5. *c* 6. *c* 7. *d* 8. *a* 9. *a* 10. *d*
CHAPTER 9
1. *b* 2. *c* 3. *a* 4. *c* 5. *b* 6. *a* 7. *d* 8. *c* 9. *b* 10. *d* 11. *a*
12. *b* 13. *c* 14. *b* 15. *b* 16. *a* 17. *b* 18. *c* 19. *b* 20. *c*
21. *b* 22. *a* 23. *b* 24. *c* 25. *d*
CHAPTER 10
1. *a* 2. *c* 3. *b* 4. *c* 5. *c* 6. *d* 7. *d* 8. *a* 9. *d* 10. *b* 11. *c*
12. *a* 13. *c* 14. *c* 15. *b*
CHAPTER 11
1. *c* 2. *c* 3. *c* 4. *b* 5. *b* 6. *c* 7. *b* 8. *d* 9. *c* 10. *a*
CHAPTER 12
1. *a* 2. *b* 3. *d* 4. *b* 5. *c* 6. *b* 7. *d* 8. *b* 9. *b* 10. *a*
CHAPTER 13
1. *b* 2. *b* 3. *c* 4. *d* 5. *a* 6. *b* 7. *b* 8. *d* 9. *c* 10. *a*
CHAPTER 14
1. *b* 2. *c* 3. *d* 4. *a* 5. *c* 6. *b* 7. *c* 8. *a*
CHAPTER 15
1. *c* 2. *c* 3. *b* 4. *b* 5. *d* 6. *d* 7. *b* 8. *c*
CHAPTER 16
1. *b* 2. *c* 3. *b* 4. *a* 5. *a* 6. *c* 7. *a*
CHAPTER 17
1. *a* 2. *b* 3. *c* 4. *c* 5. *d* 6. *c* 7. *c* 8. *a*
CHAPTER 18
1. *b* 2. *c* 3. *b* 4. *d* 5. *a* 6. *b* 7. *d* 8. *a*
CHAPTER 19
1. *d* 2. *c* 3. *c* 4. *d* 5. *a* 6. *d* 7. *b* 8. *d*
CHAPTER 20
1. *b* 2. *d* 3. *d* 4. *b* 5. *b* 6. *a* 7. *d* 8. *b*
CHAPTER 21
1. *d* 2. *c* 3. *c* 4. *a* 5. *b* 6. *d* 7. *d* 8. *a*
CHAPTER 22
1. *b* 2. *d* 3. *a* 4. *a* 5. *c* 6. *a* 7. *b* 8. *a* 9. *b* 10. *d* 11. *b*
12. *a* 13. *a*

CHAPTER 23
1. *b* 2. *d* 3. *b* 4. *a* 5. *c* 6. *a* 7. *c* 8. *a*
CHAPTER 24
1. *c* 2. *d* 3. *b* 4. *b* 5. *a* 6. *c* 7. *d* 8. *a*
CHAPTER 25
1. *b* 2. *a* 3. *d* 4. *b* 5. *c*
CHAPTER 26
1. *c* 2. *c* 3. *d* 4. *d* 5. *b* 6. *a* 7. *c* 8. *b* 9. *b* 10. *b* 11. *a*
12. *a* 13. *b* 14. *b* 15. *b* 16. *d* 17. *c* 18. *a*
CHAPTER 27
1. *b* 2. *c* 3. *d* 4. *c* 5. *c*
CHAPTER 28
1. *c* 2. *b* 3. *a* 4. *d* 5. *b* 6. *a* 7. *c* 8. *c*
CHAPTER 29
1. *d* 2. *d* 3. *c* 4. *a* 5. *a* 6. *b*
CHAPTER 30
1. *b* 2. *d* 3. *a* 4. *a* 5. *d* 6. *c* 7. *b* 8. *d*
CHAPTER 31
1. *a* 2. *c* 3. *c* 4. *a* 5. *b*
CHAPTER 32
1. *a* 2. *c* 3. *a* 4. *c* 5. *b* 6. *c* 7. *d*
CHAPTER 33
1. *b* 2. *a* 3. *d* 4. *b* 5. *d*
CHAPTER 34
1. *c* 2. *b* 3. *d* 4. *c* 5. *a*
CHAPTER 35
1. *c* 2. *d* 3. *d* 4. *d* 5. *b*
CHAPTER 36
1. *c* 2. *b* 3. *d* 4. *a* 5. *b*
CHAPTER 37
1. *c* 2. *c* 3. *d* 4. *c* 5. *a*
CHAPTER 38
1. *d* 2. *b* 3. *c* 4. *b* 5. *a* 6. *d* 7. *b*
CHAPTER 39
1. *c* 2. *a* 3. *d* 4. *c* 5. *b* 6. *c* 7. *d* 8. *a*
CHAPTER 40
1. *c* 2. *a* 3. *c* 4. *d* 5. *c*
CHAPTER 41
1. *b* 2. *c* 3. *b* 4. *a* 5. *d* 6. *d* 7. *b* 8. *b*
CHAPTER 42
1. *d* 2. *a* 3. *c* 4. *a* 5. *b* 6. *b* 7. *a*
CHAPTER 43
1. *a* 2. *a* 3. *b* 4. *a* 5. *c*
CHAPTER 44
1. *a* 2. *b* 3. *a* 4. *c* 5. *c*
CHAPTER 45
1. *b* 2. *d* 3. *d* 4. *c* 5. *a*